A HISTORY OF AUSTRALIA

VOLUME I

JAMES COOK

Portrait by John Webber in the National Portrait Gallery, London

C. M. H. CLARK

A HISTORY OF AUSTRALIA

I

FROM THE EARLIEST TIMES
TO THE
AGE OF MACQUARIE

MELBOURNE UNIVERSITY PRESS

First published 1962
Reprinted, with corrections, November 1962
Reprinted, with alterations, 1963
Reprinted 1968
Reprinted 1971
Printed in Australia by
Halstead Press Pty Ltd, Kingsgrove, N.S.W. 2208 for
Melbourne University Press, Carlton, Victoria 3053
Great Britain and Europe: ISBS Inc., London
U.S.A. and Canada: ISBS Inc., Zion, Illinois 60099
Registered in Australia for transmission by post as a book

ISBN 0 522 84008 6
Dewey Decimal Classification Number 994

For
Dymphna Clark and Barbara Penny
in gratitude

Since Copernicus man rolls from the centre into X.

—F. Nietzsche: *The Will to Power*

All the wealth of love lavished of old upon Him, who was immortal, would be turned upon the whole of nature, on the world, on men, on every blade of grass.

—F. M. Dostoevsky: *A Raw Youth*

PREFACE

SOME of the material used in the early sections of this book was collected in the Museum in Djakarta, the library of the University of Malaya in Singapore, and the National Archives in Delhi during a trip which was made possible by a grant from the Rockefeller Foundation in New York. I would like to thank the Rockefeller Foundation for making that possible. Some of it was collected in the Public Record Office and the British Museum in London, the Public Library in Dublin, and the Archives in the Hague, and I would like to thank the librarians and archivists of those institutions for their help. Some of it was collected at the Mitchell Library in Sydney, the State Library of Victoria, and the library of the Royal Society in Hobart, to all of which I owe a great debt. Most of the material was collected in the National Library in Canberra, from the great collection gathered by the librarian, H. L. White, and made available by his courteous and helpful staff. In particular I would like to thank Mrs Fanning and Miss Patricia Tiernan. I would also like to thank Jennifer Ratcliffe for typing the manuscript, and H. E. Gunther, of the Australian National University, for drawing the maps. There are also debts to Keith Hancock and Gavin Long, who taught me how to begin, and to Kurt Baier, Don Baker, Asa Briggs, David Campbell, Geoffrey Fairbairn, Bruce Grant, Ruth Knight, James McAuley and Michael Roe, who read drafts or talked on what it is all about. There is a very special debt to those students in Melbourne whom it was my great good fortune to teach in the years after the war. In their company one felt it might be possible to tackle the mighty theme of the coming of European civilization to Australia.

M. C.

CONTENTS

ILLUSTRATIONS

PLATES

MAPS

ABBREVIATIONS

Bigge: Agriculture and Trade	Report of the Commissioner of Inquiry, on the state of Agriculture and Trade in the Colony of New South Wales, 10 January 1823. Ordered by the House of Commons to be printed, 13 March 1823. *British Parliamentary Papers*, 1823, vol. X, no. 136.
Bigge: Colony of N.S.W.	Report of the Commissioner of Inquiry, into the state of the Colony of New South Wales, 6 May 1822. Ordered by the House of Commons to be printed, 19 June 1822. *British Parliamentary Papers*, 1822, vol. XX, no. 448.
Bigge: Judicial Establishments	Report of the Commissioner of Inquiry, on the Judicial Establishments of New South Wales, and Van Diemen's Land. Ordered by the House of Commons to be printed, 21 February 1823. *British Parliamentary Papers*, 1823, vol. X, no. 33.
C.J.	*Journals of the House of Commons.*
C.O.	Colonial Office.
H.O.	Home Office.
H.R.A.	*Historical Records of Australia.*
H.R.N.S.W.	*Historical Records of New South Wales.*
P.P.	*British Parliamentary Papers.*
R.A.H.S., *J. & P.*	Royal Australian Historical Society, *Journal and Proceedings.*

PART I

THE FORERUNNERS

THE EARLIEST TIMES TO CATHOLIC CHRISTENDOM

C IVILIZATION did not begin in Australia until the last quarter of the eighteenth century. The reason lies partly in the environment and way of life of the people inhabiting the continent before the coming of the European, and partly in the internal history of those Hindu, Chinese, and Muslim civilizations which colonized and traded in the archipelago of south-east Asia. The early inhabitants of the continent created cultures but not civilizations.[1] The first of these were the Negrito people—short, dark-skinned, curly-haired and broad-nosed—who were forced to migrate from their hunting grounds in south-east Asia by the movement into those areas of people of a higher material culture, at a time when Tasmania, Australia and New Guinea formed part of the land mass of Asia.

Later another people arrived—the Murrayians, who were related to the Ainu in Japan and either destroyed the Negritos or drove them into the valleys behind Cairns, and south to what is now Tasmania, the islands of Bass Strait and Kangaroo Island. Then, in turn, the Murrayians were challenged and displaced by the Carpentarians—a people probably related to the Vedda of Ceylon, who settled in the northern portion of Australia after driving the Murrayians southwards in their turn. When the ice receded in northern Asia and in Antarctica, the climate of central Australia gradually became drier. The rivers ran only in wet seasons; the inland lakes turned into salt pans; the huge animals dependent on such water died out, leaving their bones as a memorial of a time before the days of desolation. As the ice sheets melted, the levels of the ocean gradually rose till Tasmania, Kangaroo Island, Australia, New Guinea and the islands of the Indonesian and Malay archipelagos were cut off from each other by stretches of sea.[2]

[1] A distinction is made here between 'civilization' in the sense described in the *Oxford English Dictionary*, of a people brought out of a state of barbarism, and 'culture' in the sense defined in the *Grosse Brockhaus* as the sum of the efforts made by a community to satisfy and reconcile the basic human requirements of food, clothing, shelter, security, care of the weak and social cohesion by controlling its natural environment. The word 'culture' is not used in its other sense of 'the efforts made to ennoble, refine and cultivate the human personality by sublimating its instinctual nature'.

[2] This account is based on N. Tindale and J. Birdsell: 'Results of the Harvard-Adelaide Universities Anthropological Expedition 1938-9: Tasmanian Tribes in North Queensland', in *Records of the South Australian Museum*, vol. 7, Adelaide, 1941-3; and H. A. Lindsay: 'The First Australians', in *Science News*, 43 (London, 1957), pp. 54-61. Before the work of Tindale, writers attempting to explain origins were

Of the way of life of these three peoples before the coming of European civilization, little need, or indeed can, be said. On their numbers on the mainland of Australia the estimates of anthropologists, historians and missionaries have always differed; some put the figure as high as one million four hundred thousand, while others put it at approximately three hundred thousand.[3] Estimates of the number of Tasmanian aboriginals in the period before the coming of the European also differed greatly, some missionaries suggesting two hundred thousand while secular observers put the figure as low as between four thousand and seven thousand.[4] Neither the Negritos nor the Murrayians, nor indeed the Carpentarians, made the advance from barbarism to civilization. The age of belief was inclined to explain this as a special punishment for their part in the Fall, by which the snake was condemned to go on his belly all his days, the man to produce bread in the sweat of his brow, the woman to produce children in pain and anguish, and the aborigine, together with primitive people in the rest of the world, to suffer the drudgery and the wretchedness of the uncivilized.[5]

A more secular age has looked for material explanations for this failure, rather than ponder the inscrutable ways of providence, or judge a people's moral worth by its material achievements. Historians and anthropologists have written more of the aborigines' intelligent adaptation to their environment, and of the absence of suitable grain for crops or of animals to domesticate as the reasons for their failure to advance from barbarism; while in moments of doubt or spiritual sickness some have esteemed the absence of material refinements and social order as a blessing rather than a curse, as a source of happiness rather than a misery.[6] For all writings on the aborigines both on the mainland and in Tasmania, have mirrored the civilization of their authors, of those driven by the hope of salvation or the fear of damnation, as well as those in pursuit of some secular millennium, or the advancement of knowledge. But, whatever the reason may have been, the failure of the

forced back on intelligent guesses. An example of such guessing is J. Mathew: *Eaglehawk and Crow. A Study of the Australian Aborigines including an inquiry into their origin and a survey of Australian languages* (London, 1899), p. 5. See also A. P. Elkin: *The Australian Aborigines*, 2nd ed. (Sydney, 1948), pp. 4-8.

[3] R. B. Gribble: *The Problem of the Australian Aborigine* (Sydney, 1932), p. vii. The Reverend Gribble is quoting a figure given at Exeter Hall in 1840; see R. and C. Berndt: *The First Australians* (Sydney, 1952), p. 11.

[4] E. D. Cree: *The Australian Native: His Capabilities and the Power of Christianity in Mission Life* (London, 1872), p. 475; W. H. Flower: *The Aborigines of Tasmania, an Extinct Race* (London, n.d.), p. 47.

[5] T. Dove: 'Moral and Social Characteristics of the Aborigines of Tasmania', in *Tasmanian Journal of Natural Science* (1842), p. 249; D. J. Mulvaney: 'The Australian Aborigines 1606-1929: Opinion and Fieldwork', Part I, in *Historical Studies: Australia and New Zealand*, vol. 8, no. 30, May 1958; B. Smith: *European Vision and the South Pacific* (Oxford, 1960), pp. 107-9.

[6] A. P. Elkin: *The Australian Aborigines*, 3rd ed. (Sydney, 1954), p. 321 et seq.; E. J. B. Foxcroft: *Australian Native Policy: Its History, especially in Victoria* (Melbourne, 1941), p. 14 et seq. For the general problem, see V. G. Childe: *What Happened in History*, ch. 3, and *Man Makes Himself*, ch. 5.

aborigines to emerge from a state of barbarism deprived them of the material resources with which to resist an invader, and left them without the physical strength to protect their culture.

Other peoples have recovered from the destruction of their culture, but that of the aborigines was to wither when in contact with other races; for the aborigine was also endowed with a tenacious, if not unique inability to detect meaning in any way of life other than his own; and by one of those ironies in human affairs it was this very inability to live outside the framework of his own culture that prevented any subsequent invaders from using the aborigine for their own purposes. This, in turn, relieved the European from the evil consequences of reducing an indigenous population to slavery or semi-slavery. It protected the aborigine from such slavery or some form of forced labour, but at the price of the total destruction of the Tasmanian aborigine, and the gradual destruction of aboriginal culture on the mainland.[7]

The odd thing is why no invasion occurred between the end of the ice age in the twenty-fifth millennium and the coming of the European in the last quarter of the eighteenth century.[8] For even after the levels of the ocean rose there was no geographical barrier to such an invasion, as it was possible during six months of every year for people with the most primitive craft to proceed from island to island in the Indonesian archipelago, thence to New Guinea, and across the narrow straits to the north coast of Australia. At the beginning of recorded history an imaginary line on a map drawn from Timor through Banda to Macassar in the Celebes, marked the point where civilization ended and barbarism began. The very word Timor (meaning the East) suggested the end of the civilized, if not the habitable world. The two Malay migrations into the area, the first in approximately 3000 B.C. and the second beginning in approximately 200 B.C., did not cross this line, mainly because of the absence of need, but probably also because of the absence of established knowledge of those areas.[9] Then, over a period of fifteen hundred years and more, the three great colonizing movements in Asia—the Hindu-Buddhists, the Chinese, and the Muslim merchants—moved into the area, without advancing beyond Timor and Macassar. They speculated and phantasized about the lands and peoples in the unknown parts beyond in stories which were to excite curiosity when the internal weakness of the Asian states prepared the way for the coming of the European.

The Hindu-Buddhists, partly from population pressure, partly to obtain spices, fragrant woods and gold, and partly to win converts for their religious faith, began to colonize Sumatra, Java, and the islands of the archipelago in the first century of the Christian era. This was colonization by infiltration

[7] For archaeological evidence that the culture of the aborigines of the Gulf of Carpentaria and Arnhem Land areas was affected by contact with people probably from the Celebes, see P. M. Worsley: 'Early Asian contacts with Australia', in *Past and Present*, no. 7 (April, 1955).

[8] T. W. E. David: *The Geology of the Commonwealth of Australia* (London, 1950), vol. 1, pp. 648-50.

[9] For the Malay migrations see B. H. M. Vlekke: *Nusantara. A History of the East Indian Archipelago* (Harvard, 1945), p. 5 et seq.

rather than conquest. Yet the Hindu-Buddhist, despite his lust for wealth and his religious zeal, did not advance the limits of the known world. The Hindu religion (though not the Buddhist) prohibited sea voyages, as well as contact with foreigners,[10] and a queer 'geography' supplemented the teaching of religion. For the Hindu believed the world was flat and triangular; that it was composed of seven distinct habitations, each surrounded by its own peculiar sea; that one sea was of milk, another of sugar, another of butter, another of wine, and so on; that the whole of this world was supported on the heads of elephants, whose occasional motion was the cause of earthquakes.[11] But it was the advent of Islam both in the mother country and in the archipelago which ended Hindu-Buddhist colonization and evangelization by the middle of the fifteenth century.

In Java and Sumatra and the other islands of the archipelago, the Hindu-Buddhists left their memorials in stone, which represented their conception of the fate of man both in his journey across the terrible ocean of life as well as of this life as a passage from one eternity to another. In their folk stories they first created and then handed on to posterity the first speculations of a civilized people on the world to the south of Java, as well as to the south and east of Timor. The first of these was the story of the islands of gold; on the location of these islands they could give no information, but what they lacked in exact knowledge they made good by the exercise of their delightful imaginations. They put there a city, the palaces of which gleamed with fabric of gold, where men enjoyed an ineffable happiness with fair-eyed wives in charming gardens, the lakes of which had steps made out of jewels.[12] Or so the Hindu story ran. For though not all their successors were so gullible or so credulous as to accept this fruit of the Hindu imagination, all voyagers from the Indies in search of wealth were looking for the fabulous islands: the Chinese, the Muslims, the Portuguese, the Spanish, the Dutch, the French and the English, the unbeliever, the Mussulman, the Catholic and the Protestant, as well as those not touched by any vision of God's throne, were all driven on by the hope of finding the islands of gold.

By an odd irony, the Hindus, who had woven the tale which lured men to every possible fate except the discovery of gold, also handed on from generation to generation a story to deter men from exploring those areas. This was the story of the tree of Pausengi which stood with its crown above water in the seas south of Java. On its branches there lived a bird, Geruda, shaped like a griffin, which flew by night, taking in its claws an elephant, a tiger, a rhinoceros or any large animal, which it carried to its nest. In those seas the currents from all directions flowed towards this tree, and the ships which were carried along by them were sucked into an abyss, while the crews died of hunger or fell prey to the Geruda. For this reason, the

10 K. A. Nilakantasastri: *History of Sri Vijaya* (Madras, 1949), and *South Indian Influences in the Far East* (Bombay, 1949). See also K. M. Panikkar: *Asia and Western Dominance* (London, 1953), pp. 34-5.

11 Bernier's Travels. Printed in Constable's *Oriental Miscellany of Original and Selected Publications* (London, 1891), vol. 1, p. 340.

12 N. M. Penzer (ed.): *The Ocean of Story* (London, 1924), vol. 2, p. 238.

Javanese and all who lived on the south coast of the islands as far east as Timor were afraid to proceed more than three miles out of sight of land; on finding the current carrying them southward they abandoned their junks and rowed for the shore in small boats for fear of being drawn into the abyss of Pausengi from which there was no return. So attached were they to the story that later, when the Dutch told them how Tasman had discovered a great land in the south seas and had found neither abyss nor Pausengi, they could make no reply except that the tree must nevertheless stand somewhere in the south because its fruits were cast upon the south coasts of the islands. So the Hindu declared the south seas taboo, or 'pamali', or 'boejoet', an expression which they handed to the Dutch, whose equipment, knowledge and religion emancipated them from the terrors which overwhelmed the Hindu.[13]

The second colonizing power in the area was the Chinese. Their economic interests were three-fold: to establish a depot in the vicinity of the equator for their trade with India, Africa, the Middle East, and Europe; to trade with the Celebes for trepang and the bird of paradise; and to trade with Timor for sandalwood.[14] The first interest turned their backs to the south seas; the second and the third both brought them to the line that divided civilization from barbarism, and might well have caused them to look further south for the trepang as the fishing grounds in the Celebes became exhausted. The Bugis probably did the carrying trade from the islands to the Chinese depots at Djakarta and Sri-vijaya, where the goods were finally transshipped to Chinese junks. From their encyclopaedias, their dynastic histories, and the special accounts of the area published between 1300 and 1500, it is clear that the Chinese knew the Malay peninsula, Sumatra, Java, Bali, Lombok, Timor, the Moluccas, Celebes, and Borneo. On their maps they marked the rest as unknown seas, and their scholars confessed their ignorance. 'Regarding the foreign countries of the barbarians south-east of the South Sea . . . there is no means of investigating them because of their great distance . . . Those who speak of them are unable to say anything definite, while those who say something definite cannot be trusted. Hence, I am compelled to omit them here.' So wrote Chu-Ssu-Pen in the introduction to his atlas published in Peking between 1311 and 1320.[15]

13 Translated from G. E. Rumphius: *Het Amboinsche Kruid-Boek, dat is, Beschryving van de . . . Boomen, Heesters, Kruiden . . . in Amboina en de omleggende Eylanden, . . . mitsgaders van eenige Insecten en Gedierten . . . Herbarium Amboinense* (Amsterdam, 1741), vol. 1, p. 210. See also F. De Haan: *Priangan: de Preanger-Regentschappen onder het Nederlandsch bestuur tot 1811* (Batavia, 1910-12), pt. 2, p. 367n. and A.D.A. de Kat Angelino: *Colonial Policy* (Chicago, 1931), vol. 1, pp. 190-1.

14 W. W. Rockhill: 'Notes on the Relations and Trade of China', printed in *T'oung Pao* (Leiden), vols. 15 and 16; W. Forster (ed.): *Early Travels in India* (London, 1921), p. 41, and N. J. Krom: *Hindoe-Javaansche Geschiedenis* ('s-Gravenhage, 1931), pp. 431-4.

15 W. Fuchs: 'The "Mongol Atlas" of China by Chu-Ssu-Pen and the Kuang-Yü-T'u' (Peking, 1946), p. 8. See also Ma Touan Hin: *Ethnographie des Peuples Etrangers à la Chine (XIIIe siècle)*, traduit par le Marquis de Hervey de Saint Denis (1883).

Like those of the Hindus, the Chinese descriptions of the area lapsed from fact to fantasy as soon as they reached that invisible frontier on the map beyond Timor. East of Shö-P'o, ran one of their descriptions in the thirteenth century, lies the ocean sea where the waters flow downward: there is the kingdom of women. Still further east, it continued, is the Wei-Lü, a great hole in the ocean down which the waters of the oceans of the world are drained.[16] Such knowledge was not extended either by the seven voyages of Cheng Ho between 1407 and 1431, or by information from the people doing the carrying trade for the Chinese between Java, Timor, Celebes and the Moluccas. For the aim of Cheng Ho was to keep open the sea route between south China, Java, India and Africa, rather than the exploration of unknown seas. Cheng Ho set out to perform for the Chinese what da Gama at the end of the same century did for the Portuguese: to open up a sea route to the sources of wealth.[17] It was probably not till the arrival of the Dutch that the Bugis seamen began collecting trepang, a sea-slug in great demand at the Chinese court, from the shores of the Gulf of Carpentaria. So the absence of an incentive to explore the world beyond its known limits cheated the Asian both of the discovery and the colonization of Australia, for by the time any incentive to search beyond those seas was felt, the Asian colonizing powers were impotent. In 1433 the voyages of Cheng Ho were abruptly ended by a palace revolution at the Chinese court when a rival group, which despised trade and luxury and frowned on all contact with foreign barbarians, took over from the party sponsoring Cheng Ho.[18] The Chinese domination in the Indonesian archipelago withered away on the very eve of the period in which the Portuguese in Europe were making the advances in ship-building, nautical instruments and cartography which would enable their ships to leave the coasts and sail out on to the mighty ocean. So the Chinese lost their first chance to colonize the lands in the unknown seas. Yet their legacy in the archipelago was not without its influence, for their withdrawal presented the opportunity for any other people driven by greed and by a conviction that the earth and the fullness thereof was theirs both as a fact and as part of divine intention. In the 1430s it looked as though this inheritor of the Chinese would be the Muslim merchants from Persia and the Gujerati province of India.

The spread of Islam in the Indies occurred in a piecemeal fashion. Muslim

16 On the Wei-Lü, see F. Hirth and W. W. Rockhill: *Chau-Ju-Kua* (St Petersburgh, 1911), pp. 75-9.

17 J. J. L. Duyvendak: *The True Dates of the Chinese Maritime Expeditions in the Early Fifteenth Century* (Leiden, 1939), pp. 343-9; J. J. L. Duyvendak: *China's Discovery of Africa* (London, 1949), pp. 26-8; J. V. Mills: 'Notes on Early Chinese Voyages', in *Journal of the Royal Asiatic Society of Great Britain and Ireland* (1951), pp. 3-25; W. P. Groeneveldt: *Notes on the Malay Archipelago and Malacca. Compiled from Chinese Sources* (Batavia, 1876); A. Marré: *Malais et Chinois. Coup d'oeil sur leurs relations mutuelles à l'arrivée des Portugais dans les Indes Orientales* (Paris, 1892), p. 12.

18 C. P. Fitzgerald: 'A Chinese Discovery of Australia?' published in T. I. Moore (ed.): *Australia Writes* (Melbourne, 1953); P. M. Worsley: op. cit.; and W. L. Warner: 'Malay Influence on the Aboriginal Cultures of North-Eastern Arnhem Land', in *Oceania*, vol. 2, no. 4, June 1932, p. 476 et seq.

merchants and missionaries had arrived in west Java by the end of the eleventh century. From that time until 1600 the history of the Indies was in part the story of conversion, sometimes by persuasion and sometimes by force, to the religion of Islam. Political power followed in the wake of trade and religion, beginning with the creation of the Mohammedan kingdoms in Malacca and Java in the fifteenth century, and in the Moluccas early in the sixteenth century, with a long bloody war of attrition during that century to establish a Mohammedan kingdom at Macassar. This brought them to the frontiers of civilization, from which, if they had pushed further in search of gold or spices or fragrant woods, or souls for Islam, they would have moved on into New Guinea and from there across to the north coasts of Australia.[19] They had begun to do this just when the coming of the European ended the spread of Islam, for when Torres first sailed through the strait which still bears his name, he met Moors in west New Guinea.[20] That was in 1607. This marked the limits of the Muslim expansion and knowledge of the area.

Like his predecessors, the Hindu and the Chinese, the Muslim lapsed into fantasy when he described the world south and east of the line between civilization and barbarism. Before 1400 their sailors referred to it as Dedjdal or the kingdom of Antichrist. As late as 1554 they were still circulating stories calculated to deter their sailors from the waters to the south and south-east of Java, for there, according to one of their manuals for seamen, in the Mohit, or the ocean, was an island called Wak Wak on which a fruit in the shape of a human skull grew. As soon as the fruit ripened it fell to the ground, when a voice came forth from the skull crying 'Wak Wak'. The power of God, ran the refrain at the end of the story, is limitless: God, the Lord, is all-powerful.[21] So the Muslims took over the old Hindu story of Geruda and embroidered it with a puff for Allah. Yet these terrors of Geruda, of the kingdom of women, of Dedjdal, or of Wak Wak, melted as mists before the rising sun when improvements in ship-building, in aids to navigation and cartography, inspired the confidence to leave the coasts. By the time such changes had occurred, the Muslim had been superseded in the area by the Portuguese and the Dutch. The material weakness of the Asian states, their lack of sea power, together with the long and bloody struggle between Hindu and Muslim, created the conditions for the success of the European in the archipelago. One of the by-products of this was the coming of European civilization to Australia. So the internal history of the Asian states explains why

19 W. F. Stutterheim: *De Islam en zijn Komst in den Archipel* (Batavia, 1935).

20 Letter by L. V. de Torres to His Majesty, Manilla, 12 July 1607. Printed in C. Markham (ed.): *The Voyages of Pedro Fernandez de Quiros, 1595-1606* (Hakluyt Society, London, 1904), vol. 2, pp. 462-6.

21 For the text of the Mohit, see G. Ferrand (ed.): *Rélations, Voyages et Textes Géographiques Arabes, Persans et Turks Rélatifs à l'Extrême-Orient* (Paris, 1914), pp. 511-14. For the Muslim merchants as seamen and explorers, see G. T. Hourani: *Arab Seafaring in the Indian Ocean in Ancient and Early Mediaeval Times* (Princeton, 1951); G. Ferrand: 'L'élément persan', *Le Journal Asiatique* (1924), vol. 204; the articles on 'Shihab/al/din' and 'Sulaiman/al/majri' in the *Encyclopaedia of Islam*; P. K. Hitti: *History of the Arabs* (London, 1951); and M. J. de Goejoed: *Bibliotheca Geographorum Arabicorum* (Lugduni Batavorum, 1870-85).

Hindu, Chinese and Muslim did not cross that line between civilization and barbarism, just as it explains in part why not only the discovery, but also the first permanent occupation of Australia since the ice age was begun by Europeans.[22]

Like the Hindus and the Muslims, the Europeans were searching for spices, gold, and fragrant woods, as well as for souls for the true religion. Like the Hindus and the Muslims, too, the first European accounts of the area in the first century were ill-informed, and described the Malayan archipelago as the end of the habitable world. They called it an island opposite the mouth of the Ganges, adding that the regions beyond were either difficult of access because of their severe winters and great cold, or else could not be sought out because of the influence of the gods.[23] By the third century, the Europeans had copied from the Hindu the habit of reporting the fantasies about those people who lived beyond the boundaries of civilization. They wrote a delightful story of a people not more than one cubit high, with ears as large and long as themselves, one of which served for a mattress, and the other for bed clothes.[24] By the end of the thirteenth century, travellers' reports, especially those of Marco Polo, enabled their cartographers to trace a crude sketch of the islands which whetted the appetites of those interested in material gain. For Polo had written of a country abounding with rich commodities, of quantities of gold exceeding all calculation and belief, of a land where it was possible to obtain the greatest part of the spices distributed throughout the world. Polo had written enthusiastically also of a land to the south of Java, which he called Lochac or Beach.[25] When the Europeans investigated the area beyond the habitable world, the area south and east of the line from Timor through the Moluccas to Macassar, they were searching for Lochac —the islands of gold.

There were, however, two differences between the European discussion and the Asian. In the European discussion the speculation about the lands to the south or south-east of Java became tangled up and even confounded with the search for a south land, a *terra australis incognita*. The idea of a *terra australis* was as old as Pythagoras, and accepted by Greek and Roman writers who lent the authority of their name to the idea by placing the words 'terra australis incognita' on land to the south of Africa, India and Asia.[26] Then for a few centuries, they relied too literally on holy scripture for their ideas on the unknown parts of the world; Augustine had dismissed the idea of an unknown southern continent by reminding his readers that scripture said nothing of Adam's descendants in a 'terra australis', while the monk Cosmas in the sixth century dismissed the theory as blasphemous because it made Christ

[22] G. Coedes: *Les Etats Hindouisés d'Indochine et d'Indonésie* (Paris, 1948), p. 419.

[23] W. H. Schoff (ed.): *The Periplus of the Erythraean Sea* (New York, 1912), pp. 48-9.

[24] H. L. Jones (ed.): *The Geography of Strabo* (London, 1954), vol. 7, bk. 15.

[25] *The Travels of Marco Polo*, bk. 3, chs. 7 and 8. See also C. R. Beazley: *The Dawn of Modern Geography* (London, 1897), vol. 1.

[26] For Greek ideas see W. W. Hyde: *Ancient Greek Mariners* (New York, 1947); J. O. Thomson: *The Story of Ancient Geography* (Cambridge, 1948).

a liar, and His word not in us.[27] By the twelfth century, when the church learned its geography from the Greeks and the Arabs rather than from the Old Testament, the 'terra australis incognita' began to reappear on the maps of the world.

The second difference lay in the knowledge and equipment possessed by the Europeans. For in the fifteenth century improvements in ship-building, in aids to navigation and in map-making made it possible for their ships to cross the oceans. The first to move into the Indonesian archipelago were almost untouched by curiosity about a 'terra australis', but excited by the stories of islands of gold. They were the Portuguese. Vasco da Gama reached the coast of India in 1498; by 1511 Alfonso de Albuquerque had conquered Malacca, and by the end of the same year two Portuguese ships under Antonio d'Abreu reached Banda in the Moluccas.[28] Their motives probably set the limits of their expansion. For these men were both inspired and led on to their destruction by a great dream—that by winning a monopoly of the spice trade they would destroy the abominable, ignominious and false veneration of Mohammed, the head of the vain Moorish religion, and so win infinite merit before the Most High God.[29] Albuquerque put forward a scheme to divert the Nile to the Red Sea in order to make the lands of the Grand Turk sterile, and then to capture Mecca and carry away the bones of Mohammed so that, as he put it, these being reduced publicly to ashes, the votaries of so foul a sect might be confounded.[30] Whether in this grandiose, quixotic attempt to destroy Islam and obtain the monopoly of the spice trade, to save their own souls and gain the whole world, the Portuguese seamen either stumbled on the coast of Australia, or drew on their maps the outlines of a country about which they had heard from Bugis or Banda seamen, must remain an open question.[31] In any event, the answer has little bearing on the coming of European civilization to Australia.

[27] Augustine: *The City of God*, bk. 16, ch. 9; J. W. McCrindle (ed.): *The Christian Topography of Cosmas, an Egyptian Monk* (Hakluyt Society, London, 1897), pp. 7-9, 136-7.

[28] G. Collingridge: *The Discovery of Australia* (Sydney, 1895), ch. 21.

[29] A. Cortesao (ed.): *The Suma Oriental of Tomé Pires, and the Book of Francisco Rodriques* (Hakluyt Society, London, 1944), vol. 1, p. 2.

[30] W. de G. Birch (ed.): *The Commentaries of the Great Alfonso Dalboquerque* (Hakluyt Society, London, 1875-1884), vol. 3, pp. 115-19.

[31] The case for a Portuguese discovery or knowledge may be studied in the following: G. Collingridge: op. cit.; P. Leupe: 'Kaartje van de Banda-eilanden vervaardigd door Emanuel Godinho de Eredia in 1601', in *Bijdragen tot de land, taal, en volkenkunde*, 3rd series, vol. 11, 1876; R. P. Meyjes (ed.): *De Reizen van Abel Janszoon Tasman en Franchoys Jacobszoon Visscher ter nadere ontdekking van het Zuidland in 1642/3 en 1644*, Linschoten Vereeniging ('s-Gravenhage, 1919), vol. 17, p. xxi; A. Cortesao: *Historia Expansao Portuguesa no Mundo* (Lisbon, 1939), chs. 10 and 11; R. H. Major (ed.): *Early Voyages to Terra Australis [now called Australia]* (Hakluyt Society, London, 1859); O. H. K. Spate: 'Terra Australis—Cognita?', in *Historical Studies*, vol. 8, no. 29, November, 1957.

For criticism of the Portuguese claims, see G. A. Wood: *The Discovery of Australia* (London, 1922), ch. 6.

For the legacy of the Portuguese lay not in any knowledge of Australia which they handed on to their successors, the Dutch. It lay rather in their behaviour in the Indonesian archipelago, in all the behaviour to which they were driven by their greed as well as their vision of themselves as the intrepid soldiers of Christ and as the vessels for the destruction of a rival religion. They were men stained by sin, men moved by gigantic forces of good and evil, men who were tormented by the prospect that eternal damnation, and not infinite merit before the Most High God might be the prize for their behaviour in this world. Driven as they were by such religious zeal, by a dream of one fold and one shepherd for the whole of mankind, they committed deeds which to those who did not share such an aspiration stained the reputation of Catholic Christendom. The Muslim was disgusted by the apparent worship of idols, and the God eating. The Muslim was horrified by the use of the Inquisition against low-caste 'converts' on the west coast of India who had lapsed back into Hindu beliefs or practices. It seemed to him monstrous that numbers of them were consigned to the flames, and piously consigned to eternal damnation for acts of the greatest simplicity and folly.[32] The Muslim was appalled, too, by the deeds of cruelty against the Dutch heretics, by such incidents as occurred at Tidore in the Moluccas in 1599 when Portuguese seamen first cut off the arms, then the legs, and then split open the heads of some Dutch seamen who were contesting their monopoly of the spice trade as well as endangering the eternal salvation of the inhabitants.[33] It was the memory of such supercilious intolerance that survived, rather than those deeds of compassion or heroism inspired by the image of Christ in their hearts; and by one of those droll results in human history the immediate result of all their sound and fury was to prepare the way for the successes of the Dutch heretics by weakening the Muslim states in the archipelago.

This contribution of the Portuguese did not end the association of Catholic Christendom with the coming of European civilization to Australia. In 1519 a Portuguese, Magellan, in the service of the king of Spain, sailed from Seville to find a route to the wealth of China and the Indies round the south of America, as well as to contribute to the glory of Almighty God and His church by converting barbarous nations to the Christian faith. To the single-mindedness of Magellan, and to the faith which sustained him against mutiny and terrible privations till he found a strait into the Pacific, only the poets can testify. In that moment of victory when the flagship the *Vittoria* swept out on to that 'very vast sea', the captain-general began to cry, and he gave the name of Cape of Desire to this cape as a thing which had been much desired for a long time. After they entered the Pacific, they remained for three months and twenty days without taking in provisions, and believed that if Our Lord and His Mother had not aided them with good weather they would all have died of hunger, for, in the words of the priest who wrote down their experiences in words befitting the majesty of their achievement,

[32] J. H. Grose: *A Voyage to the East Indies* (London, 1766), vol. 1, p. 166.

[33] F. C. Wieder (ed.): *De Reis van Mahu en de Cordes door de Straat van Magalhaes naar Zuid-Amerika en Japan, 1598-1600* ('s-Gravenhage, 1923-5), vol. 1, pp. 303-12.

'I think that never man will undertake to perform such a voyage.' For they were men of faith. They had opened up a new route to the wealth of Asia; they had opened a route from which to search for new lands, and later for a 'terra australis', as Drake, Cavendish, Schouten, Le Maire, Roggeveen, Byron, Anson, Wallis, Carteret and Cook followed in their train. For just as the discovery of the north and west coasts of Australia was a by-product of European interest in the Indies, the discovery of the east coast was a long-term by-product of Magellan's voyage.[34] Yet neither of these discoveries was made by Catholic Christendom, for in the year that Magellan's blood was staining the sands in an island of the Philippines, the unity of Christendom was sundered. Just as the Portuguese had wasted their substance attempting to destroy the horrid sect of Mohammed, so much of the wealth, the energy and the talent of Christendom in Spain was drained by the decision of Charles V to stake his lands, his friends, his body, his blood, his life and his soul so that he and the 'noble German nation' would not be for ever disgraced by the survival of heresy.[35] Yet in the resurgence of vigour and the missionary enthusiasm stimulated by that challenge, Catholic Christendom came close to the discovery of Australia.

Between 1559 and 1607 the Spaniards based on Lima in Peru made a series of voyages in the west and south Pacific in which the hopes of finding wealthy lands close to the Indies were tangled up with the quest for a 'terra australis', a desire to win souls for Christ, and a terror lest the poison of heresy should arrive in those seas before them. As early as 1526 one of their seamen, Saavedra, had discovered the north coast of New Guinea on a return journey from Tidore in the Moluccas, and he had reported the country to abound in gold.[36] This fitted in with the Inca legend which the Spaniards picked up in Peru of two rich islands due west of Lima visited by their legendary folk-hero.[37] It also fitted in with the ideas their seamen and officials were absorbing from their geographers, who had produced their reasons for postulating a south land, which it was assumed must be wealthy. The men of God testified also that both sacred writ and philosophical reasoning pointed to there being as great a surface of land uncovered in the southern hemisphere as in the northern. Their religious expectations were to enlighten and convert to Christianity all infidels, and to lead them as labourers into the vineyard of their Lord.[38] By 1580 the spread of heresy in Europe had enlivened this religious motive with a sense of urgency, for by then all true

34 J. A. Robertson (ed.): *Magellan's Voyage around the World* (Cleveland, 1907); J. C. Beaglehole: *The Exploration of the Pacific* (London, 1934); L. Lee: *The Voyage of Magellan* (London, 1948).

35 Quoted in R. N. Bainton: *Here I Stand* (Mentor Books, New York, 1950), p. 145.

36 For Spanish voyages, see J. Burney: *A Chronological History of the Discoveries in the South Seas or Pacific Ocean* (London, 1803-17); C. Markham: *Progress of Discovery on the Coasts of New Guinea* (London, 1884); G. Greenwood: *Early American-Australian Relations* (Melbourne, 1944), ch. 1.

37 J. C. Beaglehole: op. cit., p. 48.

38 Amherst of Hackney and B. Thomson (eds.): *The Discovery of the Solomon Islands by Alvaro de Mendaña* (Hakluyt Society, London, 1901), vol. 1, pp. 3-5.

believers were tormented by the fear that the English and Dutch heretics would infect with the depravity of their apostasy countless number of Gentiles in the south seas.[39]

So for wealth, for power, for all the pomps and vanities of this world, but above all that the people in the south seas walking in darkness might see a pure light, not a light smutted by the pernicious poisons of Luther and Calvin, Mendana sailed out on to the high seas from Callao in Peru in 1567, and steered west-south-west over strange and perilous seas. Like Magellan, Mendana believed it was God who released them from perils through the intercession of His Blessed Mother whom they ever called upon to intercede for them. So they sailed west, with the crew becoming restless, as the days passed without a trace of the islands of gold, for they shared the greed, but not the vision of the men in high places. They wanted the filthy lucre, but not the agony, not the physical hardships inseparable from their mission. On 7 February 1568 they discovered a group of islands, later called the Solomons, Mendana naming the one where they anchored Santa Ysabel.[40] There, they held a council to which Mendana put the case for sailing south in search of the 'terra australis'. But the pilots, the men looking for the worldly satisfactions, voted him down. So they turned for Mexico, ensuring for Mendana the lesser honour and distinction of being the first of those who might have discovered the east coast of Australia. In 1595 he won second place in the same roll of honour, for in that year he sailed again in search of the islands of gold, of lands for his Catholic Majesty, of souls for Christ and His Church; but that land or lands which the men of science and the men of God, let alone the authority of Inca legend, had assured him were surely there, eluded him as they eluded all the searchers, whatever their faith or persuasion, till the mighty Cook. For by an extraordinary dispensation of fate those who searched by sailing west from Callao were destined to lose heart in the islands which dot that vast expanse of sea between the Marquesas and the Solomons, while those who searched after passing through the straits of Magellan were driven by mountainous seas, unfavourable winds and currents, to follow the northern or the central route across the Pacific.[41]

The last of the searchers from Callao was Pedro Ferdandez de Quiros. He was one of the flowers of the Catholic reformation, part of that movement of religious idealism and of missionary fervour which strengthened the church after the disasters of Luther and Calvin. It was a movement which inspired Francis Xavier as a most loving brother wholly in Christ to spread the holy faith in India, in Malacca, in Macao, even as far as Japan,[42] which inspired

[39] A Memorial Addressed To His Catholic Majesty Philip The Third, King of Spain, by Dr. Juan Luis Arras, Respecting the Exploration, Colonisation, and Conversion Of The Southern Land. Printed in R. H. Major (ed.): op. cit., pp. 1-3.

[40] Amherst of Hackney and B. Thomson (eds.): op. cit., vol. 1, p. 111.

[41] For the two voyages of Mendana see Amherst of Hackney and B. Thomson (eds.): op. cit.; J. C. Beaglehole: op. cit., chs. 3-4; and G. Greenwood: op. cit., pp. 15-26.

[42] C. R. Boxer: *The Christian Century in Japan 1549-1650* (Berkeley, 1951), pp. 401-5.

the Jesuit missionaries to endure the most unspeakable tortures at the hands
of the Indians in North America,[43] and inspired too the Franciscan missionaries in Central and South America.[44] Quiros was a Portuguese, born in the
territory of Evoral about the year 1565, but he spent most of his life in the
service of Spain. He had sailed with Mendana as pilot major on the voyage
of 1595. From his youth he seems to have been caught up in the missionary
enthusiasm of the age. He began to believe that he had been singled out by
God as the vessel through whom the inhabitants of 'terra australis' would be
received into the true church, and that 'terra australis' would be Austrialia
del Espiritu Santo—a land dedicated to the Holy Spirit. In 1600 he had made
his pilgrimage to Rome for inspiration; he had knelt on each step of the Santa
Scala, not tormented as Luther had been in 1510, to know 'whether it is so'.
He had knelt in joy and hope in St Peter's where he accepted the pomp and
display as appropriate to the greater glory of God and his church. He had
been received reverently by Clement VIII who blessed him, and conceded
many graces and indulgences to all who sailed with him, and, presented him
with some rosaries which had received the papal blessing as well as a piece
of the true cross.[45]

After his return to Callao he decorated the prows of his ships to symbolize
the missionary purpose, placing on each a carved statue of St Peter with his
feet resting on a globe. Just as Christ had named Peter the rock on which He
would build His church, against which the gates of hell should not prevail, so
Peter's successor, in the mind of Quiros, would be the head of all that immense
number of idolaters who, in those vast and remote provinces, were buried in
the darkness of blind ignorance. For the greater glory of the same Lord he
was anxious to win the race against the Protestants to the Indies and the south
seas, to confound those powers of false doctrine.[46] He was essentially a gentle
spirit, one of God's chosen vessels bringing the gift of his holy faith. For
Quiros, all men were the adopted children of God. Yet despite the faith,
despite the knowledge and the experience, he lacked the quality to excite awe
and reverence from his crew, for they never saw him as their mirror, light
and true guide. He was no more successful than Mendana in selecting a crew
to understand, let alone share, his aspirations. As his second-in-command
he appointed Luis Viez de Torres, a Portuguese, about whose life nothing is
known except his part in this voyage.[47]

On the eve of their departure Quiros went as a pilgrim to the virgin of
Loreto to pray that she would take so important a voyage under her protection.
On 21 December 1605, after all had taken the sacrament and gained the jubilee
promised by the Pope to those who undertook the voyage, they sailed out
on to the high seas from Callao. With that abundance of good will conferred
by their desire to serve God and spread the holy Catholic faith, and aggrandize

43 F. Parkman: 'Pioneers of France in the New World', in *Works* (Boston, 1900-1).
44 C. Markham (ed.): *The Voyages of Pedro Fernandez de Quiros.*
45 Article on 'Quiros' in *Enciclopedia Italiana* (1949); and C. Markham (ed.):
The Voyages of Pedro Fernandez de Quiros, vol. 1, pp. 163-5.
46 C. Markham (ed.): *The Voyages of Pedro Fernandez de Quiros*, vol. 2, p. 410.
47 See the article on Luis Vaez de Torres in the *Enciclopedia Italiana* (1949).

the royal crown of the king their lord, all seemed easy to them—as they believed that for them the mountains would be moved, the seas made calm, and the winds hushed.[48] They sailed west till they reached a harbour in the New Hebrides, which Quiros in the first flush of the excitement named Austrialia del Espiritu Santo—a name which, together with the errors in measuring longitude, created confusion for posterity when it plotted his voyage, and even seduced men of scholarship and learning to argue that he had landed on the east coast of Australia.[49] But Quiros did not share this delusion: for in between the religious exercises and festivals at Austrialia del Espiritu, carried on with such fervour and extravagance that all protestant historians and secular humanists have tended to treat him with a mixture of disdain and contempt as a mountebank or as a lesson in the follies of religious fanaticism,[50] Quiros was preoccupied with what to do next. With a pettiness unworthy of the cause to which he was dedicated, he began to blame earlier delays in Callao which, he argued, were robbing him of the power of following up so great an enterprise. He spoke too of the great contrary winds they would encounter if they sailed south in search of the south land, of how their present position was unknown, and how little water they had left and no meat. Then with a majestic sweep he reminded himself of his subjection to the ordinances of God, His high and secret decrees, as well as the wishes of man. Whatever it was, whether obedience to the inscrutable decrees of providence or a use of the divine commands to justify the promptings of the heart, Quiros announced in grief and sorrow that all was ended. So they sailed for home and arrived at Acapulco in Mexico on 23 November 1606 where Quiros gave part of the true cross to the priest who took it into the church and fastened it to the high altar to the ringing of bells, the sound of trumpets and the discharge of guns. All the people shouted their joy. But Quiros had hoped to go to Rome to tell the Pope that this part of the true cross had been raised in Austrialia del Espiritu Santo in honour of the Catholic Church. Fate, however, had robbed

[48] C. Markham (ed.): *The Voyages of Pedro Fernandez de Quiros*, vol. 2, pp. 323-4.

[49] The site of Austrialia del Espiritu Santo was cleared up by Cook on his second voyage. He also named the group of islands the New Hebrides. The idea that Quiros had landed on the east coast lingered in Catholic circles, and was revived by Cardinal Moran, the Catholic Archbishop of Sydney. Four times, between 1895 and 1907, he asserted that Quiros had discovered Australia. He gave his authority a wider currency by an ambiguous sentence in his *History of the Catholic Church in Australasia* (Sydney, 1895), p. 2, which could be construed as making Quiros the discoverer. Until the refutation of Dr Moran's views by E. O'Brien, children in Catholic schools were taught that Quiros discovered Australia, while in the Protestant and state schools the honour was given to the Dutch—to Jansz or Hartog—O'Brien thus followed Cook not only in his opinion of the site of Austrialia del Espiritu Santo but also in his estimate of the significance of the Dutch. So Quiros lost that sort of pre-eminence, though in recent decades the poets have rightly conferred on him another distinction. See D. Stewart: 'Terra Australis' in *Sun Orchids and other Poems* (Sydney, 1952), and J. McAuley: 'Belmonte's prologue to the 1606 Voyage of Quiros to Terra Australis' in N. Keesing (ed.): *Australian Poetry, 1959* (Sydney, 1959).

[50] C. Markham (ed.): *The Voyages of Pedro Fernandez de Quiros*, vol. 1, p. 258 et seq.; G. A. Wood: op. cit., p. 173 et seq.

him of this triumph. So in Acapulco he gave many thanks to God through whose goodness he hoped to return the cross to the place whence it came.[51] Fate cheated him of that too, though not of the glory of his ideas.

At the end of June 1607 the second-in-command, Torres, sailed from Austrialia del Espiritu Santo for Manila, proposing to call at the Moluccas on the way, and in doing so reached the east coast of New Guinea. There he found he could not weather the east point. So he coasted along to the westward on the south side, thus becoming the first European to sail along the south coast of New Guinea from the east. For before Torres, the Spaniards using the central route from Callao to the Moluccas had sailed along the north coast of New Guinea. Yet from the matter-of-fact, brief way in which Torres referred to the change it is clear that it had nothing to do with hopes of discovering new land. His mind was on other things. What he noticed was the archipelago of islands without number; he noticed too that they were inhabited by black people, very corpulent and naked, their weapons being lances, arrows and clubs of stone, which he found ill-fashioned. Further to the west he noticed a different people, a people who were better adorned, who used arrows, darts, large shields, and sticks of bamboo filled with lime, with which they blinded their enemies. When they reached the western extremity of New Guinea they found iron, Chinese bells and other things by which they knew they were near the Moluccas. They also found Mohammedans who were clothed, men who used artillery, falconets, swivel guns and arquebuses. These men, Torres reported, were conquering the people, who were called Papuas, and preaching to them the sect of Mohammed. For by 1607 Islam had reached the western end of New Guinea. So had another mighty conqueror—the Dutch.

The Moors had told Torres of Dutch ships, and added, with understandable ignorance, that none of them had come as far as New Guinea. In the previous year, however, a small Dutch ship had coasted along the south coast of New Guinea from the west in search of the same things as were interesting Torres —much gold and other good things such as pepper and nutmegs. So in 1606-7 Islam, Catholic Christendom and the Protestants had moved into the strait between New Guinea and Australia. But Torres sailed on to the Moluccas, then on to the Philippines, never once wondering about the world to the south of those islands without number, but simply tossing off the observation: 'I doubt if in ten years could be examined the coasts of all the islands we descried.'[52]

[51] C. Markham (ed.): *The Voyages of Pedro Fernandez de Quiros*, vol. 1, pp. 309-10.

[52] Letter by Luis Vaez de Torres to His Majesty, Manilla, 12 July 1607. Printed in C. Markham (ed.): *The Voyages of Pedro Fernandez de Quiros*, vol. 2, pp. 462-6. The subsequent history of this letter affected the later history of the discovery of Australia. At Madras in the 1760s Alexander Dalrymple copied an account of the voyage of Torres from W. Roberts, who had been a supercargo to Manila. Then, in London, in 1767 Dalrymple published in his *An Account of the Discoveries made in the South Pacifick Ocean, Previous to 1764*, a map tracing the course of Torres. This work was seen by Banks before Cook sailed on the *Endeavour* in 1768. The text of the Torres letter was published in R. H. Major: op. cit. For the use of the Dalrymple map of Torres' voyage by Cook, see J. C. Beaglehole (ed.): *The Journals*

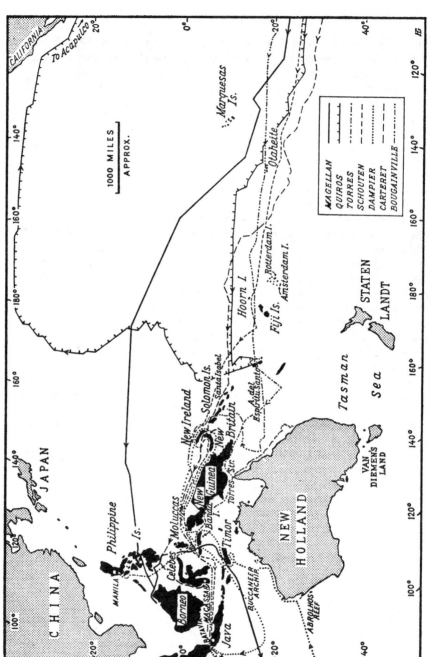

1 Pacific Voyages before Cook

The contribution of Catholic Christendom to the search for a south land was drawing to a close. Almost from the moment he returned, things began to go wrong for Quiros. The men in high places in New Spain passed him by. In Madrid, where he went for finance and support, his enemies gratified their evil passions by vilifying him. One told the council that such low and mendacious fellows ought to be of no account; another referred to him as a liar and a fraud.[53] In Madrid he began a paper war, pouring out memorial after memorial, having earlier ones printed, and then, as he sank further into poverty, copying them by hand. To the end he was sustained by the same dream of a south land dedicated to the Holy Spirit; to the end he was plagued by the fear lest the sowers of false doctrine would win the race. He had his supporters among the Franciscan monks who shared his fear that the English and the Dutch heretics would sow there the most pernicious poisons of their apostasy. The officials of Madrid, however, considered Quiros not as a dreamer, a man with a vision, but as a nuisance, a pest to be humoured, to be fobbed off with those evasions, those verbal tricks with which the men in black have generally defeated in the end the man with the big idea. Only an instruction from the council in Madrid could give Quiros another chance, but the very heresy which gave Quiros his sense of desperate urgency, was diverting much of the attention, the energy and the wealth at the disposal of the officials who might have helped him. At last, on 21 October 1614, he received a certificate from the king that he was to be equipped to sail from Callao to the southern regions, but the official who drafted this letter wrote another confidential one telling the officials in New Spain to ignore the one on which Quiros was pinning his hopes and his vision.[54] So Quiros died, lonely and defeated, at Panama in 1615, on his way to Callao. Years later, officials raised a monument to the man whom their spiritual ancestors had destroyed. Before he died he adopted the language of the prophets of the Old Testament to predict the future of a south land should Catholic Christendom vacate the field to the Dutch and English heretics, prophesying that they would sow false doctrine, convert all the blessings into great evils, and bring everything to ruin.[55]

For a season it looked as though Catholic Christendom had disquieted itself in vain, that in the search for and the use of a south land, all had been lost. For when the Europeans met under the gum-tree in February 1788 for their first ceremony in Australia, the dream of the lonely Portuguese of a land dedicated to the Holy Spirit did not sustain the mind of any of the speakers who laid bare their hearts on that day. By the end of the nineteenth century,

of Captain James Cook on his Voyages of Discovery (C.U.P. for Hakluyt Society, 1955), pp. iii, clxii. For a discussion of the course followed by Torres, see F. J. Bayldon: 'Voyage of Luis Vaez de Torres from the New Hebrides to the Moluccas, June to November 1606', in R.A.H.S., *J. & P.*, vol. 11, pt. 3, 1926.

[53] C. Markham: *The Voyages of Pedro Fernandez de Quiros*, vol. 1, pp. 310, and 512-13.

[54] Ibid., vol. 1, pp. 320-1.

[55] Eighth Memorial submitted to His Majesty by Captain Pedro Fernandez de Quiros on the Subject of his Discoveries. Quoted in C. Markham: *The Voyages of Pedro Fernandez de Quiros*, vol. 2, pp. 484-6.

the sons of the enlightenment, the believers in progress, the believers in material well-being for all, and the believers in universal brotherhood, were shouting to their fellow-countrymen that heaven and hell were priests' inventions and that they should trust the brotherhood of man. To them the vision which had sustained Quiros and the faithful for a thousand years and more seemed a chimera, to sustain man in the vale of tears before the enlightenment revealed his capacity for better things.[56]

[56] See also C. Kelly: *The Terra Australis: a Franciscan Quest* (New York, 1948); P. F. Moran: *The Discovery of Australia by De Quiros in the year 1606* (Sydney, 1906). There are useful articles on Torres and Quiros in the *Enciclopedia Italiana* (1949). There is no article on Quiros in the *Encyclopaedia Britannica* or *Chambers Encyclopaedia*, or *Der Grosse Brockhaus*. There is a brief article on him in *Larousse*, and the *Bolshaya Sovietskaya Entsiklopediya* has a useful article on his achievements, but refrains from mentioning his vision of a land dedicated to the Holy Spirit.

2

THE CONTRIBUTION OF THE
PROTESTANTS

THE ENGLISH and the Dutch Protestants were the bridge from the men of Trent to the men of 1789, from the intrepid soldiers of Christ to the sons of enlightenment. Where the soldiers of Christ testified to their desire to win souls for heaven and kingdoms for the princes of this world by discovering a south land, the Protestants saw themselves as restorers of the pristine purity of Christ's Church, men chosen by God to enlarge the bounds of the Christian religion, and to benefit trade.[1] They differed, however, from their Catholic predecessors in their conception of both God and man. To the Calvinist, the whole meaning of life was contained in two propositions in the Psalms: 'Thou art God from everlasting, and world without end. Thou turnest man to destruction: again thou sayest, Come again, ye children of men.'[2] For the Calvinist was obsessed with human depravity, obsessed with the reminder in the Book of Job of how abominable and filthy is man who drinketh iniquity like water.[3] While the motivation of the Catholic had been a mixture of greed and religious glory, with the fear of eternal damnation taking such possession of their hearts as to make them reckless of doom and destruction in this world, the Calvinists, though equally zealous for the prize of salvation, saw greed as a force with which to lay up for themselves treasures both in heaven and earth.

The Portuguese Catholics spoke of infinite merit: the Dutch Calvinists spoke of uncommonly large profit. There was something sensuous and elemental in their discussion of the uses to which they would put the spices from the Moluccas.[4] They wanted pepper for food and for a physic, ginger because it made a man go easily to the stool and restored a man's strength that is decayed, and cloves because they strengthened the liver, the mouth and the heart, furthered digestion, procured evacuation of the urine, and being put into the eyes preserved the sight, and four drams being drunk with milk, procured lust.

The early reputation of Catholic Christendom in the Indonesian archipelago was darkened by deeds of brutality and violence and by an element of supercilious religious intolerance. The behaviour of the early Protestants was tainted by sectarian prejudice. For they too had their fear—that the minds of the

---

[1] A. L. Rowse: *Sir Richard Grenville of the Revenge* (London, 1937), ch. 5.

[2] Psalm 90, vs. 2-3.

[3] Job, ch. 15, vs. 16.

[4] P. A. Tiele and A. C. Burnell (eds.): *The Voyage of John Huyghen van Linschoten to the East Indies* (Hakluyt Society, London, 1885), vol. 2, pp. 75-94.

people in the south seas might be poisoned by the unnatural and incredible absurdities of papistry. To them Catholic Christendom had been disgraced by what they called the moral depravity of the papists, who encouraged not only whoredom, but also the filthiness of Sodom from which the Pope, in the words of the Protestant clergyman who accompanied Drake on his voyage round the world in 1578, sucked no small advantage. Catholic Christendom had been disgraced too by the Pope's correction of Christ's work, that, as the same clergyman put it, the Pope and his antichristian bishops laboured with tooth and nail to deface the glory of God and to shut up in darkness the light of the gospel.[5] Such dark and monstrous prejudices soon informed their principles of behaviour. When the same clergyman on Drake's ship, the *Pelican*, first saw the natives of Patagonia, he was disgusted by one of their religious practices which consisted in offering backwards a loathsome sacrifice of their excrements to their god, accompanied by a motion of their bodies most loathsome to their beholders. Yet, as an illustration of the depth of his loathing for popery, he professed to prefer them to the papists in their religion.[6]

They were ferocious in their behaviour to each other. Whoever drew a knife in anger on a Dutch ship, in order to do bodily harm, even without injuring anybody, was nailed to the mast with a knife through his hand, and stood there until he pulled it through himself. Whoever injured anyone was keel-hauled, and forfeited six months' wages.[7] They were ferocious too in their behaviour to their rivals for the spice trade; in 1623, when the Dutch captured the English garrison at Ambon, they applied the water torture to them till their entrails burst out of their noses, their mouths and their eyes. Then they applied the fire torture to the bottoms of their feet, to their elbows, to the palms of their hands, and under their arm-pits, as worthy pupils of their own doctrine of human depravity.[8]

They were equally ferocious in their behaviour to the Catholics. At Valparaiso in Chile in 1599, for example, the Dutch burned houses and churches, and knocked off the heads of the popish images crying, 'Down go the gods of the Spaniards.'[9] Yet, unlike the Portuguese, they were not tainted by that divinely inspired folly of squandering their material resources in pursuing Muslims; they were prepared to grant toleration to the Muslim, because holy wars were not compatible with uncommonly large profit. When the Protestant

[5] R. C. Temple (ed.): *The World Encompassed by Sir Francis Drake* (London, 1926), pp. 9-10.

[6] Ibid., pp. 91-2.

[7] Articles and Ordinances issued by Prince Mauritius of Orange-Nassau for the governance of ships sailing to the East Indies. Translated from J. A. van der Chijs: *Geschiedenis der Stichting van de Vereenigde Oost Indische Compagnie* (Leiden, 1857), p. 180.

[8] John Beaumont: *Dutch Alliances: or a Plain proof of their Observance of treaties exemplify'd in the particulars of their inhuman treatment of their friends and confederates the English, at Amboyna, etc.* (London, 1712), pp. 38-9. For an example of similar behaviour by the English in 1601, this time the cruelties being practised against a Javanese, see R. Kerr (ed.): *A General History and Collection of Voyages and Travels . . .* (Edinburgh, 1811-24), vol. 8, pp. 158-9.

[9] R. Kerr: op. cit., vol. 10, p. 122.

chaplains in Batavia reminded the Dutch Governor-General that the law of Moses forbade the toleration of non-Christian religions, he replied that the laws of the old Jewish republics had no force in the territory of the Dutch East India Company.[10]

For they had all the confidence of men of achievement. In 1596 the first Dutch trading party had arrived at Djakarta; by 1600 they had traded with Atjeh, the Moluccas, Brunei in Borneo, Banda and Ambon. By 1606 they had stumbled on the north coast of Australia. By 1644 they were able to draw in outline the coast from Cape York peninsula to the eastern end of the Great Australian Bight, the southern tip of Tasmania, and part of the west coast of both the north and south islands of New Zealand. By their contemporaries they were despised and derided as are most men to whom success comes too quickly, especially men like the Dutch who did not pause to cloak their greed with the garb of spiritual aspiration. The inhabitants of the Indies despised them as merchants: the Chinese in Djakarta ridiculed them as red haired barbarians.[11]

For those who were puzzled by the problem of deserts, the distribution of rewards and prizes in this world, there was perhaps a stern justice in what the Dutch discovered in Australia. For these men who asked the Lord to forgive those who compromised the profits of the Company, because they did not practise human forgiveness for such folly, found in Australia a land of flies and sand and savages.[12] Of the four ways in which the Dutch contributed to the bringing of civilization to Australia—the search for islands of gold from the Indies, the use of a new sailing route to the Indies, the search for a 'terra australis', and teaching the Bugis seamen how to use their aids to navigation—every one of them was tinged by their insatiable covetousness.

The whole story of the Dutch contribution was contained in the scrappy accounts which have survived of the first of their seamen to sight the coast of Australia. In November 1605, the yacht *Duyfken* (Little Dove), Captain Willem Jansz, supercargo Jan Rosengeyn, sailed from Bantam for the discovery of the land called Nova Guinea which, the Dutch had been told, afforded great store of gold. They called at the islands of Key and Arou, then sailed along two hundred and twenty odd miles of the undiscovered south coast of New Guinea till they reached a cape to which they gave the name Cape Keerweer

---

10 Quoted in B. H. M. Vlekke: *Nusantara: A History of the East Indian Archipelago* (Harvard, 1945), p. 132. For an example of the Dutch granting religious toleration to the Muslims, see J. E. Heeres and F. W. Stapel: *Corpus Diplomaticum Neerlando-Indicum* ('s-Gravenhage, 1907-38), vol. 1, p. 31. See also J. Mooij: *Geschiedenis der Protestantse kerk in Nederlandsch Indië* (Weltevreden, 1923-31).

11 For the reactions of some of the inhabitants of the Indies to the Dutch, see F. De Haan: *Priangan: de Preanger-Regentschappen onder het Nederlandsch bestuur tot 1811* (Batavia, 1910-12), vol. 3.

12 Letter by J. P. Coen to Peter Direx Deucht, 25 May 1617: 'Andre dienst hadden wy van't *Wapen van Amsterdam* verhoopt. Dit is nu de tweede dutreys, daervan de Compagnie een irreparabile schade soude connen overcomen. De Heere wil't degene vergeven, die daervan oorsaecke sijn' (H. T. Colenbrander (ed.): *Jan Petersen Coen: Bescheiden omtrent zijn Bedrijf in Indie* ('s-Gravenhage, 1919-23), vol. 2, p. 247).

(Turn Again). They did not know then that this cape was not part of the island of New Guinea, but part of a land to which no civilized people had up till then given a name—that it was part of Australia. On the coast of New Guinea they had sent their men on shore to entreat of trade, and nine of their number were killed by heathen man-eaters. So, as they put it, they were constrained to return, finding no good to be done there. Although it is obscure whether these words referred to New Guinea or Cape Keerweer, they could be taken as the first cry of anguish and despair of the Dutch on seeing the land and the people of Australia.[13] By an odd irony of history, news of this voyage was reported to the Dutch at Bantam by skipper Tingall, a clingman from Banda. So an Asian reported first of all on a country in which in time his people would be insulted and then excluded as a menace to higher civilization.

Over the next thirty-eight years the Dutch found little to cause them to mute that first cry of despair. In 1623 they again despatched two ships from Bantam—the *Pera* and the *Arnhem*, skippers Jan Carstens and Dirck Melisz (succeeded by Colster), to search for gold on the south coast of New Guinea. Again, like the *Duyfken*, they ran on to Cape York peninsula, and followed its west coast to the mouth of a river in latitude 17' 8" S. which they called Staten River. There they landed, and fastened a wooden column to a tree with these words carved on it:[14]

Anno 1623 24 April sijn hier aen gecomen
twee jachten wegen de Hooge Mogende Heeren Staten Gen.

Again they were disenchanted by the land and its people. They were seeking a land which would afford great store of gold, and a people with whom to trade. They found a land without a single fruit-bearing tree or anything that could be eaten by man, and a people who were in general barbarians, who had no knowledge at all of gold, silver, tin, iron, lead, or copper, and even less of nutmegs, cloves and pepper. When the Dutch showed them all these things many times they showed neither enthusiasm nor disdain. Carstens concluded that they were a poor and miserable people, who appeared to value most coral and iron. So Carstens decided there was nothing in particular to be got there —just as the men on the *Duyfken* found there was no good to be done there.[15] Perhaps Quiros had disquieted himself in vain with that nightmare about the work that the sowers of false doctrine might perform in a south land.

[13] For the accounts which have survived see: J. E. Heeres: *The Part Borne by the Dutch in the Discovery of Australia, 1606-1765* (London, 1899), p. 4; and F. C. Wieder (ed.): *Monumenta Cartographica. Reproductions of unique and rare maps, plans and views in the actual size of the originals; accompanied by cartographical monographs* (The Hague, 1925-33), vol. 5, pp. 176-8 and plate 125.

[14] ('On 24 April in the year 1623 two yachts arrived here on behalf of the High and Mighty Lords of the States General'.) For the journal of Carstenz, see L. C. D. Dijk (ed.): *Mededeelingen uit het Oost-Indisch Archief*, no. 1, 'Twee togten Naar de Golf van Carpentaria: J. Carstenz, 1623' (Amsterdam, 1859), p. 39 et seq. See also J. E. Heeres: op. cit., pp. 29-30, and R. P. Meyjes (ed.): *De Reizen van Abel Janszoon Tasman en Franchoys Jacobszoon Visscher ter nadere ontdekking van het Zuidland in 1642/3 en 1644*, Linschoten Vereeniging, vol. 17, pp. xxxiii, lxxi, and 171.

[15] L. C. D. van Dijk (ed.): op. cit., pp. 41-2; and J. E. Heeres: op. cit., p. 22.

It was the same with the Dutch discovery of the west coast. As early as 1611 Captain Brouwer had tried a new route from the Cape of Good Hope to Djakarta. To use the trade winds he sailed due east from Cape Town for four thousand miles and then turned north. In October 1616 the ship *Eendracht* (Concord), skipper Dirk Hartog, using this route, ran on to the west coast of Australia in latitude 26° south, which the Dutch later called Eendrachtsland or Land van de Eendracht, then sailed north along the coast to 22° south latitude at Willem's River, and then on to Macassar where they almost certainly discussed what they had seen with the Bugis. But the records which have survived are tantalizingly brief on Eendrachtsland, merely stating they had come upon various islands which were, however, found to be uninhabited. On the conversations at Macassar history is silent, and after this journey Hartog sank again into anonymity till 1697 when the plate he had erected was discovered by Willem de Vlamingh.[16]

On 4 August 1616 the directors of the East India Company in Amsterdam instructed their captains to follow the route recommended by Captain Brouwer, and on 15 August 1617 the directors issued sailing instructions which prescribed the route to be followed by all Dutch ships sailing to the East Indies. In following this route a number of Dutch ships touched the west coast between Cape Leeuwin in the south and Willem's River in the north. One ship, *t'Gulden Seepaart* (the Golden Seahorse), skipper F. Thijssen or Thijszoon, was blown so far out of its course, early in 1627, that it missed Cape Leeuwin and sailed east as far as the islands of St Francis and St Peter at the eastern extremity of the Great Australian Bight, but the only memorial which survived of this achievement was a line on a map. Again the imagination of the historian may rove over the minds of those men doing their business in deep water, who believed that though the waves of the sea raged horribly yet the Lord which dwelt on high was mightier, who boasted in their national songs of their strength to destroy the princes of this world.[17] In such brief comments as have survived from the skippers who saw the land and its people, the note of disenchantment, the note of despair, predominated. When they came to sum up their impressions after *t'Gulden Seepaart* had discovered the south coast of the country which they had begun to call the great Southland, they wrote with a note of disappointment of how none of these discoveries had resulted in the obtaining of any considerable information respecting the situation and condition of this vast land. It was a land of barren and dangerous coasts and exceedingly savage, black, barbarian inhabitants.[18]

The one Dutch skipper who had a more intimate knowledge of the west

---

[16] J. E. Heeres: op. cit., p. 8; R. P. Meyjes: op. cit., p. xxix; J. W. Izzerman: 'Het schip De Eendracht voor Makassar in December 1616', in *Bijdragen tot de Taal, Land en Volkenkunde van Nederlandsch-Indie*, vol. 78 ('s-Gravenhage, 1922), p. 343 et seq. For 'Schipper' see *Woordenboek der nederlandse taal*, vol. 14, p. 73.

[17] For the history of and the text of the sailing instructions, see F. W. Stapel: *De Oostindische Compagnie en Australië* (Amsterdam, 1937), p. 18 et seq. For the voyages which touched on the west or south coasts, see J. E. Heeres: op. cit. For the Hessel Gerritz map see F. C. Wieder (ed.): op. cit., vol. 5, p. 177.

[18] J. E. Heeres: op. cit., p. 22.

coast had provided the detail for such a despondent generalization. After his ship, the *Batavia*, was wrecked on the Abrolhos reef in June 1629, Francois Pelsaert set out for Djakarta in a long boat with a small crew to obtain help, a voyage which took him along part of the west coast of the Southland. They were appalled by what they saw: they found no traces of running water; the higher ground was barren and unpromising, without trees, shrubs or grass, but with plenty of high ant hills in all directions; there were multitudes of flies which crept into their mouths and into their eyes; and the inhabitants ran off in terror on seeing the white man. The prospect did not please, and man seemed praeternaturally vile. Yet, despite it all, Pelsaert still wanted to know more about this vast land. So he sent two delinquents ashore—Wouter Loos and Jan Pelzroende—knowing that if they were picked up, their punishment would ultimately redound to the service of the Company, as they would give trustworthy information about those parts. For not even the flies, the barrenness, the dryness, the desolation, could shake the hope for better things. While the Dutch continued to entertain such expectations, their eye had already detected one singular thing about this land—its animals. Of these none was more singular than the kangaroo which carried and nourished its young in a pouch: here, at last, was something perfectly proportioned in the great Southland.[19]

So the Southland they knew was barren, while the land some of their merchants believed they would discover in the great south sea where their ships would obtain rich cargoes, eluded those who searched for it. These searches were of two kinds. On the one hand there was the private expedition from Amsterdam, such as the expedition of Le Maire and Schouten in 1614, which sailed round the Horn planning to look for a Southland, but winds, currents, and the great swell of the ocean soon persuaded them to leave the seas of danger and uncertain profit, and to sail for Java where they believed they would certainly trade with profit. So they discovered no Southland. Yet, in a sense, the experiences of this voyage had more lasting effects than the profits and losses of its promoters. As Calvinists they looked on all human beings as being stained by the original sin of their common ancestors. Yet in some of the islands of the Pacific, in the Hoorn Islands for example, they observed a people who appeared to have escaped the punishment of Adam, men who did not earn their daily bread in the sweat of their brows, women who did not bring forth their children in sorrow, a people indeed living a life free of care, who neither sowed nor mowed nor performed any kind of work as the earth gave them all they needed to support life. They noted, too, the terror stirred up in the natives by the presence of the white man—the natives being in constant fear lest the white men kill them and take their land.[20] Thus these Dutch Calvinists foreshadowed the mind of the European when plagued by doubt, and in so doing made the first scratch on the page which was to record some of the big themes of the European in the islands of the Pacific.

[19] J. E. Heeres: op. cit., p. 61.

[20] J. A. J. de Villiers (ed.): *The East and West Indian Mirror, being an account of Joris van Spielbergen's voyage round the world, and the Australian navigations of Jacob le Maire* (Hakluyt Society, London, 1906), pp. 213-14.

It was more fruitful to search for a Southland from their possessions in the Indonesian archipelago. From 1622 onwards all skippers on voyages of discovery from their Kasteel in Djakarta were given instructions which reproduced the mixture of motives, muddles and puzzles in their own minds. They were still chasing the elusive islands of gold and spices; they wanted more accurate information about the Southland than their sailors had yet discovered in order to avoid shipwrecks; they believed their sailors might still discover the Southland of the geographers—i.e. the 'terra australis incognita'. Meanwhile they were puzzled by the extent of the Southland that their seamen had discovered. How vast was it? Was it part of the 'terra australis' of the geographers? So, on 29 September 1622, the Governor-General of the Indies, Jan Pieterszoon Coen, issued orders to equip two yachts, the *Haring* and the *Hazewind*, to undertake a voyage and to discover as much of these lands as God Almighty would be pleased to allow.[21] But man, not God, delayed their departure, for the Dutch had more urgent business at hand. There were wars of conquest, wars against the Muslim merchants, wars against the Portuguese and against the English, which so taxed their time and their resources that the council in Batavia could spare neither yachts nor crews for another voyage of discovery.[22]

In 1642, when the way at last seemed clear, three documents were composed in Batavia on discovery in the south seas. The first was written by Franchoys Jacobsen Visscher—'Memoir touching the discovery of the Southland'—in which he urged that an expedition should be sent to plot the coast of the Southland from False Cape to Willem's River. Visscher believed as Carstens had believed that False Cape was part of the south coast of New Guinea.[23] The second document was a resolution of the council in Batavia of 1 August 1642 in which they announced their intention to send an expedition for the discovery of the supposed rich southern and eastern lands, by which they meant both searching for a 'terra australis' as well as clearing up their knowledge of the known Southland.[24] The third document was the instructions to the commander, as they put it, destined for the discovery and exploration of the unknown and known Southland, of the south-east coast of New Guinea, and the islands circumjacent.[25] This was a document on a grand scale. It began by reminding the commander how the invaluable treasures, profitable trade connections, useful trades, excellent territories, vast powers and dominions had enriched the kingdoms and crowns of Spain and Portugal as well as the numberless multitudes of blind heathen who had been introduced to the blessed light of the Christian religion. Then in language befitting both their achievements

21 The text of the Instructions by Coen is printed in J. E. Heeres: op. cit., pp. 18-21.
22 See, for example, the 'Dagh Register' (Museum, Djakarta), 6 May 1637, p. 204.
23 The text of the Visscher memoir is printed in J. E. Heeres: *Abel Janszoon Tasman's Journal of his discovery of Van Diemen's Land and New Zealand in 1642 with documents relating to his exploration of Australia in 1644 . . .* (Amsterdam, 1898), App. H. To distinguish between it and the other work by Heeres, this volume will be referred to as J. E. Heeres: *Abel Tasman.*
24 Ibid., App. D.
25 Ibid., App. E.

and their greed, it stated in measured periods their expectations from discovery in the south seas in a rehash of the ideas which were a commonplace of Dutch thinking at the time on the old 'terra australis' theme, after which the instructions slid over to the value of exploring the Southland known to their seamen, before concluding with the possibility of finding a short route from the Indies to Chile. For whenever 'terra australis' or the Southland was mentioned, the possibility of plundering the wealth of Spain in South America was never far from their minds.[26] So the commander was instructed to discover the unknown Southland, to explore the known Southland, and to discover a short route from Java to Chile.

Such instructions reflected the confusions in Dutch minds arising from what they knew and from what the old idea of 'terra australis' had taught them to expect. The detailed instructions to the commander sought the impossible: namely, how to achieve all three of these aims. When their author faced up to the problem of how a commander could both explore the known Southland, and at the same time discover a 'terra australis', he realized that it would be necessary to follow two quite different routes. Accordingly, instructions for two such routes were outlined: one was for the search for 'terra australis': the other was for the exploration of the coast of the known Southland. So the commander was instructed to do one of two things: either to sail to Mauritius, then south to latitude fifty-two or fifty-four in search of 'terra australis', then east to the longitude of New Guinea, again in search of 'terra australis', and then north. If he had followed this route he might have discovered Heard Island, but little else. By the second route, when sailing east in fifty-two to fifty-four degrees of south latitude, at the longitude of the islands of St Peter and St Francis, he could steer north to the south coast of the known Southland in the sight of these islands, and then follow the coast eastward to ascertain how far it extended, and whether the discovered Southland joined New Guinea near Cape Keerweer, or whether it was separated from it by channels or passages. In which case, the instructions concluded, by passing through one of the channels and continuing as far as Willem's River, the north coast might be conveniently explored sailing westward.[27] Again, as with Magellan, a tremendous 'if' leaps to the mind; if the commander had followed this route, if the Dutch had seen the east coast, would they have concluded there was no good to be done there? What if the commander had discovered the passage between New Guinea and False Cape? But such was not to be, partly because the instructions cautioned the commander against this route, warning him that winds and currents were unfavourable to it. So these chance words possibly cheated the commander of such glory, and chance and circumstance combined to strengthen their first cry of anguish and despair of achievement in such a vast land.[28]

As commander, the Council in Batavia chose Abel Janszoon Tasman. Of the man himself little is known. He was born at Lutjegast in the province of

[26] Ibid. See also L. C. Wroth: 'The Early Cartography of the Pacific' (*Papers of the Bibliographical Society of America*, vol. 38, no. 2, 1944).

[27] J. E. Heeres: *Abel Tasman*, App. E.

[28] Ibid.

Groningen, in Holland, about 1603, went to Java in 1633, became a skipper in 1634 in the service of the Dutch East India Company, returned to Holland in 1636, was back in Batavia by 1638, and in 1639 was appointed second-in-command of a Dutch expedition to Japan. There was, it seems, a dark side to his character, for the man was driven by some flaw in his make-up to take pleasure in tormenting those under his command. It is known that like his fellow-skippers he had succumbed to the temptation of pocketing the proceeds from sales of company cargoes. But the Council in Batavia was willing to forgive such peccadilloes in men of ability, while reserving the full wrath of their Calvinist Jehovah for those who by their negligence or incompetence cheated the Company of its expectations. They were expecting much from this voyage —and it may be that a man driven as Tasman was by the desire to hurt, could not fulfil such expectations; it may be that he was pitifully ill-equipped by nature to understand the vision which sustained the Council at Batavia. From the little that is known, the eye of pity looks on Tasman as one commanded to perform tasks beyond the reach and scope of the powers of any mortal, let alone a man divided as he was. For he had not been endowed by nature with either the imagination or the singlemindedness that his instructions demanded. The Council in Batavia was singularly narrow in its conception of success and singularly lacking in pity or breadth of understanding for those who failed. They were looking for the great profits.

As pilot-major, or steersman-major, they chose Franchoys Jacobsen Visscher, a man with the power and prestige to influence Tasman on that fateful question of the course to follow. He was born at Husking in Holland, and left for the Indies in 1623 where he served the Dutch East India Company.[29] For ships they had the *Heemskerk*, a small war yacht, and the *Zeehaen*, a smaller flute, with sixty of the ablest-bodied seafaring men to be found in Batavia on the *Heemskerk* and fifty of them on the *Zeehaen*. They were victualled for eighteen months, two days a week to be meat days, one a bacon day, with a ration of spirits to be served in moderation for the sake of their health. Also, both ships carried supplies of merchandise—such as coloured cloth, blankets, linen, small Chinese mirrors, pepper, elephants' teeth, sandalwood, Chinese wooden combs—for the Council in Batavia wanted to allow for every sort of trade, to allow even for all sorts of people, while hoping they would not be those exceedingly savage, black barbarian inhabitants of the Southland.[30]

They sailed from Batavia on 14 August 1642 with Tasman's mind for a moment on higher things: 'May God Almighty', he wrote in his journal, 'vouchsafe His blessing on this work.'[31] They sighted Mauritius on 5 September and dropped anchor the following day to repair their ships, to gather stores

---

[29] For what is known of the lives of Tasman and Visscher see J. E. Heeres: *Abel Tasman*, p. 1 et seq.; P. A. Leupe: 'Abel Jansz. Tasman en Franchoys Jacobsz. Visscher, 1642-1644', in *Bijdragen tot de Taal, Land en Volkenkunde van Nederlandsch-Indie*, vol. 4 ('s-Gravenhage, 1856), pp. 123-40.

[30] J. E. Heeres: *Abel Tasman*, App. G.

[31] Ibid., p. 1.

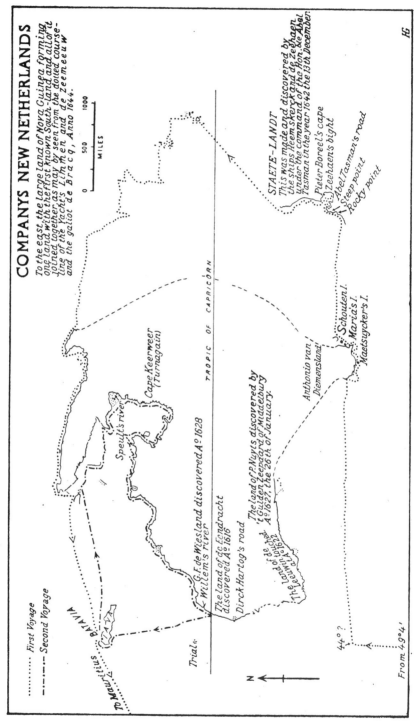

2 Tasman's Map of his Voyages (Original in the Mitchell Library, Sydney)

of wood and food, and to take on water. On 8 October they weighed anchor, and sailed out on to the high seas to the south eastwards to begin the search for the unknown Southland. By 6 November they had reached 49° 4' south latitude without sighting land, though the rock weed and manna grass floating past the ship had roused their expectations. As the seas were running very high, and the sailors were suffering very badly from the hail and snow which lashed the ships, Tasman asked Visscher to advise him. Visscher, by one of those choices which baffle posterity, counselled him to pursue neither of the two routes defined in the instructions, but to blend them. He advised Tasman to return to latitude 44° south and then sail east till they reached the longitude of the Solomons, where they should turn north, as they would then be in an open sea again, unless, as he added cautiously, they met with islands, all of which time and experience, being the best of teachers, would no doubt bring to light.[32] Whereupon Tasman decided to alter course accordingly. On 17 November he made two observations: that though they saw rock weed every day, it was not likely there was any great mainland to the south, on account of the high seas still running from that quarter. He also estimated that they had already passed the Southland known up to the present, or so far as Pieter Nuyts had run to eastward.[33] But Tasman, reticent as ever, did not mention that here was the chance to move on to course two—the course which would have made him the discoverer of the south and east coasts of Australia. His mind was clearly on the discovery of the unknown Southland—on 22 November, for example, he again noted the unlikelihood of land to the south owing to the heavy swell coming from that direction.

So it must have been a surprise on 24 November 1642 when they sighted land, though Tasman's words describing the event betrayed no emotion;— 'In the afternoon', he wrote in his journal, 'about 4 o'clock, we saw land bearing east by north of us, at about 10 miles' distance from us by estimation; the land we sighted was very high . . .' That evening there was a council on the *Heemskerk*, but again, he does not say whether there was excitement and pleasure in their hearts and minds or if they speculated whether this was part of the known or part of the unknown Southland. On 25 November there was another council of the officers from both ships on the *Heemskerk*, at which they decided on a name, but skirted the problem of what they had found:

> This land being the first land we have met with in the South Sea, and not known to any European nation, we have conferred on it the name of *Anthoony van Diemenslandt*, in honour of the Hon. Governor-General, our illustrious master, who sent us to make this discovery; the islands circumjacent, so far as known to us, we have named after the Hon. Councillors of India, as may be seen from the little chart which has been made of them.[34]

For seven days they sailed slowly, cautiously, round the coast; then, on the evening of 1 December they dropped anchor in a good harbour with white and grey fine sand, and a naturally drying bottom—for all which it behoved

---

[32] Ibid., p. 9.
[33] Ibid., pp. 10-11.
[34] J. E. Heeres: *Abel Tasman.* p. 12.

them, they believed, to thank God Almighty with grateful hearts.[35] They were then at Cape Frederick Henry Bay. It was 1 December 1642, almost the end of a decisive year in the history of the Protestant religion and of the parliamentary system of government in England, while in south-east Asia the Dutch had founded a trading station at Palembang in Sumatra, and the English and the French had extended their dominion over Hindu and Muslim in India.

They landed three times. On 2 December Tasman sent Visscher in command of a pinnace into North Bay with four musketeers and six rowers, together with the cock boat from the *Zeehaen* with a second mate and six musketeers. They found high but level land, covered with vegetation which, to their surprise, was not cultivated but growing naturally by the will of God, excellent timber, and a gently sloping water course in a barren valley. But of man there was not a sight, only indirect evidence of his presence, certain human sounds, and sounds resembling the music of a trump or small gong. The trees, sixty to sixty-five feet high, bore notches made with flint instruments, notches fully five feet apart, so they concluded that the natives must be of very tall stature. On the ground they observed footprints not unlike those of tigers' claws, and excrements from quadrupeds which they brought back to the ships. They also saw smoke from fires which, for some reason which Tasman never explained, again convinced them there must be men here of extraordinary stature. On 3 December they landed on the south-east shore of Cape Frederick Henry with supercargo Gilsemans and a number of musketeers, but they were again disappointed with the water they obtained. That afternoon Tasman, Visscher, skipper Gerrit Jansz, Isack Gilsemans, sub-cargo Abraham Coomans and the master carpenter, Pieter Jacobsz, returned to the south-east shore of the bay.[36] They carried with them a pole with the company's mark carved into it, and a prince-flag which was to be set up that those who came after them might become aware that they had been there, and had taken possession of the said land as their lawful possession.[37] When the wind began to blow stiffly, the cock boat was obliged to return to the *Zeehaen*, while further inshore the surf ran so high that Tasman ordered the carpenter to swim ashore with the flag, which he planted near four tall trees. Yet from that day to the present only the blue gums, the she-oaks, the stringy barks, the bell heather, tea-tree, and sword-grass have witnessed the site. For here was no source of the wealth for which they had endured the hardships of the mighty deep, not even a people with whom they could establish profitable connections.

Later that day Tasman wrote again with dignity though not with excitement of planting the flag as a memorial for those who came after them, and for the natives of this country. He did not speculate on what they had discovered, on whether it was part of the known or part of the unknown South-

[35] Ibid., p. 14.

[36] For the controversy on where they were, see G. H. Halligan: 'Tasman's Landing Place', the Royal Society of Tasmania, *Papers and Proceedings* (1925), pp. 195-202. For a reply, see C. Lord: 'On the Planting of the Dutch Flag in Tasmania in 1642', ibid. (1926), pp. 25-34.

[37] J. E. Heeres: *Abel Tasman*, p. 15.

land. Nor did he attempt to explore it. Indeed, the place made such a slight impression on his mind that he begged to be excused from writing a detailed description for what he called briefness' sake.[38] On 4 December he decided to weigh anchor to look for a better watering place. Next day, when the wind made it difficult for the two ships to follow the coast, Tasman convened a council at which it was decided to keep to their earlier decision to sail east till they reached the longitude of the Solomons, as though nothing of significance had happened. Indeed, so little notice was taken of this discovery that it was not for another one hundred and thirty years that a European again visited Van Diemen's Land, and then, Marion du Fresne anchored in 1772 within a mile of where the *Heemskerk* and the *Zeehaen* had cast anchor in December 1642. So ended the first visit of the Europeans to Tasmania, without disaster to the land or its people, without a hint of any desire to return.

On 5 December 1642 Tasman and Visscher sailed east, still searching for an unknown Southland, but found no signs of it; the heavy swells still continuing from the south-west convinced them there was no mainland to the southward. They sighted land again on 13 December—Tasman giving their position as latitude 42° 10′ S., longitude 188° 28′.[39] This time they celebrated the event by firing a gun and hoisting a white flag. They sailed north along the coast, looking for a suitable watering place and believed they had found one, but in a fight with the natives four of Tasman's men were murdered. So Tasman, timid as ever, sailed away without exploring the situation. He branded it a detestable deed, and one which taught him to consider the inhabitants of the country as enemies.[40] They decided to look for a watering-place further east along the coast, to call the bay Moordenaersbay or Murderers Bay, to call the country Staten Landt and to call the sea between Van Diemen's Land and Staten Landt the Tasman Sea. In this way Tasman scratched his name in the history of the coming of Europeans to Australia.

After sailing along the west coast of the north island of New Zealand, Tasman and Visscher sailed north for the Solomons, calling at the Friendly Islands where they at long last began to trade, exchanging nails for coconuts— as if to mock the Company's hopes of great profits from the voyage. That was on the island on which Tasman, without sarcasm or malice, conferred the name of Amsterdam. A few days later, on a neighbouring island which he honoured with the name of Rotterdam, he was noting the superstitions of the inhabitants—how, for example, religious scruples deterred them from killing flies, though, as Tasman put it, they caused trouble enough.[41] On their way to the Solomons they also discovered the Fiji Islands and called at the Hoorn Islands. Tasman not only failed but never even attempted to find an answer to one of the questions put to him by the Council at Batavia, whether there was a passage between New Guinea and False Cape. Again Tasman played safe and sailed along the north coast to Ceram and Batavia,

[38] Ibid., p. 16.

[39] For their position see T. M. Hocken: *Abel Tasman and His Journal* (Otago, 1895) and J. C. Beaglehole: *The Discovery of New Zealand* (Wellington, 1939).

[40] J. E. Heeres: *Abel Tasman*, p. 20.

[41] Ibid., p. 32.

where they arrived on 14 June 1643, after a voyage of ten months, whereupon Tasman, in a rare comment, wrote in his diary: 'God be praised and thanked for this happy voyage.' [42]

But the Council at Batavia was not impressed. For them Tasman was a man who had been on the high seas for ten months without finding gold, spices, trade connections or a short route to Chile, a man who had not explored the coast of the known Southland, who had not charted its dangerous west coast, a man who had not discovered the unknown Southland. So Tasman must try again. With all the testiness of men cheated of a rich prize by human frailty, with that arrogance and insolence of men who had threatened woe to those who endangered their profits, they again set him an impossible task. He was to answer all the questions raised by the Dutch voyages in the south seas from the *Duyfken* in 1606 to the *Heemskerk* and the *Zeehaen* in 1642-3. Did New Guinea join the Southland? Did Van Diemen's Land form a connected whole with these two great countries, or with either of them? What unknown islands were situated between New Guinea and the unknown Southland? In addition, he was to try to obtain ampler information concerning the nature and situation of all the known and unknown lands referred to; he was to seek a convenient place for obtaining water and refreshments for ships bound to the Indies from the Netherlands. As they realized, if Tasman had followed out these instructions then the whole of the known Southland would have been circumnavigated, and it would have been found to be the largest island of the world. So the Council wanted a great deal: and they wanted it in a hurry, for, as they put it in the concluding section of the instructions, it was of the highest importance that the commander should discover a great deal in the shortest compass of time.[43]

Yet the man from whom so much was expected was the one to whom all too little had been given. Tasman as commander, with Dirk Cornlisz Haen as second-in-command, was equipped with three ships, the yachts *Limmen* and *Zeemeeuw*, together with a small fishing boat the *Bracq*. They were manned with one hundred and eleven men all told, and a collection of elephants' teeth, mirrors, tortoise shell, porcelain, needles, knives, spices, pearls, ebony, gold, silver, and nails to be used for trade. Tasman's journal, presuming he kept one, has been lost, and the only surviving account is a letter addressed rather fulsomely on 23 December 1644 to the noble, worshipful, wise, provident and very discreet gentlemen in Amsterdam by the Council in Batavia.[44] Tasman had sailed from Batavia on 29 January 1644 for Ambon, Banda and False Cape, where, for reasons which the Council later felt reflected his lack of resolution, he did not clear up the mystery of its connection or otherwise with New Guinea, but decided instead to follow and chart the coast of the

[42] Ibid., p. 59.

[43] 'Instructions for Skipper Commander Abel Jansen Tasman, Skipper Pilot-Major Frans Jacobsz Visscher, and the Council of the Yachts Limmen, Zee-meeuw and the Quel the Brack, destined for the further discovery of Nova Guinea, and the unknown coast of the discovered East- and Southlands, together with the channels and islands presumably situated between and near the same', in ibid., App. M.

[44] Ibid., App. O.

Southland from Cape York to Willem's River, where he decided to return to Batavia. He reached Batavia on 10 August 1644, the whole voyage taking six and a half months, another example of his caution or prudence, for they had been victualled for eight months.

The Council in Batavia was bitterly disappointed. Tasman had not found an answer to any one of the questions put to him: to the connection between New Guinea and the Southland, or between the Southland and Van Diemen's Land. Tasman, they regretted, had only confirmed the gloomy accounts of their seamen about the land and its people, a land where man could not make profit by barter, where the people were naked, beach-roving wretches, destitute of rice, and not possessing any fruits worth mentioning, an excessively poor people, and of a very malignant nature. So in their despair and desolation, like the prophets of the Old Testament, they sought comfort in prophecy: 'What there is in this Southland,' they wrote, 'whether above or under the earth continues unknown, since the men have done nothing beyond sailing along the coast; he who makes it his business to find out what the land produces must walk over it.' But fate was not reserving the glory of this discovery for the Dutch.

The hope of the Council at Batavia, however, had not been entirely snuffed out by the Tasman voyages and the reports of his predecessors. They continued to entertain a Micawberish belief that something would turn up, as it could hardly be supposed that no profit of any kind should be obtainable in so vast a country. If it did not turn up in the Southland, they hoped God would grant that in the one or the other part of the world some prolific silver or gold mine would be hit upon, to the solace of the general shareholders and the signal honour of the first discoverer. Their faith in God's bounty was greater than their faith in Tasman, for they then slipped in the rebuke that such a search should be conducted by more vigilant and courageous persons than had hitherto been employed on this service.[45] On this note of spite the Council in Batavia summed up their attitude to Tasman, the man who had made the greatest voyage since Magellan, though ordered to perform tasks beyond his reach and capacity. The historian lingers over the ingratitude of men driven by greed, and the deserts of a man not endowed by nature with the power to satisfy his masters' appetite for uncommonly large profit. Within a few months of his return, however, the Council was writing more generously of Tasman as the man who had been endowed with the courage required to do additional good service to the company by seeking rich lands or forming profitable trade-connections.[46]

So the Council did not despair. There were other places where man was vile, but other prospects pleased. There was trade with China, there was that story about an island of gold near Formosa, there was the opportunity to capture booty in the West Indies, there were prospects in Chile where the way had been prepared by the Lord-General Brouwer, now, as they put it with

[45] Ibid.
[46] Ibid., App. P.

D

their accustomed confidence in things spiritual as well as things temporal, with God.[47] As for the Southland, it still had its uses as a landmark for their seamen on the route from the Cape of Good Hope to Batavia. So even as late as 1696-7 Willem de Vlamingh, to aid such navigation, charted the coast from south of the entrance to Swan River to Willem's River, finding it as all his predecessors had done, an arid, barren and wild land.[48] Their other enterprises remained much more profitable than the sand, the flies, and the savages in the Southland. When Cook arrived in Batavia in October 1770, the Council was troubled by his ill behaviour, but not by his accounts of the Southland.[49] On the day the Dutch press announced the departure of the first fleet for Botany Bay at the end of May 1787, they did not indulge in any wistful reminiscing, any sentimental recreation of those days when their men of vision, the Brouwers, the Coens, and the van Diemens, dreamed of a Southland from which there would be satisfactory returns; for on that day *La Gazette de Leyden* told their readers that nothing of great interest for public curiosity had occurred except that twelve ships had sailed from Portsmouth for New Holland. Their great interest was in the reports of the cargoes of pepper from Batavia.[50]

These Dutch seamen, these councillors at Batavia, the high and mighty in Amsterdam, the cartographers, the scribblers, and the men who conceived the ideas in the instructions to Tasman, contributed something more to the coming of European civilization to Australia than the charting of the coast from Cape York peninsula to the islands of St Francis and St Peter, something more than the honour of being the discoverers of the north, west and south coasts and Van Diemen's Land, let alone their claim to it as their property.[51] The Dutch so completed the decline in the material power of the states of Indonesia that no state in the archipelago could resist the coming of European civilization to Australia, let alone spread its own civilization to such a vast land. Above all the Dutch halted the spread of Islam in the area at a time when Muslim merchants had approached as close to Australia as the west coast of New Guinea. Their deeds of conquest and economic exploitation so stained their name and that of their civilization in the minds of the people they forced to do their will, that even Dutch writers foretold of a day when the blood of the poor people would seek revenge against such criminal and murderous behaviour.[52] Yet by not forcing the followers of Islam to embrace

[47] Ibid., App. O.

[48] J. E. Heeres: *Part Borne by the Dutch* . . . , p. 84.

[49] For Cook at Batavia, see J. C. Beaglehole (ed.): *The Journals of Captain James Cook on his Voyages of Discovery* (C.U.P. for the Hakluyt Society, 1955), p. 436 et seq.; Anon.: *James Cook in de Nederlandsche Oost-Indische Bezittingen* (Batavia, 1876).

[50] *La Gazette de Leyden*, 25 May 1787.

[51] The words were used by Cook, who struck out the reference to a Dutch property in the land discovered. See J. C. Beaglehole (ed.): *The Journals of Captain James Cook* . . . , p. 387, and n. 5.

[52] See, for example, K. M. Panikkar: *Asia and Western Dominance* (London, 1953), pp. 110-11.

Christianity they gained temporary respites from religious strife at the expense of allowing the survival of a religion which, when united with an implacable hatred of the Dutch, provided the two bonds of unity working for their ignominious expulsion. But all this was still in the womb of time when the men of the *Duyfken*, the *Eendracht*, the *Pera*, the *Arnhem*, the *Haring* and the *Hazewind*, *t'Gulden Seepaart*, the *Zeehaen* and the *Heemskerk*, the *Limmen*, the *Zeemeeuw* and the *Bracq*, explored the wonders of the mighty deep off the coasts of the Southland, believing, as good Calvinists, that the hearts of the sons of men were filled with evil and madness while they lived, believing too, as the psalmist reminded them, that the earth was the Lord's and the fullness thereof, but never doubting, never questioning their right to its fruits. As men who were driven to discover a Southland which would swell their coffers, but who, to their unquenchable anguish and despair found instead an arid, barren and wild land peopled by exceedingly savage, black barbarian inhabitants, they missed that other discovery in the Southland, the anguish of men who walked over it first as strangers and intruders and then with the passionate attachment of men who knew it as their native land. For when the Europeans gathered for the ceremony under the gum-tree in February 1788, if any of the exceedingly savage black barbarian inhabitants had been able to recognize the anthem which concluded that ceremony, they would have heard some quiet requests to God for the preservation of a king, and not of those elemental passions which had sustained the Dutch, who gushed out their glory and their guilt in their national songs.

The Dutch also probably taught one of the sea-faring people in the Indonesian archipelago how to make regular expeditions to the north coast of the Southland for trepang. They were the Bugis seamen from Macassar. Travellers described them as the modern Phoenicians of the archipelago.[53] Flinders found them at the north-western entrance to the Gulf of Carpentaria in February 1803. He described them as Mohammedans with prows from Macassar, who expressed great horror to see hogs but had no objection to port wine, and who had come to get trepang to carry to Timor for sale to the Chinese who met them there.[54] From his talks with the leader of the expedition, Pobasoo, Flinders estimated that these expeditions had begun in the 1780s.[55] Some, however, put the date much earlier, though those who wrote of them did so in such a way as not to commend themselves to those anxious to distinguish between fact and fancy. According to Dalrymple, for example, writing in 1769, the Bugis described New Holland as a gold-yielding country where the natives were Mohammedans and well inclined to commerce.[56] All

53 G. W. Earl: *The Eastern Seas, or Voyages and Adventures in the Indian Archipelago in 1832-33-34* (London, 1837), pp. 389-90. See also T. Raffles: *The History of Java* (London, 1817), vol. 2, pp. clxxxi-iii.

54 M. Flinders: *A Voyage to Terra Australis* (London, 1814), vol. 2, p. 228 et seq.

55 Ibid., vol. 2, pp. 231, 257.

56 A. Dalrymple: *A Plan of Extending the Commerce of this Kingdom and of the East India Company* (London, 1769), pp. 83-92. See also the journal of Baron van der Capelhan of his journey through the Moluccas, *Tijdschrift voor Nederlandsch Indië* (1855), vol. 17, p. 375.

observers agreed that the Bugis began these voyages after the Dutch had taught them how to use their navigation instruments and charts.[57] What has survived of their own account of their history in the palm leaf manuscript confirms this impression, but their name for the Southland—Marege, from Pamarege, a trepang fisher—and their name for its inhabitants—the Maregeka, a people engaged in trepang fishing—throw no light on the date of such contact.[58] Nor does the work of the anthropologist throw fresh light on the date.[59] One can hazard the guess that the trepang beds at Macassar and the neighbouring islands were exhausted shortly after the Dutch established a tenuous authority there.

The contribution of these Bugis seamen to the history of civilization in Australia was not negligible. They influenced the art, the social organization, the religion, and above all, the idea of the past created by the aborigine on the north coast, planting in his mind the idea of a golden age for his people before the coming of the white man.[60] Their very presence created in the minds of some Europeans the idea that the Bugis seamen might be the medium of contact if not of reconciliation and understanding between the European and the Asian, at a time when the European was free from the taint of racial insolence and arrogance, for at the same time officialdom was toying with the idea of importing women from China or from the islands as wives for the convicts.[61] So in a sense, by one of those odd sequences of events, the Dutch Calvinists became the medium or the cause of raising for the first time a theme of deeper import for the history of European civilization in Australia than that theme of despair about the land and its people which was the immediate legacy of the work of their seamen.

By the middle of the seventeenth century the Dutch had written the very first page in the history of European civilization in Australia by stating that there was no good to be done there. William Dampier popularized this idea amongst the English reading public half a century later. Dampier, who was born in England in 1652, was a widely travelled man on the eve of his first

---

[57] M. Flinders: op. cit., vol. 2, p. 228 et seq.; T. Forrest: *A Voyage from Calcutta to the Mergui Archipelago* (London, 1792), pp. 82-3; F. Péron et L. Freycinet: *Voyage de découvertes aux Terres Australes* (Paris, 1807-16), vol. 2, pp. 245-53; and F. Valentijn: *Oud en Nieuw Oost-Indie* (Amsterdam, 1724-6), vol. 4, p. 137.

[58] For an account of the palm leaf manuscripts see J. Doorduyn: 'Een Achttiende—Eeuwse Kroniek Van Wadjo', *Buginese Historiografie* ('s-Gravenhage, 1955); A. Ligtvoet: 'Transcriptie Van Het Dagboek Der Vorsten Van Gowa En Tello Met Vertaling En Aanteekingen', *Bijdragen tot de Land, Taal, en Volkenkunde* (1880), 4th series, vol. 3. For the names and their history, see the *Dutch-Macassar Dictionary*. For the trepang fishing see A. Cense: 'De Tripang-Visscherij', *Bijdragen Koninklijk Instituut*, vol. 108, 1952, pp. 248-64; and H. J. Heeren: 'Indonesische Cultuurinvloeden in Australie', *Indonesie*, vol. 6, 1952-3, pp. 149-59.

[59] For the opinions of the anthropologists, see P. M. Worsley: 'Early Asian Contacts with Australia', *Past and Present*, no. 7, April 1955; W. L. Warner: *A Black Civilisation* (New York, 1937).

[60] P. M. Worsley: op. cit.

[61] T. Forrest: op. cit., pp. 82-3.

voyage to New Holland in 1688. He had known Java as a youth of twenty, had buccaneered in the Caribbean in the 1670s, and had seen there the altars of gold raised to the greater glory of God and the degradation of the negro slaves on the sugar plantations. He was a man who believed he had seen the alpha and the omega of human achievement until he saw the land and the people of New Holland. 'Look at the face of old Dampier,' Coleridge said about his portrait, 'a rough sailor, but a man of exquisite mind. How soft is the air of his countenance, how delicate the shape of his temples.'[62] He had a mind which was quick to take over other people's ideas, a mind which delighted to play with big ideas, the broad sweeps in human history, the view of man of those who have been taken up into high mountains, but he lacked the strength to examine them closely, as he was cursed with the tendency to drift of the man of imagination. When the *Cygnet* arrived at Mindanao in the Philippines in 1686, Dampier browsed over the whole question of British trade in the Pacific, saw the possibility of using New Holland as a watering place for ships engaged in such trade, and saw too the possibility of reaching New Holland from Cape Horn; after rounding Tierra del Fuego, instead of following the northern route, a ship might stretch over towards New Holland. This idea might have enabled him to anticipate Cook.[63] But not in 1687, for Dampier sailed instead for Timor, and from there to the north-west coast of New Holland, arriving at the Buccaneer's Archipelago on 4 January 1688.

He found New Holland a very large tract of land, with a dry sandy soil, which was destitute of water. He saw no trees that bore fruit or berries. He saw no animals except one with the track of a beast as big as a great mastiff dog. He saw a few small land birds, and a few sea fowls—nor was the sea very plentifully stored with fish.[64] As for the aborigines they were the miserablest people in the world.

> The *Hodmadods* of *Monomatapa*, though a nasty People, yet for Wealth are Gentlemen to these; who have no Houses and Skin Garments, Sheep, Poultry, and Fruits of the Earth, Ostrich Eggs, &c. as the *Hodmadods* have: and setting aside their humane shape, they differ but little from Brutes. They are tall, strait bodied, and thin, with small long Limbs. They have great Heads, round Foreheads, and great Brows. Their Eye-lids are always half closed, to keep the Flies out of their Eyes: they being so troublesome here, that no fanning will keep them from coming to ones Face; and without the assistance of both hands to keep them off, they will creep into ones Nostrils; and Mouth too, if the Lips are not shut very close. So that from their Infancy being thus annoyed with these Insects, they do never open their Eyes, as other People: and therefore they cannot see far; unless they hold up their Heads, as if they were looking at somewhat over them.
>
> They have great Bottle noses, pretty full lips, and wide mouths. The two fore-teeth of their upper Jaw are wanting in all of them, men and women, old and young: whether they draw them out, I know not: Neither

62 H. Morley (ed.): *Table Talk of Samuel Taylor Coleridge* (London, 1884), p. 145.

63 W. Dampier: *A New Voyage Round the World*, 3rd ed. (London, 1698), vol. i, pp. 350-1.

64 Ibid., vol. i, pp. 462-3.

have they any Beards. They are long visaged, and of a very unpleasing aspect; having no one graceful feature in their faces. Their Hair is black, short and curl'd, like that of the Negroes: and not long and lank like the common *Indians*. The colour of their skins, both of their faces and the rest of their body, is coal black, like that of the Negroes of *Guinea*.

They have no sort of Cloaths; but a piece of the rind of a Tree ty'd like a Girdle about their wastes, and a handful of long Grass, or 2 or 4 small green Boughs, full of Leaves, thrust under their Girdle, to cover their nakedness.

They have no Houses, but lye in the open Air, without any covering; the Earth being their Bed, and the Heaven their Canopy. Whether they cohabit one Man to one Woman, or promiscuously, I know not: but they do live in Companies, 20 or 30 Men, Women, and Children together. Their only food is a small sort of Fish, which they get by making Wares of stone, across little Coves, or branches of the Sea: every Tide bringing in the small Fish, and there leaving them for a prey to these people, who constantly attend there, to search for them at low water. This small Fry I take to be the top of their Fishery: they have no Instruments to catch great Fish should they come; and such seldom stay to be left behind at low water: nor could we catch any Fish with our Hooks and Lines all the while we lay there. In other places at low water they seek for Cockles, Muscles, and Periwincles: Of these Shell-fish there are fewer still; so that their chiefest dependance is upon what the Sea leaves in their Wares; which, be it much or little, they gather up, and march to the place of their abode. There the old People, that are not able to stir abroad, by reason of their Age, and the tender Infants, wait their return; and what Providence has bestowed on them, they presently broil on the Coals, and eat it in common. Sometimes they get as many Fish as makes them a plentiful Banquet; and at other times they scarce get every one a taste: but be it little or much that they get, every one has his part, as well the young and tender, as the old and feeble, who are not able to go abroad, as the strong and lusty. When they have eaten they lye down till the next low water, and then all that are able march out, be it night or day, rain or shine, 'tis all one: they must attend the Wares, or else they must fast: For the Earth affords them no Food at all. There is neither Herb, Root, Pulse, nor any sort of Grain, for them to eat, that we saw: nor any sort of Bird, or Beast that they can catch, having no Instruments wherewithal to do so.

I did not perceive that they did worship anything. These poor Creatures have a sort of Weapon to defend their Ware, or fight with their Enemies, if they have any that will interfere with their poor Fishery. They did at first endeavour with their Weapons to frighten us, who lying ashore de-terr'd them from one of their Fishing-places. Some of them had wooden Swords, others had a sort of Lances. The Sword is a piece of Wood, shaped somewhat like a Cutlass. The Lance is a long strait pole, sharp at one end, and hardened afterwards by heat. I saw no Iron, nor any other sort of metal; therefore it is probable they use Stone-Hatchets, as some *Indians* in *America* do, described in Chap. IV.

How they get their Fire, I know not: but, probably, as *Indians* do, out of Wood. I have seen the *Indians* of *Bon-Airy* do it, and have myself tryed the experiment: They take a flat piece of Wood, that is pretty soft, and made a small dent in one side of it, then they take another hard round stick, about the bigness of ones little finger, and sharpening it at one end like a Pencil, they put that sharp end in the hole or dent of the flat soft piece, and then rubbing or twirling the hard piece between the palms of their hands, they drill the soft piece till it smoaks, and at last takes fire.

These people speak somewhat thro the throat; but we could not under-stand one word that they said. We anchored, as I said before, *January* the

5th, and seeing Men walking on the shore, we presently sent a Canoa to get some acquaintance with them: for we were in hopes to get some Provision among them. But the Inhabitants, seeing our Boat coming, run away and hid themselves. We searched afterwards 3 days in hopes to find their Houses; but found none: yet we saw many places where they had made Fires. At last, being out of hopes to find their Habitations, we searched no farther: but left a great many toys ashore; in such places where we thought that they would come. In all our search we found no water, but old Wells on the sandy Bays.[65]

Thus the first detailed description of the aborigine was written by a man who was not driven to distribute praise or blame, and who did not see the aborigines as special dispensations of the Fall, or as a people who had escaped the consequences of original sin, or as a people who through lack of animals to domesticate and suitable grasses had not progressed from barbarism to civilization. Dampier, too, had his faith—the plain man's faith that somewhere in that very large tract of land there must be something more than flies, sand, and the miserablest people in the world. He returned again in 1699, hoping to approach the east coast from Cape Horn, but a late departure from England forced him to use the Cape of Good Hope. So he ended again on the west coast, amongst the sand, the flies, and the miserablest people in the world, which, as he put it, gave him little encouragement to search further. On his return to London he popularized three views in his books on his travels: disgust with the aborigine; disgust with the land; the hope of better things somewhere in its very vastness, with the corollary that it might serve the interests of English trade.[66] The word trade, and the absence of all reference to religious motives or sectarian prejudices, indicates that Dampier belonged to a different world, a world in transition from the Protestants to the sons of enlightenment.

[65] Ibid., pp. 463-7.

[66] These ideas were popularized in the third edition of *A New Voyage Round the World*, published in London in 1698, and in the publication of *A Voyage to New Holland, &c. in the Year 1699* (vol. 3 in 1703; second edition, containing part 2, 1709).

3

THE SONS OF ENLIGHTENMENT

BY THE LAST quarter of the seventeenth century the helio-centric theory of the universe had begun to influence thinking about the meaning of life. To contemporary observers, the effect was obvious: the influence which Christianity in particular and religion in general had exercised over man's minds decayed prodigiously.[1] On the loss and gain to humanity by the decay of religious belief, historians have wrangled interminably, some stressing the blow to human pride, some the contribution to human despair by depriving man of the hope of a meeting beyond the grave, while others have welcomed the end of one of the most prolific causes of human anguish —the fear of damnation. Contemporaries, however, discussed the significance of the decay of religious belief with less concern for its cosmic meaning. They saw a new earth, one in which heaven was no longer situated in the sky above, nor hell below, in which behaviour and misfortune were not to be attributed to malign agencies, to devils, witches, or sorcerers. They recognized the unfathomable mysteries which excluded dogmatism or arrogance in questions of faith: they were aware of human ignorance, for, as a contemporary put it, all things were great darkness to them and they were so to themselves.[2]

The decay of religious belief coincided with a growing conviction of the social utility of the Christian religion, which helps to explain why in public they observed the rules of their religion with much solemnity, but in private regarded it not at all.[3] The Protestant religion served them in two ways: it was a happy instrument in the hands of Divine Providence for the propagation of the pure and unadulterated truths of Christianity unmixed with popish superstitions, and unstained by the bloody rigours of the inquisition. It preserved the higher civilization against the menace of Catholic superstition and material squalor, as well as the social dangers of infidelity.[4] They detected a connection between religious and civil liberty on the one hand and material prosperity and human behaviour on the other, for in Protestant eyes it was the Protestant religion which had rendered the meanest country, the Dutch republic, a paradise, and converted the most distressed and dejected of the

[1] T. Spratt: *The History of the Royal Society of London, for the Improving of Natural Knowledge* (London, 1702), p. 376.

[2] G. R. Cragg: *From Puritanism to the Age of Reason* (Cambridge, 1950), pp. 5, 67-8.

[3] T. Spratt: op. cit., p. 376.

[4] J. Callander: *Terra Australis Cognita: or Voyages to the Terra Australis, or Southern Hemisphere, during the Sixteenth, Seventeenth, and Eighteenth Centuries* (Edinburgh, 1766-8), vol. 1, pp. ii-v.

human race into the bravest soldiers and the most enterprising seamen.[5] In the same way Fielding saw Tom Jones as a man of heroic ingredients, because he was a hearty well-wisher of the cause of liberty and of the Protestant religion.[6]

The other source of a higher civilization was trade or commerce. It was commerce that excited and encouraged universal industry by providing that all who took pains reaped profits; it was commerce which was beneficial to society, by which application to private interests was in reality the truest testimony of public spirit; it was commerce which explained why Great Britain and Holland made so much a greater figure in Europe than Sweden or Denmark.[7] It was the promise of an extension of commerce which revived European interest in the south seas—the hope either that the Dutch had been wrong in their descriptions of New Holland, or that the unknown 'terra australis' would be discovered, or that Van Diemen's Land might be exploited, on the grounds that such countries must be extremely rich and valuable, simply because the richest and finest countries in the known world all lay within the same latitudes.[8] Improvements in ship-building, in aids to navigation, in the diet of seamen, in the knowledge of winds and currents, created more favourable circumstances for the success of such voyages.[9]

So the eighteenth century witnessed a revival of exploration in the south seas. Roggeveen, the Dutchman, sailed in 1721.[10] Bouvet, the Frenchman, presented his ideas in a memorial of 1735, some of which Bougainville tried to carry out between 1766 and 1769.[11] The Russians sent out expeditions;[12] the Spanish sent theirs.[13] In 1739 the first English expedition sailed under the command of Anson, who carried with him at least one whose hopes of immortality were not snuffed out in the general decay of religious belief, for the tablet to his memory in St Michael's Church, Cumnor, near Oxford, testifies that one of the sailors was buried in the great South Sea in hope of a joyful resurrection when the sea shall give up her dead. Byron sailed round

[5] Review of A Succinct History of the Rise, Progress and Establishment of the Dutch East India Company in J. Harris: *Navigantium atque itinerantium bibliotheca* . . . , rev. ed. (London, 1744-8), vol. 1, pp. 924-5.

[6] H. Fielding: *The History of Tom Jones. A Foundling* (Oxford, 1926), vol. 2, p. 119.

[7] J. Harris: op. cit., author's dedication, and vol. 1, p. 319.

[8] Ibid., pp. 331-4, and A. Dalrymple: *A Plan for Extending the Commerce of this Kingdom and of the East India Company* (London, 1769), pp. 8-9.

[9] J. C. Beaglehole: *The Exploration of the Pacific* (London, 1934), p. 198 et seq.

[10] F. E. Baron Mulert (ed.): *De Reis van Mr. Jacob Roggeveen ter ontdekking van het Zuidland, 1721-1722* ('s-Gravenhage, 1911), Linschoten Vereeniging, vol. 4.

[11] J. Burney: *A Chronological History of the Voyages and Discoveries in the South Sea or Pacific Ocean* (London, 1803-17), vol. 5, p. 30.

[12] For Russian exploration in the Pacific see F. A. Golder: *Russian Expansion on the Pacific 1641-1850: an Account of the earliest and later Expeditions made by the Russians along the Pacific Coast of Asia and North America; including some related Expeditions to the Arctic Regions* (Cleveland, Ohio, 1914).

[13] See B. G. Corney (ed.): *The Quest and Occupation of Tahiti by Emissaries of Spain during the years 1772-1776* (Hakluyt Society, London, 1913-19).

Cape Horn in 1764, followed by Wallis and Carteret in 1766, all in search of countries hitherto unknown to any European power to redound to the honour of the nation, the dignity of the crown, and the advancement of trade and navigation.[14] Then, in 1767, before Wallis and Carteret had returned, the British Admiralty appointed a man of stature to command an expedition to observe the transit of Venus, and to search for a continent or land of great extent to the south of the route followed by Wallis or other commanders.[15] He was Lieutenant James Cook.

Cook was born at Marton in Yorkshire on 27 October 1728, and lived his early life in Staithes and Whitby where, as a youth, he must have seen the abbey of the older faith crumbling in ruins on the bluff which overlooks the town. Behind him there were the Yorkshire moors, and in front the vast, ever restless, ever complaining sea.[16] At the age of fifteen he was bound apprentice to a coal shipping firm at Whitby, entered the navy as an able seaman in 1755, served in the Seven Years' War on the European and North American stations, helped General Wolfe in the assault on Quebec, and gained a considerable reputation both for the quality of his charts and for his care in supervising scientific observations. On 26 May 1768 he was promoted to the rank of lieutenant and given command of the expedition to observe the transit of Venus at Tahiti and to search for a continent in the south seas.

Yet on all this, on the cradle of the man, he remained silent all his life, as indeed he held his tongue and pen on most questions affecting the inner man. This has forced posterity to repeat the platitudes of the obituary notices, of those prose writers who have told us that the constitution of his body was robust, inured to labour, and capable of undergoing the severest hardships, or how his stomach bore without difficulty the coarsest and most ungrateful food.[17] Others wrote panegyrics of him as a brave and deserving sailor. A letter writer to the *Gentleman's Magazine*, in 1803,[18] using appropriately as

[14] For the text of the Admiralty instructions to Byron see J. Hawkesworth: *An Account of the Voyages undertaken by the order of his present Majesty, for making Discoveries in the Southern Hemisphere, And Successively performed by Commodore Byron, Captain Wallis, Captain Carteret, and Captain Cook, in The Dolphin, The Swallow, and The Endeavour: drawn up from the Journals which were kept by the several Commanders, and from the Papers of Joseph Banks, Esq.* (Dublin, 1773), vol. 1, pp. i-ii. For a comment on these instructions and comparison with the instructions to Wallis, Carteret and Cook, see V. T. Harlow: *The Founding of the Second British Empire* (London, 1952), vol. 1, p. 43.

[15] For the observation of the transit of Venus see H. Lyons: *The Royal Society 1660-1940. A History of its Administration under its Charters* (Cambridge, 1944), pp. 183-7. The instructions to Cook are printed in J. C. Beaglehole (ed.): *The Journals of Captain James Cook on his Voyages of Discovery* (C.U.P., for the Hakluyt Society, 1955), p. cclxxix et seq. The manuscript of the instructions, Cook's journal and log, are in the National Library, Canberra. For convenience, Beaglehole's monumental edition of these texts has been used.

[16] For the early life of Cook see C. Lloyd: *Captain Cook* (London, 1952). For the sea, see C. J. Brennan: 'The Wanderer', in his *Poems* (Sydney, 1913).

[17] Quoted in the *Annual Register*, 1784-5, vol. 24, from vol. 3 (written by Captain King) of the official account of Cook's third voyage to the Pacific.

[18] *Gentleman's Magazine*, May 1803, vol. 73, pt. 1, p. 396.

his pen name 'An Old Briton', thought that one modest stone in Westminster Abbey, with his name and a short account of his merits, would impart greater delight to a feeling mind than all the expensive monuments raised in honour of fiddlers and players, which occupied so much space there. A poet wrote rather fulsomely of how 'HUMANITY' had motivated him, while another eulogized him as the world's great friend, who had taken to foreign climes and rude, the sheep, the heifer, the stately steed, the plough, commerce and fair science.[19]

Cook comes alive however, as a man, in the descriptions by men who travelled with him on his voyages. Heinrich Zimmermann, who travelled with him on the third voyage in 1777-9, saw him as a tall, handsome, strong, rather lean man, with dark brown hair, dark skinned and rather squat. He saw him as very stern, and hot-tempered—indeed so much so that the least opposition on the part of an officer or a seaman upset him completely. No one was bold enough to gainsay him. He often sat at table with his officers without saying a word, and yet at times he was very friendly towards his crew. He never spoke of religion; he would tolerate no parson on board the ship; he very seldom observed the Sabbath. Yet in other respects he was a righteous man: he never cursed, not even in the greatest rage; he encouraged his men to wear clean clothes on Sundays; moderation was a cardinal virtue with him, for none ever saw him drunk, while he punished drunkenness in others with the greatest severity. On Saturdays he was more kindly than on other days for then he would take a glass of punch more than was his wont, and drink to the health of all pretty women and girls, while preserving strictly his own chastity. On the island of Tahiti, where other men yielded to the attractions of the women folk, he alone was above reproach.

He was brave, a man of indomitable courage, and sensitive of his own honour and respect. When the natives forgot their respect for him or mocked him, he burned with rage, and was sometimes immoderate in his vengeance. No wonder then that Zimmermann should add that on the day he died every one was silent and depressed, for Cook was a fine representative of the righteous and upright man not sustained by the consolations of religion.[20] Yet one thing was lacking from the picture drawn by his contemporaries: that tare which led him to his destruction, that inner confidence which chance and circumstance puffed into an overweening pride and belief in his own powers. But in the beginning the abilities, the native talents, the power gained by self-discipline

[19] Eulogium on Capt. Cook. From the French of the Abbé de Lisle, by W. J. D., *Gentleman's Magazine*, December 1783, vol. 53, pt. 2, pp. 1044-5. For other references see *Gentleman's Magazine*, May 1787, vol. 57, pt. 1, p. 386; June 1789, vol. 59, pt. 1, pp. 509-510; April 1791, vol. 61, pt. 1, pp. 318-19; June 1800, vol. 70, pt. 1, pp. 516-17; March 1803, vol. 73, pt. 1, p. 206; May 1803, vol. 73, pt. 1, p. 396; May 1807, vol. 77, pt. 1, p. 424.

[20] I have followed the German text: H. Zimmermann: *Reise um die Welt mit Capitain Cook* (Mannheim, 1781). For an English translation, see U. Tewsley and J. C. Andersen (eds.): Zimmermann's *Account of the third voyage of Captain Cook, 1776-1780* (Wellington, 1926). There is also a Dutch version: H. Zimmermann: *Reize rondom de Waereld, met Kapitein Cook. Uit het Hoogduitsch Vertaald* (Leyden, 1784).

and control prepared him for his role as one of the greatest navigators of all time, before the tare led him to his destruction at the very moment he had climbed the pinnacles of human achievement.

With him, on the *Endeavour*, he took Joseph Banks. Banks was born in London on 2 February 1743, and educated at Harrow and Eton where his tutor described him as being well disposed and good tempered but so im-moderately fond of play that his attention could not be fixed to study. At fourteen, however, he discovered the passion of his life when walking along a lane the sides of which were enamelled with flowers. It was more natural, he believed, to be taught to know all those productions of nature in preference to Greek and Latin. It remained the ruling passion of his life, and lingered long after the fires of love and ambition had died in his breast. In 1766 he became a member of the Royal Society on the eve of departing on an expedi-tion to Newfoundland, during which he became so sick that he tied himself to a gun on the deck to defeat the weakness. On his return he offered to sail with Cook and so Banks, who believed that every consideration a man made of the works of the Almighty increased a man's admiration of his Creator, joined a man who found the mysteries of all religions very dark.[21]

The *Endeavour* sailed from Plymouth on 26 August 1768, for which day the entry Cook wrote in his diary sharpens the contrast between him and his predecessors, whether from Catholic or Protestant Christendom. For where Magellan's and Quiros' men had taken the sacrament, and Tasman had beseeched God Almighty to vouchsafe His blessing on his work, Cook recorded the facts: 'At 2 p.m. got under sail and put to sea . . .'[22] They rounded the Horn and sailed for Tahiti, arriving there on 12 April 1769. While the scientists observed the transit of Venus, Cook spent much of his time observing the life of the natives, measuring it as he put it against the first principles of human nature.[23] For Cook wrote of this people, not with that enthusiasm or delight of a man who believed civilization was an evil, or that noble savages had preserved the secret of human happiness, but rather with a strong inclination to insert in his journal every scrap of knowledge he could obtain of a people who for many centuries had been shut off from almost every other part of the world.

All the early observers of the Tahitians tended to project on to them the tensions in their own minds. Bougainville, who was less driven than Cook to dispense praise or blame, noted their addiction to spending their whole lives in pleasure, which gave them a marked taste for that gentle raillery born of ease and joy. It also gave their character a degree of levity which astonished the Frenchmen daily, for the slightest degree of reflection seemed unbearable toil to them, and they avoided fatigue of the mind even more than fatigue of the body.[24] The missionaries on the *Duff*, who arrived at Tahiti in 1797, saw

[21] H. C. Cameron: *Sir Joseph Banks* (London, 1952); G. Mackaness: *Sir Joseph Banks. His Relations with Australia* (Sydney, 1936).

[22] J. C. Beaglehole (ed.): *The Journals of Captain James Cook* . . . , p. 4.

[23] Ibid., p. 128.

[24] de Bougainville: *Voyage autour du monde, par la frégate du roi La Boudeuse, et la flûte l'Etoile; en 1766, 1767, 1768 & 1769* (Paris, 1771), pp. 219-21.

them in quite a different light. These men believed that man at the beginning of the world had been seduced by Satan to eat of the fruit of a tree and, having thereby lost the image of God, had involved the whole human race in ruin and imparted to it a nature wholly corrupted and depraved. They found the Tahitians dissolute, and their society a sink of lewdness and cruelty. On the day they first mentioned the name of the saviour of mankind from the consequences of this transgression, they sang to them the hymn: 'O'er the gloomy hills of darkness.'[25]

Some of these missionaries settled in Sydney in 1798, where they influenced Protestant attitudes to primitive people—to the aborigines, the Maoris, and the Pacific islanders. It was not until Cook reached the east coast of New Holland that he was ready to put down on paper his thoughts on the advantages of the life of a savage over those of a civilized human being. While at Tahiti he confined himself to such a generalization as that the mysteries of most religions were very dark and not easily understood even by those who professed them.[26]

On 15 August 1769 he decided to stand directly to the southward from Tahiti in search of the southern continent, though not expecting to find one, for paradoxically enough, Cook was one of the greatest sceptics concerning its very existence.[27] From 15 August on they sighted nothing till 7 October, when Cook, the man of coolness and precision, noted in his journal: 'At 2 p.m. saw land from the mast head bearing WBN.'[28] That was Poverty Bay, on the south-east coast of the north island of New Zealand. Cook spent from October 1769 to March 1770 charting the coasts of the two islands of New Zealand, and making occasional entries in his journal on the way of life and beliefs of the Maoris, though again, as at Tahiti, the experience did not stimulate in his mind any comparison between the savage and the civilized. By March, having finished his work on the coasts of New Zealand, he began to turn over in his mind the route to be followed on the way home.

To go by Cape Horn had its attractions as by taking this route he would have been able to prove or disprove the existence of a southern continent, which, he added with his customary dry scepticism on that point, yet remained doubtful. But the Cape Horn route would have meant sailing in a high latitude in the very depth of winter, and the condition of the ship was not thought sufficient for such an undertaking. No human discomfort could influence the intrepid Cook. To sail direct to the Cape of Good Hope was laid aside as no discovery of any moment could be hoped for in that route. After consulting the officers, Cook resolved to return by way of the East Indies, by the following route: to steer westward until they fell in with the east coast of New Holland (a name also used by the Dutch for the Southland from as early as the 1630s). He was then to follow the direction of that coast till they arrived

[25] *A Missionary Voyage to the Southern Pacific Ocean, performed in the years 1796, 1797, 1798, in the ship Duff, commanded by Captain Wilson. Compiled from journals of the officers and the missionaries* (London, 1799), pp. 408-9, and 411-15.

[26] J. C. Beaglehole (ed.): *The Journals of Captain James Cook . . .* , p. 84.

[27] Ibid., p. 159.

[28] Ibid., p. 167.

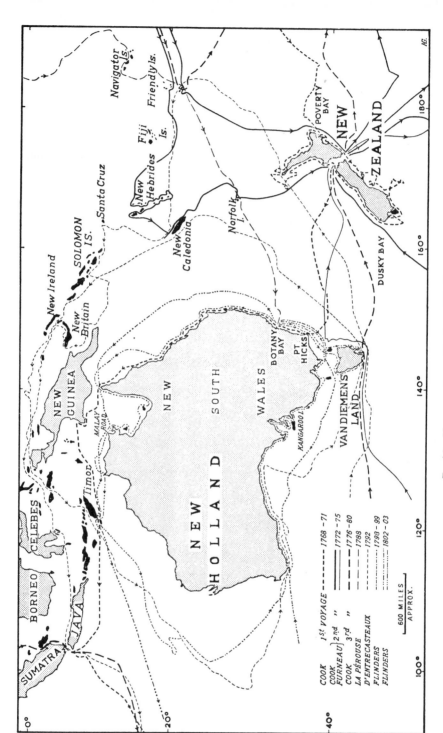

3 *Pacific Voyages from Cook to Flinders*

at its northern extremity, or if this were found to be impracticable, to fall in with the lands or islands discovered by Quiros.[29]

So Cook sailed westward. One fact which he omitted to mention in his discussion of his motives, was that on the *Endeavour* he had a map on which a dotted line traced the course of Torres in 1607,[30] for just as the mysteries of religions may be very dark, so are the motives which move men to those decisions from which flow such singular events as the coming of European civilization to Australia.

Again chance played its part. Cook was sailing for the east coast of Van Diemen's Land, but the great swell of the ocean nudged the *Endeavour* northwards. On 17 April 1770 a small land bird was seen to perch upon the rigging, but Cook, as unromantic as ever about significance or possibility, sandwiched this in between his nautical observations. Two days later they sighted land, but again Cook restricted himself to a typical cautious aside on the unlikelihood of land between Van Diemen's Land and New Holland, adding modestly that anyone who compared his journal with that of Tasman would be as good a judge as he. 'I have Named it *Point* Hicks,' Cook wrote in his journal, 'because Leuit[t] [*sic*] Hicks was the first who discover'd this land.'[31] Again he used the simple language of the observer; for Cook, the occasion demanded neither majesty of language nor sanguine sentiments. He then sailed northward looking for a place to land, and on 28 April at last decided on a place which appeared to be tolerably well sheltered from the winds, but ran into difficulty in deciding on a name. He plumped first for Sting-ray's Harbour, Botanist Harbour, and Botanist Bay, before finally choosing Botany Bay on Sunday, 6 May.[32]

On 29 April, just after one of the aborigines threw a stone at the small boat as a mark of their resolution to oppose a landing, Cook replied with light musket shot, while the wives and children of the aborigines on the beaches set up a most horrid howl. In this way the European began his tragic association with the aborigines on the east coast. A few minutes later Cook turned to Isaac Smith: 'Isaac, you shall land first', and the white man waded ashore.[33]

From 29 April to 6 May they examined the hinterland of Botany Bay, finding in many places a deep black soil which produced, besides timber, as fine meadow as ever was seen and which Cook believed was capable of producing any kind of grain. This burst of enthusiasm was to perplex all subsequent visitors to Botany Bay as well as to embarrass those who wanted to raise Cook above criticism as an observer,[34] though this temporary aberration was destined to carry more weight than his cautious summing up after passing the northern

[29] Ibid., pp. 272-3.

[30] Ibid., pp. clvii-clxiv.

[31] Ibid., pp. 298-9. For the position of Point Hicks, and the probability that it is the present Cape Everard, see also E. Scott: 'English and French Navigators on the Victorian Coast', in *Victorian Historical Magazine*, vol. 11 (1912), pp. 146-51.

[32] J. C. Beaglehole (ed.): *The Journals of Captain James Cook . . .* , p. 310 and *n*.

[33] Ibid., pp. 304-5, and S. Parkinson: *A Journal of a Voyage to the South Seas, In His Majesty's Ship, The Endeavour* (London, 1773), p. 134.

[34] J. C. Beaglehole (ed.): *The Journals of Captain James Cook . . .* , p. 309.

extremity of the coast. During his stay in Botany Bay, Cook caused the English colours to be displayed ashore every day and an inscription to be cut upon one of the trees near the watering place setting forth the ship's name, and the date of their arrival. So the English began their ceremonies in Australia, though, apart from Cook's own words and the diaries of his companions, the sole memorial of their coming lived on in the minds of the aborigines, who weaved into the songs in which they commemorated the story of their people the memory of the winged bird which came over the mighty ocean, and, they believed, would one day return. But they were the only ones to entertain such a faith at the time.

For on 6 May, having decided that they had seen everything this place afforded, Cook weighed anchor and sailed north, noting that at latitude 33° 50′ by observation they were abreast of a bay or harbour wherein there appeared to be safe anchorage, which he called Port Jackson.[35] Between Botany Bay and the northern extremity they landed at Bustard Bay, Thirsty Sound and Endeavour River, by which time the rigour of their experiences, the harshness of the country and the implacable hostility of the aborigines almost certainly caused those more unfavourable comments by Cook which contrast sharply with the cry of delight he had allowed himself during those halcyon autumn days at Botany Bay, when they were recuperating after the green swell and swing of the Tasman Sea.

On 22 August 1770 at Possession Island, off the northern tip of Cape York peninsula, having satisfied himself that New Guinea was separate from New Holland, acknowledging he could make no new discoveries on the west coast the honour of which belonged to the Dutch navigators, and being confident that the eastern coast had never been seen or visited by any European before them, Cook hoisted the English colours and in the name of His Majesty King George III took possession of the whole eastern coast from the latitude of 38° south to Possession Island by the name of New South Wales, and fired three volleys of small arms which were answered by a like number from the ship.[36] From that day the western half of Australia was known as New Holland, and the eastern half as New South Wales; it was still unknown whether a passage divided them, or whether a passage divided Van Diemen's Land from New South Wales.

Between Cape York and Timor, Cook summed up in his journal his impressions of the country and the aborigines. In his remarks on the country he distinguished between its condition in a state of nature, and what it might become at the hand of industry. In its state of nature the land was indifferently watered and indifferently fertile; the trees were hard and ponderous and could not be applied to many purposes. By nature the land produced hardly anything fit for man to eat; nor did it produce any one thing that could become an article in trade to invite Europeans to fix a settlement upon it. Yet to Cook this eastern side was not that barren and miserable country that Dampier and

[35] Ibid., pp. 312-13.

[36] Ibid., pp. 387-8. For a discussion of the name, see also G. A. Wood: *The Discovery of Australia* (Sydney, 1922), pp. 442-4.

others had described the western side to be. Fruits and roots of every kind would flourish were they once brought thither and planted and cultivated by the hand of industry, as there was provender for more cattle at all seasons of the year than ever could be brought into the country.[37] Substitute sheep for cattle, and this becomes a prophecy in broad outline of the pastoral period in the history of Australia.

At that time, however, Cook alone entertained hopes of turning the hard rock into a standing water by the hand of industry. The sameness and the barrenness had overwhelmed the other articulate ones on the *Endeavour*. Banks complained of the sameness to be observed in the face of the country, that its soil was uncommon barren and so far devoid of the helps derived from cultivation as not to be supposed to yield much towards the support of man.[38] Another man on the *Endeavour* described the shore as barbarous and inhospitable.[39]

To the aborigines they felt more kindly. Of their character Cook wrote with surprising fondness: a timorous and inoffensive race, he found them, in no ways inclinable to cruelty. Of their achievements in culture he wrote more unfavourably, finding their tools very bad, their houses mean small hovels not much bigger than an oven, and their canoes very bad and mean. Then, in a passage for which the reader of his journal is not prepared by any previous hints, Cook, in words befitting the majesty of his theme, reflected on the connection between the way of life of the aborigines and human happiness:

> From what I have seen of the Natives of New-Holland, they may appear to some to be the most wretched people upon Earth, but in reality they are far more happier than we Europeans; being wholy unacquainted not only with the superfluous but the necessary Conveniencies so much sought after in Europe, they are happy in not knowing the use of them. They live in a Tranquillity which is not disturb'd by the Inequality of Condition: The Earth and sea of their own accord furnishes them with all things necessary for life, they covet not Magnificent Houses, Household-stuff &c[a], they live in a warm and fine Climate and enjoy a very wholesome Air, so that they have very little need of Clothing and this they seem to be fully sencible of, for many to whome we gave Cloth &c[a] to, left it carlessly upon the Sea beach and in the woods as a thing they had no manner of use for. In short they seem'd to set no Value upon any thing we gave them, nor would they ever part with any thing of their own for any one article we could offer them; this in my opinion argues that they think themselves provided with all the necessarys of Life and that they have no superfluities.[40]

Cook wrote these words on the eve of a declaration in another place that all men had a right to pursue happiness, when the high-minded were dreaming

[37] J. C. Beaglehole (ed.): *The Journals of Captain James Cook . . .*, pp. 392-7.

[38] J. D. Hooker (ed.): *Journal of the Right Hon. Sir Joseph Banks during Captain Cook's First Voyage in H.M.S. Endeavour in 1768-71 to Terra del Fuego, Otaheite, New Zealand, Australia, the Dutch East Indies etc.* (London, 1896), p. 297 et seq.

[39] Quoted in J. C. Beaglehole (ed.): *The Journals of Captain James Cook . . .*, p. 654.

[40] Ibid., pp. 395-9.

E

of those better things in what had hitherto been accepted as a vale of tears, while others subscribed to the view that civilization was the enemy of human happiness. For the achievement has informed his words with an occasional majesty, just as it has puffed up that flaw in his make-up, that point where the hand of the potter faltered.

On 22 October 1770 they arrived at Batavia, where Cook again essayed a generalization that whoever gave a faithful account of this place must in many things contradict all the authors he had had the opportunity to consult.[41] But most of the time there his mind was on quite other things: on repairs to the ship, and on the well-being of his crew, for Batavia threatened to take a terrible toll on health, even on life. They left at last on 26 December for the Cape of Good Hope. As the ship rose and fell on the green swell of the Indian Ocean, events in Asia and North America were preparing the way for the voyage to acquire a significance which no member of the crew could ever have pondered. In India and the Indonesian archipelago a new era of territorial conquest and occupation had begun in response to the change in the economic use of those areas to the commercial companies exploiting their wealth.[42] During the long pull home after rounding the Cape of Good Hope they heard again of news from the English colonies in America, as they had heard earlier in Batavia that the American disputes were made up.[43] So Cook, almost at journey's end, brushed up against an event, or the prelude to an event, which was to lead to an attempt to found a penal colony at Botany Bay, on the site of that meadow as fine as ever was seen. He was brushing up against the prelude to an event in which a new vision of human life was to be brought to birth. In this vision all men were born equal, and all men had a right to life, liberty and the pursuit of happiness. By which they did not mean that happiness, that hope of re-union with God, which had inspired Quiros, nor that happiness which Cook had detected in the aborigine, but a happiness here on earth, a vision of a day when men should neither hurt nor destroy. This new vision of human life was emerging as Cook sailed home from a country in which the European would in time rejoice in its promise, and dream that this millennial Eden was actually drawing nigh.[44]

But no such thoughts, no such hopes, crossed Cook's mind as he anchored in the Downs on Saturday 13 July 1771 and, as he put it, 'soon after I landed in order to repair to London.'[45] With this simple statement he characteristically ended his journal, adding later a postscript on how to search for a southern continent, supposing it were to exist.[46]

For Cook did not predict any significance for his discoveries. The first time he discussed them, in a letter to the Admiralty from Batavia in October 1770, he had written of them with modesty, with an almost apologetic tone, perhaps

[41] Ibid., p. 442.
[42] K. M. Panikkar: *Asia and Western Dominance* (London, 1953), pp. 93-5.
[43] J. C. Beaglehole (ed.): *The Journals of Captain James Cook . . .* , p. 474.
[44] B. O'Dowd: 'Australia', in his *Poems* (Melbourne).
[45] J. C. Beaglehole (ed.): *The Journals of Captain James Cook . . .* , p. 477.
[46] Ibid., pp. 478-9.

even with a note of disappointment. Although the discoveries were not great, yet he flattered himself they might merit the attention of their lordships, although he had failed to discover the so much talked of southern continent (slipping in between brackets a Cookism that perhaps it did not exist) before concluding that though he himself had this discovery much at heart, yet he was confident that no part of the failure of such discovery could be laid to his charge.[47] He wrote in much the same vein after his return to England, that he had made no very great discoveries, then adding that he had explored more of the great south sea than all that had gone before him.[48] At no time did he foresee the coming of European civilization to New South Wales. Nor were the scribblers in the London press any more prescient, except possibly for one chance peep into the future in the *Public Advertiser* on 21 August 1771, where the writer predicted that it was to be expected that the territories of Great Britain would be widely extended in consequence of those discoveries.[49] But in general the press titillated its readers with hints of sexual licence on the islands in the south seas, which was a much more likely subject of human interest than the barbarisms and inhospitable shores of New South Wales, or that meadow at Botany Bay.[50]

The coffee house wits and pamphleteers mocked and ridiculed the enthusiasm of Cook and his fellow-officers for the way of life of the south sea islanders. The reports prompted a blast from Dr Johnson that just because ignorant savages laughed at some of the follies of civilized life it did not follow that men were better without houses.[51] One mocked at the supposed beauties of the Tahitian language, and at the claims of Banks as an amoroso;[52] another mocked at the manners of a country where bottom waggling was the royal salute.[53] A solitary verse-monger posed the question which had bothered Cook after seeing the aborigine:

> Can *Europe* boast, with all her pilfer'd wealth,
> A larger share of happiness, or health?[54]

[47] Ibid., p. 501.

[48] Ibid., p. 505.

[49] Quoted, ibid., p. 652.

[50] Ibid., pp. 650-2, for the comments in the London press.

[51] J. Boswell: *The Life of Samuel Johnson* (London, 1867), p. 193. Johnson was replying to the garbled account of Cook's reaction to Tahiti in J. Hawkesworth: op. cit. For a comment on Hawkesworth as an editor, see J. C. Beaglehole (ed.): *The Journals of Captain James Cook*, p. ccxlvi and *passim*.

[52] Anon.: *An Epistle from Oberea, Queen of Otaheite to Joseph Banks, Esq.* Translated by T. Q. Z. Esq., 3rd ed. (London, 1774). Anon.: *An Epistle from Mr. Banks, Voyager, Monster-hunter, and Amoroso, to Oberea, Queen of Otaheite.* Transferred by A. B. C. Esq. Second Professor of the Otaheite and of every other *unknown* Tongue. Enriched with the finest Passages of the Queen's Letter to Mr. Banks, 2nd ed. Printed at Batavia and sold in London (n.d.).

[53] Anon.: *An Epistle (Moral and Philosophical) from an officer at Otaheite to Lady Gr-s-n-r.* With Notes, Critical and Historical by the author of the rape of Pomona (London, 1774).

[54] Anon.: *An Historic Epistle, from Omiah, to the Queen of Otaheite; being his Remarks on the English Nation.* With Notes by the Editor (London, 1775).

But the majority dismissed it as a huge joke, though it may be a tribute to the stature of Cook that the scribblers left him out of their mockery. Official-dom also recognized his achievement, for on 14 August 1771 Cook was given his captain's commission.

The one result taken seriously was Cook's own suggestion that another expedition should be sent to search for the southern continent so that the discoveries in the south seas would be complete.[55] On 23 June 1772 the Admiralty commissioned Cook to proceed on further discoveries towards the South Pole in search of the southern continent.[56] As second-in-command they appointed Tobias Furneaux, who was born near Plymouth in August 1735, joined the navy and served off the French coast, the coast of Africa and the West India station till 1766 when he sailed with Captain Wallis in the *Dolphin* on a voyage of discovery. Cook and Furneaux left Plymouth Sound in the *Resolution* and the *Adventure* on 13 July 1772, sailing first to Madeira, then to the Cape of Good Hope. From there they sailed south, passing between innumerable high ice islands, but without finding any land.[57] So, on 16 March 1773, Cook turned north, hoping to test whether Van Diemen's Land was joined to the east coast of New South Wales, but strong winds drove him on to New Zealand, reaching Dusky Bay on 25 March 1773. In the meantime Furneaux, who had become separated from Cook in high latitudes, called at Frederick Henry Bay before rejoining Cook at Dusky Bay.[58]

For the rest of the voyage, suffice it to say that Cook, after many weeks in high latitudes, concluded there was not the least possibility of there being a continent unless near the Pole.[59] Two weeks earlier he had written with a strange beauty on the same point:[60]

> It is however true, that the greatest part of this Southern Continent (supposing there is one) must lay with the Polar Circle where the Sea is so pestered with Ice, that the Land is thereby inaccessible. The risque one runs in exploring a Coast in these unknown and Icy Seas, is so very great, that I can be bold to say, that no Man will ever venture farther than I have done and that the lands which may lie to the South will never be explored. Thick fogs, Snow Storms, Intence Cold and every other thing that can render Navigation dangerous, one had to encounter and which are greatly heighten'd by the inexpressable horrid aspect of the Country, a Country doomed by Nature never once to feel the warmth of the Suns rays, but to lie for ever buried under everlasting Snow and Ice.

To Cook this meant, as he put it, that a final end had been put to that search after a southern continent which had at times engrossed the attention

[55] J. C. Beaglehole (ed.): *The Journals of Captain James Cook . . .* , p. 479.

[56] Secret Instructions for Capt[n] James Cook. By the Commissioners for executing the Office of Lord High Admiral of Great Britain & Ireland &c[a], 23 June 1772 (National Library, Canberra).

[57] Journal of Capt. Cook's Voyage in H.M.S. *Resolution*, 1772-1775, 17 December 1772. Original in National Maritime Museum, Greenwich, England. The extracts are taken from the microfilm copy in the National Library, Canberra, henceforth referred to as Cook's Journal.

[58] Cook's Journal, 18 May 1773.

[59] Ibid., 21 February 1775.

[60] Ibid., 6 February 1775.

of some of the maritime powers for near two centuries past and the geographers of all ages.[61] Perhaps bitterness caused him to add that his fastidious attention to cleanliness would make the voyage remarkable after disputes about a southern continent had ceased to engage attention.[62] The ships returned to Spithead on 29 July 1775, Cook's characteristic last entry in his journal being on the small error in Mr Kendal's watch.[63]

This time the mockers were silent, perhaps in awe of the achievement of a man who had seen the vision of a country doomed to lie forever buried under everlasting snow and ice. The serious-minded La Pérouse summed this up simply in a conversation with one of the captains of the first fleet: 'Enfin Monsieur Cook a tant fait, qu'il ne m'a rien laissé à faire, que d'admirer ses oeuvres.'[64] An anonymous poet rejoiced to read again of the life of men liberated from some of the evils of civilization: how Europe had been overwhelmed too long by a superstitious dream; how he welcomed with relish a new religion for a sceptic age, a creed which spared vices because it had been purged from priestcraft and from prayer.[65] One of the members of Cook's crew asked his readers to acknowledge with a thankful heart those blessings of civilization and revealed religion, which had given him a distinguished superiority over so many of his fellow creatures, who followed the impulse of their senses, without knowing the nature or name of virtue, without also being able to form that great idea of general order which could alone convey to them a just conception of the Creator.[66] These resembled more the sentiments of the men who brought civilization to Australia than those somewhat heady sentiments of the men on the first voyage. But on the possible uses of his discoveries no one uttered a word.

So it looked in 1775 as though Cook had been the grave-digger of 'terra australis', though neither mourners, nor prophets, nor mockers performed at its funeral. It looked as though all who had believed in or searched for a 'terra australis' had disquieted themselves in vain. It looked as though the only result of an infinity of human effort and anguish—by the Hindus with their stories of islands of gold, the Chinese with their kingdoms of women, the Muslim merchants with their kingdom of Antichrist, the Catholics with their dream of a land dedicated to the Holy Spirit, the Protestants with their

[61] Ibid., 21 February 1775.

[62] Ibid., 21 February 1775.

[63] Ibid., 29 July 1775.

[64] J. Hunter: *An Historical Journal of the Transactions at Port Jackson and Norfolk Island, with the Discoveries which have been made in New South Wales and in the Southern Ocean, since the publication of Phillip's Voyage, compiled from the Official Papers; Including the Journals of Governors Phillip and King, and of Lieut. Ball* . . . (London, 1793), p. 292.

[65] Anon.: *Seventeen Hundred and Seventy-Seven, Or, A Picture of the Manners and Character of the Age*. In a poetical epistle from a lady of quality (London, 1777).

[66] G. Forster: *A Voyage round the World, in His Britannic Majesty's Sloop, Resolution, commanded by Capt. James Cook, during the Years 1772, 3, 4 and 5* (London, 1777), vol. 2, pp. 604-7. For a discussion on the author, see the article on Johann Reinhold Forster in the *Australian Encyclopaedia* (Sydney, 1958), vol. 4, pp. 163-4.

Jehovah and their view of human depravity, and the sons of enlightenment with their message of hope for better things—had been the sight of a barbarous and inhospitable shore and the sight of the miserablest people in the world. But four years later, when the fatal flaw in Cook was leading him on to his destruction at the hands of the savages he loved, a man who had sailed with him on the *Endeavour* was urging the British government to found a penal colony at Botany Bay.

PART II

THE FOUNDATION

4

THE CHOICE OF BOTANY BAY

THE PROPOSALS for the use of a southern continent had a history almost as long though by no means so distinguished as the history of its discovery. Some saw it as land dedicated to the Holy Spirit; some saw it as a land fit only for the refuse of society, on the principle that the political body, like the human body, is often troubled with vicious humours, which one must often evacuate.[1] Just as the quest for a southern continent promoted the alpha and the omega of human behaviour, so the discussion of its use revealed all the bewildering variety of human aspirations. In the reign of Elizabeth two proposals were made for trade in the south seas. In 1625 an eminent London merchant petitioned the king for the privilege of erecting colonies in 'terra australis' in return for granting land to him, his heirs and assigns. Early in the eighteenth century Captain John Webbe proposed to form a company to carry on trade with 'terra australis'. In 1718 Jean Pierre Purry urged the Governor-General of the Dutch East India Company in Batavia to begin a colony in Pieter Nuyt's land, pointing to the advantages for their commerce.[2] But all such schemes came to nought, only to be resurrected from the waste-paper basket of history by the actual coming of European civilization to Australia.

The preoccupation with the material benefits of trade in the second quarter of the eighteenth century quickened European interest in the south seas. Campbell, who published an edition of Harris' *Collection of Voyages and Travels* in 1744, believed labour might improve, arms might extend, but that only commerce could enrich a country. He urged the English to establish a colony at New Britain in the Solomons to open up trade with 'terra australis'.[3] In 1756 de Brosses had urged the use of New Holland as a receptacle for criminals, on the grounds that in every society there was a proportion of men whose only occupation was to harm others.[4] In 1766 J. Callander plagiarized part of the book in his *Terra Australis Cognita*. When he plagiarized the other

---

[1] The point was made by C. de Brosses: *Histoire des Navigations aux Terres Australes* (Paris, 1756), vol. 1, p. 29 and borrowed by J. Callander: *Terra Australis Cognita; or Voyages to the Terra Australis, or Southern Hemisphere, during the Sixteenth, Seventeenth and Eighteenth Centuries* (Edinburgh, 1766-8), vol. 1, p. 20.

[2] For the history of these proposals see G. Mackaness: 'Some Proposals for Establishing Colonies in the South Seas', in R.A.H.S., *J. & P.*, vol. 29, pt. 4 (1943), pp. 263-80.

[3] J. Harris: *Navigatium atque itinerantium bibliotheca . . .*, rev. ed. (London, 1744-8), vol. 1, p. 334.

[4] C. de Brosses: op. cit., vol. 1, p. 29 et seq.

volume in 1768 he added a sectarian motive and some thoughts on trade to make sure the English took notice.[5] The first two voyages of Cook put New Holland or New South Wales as names in the pamphlet literature on the possible uses of lands in the south seas, in which the authors explored the possibilities of beneficial commerce and tossed off the idea that such lands might be used as bases from which to tap the wealth of the Indies, or to plunder Spanish trade in the south seas, or to begin trade with Chile.[6]

So the idea of using New Holland was canvassed at the unofficial level, in coffee houses, press and pamphlet, till 1776, when the enthusiasm of its supporters, which had been tempered by the counter drift of opinion against colonization, languished into silence in response to the revolt of the thirteen colonies in North America. For a season it looked as though the revolt had strengthened the hand of those who advanced moral scruples against colonization and trade, who were uneasy to accumulate profits by stealth, by the violence of rapine, or dexterity of fraud.[7] It looked too as though the wisdom of the political economist would be heeded, that wisdom which prompted Adam Smith to remind people that the same passion of human avidity which had suggested to so many people the absurd idea of the philosophers' stone had suggested to others the equally absurd one of immense riches of gold and silver in the new world.[8] These words were written in 1776. In the same year other human passions played their part in transferring the discussions about New Holland and New South Wales from the wits in the coffee house and the scribblers in Grub Street to the men who advised His Majesty's government. For in July of that year, with a firm reliance on the protection of Divine Providence, the Americans revolted, proclaiming to the world that all men were endowed by their Creator with certain unalienable rights, and that among these were life, liberty and the pursuit of happiness.[9] They proclaimed, too, their decision that their soil should no longer be polluted by British criminals.[10]

In 1717 a system of transporting convicts from the British Isles to the

[5] J. Callander: op. cit., vol. 1, pp. 20-2.

[6] See, for example, A. Dalrymple: *An Historical Collection of the Several Voyages and Discoveries in the South Pacific Ocean* (London, 1770), vol. 1, p. xxvi; and: *A Plan for Extending the Commerce of this Kingdom and of the East India Company* (London, 1769), pp. 8-9.

[7] S. Johnson: *Thoughts on the Late Transactions respecting Falkland's Islands*, 2nd ed. (London, 1771), p. 9. For English opinion on colonies, see A. Smith: *The Wealth of Nations*, Everyman ed. (London, 1954), bk. iv, ch. 7; and R. L. Schuyler (ed.): *Josiah Tucker, A Selection From his Economic and Political Writings* (New York, 1931).

[8] A. Smith: op. cit., bk. ii, p. 61.

[9] Quoted in S. E. Morison (ed.): *Sources and Documents Illustrating the American Revolution, 1764-1788, and the Formation of the Federal Constitution* (Oxford, 1929), p. 157.

[10] W. Oldham: 'The Administration of the System of Transportation of British Convicts, 1763-1793' (Ph.D. thesis submitted to the University of London, King's College, 1933; copy in Australian National University Library), pp. 78-80. See also A. E. Smith: *Colonists in Bondage. White Servitude and Convict Labour in America 1607-1776* (Chapel Hill, 1947), p. 115 et seq.

North American colonies had been begun to deter wicked and evil disposed persons from committing crimes, and to provide labour for the colonies. Convicts sentenced to transportation were sold by their gaolers to shipping contractors who shipped them to the West Indies or the southern American colonies, where they were sold again to plantation owners who acquired a property in their labour for the term of their sentence. All told, between 1717 and 1776, approximately thirty thousand convicts from England and Scotland, and ten thousand from Ireland, were transported to the colonies in America. By the end of 1775, when the opposition to convicts in America became confounded with the opposition to political oppression, demand slackened, and in that wave of righteous anger which possesses people resisting an oppressor, the convicts were not permitted to land. This forced the British government to look for alternative destinations.

On 1 April 1776, in an exhibition of the skill of the politicians, Lord North told the House of Commons that transportation had been found to be attended with various inconveniences, that in particular it had deprived the kingdom of many subjects whose labour might be useful to the community, and who, indeed, by proper care and attention might be reclaimed from their evil courses. To retain the value of their labour, and assist in their reclamation, the government had decided to institute prison hulks. Under this system, convicts sentenced to transportation were accommodated on hulks on the Thames or in the naval harbours on the south coast, and forced to labour by day on such public works as dredging sand and silt. In the beginning the system worked tolerably well despite outbreaks of gaol distemper and lamentations by prison reformers about the effect on profanity and morality of herding convicts together. These lamentations seduced the unwary to infer an indifference, even a callousness and a brutality, amongst those in power to the sufferings of the criminal classes.[11]

It was, however, neither unsavoury conditions nor talk of Sodom and Gomorrah which persuaded the British government to think again about the use of convicts sentenced to transportation, but rather the failure of the hulks to accommodate the number under sentence. A committee of the House of Commons was appointed in 1779 to examine this pressure on accommodation, and to consider whether transportation was practicable to other parts of the world.[12] The committee reported on the pressing want of some adequate provision for convicts sentenced to transportation—estimating the number to be near one thousand annually. They also reported that they had taken evidence on possible sites. One witness recommended Gambia on the west coast of Africa; another recommended Gibraltar; many expatiated eloquently on the value of convict labour, and the moral benefits of transportation to English society.

[11] The prison reformer Howard was the only witness to criticize the living conditions and morality of convicts on the hulks. See 'Report of the Select Committee on the Hulks, 15 April 1778', *C. J.*, 1776-8, vol. 36, col. 926 et seq.

[12] Resolution of Sir C. Bunbury in the House of Commons, 5 February 1779, *Parliamentary Register*, vol. 10, pp. 233-4; see also 'Report of Select Committee on the Returns of Felons', *C. J.*, 1778-80, vol. 37, col. 313.

Joseph Banks told the committee that the place which appeared to him best adapted for such a purpose was Botany Bay on the coast of New Holland in the Indian Ocean, which was about seven months' voyage from England; that he apprehended little probability of opposition from the natives as those he had seen were naked, treacherous, and armed with lances, but extremely cowardly; that the climate was moderate; that the proportion of rich soil was small in comparison to the barren, but sufficient to support a very large number of people; there were no tame animals, no beast of prey, but he did not doubt that oxen and sheep if carried there would thrive and increase; there was great plenty of fish; the grass was long and luxuriant; there were some eatable vegetables; the country was well supplied with water; and there was abundance of timber and fuel.

In the beginning they must be furnished with a full year's allowance of victuals, raiment and drink, with all kinds of tools for labouring the earth, with cattle, sheep, hogs and poultry, with seeds of all kinds, with arms and ammunition, with small boats, nets and fishing tackle; but afterwards, with a moderate portion of industry, they might undoubtedly maintain themselves without any assistance from England. On being asked whether the mother country were likely to reap any benefit from a colony established in Botany Bay, he replied that the people would necessarily increase and find occasion for many European commodities, adding it was not to be doubted that a tract of land such as New Holland, which was larger than the whole of Europe, would furnish matter of advantageous return.[13]

So time had brushed the impression of sameness and harshness from his mind, or maybe the desire to confer an imperishable name on the lands where he had had the big experience of his life caused his memory to play tricks. The committee, unlike the historian, showed no interest in the secrets of his heart. They agreed that a change should be made in the existing system for the maintenance and employment of convicted felons, and that it might be of public utility if the laws authorizing transportation to the colonies in North America were made to authorize the same to any part of the globe that may be found expedient. But they were not yet prepared to say where that would be.[14]

In the meantime Cook was making his last contribution to the debate on the possible uses of New Holland. In July 1776, the Admiralty commissioned him to attempt to find a northern passage by sea from the Pacific to the Atlantic Ocean, to return Omiah to Tahiti, and to distribute presents among the chiefs of the Friendly Islands and the natives of the countries they might discover in the northern hemisphere.[15] Two ships—the *Resolution* and the

[13] C. J., 1778-80, vol. 37, col. 311.

[14] Ibid., col. 314.

[15] J. Cook and J. King: *A Voyage to the Pacific Ocean. Undertaken, by the Command of his Majesty, for making Discoveries in the Northern Hemisphere . . . In the Years 1776, 1777, 1778, 1779 and 1780*, 3rd ed. (London, 1785), vol. 1, pp. xxxi-v. Vols. 1 and 2 were written by Captain James Cook, vol. 3 by Captain James King.

Discovery—were fitted out for the voyage, with Captain Charles Clerke in command of the *Discovery*. Cook sailed from England in the *Resolution* on 12 July 1776. Clerke, who was a sick man, followed later in the *Discovery* and met him in Table Bay, South Africa, from where they sailed south in a fruitless search for the continent Kerguelen claimed he had seen. Then, briefly, they refreshed the crews and gathered supplies in Adventure Bay on the south coast of Van Diemen's Land. The year 1777 was spent exploring the Friendly Islands and the Society group. During 1778 they sailed to the Sandwich Islands and then to Nootka Sound, near Vancouver, where Cook scribbled in his journal some reflections on the fur trade before attempting to find the northern passage from the Pacific to the Atlantic. This attempt took him deep into the Behring Strait and to Kamchatka, on deeds of heroism and exploits of navigation which earned him the highest praise from Russian writers on Pacific exploration. From Kamchatka he sailed once again to the Behring Strait before returning to the Sandwich Islands to avoid the rigours of the northern winter.

On 14 February 1779 at Karakakoa Bay on Hawaii Island, some natives stole the cutter of the *Discovery*. Cook determined to recover it and punish the thieves. Then chance and that tare of the potter combined for the destruction of one of the giants of this world. As Cook was returning to the boats off shore, one of his boatmen, on his own initiative, fired at some natives in canoes, and by chance killed a chief of the first rank. The natives were incensed, and by gesticulations and chants made plain that they would avenge his death. But Cook would not believe that anything could touch him. The sergeant of marines warned him of his danger, but, as one eye-witness put it, there seemed to be a degree of infatuation attending him which rendered him deaf to everything. The natives pressed upon him, and he was last seen to push them back, exclaiming 'Get away, get away!' He fell beneath their clubs and stones, and his body was hacked.[16]

One witness of the disaster was the master of the *Resolution*, who spent the day in terrible rages. His name was William Bligh. Others who witnessed the scene recognized that a giant had been cut down, that a man who had settled the boundaries of the earth and the sea and had looked death in the face in a thousand forms had at last been cut off by the hands of a cowardly savage, who, dreading the impetuosity of his rage, came behind him and stabbed him in the back.[17] In the same year Banks, whom nature had endowed with more of the power to survive, was urging in London that a tract of land such as New Holland would furnish matter of advantageous return, while a few years later a solitary writer urged the government to use New Holland as a base for English ships proceeding to Nootka Sound in pursuit of the

[16] For eye-witness accounts see W. Ellis: *An authentic Narrative of a Voyage performed by Captain Cook and Captain Clerke, in his Majesty's ships Resolution and Discovery During the Years 1776, 1777, 1778, 1779 and 1780* ... (London, 1782), vol. 2, pp. 108-9; and Anon.: *Journal of Captain Cook's last Voyage to the Pacific Ocean* ... (London, 1781), pp. 318-20.

[17] Anon.: *Journal of Captain Cook's last Voyage to the Pacific Ocean* ... (London, 1781), p. 320.

tremendous fortune to be made from selling furs from Nootka Sound to the Chinese.[18]

When the *Resolution* and the *Discovery* returned to Deptford on 6 October 1780, with the melancholy news of the death of their two commanders (for the ailing Clerke had died on 22 August of the same year), officialdom was caught up with the American revolt and its irritating by-product, the overcrowding of the hulks and the gaols caused by the suspension of transportation. So long as the War of Independence lasted the official policy was to make do with such expedients as the hulks, until such time as an American surrender permitted transportation to be renewed. On this the British remained doggedly sanguine. As late as July 1783 George III was writing rather waspishly on this theme to Lord North. 'Undoubtedly,' he wrote, 'the Americans cannot expect nor ever will receive any favour from Me, but the permitting them to obtain Men unworthy to remain in this Island I shall certainly consent to.'[19] Within a month, with such dignity as a man can muster when confronted with disaster after predicting triumph, he had accepted the Treaty of Versailles, the first article of which stated simply: 'His Britannick Majesty acknowledges the said United States.'

From September 1783 to March 1784 the government spasmodically attempted to persuade the planters in the southern states to buy convicts, until finally the contractor, Duncan Campbell, admitted defeat and added his own name to the tiny band of philanthropists and interested parties who were pestering the government to consider a permanent solution to the problem of what to do with the felons sentenced to transportation.[20] By then the escapes of felons from the hulks, as well as anxiety about the spread of gaol distemper and smallpox, enabled the philanthropists and charity workers to play on the fears of those in high places, while hints and complaints of the hulks as schools of villainy and vice tweaked consciences into action.

While the philanthropists and charity workers clamoured for action, men with solutions began to submit their plans to the Home Office. On 23 August 1783 one James Matra, who had sailed with Cook on the *Endeavour*, dropped in his plan in which he sketched the possible uses for New Holland. Matra had picked the minds of other people on trade with China, furs from Nootka Sound, spices from the Moluccas, and the cultivation of the flax plant. When the Secretary of the Home Office, Lord Sydney, got round to granting Matra an interview eight months later, in April 1784, he told him that what he was really looking for was a solution to the problem of felons sentenced to transportation. So Matra went away and tacked the idea of New Holland as a convict colony on to his first draft. To justify this union of the trade arguments with the solution to the transportation problem he reminded the Home Office

[18] *Whitehall Evening Post*, 19-21 September 1786. For Nootka Sound, see V. T. Harlow: *The Founding of the Second British Empire, 1763-1793* (London, 1952), vol. 1, pp. 8 and 18.

[19] J. Fortescue (ed.): *The Correspondence of King George the Third* (London, 1928), vol. 6, p. 415 et seq.

[20] A. E. Smith: op. cit., pp. 123-4.

that good policy and humanity were thereby united.[21] But the Admiralty, to whom the Home Office had passed on the Matra plan for comment, was not impressed; the length of the navigation did not encourage them to hope for many of the advantages in commerce or war which Mr Matra had in contemplation—a conclusion they reached eight months after Matra submitted his revised plan.[22]

In the meantime the philanthropists, charity workers, and other interested groups were addressing their demand for a permanent solution to a wider and more powerful audience. Early in 1784 the House of Commons had debated a bill to renew transportation, in which the words of the preamble made it clear that while people agreed on the need to renew transportation, no thinking had been done so far on the site.[23] In the short debate on the bill only one speaker, a Mr Hussey, mentioned a place: he said he meant New Zealand, lately discovered in the south seas.[24] As the year wore on however, all sorts and conditions badgered the Home Office to name a site. At the end of that year the Lord Mayor of London wrote to the Under-Secretary for the Home Office about the increase of men escaping from the hulks.[25] In January 1785 Sir George Young, a naval officer of distinction, submitted his solution, which was to use New Holland both to advance English trade and to solve the convict problem.[26] In March, with that reckless and irresponsible talk which the Anglo-Irish were prone to use to prod the more phlegmatic English into action, Burke told the House of Commons that there were one hundred thousand languishing in English gaols. Burke went on to plead against the use of Gambia for there, he put it to the house, was the capital seat of plague, pestilence and famine; there, he concluded, all life dies and all death lives.[27] On 20 April 1785 the House of Commons set up a committee under the chairmanship of Lord Beauchamp to inquire into the operation of the transportation act of 1784 and what further measures might be necessary to carry the purposes of the said act into effect: that is, they were asked to report on a site.[28]

This committee presented persuasively the case for a decision by the government. The extraordinary fullness of the gaols encouraged that constant intercourse between offenders by which they corrupted and confirmed each other in every practice of villainy. The hulks had contributed singularly to these mischievous effects by the forming of distinct societies for the more complete instruction of all newcomers; they did not reform, but confirmed offenders in every vicious habit. Crimes still multiplied in defiance of the severest exertions of justice. The hulks were a dead charge to the public, ex-

[21] *H.R.N.S.W.*, vol. 1, pt. 2, pp. 1-8.

[22] Lord Howe to Lord Sydney, 26 December 1784 (ibid., p. 10).

[23] An Act for the Effectual Transportation of Felons and other Offenders, 24 Geo. III, c. 56, *Statutes at Large*, vol. 14.

[24] *Parliamentary History*, vol. 24, cols. 755-8.

[25] Fraser to Nepean, 21 November 1784 (H.O. 32).

[26] *H.R.N.S.W.*, vol. 1, pt. 2, pp. 10-13.

[27] *Parliamentary History*, vol. 25, cols. 391-2. Burke borrowed this phrase from Milton's *Paradise Lost*.

[28] *C. J.*, vol. 40, col. 116:.

cept for the small return made by their work at Woolwich Warren. The committee then went on to declare that these mischiefs were in great measure to be attributed to the want of a proper place for the transportation of criminals. For members believed that the old system of transporting offenders to America had answered every purpose which could be expected of it; it had reclaimed them, it had tended to break gangs and combinations of criminals, it was not attended with much expense to the public, it had benefited the colonies, it had removed the convicts into back country where they found none of those temptations which occasioned their offence at home.

They were just as unequivocal on the type of colony to be established. They rejected the idea of composing an entire colony of male and female convicts, partly because such an experiment had never been made in the history of mankind, and partly because outcasts of an old society would not serve as the foundation for a new one. Society could not exist without justice, without order, and without subordination, to which convicts must of necessity be strangers. The labour of convicts could be put to most useful purposes: to establish a new settlement for enlarging commerce, as well as to defend the settlement. In a new society that aversion to labour and that inequality of fortunes which stimulated men to crime in the old world would have no force. The convicts would remain honest for want of a temptation to be otherwise, while the hope of being restored to freedom might reform even the most refractory.

They were not quite so confident in recommending where such a colony should be established. Lord Sydney had told them at the beginning of their inquiry that different ideas had been suggested on the subject, but that such suggestions were either made in conversation or appeared unworthy of the attention of the committee, and that no such plan as was required existed in his office. But others came forward with suggestions. Some argued for a site on the west coast of Africa as an aid to British commerce with India and the east. Others condemned this because climate, hostile and treacherous natives and man-eating animals in the rivers would promote riot and confusion. Matra and Banks again recommended New Holland or Botany Bay, the latter once more eulogizing the fertility of the soil, the timid disposition of the inhabitants, and the climate, adding this time the suggestion that a supply of women could be obtained for five hundred convicts from the islands of the Pacific. The committee boggled at the expense, however, when the shipping contractor, Duncan Campbell, informed them that the voyage to Botany Bay could not be undertaken for less than thirty pounds a man, or six times the cost of transporting a convict to America. Nor had they been seduced by the expectations of Banks on the commercial possibilities of Botany Bay, for in putting the question to Campbell about expense, they spoke of Botany Bay as a place where no kind of trade was carried on.[29]

The committee, however, was not prepared to commit itself. All it was prepared to say was that it had been induced to turn its thoughts towards Africa, as it was incumbent on the public to provide a place of transportation

[29] Evidence of D. Campbell (ibid.).

without delay or resort to some more practicable system of punishment, for otherwise the respect for the administration of criminal justice would be lessened.[30] In August 1785 the Admiralty commissioned the sloop, *Nautilus*, to examine the west coast of Africa. When its officers reported the entire region as unfit for a settlement of that description,[31] the situation at the end of 1785 was the same as at the beginning. The government was committed to a renewal of transportation, while parliament, press, pamphlet, and pulpit were pestering them about overcrowding in the gaols and the mischiefs likely to ensue from such a situation.[32]

At the beginning of 1786, members of parliament were needling Pitt, arguing that the suspension of transportation had caused numerous daring and dangerous gangs of villains to assemble to the great annoyance of the public. For by then the press and more irresponsible members of parliament were infusing their campaign for a decision with a shrill note of hysteria. On the morning of 24 March 1786 the convicts on board the hulk at Plymouth rose upon their keepers, and were not subdued until eight were shot dead, and thirty-six wounded.[33] In the previous year a pamphleteer had drawn a picture of crime: 'Highway robberies,' he wrote, 'threaten the traveller, whether by night or by day—the lurking foot-pad lies, like a dangerous adder, in our roads and streets—the horrid burglar, like an evil spirit, haunts our dwellings, *making night hideous.*' All through 1784, 1785, 1786 and 1787 the press of the metropolis and the provinces was filled with stories of unhappy wretches being launched into eternity, of others labouring under real or artificial disorders and showing them unasked to the public, strolling in the streets with impunity, rendering the air noxious with their stench and endangering the health of the respectable members of society.[34] Pitt restrained all such emotional stampedes with a becoming and, indeed, a singular dignity, reminding the zealots that it was easier for a gentleman to state and complain of the grievance than for government to find out and apply an adequate remedy, and adding that the government would continue maturely to weigh a great variety of proposals.[35]

He was then just twenty-seven years old, tall and slender, but without elegance or grace, for his features were prominent and coarse. In manner he was cold and stiff, a man who seemed never to invite approach, or to encourage acquaintance.[36] His opponents called him unkindly the boy statesman, whispered that he was intemperately addicted to the bottle, and compared his

[30] Beauchamp Committee, *C. J.*, vol. 40, col. 1164.

[31] *Dropmore Papers*, vol. 1, pp. 256-7; evidence of E. Nepean to the Beauchamp Committee, 27 April 1785 (H.O. 7/1); G. B. Barton and A. Britton: *History of New South Wales from the Records* (Sydney, 1889-1894), vol. 1, pp. 494-5.

[32] *Gentleman's Magazine*, 12 December 1785.

[33] *Annual Register*, 1786, vol. 28, p. 198.

[34] M. Madan: *Thoughts on Executive Justice, with respect to our Criminal Laws, particularly on the circuits* (London, 1785), pp. 14-15; *Morning Post and London Advertiser*, 13 October 1787; *Scots Magazine*, vol. 49 (1787), p. 407.

[35] *Parliamentary Register*, vol. 51, pp. 53-4.

[36] Quoted in P. H. Stanhope: *The Life of the Rt. Hon. William Pitt* (London, 1861-2), vol. 1, pp. 240-1; *Gentleman's Magazine*, 1806, vol. 76, pt. 1, pp. 125-31; *Annual Register*, 1807, vol. 49, pp. 790-5.

F

ardent public declamations in favour of religion with his unsound private convictions. He had too, according to his enemies, an insurmountable jealousy of place and honour which led him to prefer instruments to associates and to commit the execution of his plans to those who were unworthy of them. His admirers, who included the historian Gibbon, retorted that he had raised himself to the government of an empire by the power of genius and the reputation of virtue, and that before him the opposition was as chaff before the wind. They saw him as a man who went into the House of Commons not to cringe and bow but to do the business of the nation.[37] Behind the cold and rather forbidding exterior there lay that inner man who loved his sister, the man who declined the sacrament on his death-bed because of a sense of his own unworthiness.[38]

But only those who knew and loved him in 1786 were aware of such wells of warmth and compassion. Only the few perceived that his reluctance to commit himself on the problem of felons sentenced to transportation proceeded from the profound conviction that all human interference with the body politic was fraught with disaster. To his opponents, this reluctance flowed from laziness and a callous indifference to the sufferings of the human wretches in the gaols and the hulks. They forgot the other problems with which he was besieged—the debts of the Prince of Wales, the negotiations for a treaty with France, the impeachment of Warren Hastings, and the agitation against the slave trade, beside which the convict problem appeared as a gnat to an elephant.[39]

The drift on the convict question was caused as much by the pressure of other business, as by the character of the man responsible for submitting a solution to cabinet—Lord Sydney. Mr Thomas Townshend, commonly denominated Tommy Townshend, owed his political career to a very independent fortune and a considerable parliamentary interest, which contributed to his personal no less than to his political elevation, for his abilities, though respectable, scarcely rose above mediocrity.[40] The poet Goldsmith saw him exclusively as a dispenser of political interest, imputing a rottenness to a political system which exacted that a man of the learning of Edmund Burke should be obliged to strain his throat to persuade Tommy Townshend to lend him a vote.[41] He had been raised to the peerage in 1783 for his part in concluding the treaty with America, and given the Home Office. He enjoyed the esteem of Charles James Fox, who was happy to see him loaded with honours; he enjoyed, too, amongst his friends a reputation for oratory and energy through which he maintained a conspicuous place in the front ranks of his group or faction.[42] The labours and anxieties associated with this possession

37 P. H. Stanhope: op. cit., vol. 1, p. 237.

38 Ibid., vol. 1, pp. 313-15, and vol. 4, pp. 383-4.

39 See *Gentleman's Magazine*, February 1806, vol. lxxvi, pt. 1, pp. 125-31; and Supplement for 1807, vol. lxxvii, pt. 2, p. 1219.

40 N. W. Wraxall: *Historical Memoirs of His Own Time* (London, 1836), vol. 2, pp. 291-2.

41 O. Goldsmith: 'Retaliation'.

42 N. W. Wraxall: op. cit., vol. 2, p. 292, and vol. 3, pp. 312-13.

of political interest, rather than any innate tendency to drift and procrastinate, contributed much to that gap of two years between the decision to renew transportation and the choice of a site.

In June 1786 cabinet discussed proposals to send convicts to the West Indies, to Canada and to the west coast of Africa, but once again no decision was reached.[43] Then, on 18 August 1786, Sydney finally announced the decision in a letter to the Lords of the Treasury. One factor alone had convinced him of the need for a definite decision: the several gaols and places for the confinement of felons were so crowded that the greatest danger was to be apprehended not only from their escape, but from infectious distempers. As the coast of Africa had been found unfit for a settlement, His Majesty had thought it advisable to fix upon Botany Bay which, according to the accounts given by Captain Cook, as well as the representations of persons who accompanied him during his last voyage and who had been consulted upon the subject, was looked upon as a place likely to answer these purposes. After sketching plans to preserve a proper degree of subordination and regularity by the despatch of officers and three companies of the marine corps, and to provide women from the islands, provisions for two years, and cattle and seed to make them independent (though making no provision for their spiritual comfort and instruction), Sydney requested the Lords Commissioners of the Treasury to prepare shipping to transport supplies, provisions and men to Botany Bay.[44]

The same motive was repeated in the heads of a plan sent to the Treasury as an enclosure with this letter, where the plan was described as a remedy for the late alarming and numerous increase in felons in the country and more particularly in the metropolis.[45] Indeed, everyone associated with the execution of the decision named the overcrowding in the gaols as the only motive, some, however, adding the hope that the colony might also be useful to the mother country.[46] In general the heads of a plan repeated the points made in the letter. For their lordships at the Treasury, it added an assurance that the difference in the expense between this mode of disposing of convicts and the usual ineffectual one was too trivial to be a consideration with government, at least in comparison with the great benefit to be gained from it, as the evil had increased to such an alarming degree. It also added the bait of potential advantages—the cultivation of the New Zealand flax, the cultivation of Asiatic products, and timber from New Zealand for the navy.[47] So in a perfunctory, slapdash way, some of the commercial arguments for New Holland were tacked on to the Botany Bay solution for the evil of over-crowded gaols.

The government's decision was made known to parliament in the speech from the throne on 23 January 1787. On that day, Pitt entered the House of

[43] Report of cabinet agenda in *Edinburgh Magazine*, June 1786, p. 278.

[44] Lord Sydney to the Lords Commissioners of the Treasury, 18 August 1786, *H.R.N.S.W.*, vol. 1, pt. 2, pp. 14-16.

[45] Heads of a Plan, ibid., pp. 17-20.

[46] See, for example, the journal of P. G. King, 1786-1790 (MS. in Mitchell Library); Heads of a Plan, *H.R.N.S.W.*, vol. 1, pt. 2, p. 17.

[47] Ibid., p. 19.

Commons with a quick and firm step, his head erect and thrown back. He looked neither to the right nor to the left, nor favoured with a nod or a glance the men of property among whom were many who would have been gratified by so slight a mark of attention by the greatest subject that England had seen during many generations.[48] He heard the Speaker of the house read the decision of the government: 'A plan has been formed by my direction, for transporting a number of convicts, in order to remove the inconvenience which arose from the crowded state of the gaols in different parts of the kingdom.' In the debate on the address in reply only one speaker mentioned the proposed transportation of convicts, calling it a measure of absolute necessity arising from the crowded state of the gaols. The others spoke on subjects of greater moment.[49]

More notice was taken of the proposal in books and in the press. Late in 1786 an anonymous author published *An Historical Narrative of the Discovery of New Holland and New South Wales* in which the commercial and strategic advantages were stressed side by side with the solution to the overcrowding of the gaols. Early in 1787 another anonymous author published the *History of New Holland, from its first discovery in 1616 to the present time.*[50] This discussed the wishes entertained by the sober part of the community on the Botany Bay experiment, then contemplated a grander vision of Botany Bay as a settlement which would enhance the comforts and add to the lights of polished society, as well as of its own still uncivilized possessors, and tend to the general happiness of mankind and the glory of that Being whose providence had reserved their discovery to the present generation. Such speculations inspired at least one eighteenth-century reader to an even grander vision, for one man scribbled on the end pages his belief that at Botany Bay the perfection of the present race of men appeared destined to be consummated.[51] So at least one son of enlightenment apotheosed convicts into the vessels of human perfection, and dreamed of a consummation in New Holland clean different from the Dampier picture of it as a cradle for the most miserable people in the world. Another pinned his hopes on the offspring of the convicts and the women from the Pacific Islands. From this union of the convicts with a set of the most beautifully formed women that the sun beholds, he wrote in a letter to Joseph Banks on 13 December 1786, Botany Bay might be peopled with beings that would be an ornament to human nature, and a generation of social benevolent beings might arise.[52]

The poets took up the idea. One W. Sotheby hoped a tear of penitence might drop on the soil and turn to blessing that dread curse of God which had

[48] N. W. Wraxall: op. cit., vol. 4, p. 633, and P. H. Stanhope: op. cit., vol. 1, pp. 237 and 241.

[49] *Parliamentary Register*, vol. xxi, pp. 1-4.

[50] This work is often attributed, in error, to William Eden, Lord Auckland, because of the inclusion of the fourth chapter of Eden's *Principles of Penal Law*; while the second edition (1808) has been incorrectly attributed to George Barrington. See J. Ferguson: *Bibliography of Australia* (Sydney, 1941), vol. 1, p. 12.

[51] Scribbled on the copy in the National Library, Canberra.

[52] R. H. to J. Banks, 13 December 1786 (Banks Papers, Mitchell Library).

smitten that ground.[53] Erasmus Darwin dreamed of a day when hope stood sublime, when embellished villas crowned the landscape scene, farms waved with gold, orchards blushed between, and joy's loud voice was heard from shore to shore.[54] The London press called it a colony in New Holland in the Indian Seas at Botany Bay on the west-side of the island—an error which was copied by the press in the other capitals of Europe.[55] The Irish press started a quite unfounded rumour that the Dutch had protested against the British planting a settlement on a territory which they asserted belonged to another country.[56] By December 1786 the press in London had settled down to accepting the scheme as a solution to the overcrowding in the gaols. The more imaginative conjured up pictures of what it would be like if the spirit of reformation began to leaven that society, and thieves began to flourish and be respectable,[57] while others wrote of it as both providing a place for the convicts as well as a settlement which might be made highly beneficial to Asiatic commerce.[58] At another level the proposal caught the popular fancy. On 24 April 1787 a theatre proprietor begged leave to acquaint the nobility, gentry, and public that at the Royal Circus they could see the opera 'Botany Bay', along with such other entertainment as rope dancing, conjuring, and displays of horsemanship.[59]

The convicts, however, did not share the amusement of the nobility, gentry, clergy and the public at the proposal. Some of them were terrified, choosing death rather than a removal from their old connections.[60] Some were mournful:

> All you that's in England, and live at home at ease
> Be warn'd by us poor lads, that are forc'd to cross the seas,
> That are forc'd to cross the seas, among the savages to go
> To leave friends and relations to work at the hoe.[61]

Some were light-hearted:

> 'Taint leavin' old England we cares about.[62]

Others petitioned friends in high places to hear their sighs and groans. They

---

53 W. Sotheby: 'On the Ships sailing for Botany Bay', in his *A Tour Through Parts of Wales, Sonnets, Odes, and Other Poems* (London, 1794), reproduced in J. Ferguson: *Bibliography of Australia*, vol. 4, p. 473.

54 E. Darwin: 'Visit of Hope to Sydney-Cove, near Botany Bay', in Anon.: *The Voyage of Governor Phillip to Botany Bay; with an Account of the Establishment of the Colonies of Port Jackson and Norfolk Island . . .* (London, 1789), p. iv.

55 *London Chronicle*, 12-14 September 1786; *La Gazette de Leyden*, 26 September 1786.

56 *Dublin Evening Herald*, 30 October 1786. Quoted in the *H.R.N.S.W.*, vol. 2, p. 737.

57 *Gentleman's Magazine*, 4 December 1786, vol. lvi, p. 1019.

58 *Whitehall Evening Post*, 16-19 September 1786; *Morning Post and London Advertiser*, 13 October 1787.

59 *Morning Chronicle and London Advertiser*, 24 April 1787.

60 *The Lady's Magazine or Entertaining Companion for the Fair Sex*, vol. 20, 1789, pp. 275-6.

61 Anon.: *The History of Botany Bay in New Holland* (London, 1790).

62 'Botany Bay' in H. Anderson: *Colonial Ballads* (Ferntree Gully, 1955), p. 18.

saw themselves caught between death in England, or perpetual exile and arbitrary government in a barbarous country where the remainder of their lives would be made bitter with hard bondage. They pleaded for the reduction of the number of crimes carrying the death penalty, for in England thieves were accounted as sheep for slaughter, and the life of a man had grown continually cheaper. The ideas of reformers such as Sir Thomas More, they believed, were closer to the infallible laws of God than the sanguinary statutes of the Christian kingdoms of their day.[63]

The convicts were not the only ones to dwell on the possible evil consequences of the decision. Alexander Dalrymple listed the many dangerous consequences to be dreaded from this 'thievish plan', from the moral evil of surrounding men undergoing punishment with creature comforts to jeremiads about the effect of the thieves on the reputation of British commerce in Asia.[64] But the worm of failure had been feeding on him ever since that day in 1768 when he learned that Cook and not he would command the *Endeavour* on its voyage to the south seas. Others shrank in horror from the darkness of the scheme, condemning it as beneath the disquisition of reason, and below the efforts of ridicule.[65] Some shrank from conferring the respectable station of landholder on a felon, from sowing some of the worst seeds in the world upon some of its best land,[66] while others painted pictures of convicts in succeeding times filling the Chinese and Indian seas with slaughter and depredation.[67] In Scotland there was anxiety about the scheme because trial and transportation would cost the public four times the value of the articles stolen. To one Scot the Botany Bay scheme was the most absurd, prodigal and impracticable vision that ever intoxicated the mind of man.[68]

In general the critics lacked the vision of the supporters. No one paused to ponder the effect on the aborigine: no one questioned the wisdom or pondered the effects of transplanting European civilization to the vast south land for the simple reason that the critics concentrated on the thieves. At least the supporters had their hopes. For them the settlement would solve overcrowding in the gaols, effect mundane benefits by an expansion of commerce, or even create a new society in which the great dream of the enlightenment would come to pass—the perfection of the human race. For them these victims of the overcrowding of the gaols were making the voyage across the oceans of the world as exiles not only from their families and their country, but also from God.

[63] *General Evening Post*, 4-6 January 1787.

[64] A. Dalrymple: *A Serious Admonition to the Public, on the Intended Thief-Colony at Botany Bay* (London, 1786).

[65] N. W. Wraxall: *A Short Review of the Political State of Great Britain* (London, 1787), pp. 77-83.

[66] K—— G——: *Proposals for employing convicts within this Kingdom* (London, 1787), pp. 90 and 92.

[67] Anon.: *A Short Review of the Political State of Great Britain at the Commencement of the Year One Thousand and Seven Hundred and Eighty-Seven*, 6th ed. (London, 1787), p. 83; and F. W. Gardenstone: *Miscellanies in Prose and Verse*, 2nd ed. (Edinburgh, 1792).

[68] F. W. Gardenstone: op. cit.

5

THE BEGINNING OF SYDNEY COVE

IN THE MEANTIME, the Home Office and the Admiralty began to prepare for the departure of the first fleet for Botany Bay: to choose the officers, select the convicts, equip the ships, and purchase supplies to support them during the voyage and till such time as they could support themselves or receive more supplies from England. As Captain General and Governor-in-Chief, the Home Office chose a retired naval officer—Captain Arthur Phillip. He was then forty-eight years old. He was born in London on 11 October 1738, the son of Jacob Phillip, a teacher of languages from Frankfurt in Germany, and of Elizabeth Phillip, née Breach. He entered the navy at the age of fifteen, saw active service in the Seven Years' War, was commissioned as a lieutenant in 1762, retired on half pay in 1763 on the conclusion of peace, and married, but not happily, for in 1769 he made an agreement of separation with his wife before he began farming near Lyndhurst in Hampshire in the south of England. He served again in the navy from 1770-1, and received permission to enlist in the Portuguese navy in 1774 where he was promoted to the rank of captain. He returned to the English navy in 1778, became a post captain in 1781 and in 1782 commanded the *Europe* on which by chance one of the lieutenants was Philip Gidley King. Phillip retired on half pay in 1784, and was again farming at Lyndhurst when Lord Sydney offered him the position of Governor of New South Wales.[1]

Of the motives which prompted Lord Sydney to make the offer, and Phillip to accept, but little is known. For on these motives, as so often in human history, what has survived has been the malice of his detractors, who whispered that Phillip had so long pestered those in high places for some such preferment that in desperation they silenced him with Botany Bay; or of those more skilled in the art of the character assassination of men climbing the ladder of official preferment, who dropped the hint that the little they knew of Captain Phillip would not have led them to select him for a service of that complicated nature.[2] But the stature of the man who won the battle for survival in New South Wales cannot be expected to emerge from the malice of the mockers, if only because in attributing ambition they missed out on that vision which sustained him through the days of unleavened bread in New South Wales. This vision

[1] For the early life of Phillip see 'Biographical Memoir of Arthur Phillip Esq., Vice-Admiral of the Red Squadron', in *Naval Chronicle*, vol. 28, 1812. See also M. Barnard Eldershaw: *Phillip of Australia, An Account of the Settlement of Sydney Cove, 1788-1792* (London, 1938), and H. J. Rumsey: 'Governor Phillip's Wife', *Australian Genealogist*, vol. 2, pt. 2, July 1938, pp. 189-90.

[2] Howe to Sydney, 3 September 1786. *H.R.N.S.W.*, vol. 1, pt. 2, pp. 22-3 and C.O. 201/2.

began to form in his mind as he fussed and fretted over the preparation for departure. He was not sustained by either of the great faiths of his age, either by the vision of God's throne, or by the vision of human perfection here on earth. From his actions from the moment he accepted the offer in September of 1786 it is clear that he had been endowed by nature with an inner dignity though, if one may judge from the portraits, he was somewhat careless if not indifferent to questions of personal appearance.

The face also suggests belief in the Roman or stoical virtues of courage, duty, discipline and self-control, the strength to stand firm when the world rocks, while the loose-fitting jacket suggests a person sterner with the inner than the outer man. The face suggests, too, what all who were to be associated with him testified to abundantly—that he had a power to evoke the affection of the men who worked under him, to inspire them to give of their best in his service, and the gift of making inferiors feel their baser motives and behaviour were not worthy of their Governor. The eyes in the portrait suggest some pain, some wound about which history and his biographers have perforce been silent. By chance he was endowed with one singularity in his appearance which contributed to the success of his relations with the aborigines. For a front tooth in his upper jaw was missing; so what partially disfigured him in polite society, became for the aborigine a sign that he was one of them.

As Lieutenant-Governor the Home Office appointed Major Robert Ross on 24 October 1786. He had joined the marines in 1756, became a captain-lieutenant in 1773, served in America, was promoted captain in 1774, and brevet-major in 1783. In this way a man so indifferent to outward form as to allow a sock to tumble down his legs served with a man who signed every official letter—Robert Ross, Major.[3] As Judge Advocate, the Home Office appointed Captain David Collins. He was born probably in 1754 (though some say 1756),[4] educated at Exeter Grammar School, entered the army, became a lieutenant in 1771, fought in America where he was married and promoted to the rank of captain in 1779, took part in the relief of Gibraltar in 1782, and then retired on half pay to Rochester in Kent. In person he was remarkably handsome, and his manners extremely prepossessing, while to a cultivated understanding and an early fondness for the belles-lettres he joined the most cheerful and social disposition.[5] So he appeared to the outside world, who did not detect how the inner man was tormented by ambition, both his own and his wife's, nor that preoccupation with evil and retribution, that fear of damnation which gave an Old Testament flavour and dignity to his pronouncements on his fellow human beings. Time and circumstance were to ravage him, for at the end of his days the remarkably handsome, prepossessing and cultivated young man of thirty-two had developed into the Lieutenant-Governor at Hobart Town who took snuff in handfuls while watching men flogged.[6]

[3] See the letters of Ross in C.O. 201/2.

[4] For a discussion on the date of the birth of Collins see P. Serle: *Dictionary of Australian Biography* (Sydney, 1949), vol. 1, p. 184.

[5] Memoir of the late Colonel Collins, in *Gentleman's Magazine*, November 1810, vol. lxxx, pt. 2, pp. 489-90.

[6] J. P. Fawkner: Rough Note Book, p. 30 (MS. in the State Library of Victoria).

As Chaplain, the Home Office appointed the Reverend Richard Johnson, who had been recommended by the Society for the Propagation of the Gospel. He was born, probably in 1753, in Norfolk and educated at the grammar school at Kingston-upon-Hull, from where he won a sizarship to Magdalene College where he absorbed the principles of the evangelicals. He graduated in 1784 and, with the help of influence from Wilberforce and the Society for the Propagation of the Gospel, was offered the chaplaincy of New South Wales in October 1786.[7] His sponsors entertained great hopes for the success of his work, that he would prove a blessing to lost creatures, and hasten the coming of that day when the wilderness became a fruitful field, when the heathen would put off their savageness, and put on the graces of the spirit.[8] To assist him the Society provided a library of tracts and books, the very titles of which uncover that gap between intention and performance in the men whose principles condemned them to a dependence on the Word. In addition to Bibles, Books of Common Prayer, and Psalters, Johnson took with him copies of Osterwald on the necessity for reading the scriptures, Kettlewell's offices for the penitent, copies of exercises against lying, of cautions to profane swearers, of exhortations to chastity, of dissuasions from stealing together with the most fervent wishes from the board of the Society that the divine blessing might go with him.[9] For Johnson was a most worthy man, but trapped by the pitiful equipment with which he was endowed for the execution of his noble purpose, as so many men have been. He was trapped too by the conflict between his own and the Governor's conception of the utility of religion. Where he saw religion as the divine medium for eternal salvation, the Governor treasured it as a medium of subordination, and esteemed a chaplain according of the efficacy of his work as a moral policeman. So Johnson, like all the evangelicals, spent his days torn between the temptation to hold the depravity of his charges responsible for the failure of his work, and that other temptation to lacerate himself for his own unworthiness to serve the Lord.

As surgeon, the Home Office chose John White, a young man of thirty years, a man of much credit in his profession, and of that tenacity of temper that rendered him a very proper person for such an establishment.[10] Similar encomiums were made on the talent and experience of the other civil and military officers. Amongst the naval officers there were John Hunter and Philip Gidley King, whose lives and fortunes thus began to be associated for good and evil with the history of the colony of New South Wales. Amongst the army officers, all of whom were volunteers, were men such as Lieutenant William Dawes, a man of such distinction as an astronomer that the Astrono-

7 F. T. Whitington: *William Grant Broughton, Bishop of Australia* (Sydney, 1936), pp. 3-11; J. Bonwick: *Australia's First Preacher* (London, 1898); and G. A. Wood: 'The Reverend Richard Johnson, Australia's First Clergyman', in R.A.H.S., J. & P., vol. 12, pt. 5 (1926), pp. 237-70.

8 H. Venn to J. Venn, 28 October 1786 (Bonwick Transcripts, box 49, vol. 1, pp. 13-15).

9 Report of the Meeting of the S.P.G., 28 November 1786 (Bonwick Transcripts, box 56, pp. 29-31).

10 A. S. Hammond to E. Nepean, 16 October 1786 (C.O. 201/1).

mer Royal commended him as a man worthy to observe a comet which was expected to be seen in south latitudes in 1788. Indeed, so engaged was Dawes with the stars that to mortal eye he was not always visible.[11] There was Watkin Tench, who had joined the marines as a second lieutenant in 1776, and was promoted to captain-lieutenant in 1782—a rank he held when in 1786 he volunteered to serve in New South Wales. Tench was a man who found it easy to like his fellow human beings, a man who wrote of their motives with an insight sweetened by charity, a man who delighted in the beauty of the world, who looked confidently to its improvement rather than brooded sombrely over any darkness in the hearts of men. Except for Dawes and Hunter, who shared the convictions and the aspirations of the reverend chaplain, these officers were characterized by their faith in commonsense, men who disdained enthusiasm either for the religion of the Established Church, or the faith of the enlightenment, or the belief in the noble savage. They accepted the Protestant religion very much as Tom Jones had accepted it, for its contribution to higher civilization and liberty, for its services in emancipating mankind from priestcraft and superstition, while remaining discreetly silent about their attitude to the Thirty-nine Articles of the Church of England. They were men of talent, men of experience, men who had volunteered from motives of ambition, curiosity and a desire to serve, but they were not aware of those gigantic forces of good and evil which had driven their predecessors in the great south seas to glory or damnation. They belonged to a climate of opinion which encouraged restraint and moderation. Yet at least one of their number was passion's slave. He was Ralph Clark, a second officer of the marines, who shortly after the first fleet weighed anchor began a diary in which he gushed out all the anguish and torment of his daily life.

All told, nineteen officers were appointed. With them went twenty-four non-commissioned officers, eight drummers, one hundred and sixty privates, thirty wives, and twelve children. On the number of convicts estimates vary. Just on three weeks before sailing an official return put the number at five hundred and sixty-five men, one hundred and fifty-three women, six boys and five girls, or seven hundred and twenty-nine all told.[12] Towards the end of 1786, the Admiralty commissioned two ships to convoy the convict transports— H.M. *Sirius* and the tender ship *Supply*. At the same time the Home Office contracted with shipowners to make available, equip and victual as transports and storeships for the convicts the *Alexander*, the *Charlotte*, the *Scarborough*, the *Friendship*, the *Prince of Wales*, and the *Lady Penrhyn*, together with the storeships *Borrowdale*, *Golden Grove*, and *Fishburn*. In the winter of 1786-7

[11] A remark by Elizabeth Macarthur, quoted in S. M. Onslow (ed.): *Some Early Records of the Macarthurs of Camden* (Sydney, 1914), p. 28.

[12] Return of the Botany Bay detachment of Marines, the number of wives and children, and the names of the ships on board of which they are embarked, with the number on board of each ship, April 15th, 1787; and Return of the male, female and children convicts embarked for Botany Bay, distinguishing the number of each on board each transport, April 15th, 1787; in *H.R.N.S.W.*, vol. 1, pt. 2, p. 79. For a discussion of the number of convicts embarked, see E. O'Brien: *The Foundation of Australia*, 2nd ed. (Sydney, 1950), App. B, pp. 279-84, and C. Bateson: *The Convict Ships 1787-1868* (Glasgow, 1959), pp. 82-5.

the officers (without their wives), the marines (with their wives and children), and the men and women convicts, with the children of the women, assembled at Portsmouth to prepare for departure.

In the beginning an indescribable hopelessness and confusion dominated the scene. The shop-keepers, in terror, lowered their shutters; the householders barred their doors; the convicts overcrowded the transports; the women convicts lolled on the decks in indescribable filth and their all too scanty clothing. Food was very short; medical supplies were non-existent; there was no provision to pay the marines; tools and ammunition were scarce.[13] In the terror and anxiety of impending exile, rumours began to circulate to add to the confusion. Some whispered that the fleet would sail within three weeks;[14] some said they knew for certain the unemployed had petitioned the Home Office for permission to accompany the convicts to Botany Bay.[15] No sooner had the latter rumour started than the wives of the convicts began to pour into Portsmouth from all parts of the country, but especially from London, to badger the officials in the name of humanity to permit them to travel with their husbands.[16]

But Phillip did not despair, nor did he succumb to the temptation to question the humanity of the people responsible for such a mess. With a becoming dignity he set down on paper the vision by which he would guide his behaviour in New South Wales. He wrote first of his intention to furnish the aborigines with everything that could tend to civilize them, and to give them a high opinion of their new guests. He then uncovered his values by declaring that as convicts could not be used to lay the foundations of an empire they should ever remain separated from the garrison, for on the convict question he always allowed personal prejudice to suppress all reference to their economic use, as well as their possible restoration to society. What was taking shape before his eyes was the future of the territory as a free society. He wrote of it in the grand manner: 'There can be no slavery in a free land, and consequently no slaves.' At that time he was harbouring neither illusions nor kindly feelings towards the convicts. The only two crimes which he believed merited death were murder and sodomy. For either of these crimes he would deliver the criminal to the natives in New Zealand and let them eat him, as the dread of this would operate much more strongly than the fear of death. For the rest, his mind was turning over the problems of food, clothing, and shelter in the new settlement. On goods of barter for the aborigines, his ideas were the commonplace ones of hatchets, beads, and a few small grindstones for the chiefs, though he added one queer idea—that as he understood the aborigines used a light, small tin lamps must be very acceptable.[17]

At the same time he appealed to the Admiralty and to the Home Office to

[13] See correspondence in C.O. 201/2.

[14] *Whitehall Evening Post*, 28-30 November 1786.

[15] *General Evening Post*, 4-6 January 1786.

[16] Ibid.

[17] This undated memorandum is in C.O. 201/2. It is reprinted in *H.R.N.S.W.*, vol. 1, pt. 2, pp. 50-4, without Phillip's capitals, and with some minor differences in words.

ease the overcrowding, increase the rations, clothe the half-naked women, and provide medicines for those distressed in mind or body. By the middle of March 1787 he had so sharpened his language, that he was telling Nepean: 'If you don't do what I ask, at least let the world know I was asking,'[18] and adding he was certain it was not the intention of His Majesty's ministers to send the marines out of the country in a worse state than troops were ever before sent out of the kingdom.[19] All round him high-minded motives jostled in his fellow-officers with the base and the petty. White laboured to obtain fresh food and wine for the sick; the same White pestered the Home Office to provide him with a servant, as without a servant his situation would, he believed, be truly uncomfortable.[20] The marines petitioned for a free ration of grog on the grounds that it was one of the principal necessaries of life.[21] Higher aspirations swayed the behaviour of others who swept swiftly across these early pages of the history of New South Wales. A Catholic priest, the Reverend Thomas Walsh, told Lord Sydney that if the ignorance of the Catholic convicts were removed, and their obligations as men and Christians forcibly inculcated, this might be a means of their becoming useful to themselves and perhaps afterwards to their country, and the practice of their religion might bring them out of the wretched state of depravity into which they had fallen.[22] For where the evangelical trusted in the Word to work an amendment of life, the Catholic trusted in the efficacy of the sacraments. But on all questions touching the Protestant ascendancy Sydney, like Tom Jones, behaved as a man of heroic ingredients. So the Catholic convicts were deprived of their means of grace and their hope of glory, simply because Lord Sydney believed sincerely that their means of grace could only be ministered to them at the risk of weakening the Protestant ascendancy.

The minds of those responsible for the success of the scheme did not linger long over problems of eternal salvation. Their minds were dwelling on the more mundane problems of how to feed, clothe and keep alive the marines and convicts under their charge. Such prospects improved in April and May. In April, the government got round to issuing a more detailed commission and instructions to Phillip and providing him with a semblance of a constitution. His first commission, issued on 12 October 1786, had done little more than appoint him Governor of the territory called New South Wales, and define the boundaries of that territory to extend from Cape York in latitude 10° 37' to the southern extremity of the said territory of New South Wales in the latitude of 43° 39' south, and all the country inland to the westward as far as the one hundred and thirty-fifth degree of longitude, including all

18 Phillip to Nepean, 18 March 1787 (C.O. 201/2).

19 Ibid.

20 White to Phillip, 7 February 1787, and White to Nepean, 27 February 1787 (C.O. 201/2).

21 Petition to Major Ross from the Detachment of Marines on Board the *Scarborough* transport, 7 May 1787 (C.O. 201/2). See similar petitions from Marines on the *Alexander*, 7 April 1787, on the *Prince of Wales*, 4 May 1787, and the *Charlotte*, 7 May 1787.

22 T. Walsh to Lord Sydney, not dated (C.O. 201/2).

the islands adjacent in the Pacific Ocean. It also required him carefully and diligently to discharge the duty of governor in and over the said territory by doing and performing all and all manner of things thereunto belonging. It required the officers, soldiers and all others to obey him, and the Governor to observe and follow the orders and directions he received under the signet and royal sign manual.[23] On 2 April 1787 a second commission was issued which began by styling Phillip Captain-General and Governor-in-Chief of the territory of New South Wales, defined the same boundaries as in the first commission, recited the oaths to be taken on assuming office, and then proceeded to spell out some of his powers. He was to administer oaths of allegiance, to appoint justices of the peace and other officers of the law, to pardon and reprieve, to provide for the cure and custody of idiots and lunatics, to levy armed forces, to proclaim martial law, to erect fortifications, to exercise certain naval powers, to control public moneys, to grant land, to control commerce, to require civil and military officers and the other inhabitants to assist him in executing the commission and powers conferred on him, to hold execute and enjoy the office and place of Captain-General and Governor-in-Chief, together with the powers and authorities pertaining thereto for and during the royal will and pleasure.[24]

On 25 April the government issued his instructions. These began by repeating the definition of the boundaries of the territory, then instructed him to have his commission read in public, and to proceed with the naval ship, the tender and the transports with about six hundred male and one hundred and eighty female convicts on board to Botany Bay. If necessary and expedient he was to call at Teneriffe, Rio de Janeiro, and the Cape of Good Hope, where he was to put corn and seed grain on the ships, and to take on board any number of black cattle, sheep, goats, or hogs. On arrival at Botany Bay he was to discharge the transports promptly to enable those engaged by the East India Company to proceed to trade with China, then to found the settlement at Botany Bay where, after securing the company from any attacks by the natives, he was to proceed to the cultivation of the land, distributing the convicts for that purpose in such manner and under such inspectors or overseers and regulations as might appear to be necessary and best calculated for procuring supplies of grain and ground provisions. He was to use every proper degree of economy, and transmit a copy of all expenditure to the Commissioners of the Treasury who would judge its propriety or expediency. He was to account also for clothing and provisions issued to convicts or civil and military officers in the same manner. The productions acquired by the labour of the convicts were to be considered a public stock, the disposal of which was to be left to him for the subsistence of the convicts and their families or the civil and military establishments. He was to reserve some for the subsistence of a further number of convicts. As all the convicts would not be employed in the production of food, he should use some to cultivate the flax plant. In addition, he was to send expeditions to explore the coast, to colonize Norfolk Island, to

23 *H.R.A.*, I, 1, pp. 1-2.
24 Ibid., pp. 2-8.

open an intercourse with the natives, and to conciliate their affections, enjoining all subjects to live in amity and kindness with them, to ascertain their numbers, to punish those who wantonly destroyed the natives or interrupted their several occupations, and report in what manner intercourse with them might be turned to the advantage of the colony.

He was to enforce a due observance of religion and good order among the inhabitants, and take such steps for the due celebration of public worship as circumstances would permit. In the first draft of these instructions he was to grant full liberty of conscience, and the free exercise of all modes of religious worship not prohibited by law, provided his charges were content with a quiet and peaceable enjoyment of the same, not giving offence or scandal to government; he was to cause the laws against blasphemy, profaneness, adultery, fornication, polygamy, incest, profanation of the Lord's Day, swearing and drunkenness to be rigorously executed. He was not to admit to the office of justice of the peace any person whose ill-fame or conversation might occasion scandal; he was to take care that the Book of Common Prayer as by law established be read each Sunday and Holy Day, and that the Blessed Sacrament be administered according to the rites of the Church of England.[25] Because of the great disproportion of female to male convicts, he was to take on board at any of the islands any women who might be disposed to come, taking care not to make use of any compulsive measures or fallacious pretences. He was to emancipate from their servitude any of the convicts who should, from their good conduct and a disposition to industry, be deserving of favour, and to grant them land, victual them for twelve months and equip them with tools, grain, and such cattle, sheep and hogs as might be proper, and could be spared. As the military officers and others might be disposed to cultivate the land, he was to afford them every encouragement. To prevent trade between New South Wales and the settlements of the East India Company in India or the coast of China he was to prohibit the building of boats as well as such trading by vessels arriving at the settlement.[26]

At the same time the government passed through parliament an act to authorize the Governor to create a court of criminal jurisdiction in New South Wales.[27] In the measured language of this statute, officialdom acknowledged that something more might be created in New South Wales than a place for the punishment and reformation of British criminals—that, as the preamble put it, it might be found necessary that a colony and a civil government should be established in the place to which the convicts were to be transported. This fell very short of that vision of empire which was taking shape in Phillip's mind, but then the purpose of the statute was more sombre. It stated simply that all outrages and misbehaviours were to be tried by a court of judicature consisting of the Judge Advocate together with six officers

[25] Original text of Instructions to Phillip, 25 April 1787 (C.O. 201/1). According to a heading on the outside sheet, these were referred to a committee on 20 April who presumably altered them as above.

[26] *H.R.A.*, I, 1, pp. 9-16.

[27] 27 Geo. III, c. 11. The text is printed in *H.R.A.*, IV, 1, pp. 3-5.

of His Majesty's forces by sea or land.[28] The warrant to create the court of civil jurisdiction put the point more positively: 'Wee find it Necessary that a Colony and Civil Government should be Established in the place.'[29] For the recovery of debts and the determining of private causes a court of civil jurisdiction should be created, consisting of the Judge Advocate together with two fit and proper persons appointed by the Governor, with the Governor or Lieutenant-Governor sitting as a court of appeal, with a right of appeal to the Privy Council in any case where the debt or the thing in demand exceeded the value of three hundred pounds.[30]

In the meantime the conditions on board the convict transports began to improve. Overcrowding was eased; surgeon White received his fresh food and his hospital wines for which he thanked the humanity of Lord Sydney.[31] A free allowance of grog was provided for the marines, for Sydney was a man too and anxious as he put it to remove every possible cause of dissatisfaction;[32] and clothing was issued for the men, including a number of worsted night caps for such of the convicts whose hair it might be necessary to cut off.[33] But the clothing for the women did not arrive, nor did the ammunition for the guns. On both, Phillip fussed and fretted as sailing day drew near. But, as that day approached, the desperate frantic note of the February and March letters to the Home Office mellowed into gratitude and affection, when the awareness of the momentousness of their business brushed aside the petty and the trivial, and his mind rose to the dignity of the occasion as he wrote to Evan Nepean, under-secretary at the Home Office.[34]

> Once more, I take my leave of you, fully sensible of the trouble you have had in this business, for which at present I can only thank you; but at a future period, when this Country feels the advantages that are to be drawn from our intended settlement, you will enjoy a satisfaction, that will I am sure make you ample amends. Wishing you health, I remain Dear Sir, your very sincere & obliged Friend, A. PHILLIP.

That was written on Friday, 11 May 1787. On the Saturday the final performance of the opera *Botany Bay* was given at the Royal Circus Theatre in London.[35]

Early on the golden Sunday morning of 13 May, the fleet of eight ships, the *Sirius*, the *Supply*, the *Alexander*, the *Charlotte*, the *Scarborough*, the *Friendship*, the *Prince of Wales*, and the *Lady Penrhyn*, together with the three storeships, weighed anchor in Portsmouth harbour, and sailed down the

[28] *H.R.A.*, IV, 1, pp. 3-5.

[29] Ibid., pp. 6-12.

[30] Ibid., pp. 6-8.

[31] J. White: *Journal of a Voyage to New South Wales* (London, 1790), p. 8.

[32] Nepean (for Sydney) to Phillip, 10 May 1787 (C.O. 201/2).

[33] Nepean to Middleton, 18 April 1787 (C.O. 201/2).

[34] Phillip to Nepean, 11 May 1787 (C.O. 201/2). For another version of this letter see *H.R.N.S.W.*, vol. 1, pt. 2, pp. 102-3. For another example of gratitude to Nepean, see the attitude of Nelson in N. H. Nicolas (ed.): *The Dispatches and Letters of Vice Admiral Lord Viscount Nelson*, 2nd ed. (London, 1845-6), vols. 5 and 6 *passim*.

[35] *Morning Chronicle and London Advertiser*, 14 May 1787.

channel for the high seas. In the town the shutters in the shops were still
lowered, and one clergyman on shore went down on his knees to ask God's
forgiveness on all of them. Otherwise no one noticed their departure. In
London, the home of over a third of the convicts, and of most of the men
responsible for their departure, the weather that day favoured the lovers of
riding and walking. The parks presented a fine show of carriages, of smart
beaux and nags. The weather favoured too the display of summer dresses, and
as the tartan was all the fashion, nothing but highland ladies and lasses were
to be seen in the parks.[36] At Carlton House, Mr Pitt was closeted for three
hours with the Prince of Wales, discussing the problems of the latter's debts
which had by then reached one hundred and sixty-one thousand pounds. On
the movements of Lord Sydney on 13 May history is silent, though there is
no reason to suppose that a man for whom votes were the stuff of life pondered what had happened at Portsmouth on that morning.

The press, too, both in the British Isles and western Europe confined itself
to the facts without comment. The *London Chronicle* announced the departure
on 15 May, contenting itself with the simple statement that early on Sunday
13 May the transports and convict ships had sailed for Botany Bay. The
Dutch press reported the facts likewise: 'Den 13 deezer is het Eskader, naar de
Botany-Bai in Nieuw Holland bestemd, en uit elf Zeilen bestaande, van Portsmouth derwards onder zeil gegaan',[37] but did not mention that it was to be a
settlement for the punishment and reformation of convicts. In this matter-of-
fact way the Dutch announced the first step in the colonization of that
'Zuidland' in which their ancestors had searched for gold and spices and
precious timbers and found only a land where the flies crawled into the eyes,
and the inhabitants were very black and very barbarian. But the minds of the
Dutch as ever were on such things as the consignments of spices arriving from
Java.[38] The minds of the Parisians too were on other things, for there nothing
was talked of so much as reform.[39]

According to Tench the faces of the convicts indicated a high degree of
satisfaction as the ships moved down the channel, though in some the pangs
of separation from their native land could not be wholly suppressed. Marks of
distress were more perceptible among the men than among the women. One
woman dropped some tears, but soon wiped them. After that the accent of
sorrow was no longer heard as more genial skies and a change of scene
banished repining and discontent, and introduced in their stead cheerfulness
and acquiescence in their lot, now not to be altered.[40] On that evening Ralph
Clark scribbled his first entry in his diary:

> May the 13th. 1787. 5 O'clock in the morning. The Sirius made the signal
> for the whole fleet to get under way, O gracious God send that we may

[36] *London General Evening Post*, 12-15 May 1787.

[37] *Haarlemse Courant*, 24 May 1787. See also *Amsterdamsche Courant*, 24 May
1787, and *La Gazette de Leyden*, 25 May 1787.

[38] Ibid.

[39] See, for example, the report in the *Gentleman's Magazine* (1788), vol. lviii, p. 174.

[40] W. Tench: *A Narrative of the Expedition to Botany Bay* (London 1789),
pp. 6-7.

put in to Plymouth or Torbay on our way down Channel that I may see our dear and fond affectionate Alicia and our sweet son before I leave them for this long absence. O Almighty God heer my prayer and grant me this request . . . what makes me so happy this day is it because that I am in hoppes the fleet will put into Plym^th Oh my fond heart lay still for you may be disappointed I trust in God you will not.[41]

But the fleet did not put in to Plymouth; and on 14 May Clark wrote: 'Oh my God all my hoppes are over of seeing my beloved wife and son.'

The Reverend Richard Johnson was troubled too. He found the captain of his ship close, unsociable and ill-natured; and the ship's company very profane. On the second Sunday, after he preached to the convicts on the heinous evil of common swearing, he was pleased to note for days afterwards that no coarsenesses passed their lips. So he knelt down in his cabin and beseeched his God to convince them of the folly and wickedness of such conduct. On that same Sunday a design by some convicts on the *Scarborough* to mutiny and take possession of the ship was discovered, the two ring-leaders being punished with two dozen lashes each.[42] These things, however, did not trouble Johnson. He felt a warm desire of soul to pour out his sins and sorrows before the Lord.

When they arrived at Teneriffe at the end of May he and his wife watched a procession of people carrying a statue of the Virgin. Johnson was shocked: 'Alas! Alas!' he wrote to a friend in England, 'what superstition and idolatry is all this—God make us thankful.'[43] The procession stimulated quite different thoughts in the mind of Collins, who believed the same great Creator of the universe was worshipped alike by Protestant and Catholic. He therefore felt no difficulty in divesting the pageant of its tinsel, its trappings and its censers, and joining with sincerity in offering the purest incense, that of a grateful heart.[44] While Johnson was thus thanking God for conferring on Englishmen the blessings of the Protestant religion, Phillip was fussing over such mundane affairs as procuring fresh meat and water, but not bread, as the latter was most expensive.[45]

On the voyage from Teneriffe to Rio de Janeiro the same pattern of behaviour was repeated. The convicts seemed incapable of experiencing that remorse and contrition which the pangs of exile were intended to rouse in their breasts, but displayed the depravity of their hearts. Some used their ingenuity to gain admission into the apartment of the female convicts, while another coined quarter dollars out of old buckles, buttons and pewter spoons with such cunning and address that White wished these qualities had been employed to more laudable purposes.[46] Johnson was torn between the temp-

[41] Journal of Ralph Clark, 13 May 1787 (MS. in Mitchell Library, Sydney).

[42] D. Collins: op. cit., vol. i, p. v.

[43] R. Johnson to Mr Fricker, Teneriffe, 30 May 1787 (original in the library of St Paul's Cathedral, Melbourne).

[44] D. Collins: *An Account of the English Colony in New South Wales* (London, 1798-1802), vol. i, p. vii.

[45] Phillip to Nepean, 5 June 1787, *H.R.N.S.W.*, vol. i, pt. 2, p. 108.

[46] J. White: op. cit., pp. 30-1 and 40-5.

G

tation to blame their depravity and the temptation to blame his own poor powers for his failure to communicate his message of hope. Clark gushed his guilt about drinking and gambling on to the pages of his diary, interspersed with words of tenderness for his fond Alicia and his darling son, and some angry words about the damned whores on board the ship, and how he was very glad to see that when a corporal flogged one of them he did not play with her but laid it home, for sentimentality and cruelty lived together in him too.[47]

The mind of Phillip was on quite different things, sometimes on such mundane matters as adequate clothing for the women, and sometimes on the type of civilization they would create in New South Wales. The arrival at Rio de Janeiro on 7 August 1787 prompted thoughts on what could be achieved with convict labour, for Rio de Janeiro had been built by convicts. One officer wrote back to London saying that his spirits had soared on reflecting that this flourishing and important colony was originally settled and peopled on a plan exactly similar to that of the present expedition.[48] But Phillip would have none of this: he was confident he would see the time when Botany Bay would be of more use to England than as a drain for its more degraded inhabitants.[49] Others drew quite a different sort of lesson from their experiences in Rio de Janeiro—Tench thought that any man who wanted to give his son a distaste for popery should point out to him the sloth, the ignorance, and the bigotry at Rio de Janeiro, while some of the other officers reflected on the superiority of Protestant over Catholic civilization.[50] At the same time rum was laid in, and all such seeds and plants procured as were thought likely to flourish on the coast of New South Wales—coffee, cocoa, cotton, banana, orange, lemon, guava, tamarind, prickly pear, eugenia, and the ipecacuanha.[51] On 4 September they sailed for the Cape of Good Hope.

They arrived at Table Bay on 13 October 1787. Here again the serious minded reflected on their future. A captain on an American ship, learning of their destination, suggested that in time free settlers would migrate to New South Wales not only from the old continent of Europe but also from the new continent of America, where the spirit of adventure and the thirst for novelty were, he believed, excessive.[52] Some of the convicts were beginning to hope that the disgrace they had suffered in England, due to their crimes, would by good behaviour at Botany Bay be buried in oblivion; that removed from their

[47] Journal of Ralph Clark, 22 June 1787.

[48] Letter written at Rio de Janeiro on 1 September 1787, and printed in the *London Chronicle* 26-9 January 1788. For a discussion of the employment of convicts in the formation of new colonies, see G. B. Barton: *History of New South Wales from the Records* (Sydney, 1889-94), vol. 1, pp. 12-13.

[49] *London Chronicle*, 3-5 January 1788.

[50] W. Tench: op. cit., pp. 28-9; Anon.: *The Voyage of Governor Phillip to Botany Bay: with an Account of the Establishment of the colonies of Port Jackson and Norfolk Island*, . . . (London, 1789), p. 34, and J. White: op. cit., p. 47 et seq.

[51] D. Collins: op. cit., vol. 1, p. xxviii; and *The Voyage of Governor Phillip* . . . , p. 33.

[52] W. Tench: op. cit., pp. 39-40.

wicked companions in London they would have no seducing opportunities to swerve them from the course of virtue; that in all probability they might be the founders of an empire greater than that from which they were banished.[53] So the germ of the idea that the colony belonged to the convicts and their posterity began to form in the anonymous minds of the convicts during the voyage of the first fleet. At the same time Phillip and the officers purchased more plants and seeds and animals—fig, bamboo, spanish reed, sugar cane, vines, quince, apple, pear, strawberry, oak, myrtle, rice, wheat, barley, Indian corn, a stallion, mares, a bull, a bull calf, cows, sheep, goats, hogs, and poultry, so that as sailing day approached the ships, having on board not less than five hundred animals of different kinds, chiefly poultry, put on an appearance which suggested the idea of Noah's ark.[54]

As the fleet sailed from Table Bay on 12 November, a melancholy reflection obtruded itself on the minds of a few. The land behind them was the abode of a civilized people; before them was the residence of savages. The refreshments and pleasures were to be exchanged for coarse fare and hard labour at New South Wales. All communication with families and friends was now cut off as they were leaving the world behind them to enter on a state unknown. To imprint this idea more firmly on their minds, and render the sensation still more poignant, that evening they spoke a ship from London.[55] To some this was an attractive challenge: this leaving behind civilization, this task of exploring a remote and barbarous land, and planting in it the arts of civilization.[56] Others were so overwhelmed by their private anguish that their minds could not soar to such a theme. Months earlier Clark had written in his diary: 'If I thought I should have been so unhappy at leaving my family behind I should never have come away from them, I did not know half how much I love them all or all the gains in earth should never have made me leave them.'[57]

They sailed for Botany Bay with a very unfavourable wind and a heavy southerly swell which buffeted the ships so much that on Christmas Day the weather was too rough to permit them much enjoyment in their Christmas dinner, which, as Collins put it, they complied with in the good old English custom. After rounding Van Diemen's Land they sighted the land of New Holland. By 19 January they were gratified with the sight of the entrance into Botany Bay.[58]

By 20 January 1788 the whole fleet had cast anchor in Botany Bay.[59] In the next few days most were disappointed by what they saw—'I cannot say

[53] *London Chronicle*, 29-31 May 1788.

[54] Anon.: *The Voyage of Governor Phillip . . .*, p. 41; D. Collins: op. cit., vol. 1, p. xxviii and *H.R.A.*, I, 1, p. 716, note 15.

[55] D. Collins: op. cit., vol. 1, p. xxxiv.

[56] W. Tench: op. cit., pp. 37-8.

[57] Journal of Ralph Clark, 22 June 1787.

[58] W. Tench: op. cit., pp. 10-11; D. Collins: op. cit., vol. 1, pp. xxxv-viii.

[59] For the arrival of the various ships see J. White: op. cit., p. 114; J. Hunter: *An Historical Journal of Transactions at Port Jackson and Norfolk Island* (London, 1793), pp. 41-2; Anon.: *The Voyage of Governor Phillip . . .*, p. 46.

from the appearance of the shore,' wrote Clark, 'that I will like it.'[60] Surgeon White looked in vain for the fine meadows talked of in Captain Cook's account, and concluded that that great navigator, notwithstanding his usual accuracy and candour, was certainly too lavish in his praises of Botany Bay.[61] King noted that the soil was nothing but sand.[62] Only the irrepressible Tench detected joy sparkling in every countenance, and risked the prediction that from this great day, the foundation, not the fall, of an empire would be dated.[63] Collins had an eye for the achievement: how under the blessing of God the voyage had been completed in eight months and one week, in which they had sailed five thousand and twenty-one leagues, had touched at the American and African continents, and had at last rested at the antipodes of their native country without meeting any accident, and with the loss of only thirty-two from sickness.[64]

In the meantime Phillip was just as quickly convinced as most of his fellow-officers that Botany Bay did not enjoy that commodious harbour and those other advantages to which his instructions had so confidently referred, for he found nothing there to recommend it as a place for settlement. On 21 January, accompanied by Captain John Hunter, two other officers and sailors, Phillip embarked with three boats for Broken Bay, hoping to discover a better harbour as well as a better country.[65] Early that afternoon they had the satisfaction of finding, as Phillip put it, the finest harbour in the world, in which a thousand sail of the line might ride in the most perfect security. Hunter put it more prosaically: 'The governor being satisfied with the eligibility of this situation, determined to fix his residence here.'[66] The next day Phillip examined the coves in the harbour, fixed on the one with the best spring of water, and honoured it with the name of Sydney before returning to Botany Bay in the evening of 23 January.[67]

On 25 January he sailed again in the *Supply* from Botany Bay, the rest of the transports following next day. As the ships sailed up the harbour to Sydney Cove the natives on the shore hollered 'Walla Walla Wha', or something to that effect, and brandished their spears as if vexed at the approach.[68] Mrs Whittle, the wife of Thomas Whittle, was delivered of a son on that day as the

[60] Journal of Ralph Clark, 20 January 1788.

[61] J. White: op. cit., p. 116, and p. 179.

[62] Journal of P. G. King, 1786-1790 (MS. in the Mitchell Library, Sydney).

[63] W. Tench: op. cit., p. 45.

[64] D. Collins: op. cit., vol. 1, pp. 1-2.

[65] J. Hunter: op. cit., pp. 142-3, and compare with Phillip to Sydney, 15 May 1788, *H.R.A.* I, 1, pp. 17-18, which states they were looking for Port Jackson, and with J. White: op. cit., p. 115, which states that Phillip, Hunter, and two masters of the men of war, and a party of marines set off on the morning of 21 January in two rigged long boats to examine Port Jackson.

[66] Phillip to Sydney, 15 May 1788, *H.R.A.*, I, 1, p. 18, and J. Hunter: op. cit., p. 43.

[67] J. White: op. cit., p. 115, and Anon.: *The Voyage of Governor Phillip . . .*, pp. 47-51.

[68] Log of Captain Robert Browne of the *Fishburn*, 26 January 1788 (Mitchell Library).

ship on which she was sailing edged towards Sydney Cove.[69] In the afternoon, the officers and marines having landed, the flag was hoisted on shore, while four glasses of porter were drunk to the health of their Majesties and the Prince of Wales, with success to the colony. Then the marines fired a *feu de joie*. The whole group gave three cheers, which was returned by the men on the *Supply*.[70] So, as one observer put it, the new town was 'crisned'.[71] Such was the display to enliven spirits, and fill the imagination with pleasing presages on the day European society conducted its first ceremony in Australia.[72]

On 27 and 28 January the male convicts and the rest of the marines landed. Some cleared ground for the different encampments; some pitched tents; some landed the stores; a party of convicts erected the portable house brought from England for the Governor on the east side of the cove. So, as Collins put it, the spot which had so lately been the abode of silence and tranquillity was now changed to that of noise, clamour and confusion, though after a time order gradually prevailed everywhere.[73] Very soon the old habits of depravity amongst the convicts began to recur.[74] This bothered Collins who had hoped that in taking possession of nature in her simplest, purest garb, they might not sully that purity by the introduction of vice, profaneness, and immorality.[75] Tench remained as sanguine as ever, believing the prospect before them justified expectation.[76]

On Sunday, 3 February, Johnson preached his first sermon under a great tree to a congregation of troops and convicts whose behaviour, according to one eye witness, was equally regular and attentive. He took for his text verse 12 of psalm 116: 'What shall I render unto the Lord for all his benefits toward me?' From the beginning of the voyage Johnson had laboured for their salvation, and to reclaim them from vice and depravity. He had furnished them with those books which tended to promote instruction and piety.[77] Yet from the day of the landing, if not earlier, a hopelessness and despair, a sense of failure, informed his language whenever he discussed the progress of his sacred mission—a sense of the hopelessness of his task, and an even livelier one of the depravity of his charges.[78]

[69] *Australian Genealogist*, 1936, vol. 2, pt. 3, p. 33.

[70] Journal of P. G. King, 1786-1790.

[71] Quoted in G. Mackaness: 'Australia Day', in R.A.H.S. *J. & P.*, 1960, vol. 45, pt. 5, p. 267.

[72] Anon.: *The Voyage of Governor Phillip . . .* , p. 58. For a discussion of the site of Sydney Cove and other details associated with the landing, see A. Lee: 'The Landing of Governor Phillip in Port Jackson', in R.A.H.S., *J. & P.*, 1901, vol. 1, pt. 1, p. 2 et seq. W. H. Yarrington: 'Some particulars concerning Phillip's arrival', in R.A.H.S., *J. & P.*, 1918, vol. 4, pt. 6, p. 310 et seq.; W. Dixon: 'The official Landing Place of Governor Phillip' (extract), in R.A.H.S., *J. & P.*, 1920, vol. 6, p. 292; and W. Dixon: 'The First Landing' (extract), in R.A.H.S., *J. & P.*, 1923, vol. 9, pt. 2, p. 112.

[73] Based on D. Collins: op. cit., vol. 1, p. 6 and W. Tench: op. cit., p. 60.

[74] W. Tench: op. cit., pp. 62-3.

[75] D. Collins: op. cit., vol. 1, p. 5.

[76] W. Tench: op. cit., p. 59.

[77] Ibid., p. 63.

[78] R. Johnson to J. Stonard, 8 May 1788 (MS. in St Paul's Cathedral, Melbourne).

At five o'clock on the morning of 6 February all things were in order for the landing of the women. All day the disembarkation went on, and about six in the evening at least one officer, Bowes, was enjoying the long wished for pleasure of seeing the last of them leave the ship. But what was one man's pleasure was as ever another man's pain, for one young seaman who impulsively swam ashore to visit the woman he had lived with on the ship, caught a chill and died. The women, we are told, were in general dressed very clean, and some few amongst them could be said to be well dressed. That night the sailors asked for some rum to make merry with upon the women quitting the ships. Soon, as one observer put it, they began to be elevated, and all that night there were scenes of debauchery and riot, which beggared description. To add to the confusion, a thunder-storm drenched the revellers.[79]

The next morning the convicts, both men and women, were gathered in a special clearing near Sydney Cove. The marines formed an outer circle. In the middle of the circle there was a camp table, with two red leather cases containing the texts of Phillip's two commissions. Then, to the music of the band of the marines, Phillip, Lieutenant-Governor Robert Ross, Judge Advocate David Collins, and the other civil and military officers, marched into the clearing and gathered round the table. The Judge Advocate read the two commissions appointing Arthur Phillip Captain General and Governor-in-Chief of the colony of New South Wales, the text of the act of parliament creating a court of civil jurisdiction, and the letters patent of 5 May constituting the vice-admiralty court. When the reading finished, the marines fired three volleys, while the band of the marines played the first bars of 'God Save the King' between each volley.[80]

Then Phillip harangued the convicts. The accounts of those who listened to what he had to say differed somewhat as attention was bound to wander after the tedious reading, the activities of the previous night, and the hot, sticky day. All agreed that he addressed himself to the behaviour of the convicts, saying that he would ever be ready to show approbation and encouragement to those who proved themselves worthy of them by good conduct, while those who acted in opposition to propriety would meet with the punishment they deserved. Some said he spoke more severely: that he described the greater part of the convicts as innate villains and people of the most abandoned principles, that for offences they would be punished most severely, that lenity had been tried and that to give it further trial would be vain, as he was no stranger to the use they made of every indulgence, and that a vigorous execution, whatever it might cost his feeling, would follow close upon the heels of every offender.[81] The sentry, he warned them, had orders to

[79] Diary of Lieut. Bowes, 6 February 1788 (Mitchell Library, Sydney).

[80] W. Tench: op. cit., pp. 65-6. See also diaries of Bowes and Clark, and the Journal of G. B. Worgan, Surgeon of the *Sirius* (Mitchell Library) for that day; D. Collins: op. cit., vol. 1, pp. 7-8; and C. H. Currey: 'An argument for the Observance of Australia Day on the Seventh Day of February and An Account of the Ceremony at Sydney Cove February 7, 1788', in R.A.H.S., *J. & P.*, 1957, vol. 43, pt. 4, pp. 153-74.

[81] Southwell Papers, 7 February 1788 (Mitchell Library). Printed in *H.R.N.S.W.*, vol. 2, App. D, p. 665.

fire with ball at any man seen in the women's camp in the evening, and all men practising promiscuous intercourse would be punished severely.[82] So perhaps Tench was displaying his characteristic charity when he described Phillip's words as a pointed and judicious speech,[83] while the others chose the right word when they called it a harangue. Some added that Phillip concluded by recommending marriage as an estate which would contribute to the convicts' happiness and comfort.[84]

After the ceremony, Phillip invited the officers to celebrate the occasion at a cold collation in his canvas house. Bowes noted with resentment that Phillip had not invited the captains of the ships and that he took no more notice of them than he did of the convicts.[85] Clark, with that unerring malice of the unquiet towards men in high places, scribbled in his diary his uneasiness about the powers of the Governor, how he had never heard of any one single person having so great a power vested in him as Phillip had by his commissions.[86] The minds of others were on the many loyal and public toasts drunk after the cloth was removed.[87]

On Sunday, 10 February, Johnson joined fourteen couples together in holy matrimony. Then, on 13 February, in the presence of the Judge Advocate, Phillip swore on the Bible: 'I, Arthur Phillip, do declare That I do believe that there is not any Transubstantiation in the Sacrament of the Lord's Supper or in the Elements of Bread and Wine at or after the Consecration thereof by any Person whatsoever.'[88] After which he acknowledged and declared George III to be the only lawful and undoubted sovereign of this realm, and that he abjured allegiance to the descendants of the person who pretended to be the Prince of Wales during the reign of James II.[89] He could not have known then that that descendant, Charles Edward Stuart, had died of alcoholic poisoning in Rome on 31 January 1788. With minds fortified by such a reminder of the Protestant ascendancy, they gathered again in the marquee of Lieutenant Ralph Clark on Sunday, 17 February, where Johnson celebrated the sacrament of the Lord's Supper, and Clark was so carried away by the solemn occasion that he vowed to keep the table as long as he lived, as it was the first table that ever the Lord's Supper was taken from in this country.[90]

[82] Journal of G. B. Worgan, Surgeon on the *Sirius*, 9 February 1788.

[83] W. Tench: op. cit., p. 66; D. Collins: op. cit., vol. 1, p. 8; and J. White: op. cit., pp. 124-5.

[84] J. White: op. cit., p. 124.

[85] Diary of Bowes, 7 February 1788.

[86] Diary of Ralph Clark, 7 February 1788.

[87] W. Tench: op. cit., pp. 66-7.

[88] *H.R.A.*, IV, 1, p. 21.

[89] Ibid., pp. 19-20. Oaths of Abjuration and Assurance.

[90] Journal of Ralph Clark, 17 February 1788.

6

CONVICTS AND THE FAITH OF
THE FOUNDERS

THIS FIRST FLEET arrived in January 1788. The *Lady Juliana* brought another two hundred and twenty-one women convicts early in June 1790; then, later in the same month, the second fleet arrived bringing another seven hundred and fifty-seven convicts. Over two thousand convicts arrived during 1791, and every year from 1792 to 1813, except for 1794-6 and 1805, between three and seven hundred convicts arrived each year; in 1814 the number rose into the thousands. Between 26 January 1788 and 20 November 1823, thirty-seven thousand, six hundred and six convicts embarked for Sydney Cove or one of the outer settlements of New South Wales.

The gap of two years and five months between the arrival of the first and second fleets provided the setting for the early struggle for survival. The low numbers in 1794-6 were in the main the consequence of war at home, though unwittingly they subsequently lent weight to the nationalists who pored over the early history for evidence of neglect or indifference in high places in London. The sudden increase in numbers between 1817 and 1819 created conditions which influenced the British government to abandon the use of New South Wales as a settlement for the punishment and reformation of British criminals, and to use the convicts as the labour force with which to build the material foundations of European society in Australia. Throughout the whole period, the men outnumbered the women; all told, thirty-one thousand, nine hundred and twenty-six men were transported and five thousand six hundred and eighty women, or a proportion of 5.6 men to every woman—a proportion which was increasing rather than decreasing by 1823. So, during the period, there were various schemes to import women for the men, and many denunciations of the behaviour caused by the absence of women, such as drinking, whoring, and crimes against nature.

One thousand four hundred and fifteen Irish convicts (1,140 men and 275 women) were embarked from Irish ports between 1791 and 1800; seven hundred and one (610 men and 91 women) between 1801 and 1802; five hundred and forty-six (409 men and 137 women) between 1803 and 1810; and five thousand, eight hundred and forty-seven (5,069 men and 778 women) between 1811 and 1823—or eight thousand, five hundred and nine (7,228 men, 1,281 women) all told.[1] In the same periods, seventy Scots (58 men, 12 women) were

[1] From figures compiled by Mrs Barbara Penny from C.O. 207/1; Accounts and Papers relating to Convicts on Board the Hulks and those transported to New South Wales, Ordered to be printed 10 and 26 March 1792; *H.R.A.*, *passim*; T. J. Kiernan: *Transportation from Ireland to Sydney, 1791-1816* (Canberra 1954); and C. Bateson: *The Convict Ships, 1787-1868* (Glasgow 1959).

embarked between 1788 and 1800; five Scots, all men, between 1801 and 1802; forty-three Scots (31 men, 12 women) between 1803 and 1810; and seven hundred and thirty-seven (670 men, 67 women) between 1811 and 1823—or eight hundred and fifty-five all told, of whom seven hundred and sixty-four were men and ninety-one were women. Only three and a half per cent of the convicts embarked from England and Scotland between 1801 and 1823 were Scots.[2] By a rough and ready calculation, approximately two hundred and seventy of the seven hundred and eighty odd convicts on the first fleet came from London—a proportion roughly preserved in all the ships with English and Scots convicts on board between 1788 and 1823, except for such odd years as 1812 and 1813—when special crimes caused by economic distress upset that proportion. The other main area from which convicts were transported was Warwickshire.[3]

These were the men, women and children who had been found guilty of a crime punishable by transportation in either the British Isles or, in rare cases, a British possession overseas. Transportation was, next to death, the most severe punishment known to the criminal law and as such was intended to serve the ends of all punishment—namely to purge, to deter, and to reform. Of these three, the contemporaries responsible for the execution of the law believed the deterrent to be the principal aim. They believed the greater the terror the greater the deterrent, the greater the physical and mental sufferings, the greater the deterrent.[4] The preamble to the act introducing transportation as a punishment defined its purposes as to deter wicked and evil-disposed persons from being guilty of crimes, and to supply servants to the colonies and plantations who by their labour and industry might be the means of improving and making the colonies and plantations useful to the nation.[5] By the 1780s official comments added the aim of reformation, an addition acclaimed by the criminal law reformers, the philanthropists, and the charity workers, but treated with indifference by officials. Transportation, they said, was a deterrent, intended to be an object of the greatest apprehension to those who looked upon strict discipline and regular labour as the most severe and least

[2] Compiled by Mrs Barbara Penny from H.O. 11/1, 11/2, 11/3, 11/4 and 11/5.

[3] Taken from returns in C.O. 201/2 (first fleet); C.O. 201/4 (*Lady Juliana* and second fleet); and H.O. 11/1, 11/2, 11/3, 11/4, 11/5 (third fleet and to 1823).

[4] W. Blackstone: *Commentaries on the Laws of England* 13th ed. (London, 1800), vol. 4, pp. 251-2. Compare this passage with the statement by Lord Swinton at the trial of Thomas Muir in 1793: 'The sole object of punishment among us is only to deter others from committing like crimes in time coming.' T. B. Howell: *State Trials* (London, 1809), vol. 23, p. 234. See also the statement by Archbishop Whately in 1832: 'No axiom in Euclid can be more evident than that the object of the legislator in enacting that murderers shall be hanged and pilferers imprisoned or transported, is, not to load the gallows, fill the jails, and people New Holland, but to prevent the commission of murder and theft.' R. Whately: *Thoughts on Secondary Punishment* (London, 1832), p. 61.

[5] An Act for the further preventing Robbery, Burglary, and other Felonies, and for the more effectual Transportation of Felons, and unlawful Exporters of Wool; and for declaring the Law upon some Points relating to Pirates, 4 Geo. I, c. 11, 1717, *Statutes at Large*, vol. 5.

tolerable of evils, to reform the convicts and to provide labour for the colonies.[6] Some claimed that the greatest benefit of transportation was that it removed the criminal to a place where he could do no further harm.[7] The interest of the mother country lay in the reduction of crime and in protecting citizens from harm, while the interests of a colony lay in the supply and quality of labour.

The length of the sentence and the type of crimes punished by transportation varied between England, Scotland and Ireland. In England sentences were for seven years, fourteen years or life between 1788 and 1823, though there were isolated examples of ten-year sentences. A person could be sentenced to transportation either by the commutation of a death sentence to transportation for a stated period, or for a breach of law for which the punishment prescribed by statute was transportation, or for an offence against the army or navy codes. Wrongs to property, wrongs to the person, piracy, offences relating to the coinage (such as counterfeiting, gaming and lotteries), offences against the game laws, offences against the machinery of justice, offences against public order (such as framebreaking), offences against the state (such as riot or sedition), offences against army or navy law, and many miscellaneous offences—such as opening places of amusement or entertainment on Sunday evenings, the holding of debates on texts of Holy Scripture by incompetent persons such as a Jesuit or a member of a religious order coming into England without a licence to reside therein, solemnizing a marriage clandestinely, or stealing a shroud out of a grave—were all punished by transportation.[8] The law changed in some details from year to year, as did the disposition of juries to convict and the mood of the judges, but such changes, decisive as they were in the lives of individuals, affected very little either the numbers sentenced or the types boarding the convict ships.

An act of 1785 authorized the King-in-Council to name a place or places to which persons sentenced to transportation, or to banishment from Scotland, might be sent.[9] The Scots criminal law differed from the English, however, in two ways. Sentences, in the main for three, five or ten years, were milder, the judges being given discretionary power to modify the sentence according to the youth, the condition or the temptation of the prisoner. So where the English were hanging ten to twelve in a day during the legal year, the Scots were launching a mere six a year into eternity, and transporting only three and a half per cent of the number despatched from England and Scotland between 1787 and 1823. The teachings of Calvin and the Puritans on human relations still tainted their criminal law, investing it with a cruelty on questions affecting the human heart to match the ferocity of the English laws to pro-

---

[6] C. J., vol. 40, col. 1161.

[7] Lord Henderland at the trial of Thomas Muir in 1793, T. B. Howell: op. cit., vol. 28, p. 233.

[8] Based on W. Holdsworth: *A History of English Law* (London, 1932-52), vol. 11, pp. 530-47; and P. Colquhoun: *A Treatise on the Police of the Metropolis*, 1st ed. (London, 1796), pp. 261-3.

[9] An Act for the more effectual Transportation of Felons and other Offenders, in that part of *Great Britain* called *Scotland*, and to authorize the Removal of Prisoners in certain Cases, 25 Geo. III, c. 46, *Statutes at Large*, vol. 35.

tect property and the existing social order. Women who bore illegitimate children, men who committed adultery, men or women who denied the existence of God, and all desecrators of the Lord's Day, could be exposed to public derision and abuse; the adulterers could be sentenced to stand in a public place with a placard suspended from their necks bearing the words— 'These are adulterers.' So the Scots criminal law conferred the prestige of the law on the Calvinist notion of the upright man, while endowing the malice of the improver and the cruelty of the upright against the weak with all the might, majesty and power of the law.[10]

For a brief period, in 1793, the laws against sedition in Scotland were used to prevent the spread of what one contemporary described as the itch of Jacobinism. In the first flush of panic the judges sentenced to transportation five men who propagated the teachings of the enlightenment on politics. Their numbers were few, while some of them were unworthy of the noble view of man, for testifying to which their gaolers were prepared to allow them to rot away their lives on a barbarous and inhospitable shore. Yet it was these two accidents of the Scottish criminal law—the Calvinist-dominated moral code, and the punishment for sedition—which brought together an association of great moment in the history of civilization in Australia: the association between men whose minds were steeped in Calvinist traditions and men whose minds were fashioned by the teachings of the enlightenment.

The criminal law also provided the occasion for the coming of another great creative force in the shaping of that civilization—Irish Catholicism and the Irish character. In 1790 an act passed by the Irish Parliament empowered the Lord-Lieutenant or Chief Governor to name a place or places to which felons and vagabonds could be transported. By an order of 1790 the Lord-Lieutenant named New Holland.[11] In its sentences, between 1788 and the act of union in 1801, the Irish law copied the English—the sentences being for seven years, fourteen years or life. Because of the more inflammatory political situation, caused by an alien political domination and the Protestant ascendancy, and fed by the Irish gift for nursing an ancient wrong, the laws to protect property, the person and the state were more draconian than in England. Vagrancy could be punished by transportation for seven years; agrarian outrage could be punished by death or transportation; after 1796, associating to end English rule could be punished by transportation for life.[12] So the ancient wrong and the laws to perpetuate that wrong drove on to the convict ships sailing from

10 J. Galt: *Annals of the Parish* (Edinburgh, 1936), 1st ed. 1821; H. G. Graham: *The Social Life of Scotland in the Eighteenth Century* (London, 1937), pp. 485-501.

11 An Act for rendering the Transportation of Felons and other Vagabonds more Easy, 30 Geo. III, c. 32, 1790, *Statutes Revised, Northen Ireland* (Belfast, 1956), vol. 1. See E. O'Brien: *The Foundation of Australia*, 2nd ed. (Sydney, 1950), pp. 130-3; and E. Curtis and R. B. McDowell: *Irish Historical Documents, 1172-1922* (London, 1943), pp. 204-5, and 238-9.

12 An Act to prevent and punish tumultuous risings of persons within this kingdom, and for other purposes therein mentioned. 15 & 16 Geo. III, c. 21, 1775, *Statutes Revised, Northern Ireland* (Belfast, 1956), vol. 1; G. C. Lewis: *Our Local Disturbances in Ireland, and on the Irish Church Question* (London 1836), pp. 6-7; E. Curtis and R. B. McDowell: op. cit., p. 205.

Irish ports a higher proportion of people not dependent on crime for a living than similar ships from England and Scotland.

For all the evidence suggests that a very high proportion of the men and women transported to New South Wales from England and Scotland between 1788 and 1823 were dependent on crime for a living: that is to say, they belonged by taste and circumstance to the criminal classes. This conclusion emerges from an examination of the official and unofficial descriptions of the convicts. The official descriptions do not tell very much. Up to 1813, they merely give the numbers embarking, the numbers landing, and the length of the sentences. From 1813 on, they begin to give information on age and religion. From 1813 to 1823, the average age of the men on the convict ships was between twenty-four and twenty-nine, the youngest age recorded being eleven years. The custom was to select men under fifty years of age.[13] In the same years, the average age of the women was from twenty-three to twenty-five. Again, it was customary to select women below the age of forty-five from the women sentenced to transportation.[14] The men also greatly outnumbered the women; 586 to 192 on the first fleet, 939 to 304 on the second (*i.e.* including the *Lady Juliana*), 1,736 men to 150 women on the third. All told, as we have seen, 24,698 men and 4,399 women were transported from England and Scotland between 1787 and 1823, or some 85% men and 15% women. Of their religion we have only snatches of the answer. On the first fleet, approximately two-thirds classified themselves as Church of England and one-third as Catholic. Over the whole period, Protestants outnumbered Catholics from England and Scotland by approximately twenty to one. Representatives of other faiths on the convict ships were few: there were a few Jews on the first fleet, and a few on most of the ships down to the end of the convict period; there was one Ukranian; there were negroes; and there were Indians and Anglo-Indians from the British possessions in India.[15]

All sorts of occupations were represented—butchers, brass-founders, hatters, factory boys, grocers, errand boys, carpenters, needlemakers, shoemakers, cabinet makers, tailors, painters, clergymen, priests, boiler-makers, wool-sorters, hair-dressers, pot-boys, waiters, linen-weavers, curriers, cooks, coal-miners, tobacconists, machine-turners, silk-twisters, jockeys, cork-cutters, saddlers, ostlers, bargemen, commercial travellers, clerks, domestic servants, spinners, weavers, needlewomen, dairy-maids, and barmaids. But such a variety deceives, for it cloaks with a respectable trade many of the men and women whose very aversion to labour had driven them to crime in order to escape the punishment of earning their living in the sweat of their brow.

13 Compiled from information in Indents of Convict Ships, 1813-1823 (MS. in Mitchell Library, Sydney). See also Report of the Select Committee on Transportation, 1812, pp. 9-10, and evidence of J. H. Capper, ibid., *P.P.* 1812, II, 341; his evidence to the Select Committee on the State of the Gaols, 1819, p. 300, *P.P.* 1819, VII, 579; and H. G. Bennet: *Letter to Viscount Sidmouth, Secretary of State for the Home Department, on the Transportation Laws, the State of the Hulks, and of the Colonies in New South Wales* (London, 1819), pp. 10, 19, 24.

14 Ibid.

15 Based on figures taken from the *H.R.A.*, I, vols. 1-10; H.O. 11/1, 11/2, 11/3, 11/4, 11/5; and C. Bateson: op. cit., *passim.*

From the year 1826, when the indents of convict ships began to publish the crimes for which convicts were transported, down to the end of transportation to eastern Australia in 1853, the thieves predominated, as two examples from 1826 can show.[16] Of the 147 transported on the *Sesostris* no fewer than 123 had been convicted for theft, as distinct from highway robbery which accounted for another eleven. On the *Marquis of Huntley*, the numbers transported for theft and highway robbery were 163 and 17 respectively, in a total of 196. There is no reason to believe these proportions differed in the period before 1826.

Most observers distinguished between the regular thieves, whom they found by character and disposition reckless of the future, and the receivers of stolen goods and the forgers who generally belonged to a higher rank in society and were possessed of some education.[17] All other descriptions accept this classification, some adding bizarre characters such as itinerant Jews, who wandered from street to street holding out temptations to pilfer and steal, spendthrifts, rakes, giddy young men, profligate, loose and dissolute characters who seduced others to intemperance, lewdness, debauchery, gambling and excess, bawds who kept houses of ill-fame, brothels or lodging houses for prostitutes, unfortunate females of all descriptions who supported themselves by prostitution and theft, strolling minstrels, ballad singers, showmen, trumpeters, gipsies, gin-drinking dissolute women, and destitute boys and girls who wandered and prowled about the streets. It has been estimated that in London at the end of the eighteenth century one hundred and fifteen thousand depended on crime for a living.[18]

When these men and women spoke for themselves before their judges, they seemed to be liars, drunkards and cheats, flash and vulgar in dress, cheeky in addressing their gaolers when on top, but quick to cringe and whine when retribution struck. With hearts and minds unsustained by any of the great hopes of mankind, driven on by the terror of detection, strangers to loyalty, parasites preying on society, fit objects for that eye of pity with which the historian contemplates those on whom the hand of the potter blundered, they were men and women who roused their contemporaries to disgust and to apprehension, but rarely to compassion, and never to hope. Some of them can be seen before their judges.

Here is a man charged with theft at the Old Bailey in December of 1787:[19]

Prisoner: I have a witness in Court, who is the keeper of Tothill-fields, who can prove that I was so much intoxicated, that I even fell out of the

[16] Indents of convict ships, 1826 (Mitchell Library).

[17] See, for example, E. G. Wakefield: *Facts Relating to the Punishment of Death in the Metropolis* (London, 1831), pp. 185-6.

[18] P. Colquhoun: *A Treatise on the Police of the Metropolis*, 4th ed. (London, 1797), pp. vii-xi, 88-90, and 158-9.

[19] *The Whole Proceedings on the King's Commission of the Peace, Oyer and Terminer, and Gaol Delivery for the City of LONDON, and also the Gaol Delivery for the County of Middlesex, held at Justice Hall in the Old Bailey,* 12 December 1787, no. 1, pt. 1, pp. 13-14.

coach as they carried me to prison, and that I did not know I was in prison till the next day.

Court: I do not think that will be of any use to you; if you was to prove that you was ever so much intoxicated; because an honest man, if he was ever so drunk, would not steal.

Prisoner: Very just, my Lord.   GUILTY   DEATH

He was humbly recommended to mercy by the Jury and Prosecutor.

The Crown graciously listened to his appeal for mercy, and he went on his long journey to New South Wales.

Here is a young man of eighteen years defending himself against a charge of stealing spoons:[20]

> I went into this shop to buy a black pudding for my breakfast, I knocked several times and nobody came to me; I went to the parlour door and cried out halloo! is there nobody here? while I was standing there, this man came, and said I wanted to steal those spoons that laid in the chair, and charged me with a constable.   GUILTY
>
> *Court:* The sentence of the court upon you is, that you be transported beyond the seas, for the term of seven years.
>
> *Prisoner:* I am very much obliged to you gentlemen, I shall make a bright man yet.

He at least entertained hopes for his future.

An odd one or two pleaded hunger as the motive for their crime. William Constable, for example, accused in February 1788 of stealing a linen frock, a printed book valued at 6d., two other printed books valued at 12d., and another printed book valued at 6d., pleaded he had been two or three days without food, went to get some victuals, and found these odd sources of human refreshment, for which the court transported him for seven years.[21] Sarah Sophia Ann Brown was accused in December 1787 of stealing nine guineas and three shillings from a Mr Redmond who had drunk with her at a hotel (which was a house of ill-fame), had gone up to bed, and fallen asleep. 'My Lord,' Sarah Sophia Ann Brown told her judge, 'I live in Mrs Foy's house, as a girl, an unfortunate girl . . .'[22]

There was Samuel Burt, sentenced to death for forgery, who, when told that His Majesty, whose humanity could only be equalled by his love of virtue, had extended his mercy, told the court he was so sunk and degraded in society that he was insensible to such a blessing. He told them too that as it was impossible for him to be united with the person who was dearer to him than life itself, he preferred death to the prolongation of a life which could not be otherwise than truly miserable. The court, we are told, was astonished at this address. But within a month Burt wrote to the court recorder expressing his sorrow for his obstinacy and presumption, and entreated to be sent to Botany Bay.[23] So he made the long journey across the oceans.

[20] Ibid., 25 June 1788, no. 6, pt. 4, p. 594.

[21] Ibid., 27 February 1788, no. 3, pt. 5, p. 318.

[22] Ibid., 10 September 1788, no. 7, pt. 7, pp. 770-1.

[23] *Gentleman's Magazine*, January 1787, vol. 57, pt. 1, p. 87; and February 1787, vol. 57, pt. 1, p. 180.

There was John ——, who was convicted of a capital crime in 1793, sentenced to death, and returned to a prison whose keeper, observing signs of contrition in him, was distressed that a man in such a deplorable situation should have such faint ideas of a supreme being and fainter still about a future state. The keeper was distressed, too, to find the man tortured almost to madness by gloomy apprehensions of misery after death. So he arranged to discourse and pray with him each day, and conceived the idea of teaching the man how to read. But the man made little progress, and in desperation he fell on his knees: 'Good God!' he cried, 'you know what a blockhead I am, and that I never can learn this hard thing; but you know also that you made everything, and see every thing, and can look into our thoughts; look into mine, and, as you are wiser than any man, do me a favour . . . Take I pray you, these cards [*i.e.* the letters of the alphabet] and make the best prayer you can for me: then read it out to yourself, and think as if I made it, for I promise you, I will try to be a good man. Only let me know what you have written, that I may be as good as my word.' He was pardoned on condition that he went to Botany Bay for fourteen years.[24]

Not all the men and women sentenced to transportation embarked for New South Wales. The regulations instructed the officials to select in the first instance all the male convicts under the age of fifty who were sentenced to transportation for life or fourteen years, and to fill the numbers up with such seven-year men as were most unruly in the hulks, or were convicted of the most atrocious crimes. It was customary to send without any exception all women whose health would permit it and whose age did not exceed forty-five.[25] Those who were shocked by the appearance and character of the men on the hulks, who found many of them scarce a degree above brute creation and branded them as drunkards, as men who shocked the ears of the passers-by with blasphemy, oaths and songs most offensive to modesty, continued to be shocked and revolted by the men and women on the convict ships.[26]

Most of those who worked with them on the ships—the captains, the chaplains, the surgeons, the charity workers—have testified to their degradation and spiritual wretchedness. They denounced them as liars, as men driven to lying as the weak from time immemorial have been driven to behaviour which provides the occasion and the pretext for the strong to torment them. They denounced them as treacherous. In 1816 a wife visited her husband at Portsmouth. During a tender and distressing farewell he stole from her the money for her return fare to London and her wedding ring; on being accused of the theft he refused to see his wife again, on the pretence that his feelings had been so lacerated by the farewell that he would not be able to endure a repetition of the conflict.

24 Ibid., May 1798, vol. 68, pt. 1, pp. 395-6.

25 Report of the Select Committee on Transportation, 1812, pp. 9-10, *P.P.* 1812, II, 341.

26 G. Barrington: *An Account of a Voyage to New South Wales* (London, 1810). p. 74.

They denounced them as hypocrites who performed to admiration the mimicry of repentance. They denounced them as men who used their idleness to sink deeper into vice, debauchery, and depravity, men who drowned the admonitions of the improvers—the chaplains, the charity workers, the surgeons with a self-appointed bent for the cure of souls—in a roar of blasphemy; men who wore on their faces the most deplorable and hideous features of drunkenness and depravity. Yet out of such wretchedness and degradation was conceived that desperate song of defiance:

> I'll kill them tyrants one by one and shoot the floggers down;
> I'll give the law a little shock, remember what I say,
> They'll yet regret they sent Jim Jones in chains to Botany Bay.[27]

For what the improvers did not detect was the source of their future power and glory, the strength in their hands and their brains to create wealth, the drive to use that wealth to buy property, to acquire that degree of respectability which their society attached to property, to found families and so experience those nobler human emotions to which their pursuit of crime had left them a stranger.

The improvers were just as purblind on the behaviour of the women. They recorded their disgust with the drunkenness, the coarse language, the brawls between these consorts of thieves, the women who hawked the body to supplement the takings from theft. There were women such as Mrs Pryor who visited the convict women ships to distribute haberdashery and to read to them from the Word, to be greeted by drunken women shrieking their intention to murder one another.[28] But again the improvers missed the variety —that presence on the same ship of the alpha and omega of human behaviour —of the woman who died from a broken heart before the ship sailed; of Jewesses who masqueraded as Roman Catholics at Rio de Janeiro to increase their takings in the pursuit of one of the oldest professions known to mankind, while on the same boat there was a woman named Mary Bryant who, three years after her arrival in New South Wales, made a voyage in a small open boat from Sydney to Batavia.[29] Some convicts surprised their surgeon by shedding tears, for these drunkards, these liars, these informers could weep, as they too had been made in the image of God, and were inheritors of His kingdom, or that other kingdom which the sons of the enlightenment were confident of man's capacity to create.

Not all of the men and the women, however, were recruited from the criminal classes. Between 1787 and 1823 four hundred and fourteen men were transported from the army and the navy for offences punishable by transportation in their regulations. At least ninety-nine per cent of these came from

[27] See for example, J. Haslam: *Convict Ships. A Narrative of a Voyage to New South Wales, in the year 1816* . . . (London, 1819), pp. 16-21; and T. Reid: *Two Voyages to New South Wales and Van Diemen's Land, with a description of the present condition of that interesting colony* . . . (London, 1822), p. 24 et seq. and 136-8. Jim Jones at Botany Bay in D. Stewart and N. Keesing: *Old Bush Songs* (Sydney, 1957), p. 17.

[28] T. Reid: op. cit., pp. 116-17.

[29] G. Rawson: *The Strange Case of Mary Bryant* (London, 1938).

the rank and file though, as with so much in the history of the convict system, one exception survived as a person in the history books. For amongst them was William Redfern, a surgeon in the navy, who as a young man of nineteen had joined in the mutiny of the Nore in 1797, for which he was sentenced to death, the sentence being commuted to transportation for life. In 1812-13, fifty-five men were transported for their behaviour during the Luddite riots. For offences committed during the upheavals following the Napoleonic wars —the march of the Blanketeers, the Pentridge revolution, the Huddersfield rising—one hundred and sixty were transported to New South Wales or Van Diemen's Land.[30]

There were the gentlemen criminals, who were willing to confess to crime for their daily bread, but disdained to be confounded with the common thief. On the contrary these men prided themselves on their superior accomplishments, on their culture and their refinement. 'Though I lived by depredation,' said James Hardy Vaux, who was transported for stealing in 1801, 'yet I did not, like the abandoned class of common thieves, waste my money and leisure time in profligate debauchery, but applied myself to the perusal of instructive and amusing books, my stock of which I daily increased.'[31] George Barrington, who was transported for removing a gold watch, chain and seals from the pocket of Henry Hare Townsend on 1 September 1790, was a gentleman pickpocket, who resented the ignominy of being mingled with felons. His creator had endowed him not only with such a fatal flaw, but also with a fulsomeness, an extravagance of speech and gesture, which exposed him to the ridicule as well as the persecution of the law. His histrionic appeals to his judges in 1790 to extend to him that supreme felicity of having comfort administered to his wounded spirit, roused a cackle of laughter rather than pity.[32]

There were also the casual criminals, the men and women pushed by chance and circumstance into the clutches of the criminal law. There was Dr Halloran, who was transported in 1818 for forging a frank, and thus depriving the revenue of ten pence. Such a trifle provided New South Wales with the man to pioneer schools for the education of the sons of the men of property and respectability.[33] There was Francis Howard Greenway, who was transported in 1813 for having forged an endorsement on a contract. Greenway's Sydney is the monument to that transgression.[34] There was George Howe, who was transported in 1800, probably for a political offence, a transgression which provided New South Wales with an editor for its first gazette.[35] For while

30 See F. O. Darvall: *Popular Disturbances and Public Order in Regency England*, (London, 1934), pp. 2-3; E. O'Brien: op. cit., p. 21 et seq.; J. H. Clapham: *Economic History of Modern Britain* (Cambridge, 1926), vol. 1, p. 602; M. Clark: 'The Origins of the Convicts transported to Eastern Australia, 1787-1852', in *Historical Studies*, vol. 7, no. 26, May 1956, pp. 121-35, and vol. 7, no. 27, November 1956, pp. 314-27.

31 J. H. Vaux: *Memoirs* (London, 1819), vol. 2, p. 24 and B. Elliott: *James Hardy Vaux. A Literary Rogue in Australia* (Adelaide, 1944), pp. 18-20.

32 G. Barrington: op. cit., pp. 59-72; and *Scots Magazine*, 1790, vol. 52, pp. 455-6.

33 H. G. Bennet: *Letter to Viscount Sidmouth* . . . , note (f), pp. 116-18.

34 M. H. Ellis: *Francis Greenway, His Life and Times* (Sydney, 1953). .

35 J. A. Ferguson, A. G. Foster and H. M. Green: *The Howes and Their Press* (Sydney, 1936).

the casuals were few in numbers, they were rich in talents. Amongst them were lawyers, clergymen, priests, teachers, journalists and clerks—whose knowledge and gifts were to provide some of the adornments of civilization in a society otherwise limited to the search for food, shelter and clothing.

There was also a sprinkling of bizarre characters. James Lara (or Larra), when charged in December 1787 with feloniously stealing one silver tankard, told the court: 'My Lord, to deny the fact would be very horrid; at the same time I leave myself entirely to your mercy; at the time the fact was committed, which my witness will prove, I was very much intoxicated, or else no man in the world could attempt to do a thing of the kind, to put a tankard in his pocket where there was forty or fifty people in the room; as such I leave myself entirely to your mercy; I never was guilty of such a crime before; I never was at the house before in my life.'[36] In London he had followed the profession of thief and forger of bank notes; within a few years he was known as the honest Jew of Parramatta.[37] There was John Hyam who, when charged with receiving stolen goods in January 1790, had told the court he had not got a friend in the world, but God above and the mercy of the court. He was transported—to become with Lara a founder of the Jewish community in New South Wales.[38] Such oddities, such surprises amongst the men sentenced to forced labour in an unknown and barbarous land, ensured their rescue from that anonymity to which their partners in crime and misfortune were condemned.

It was the same with the convicts from Scotland, where the professional criminals, the common thieves and the gentlemen criminals greatly outnumbered the trickle of casuals. Amongst the latter there were the five Scottish martyrs: Muir, Palmer, Margarot, Skirving and Gerrald. In December 1792, Thomas Muir, a legal advocate, presented an address from the United Irishmen in Dublin to a convention in Edinburgh which recommended fundamental changes in the political system. For this he was tried at Edinburgh and sentenced to transportation for fourteen years. In 1793 the Reverend Thomas Fyshe Palmer transcribed and circulated the pamphlet 'An Address to the People'—for which he was transported for five years. In November 1793, Skirving, Gerrald, and Margarot were sentenced to transportation for fourteen years for the opinions they had expressed at the Edinburgh convention on political reform.

The motives and characters of these men illustrated the observation that all great movements for the improvement of mankind attract both those who are too good and those who are too bad for existing society. Gerrald was thirty-two years of age, five feet eight inches in height, endowed by nature

36 *The Whole Proceedings on the King's Commission of the Peace* . . . , 12 December 1787, no. 1, pt. 1, pp. 13-14.

37 D. Collins: *An Account of the English Colony in New South Wales* (London, 1798 and 1802), vol. 1, p. 391; T. C. Croker (ed.): *Memoirs of Joseph Holt* (London, 1838), vol. 2, p. 123; F. Péron and L. Freycinet: *Voyage de découvertes aux Terres Australes* (Paris, 1807-16), vol. 1, pp. 407-9.

38 *The Whole Proceedings on the King's Commission of the Peace* . . . , 13 January 1790, no. 2, pt. 5, p. 210.

with a slender frame and a puny constitution, but sustained by a belief in the light of reason and philosophy. Some of his contemporaries considered him a misguided individual, because the hearts of men never could be so inclined to the practice of virtue as he imagined.[39] Muir, too, was high-minded: 'I have devoted myself,' he told his judges, 'to the cause of the people. It is a good cause—it shall ultimately prevail.'[40] Palmer also was sustained by his vision—the union of the sermon on the mount with the rights of man, or that alliance between evangelical Christianity and liberalism which was later to sustain and yet bemuse Protestant civilization in Australia. Palmer believed he had borne shame, odium, disgrace and the loss of fortune for the cause of mankind and of human happiness, that his sufferings would not be lost but would, with the blessing of God, prove efficacious in accomplishing what he had laboured for.[41] By contrast the motives of Margarot were spiteful and malicious: to unseat and discomfit people in high places, not to the greater glory of God or the advancement and happiness of the people, but for the pleasure of hurting the rich and the mighty. For Margarot had been rejected and expelled from the society of the reformers as unworthy of the cause he represented,[42] and in the colony of New South Wales no one would infer from the behaviour of Maurice Margarot that he believed in a day when men would neither hurt nor destroy.

Contemporaries judged them according to their political opinions. Opponents spoke and wrote of them as men who were propagating that monstrous doctrine of the rights of man, by which, as they put it, the weak and ignorant who were most susceptible of impressions from such barren abstract positions, were seduced to overturn government, law, property, security, religion, order and everything valuable in the country. To protect the weak and the ignorant against such delusions they agreed with their removal to a place from which they could do no further harm.[43] Their supporters offered them the consolation enjoyed by all martyrs in the cause of liberty: the consolation that they would not, that they could not suffer in vain, for truth, as they conceived it, must prevail, and neither persecution nor banishment nor death itself could finally injure the progress of those principles which involved the general happiness of man.[44] Their eye lingered on such scenes as happened at Newgate in May 1794 when Gerrald, being much indisposed, laid down to rest. The turnkey

[39] Anon.: *Authentic Biographical Anecdotes of Joseph Gerrald, a delegate to the British Convention in Scotland from the London Corresponding Society* . . . , 2nd ed. (London, 1795), p. 24.

[40] T. B. Howell: op. cit., vol. 23, p. 228.

[41] Anon.: *An Account of The Trial of Thomas Fyshe Palmer, Unitarian Minister, Dundee* . . . (Perth, n.d.), p. 110.

[42] Anon.: *The Trial of Maurice Margarot* . . . (London, 1794), pp. 176-8 and *passim*.

[43] T. B. Howell: op. cit., vol. 23, p. 132; *Parliamentary History*, vol. 31, pp. 498-9.

[44] Address from the Society for Constitutional Information in London, 1794, quoted in T. F. Palmer: *A Narrative of the Sufferings of T. F. Palmer, and W. Skirving, during a voyage to New South Wales, 1794, on board the Surprize Transport* (Cambridge, 1797), pp. 52-3.

sent for him, handcuffed him and shackled him, and hurried him off in a chaise to join the convict transport *Sovereign*,[45] which finally sailed in January 1795. Muir, Palmer, Skirving and Margarot had sailed on the *Surprize* in February of 1794.

Contemporaries viewed them as martyrs in the cause of liberty and human happiness, just as historians who shared their aspirations esteemed them as the forerunners of those men who at the end of the nineteenth century declared man's power to make and unmake social conditions. So history became not so much half guess and half lies[46] as a support for a political creed, in which process not only was the character of the men lost, but their immediate contribution suppressed.

In the same way the contribution of the Irish convicts lay not so much in their numbers, but in the transporting to New South Wales of the sense of their melancholy history, and Irish Catholicism. The melancholy history was reflected in the types transported; for whereas in England and Scotland the thieves predominated, of the two thousand and eighty-six transported from Ireland between 1791 and 1803, about six hundred were convicted for riot and sedition.[47] The religious persuasions proportions were reversed too, for on the Irish ships the Catholics outnumbered the Protestants by about twenty-three to one.[48]

One curious accident of that melancholy history was the absence of any selection among the convicts from Ireland. All were transported without reference to age, health or crime. In the northern counties, the men and women sentenced to transportation were brought first to Dublin, where they were examined by a doctor, shaved, bathed, clothed and then shipped to Cork to board the convict transport at Cobh. The sheriffs in the southern counties dispatched their men and women direct to Cork.[49] The quantity of food, the standards of cleanliness, and the clothing issued were the first taste some of the Irish had enjoyed of that higher civilization which the English never wearied from reminding them was the blessing of the Protestant religion and British political institutions. The Irish convicts generally arrived in New South Wales in sound health, and many of them expressed the wish that their passage could last forever![50]

[45] Anon.: *Gerrald. A Fragment; containing some account of the life of . . . a Delegate to the British Convention, at Edinburgh . . . Transported to Botany Bay for Fourteen Years!!!* (London, n.d. [1795]), pp. 16-17.

[46] R. D. Fitzgerald: 'Essay on Memory', in *Moonlight Acre*, 3rd ed. (Melbourne, 1944), p. 43.

[47] T. J. Kiernan: op. cit., *passim*; and A. G. L. Shaw: Review of T. J. Kiernan: *Transportation from Ireland to Sydney, 1791-1816*, in *Historical Studies*, vol. 7, no. 25, November 1955, pp. 83-8.

[48] Information in indents of convict ships (Mitchell Library).

[49] T. C. Croker (ed.): op. cit., vol. 2, pp. 6-25; Appendix 38 to the Report of the Select Committee on Transportation, 1812, *P.P.*, 1812, II, 341; evidence of Rev. F. Archer, Inspector-General of the Prisons in Ireland, to the Select Committee on the State of the Gaols, 1819, pp. 207-8, *P.P.* 1819, VII, 579.

[50] J. T. Bigge: *The Colony of New South Wales*, pp. 9-10; T. C. Croker (ed.): op. cit., vol. 2, pp. 43-5. But compare with T. J. Kiernan: op. cit., pp. 17-18.

Observers of these thieves dwelt on their drunkenness, their whoring, their filth, their degradation and wretchedness.[51] So the eye of disgust and loathing rather than of pity dwelt on scenes enacted by Irish thieves on convict ships. Grief and sympathy flowed, however, towards the victims of Ireland's melancholy history—to the three priests, James Dixon, James Harrold and Peter O'Neill, who were transported for their participation in the troubles of 1798, to the three Protestant clergymen, Birch, Fulton and Simpson, for their part in the same upheaval, to a landowner such as Joseph Holt, a physician such as Bryan O'Connor, who were engulfed in those muddy waters. Indeed, the gap between the wealth and the respectability of such men and the poverty and lack of respectability of the common thief caused one of the early manifestations of social exclusiveness in New South Wales. For the casual criminal disdained the professional much as the gentleman criminal disdained the petty thief. Ireland, too, contributed her quota of queer cases. There was, for example, Sir Henry Browne Hayes, an ex-mayor of the city of Cork, who was charged in 1801 with abducting a Quaker lady of large fortune, and sentenced to death, a sentence later commuted to transportation for life. The fate of Sir Henry, as a contemporary balladist noted, was sure a hard case,[52] but what was singular to him was not so much the horror of his sentence, or its savagery, because that applied to many, but rather the trials to which he was exposed in the colony, the intermingling of his fortunes with the petty squabbles of New South Wales—for chance and destiny were conspiring to inflict on him greater sufferings than the pangs of exile for an act of folly and passion. Hayes sailed on the *Atlas* in November 1801, and paid the master some hundreds of pounds for the privilege of messing with him, an extravagant gesture in keeping with his earlier folly and passion. During the voyage he insulted a surgeon on the ship, for which temporary gratification of his feelings he was sentenced to six months on arrival in the colony.[53]

The Irish sense of wonder, the awareness of magic in the world, and their quaint twists to the Christian hope of the life of the world to come, preceded that Protestant ascendancy, the occasion of their nursing a melancholy history.[54] For the Irish not only looked for the resurrection of the dead, but used their imagination to explore the delights of such a life:

> I would like to have a great lake of beer
> For the King of Kings.
> I'd love to be watching the family of heaven
> Drinking it through all eternity.[55]

They were a people whose holy faith and family affections lent a charm to and softened the harshness of their lives in their wretched cabins, and com-

[51] T. C. Croker (ed.): op. cit., vol. 2, pp. 122-3.

[52] Quoted in T. C. Croker (ed.): op. cit., vol. 2, pp. 122-3.

[53] *H.R.A.*, I, 3, p. 584, p. 718 and note 227 on p. 801.

[54] The phrase comes from J. A. Froude: *The English in Ireland in the Eighteenth Century*, 2nd ed. (London, 1881), vol. 3, p. 123.

[55] S. O'Faolain: *The Irish* (West Drayton, 1947), pp. 23, 50 and 78.

pensated them for their worldly privations.[56] The wretchedness of their lives contributed to the extremes in their behaviour, to the creation of a type who one hour was dignified with every kind and noble sentiment, only to be degraded the next by acts of the most brutal malevolence.[57]

Misery and idleness encouraged drunkenness and feuds, and created too the conditions in which loyalty to their own groups and treachery to their eternal enemies governed standards of conduct. Lying, deceit, double-dealing, perjury, subornation of witnesses, violence, even murder, ceased to be reprehensible or damnable if perpetrated against the Protestant ascendancy. They refused to believe in justice for Irish Catholics in British law courts: they despised their laws, defied their administration, and cursed all who collaborated with their oppressors.[58] The poverty contributed to the gross and sordid ignorance of the largest part of the population, which brought in its train barbarous habits and tastes, an ill-equipped agriculture, and improvident marriages, and aggravated that tendency to anarchy and violence.[59] People without any interest in or sympathy for the sense of magic, but with an angry contempt for the liar and the drunkard, tended to judge them harshly, tended to rush over the charm, the wit, and the lugubrious cheerfulness, and to draw attention to the garrulousness, the torrent of words, the delight in extremes, the absence of moderation, that vanity which, as with the French, flowed from entertaining a high idea of themselves, and which endowed them with an unbounded appetite for praise, and a character in which censure always mortified their pride and irritated their feelings. Such observers lamented the unsteadiness in their conduct, their grasping at objects which when attained did not afford the expected gratification.[60] So the mind stuffed with Protestant ideas of upright behaviour, readily dismissed them as despicable and contemptible.

One other effect of the Protestant ascendancy was the power and prestige of the priest in the Catholic sections of Irish society. The Protestant ascendancy had evicted the Catholic landlord and replaced him with a resident or an absentee Protestant landlord, whom the Catholic tenant despised as an alien and a reprobate.[61] The tenant turned to the priest not only for the consolations of religion, but as a guide and leader in the fight against poverty and oppression. The priest looked to the tenant as the sole support for the maintenance and welfare of the church: so the priest was obliged to ride the popular wave, or be left on the beach to perish. The peasant radicalized and barbarized the church.[62] To the Protestant, this dependence of the Catholic

---

[56] J. C. Curwen: *Observations on the State of Ireland, principally directed to its Agriculture and Rural Population . . .* (London, 1818), vol. 2, pp. 276-7.

[57] Ibid.

[58] E. Wakefield: *An Account of Ireland, Statistical and Political* (London, 1812), vol. 2, p. 813; W. E. H. Lecky: *A History of Ireland in the Eighteenth Century*, vol. 5, p. 485 et seq. (London, 1902-6); R. B. McDowell: *Irish Public Opinion, 1750-1800* (London, 1944), p. 122.

[59] W. E. H. Lecky: op. cit., vol. 5, p. 423 et seq.

[60] E. Wakefield: *An Account of Ireland . . .*, vol. 2, p. 794.

[61] W. E. H. Lecky: op. cit., vol. 5, p. 280 et seq.

[62] J. Gordon: *A History of the Rebellion in Ireland in the Year 1798* (Dublin, 1801), pp. 286-7.

on the priest tended to perpetrate that ignorance, superstition, priestcraft, servility, poverty, filth, disease, drunkenness and lying which in Protestant eyes followed Catholicism as night followed day. For the Protestant believed passionately that Protestantism represented the higher level or order—industry, intelligence, and civilization, that the Catholic religion was calculated to promote arbitrary power, that father confessors taught their flocks to hold no faith with Protestants, that the inclinations of Catholics to enslave mankind were universal, and their abilities and power to do it very great.[63] On 21 September 1795, the Protestants in Ireland formed the Orange Society to defend the king and his heirs so long as he or they supported the Protestant ascendancy.[64] So, too, in Australia, the great nightmare of the defenders of the Protestant ascendancy was that the Protestant dyke against poverty, superstition and a priest-ridden society might be pierced by waves of immigrants, both bond and free, from Catholic Ireland. What the Protestant suppressed or found inscrutable was that to the Catholic his holy faith was the means of eternal salvation, and the priest the divinely ordained dispenser of those sacraments through which alone he could gain such a prize.

While the Protestant nursed in his mind the dark and monstrous suspicion that the priests were conspiring to enslave mankind, other observers wrote and talked of the two sections within the Catholic Church. One, to which history has attached the doubtful distinction of being named the Castle Catholics, favoured English rule in Ireland after 1789 as a protection against those principles of the rights of man which they believed were uniformly marked with hostility to the rights of God and to the ministers of revealed religion.[65] They asked the faithful to go down on their knees at the end of the mass to pray for the eternal salvation of a heretic—George III by the grace of God of England, Ireland and Scotland king. They warned the faithful against the ideas of the Jacobins, and against liberty and equality, which they characterized as charms operating on the too credulous poor, maddening them and deluding them to procure property by the pillage of their opulent neighbours.[66] They hailed the return of the Pope to Rome in 1800 as evidence of divine approval for their stand, that the defenceless successor of the Galilean fisherman had won a lasting victory over the men who muddied the waters, as evidence that Christ still walked on the waves, and that the gates of hell would not prevail against His Church.[67] But the numbers who understood the lofty, indeed the cosmic, significance of this position were few. Educated in Catholic schools and seminaries on the continent, where they ac-

63 W. E. H. Lecky: op. cit., vol. 5, pp. 56-7; J. Barrow: *Serious Reflections on the Present State of Domestic and Foreign Affairs* (London, 1757), p. 48.

64 W. E. H. Lecky: op. cit., vol. 3, p. 426; R. Lilburn: *Orangeism, its Origin, Constitution and Objects* (London, 1866), *passim*.

65 J. T. Troy: *Pastoral Instruction to the Roman Catholics of the Archdiocese of Dublin* (Dublin, 1798), p. 5.

66 J. T. Troy: *To the Reverend Pastors and other Roman Catholic Clergy of the Archdiocese of Dublin* (Dublin, 1798), pp. 7-11.

67 Based on L. F. von Pastor: *The History of the Popes from the Close of the Middle Ages* (London, 1923-53), vol. 40, pp. 396-7.

quired a refinement, an urbanity and a sophistication which distinguished them from the ruck of the population, they were to be found only in the higher ranks of the ecclesiastical hierarchy and the cultivated laity.

By contrast, the priests who ministered to the peasants had all the tastes, passions and prejudices of that group. They preached a fanatical Catholicism, and a credulous Catholicism, in coarse, violent and grotesque language. Most of them claimed supernatural powers, especially the healing powers of participation in the sacraments, of the veneration of relics, and of the intercession of the Irish saints. They sympathized with the aspirations of the peasants. They encouraged their conception of the English as the hereditary oppressors of their co-religionists and fellow-countrymen, as the men who had made the most beautiful island under the sun a land of skulls or of ghastly spectres. They nourished in their hearts the longing for that day when the mighty would be taken down from their seats and the rich sent empty away. They shared the dreams sketched in the popular songs which assured the faithful that though the Protestant boys had gained the day, they would not gain the night.[68]

They passed on in an intelligible form the main teachings of the Jansenists, who supported the claims of the papacy. They passed on, too, their Puritanism, which in that ill-digested form degenerated into prudishness, and into all those degradations resorted to by human beings who have been taught to believe the sins of the flesh condemned a man to eternal damnation. These in turn encouraged drunkenness and a man-dominated society. They passed on the Jansenist teaching that there was no salvation outside the Church of Rome, that through heresy a man destroyed his faith, extinguished the light in his soul, and knew not whither he went, as he wandered from darkness into darkness until he fell into the abyss of eternal despair. To the Protestant their claim to the exclusive possession of God's favour was proof in abundance that they were morally mad, that this deadly sentiment darkened their minds, and turned the very milk of human kindness into the venom of vipers. The Protestant believed one must fight such bigots as would warn a fifer that damnation was the penalty for playing the flute at a Protestant religious service.[69] While the Protestant perceived the mote, he was yet blind to the achievement, as he did not pause to ask why, granted such bigotry and superstition, the Irish had managed to create and keep alive an image of Christ and the holy mother of God, nor why they treasured their faith as a priceless possession. Nor did he pause to ponder over the experience of a people whose melancholy

68 W. E. H. Lecky: op. cit., vol. 3, p. 356; O. Macdonagh: 'The Irish Catholic Clergy and Emigration During the Great Famine' in *Irish Historical Studies*, 1946-7, vol. 5, p. 292; D. Trant: *Considerations on the Present Disturbances in the Province of Munster, their Causes, Extent, Probable Consequences, and Remedies*, 2nd ed. (Dublin, 1787), p. 6; and J. Alexander: *Some Account of the late Rebellion in the County of Kildare, and an adjoining part of the King's County* (Dublin, 1800), *passim*.

69 R. B. McDowell: op. cit., p. 184; Anon.: *An Answer to the Right Hon. P. Digenan's Two Great Arguments against the full enfranchisement of the Irish Roman Catholics. By a Member of the Establishment* (Dublin, 1810); Anon.: *A Test of Roman Catholic Liberality, submitted to the Consideration of both Roman Catholics and Protestants* (London Derry, 1792).

history had taught them that the race was not to the swift, nor the battle to the strong, who had learned to esteem the man of compassion above the man who gained the whole world, who believed in the communion of saints, and looked for the resurrection of the dead, when all the faithful members of their church, all those in a state of grace, would enjoy their eternal salvation, while all others went to their eternal damnation. For what endeared them to their priests, and their future judges, deprived them of the confidence and respect of all other members of the community.

By contrast the Protestants presented not so much a problem of description, but rather a problem of identification. For the historian may well be dismayed by the bewildering variety of Christian persuasions—of Anglicans, Presbyterians, Methodists, and the various dissenting sects. Within each persuasion there was further variety of opinion, both on questions of religious doctrine as well as of social and political opinions. The tone of the official religious life in the colony, with the exception of the Catholics, was set by chaplains and officers who preached and taught, both bond and free, the principles of the evangelicals. Fortunately, like most groups who believed the Lord had singled them out as vessels of human salvation, they were not at all diffident in talking and writing about themselves. Like the Catholic, they believed in eternal salvation, but differed in their idea of ways and means. For where the Catholic taught the sacraments as the means of grace and the hope of glory, the evangelical taught the Word, and the cultivation of the moral qualities. It was in the cultivation of these moral qualities that they developed their idea of the good man, or rather to borrow one of their own phrases, the idea of the upright man. Passionately convinced that man was made in the image of God, they devoted much of their energy to campaigns against all human activity which degraded or besmirched that image. They preached against duelling, against all brutal amusements such as cock-fights, bear-baiting, bull-fighting, flogging in the army, the slave trade and slavery. They strove to protect children against oppressive employers, to improve the condition of the prisons, and the condition of the hospitals, to end heathen blindness, idolatry and other revolting practices. They discouraged the profanation of the sabbath, swearing, drunkenness, licentious publications, unlicensed places of public amusement, and the regulation of licensed places, on the principle that once the temptation had been removed, the appetite might not be provoked.[70]

On life in this world they counselled resignation. They instructed the lower orders to be diligent, humble and patient; they rebuked the upper classes for their drinking, their gambling, and their whoring, but not for their possession of wealth. They reminded the poor that their more lowly path had been allotted to them by the hand of God. They reminded them that the present state of things was very short, that if their superiors enjoyed more abundant comforts, they were also exposed to many temptations from which the inferior classes were happily exempted. They reminded them that their

70 E. Halevy: *A History of the English People in the Nineteenth Century* (London, 1949-52), vol. 1, pp. 451-5; R. I. and S. Wilberforce: *The Life of William Wilberforce* (London, 1881), vol. 1, p. 131.

situation in life with its evils was better than they deserved at the hand of God, that all human distinctions would soon be done away and the true followers of Christ would all, as children of the same father, be alike admitted to the possession of the same heavenly inheritance.[71] They preached the ideal of the upright man, the man who obeyed without protest the will of God, not from pity or sympathy with the fate of man, or any humanitarian motive, but because it was the will of God. To them God was all, the thought of Him all in all, and a man almost as nothing before Him. As he had made man for Himself and not for man's pleasure, the evangelicals frowned on pleasure, frowned on all the passionate emotions as insidious incitements to worldly pleasure, professed the greatest contempt for all who had written in exaltation of them, and regarded them as a form of madness.[72]

For them life was stern, a vale of tears, and a trial. Their great difficulty was to persuade their fellow human beings that the gratification of their appetites paved the way to their eternal damnation. Their other great diffi- culty was how to persuade men in high places that theirs was not merely a religion of social utility, that theirs was a divine mission, and not the con- temptible, servile, hypocritical function of acting as moral policemen, or sanctimonious spies, for the established social order. They entertained, too, an inordinate suspicion of Rome. They did not believe Rome's views on sal- vation were a form of moral madness, for English Catholic priests were not touched by Jansenist views. Their own madness was to believe that the Catholic Church was a gigantic conspiracy to enslave the mind of man, to upset the revolution settlement of 1688, to replace the British constitution by a con- tinental despotism, to destroy the rights of conscience, and the sacred in- terests of political and civil liberty, and to reduce the material standard of their civilization to the level of the Irish or the Spanish peasant.[73] On this question they were not only provincials, but men exposed to an enormous

71 W. Wilberforce: *A Practical View of the Prevailing Religious System of Pro- fessed Christians* (London, 1797), pp. 403-6; J. Bean: *Zeal Without Innovation* (Lon- don, 1808), pp. 285-7; H. More: *An Estimate of the Religion of the Fashionable World, By one of the laity*, 3rd ed. (Dublin, 1791); H. More: *Modern Politicians: a word to the working classes of Great Britain, by Will Chip, a country carpenter. Newly edited for the present time by his grandson*, 2nd ed. (London, 1848), p. 11 et seq.

72 E. Halevy: op. cit., vol. 1, p. 466; J. S. Mill: *Autobiography* (World's Classics, London, 1924), pp. 48-9; A. Dakin: *Calvinism* (London, 1940), p. 210; Anon.: *The Life and Dreadful Sufferings of Captain James Wilson* (Portsea, 1810), pp. 34-5.

73 *Morning Chronicle and London Advertiser*, 15 May 1787: 'A young nobleman (Lord Gormanston) had been clandestinely carried to Liege to be educated "in the principles of the Popish religion". The Court of Chancery issued a writ for his return, which was rejected by his uncle "in the most insolent and imperious language." A threat was made to disinherit the uncle. "Now, if those persons should think proper rather to destroy the child, than suffer him to be brought up in the principles of the British constitution, and in the protestant religion . . ."'
Anon.: *The Dispute Adjusted, about the Proper Time of Applying for a Repeal of the Corporation and Test Acts, by shewing That No Time Is Proper*, 2nd ed. (Oxford, 1790); A. Kippis: *A Sermon preached at the Old Jury, on the Fourth of November, 1788, before the Society for Commemorating the Glorious Revolution* (London, 1788), p. 46.

temptation to use the latitudinarians and the opponents of religion to defeat the agents of what they believed to be a satanic delusion.

The tone of early civilization in New South Wales was fashioned by the evangelicals, for amongst their adherents were the chaplains, governors—such as Hunter and Macquarie, a number of the officials, the editor of the first newspaper, and the school teachers. They were the ones in the colony with power both to persuade and compel. For a moment the Protestant religion enjoyed the opportunity of belonging to an establishment, but in succeeding generations its power melted like the snowdrift, possibly because the fundamental poverty of its position was hidden in a maze of words, possibly because it did not stand on entrenched ground, possibly because what it fondly believed to be its strength, its occupation of the space midway between the Catholic Church and the rationalists, proved its undoing in the coming encounter between belief and unbelief, but possibly also because of the disappearance of that social situation which it was designed to serve. In our period they were men of achievement: only the sorry farce in their subsequent history drives the historian to search for their worm of failure.[74]

The other faith with a vision of the future of mankind was the enlightenment. Catholic and Protestant encouraged 'that-sidedness': the enlightenment taught 'this-sidedness,' or the capacity of man to achieve happiness here on earth. Catholic and Protestant pointed to the Fall as the cause of evil. The enlightenment taught evil as the product of economic and material environment; that bad conditions, not innate depravity, were the cause of human vileness; that it was within man's power to create a society from which war, plague, famine, and all the other manifestations of human evil had disappeared; that these scourges were not the ineradicable punishment for original sin, but the consequence of ignorance and environment. The enlightenment taught that the end of the belief in immortality would develop in human beings a compassion and a tenderness for each other.[75] Those who condemned them as pitifully inadequate on the origins and nature of human evil described them as arid souls.[76] Their numbers were few, and their opportunities to gain converts negligible. Before the nineteenth century was out they had begun the struggle between belief and unbelief. In association with some of the Protestants they had secularized the state, and had created a society unique in the history of mankind, a society of men holding no firm beliefs on the existence of God or survival after death.

Finally there were the men and the women who were untouched by any one of these enthusiasms—the men of common-sense. They accepted the Roman virtues of courage, stoicism, endurance; they disdained religion as a consolation for human suffering, and condemned its followers for their lack of

[74] J. H. Newman: *History of My Religious Opinions* (London, 1865), p. 102.

[75] E. Condorcet: *Esquisse d'un Tableau Historique du Progrès de l'Esprit Humain* (Paris, 1933), pp. 203-4; J. B. Bury: *The Idea of Progress* (London, 1920); H. R. Murphy: 'The Ethical Revolt against Christian Orthodoxy in Early Victorian England', in *American Historical Review*, vol. 60, no. 4, July 1955.

[76] P. Hazard: *La Pensée Européenne en XVIIIème Siècle de Montesquieu à Lessing* (Paris, 1946), vol. 1, pp. iv-v.

strength and courage. They supported the established church, provided it effected subordination in society, and encouraged its clergymen to act as moral policemen. They approved of candour, of benevolence, of charity to those distressed in mind, body or estate; they believed in the moral and beneficent role of their civilization, its contribution to human progress and to the reduction of superstition and ignorance; they believed in the progress of the human race, but not its perfectibility; they believed with a quiet optimism that they were advancing towards a unique era in the history of mankind, in which improvements in science, liberal ideas in politics and religion, the abolition of the slave trade, and the genius of commerce would bring peace, plenty and freedom in their train, and gradually spread European civilization over the whole world.[77]

All of them bore the taint of supercilious intolerance towards all other forms of civilization. They bore too that other taint of European civilization—its destructive effect on all primitive cultures with which it came into contact. Not one of the faiths sustaining these men—neither the Christian religion, the enlightenment, nor romantic notions about noble savages—could restrain the rapacity and greed of the white man, nor afford him a workable explanation for the backwardness and material weakness of the aborigine. So when those aboriginal women uttered their horrid howl on first seeing the white man at Botany Bay in April 1770, that howl contained in it a prophecy of doom[78]— that terrible sense of doom and disaster which pervaded the air whenever the European occupied the land of a primitive people. For the culture, the way of life of the aborigine was doomed, though, on the mainland, some of them survived the coming of the white man. That land, on which man so far had scarcely scratched his presence, had, unlike the aborigine, a strength of its own with which to adapt itself to the invader.

[77] H. More: *An Estimate of the Religion of the Fashionable World* . . . , pp. 43-4; D. Collins: op. cit., vol. 1, p. 6; *Scots Magazine*, 1789, vol. 51, p. 475. But compare with the opinions of a letter-writer in ibid., pp. 475-6, who predicted that infidelity, heterodoxy, luxury, dissipation, debauchery, excess, extravagance of every kind, total want of principle, impurity of crimes, and mistaken pretences and pleas for humanity: in short, the pride of human wit, human wickedness and an universal passion to do what everyone likes, were preparing the way for the dissolution of the world.

[78] S. Parkinson: *A Journal of a Voyage to the South Seas, in his Majesty's Ship, The Endeavour* (London, 1773), p. 134.

PART III

PHILLIP TO BLIGH

7

PHILLIP

BY THE MIDDLE of February 1788 the secular and religious ceremonies to mark the beginning of the colony had been completed. Then the elementary task of housing, feeding, and preserving law and order was begun. In observing their behaviour in those early years when the foundations of civilization were hacked out in that rude and barbarous land, posterity has detected two patterns: how a settlement designed for the punishment and reformation of criminals developed within four years into a colony using convict labour, and how in transplanting a civilization changes quickly emerged in the character of that civilization. Such patterns escaped the minds of those on the spot. They were too pre-occupied with the struggle for survival, dismayed by the difficulties of creating any civilization at all in such an alien environment and with such unpromising human material.

In the beginning, all were housed in tents, the Governor in a pre-cut canvas house constructed in London, the sick, the civil and military officers, the marines and the convicts in tents, and the stores under wretched covers of thatch. By July some of the convicts were housed in huts, though the Governor, the civil and military officers and the marines remained under canvas. Some grumbled that a mere fold of canvas should be their sole check against the rays of the sun in summer or the chilling blasts from the south in the winter. In the meantime, they continued the slow business of building first with canvas, then with wood, and finally with stone, but in all this the unexpected daunted them: the hard wood blunted and bent their tools; there was no suitable lime with which to mix cement; there were too few skilled workers. So they improvised, and made do with what they had.[1]

It was the same with the planting of seed to grow crops and vegetables. The Governor established a government farm under the supervision of a member of his own staff, using the convicts to till the soil. In addition, he granted small plots of land to the civil and military officers, and assigned convicts to work the soil, supplying them with seed and tools to raise grain and vegetables. But again the trees blunted the blades of the axes, the soil blunted the spades and the picks, and the men whose very aversion to labour had been the occasion of their pursuing the profession of crime had to be driven to labour. Until such time as they could master the problems of husbandry in their new environment, they were dependent on the flour, the meat, the pease and the butter brought from England and the Cape of Good Hope. So long as supplies lasted, these kept them alive, while exposing them to all

---

[1] W. Tench: *A Complete Account of the Settlement at Port Jackson in New South Wales* (London, 1793), pp. 1-3; J. White: *Journal of a Voyage to New South Wales* (London, 1790), p. 121 et seq.

those disorders to which men subsisting without green vegetables and fruits were liable. By May, the camp on the banks of Sydney Cove began to wear aspects of distress, as great numbers of scorbutic patients were daily seen creeping to and from the hospital tents.[2] Some died, and the Reverend Richard Johnson read over their shallow graves the solemn words 'Man that is born of woman hath but a short time to live'—and reminded those who cocked an ear that hope of a glorious resurrection awaited the dead. By May, Tench had noted that fresh provisions were becoming scarcer than in a blockaded town.[3] The weather in the late summer was oppressive with much rain, thunder and lightning.[4] Flies which bred large living maggots nauseated them; ants bit them severely.[5]

The behaviour of the convicts disgusted and appalled them. To their surprise, neither the convicts nor the aborigines challenged that subordination they prized as the foundation of order in society. Indeed, as early as the end of February, one observer found the colonists in such subordination as to make the presence of so large a military force unnecessary.[6] Johnson, however, continued to urge the convicts in his Sunday sermons to pay due respect, submission and obedience to their superiors, reminding them that it was the good pleasure of God that some men should be placed in a more exalted and others in a more humble station, and that such was a proof of His wisdom and His goodness.[7] But such was the depravity of human nature that neither lenient measures nor whippings, imprisonments nor degradations could apparently operate upon callous hearts to prevent theft.[8] Some of the convicts had taken advantage of the festivities on 7 February to steal food; for this some were flogged, and one sent to a barren rock in the harbour to live on a diet of bread and water. Thefts from the public stores continued. On 27 February Thomas Barrett, Henry Lovel, and Joseph Hall were tried by the court of criminal jurisdiction, found guilty, and sentenced to death. The same evening Barrett confessed to the Reverend Richard Johnson at the foot of the ladder that bad company and evil example had been his ruin, before being launched into eternity. Lovel and Hall were reprieved the next morning on condition of being exiled to an uninhabited place.[9] But so hardened in wickedness and

[2] D. Collins: *An Account of the English Colony in New South Wales* (London, 1798 and 1802), vol. 1, p. 25.

[3] W. Tench: *A Narrative of the Expedition to Botany Bay* (London, 1789), p. 106.

[4] D. Collins: op. cit., vol. 1, pp. 18-19.

[5] W. Tench: *A Complete Account* . . . , p. 177.

[6] W. Tench: *A Narrative of the Expedition to Botany Bay*, p. 71.

[7] R. Johnson: *An Address to the Inhabitants of the Colonies, established in New South Wales and Norfolk Island* (London, 1794), pp. 62-3.

[8] Anon.: *An Authentic and Interesting Narrative of the late expedition to Botany Bay . . . Written by an Officer . . . who visited that Spot with Captain Cook and Dr Solander . . .* (London, 1789), p. 22.

[9] Based on J. White: op. cit., pp. 127-8; D. Collins: op. cit., vol. 1, pp. 9-10, and W. Tench: *A Narrative of the Expedition to Botany Bay*, pp. 72-3. Tench's account differs from the other two as he reported that Barrett (whom he spelt with one 't') died with that hardy spirit which too often is found in the worst and most abandoned class of men.

depravity were some of them that they seemed insensible to the fear of corporal punishment, or even death itself.[10] By May, Phillip expressed regret that so little labour was drawn from them in a country which required the greatest exertions, while the return was diminished daily as the number made unfit for work by scurvy increased. He estimated that of those assigned to manual labour, two hundred had become unfit.[11] Yet the convicts were conducting themselves with more propriety than could have been expected from people of their description.[12]

For a while it looked as though all the more noble aspirations of Phillip turned to the squalid, the sordid and the wretched in their hands. In February Phillip sent a party of convicts under the command of Lieutenant Philip Gidley King in the *Supply* to occupy Norfolk Island, which had been discovered by Cook during his second voyage in the Pacific. They arrived there on 29 February, and on 9 March gathered for divine service. King's commission was then read, and King spoke of how he would punish wickedness and vice, but reward those who behaved with propriety and industry. At first the convicts behaved well, but as more arrived from Sydney Cove, they renewed their wicked practices. A few responded to the advantages arising from industry and good behaviour by clearing the ground, sowing corn and potatoes, and becoming respectable. The greater part, however, remained idle and miserable wretches despite the climate, and their isolation from previous haunts of crime.[13]

In April Phillip instructed his Surveyor-General, Augustus Alt, to draft a plan for a town on the principle that extent of empire demanded grandeur of design. In Alt's plan the main street was to be two hundred feet in width. The very grandeur of the plan, as well as the need to use available labour on the production of food and shelter, caused it to be shelved. So the town of Sydney grew in a slap-dash way until Macquarie arrived and restored some of the original grandeur when he redesigned the streets.[14] In the meantime, when Phillip looked to the military officers for an example and to assist in the administration of justice, they responded with petty squabbles about rank, or complained of the hardship of being called on to serve on the court of criminal jurisdiction.[15]

It was the same with the aborigine. The white man came bearing his civilization as his offering, expecting the aborigine to perceive the great benefits he would receive at its hand, including that benefit of being received into the Church of England, which was believed to contain all that was

10 J. White: op. cit., pp. 132-3.

11 Phillip to Sydney, 15 May 1788, *H.R.A.*, I, 1, p. 32, and Phillip to Sydney, 16 May 1788, *H.R.A.*, I, 1, p. 35.

12 D. Collins: op. cit., vol. 1, p. 25.

13 J. Hunter: *An Historical Journal of the Transactions at Port Jackson and Norfolk Island ... since the publication of Phillip's Voyage, ...* (London, 1793), p. 302, and pp. 398-401.

14 W. Tench: *A Narrative of the Expedition to Botany Bay*, pp. 103-4.

15 Phillip to Sydney, 16 May 1788, *H.R.A.*, I, 1, p. 35, and Phillip to Nepean, 9 July 1788, *H.R.A.*, I, 1, p. 56.

1

necessary to salvation. Phillip had been instructed to conciliate their affections, and to enjoin all subjects to live in amity and kindness with them.[16] In the beginning Phillip made all the traditional gestures of goodwill: he smiled with compassion; he gave them presents of hatchets and other articles; he ordered his men not to fire on them except when absolutely necessary.[17] For a season the aborigines responded with affection, and even with veneration as the white skin, the material power, his status as leader, and that quite fortuitous gap in his front teeth gave him some little merit in their opinion.[18]

Yet the aborigine remained aloof, out of reach, elusive, practising a stand-offishness which puzzled and exasperated the bearers of such gifts. They remained shy in the company of the white man, though they had been treated with kindness and loaded with presents. They seemed either to fear or to despise the white man too much to be anxious for a closer connection. The more the white men learned of their way of life and view of the world, the more they were puzzled: they observed no degree of subordination in their society; they remained strangers to their religious rites and opinions.[19] By the end of February, however, the aborigines inferred from the building that the white man intended to stay. At the end of that month they stoned white men who attempted to land in one of the coves of the harbour; they stole the white man's tools; they stole his food; on 30 May they murdered two rush-cutters and mutilated their bodies in a shocking manner. Such behaviour quickly changed the white man from a delighted observer of the picturesque and the quaint into a partisan defending his civilization. After six months, one of them wrote of the aborigine as a creature deformed by all those passions which afflicted and degraded human nature, unsoftened by the influence of religion, philosophy and legal restriction.[20] The behaviour of the white man was equally disgusting to the aborigine. To teach the aborigine the ways of the civilized, Phillip instructed his men to gather as many as possible to witness a flogging. The few aborigines who watched manifested only symptoms of disgust and terror.[21] In this way, the efforts to conciliate their affections and to diffuse amity and kindness degenerated into theft and murder, as goodwill was pushed aside by the more primitive passions of an eye for an eye and a tooth for a tooth.

By June and July most of the officers began to despair. The Reverend Johnson wrote to his mentors in England that he could not entertain any very genuine expectations that the colony would ever turn to any very great account. God alone knew the hereafter, but appearances were against them.[22] Clark wrote of it as the poorest country in the world, and the aborigines as

[16] *H.R.A.*, I, 1, pp. 13-14.

[17] *The Voyage of Governor Phillip to Botany Bay; with an Account of the Establishment of the Colonies of Port Jackson and Norfolk Island* (London, 1789), pp. 44-5, 48-51, and p. 68.

[18] Phillip to Sydney, 15 May 1788, *H.R.A.*, I, 1, p. 27.

[19] W. Tench: *A Narrative of the Expedition to Botany Bay*, pp. 89-90.

[20] W. Tench: *A Complete Account . . .* , pp. 200-1.

[21] Ibid., p. 17.

[22] R. Johnson to J. Banks, 8 July 1788 (original in St Paul's Cathedral, Melbourne).

the most miserable set of wretches under the sun.[23] To add to the general anxiety and despair, by unpardonable neglect the convict in charge of the government herd allowed two bulls and four cows to be lost.[24] Some things, however, delighted them. When they began to explore the hinterland between February and April, they found to their delight an extensive tract of ground capable of producing everything which a happy soil and genial climate could bring forth.[25] When Phillip sat down in his canvas house to write his fourth despatch to Lord Sydney, in July 1788, the promise of such better things prompted him to prophesy that the country would prove the most valuable acquisition Great Britain ever made. But remembering the thunderstorms, the nauseous flies, the ants which bit severely, the blunted tools, all the depravity and wickedness, the thieving, the whoring, the drinking and the gambling, and conscious too of the wound in his shoulder from the spear of an aborigine, he added rather ruefully that no country offered less assistance to the first settlers than this did.[26]

On 4 June they celebrated the birthday of the King with cheerfulness and good humour. At sunrise the *Sirius* and the *Supply* fired off a twenty-gun salute, which was repeated at noon and sunset. From one till two in the afternoon there were more salutes from the guns before the officers dined as the guests of Phillip, while the band of the marines played 'God Save the King' and several excellent marches. At the end of the dinner toasts were drunk to His Majesty, the Prince of Wales, the Queen and the royal family, the Cumberland family, Prince William Henry, and His Majesty's ministers, who, as one man punned, could be pitted against any that ever conducted the affairs of Great Britain. In the evening there was a bonfire and a special supper for the officers. During the day every marine was given a pint of porter and every convict half a pint of spirits in which to drink the health of their sovereign. At the end of the day Phillip expressed the hope that there was not a single heavy heart in that part of His Majesty's dominions. To add to the spirit of goodwill he pardoned some sailors and some convicts. With a display of that self-control which won him the respect and admiration of his fellow-officers, he attempted to conceal the suffering inflicted by the pain in his side lest it should break in upon the feasting and harmony of the day.[27] On that day, some convicts had exploited the added opportunity to thieve from the public stores. A few days earlier, a convict made his week's allowance of flour into eighteen cakes which he devoured in one meal. Soon after he became senseless and speechless, and died the following day at the hospital, a loathsome putrid object.[28]

23 R. Clark to Kempster, 11 July 1788 (Clark Letters, Mitchell Library, Sydney).

24 D. Collins: op. cit., vol. 1, p. 33.

25 *The Voyage of Governor Phillip* . . . , pp. 100-2; W. Tench: *A Narrative of the Expedition to Botany Bay*, p. 105; Phillip to Sydney, 15 May 1788, H.R.A., I, 1, pp. 29-30.

26 Phillip to Sydney, 9 July 1788, H.R.A., I, 1, p. 51.

27 J. White: op. cit., pp. 169-72; *The Voyage of Governor Phillip* . . . , pp. 116-17; D. Collins: op. cit., vol. 1, pp. 31-2; J. Hunter: op. cit., p. 79.

28 D. Collins: op. cit., vol. 1, p. 33.

By July Phillip had conceived a policy for the future of the colony. To feed them until such time as the government farm and the plots of the officers produced enough food, he sent the *Sirius* to the Cape of Good Hope to purchase supplies.[29] He also wrote to Lord Sydney for better axes, better spades, and better shovels, as those they had were the worst that ever were seen.[30] The difficulty was to find people interested in growing food, as all attempts to bully, cajole, flatter, or coax the convicts to work had failed. Phillip's solution was to encourage the migration of settlers who would be interested in the labour of the convicts, and in the cultivation of the country, for with a few families who had been used to the cultivation of land he believed that the country would wear a more pleasing aspect, and make amends for being surrounded by the most infamous of mankind.[31] As for the aborigines, his faith in the fruits of treating them with amity and kindness remained unshaken; he looked forward to the day when they were reconciled to living among the white men, to the day when the white men had taught them how to cultivate the land.[32] The plans to grow food were still dogged with misfortune, however; very little of the English wheat germinated, while the barley rotted in the ground and the weevil destroyed the seed. By September Phillip was reporting the failure of the first crop.[33]

Hope still ran high, nevertheless, for in November he had established a second settlement at Rose Hill which, after 2 June 1791, was known by the aboriginal word Parramatta (the head of the river or the place where eels lie down) where the soil was free from the rock which covered the top soil at Sydney Cove.[34] The aborigines, however, responded to all their advances, to their benevolence, their amity, and their kindness, with such deeds of violence, that by October it was decided to compel them to keep at a greater distance from the settlement.[35] The year drew to a close with food supplies and health causing grave anxiety, and the behaviour of the aborigines a measure of irritation. The behaviour of most of the convicts was a disgrace; few attended to their labour and obeyed their masters. For comfort, there was the prospect of better land to the west of Parramatta: there was also the climate which continued to delight them as sea breezes moderated the heat of summer and the cold in winter was too slight to cause any inconvenience.[36] The faint-hearted were tempted to despair, or to dismiss as a cruel mockery or a malicious irrelevance the Reverend Richard Johnson's message of peace on earth and goodwill towards men on the first Christmas Day. But Phillip, the one man who did not share the Christian hope, stood firm in his faith, that in time civilization would yet flourish in New South Wales without the labour of the most infamous of mankind.

[29] D. Collins: op. cit., vol. 1, pp. 41-2.
[30] Phillip to Nepean, 9 July 1788, *H.R.A.*, I, 1, p. 56.
[31] Phillip to Sydney, July 1788, *H.R.A.*, I, 1, p. 67.
[32] Phillip to Sydney, 10 July 1788, *H.R.A.*, I, 1, p. 65.
[33] Phillip to Sydney, 28 September 1788, *H.R.A.*, I, 1, pp. 72-3.
[34] D. Collins: op. cit., vol. 1, p. 45 and p. 165.
[35] Ibid., vol. 1, pp. 44-5.
[36] W. Tench: *A Narrative of the Expedition to Botany Bay*, pp. 130-1.

The same problems, the same anxieties, the same irritations dominated their lives all through 1789. They attempted to grow enough food when out of a work force of seven hundred and fifty odd convicts, only two hundred and fifty were employed in agriculture, the rest being either used on public works, building stores, houses, or wharfs, or incapable because of age or illness. They attempted to coax men to work who were born with an aversion to labour. They tilled the soil with hoe and spade and shovel, as they possessed neither a plough nor an animal to draw it; they planted seed in the autumn for a spring harvest in a country where even the seasons had lost their distinctive signs. The convicts remained as refractory and wayward as before: they drank, they robbed the stores, they consorted with the women, they informed on each other even at the foot of the gallows—revelations that led to more floggings, and to more hangings. The aborigines pestered them. While the prospects of place and climate pleased, man remain vile. In such unpromising circumstances the battle for survival continued.

In the meantime, events were happening in Europe which would fashion their way of life for generations to come. On 14 July Phillip returned to Sydney Cove from one of his journeys in the discovery of his new land. On that day at Sydney Cove all was quiet and stupid, the inhabitants were suffering from boredom, or dreaming of being transported to happier climes. On that day in Paris the crowd stormed the Bastille to begin a revolution to prove the capacity for and the rudiments of better things in man.[37] In August at Sydney Cove the conversation was on food, and the prospects of relief from London. In London Lord Grenville, who had taken over the seals of office from Lord Sydney, had dictated a letter which agreed with Phillip's policy for the future of the colony: land grants were to be made to officers, non-commissioned officers, privates and persons disposed to become settlers; convicts were to be assigned to work for persons with land grants; nine persons to act as superintendents of convicts were to be sent, and twenty-five convict artificers to provide the urgently needed skilled workers.[38] In July the *Lady Juliana* sailed for Botany Bay with female convicts and stores. In September of 1789 the *Guardian*, a converted warship, sailed with stores and twenty-five convict artificers and the superintendents. She struck an iceberg and sank off the Cape of Good Hope on Christmas eve of 1789. In December 1789, the *Surprize*, the *Neptune* and the *Scarborough* sailed with more convicts and stores.[39] In March 1790, Grenville wrote to inform Phillip that the *Gorgon* would sail to New South Wales, discharge its troops and cargo, and then sail to the north-west coast of America to engage in the trade in furs.[40] In this way the colony of New South Wales would begin to serve one of those functions mentioned in the earlier debate on the uses of New Holland, by being used as a base for the expansion of British trade and commerce in the Pacific.

As the convict transport *Neptune* sailed down the English Channel in the late autumn of 1789, a young lieutenant on board complained to his superior

37 D. Collins: op. cit., vol. 1, pp. 72-3.
38 Grenville to Phillip, 22 August 1789, and 24 August 1789, *H.R.A.*, I, 1, pp. 124-30.
39 *H.R.N.S.W.*, vol. 1, pt. 2, p. 334 et seq.
40 Grenville to Phillip, March 1790, *H.R.A.*, I, 1, p. 162.

officer, Captain Nepean, that his wife was exposed on board the ship to the stench from the sanitary buckets of the convict women, as well as their foul language and behaviour. When Nepean passed on the complaints to the master of the ship, Captain Gilbert made light of the matter. A few days later, on deck, the young lieutenant told the captain he was an insolent fellow, and the captain pushed the lieutenant in the chest. By the time the ship arrived at Land's End, the lieutenant had called the captain a great scoundrel; the captain replied that he had settled many a better man than him, and that he was to be seen ashore. After missing each other twice they returned to the ship, where the young lieutenant testified that Captain Gilbert's conduct was in every respect that of a gentleman and a man of honour. So ended the first scene in this young lieutenant's association with the history of New South Wales.[41] He was Lieutenant John Macarthur, born on 3 September 1767 of parents whose trade or profession remains obscure, educated at a grammar school till 1782 when he secured an ensign's commission in the army for service in America. He retired on half pay in 1783 to live at a farm house at Holdsworthy in Devonshire, where, according to the Botany Bay wits who were renowned more for their malice than their love of truth, he was employed as a stay-maker's assistant. While living in Devon, probably at the age of twenty-one, he married Elizabeth Veale, a woman of Cornish descent. He was commissioned again as an ensign in 1788, and in 1789 volunteered for service as a lieutenant in the New South Wales Corps. On his motives for this decision he remained reticent throughout his life, though his wife wrote to her mother on the eve of departure of their expectation of reaping the most material advantages, and of her faith that Providence would watch over and protect them.[42] Of the faith by which John Macarthur lived, of any comforts to console him for the anguish he brought on himself and others by his stormy, wayward, vagrant spirit, we know nothing. The insults, the execrations and the abuse continued all the way to the Cape of Good Hope, for Macarthur had the fatal power to provoke the baser passions in the men and women with whom he associated.[43] But the time came when the pride, the honour, the ambitions of the man were to be engaged over greater issues than the stench from the sanitary buckets of convict women, when his talents and his passions were to influence the economic organization of the colony at a time when the seeds of his own destruction cheated him of the power to enjoy the fruit of his work.

　　While the second fleet with its cargo of relief was proceeding slowly to Sydney Cove, the supplies of food were sinking lower and lower. In September 1789 the supply of butter was exhausted; in November the ration of every item of food was reduced to two-thirds, except for spirits;[44] in January 1790 the flour from England was exhausted, and they began to use the flour

41 M. H. Ellis: *John Macarthur* (Sydney, 1955), pp. 18-19. See also the eye-witness account by the surgeon's mate Harris, in the *Morning Post*, 2 December 1789.

42 M. H. Ellis: op. cit., pp. 5-13.

43 S. M. Onslow (ed.): *Some Early Records of the Macarthurs of Camden*, (Sydney, 1914), pp. 9-12.

44 D. Collins: op. cit., vol. 1, p. 83.

from the Cape of Good Hope, calculating that it would last four months;[45] in February Phillip again sent the *Sirius* to the Cape of Good Hope for provisions; on 1 March the ration of spirits was reduced, and so the gradual decrease in the stores was followed by a diminution of their daily comforts and necessaries.[46] As food and liquor dwindled, the comments on New South Wales became more bilious: one officer described it in a letter to London as past all dispute a very wretched country and totally incapable of yielding to Great Britain a return for colonizing it.[47] Collins, however, retained his faith in their mission to establish civilization in the savage world, to animate the children of idleness and vice to habits of laborious and honest industry, and show the world that no difficulties were insuperable to Englishmen.[48] Phillip was more laconic. They would not starve, he wrote to Nepean, though seven-eighths of the colony deserved nothing better.[49] To solace him for the despair caused by the convicts, his mind from time to time wandered off into contemplating a future when there was a settlement on the banks of so noble a river as the Hawkesbury.[50]

On 5 April, to their unspeakable consternation, they learned of the wreck of the *Sirius* at Norfolk Island. On that day dismay was painted on every countenance when the news was passed around at Sydney Cove.[51] That night all the officers were summoned to meet the Governor-in-Council where, on being told that their salt meat would last till 2 July, the flour till 20 August, and the rice and pease till 1 October, they decided to reduce the weekly rations still further, to strengthen the precautions against theft, and to send the *Supply* to Batavia for provisions.[52] Divine service on the next day was held in one of the empty storehouses.[53] People invited out to dine were instructed to bring their own bread. The lack of food so weakened the workers that the hours of compulsory labour were shortened. A convict caught stealing food was flogged with three hundred lashes, chained for six months to two other criminals, and had his rations reduced for six months. Still the thieving of food continued.[54] A woman overloaded her stomach with flour and greens and died. An old man fainted while waiting to collect his ration at the store, and died the next morning. When his stomach was opened it was found to be quite empty.[55] The convict men and women were short of clothing; the marines were so short of shoes that the majority did guard duty in bare feet. Phillip,

---

[45] Ibid., vol. 1, p. 93.

[46] Ibid., vol. 1, p. 98.

[47] Letter from an officer to Joseph Banks, 14 April 1790 (Banks Papers, Brabourne Collection, vol. 3, p. 60, Mitchell Library, Sydney).

[48] D. Collins: op. cit., vol. 1, p. 67.

[49] Phillip to Nepean, 15 April 1790, *H.R.A.*, I, 1, p. 172.

[50] Phillip to Sydney, 13 February 1790, ibid., I, 1, p. 156.

[51] W. Tench: *A Complete Account* . . . , pp. 39-40.

[52] D. Collins: op. cit., vol. 1, pp. 105-6; W. Tench: *A Complete Account* . . . , p. 40.

[53] Ibid.

[54] D. Collins: op. cit., vol. 1, p. 109

[55] Ibid., vol. 1, p. 110.

from a motive that did him immortal honour, put his private food reserves into the common pool.[56]

On the evening of 3 June they were preparing for a melancholy celebration of the King's Birthday. On that evening even Tench was musing on their fate in his tent, when he heard the joyful sound, 'The flag's up!' He opened the door and saw several women with children in their arms running to and fro with distracted looks kissing their babies with the most passionate and extravagant marks of fondness. He ran down the hill, put a pocket glass to his eye—and saw the sign for which they had so desperately waited. By that time his next-door neighbour, another officer, had joined him, but as they were too deeply moved to speak, they wrung each other by the hand, with eyes and hearts overflowing. He then begged to be allowed to join the Governor in the small boat in which Phillip proposed to go down the harbour. As they rowed they saw a large ship with English colours flying, working her way in between the entrance of the harbour. So tumultuous were their minds that for a moment they imagined the ship in danger, and they were in agony, but needlessly so. As soon as he learned what the ship was, Phillip stepped into a fishing boat to return to Sydney Cove. The others rowed on through wind and rain till at last they read the word London on her stern—'Pull away, my lads! she's from old England!' they cried, 'a few strokes more and we shall be aboard! hurrah for a belly-ful, and news from our friends!'

In a few minutes they had climbed on board the *Lady Juliana* transport to learn that she had been almost eleven months on her passage from Plymouth. They questioned the men on the *Lady Juliana*, asked a thousand questions on a breath; the men on the ship questioned them, but Tench and his party thought the right of being first answered lay on their side. 'Letters! Letters!' they cried. They were produced and torn open in trembling agitation. News burst upon them like meridian splendour on a blind man; they were overwhelmed by it, and many days elapsed before they were able to absorb it all.[57] They read of the loss of the *Guardian*, of the liberal and enlarged plan for the future of the colony, of the stores on the ships of the second fleet which ended the threat of death by starvation, of the coming of free settlers, of the use of convicts to grow food on the land granted to officers, soldiers and settlers.[58] They read of the outbreak of revolution in France. To Tench, this was a wonderful and unexpected event;[59] to Collins it was one which was not likely to interrupt the tranquillity of their own nation which he was proud to say was happy in a constitution that might well excite the admiration and become the model of other states not so free.[60]

Phillip opened the despatches from London, to learn that Grenville had taken over the seals of office from Lord Sydney.[61] Grenville was born in 1759,

56 D. Collins: op. cit., vol. 1, pp. 108-9.
57 W. Tench: *A Complete Account* . . . , pp. 45-6.
58 Ibid., pp. 47-9.
59 Ibid., p. 47.
60 D. Collins: op cit., vol. 1, p. 120.
61 Grenville to Phillip, circular despatch of 5 June 1789, H.R.A., I, 1, p. 119.

the son of a prime minister, educated at Eton and Christ Church Oxford, was skilled in all the details of Europe, had studied deeply the law of nations, was acquainted with ancient and modern languages, could endure fatigue, never allowed an avocation or a pleasure to interrupt his attention, was not eclipsed in the presence of some of the greatest men that ever adorned English public life, but was utterly without feelings for anyone, even for those to whom such feelings were most due.[62] Yet this man of parts wrote a few words in his second despatch which pleased Phillip deeply: 'His Majesty is graciously pleased,' he told him, 'to approve of your conduct in the execution of the arduous and important service which has been committed to your care.'[63] Phillip replied, telling Grenville he had been honoured with this mark of attention from his royal master, and asking him to make known his grateful sense of His Majesty's bounty.[64]

The Reverend Richard Johnson, conscious as ever of his responsibility to answer for the behaviour of the souls committed to his charge at the day of judgment, preached a special sermon to the recently arrived female convicts. With much propriety he touched upon their situation, and described it so forcibly as to draw tears from the least hardened amongst them.[65]

On 26 June, the transport *Surprize* arrived with two hundred and eighteen male convicts as well as various officers, non-commissioned officers and privates of the newly formed New South Wales Corps. It was followed on 28 June by the transports *Scarborough* and *Neptune*, with one hundred and eighty-eight male convicts on the former, and two hundred and eighty-six males and sixty-seven females on the latter, and the remainder of the New South Wales Corps.[66] Thirty-six had died on the *Surprize*, seventy-three on the *Scarborough*, and one hundred and fifty-eight on the *Neptune*, a total of two hundred and sixty-seven out of the one thousand and twenty-six who had sailed from England, while four hundred and eighty-eight arrived sick and unfit for work—victims of the cruelty and greed of the commanders of the ships.[67] For days after the landing the west side of Sydney Cove afforded a scene truly distressing and miserable: more than thirty tents were pitched in front of the hospital, all of which were quickly filled with people suffering from scurvy, dysentery, or an infectious fever.[68] Naked, filthy, dirty, lousy wretches, many of them unable to stand, to creep, or even to stir hand or foot,

[62] *Gentleman's Magazine*, March 1834, vol. 1, pp. 327-9; Henry Lord Brougham: *Historical Sketches of Statesmen who flourished in the time of George III*, first series, 2nd ed. (London, 1839), pp. 254-9; *Journal and Correspondence of William, Lord Auckland* (London, 1861-2), vol. 4, p. 308.

[63] Grenville to Phillip, 19 June 1789, *H.R.A.*, I, 1, p. 120.

[64] Phillip to Grenville, 14 June 1790, *H.R.A.*, I, 1, p. 175.

[65] D. Collins: op. cit., vol. 1, p. 121.

[66] Ibid., pp. 122-3; E. O'Brien: *The Foundation of Australia*, 2nd ed. (Sydney, 1950), pp. 284-5; C. Bateson: *The Convict Ships, 1787-1868* (Glasgow, 1959), pp. 110-15; *H.R.A.*, I, 1, p. 189 and n. 139, p. 750.

[67] Ibid.

[68] D. Collins: op. cit., vol. 1, pp. 122-3; W. Tench: *A Complete Account . . .*, pp. 50-1; *H.R.N.S.W.*, vol. 1, pt. 2, p. 367 et seq.

were moved from the ships to the improvised hospital. The Reverend Richard Johnson spent so much time amongst them that he became quite ill.[69]

There came out in the *Neptune* a person of the name of D'Arcy Wentworth, a tall, handsome and burly person, who was born in County Down in 1764. He was descended from the Strafford family, and distantly related to the Anglo-Irish family of Fitzwilliam. He had travelled to London in 1785 to learn the trade of a surgeon, where he lived on the fringe of high society, but the gap between his own income and the expenses of his way of life, or some flaw in his clay, seemed to push him towards crime. On 12 December 1787 he was tried at the Old Bailey on three charges of felonious assault on the king's highway, putting a person in corporal fear and danger of his life, and feloniously taking from the person and against his will such goods as a watch, or a purse. On all three he was acquitted. The Fitzwilliam family then arranged for him to serve as a surgeon at Sydney Cove. Also on the *Neptune* was Catherine Crowley, who had lived on the Fitzwilliam estates in Staffordshire, where she was sentenced to transportation for some minor offence. On the *Neptune* she became the mistress of D'Arcy Wentworth.[70] The Macarthurs landed from the *Scarborough*, but no one noted their arrival, nor did either of them record their feelings on first landing in the country whose early history was henceforth to be tangled inextricably with the vicissitudes of their own and the Wentworth family.

The material fortunes of the colony improved quickly after the arrival of the second fleet. The climate exercised its beneficent influence on the sick; the old hours of compulsory labour were restored as food rations returned to normal; new buildings were planned; large tracts of land were cleared at Sydney and Parramatta; a pair of shoes was issued to each convict; some women began to make slops; in October the *Supply* returned with supplies from Batavia, to be followed in December by the Dutch ship *Waaksamheyd*; by March 1791, three brick buildings for stores had been finished at Sydney Cove and Parramatta, and a brick barracks for the soldiers.[71] Gradually the material setting began to take a more permanent form.

Johnson was uneasy with the indifference to religion. So low was the attendance by the convicts at divine service each Sunday that their rations were reduced for non-attendance.[72] What Johnson craved, however, and what it was not within Phillip's power to grant, was a recognition of his divine mission, not its degradation to the level of a moral policeman. Johnson believed he had been called by God to higher work than a mere means to

[69] R. Johnson to H. Fricker, 21 August 1790 (original in St Paul's Cathedral, Melbourne).

[70] D. Collins: op. cit., vol. 1, p. 130; *The Whole Proceedings on the King's Commission of the Peace, Oyer and Terminer, and Gaol Delivery for the City of London; and also the Gaol Delivery for the County of Middlesex, held at Justice Hall in the Old Bailey*, 12 December 1787, no. 1, pt. 1, pp. 15-20.

[71] D. Collins: op. cit., vol. 1, pp. 132-45, 149, 160 and 174; Phillip to Grenville, 1 March 1791, *H.R.A.*, I, 1, p. 226; Phillip to Grenville, 4 March 1791, *H.R.A.*, I, 1, p. 247.

[72] D. Collins: op. cit., vol. 1, p. 131.

deter convicts from further crime, or a servant to the law in its two most extreme and savage activities, the flogging triangles and the scaffold.[73] Phillip was still trying to make men industrious who had passed their lives in habits of vice and indolence and who dreaded punishment less than they feared labour.[74] The more dissatisfied he became with their labour, the more disgusted with their vices and their appearance, the more he pinned his faith in the future of the colony on the coming of free settlers.[75]

Towards the end of 1790, Grenville agreed with Phillip's point of view on the future of the colony. In November 1790 he despatched the text of the act conferring on the Governor the power to grant absolute or conditional pardons. An absolute pardon conferred full restitution of legal rights: a conditional pardon prohibited the emancipist to leave the colony until the original sentence had expired.[76] In February 1791 he informed Phillip that two fleets of convicts and supplies would be sent each year to ensure adequate food supplies. In the same despatch he suggested that Phillip might also obtain supplies from Calcutta.[77] In July, Grenville's successor, Dundas, promised that in future only potentially useful convicts would be sent.[78]

In the meantime the news of their arrival and the reports and rumours circulating in London led to the whole future of the Botany Bay scheme coming up for public debate. In March 1789 their arrival had been announced in the London press. It was rumoured in London that several were committing robberies in order to be transported to Botany Bay.[79] In April the London press reviewed cautiously Tench's *A Narrative of the Expedition to Botany Bay*, calling it a well-written informing account, and drawing attention to Tench's view that as a receptacle for convicts it stood unequalled, but that when viewed in a commercial light he feared its insignificance would be very striking.[80] Throughout 1789 and 1790 the newspapers occasionally published the gossip from the colony. But it was not till the beginning of 1791 that they published the hardships of the struggle for survival. In January 1791 the *Gentleman's Magazine* printed the letter by Surgeon White, written in April 1790, in which he described New South Wales as a country and place so forbidding and so hateful as only to merit execrations and curses—a source of expense to the mother country, and of evil and misfortune to its inhabitants, without the smallest likelihood of its repaying or recompensing either. In

---

[73] R. Johnson to H. Fricker, 18 March 1791 (original in St Paul's Cathedral, Melbourne).

[74] Phillip to Grenville, 17 July 1790, *H.R.A.*, I, 1, p. 195.

[75] Ibid., pp. 195-6.

[76] Grenville to Phillip, 13 November 1790, *H.R.A.*, I, 1, p. 208 et seq.; An Act for enabling his Majesty to authorize his Governor or Lieutenant Governor of such Places beyond the Seas, to which Felons or other Offenders may be transported, to remit the Sentence of such Offenders, 30 Geo. III, c. 47, 1790, *Statutes at Large*, vol. 16.

[77] Grenville to Phillip, 19 February 1791, *H.R.A.*, I, 1, pp. 214-19.

[78] Dundas to Phillip, 5 July 1791, *H.R.A.*, I, 1, p. 266.

[79] Anon.: *An Authentic and Interesting Narrative of the Late Expedition to Botany Bay* . . . (London, 1789), p. 1.

[80] *Gentleman's Magazine*, April 1789, vol. 59, pt. 1, p. 340.

the name of heaven, asked White, what had the ministry been about? Surely, he went on, they have quite forgotten or neglected us.[81] In February, Sir Charles Bunbury asked Pitt to comment on reports that the settlements in New South Wales were not fit for their purpose and a Mr Jeckyll added that he had heard that the soil was sterile, and unproductive of anything for the nourishment of man and the support of human nature. To which Pitt replied that there was no reason whatever for any such apprehensions, and that the system was the cheapest mode of disposing of the convicts, winding up with a blast against the irresponsibles who had branded it as a luxury to exiles, and against the criminal law reformers for pretending that severity of punishment was incompatible with humanity.[82]

By an odd irony, while the scribblers and politicians of London were debating the success or failure of the scheme, the men in the colony were confident that at least the battle for material survival had been won. That great labour, Phillip reported to Grenville in March 1791, might be said to be past.[83] The arrival of two fleets in the second half of 1791 again reminded them that they were neither forgotten nor neglected in London. In July the third fleet began to arrive, bringing one thousand, eight hundred and sixty-three convicts, as well as soldiers but, to their unspeakable anguish, neither letters nor newspapers.[84] In September the first convict ship from Ireland, the *Queen*, arrived with one hundred and twenty-six men and twenty-two women convicts on board, most of whom were in an emaciated and feeble condition because of the greed and rapacity of the master who had kept them short of food to increase his profits from the journey.[85]

All attempts to convert the aborigine to their civilization had proved as futile as ever. In May 1791 a convict had been caught stealing fishing tackle from the aborigines. Phillip decided to have him flogged in the presence of the aborigines that they might again see that British law governed the relations between white man and aborigine and that there was not one law for the white man and another for the white man's relations with the aborigine. Again, as with their aversion to the first flogging, the aborigines were shocked. By nature they were not of a sanguinary and implacable temper; though quick to bear resentment, they were not nevertheless unforgiving of injury. The women were particularly affected: one of them shed tears, another snatched a stick and menaced the flogger.[86] The spirit of the place continued to depress. In April 1791 Tench gazed over the country near Richmond Hill: dreary wilds, he found it, for as far as the eye could reach he could not detect a single gleam of change which could encourage hope or stimulate industry to attempt its culture.[87]

[81] *Gentleman's Magazine*, January 1791, vol. 61, pt. 1, pp. 79-80.
[82] *Parliamentary History*, vol. 28, pp. 1222-4.
[83] Phillip to Grenville, 25 March 1791, *H.R.A.*, I, 1, p. 262.
[84] D. Collins: op. cit., vol. 1, p. 168; *H.R.N.S.W.*, vol. 1, pt. 2, p. 538.
[85] Ibid., vol. 1, pp. 179-80.
[86] W. Tench: *A Complete Account . . .* , p. 111.
[87] Ibid., p. 118.

So though the battle for survival had been won, few wanted to stay in the country. In July 1791 the expirees could choose between taking up land grants, working for wages, or returning to England. A few accepted land grants, a few worked for wages, but the majority chose to return to England.[88] The officers and the marines were just as nostalgic. Johnson was weary of being tied with the crooked and ungodly ways of sinners, as well as the great trials in worldly matters unappropriate to his station and office. But as he was where God intended him to be, he believed it his duty to abide where he was.[89] In November Phillip resigned on account of ill-health, adding that every doubt respecting its future independence as to the necessities of life was fully done away, and his wish to return to England in hopes of finding that relief from his pain which this country did not afford.[90] When the *Supply* and the *Gorgon* sailed out on to the high seas for England in November and December, those left behind turned with an understandable lack of enthusiasm to that dull uniformity of uninteresting circumstances. Yet those left behind were not without mettle. On 31 December they assembled in a tumultuous manner to demand that their rations continue to be issued once a week and not, as had been proposed, every day. In a sense this was an historic moment, for it was the first example of people associating for a political purpose. Appropriately enough the veterans from the first fleet were not happy about it, ascribing it to the spirit of resistance and villainy lately imported by the newcomers from England and Ireland.[91]

By the beginning of 1792 the life of the colony had begun to assume a pattern. Phillip was as disgusted and dissatisfied as ever with the convicts and all their works. He began to feel the same contempt and loathing for them as settlers that from the very beginning of the colony he had felt for them as workers and men. As he saw it, very few of them were equipped for the life they must necessarily lead in the country where they were so entirely cut off from the gratifications in which most of them had always sought their happiness. He was just as dissatisfied with the ex-convict as a worker for wages, finding him infinitely more troublesome than the convicts.[92] By the middle of 1792 he wanted neither a convict nor an ex-convict's colony, but a colony of free settlers using convict labour. Again, Dundas, like his predecessors Grenville and Sydney, was converted to Phillip's views, for in January 1792 he announced that he would give every encouragement to induce certain settlers to embark for New South Wales.[93]

Dundas had taken over the seals of office from Grenville on 8 June 1791. Born in 1742, educated in Edinburgh, he spoke English with a pronounced Scots accent. Lacking the urbanity, the cultivation and refinement of Gren-

[88] D. Collins: op. cit., vol. 1, p. 169.
[89] R. Johnson to H. Fricker, 4 October 1791 (original in St Paul's Cathedral, Melbourne).
[90] Phillip to Grenville, 21 November 1791, *H.R.A.*, I, 1, p. 313.
[91] D. Collins: op. cit., vol. 1, pp. 192-3.
[92] Phillip to Dundas, 19 March 1792, 2 October 1792, 4 October 1792, *H.R.A.*, I, 1, pp. 338-9, 371-3, and 385.
[93] Dundas to Phillip, 10 January 1792, *H.R.A.*, I, 1, p. 332.

ville, he relied for his effect as a speaker on broad and coarse appeals to popular prejudices, or exploited the inveterate habit of official assertion. He owed his political career in part to Pitt, who used him as an accomplice; and Dundas stuck to him, as one contemporary put it, as fast as a barnacle to an oyster shell. The two were drinking partners. He was as well a promiscuous and a successful lover:

> What various tastes divide the fickle town!
> One likes the fair, and one admires the brown,
> The stately, Queensb'ry; Hinchinbrook the small;
> Thurlow loves servant maids; Dundas loves all.

It seemed to be the object of his life to employ his talents to the greatest personal advantage. In society he was easy, frank, and convivial, ready to do kind offices, and affectionate in his private life.[94] On such a man hung for the next three years the decisions on the future of New South Wales.

In the meantime the way of life of the convicts had already hardened into a pattern. Working in the summer on the government farms, or on the plots of the officers, from five in the morning till eleven, and again from two till sunset, felling trees, digging up stumps, rooting up shrubs and grass and turning the ground with spades or hoes, the heat of the sun, the short allowance of food, and the ill-treatment from their merciless overseers rendered their lives truly miserable. At night they were housed in huts which accommodated fourteen to eighteen, with one woman whose duty it was to keep the hut clean and provide food for the men at work. They were without the comforts of either beds or blankets. At meal-time they had neither bowl nor plate, and only such crude implements as they had fashioned out of the green wood of the country. In short, they were strangers to all the necessary conveniences, let alone the adornments of life. The women enjoyed a more comfortable life than the men. The fortunate were selected as wives to the officers and soldiers; others were made hut-keepers; the rest were set to work to make spirits, frocks and trousers, or to pick in the fields. The convicts enjoyed the advantages of the laws as well as others: they could only be punished after trial; no person was allowed to strike them or ill-use them, and all complaints against or by convicts, had to be referred to a magistrate.[95]

The convicts, too, were beginning to develop a way of life of their own. They had transplanted with them the language in currency in the profession of crime, that flash or *kiddy* language which differed so sharply from standard English that an interpreter was frequently necessary in the law courts at Sydney Cove to translate the deposition of a witness. The language irritated the officers, some of whom asserted that indulgence in such an infatuating cant was more deeply associated with depravity and continuance in vice than was generally supposed.[96] Most of the officers contented themselves with some

[94] P. H. Stanhope: *Life of the Right Honourable William Pitt* (London, 1861-2), vol. 1, pp. 309-11; *Gentleman's Magazine*, 1811, vol. 81, pt. 1, pp. 676-7.

[95] G. Thomson: *Slavery and Famine, Punishments for Sedition; or, an Account of the Miseries and Starvation at Botany Bay* (London, 1794), pp. 5-9.

[96] W. Tench: *A Complete Account . . .* , pp. 205-8.

such disapproval of the madness and wickedness of the convicts without exploring the possibility of doing anything about it. There was only one who consistently tried to wean them from the ways of the ungodly, and his prescription never varied: read the Bible, he urged them each Sunday; observe and reverence the sabbath day; pray constantly and diligently to God, for as weak and needy creatures men were dependent on God; avoid profane swearing, an unclean and adulterous course of life, theft, dishonesty, villainy and idleness; pay due respect, submission and obedience to superiors.[97] For Johnson looked to God to perform the miracle, not to man in his new environment. He felt such rheumatic pains and weakness that he could scarcely go through the duties of his office.[98]

The officers and their families, too, were beginning to define their attitude to the country and the way of life slowly taking shape. Some continued to be oppressed and appalled by its sameness, its dreary barren appearance, the vista from high places of ridge beyond ridge of mountains covered with trees, and to despair of man's powers to touch it in any way.[99] Some, however, were finding things which delighted and pleased them. Elizabeth Macarthur had discovered how to pass the time cheerfully if not gaily, despite the oppressive heat in the summer and the absence of any female friend, as from the society of the clergyman's wife she could reap neither profit nor pleasure. She learned astronomy and botany from Mr Dawes, or chatted gaily with Captain Tench. Life indeed, as she put it, had become very amusing to her, more so than at any time since she had the powers of reason and reflection, so that believing as she did that life in this world was not a state of perfection she was abundantly content.[100] In June 1791 her family moved to Parramatta from where she spent pleasant days in boating parties up and down the various inlets of the harbour, took refreshments and dined out under an awning on some pleasant point of land, or in one of the necks or coves in which the waters of that harbour abounded. With the arrival of the third fleet there were so many ladies in the regiment that she no longer felt the want of female society as at first.[1] So by the end of 1792 some of the refinements of civilization such as conversation, reading, music, and delight in scenery, had thrown out their first tender shoots in a society hitherto compelled by stern necessity to devote all its energies to preserving life rather than adorning it.

The economic developments in 1791 and 1792 had laid the foundations for the beginnings of such civilized life. Trade with the outside world began: in June 1792 the storeship *Atlantic* arrived from Calcutta;[2] in October the first ships of the East India Company arrived;[3] in November a ship arrived

97 R. Johnson: op. cit., pp. 37-63.
98 R. Johnson to Phillip, 23 March 1792, *H.R.N.S.W.*, vol. 1, pt. 2, p. 602.
99 W. Tench: *A Complete Account* . . . , frontispiece—A Map of the hitherto explored country contiguous to Port Jackson; laid down from Actual Survey.
100 E. Macarthur to Miss Kingdon, 7 March 1791, S. M. Onslow (ed.): op. cit., pp. 28-39.
1 E. Macarthur to her mother, 18 November 1791, ibid., p. 42.
2 D. Collins: op. cit., vol. 1, pp. 227-8.
3 Phillip to Dundas, 11 October 1792, *H.R.A.*, I, 1, pp. 397-8.

from England with silver coin supplies. Earlier, in July, the government had begun a new farm at Toongabbe to increase the production of food. Housing proceeded apace; in November the brick hospital at Parramatta was occupied.[4] By the end of 1792 there were government farms at Sydney Cove, Parramatta and Toongabbe; the colony traded with England, Ireland, Calcutta, Batavia, Chinese ports, and the United States of America; whalers and sealers had used Sydney Cove as a base from which to fish in the south seas; the arrival of free settlers had been promised. The population had increased to three thousand one hundred and eight in New South Wales, and one thousand, one hundred and fifteen at Norfolk Island, made up as follows:

Numbers at Sydney, Parramatta, and Toongabbe, 12 October 1792[5]

	Men	Women	Children
Civil department	23	3	4
Military department	351	31	34
Vice-Admiralty Court	4	—	—
People not victualled from the public stores	62	4	1
Free people	5	24	—
Settlers from free people	11	—	—
Settlers from convicts	52	—	—
Emancipists	8	2	—
Convicts	1948	414	—
Children	—	—	127
Total numbers in the settlements	2464	478	166

i.e. 3108 in the settlements, not including natives who were victualled.

Numbers on Norfolk Island, September 1792[6]

Officers, civil and military, non-commissioned officers, and free people, with their wives and children	121
Settlers from the marines, seamen and convicts	123
Wives, women and children belonging to the above	179
Convicts taken off the stores by settlers, or expirees off the stores (59 men, 17 women)	76
Other servants of officers and settlers, being victualled	161
Invalids	91
Women living with officers as washerwomen, and children ..	137
	888
Convicts available to do public labour (5 women, 222 men) ..	227
Total number in the settlement	1115

When Major Grose arrived on 14 February 1792 to take up his duties as Lieutenant-Governor, he found to his great comfort and astonishment that there was neither the scarcity that had been represented to him, nor the barren sands he had been taught to imagine he would see. On the contrary, he saw

[4] D. Collins: op. cit., vol. 1, p. 247.
[5] Phillip to Dundas, 12 October 1792, *H.R.A.*, I, 1, p. 399.
[6] King to Phillip, 19 September 1792, *H.R.A.*, I, 1, p. 388.

the whole place as a garden in which fruit and vegetables of every description grew in the greatest luxuriance. He found a good house, a not unwholesome climate, plenty of fishing and good shooting. His one complaint was that he was further from England than he would desire to be. As for hunger and misery, they attacked only those who were too idle to help themselves.[7]

On 10 December 1792 Phillip went on board the *Atlantic* transport to sail for England. Voluntarily and cheerfully Bennilong and Yem-mer-ra-wan-nie, two natives who were much attached to his person, boarded the ship with him. Two convicts who had conducted themselves to his satisfaction also joined the party.[8] For Phillip had in abundance that power to attach people to his person. Some of those who were left behind remembered him tenderly for his little acts of kindness, his habit of sending those for whom he felt such fondness some little thing or other every day.[9] Others paused to praise the zeal and perseverance which had enabled him to surmount the natural and artificial obstacles which the country had thrown in his way.[10] All agreed that his role had been paramount if not decisive in winning the battle for survival. Yet by one of those ironies in human history, the other achievement of his term as Governor, the conversion of the British government to policies which would transform the gaol into a colony of free settlers using convict labour, sprang as much from his prejudices and idiosyncrasies as from any vision he entertained for the future of European civilization in New South Wales.

On his return to England he again served with distinction in the navy, was promoted rear admiral of the blue in 1801, and rear admiral of the white in 1804. In 1805 he retired from active service, and lived at Bath on a pension, becoming an admiral of the blue in June 1814. He gradually assumed the role of a benevolent father confessor and adviser for those associated with the colony.[11] Before his retirement to Bath he had risked marriage again in 1794.[12] After his retirement he behaved sufficiently oddly for the gossips to prattle about suicide as the cause of his death in 1814.[13] As though to keep the historians guessing, he was buried at Bathampton, and not in the grounds of his parish church at Bath. For within Phillip two men survived to the end. There was the man who with grace, dignity, industry and great self-control had won the battle for survival: there was also the man who had once wanted to hand over murderers and sodomites to be eaten by cannibals.

---

[7] Extract from a letter from Major Grose, dated Sydney, 2 April 1792, in *Gentleman's Magazine*, February 1793, vol. 63, pt. 1, p. 176.

[8] D. Collins: op. cit., vol. 1, p. 251.

[9] E. Macarthur to her mother, 18 March 1791, S. M. Onslow (ed.): op. cit., p. 40.

[10] D. Collins: op. cit., vol. 1, p. 248.

[11] M. Barnard Eldershaw: *Phillip of Australia: an account of the settlement at Sydney Cove, 1788-92* (London, 1938), *passim*; *Australian Encyclopaedia* (Sydney, 1958), vol. 7.

[12] *Australian Genealogist*, vol. 2, pp. 189-90.

[13] G. Mackaness: *Admiral Arthur Phillip, Founder of New South Wales, 1738-1814* (Sydney, 1937), ch. 22.

8

GROSE, PATERSON AND HUNTER

THE BATTLE for survival was followed by the traditional battles of societies with a European civilization. In the battle for economic and social power, the ownership of wealth was gradually concentrated in the hands of the few. In the collision of opinion, there was a never-ending debate between conflicting views of the nature of man and his destiny. There was all that hubbub and uproar of human intercourse, which some have taken as evidence of the follies and passions of the human heart, some of its evil imagination, and others of its madness. By another of the ironies of history, the man who took these momentous steps was a man singularly lacking in distinction or any power to perceive the significance of his actions.

Major Francis Grose assumed the office of Acting Governor when Phillip sailed for England on the *Atlantic* in December 1792. He was born in 1754, entered the army, received a commission as an ensign in 1775, fought in the War of Independence and remained in America sick of his wounds, till he was repatriated and promoted to the rank of major, retired on half pay in 1783, and rejoined the army in 1789 when he was appointed to command the New South Wales Corps. He arrived in Sydney on 14 February 1792.[1] Those whom he met noted the lack of distinction, the amiability, the joviality, but the lack of the talents of a leader. Bligh, who met him at Cape Town on his way out to assume command of the New South Wales Corps, wrote of him as a man not blessed with any moderate share of good knowledge to give much stability to the new settlement.[2] For Grose was a man of little cultivation, a man who on his own confession spoke French indifferently and was not acquainted with any other foreign language, a man to whom the obscurity of second-in-command ministered both to his distaste for the burdens of command as well as to the complete absence of that power to command.[3] Chance, however, presented him with a situation he had not coveted.

He decided to increase the quantity of foods and goods available. To achieve this he allotted one hundred acres of land to every officer who asked for it, because work on government farms proceeded slowly and never with that spirit and energy which were created by private interest.[4] This policy

[1] Statement of the service of Major General Grose (Bonwick Transcripts, Biography, vol. 2, pp. 452-4, Mitchell Library, Sydney).

[2] Bligh to Banks, Cape of Good Hope, 17 December 1791 (Banks Papers, Brabourne Collection, vol. 5, pp. 166-9, Mitchell Library, Sydney).

[3] Statement of the service of Major General Grose (Bonwick Transcripts, Biography, vol. 2, pp. 452-4, Mitchell Library, Sydney).

[4] Grose to Dundas, 16 February 1793, *H.R.A.*, I, 1, p. 416; D. Collins: *An Account of the English Colony in New South Wales* (London, 1798 and 1802), vol. 1, p. 368.

affected the private fortunes of most of the officers in the settlement. John Macarthur received one hundred acres of some of the best ground that had been discovered at Parramatta, and the labour of ten convicts to clear and cultivate it.[5] The Reverend Richard Johnson, after some compunction, accepted one hundred acres, cultivated it at great expense, not to lay up any treasures on earth, but simply to make his family more comfortable.[6] In addition Grose granted land to non-commissioned officers, to privates, to emancipists and to expirees, the number of acres being decided not by any abstract principle of ability or needs, but by their station in society.[7] At the Liberty Plains near Parramatta, Grose granted land to the free settlers who had arrived on the *Bellona* in January of 1793. To the most respectable of these, Thomas Rose, a farmer from Dorsetshire, he allotted one hundred and twenty acres, and to Frederic Meredith and Thomas Webb, who had come to New South Wales on the *Sirius*, and to Edward Powell, who had been there before on the *Lady Juliana*, allotments of eighty acres each. All of them received seed and tools from the public stores, supplies for two years, and the services of convicts free of charge. They and the officers began their settlement in high spirits, as from their efforts Grose was confident of increasing considerably the cultivation of the country.[8]

At the same time Grose encouraged the officers to engage in trade. At first he encouraged them to purchase goods in bulk for re-sale to the public. Then he permitted them to negotiate directly with captains of ships for their cargo, believing, as with the land grants, that a free play to the incentive of material gain would hasten the transition from near starvation to abundance.[9] The licence in questions of morality which accompanied the increase in material wealth, together with the increasing opulence of the officers, caused the envious and the malicious to gossip about darker motives governing his policy. His critics said that he was indifferent to the well-being of religion and morality, that he aimed to make a joke of them, and that he was hostile to the sacred principles of the British constitution because he promoted the wealth and power of army officers at the expense of civilians.[10] His vilifiers succeeded more with the historians than with their contemporaries, who judged him by his own declaration of policy and by its success.

As early as May 1793 observers were commenting on the improvement as many advanced fast towards the comfortable situation of independent farmers.[11] A year later they were again commenting on how the permission given

[5] S. M. Onslow (ed.): *Some Early Records of the Macarthurs of Camden* (Sydney, 1914), p. 44.

[6] Johnson to Thomas Gill, 29 July 1794 (original in St Paul's Cathedral, Melbourne).

[7] Return of lands granted in New South Wales, December 1794 to September 1796, in *Historical Studies*, November 1951, vol. 5, no. 17, pp. 69-75.

[8] D. Collins: op. cit., vol. 1, pp. 267-8.

[9] Grose to Dundas, 9 January 1793, *H.R.A.*, I, 1, pp. 413-14.

[10] Diary of Richard Atkins, 15 December 1794 (MS. in National Library, Canberra).

[11] G. Barrington: *The History of New South Wales . . . from the Original Discovery of the Island . . . to the Present Time* (London, 1802), pp. 188-9.

to officers to hold land had operated powerfully in favour of the colony.[12] By August 1794 John Macarthur too was referring to those great and extra-ordinary changes by which the colony had been raised from a state of des-ponding poverty and threatened famine to affluence. By then he had a farm of nearly two hundred and fifty acres at Parramatta, of which one hundred acres were under cultivation. He had sold four hundred pounds worth of his produce that year, and had one thousand eight hundred bushels of corn in his granaries. He had twenty acres of fine wheat growing and eighty acres prepared for Indian corn and potatoes. Of livestock he had a horse, two mares, two cows, one hundred and thirty goats, one hundred hogs, and poultry of all kinds in the greatest abundance. His table was constantly filled with wild duck and kangaroo, the dogs killing three hundred pound weight a week. He had built a most excellent brick house, sixty-eight feet in length and eighteen feet in breadth, consisting of four rooms, a large hall, closets, and cellar, with a kitchen, servants' apartments and other necessary offices adjoin-ing. The house was surrounded by a vineyard and garden of about three acres, the former full of vines and fruit trees, and the latter abounding with most excellent vegetables. As the farm was conveniently near the barracks, Mac-arthur could without difficulty attend to the duties of his profession.[13]

Profits were also being made from trade. All through 1793 and in 1794, according to the Reverend Richard Johnson, little other conversation was heard but buying, selling, and bartering, as many of the civil and military officers had turned merchants and wholesale and retail dealers in spirituous liquors. Even a convict could go and purchase a pint of rum from an officer and a gentleman, while some employed their wash-women or others as sales-women. Many were making their fortunes. Such conduct, however, was un-accountable to Johnson, who was proud to say he had no hand whatsoever in the affair, as he thought it unbecoming to him as a minister and beneath him as a gentleman. He proposed to stick to farming, where he believed he would be able to do pretty well.[14] Another clergyman, the Reverend Thomas Fyshe Palmer, was predicting it would soon be a region of plenty, and wanted only virtue and liberty to be another America, for he had never seen a place where a man could so soon make a fortune. It was even within the grasp of the con-victs, so much so, indeed, that he prophesied that with a little more good sense, transportation would become a blessing. He heartily wished all the paupers of Great Britain would make efforts to be sent to New South Wales.[15]

The way of life of the successful became more comfortable. With one of the finest climates in the world and abundance of the necessaries of life—gardens and orchards laden with vegetables and fruit, animals to provide meat,

[12] D. Collins: op. cit., vol. 1, pp. 367-8.

[13] Quoted in a letter by Mrs Macarthur to Miss Kingdon, 23 August 1794, S. M. Onslow (ed.): op. cit., pp. 45-6.

[14] Johnson to J. Stonard, 11 August 1794 (original in St Paul's Cathedral, Mel-bourne).

[15] T. F. Palmer to J. Joyce, 15 December 1794, quoted in T. F. Palmer: *A Nar-rative of the sufferings of T. F. Palmer and W. Skirving, during a voyage to New South Wales, 1794, on board the Surprize Transport* (Cambridge, 1797), pp. vi-vii.

cheap convict servants to relieve them of drudgery, good dairies to supply milk, cream and butter—one of the few anxieties for the successful was how to educate their children. Elizabeth Macarthur believed it would be unjust to confine her children to so narrow a society. She wanted them to see a little more of the world so that they would learn to appreciate better their retirement. All children spoke of going home to England with rapture. Her own dear Edward had quitted her almost without a tear, for the children had imbibed the idea that England was the seat of happiness and delight, that it contained all that could be gratifying to their senses; yet, she added, she would not wonder if some of them made this place the object of their choice.[16] So prosperity created the setting for that complex fate of people with intellectual interests in a colonial society, where the country of their birth provided material comforts in abundance while Europe provided everything which they associated with civilization.

The officers very soon used their power to preserve a monopoly in trade for themselves. They allowed no one but themselves to board ships as they arrived. They alone bought the cargoes and sold them at anything between one hundred and one thousand per cent profit. They ordered into confinement a Mr Ellis and a Mr Boston who boarded a ship to purchase things for their own use. When Ellis and Boston, with great respect but firmness, remonstrated against this invasion of the common rights of British subjects, this was construed into an audacious attack upon the privileges and interests of these military monopolists who promptly crushed them. The critics and opponents of the officers were commanded to doff their hats to the officers or they would be confined to the cells and punished.[17] By such ceremonies as the capping of officers, these men symbolized the concentration of wealth and power in the hands of the few.

Yet in other respects Grose had no eye for ceremony, none of Phillip's sense of the Governor as a stern, forbidding, but generous father of his people. On all previous King's Birthdays Phillip sent some mutton and some wine to the gentlemen, and a pint of rum each to the convicts. In the evening there had been a bonfire where the people expressed their loyalty in the best way they were able. Phillip also usually extended mercy to all the convicts in irons except the very hardened wretches. On 4 June 1793 Grose cut these ceremonies to the bone, and characteristically invited a few officers to dine with him.[18] Grose, however, had succeeded on one point where all Phillip's efforts had failed. He had found an incentive to induce the convicts to work on the farms of the officers by permitting the latter to pay the convicts in rum on those days or during those hours when they were not employed on government work.[19] So the rum worked where kindness and the lash had failed. While Grose and most of the officers seemed indifferent to the effects on behaviour

16 Mrs Macarthur to Miss Kingdon, 1 September 1795, S. M. Onslow (ed.): op. cit., pp. 46-7.

17 T. F. Palmer to the Reverend Disney, 13 June 1795 (broadside in the National Library, Canberra).

18 Diary of Richard Atkins, 4 June 1793.

19 D. Collins: op. cit., vol. 1, p. 268.

of that mode of payment for such extra labour, the Reverend Richard Johnson grieved that in the evening the convict camps became scenes of intoxication, riots and disturbances.[20]

The transition from scarcity to comparative affluence affected the way of life of the convicts and the emancipists in other ways. Charles Williams had been granted thirty acres of land at Parramatta in April 1791, in recognition of the extraordinary propriety of his conduct as a convict overseer.[21] In October 1792, Williams and another convict, Richard Sutton, bound each other by a horrid ceremony in which they cut each other on the cheek with their knives before swearing not to betray their intentions to rob the master of the *Britannia* in his hut and to share the proceeds with each other. When the takings of the robbery proved valueless, Williams informed on Sutton. Until then he had been remarkable for the propriety of his conduct, but after taking up his land he had given himself up to idleness and dissipation, and went away from the court in which he had given his testimony, and so exposed his treachery, much degraded in the opinion of every man who heard him.[22]

On 18 January 1793, Williams, his wife Eleanor M'Cave, their child, and a woman by the name of Green, spent the day drinking and revelling in Sydney, then staggered rioting and fighting with each other to the water's edge, where Mrs Williams imprecated every evil to befall her and the child she carried in her womb if they accompanied Williams to Parramatta. But they did board a small boat, which capsized near Breakfast Point, and the two women and the child were drowned. A short time after Williams had buried his wife within a few feet of his own door, he was seen sitting at that door with a bottle of rum in his hand, drinking one glass and pouring the other on her grave until it was emptied, prefacing every libation by declaring how well she had loved it during her life.[23] In May 1793 a convict settler, Lisk, drank at the house of Williams with Rose Burk until they were very much intoxicated. On the way home a gun discharged, shattering the bones in the woman's arms in a dreadful manner. This incident only established Williams more firmly in the opinion of those who judged his conduct as a public nuisance.[24] In October 1793, wearied, we are told, of being in a state of independence, Williams sold his farm with the house, crop and stock for something less than one hundred pounds to an officer of the New South Wales Corps, and was forced to work as an hireling upon the ground of which he had been the master. His judges asserted he was a stranger to the feelings which would have rendered this circumstance disagreeable to him, as the land itself came into the possession of people with the incentive and the steadiness to raise plentiful crops for the market.[25] This reads like a story of evil and retribution. But having got rid of the money he had received for his farm in three or four

[20] R. Johnson to J. Hunter, 5 July 1798, *H.R.A.*, I, 2, p. 179.

[21] D. Collins: op. cit., vol. 1, p. 160.

[22] Ibid., pp. 239-40.

[23] Ibid., p. 264.

[24] Ibid., p. 287.

[25] Ibid., p. 320.

months of dissipation, Williams took up land on the Hawkesbury in January 1794, and began with much spirit to clear several acres.[26] So Williams once again enjoyed a measure of material success, not that doom and disaster to which his judges believed his waywardness and debauchery would condemn him.

James Ruse, born in 1760 and bred to the business of a farmer, had been sentenced to transportation at the Bodmin assizes in July 1782. He arrived at Sydney Cove on the first fleet. As a convict he had shown such a strong inclination to be industrious and to return to honest habits and pursuits that Phillip, wishing to hold him up as a deserving character, granted him land on 21 November 1789, together with the tools, the seed and the stock necessary to begin life as a farmer. At that time an opinion prevailed that a man could not live off the country; but Ruse burned the fallen timber on his plot, dug in the ashes, clod-moulded it, dug in the grass and weeds, exposed the soil to air and sun, and dug it again before sowing his crop. By February 1791 he was able to maintain himself, and relinquished his claim to any further provisions from the government store. As a reward for his industry Phillip allotted him thirty acres of land. In the second half of 1790 he married Elizabeth Perry who had arrived on the *Neptune*. In July 1792, as a reward for the good conduct of the wife and the industry of the husband, Phillip pardoned her absolutely; by that time Ruse was maintaining himself, his wife, a child and two convicts. In October 1793 Ruse, who was anxious to return to England, and being disappointed in the crop of that year, sold his farm for forty pounds, and became a hireling for wages until he could get away. But he never sailed. In January 1794 he took up land on the Hawkesbury, and he began with much spirit and industry to clear it. In 1810 he was granted one hundred acres in the Bankstown district, but for reasons which remain unknown, he again lost his independence and worked as an overseer for a settler. He died in 1837, and lies in the churchyard at St John's, Campbelltown, under a tombstone which bears an inscription summing up his story:

> My Mother Reread Me Tenderley
> With Me She Took Much Paines
> And When I Arrivd In This Coelney
> I sowd The Forst Grain And Now
> With My Hevenly Father I hope
> For Ever To Remain.[27]

As for the convicts, they coveted money as the means of gratifying themselves in gambling and drinking, or sold their labour not for a mess of pottage but for buckets of rum. To obtain the means to gamble the convicts were

26 Ibid., p. 340.

27 Ibid., pp. 92-3, 158-60, 225, 249, 320 and 340. W. Tench: *A Complete Account of the Settlement at Port Jackson in New South Wales* (London, 1793), pp. 80-1, 155-6; J. Hunter: *An Historical Journal of the Transactions at Port Jackson and Norfolk Island* (London, 1793), pp. 452, 531 and 550; *H.R.A.*, I, 1, pp. 183, 271, 277-9, 341 and 749-50; *H.R.N.S.W.*, vol. 1, pt. 2, pp. 349, 592-3; *Sydney Gazette*, 12 December 1818, 15 June 1827; *R.A.H.S., J. & P.*, vol. 3, pt. 1, p. 27; vol. 3, pt. 2, pp. 33-4; *Australian Encyclopaedia*, vol. 7.

prepared to lose the very clothes on their backs. They played cribbage, and all fours for six, eight or ten dollars a game, or tossed up for dollars. At such games, they quarrelled, swore, and blasphemed, while the gambling goaded them to rob, steal, profane the sabbath, and even to murder.[28] In January 1794 the first murder was committed in the colony when an imprudent convict boasted he was worth much money.[29] They were just as desperately driven by their passion for liquor, there being nothing which they would not risk to obtain it.[30] In the eyes of the moralizers, gaming, whoring, and drunkenness stalked in broad daylight without the least check; religion was laughed at, the sabbath profaned. The more elemental passions went unrestrained.[31] In October 1794 a convict named Hill, a butcher by trade, who had long borne animosity towards an emancipist, Simon Burn, drank with him and a woman with whom he cohabited all one Sunday. When Burn attempted to protect the woman from a beating by Hill, Hill stabbed him to the heart. Burn was an Irish Catholic, and his widow celebrated the funeral rites, a contemporary observed, with orgies suitable to the disposition and habits of her husband and his fellow countrymen.[32]

The Reverend Richard Johnson continued his efforts to persuade the convicts, the ex-convicts and the soldiers to restrain the evil passions of their hearts, telling them of the manifestation of the glory of God's mercy in the eternal salvation of the elect, and of his justice in the damnation of the wicked and disobedient. He reminded them of the day when the righteous would go into everlasting life and the wicked, who knew not God and obeyed not the gospel of Jesus Christ, would be cast into everlasting burnings, and be punished with eternal destruction from the presence of the Lord, and from the glory of His power.[33] Such a message fell on debauched ears. Besides, to his mortification and chagrin Grose displayed openly his contempt for Johnson and all his works, ordering him to conduct the service at six in the morning, and to cut the service down to three-quarters of an hour, including the sermon. The opening of the first church on 25 August 1793 passed almost without official notice, while on Christmas Day only thirty to forty attended divine service in a church built to accommodate five hundred.[34] Grose was prepared to use a parson as a moral policeman, but harboured a suspicion that Johnson was one of the people called Methodists, which he probably equated with sedition, and consequently viewed him as a very troublesome, discontented character, against whom he would have made formal representations about

[28] D. Collins: op. cit., vol. 1, pp. 336-7; Anon.: *A Concise History of the English Colony in New South Wales, from the Landing of Governor Phillip in January 1788, to May 1803* (London, 1804), pp. l-li.

[29] D. Collins: op. cit., vol. 1, pp. 335-6.

[30] Ibid., p. 327.

[31] Diary of Richard Atkins, 17 June 1794.

[32] D. Collins: op. cit., vol. 1, pp. 392-3.

[33] Anon.: *A Missionary Voyage to the Southern Pacific Ocean, performed in the years 1796, 1797, 1798, in the Ship Duff. Commanded by Captain James Wilson* (London, 1799), p. 415.

[34] *H.R.A.*, I, 2, p. 179; and D. Collins: op. cit., vol. 1, p. 307.

disorderly behaviour had he not been touched by pity for Johnson's large family.[35]

In the meantime, in England, the press was happy to report they had heard from respectable quarters in the colony that it was in a very flourishing state. It also continued to publish the bizarre and the sensational, writing of how the celebrated Barrington was likely to become a man of some consequence at last, and adding the hope that he had tasted enough of the bad effects of vicious courses to abandon them entirely. They wrote of how the aborigines stole cabbages, or how a convict had built a comfortable house, cultivated his ground, and refused to return to England.[36] English interest, both public and official, continued to centre on the bizarre, on the expense, or the influence on crime, or the effect on morals. In June 1793 Dundas, who in his private life had scorned the Biblical injunctions neither to look into the wine cup when it was red nor to covet his neighbour's wife, informed Grose of the appointment of the Reverend Samuel Marsden as assistant chaplain to the colony, and urged Grose to attend to his comfort and well-being as whatever tended to increase the respect for the clerical station and character was highly important and necessary on all occasions.[37]

By education and persuasion, Marsden belonged to the same evangelical wing in the Church of England as the Reverend Richard Johnson. Born at Farsley in Yorkshire in 1764, he was educated at Hull Grammar School with help from the Elland Missionary Society, then proceeded to Magdalene College, Cambridge, to study theology as a sizar—an undergraduate who received his education in return for waiting at table and cleaning rooms. In that nest of Methodists his evangelical tendencies were strengthened. Before completing his degree, God appeared to be opening the way for Marsden to carry the gospel of His Son to distant lands. At the same time he had offered his heart, as far as it was proper to give it to any creature, and all he had, to Elizabeth Fristan, the only daughter of Thomas Fristan of Hull, a grand-niece of Admiral Sir Clowdesley Shovell. In his letter of proposal he told her he believed it to be for his good and God's glory that he should be provided with a helpmate, and added that if she declined he was confident God would give him a mind resigned to His will. She did not decline, and the two were married on 21 April. A month later Marsden was ordained a priest by the Bishop of Exeter, and on 1 July the two left England on the *William* for New South Wales.[38]

On the voyage Marsden was so much tried by the wicked conduct of those around him that he lent his ear to hear the testimony of the respectable against the vices of the master of the ship. When the master upbraided him, Marsden, with that fecklessness which he displayed to the end of his days whenever the principles of his religion clashed with the interests or passions

35 Grose to Dundas, 4 September 1793 and 29 April 1794, *H.R.A.*, I, 1, p. 451 and p. 469.

36 *Annual Register*, 1793, vol. 35, pp. 28-9.

37 Dundas to Grose, 31 June 1793, *H.R.A.*, I, 1, p. 441.

38 J. R. Elder (ed.): *The Letters and Journals of Samuel Marsden, 1765-1838* (Dunedin, 1932), pp. 1-23.

of men in high places, decided to come to more amicable terms with the master. Characteristically, he added in his private diary the fervent wish that the Lord would help him always to be faithful, that at the last he might be able to say with St Paul: 'I am clear from the Blood of all men.'[39] On 22 November they landed at Rio de Janeiro, where Marsden saw slaves for the first time. 'My bowels yearned over them,' he wrote in his diary. 'The L^d send them deliverance.'[40] On Sunday, 2 March 1794, while the ship was being buffeted by high seas off the east coast of Van Diemen's Land, Mrs Marsden began to be unwell. As Marsden put it, he had hoped and prayed the ship would arrive at their desired port in time, but now he saw that it could not be. He therefore endeavoured to prepare his mind for the trial as well as he could, writing later in gratitude how the Lord had given him strength equal to his day. For on that ship he could expect no assistance from man; the wind blew; the rain poured down. Marsden was not cast down, however; he knew God would be with them and bless them. Besides, as he added, Mrs M. was also in better spirits than could be expected. About half past ten Mrs Marsden was brought to bed of a fine girl; she had, Marsden thought, an exceeding good time, and suffered as little as if she had had all the assistance in the world. The child was no sooner born than a great wave washed over the quarter deck, forced its way into their little cabin through the port hole, fell upon the little child, and wet their linen, which Marsden then dried by placing it between his shirt and his skin. Having got the child dressed and their little place put to rights, he knelt down to return God thanks for the great deliverance He had brought to them, and hoped that this was done in spirit and truth. Then he began his entry in his diary for the day: 'This,' he wrote, 'hath been a day much to be remembered by me and mine.'[41]

They arrived at Sydney Cove in March 1794, where Marsden quickly took up his duties as assistant chaplain, assuming responsibility for the parish of Parramatta, where his duties were to preach to the military on the morning of his first Sunday on shore, and to the convicts in the afternoon.[42] Like the Reverend Richard Johnson he was appalled by the vice and depravity. He was shocked to find that the convicts condemned to death were greatly alarmed, and had no idea of a God of grace and mercy.[43] He suffered acutely the pangs of exile; he missed that happiness and conversation he had enjoyed in England in the company of God's people. His faith strengthened him to endure all these privations, for he believed in that day when the saints of every clime and nation would meet to part no more, a joyful hope that made present inconveniences and separations easy and tolerable.[44] But the duty to God embarrassed him in his relations with the men in power. In

[39] Diary of S. Marsden, 4 November 1793 (Marsden Papers, Mitchell Library, Sydney).

[40] Ibid., 22 November 1793.

[41] Ibid., 2 March 1794.

[42] D. Collins: op. cit., vol. 1, p. 359.

[43] Diary of S. Marsden, 13 July 1794.

[44] Marsden to the Reverend M. Atkinson, 16 September 1796, in J. R. Elder (ed.): op. cit., p. 29.

July 1794, two men were to be hanged in Sydney. Out of pique, Grose refused permission for Johnson to minister to their spiritual needs, a refusal which Johnson warmly resented, and said so. When Johnson suggested to Marsden that he should seek permission from Grose to see the prisoners, Marsden, after prayer and meditation, decided it was not his duty to remonstrate with the Lieutenant-Governor upon this affair as he was not stationed at Sydney, and the prisoners were more peculiarly Mr Johnson's charge than his. 'It gives me much uneasiness to see these differences prevail,' he wrote that night in his diary. 'O that they might be brought to an end!'[45]

He also decided to become a farmer, to till the soil and breed sheep. Again he felt called on to justify his conduct; he had entered the country when it was in a state of nature, and was obliged to plant and sow or starve. Besides, he added, just as St Paul's own hands had ministered to his wants in a cultivated nation, so his hands had ministered to his wants in an uncultivated one.[46] It was more than want, however, which drove him to accumulate 1720 acres of land, 1200 sheep, as well as unspecified numbers of cattle, pigs and horses, within ten years of his arrival. This laying up of treasures on earth could only arouse the suspicion that he was, to say the least, putting a very literal interpretation on Christ's injunction to feed his sheep, or encouraging the uncharitable to dismiss him as a contemptible hypocrite. It was not calculated to win him that respect for the mission which touched him most deeply—the salvation of the souls committed to his charge.

In September 1795 circumstances in the colony became more propitious for the high-minded. Grose had resigned in May 1794 because he could no longer endure the pains from his wounds,[47] and sailed for England on the *Daedalus* on 17 December following, leaving Captain Paterson to direct the settlements of New South Wales with the title of Administrator.[48] Even those most shocked and repelled by the moral quagmire, by which they claimed that Grose himself was untouched, had the grace to acknowledge that if he had not adopted the wise, humane and effective measure of encouraging private enterprise, and if the officers had not supported his liberal views with their best exertions, the inhabitants must have perished from want.[49]

Paterson was born on 17 August 1755, entered the army at an early age, served in Cape Town in 1777 from where he explored the country of the Hottentots, served in India in 1781, received a commission as lieutenant in 1787, and was promoted to the rank of captain in 1789 when he volunteered to serve in the New South Wales Corps. He sailed for New South Wales on the *Gorgon*, arriving in September 1791. He served in Norfolk Island till

45 Diary of S. Marsden, 15 July 1794.
46 S. Marsden: *An Answer to Certain Calumnies in the late Governor Macquarie's Pamphlet, and the Third Edition of Mr. Wentworth's Account of Australasia* (London, 1826), p. 9.
47 Grose to Dundas, 3 May 1794, *H.R.A.*, I, 1, p. 474.
48 Paterson to Dundas, 21 March 1795, *H.R.A.*, I, 1, p. 489.
49 S. Marsden: *An Answer to Certain Calumnies*, p. 9.

1793, then at Sydney Cove till December 1794, when, as the senior officer remaining on the departure of the Lieutenant-Governor, he assumed the office of Administrator. Paterson was that by no means singular example of an officer serving in one of the outer settlements of the British Empire whose talents were considerable and whose interests were as diverse as his experience, for he had dabbled in botany, exploring, soldiering and administration. He was brought to his destruction by an amiable, undecided temperament in a profession where amiability was branded as weakness, and by that love of the bottle which aggravated his innate tendency to procrastinate rather than make up his mind.[50] For he had the gifts to serve with distinction, but the temperament to destroy him if called on to lead. At the end of 1794 the time of responsibility was too brief for the weaknesses to make him aware of this worm of failure in his clay. He continued the policy of his predecessor: granting land to the officers, the non-commissioned officers, the privates, and the emancipists, and permitting the military officers to trade. In this way he promoted the party of the officers in what one observer called their 'dirty pecuniary views'.[51]

The hopes of those who believed that a new Governor would make the good of the community at large his particular care ran high in September 1795. For in that month a man of incorruptible integrity, unceasing zeal, and a sound and impartial judgment assumed the office of Captain-General and Governor-in-Chief of the colony of New South Wales. He was John Hunter, a captain in His Majesty's navy. Age and experience were on his side. Born at Leith, Scotland, in 1737, he was 58 when he took up the Governorship. In his early years he knew the two loves of the sea and music. At the age of sixteen he took to the sea, and served in North America before being appointed second captain on the *Sirius* with the rank of post captain for the voyage to Botany Bay in 1787. It was Hunter who had first sailed with Phillip into Port Jackson in January 1788, who first charted Sydney Harbour, who sailed in the *Sirius* for supplies to the Cape of Good Hope, by way of Cape Horn, in October 1788, so that when the vessel returned to Port Jackson in May 1789, it had circumnavigated the globe. It was Hunter who sailed the *Sirius* to Norfolk Island in February 1790, was wrecked on one of its reefs, and lay stranded there for eleven months, returned to Sydney Cove in December 1790, and sailed for England by way of Batavia in March 1791. After calling at Batavia, though the mate, the captain and some sailors died, Hunter arrived in England in April 1792 quite unaffected, for nature had endowed him with a toughness which strengthened his power to endure hardships and pain. Years before, on the West Indies station, when his ship ran ashore, Hunter's leg had been caught in a cable, his right hand severely wounded, and a blood vessel in the lung burst from his extreme physical exertions. These injuries were sufficient to kill most men, but Hunter survived them all. By a strange paradox he was endowed too with some of the gifts of the artist. He drew with competence, though not with distinction;

[50] Bonwick Transcripts, Biography, vol. 4, pp. 953-4, Mitchell Library, Sydney.
[51] Diary of Richard Atkins, 13 September 1795.

he was familiar with music, and had had some training in it; he looked to Providence as a prop and support; he wrote and spoke of Christ as his saviour, by which again he meant a protection against the cruelties and injustices of other men; and he was as unaware of women as they were of him. Had he been blessed with greater powers he might have found solace and satisfaction in artistic creation. But fate had been unkind to John Hunter, for it had given him neither the strength of the men of power, nor enough of the gifts of the creative artist. From him there were none of those dazzling achievements which, like passing meteors, could astonish an admiring world.[52] In 1793 he published his journal, and served on the *Queen Charlotte* till 1794. He might have retired with honour, but chance and ambition pushed him at the age of fifty-seven and under the patronage of Howe into the office of Captain-General and Governor-in-Chief of the colony of New South Wales.

He sailed on the *Reliance*, which dropped anchor in Sydney Cove on 7 September 1795. On 11 September at the ceremony at which the Judge Advocate read his commission of office, he spoke with much delicacy of the persons sent to the colony for a certain offence, who, as chance would have it, kept at too great a distance to hear him.[53] Then he addressed the convicts directly, telling them that he would always countenance good conduct, and concluded by telling the gathering at large that as he had come there for the general good, he hoped that no individual would take it ill if he made that the rule of his conduct.[54]

He had brought Bennilong back with him from London, to display to other aborigines the benefits of civilization. On his first appearance, Bennilong conducted himself with a polished familiarity towards the members of his family. To his acquaintances he was distant, and quite the man of consequence, telling them he would not permit them to fight and cut each other's throats as they had done in the past, for he would introduce peace amongst them and make them love one another. He conducted himself with the greatest propriety at the dining table, wore the clothes of his civilizers, and extended their courtesies to women. He presented his wife with a very fashionable rose-coloured petticoat and a jacket made of a coarse stuff to persuade her to put on the white man's clothes and abandon her lover. When she discarded her clothes and returned to her lover, Bennilong fought him, insisting on using fists instead of using the weapons of his country. Soon Bennilong's absences from the Governor's house became more and more frequent, and when he went out he usually left his clothes behind.[55]

At the same time the Reverend Samuel Marsden was lost in wonder and astonishment at the various changes through which a kind Providence had led him. He was not of noble birth, nor heir to any great inheritance, and had in the beginning only the prospect of hard labour and toil before him. Yet,

[52] *Naval Chronicle*, vol. 6, pp. 350-67; J. Hunter: op. cit., *passim.*
[53] D. Collins: op. cit., vol. 1, pp. 428-9.
[54] Diary of Richard Atkins, 13 September 1795.
[55] D. Collins: op. cit., vol. 1, pp. 439-40.

to his surprise, God had exalted him from his low station and rank to minister before Him in holy things. He had accepted a grant of land for the support of his family and himself to help render the colony independent as well as to prevent the convicts and probably the government also saying that the clergyman was an idle, lazy fellow. Now Hunter offered him the position of magistrate, and Marsden went down on his knees again to seek divine guidance to answer the question: how far was the duty of a clergyman incompatible with the duty of a civil magistrate? Hunter had presented the reasons for accepting—the want of general officers in the colony, the general distracted state of the settlement, the opportunity to report crimes and abuses as a magistrate which he could not do as a clergyman. Marsden, for his part, did not wish to offend the governor; he was rather willing to cultivate his good opinion, as well as to convince the people under his charge that he wished to promote their temporal as well as their spiritual interests. In the meantime he would continue to preach repentance towards God and faith in our Lord Jesus Christ, believing it would redound to his eternal honour to plant the gospel in this distant part of the known world, for this afforded him the most exalted idea of the dignity of his own situation, and made it lawful for him to glory in the gospel of Christ.[56] So Marsden justified to himself, to his God, and to his superiors in London, those decisions which were to cause him an infinity of anguish, and deprive him of the very respect he so desperately craved, the respect of his fellow-men.

At the same time another man in the colony was examining his conscience. He was Richard Atkins, who had arrived in the colony with Major Grose in February 1792. Born in 1745, the fifth son of Sir George Bowyer, he had changed his name to Atkins to conform with a will, and served in the army till he volunteered to go to New South Wales, where Phillip made him registrar of the Vice Admiralty Court in February 1792. At the beginning of each new year Atkins resolved to give up that inveterate love of the bottle which was ruining his reputation with his fellow-men, as well as destroying his self-respect. Each new year's eve he recorded his trust in his fortitude and resolution to resist all temptation. On 1 January 1796 he recorded once again his failures during the previous year to achieve anything praiseworthy, and his hope that 1796 would bring forth good fruit. By 11 February he was recording failure. This was a private failure, bringing anguish and suffering to himself and his family, and to those few who cared for him. Hunter's failure on the other hand was a public one, written over the pages of the history of New South Wales, the impotence of the good man before men with evil and malice and madness in their hearts. For Hunter believed with the psalmist that when many dogs came about a man, and the council of the wicked laid siege against him, and imagined mischief in their hearts, the Lord would reward them according to their deeds, and according to the wickedness of their own inventions.

Events in New South Wales simply did not correspond with Hunter's view of the world. Like Phillip, he had been instructed to conciliate the

56 S. Marsden to the Reverend M. Atkinson, 16 September 1796, in J. R. Elder (ed.): op. cit., pp. 29-31.

affections of the aborigine, to live in amity and kindness with them, and to prepare them for civilization. But the closer his contact with civilization, the more the aborigine was degraded. Bennilong became so fond of drinking that whenever he was invited to an officer's house he was eager to be intoxicated, and in that state was so savage and violent as to be capable of any mischief. At the same time, he began to lose the respect of his own people. In one of his many fights with his wife's lover he received a severe blow on the head, whereupon the lady and her lover laughed at the rage which it caused.[57] So Bennilong disgusted his civilizers and became an exile from his own people, and rushed headlong to his dissolution as a man without the eye of pity from the former, or affection from the latter. As a mark of that terror which the ways of the white man had provoked in the minds of the aborigines, an aboriginal woman who had given birth to a half-caste in 1796 was seen holding the baby over a fire in a desperate attempt to darken its skin.[58]

At the same time a harsher angrier note began to appear in the white man's description of the aborigines. He began to write of them as people who seemed to delight in exhibiting themselves as monsters of the greatest cruelty, devoid of reason, and guided solely by the worst passions.[59] During 1796 the parents of an aboriginal girl were murdered by Europeans, who then adopted the girl, lavished on her their amity and kindness, and trained her in their ways. This angered the aborigines, who lured her into the woods, murdered her, cut off her arms, and mutilated her body.[60] The Europeans complained that the aborigines repaid kind treatment with base ingratitude; that they thieved, burned and plundered the white man's property. In 1799, five white settlers on the Hawkesbury, angered by such thefts, burnings and a murder, met in the home of the widow of the murdered man to exact revenge, captured two suspected aboriginal boys, tied their hands behind their backs with rope used ordinarily to tie up the dogs in the yard, marched them outside and shot them.[61]

Hunter was horrified. He charged the five men with murder. In their defence the accused pleaded vengeance and justified murder of black men on the grounds that the aborigines were a treacherous, evil-minded, bloodthirsty set of men.[62] When the court returned a verdict of guilty, Hunter appealed to London for guidance. By the time the reply came he had left the colony, for by then the same professions of goodness had been tried and found wanting in an encounter with his fellow-Europeans. In the beginning of 1796 Macarthur made suggestions for the administration of the commissary at Parramatta which Hunter, with dignity, declined to accept. Some-

---

[57] D. Collins: op. cit., vol. 2, p. 85.

[58] Ibid., vol. 1, pp. 596-7; G. Barrington: op. cit., p. 32; Anon.: *A Concise History of the English Colony in New South Wales*, p. 23.

[59] D. Collins: op. cit., vol. 2, pp. 12-13.

[60] G. Barrington: op cit., pp. 186-7.

[61] Hunter to Portland, 2 January 1800, *H.R.A.*, I, 2, p. 401 et seq.

[62] Ibid., pp. 413-16.

one whispered into Macarthur's ears words which he claimed to have heard
Atkins use at the Governor's table, namely, that glaring partiality had been
exercised by Macarthur in the receiving of maize into the commissary's store
at Parramatta, whereupon Macarthur demanded an explanation from Hunter
why he had not rebuked Atkins there and then. When Hunter replied with
dignity that it was not his custom to encourage story-tellers, let alone those
who promoted distrust and discord rather than confidence and harmony, the
implied rebuff provoked Macarthur to look for the first opportunity to
settle his score with Atkins. He found it in a trifle. Atkins had refused to
reveal to him the name of the convict whom he had seen stealing turnips
from the Governor's garden at Parramatta, on the principle that if rigid
justice were to be the order of the day, then the Lord have mercy on all
of us. Atkins knew that if every man were used after his deserts none would
escape a whipping. But Atkins had his pettinesses too; his vanity had been
hurt when Macarthur did not extend to him the respect of writing Esq. after
his name in a letter he wrote to him.[63]

Macarthur then savaged the weaknesses of Atkins, calling him a man
deeply plunged in infamy, a public cheater, a man who lived in the most
boundless dissipation, a man from whom drunkenness and indecency were
almost inseparable, and a man who had exposed himself in the public streets in
the most disgracing state of intoxication. When Hunter protected Atkins from
being crushed by Macarthur, Macarthur then turned to destroy Hunter,
choosing as his method a letter to the Duke of Portland. In this letter, he
charged Hunter with extravagance in the expenditure of government money;
he charged him with putting men on the land who could not cultivate it,
men who should be in the service of an industrious and vigilant master. In
his private rage and thirst for revenge he was assuming the role of spokesman for the more opulent landholders. He concluded with an attack on the
moral condition of the colony, in which he asserted that vice of every description was openly encouraged, while positions of trust were held by men
whose characters were disgraceful to the British nation.[64] So wounded pride
burgeoned into that higher purpose of cleansing the colony of its moral
filth, and of protecting society from contamination by guarding the honour
of his family.

Hunter was astounded that anyone, let alone an officer and a gentleman,
should conceive of him as a man possessing a violent or a peevish disposition.
He was astounded, too, that any man should perpetrate such an impertinent,
indirect and highly censurable interference in the duties of the Governor of
the colony.[65] He was also deeply hurt, and deeply puzzled why he, a self-
declared evangelist for goodness, for religion and morality, should be singled
out for such an attack. All through 1797 he brooded over the paradox of this
man Macarthur who was drawing part of his income from the traffic in

[63] *H.R.A.*, I, 2, pp. 89-106.

[64] Macarthur to Portland, 15 September 1796, enclosure in Portland to Hunter,
30 August 1797, *H.R.A.*, I, 2, pp. 89-93.

[65] Hunter to Portland, 14 September 1796, *H.R.A.*, I, 1, pp. 661-3.

ARTHUR PHILLIP

Miniature by Francis Wheatley, c. 1786, in the Mitchell Gallery, Sydney

And he said unto them I beheld Satan as lightening fall from Heaven. Luke x.18

G. Terry Pinx.

G. Terry Sculpt Paternoster Row

Published as the Act directs Feby 8. 1787 by Goff & Co. No 8 Ivey Lane, Paternoster Row St Pauls Lon

THE REVEREND RICHARD JOHNSON

Engraving by G. Terry in the Mitchell Library, Sydney

spirits, who was a member of the officers' ring and therefore in part responsible for such moral filth as existed in the colony, yet who dared to accuse him of encouraging wickedness. By the middle of that year he saw Macarthur as a busybody who covered his self-interested motives under the most specious and plausible of opinions.[66] By the middle of 1798 he was contrasting the nobility of his own motives, the consideration for the public interest, with the horrid depravity and wickedness of Macarthur's heart. The more he protested the purity of his motives and his intentions, the more extravagant became his conception of Macarthur, until in July 1798 he told the Duke of Portland that even the sacred character of the Saviour, were He to appear in the colony in its present state, would not be secure from the dark attack of those whose private views He might oppose in favour of the public interest. There were people in the colony, Hunter believed, who would most readily prepare for His sacred head another crown of thorns, and erect another cross for His second crucifixion, and none more so than the person of whom he had complained.[67] This conviction of the horrid depravity and wickedness of Macarthur's heart cheated Hunter of the chance to see Macarthur as others saw him: to see him, for example, as his wife saw him, as a tender and affectionate husband, as an instructive and cheerful companion, an indulgent father and a beloved master, who was universally respected for the integrity of his character.[68] So the conviction of the righteousness of his own position warped Hunter's attitude to Macarthur as a man, and cut him off from the man with the mind and the drive to shape the future of society in New South Wales.

The man to whom Hunter was appealing in London for sympathy and understanding was not endowed by nature with the capacity to extend either. William Henry Cavendish Bentinck, Duke of Portland, was born in 1738, a man of high birth, of princely fortune, of honourable character, of nervous shyness and of very moderate abilities.[69] On his first assuming office in 1782, Horace Walpole described him rather maliciously as a head without a tongue; the more charitable observed that though he was swayed by most honourable motives, reluctance to make up his mind left him like a tennis ball, to be tossed from side to side. On 16 December 1792, friends called on him to entreat him not to lend his name to Fox's move to acknowledge the French republic. To all their entreaties Portland replied nothing. Neither would he answer a word when they repeatedly asked him what was to be done, or what were his opinions. All was dead silence on Portland's part; he seemed as in a trance. His friends spent a painful two hours with him, in which the intervals of silence were as long as ten to fifteen minutes.[70] To such a man Hunter had

[66] Hunter to King, 1 June 1797, *H.R.A.*, I, 2, p. 11.

[67] Hunter to Portland, 25 July 1798, *H.R.A.*, I, 2, p. 171.

[68] Mrs Macarthur to Miss Kingdon, 1 September 1795, S. M. Onslow (ed.): op. cit., p. 52.

[69] P. H. Stanhope: *Life of the Right Honourable William Pitt* (London, 1861-2), vol. 1, pp. 78-9.

[70] Ibid., vol. 2, p. 183; *Dairies and Correspondence of James Harris, First Earl of Malmesbury, edited by his grandson* (London, 1844), vol. 2, pp. 477-8.

L

appealed for action on a petty feud in one of the most remote provinces of the British empire.

While he waited for Portland's reply, Hunter continued to explain developments in the colony in terms of his religious view of the world. All through his term of office a number of small land-grant holders were obliged to sell their lots. By 1798 only twenty-one out of the seventy-three who had received grants remained on their blocks. The holders explained their loss of independence by the high price of labour and the high prices for goods caused by the officers' monopoly.[71] Hunter would have none of this. He preached to them, and reproached them for reducing their families to beggary by indulging in spirits, by their idleness, and by their speculation in traffic.[72] He came down on the side of those who told the evicted that the loss of their land was a punishment for contracting debts to raise money for the temporary gratification of beastly intoxication.[73] On this Hunter was more parsonical than the parsons, for while the clergy and missionaries were contending with what they called the depravity and corruption of the human heart in a colony where each man countenanced his neighbour in the pursuit of sensual gratifications, even the parsons acknowledged that the impoverishment of the small land-grant holders was caused by high prices, poor soil, vagaries of weather, and lack of both capital and a market, rather than the aggravation of their innate depravity by the peculiar composition of the society of New South Wales.[74] The peculiar religious view of the world to which Hunter was implacably attached prevented him from perceiving the empirical causes of their failure, just as his values concealed from him the significance of the developments in that world of buying and selling which he disdained.

Economic life continued to develop as rapidly under Hunter as under Grose and Paterson. The convicts continued to be divided on arrival between the government and private employers. Those in government service were organized in gangs of twenty according to their previous vocations. Blacksmiths were employed in making up iron work and tools of agriculture, carpenters and bricklayers in building, some as tillers of the soil in the government farms, and some as junior civil servants. Each gang was placed under an overseer who was generally a convict, while every two or three gangs worked under superintendents, who were responsible to the government and the officers for the labour and conduct of the convicts, as well as their proper treatment. The hours of labour in summer were from daylight to eleven a.m., and from two p.m. to five p.m., and in winter from daylight to three p.m. The convicts were lodged in small wooden huts built for the purpose at Sydney, Parramatta, Toongabbe and on the government farms at those settlements, and they messed together. They were supposed to wear a regulation uniform,

---

[71] See, for example, the petition by the settlers at Parramatta and adjacent districts to the Duke of Portland, 9 January 1800, *H.R.A.*, I, 2, pp. 441-4, and the petition of Hawkesbury settlers to Hunter, 1 February 1800, *H.R.A.*, I, 2, pp. 445-6.

[72] Hunter to the Hawkesbury settlers, 8 February 1800, *H.R.A.*, I, 2, pp. 446-50.

[73] D. Collins: op. cit., vol. 2, pp. 21-2.

[74] L. Becke and W. Jeffrey: *The Naval Pioneers of Australia* (London, 1899), pp. 105-6; and *H.R.A.*, I, 2, pp. 183-8 and 142-6.

but as supplies were infrequent they wore different colours, and sometimes no clothing at all, for the labouring men worked in the field and other places as naked as the natives of the country. As they had no blankets they experienced great distress by night.[75] The convicts assigned to the private employers, either as workers on the farms of officers or settlers, or as domestic servants, were at first clothed and fed by the government, but after May 1798 orders were issued in an attempt to ensure that all but a few assigned convicts would be maintained by the officers and settlers, and thus not be a charge on government.[76] They were lodged on the premises of their masters.

The women in government service worked as menders and washers of clothes and in spinning linen. In this the Irish women specialized, as even before 1800 they had established a reputation in this trade. Some were assigned as domestic servants, in which occupation after November 1798 they were fed, clothed and housed by their masters.[77] All convicts, whether in government service or assigned, could only be tried by a magistrate for a breach of convict regulations or the law, though the master had the same authority, the same power, over a convict as a master over a servant, as indeed did an overseer or a superintendent. In addition, there were the free workers, the men and women whose terms had expired, or who had been pardoned either conditionally or absolutely, who had never taken up grants on emancipation or had, like Williams, taken them up and been obliged to sell them either because fate, economic circumstances or an innate disposition to indolence and indulgence combined to defeat them.

By 1798 the demand for labour, either bond or free, by both government and settlers, exceeded the supply. This scarcity contributed to the high price of labour in the colony, as well as the high payments to convicts for work done outside regulation hours, and the high payments to free workers who, as Mrs Macarthur regretted in 1798, were demanding the enormous price of four or five shillings a day.[78] These high wages contributed in turn to the economic difficulties of many of the settlers. In addition, the settlers were obliged to employ an inordinate quantity of labour, as all agricultural work was still done by hand, without assistance from either horses or oxen.[79]

The payments of those ex-convicts who hired themselves out as labourers were both complex and diverse. On the large estates the settlers kept on hand large supplies of articles most needed by their workers, for shops there were none. The value of the articles purchased was then deducted from the wages. Most employers provided board and lodging for their workers, and either bartered goods such as sugar, tea and rum for their labour, and so provided them with both the necessaries and the luxuries, or paid them in coin. Rum was by no means the only form of such barter, despite the attempt of some

[75] Hunter to Portland, 10 July 1799, *H.R.A.*, I, 2, p. 371.

[76] *H.R.A.*, I, 2, pp. 215 and 219.

[77] Ibid., p. 360.

[78] Mrs Macarthur to Miss Kingdon, 1 September 1798, in S. M. Onslow (ed.): op. cit., p. 51, as 1795. For disputed date see Macarthur Papers, A2908, Mitchell Library.

[79] Petition by settlers of Parramatta to the Secretary of State, enclosure no. 2 in Hunter to Portland, 1 February 1800, *H.R.A.*, I, 2, p. 441 et seq.

contemporaries to delude posterity into believing that the whole of the working class of New South Wales was debauched to placate the greed of the officers of the New South Wales Corps.[80]

The buying, selling and distribution of agricultural produce, seed and live stock was performed in the main by the commissary, which had branches in both Sydney and Parramatta. Until 1798 all the workers, both bond and free, as well as the military and civil officers and their wives and families, were victualled from the commissary, while all settlers with land grants, both the ex-convicts and the free, received seed and stock and were victualled by government for two years. After 1798 assigned convicts both male and female were victualled by their masters. The commissary obtained its supplies from ships arriving from England and from other ports, from the government farms, and from the farms of the settlers. For each item purchased from a settler, the commissary issued a receipt, and these passed current as coin or could be exchanged for a bill on the treasury in England.[81]

So long as masters of ships, settlers, and others dealt exclusively with the commissary, the prices of goods were high but not exorbitant. When the officers entered trade under Grose, exorbitance degenerated into a mystery of iniquity and extortion. For the officers began quickly to make profits of one hundred to two hundred per cent in the simple transaction of buying a cargo and marketing it. Rum bought at eight shillings a gallon was retailed at twenty shillings, thirty shillings, forty shillings, eighty shillings and even as high as eight pounds a gallon. The prices of all luxuries and necessaries were correspondingly high. The settlers groaned under this load of oppression; some were forced to sell their holdings and so became dependent on the government to victual themselves and their families, which in turn increased the expenses of government. Hunter continued to attribute this increase in expenditure to their desire to be steeped in beastly intoxication, while the officers believed they were performing a public service by preventing the masters of ships imposing a more extortionate type of monopoly. They were soiling their hands in trade not for the love of filthy material gain, but to protect the weak against those whose greed was not restrained by a gentleman's code of honour.[82]

Trade with the outside world contributed to the transformation of the former years of famine, toil and difficulty into years of plenty, ease and pleasure. Ships from England found it well worth while to gratify the inhabitants of Sydney Cove with many elegant articles of dress from Bond Street and other fashionable repositories of London. American ships began to call at Sydney for refreshments and sale of cargoes; whalers and sealers began to use it as a base for their fishing in the south seas; traders from Indian ports

[80] S. M. Onslow (ed.): op cit., pp. 50-1; *H.R.N.S.W.*, vol. 3, p. 486; S. J. Butlin: *Foundations of the Australian Monetary System, 1788-1851* (Melbourne, 1953), p. 18 et seq.

[81] S. M. Onslow (ed.): op. cit., p. 50; the evidence of John Palmer to the Select Committee on Transportation, 1812, p. 64, *P.P.*, 1812, II, 341.

[82] *H.R.A.*, I, 2, pp. 442-3; the evidence of M. Margarot to the Select Committee on Transportation, 1812, pp. 52-3, *P.P.*, 1812, II, 341; and S. M. Onslow (ed.): op. cit., p. 51.

were beginning to examine prospects in the colony.[83] An improvement in farming practice of some moment was begun when, in September 1795, John Macarthur set a plough drawn by horses and oxen to work on his farm at Parramatta, and Mrs Macarthur wrote with pride of this proof of the progressive state of their infant settlement.[84] The area under cultivation continued to increase, reaching 8,690½ acres by August 1799;[85] so did the proportion of land cultivated by settlers in proportion to land cultivated by government—by August 1799 there were 280 acres under cultivation by government, 1,243½ acres by officers, and 7,167 acres by settlers.[86]

By September 1800 there were four thousand nine hundred and thirty Europeans in the settlements in New South Wales:

	Men	Women	Children
Civil	26	9	8
Military	443	69	113
Free people and settlers victualled	82	41	111
Free people and settlers not victualled ..	1777	200	—
Convicts	1230	328	459
Orphans victualled			34

In addition six aborigines were receiving victuals. By then there were five and a half men to every woman in the settlements; forty-one per cent were convicts, and fifty-nine per cent were free or freed.[87]

In the late 1790s John Macarthur, Isaac Nichols and the Reverend Samuel Marsden experimented in sheep breeding. By crossing Bengal and Irish breeds Macarthur produced a mingled fleece of hair and wool, a result which suggested to him the idea of producing fine wool in New South Wales. In 1796 he imported four merino ewes and two rams from the Cape of Good Hope and continued his experiments till, by 1801, he had produced a merino with wool the equal of any Spanish wool and a cross-breed of considerable value. While he was turning over in his mind ideas of how this could be used to the advantage of the settlers of New South Wales,[88] Hunter was still brooding over the horrid depravity of Macarthur's heart and the gratifications of the smaller settlers in beastly intoxication.

In June 1796 some fishermen who had been forced by bad weather to shelter in a bay near Port Stephens discovered coal. For several years the river was known as the Coal River. Even after 1797, when it was formally named the Hunter, Hunter himself maintained a characteristic attitude of indifference

[83] D. Collins: op. cit., vol. 1, p. 496, and vol. 2, pp. 279-80 and p. 296.

[84] S. M. Onslow (ed.): op. cit., p. 49.

[85] An account of live stock and ground in cultivation in his Majesty's settlement in New South Wales, in August 1799, *H.R.A.*, I, 2, p. 384. Government had 200 acres in wheat and 80 acres in maize; the officers had 873 acres in wheat, 296 acres in maize, 67 acres in barley, 3½ acres in oats and 4 acres in potatoes; the settlers had 4,992 acres in wheat, 2,156 acres in maize, 15 acres in barley, and 4 acres in oats.

[86] Ibid.

[87] Encl. no. 1, in Hunter to Portland, 30 September 1800, *H.R.A.*, I, 2, pp. 679-80.

[88] J. T. Bigge: Agriculture and Trade, p. 16, *P.P.*, 1823, X, 136.

to its significance.[89] In September 1795, a Mr George Bass, a surgeon by profession, who possessed by nature a strong and vigorous body and was endowed also by nature with great good sense, ingenuity and observation, had arrived in the colony with Hunter on the *Reliance*. In 1797 he discovered coal to the south of Port Hacking. Between October 1795 and June 1797, Bass and Matthew Flinders explored Botany Bay, George's River and the coast south of Port Hacking in a craft eight feet in the keel and five feet in the beam, which they named appropriately the *Tom Thumb*. On 3 December 1797 Bass set out with a crew of six volunteers from the navy in a whaleboat twenty-eight feet seven inches long, to examine the coast to the south, and in so doing to ascertain the existence of a strait between New South Wales and Van Diemen's Land. They reached Phillip Island in Westernport by 5 January 1798. They were satisfied from the rapidity of the tide and the long south-west swell of the existence of a strait but were depressed by the appearance of the land, having found in general a barren, unpromising country whose want of harbours rendered it even less valuable. When their provisions ran short after a stay of twelve days, they turned for Sydney, which they reached on 25 February.[90]

To remove all doubts about the existence of a strait, as well as to chart the coasts of Van Diemen's Land, Bass and Flinders set out in the *Norfolk* in October 1798 on a voyage in which they passed through the strait and circumnavigated Van Diemen's Land. Hunter decided to name the strait Bass Strait as a tribute to the correctness of judgment of Mr Bass in the earlier voyage, though he took an unconscionable seven months to report the voyage to the Duke of Portland, and rather ungenerously refrained from assessing the significance of their work.[91] It was left to others to point out how the voyage from the Cape of Good Hope to Sydney would be expedited by using the strait, and the value of the harbours in the strait as a haven from the storms in the Great Australian Bight,[92] and to prophesy the proper elevation of the navigators' names in the temple of fame.[93]

For a people who believed the body to be more than raiment, those in high places were unaccountably slow in providing for religion and education. In September 1796 Marsden opened a temporary church at Parramatta formed out of the materials of two old huts.[94] In October 1798 the foundation stone for a stone church was laid in Sydney. To save the children from that ruin in which the infamous examples of their abandoned parents were but too likely to plunge them, the Reverend Richard Johnson began a Sunday school in January 1797, hoping to lead the children into the paths of righteousness.[95]

[89] D. Collins: op. cit., vol. 1, pp. 484-5; Hunter to Portland, 10 January 1798, *H.R.A.*, I, 2, p. 118 and n. 50, p. 713.

[90] M. Flinders: *A Voyage to Terra Australis* (London, 1814), vol. I, pp. cvi-cxx; Hunter to Portland, 1 March 1798, *H.R.A.*, I, 2, p. 133; and D. Collins: op. cit., vol. 2, pp. 93-4.

[91] Hunter to Portland, 15 August 1799, *H.R.A.*, I, 2, p. 381.

[92] D. Collins: op. cit., vol. 2, pp. 192-3.

[93] G. Barrington: op. cit., pp. 303-4.

[94] D. Collins: op. cit., vol. 1, pp. 493-4.

[95] Ibid., vol. 2, p. 19.

At the same time two schools were opened for the instruction of the young, more in the belief that literacy was an aid to salvation than in any hopes of the worldly uses of knowledge.[96] A printing press which had been brought out with the first fleet began to print government notices in November 1795, while on 31 January 1798, on the tower of the second windmill in Sydney, a public clock was set up and announced the hour to the inhabitants.[97]

On the night of 16 January 1796 the first play-house was opened in Sydney, when some of the more decent class of prisoners put on the play 'The Revenge' and the entertainment 'The Hotel'. As a motto, they chose the words: 'We cannot command success, but will endeavour to deserve it.' When they applied for a licence they were informed that the slightest impropriety would be noticed, and a repetition punished by the banishment of their company to the outer settlements. For admission they charged one shilling for a seat in the gallery, but the management also accepted flour, meat, or rum as payment. Somewhat to the surprise of their judges, they fitted up the theatre with more propriety than these judges had expected, while their performance too was far above contempt. But the worst of the convicts broke into the houses of families who were enjoying themselves in the gallery. When the news was reported, their judges reflected that though thieves might surprise with their talents, their morals remained constant.[98] The most popular pastime for the convicts remained gaming, in which, in the eyes of their judges, they continued to indulge themselves to a deplorable degree. The women convicts consorted with them in their drinking and gaming, while the free women, the dashing belles of the settlement, promenaded at the Rocks, having spared, we are told, no expense in ornamenting their persons, or gossiped and haggled at the shops where they greedily purchased articles of ornament and apparel.

A few took an interest in what was happening in Europe. All through 1793 and 1794, during each long interval between the arrival of ships, fear gripped their hearts lest England, like France, had been convulsed by revolution, or had been invaded by the French. They had had news of the upheavals in the Dutch community in Batavia; they had heard of officers on French ships in the Pacific being deposed, and revolutionary committees taking over. To their unspeakable relief their own little community remained free from civil commotion, and they even began to think of it as a recommendation that it was the only part of the globe where quiet was to be expected.[99] So at Sydney Cove and Parramatta articulate opinion remained steady for altar and throne. The Reverend Richard Johnson believed that the principles the Scottish martyrs had espoused and so strenuously propagated in such perilous times were no good recommendation to any who loved their king and wished well to their country,[100] while Collins, who somewhat to his surprise had found one of them, Skirving, a pious, honest and worthy man, nevertheless characterized

---

[96] See below pp. 204-5.

[97] D. Collins: op. cit., vol. 1, p. 435, and vol. 2, pp. 83-4.

[98] Ibid., vol. 1, pp. 448-9.

[99] S. M. Onslow (ed.): op. cit., p. 46.

[100] Johnson to Stonard, 27 November 1795 (original in St Paul's Cathedral, Melbourne).

him as another victim of mistaken opinions.[1] This naive if enthusiastic conservatism was nourished by a narrow patriotism, which greeted every English success in the revolutionary wars against France with relief and joy. When the whaler *Rebecca* brought news of Nelson's victory at the Nile in March 1799, the people burst into rejoicing; Hunter issued a public order and all the artillery in the colony was discharged, while the Reverend Richard Johnson offered up the thanks of a grateful community.[2]

Side by side with these public occasions of grief and joy, men and women lived and suffered and died. In 1795 a Mr Barrow who had arrived in the colony as a midshipman on the first fleet, heard the Reverend Richard Johnson preach on the uncertainty of human life, how death stole up like a thief in the night. The next week he died of an obstruction in the bowels, brought on by bathing when much heated and full.[3] The Reverend Samuel Marsden was finding it easier to get on in the world than with the world. His worldly fortunes flourished; but, like Hunter, he was finding his religion and his sacred calling an ineffectual protection against the violent and shameful attempts by Macarthur to ruin him for ever in the opinion of the inhabitants of the settlement.[4] When Marsden failed to impress the strong, or was wounded by their contempt, he soothed his outraged vanity by bullying the weak. In 1800 he used his power as a magistrate to bully Joseph Holt, a victim of the 1798 upheaval in Ireland, and tried to force him to work on a government farm, but Holt told him not to meddle in his affairs. Marsden withdrew in defeat, leaving in Holt the impression that he was a fussy meddling man of but shallow understanding.[5]

To mark the beginning of the new year, in January 1799, Atkins asked Holt into his house, and Barrington followed. A bottle of rum was produced, which induced some pleasant conversation about Ireland. When Holt expressed a wish to retire, Atkins detained him saying he never allowed any bottle off his table till he saw it emptied. They finished a half-gallon bottle, being then, according to Holt, each as full of chatter as a hen magpie in May. For despite his new year resolutions, when spirits were plentiful in the colony Atkins was generally indisposed. In February 1800 the woman who had put up for years with such degradation decided not to live through the humiliation of another broken promise. On 26 February his Kitty left him, and went on board the *Reliance* to sail for England on 3 March, and Atkins was left to endure his squalor alone.[6]

In March 1799 the aborigines on the Hawkesbury warned the settlers of an impending flood but, not liking to be taught by untutored savages, the settlers treated their warnings with contempt. Soon a prodigious swelling of the waters began. The ground on which the settlers had erected their houses

---

[1] D. Collins: op. cit., vol. 1, pp. 469-70.

[2] Ibid., vol. 2, p. 201.

[3] Ibid., vol. 1, p. 446.

[4] Marsden to Hunter, 11 August 1798, encl. in Hunter to Portland, 25 July 1798, *H.R.A.*, I, 2, p. 187.

[5] T. C. Croker (ed.): *The Memoirs of Joseph Holt* (London, 1838), vol. 2, pp. 87-8.

[6] Diary of Richard Atkins, 26 February 1800.

and farm buildings was soon inundated and their retreat cut off. Some in despair and dismay climbed to the ridges of their dwelling; some took to boats; some improvised rafts. All that night nothing was to be heard but the firing of muskets and the cries of women and children, together with the noise of the torrent. In the morning the country appeared like an extensive sea, with here and there the top of a hill or the ridge of a house appearing above the surface; fragments of houses, swimming hogs, stacks of wheat, and dead poultry were seen driven before the torrent. Fortunately, only one man was lost.[7]

The parsons, the moralizers, and all those in high places who had been touched by the evangelical view of the world, pointed to such disasters as a divine punishment for the beastly indulgences of the ex-convict settlers on the banks of the Hawkesbury. The same people pointed to all deaths from excessive drinking as examples both just and dreadful of divine wrath for those who proved their unfitness to exist by sousing their minds into a state where they were incapable of preserving a proper sense of their Creator.[8] The parsons pointed to all misfortunes and privations as evidence of divine displeasure for the obliteration in the colony of all idea of a supreme being and that absence of respect for everything decent, moral and sacred.[9] Or so Marsden warned Hunter, but by then his eyes were so misted by the evangelical view of the world that they could not see the economic developments, the signs of growth and development, which had convinced even *The Times* in London that the condition of the colony was most promising.[10]

Prejudices and fears likewise stained the early relations between government and the Irish convicts with blood and tragedy. The first Irish convicts had arrived at Sydney Cove on the *Queen* in September 1791, and by October of 1800 there were one thousand two hundred and seven of them in the colony.[11] From the beginning Hunter's comments on them were unfavourable. He described them as a desperate set of villains, accused them of encouraging perjury in the law courts, and pleaded for fewer Irish convicts lest the colony be filled up wholly with the very worst of characters.[12] The superstition of the Irish, which Hunter believed to be one of the many prices of their fatuous religious beliefs, exposed them to the wildest and the cruellest flights of fancy. They believed, for example, that there was a colony of white people three to four hundred miles to the south-west of Sydney, where they could indulge in all the comforts of life without labouring for them; they cherished the delusion that it was possible to walk from Sydney Cove to China.[13] Hunter, for the sake of humanity, as he put it, as well as from a strong desire to save them,

7 Hunter to Banks, 1 June 1799 (MS. in National Library, Canberra).

8 G. Barrington: op. cit., p. 308.

9 Marsden to Hunter, 11 August 1798, encl. in Hunter to Portland, 25 July 1798, *H.R.A.*, I, 2, p. 187.

10 *The Times*, 27 October 1800.

11 T. J. Kiernan: *Transportation from Ireland to Sydney, 1791-1816* (Canberra, 1954), p. 28.

12 Hunter to King, 30 April 1796, *H.R.A.*, I, 1; p. 565, and Hunter to Portland, 10 January 1798, *H.R.A.*, I, 2, p. 118.

13 D. Collins: op. cit., vol. 2, p. 75.

worthless as they were, from death, tried to scotch the story. The Irish clung tenaciously to their delusions, as only men whose sole experiences of the world were poverty-stricken Ireland or the rude convict huts of Sydney Cove and Parramatta could believe. They nourished these beliefs as comforts to make the world bearable, just as they nourished the hope that the Irish would be rescued from the colony by French frigates. An old convict woman wandered round Sydney Cove as their sooth-sayer, comforting them with the picture of that glorious day when the French would liberate them from their barbarous Anglo-Saxon oppressors.[14]

But whereas the French landing in Ireland in September 1798 had ended in a cruel farce with the Irish leader Napper Tandy so drunk that he had to be carried back on board the French ships on the shoulders of his slightly less bibulous fellow-countrymen, the attempt at liberation in New South Wales ended in cruelty and degradation.[15] In April 1798 a convict working in a gang at Toongabbe threw down his hoe and gave three cheers for liberty. He was taken promptly before a magistrate, sentenced, tied up in the field where he had been working, and severely flogged.[16] The Anglo-Saxon did not pause to sort out the muddle and terror in his mind. Protestant ascendancy succumbing to Catholic tyranny or Jacobin anarchy was a ghoulish nightmare to him.

In September 1800, having received information that certain seditious assemblies had been held in different parts of the colony to the great danger of His Majesty's government and the public peace, Hunter decided to hold an inquiry. But the Irish, to the despair of their Protestant inquisitors, proved evasive, equivocal and jesuitical, and not prepared to inform on each other, or to be treacherous to their sacred oath to be a friend to each other till death. Richard Atkins and Samuel Marsden ordered one of their number, Galvin, to be flogged until he revealed where the pikes of the conspirators were concealed. They flogged him on the back till he was raw; they flogged him on the bottom; they flogged him again on the back. When he still refused to inform, even Marsden admitted that Galvin would die rather than reveal anything. But Marsden as a magistrate had stooped to the temptation that the truth could be flogged out of a man, just as in other quarters he had stooped to the idea that souls could be flogged away from damnation. The man who wanted to be known as the dispenser of divine love became identified with one of the most savage punishments in the early history of the colony. To restore order and recall these deluded Irish to their senses, some were sentenced to one thousand lashes, some to five hundred, some to two hundred, and some to transportation to Norfolk Island where the baneful influence of their example could not be experienced.[17] To the Irish the floggings to extract confessions and the one thousand lashes, were more evidence of that barbarity and savagery which the Anglo-Saxon was all too ready to use to maintain the Protestant ascendancy against Catholic tyranny and Jacobin anarchy. New

[14] Ibid., vol. 2, pp. 106-7.

[15] W. E. H. Lecky: *A History of England in the Eighteenth Century* (London, 1890), vol. 8, pp. 227-8.

[16] G. Barrington: op. cit., p. 230.

[17] *H.R.A.*, I, 2, pp. 575-83, and 639-51.

South Wales had contributed its first page to that book on the melancholy history of the Irish.

Prejudices against the Irish however could not bring Hunter into disrepute in London. What damaged him there was his response to criticism. From the beginning in his correspondence with the Duke of Portland he adopted a tone of deference which slid almost into a cringe when he was responding to criticism—'I will not fatigue your Grace . . . It may not be improper to remind your Grace . . . I will venture to assure your Grace . . . I hope your Grace may approve of this measure.'[18] Such posturings came strangely from a man who had endured the perils of the sea. At other times he consoled himself with the myth which has sustained seamen down the ages, that he was a very plain man bred to the honourable and respectable profession of a seaman in His Majesty's navy, that on the sea the hearts of men were cleansed from evil and madness, but on land, as Hunter pathetically asked, what character could be safe?[19]

His own character was never safe on land in New South Wales. In August of 1797 Thomas Fyshe Palmer wrote a chatty letter to England which, as Palmer intended, reached the Duke of Portland. In the letter the malice against Hunter was conveyed in the innuendoes. He explained the reasons for the high prices in the colony, dwelt on the consequent immense expense for the government in victualling its charges, and stressed that this served no other purpose than to put money into the pockets of the officers. Of course, he went on, he could not say whether the Governor knew it or not, but the greatest and most extortionate shop in the colony had been that of Government House.[20] Hunter was astounded that any one could conceive that a man such as himself, who had spent forty-six years in the service of his sovereign, who had risen through all the ranks and grades of his profession, and at last arrived at the highly flattering and exalted office of being appointed the representative of His Majesty in this remote part of his dominions, could be prevailed on to bring disgrace upon that elevated situation by such a mean, low and contemptible act. For himself he would prefer to live on bread and water with a pure and unpolluted conscience, as well as his fair and respectable character, in preference to rolling in wealth obtained by such infamous, such shameful, such ignominious means. He ended on a pathetic note: 'I have no turn for traffic, my Lord; I never had.' That was written in November 1799.[21]

It was too late; the damage had been done. On 15 April 1800 Hunter opened a despatch from the Duke of Portland who, for once in his life, had passed judgment in no uncertain way. As Hunter read through the despatch he found to his mortification that Portland had accepted the slanders of his traducers; that he had sanctioned the officers engaging in a traffic which had

[18] Hunter to Portland, 6 July 1797, *H.R.A.*, I, 2, pp. 34-5.

[19] Hunter to Portland, 5 January 1800, *H.R.A.*, I, 2, p. 429.

[20] T. F. Palmer to friends in England, 14 August 1797 (broadside in the National Library, Canberra). For the writing of the letter see J. Ferguson: *Bibliography of Australia* (Sydney, 1941-55), vol. 1, pp. 88 and 106; and M. H. Ellis: *John Macarthur* (Sydney, 1955), pp. 149 and 549.

[21] Hunter to Portland, 15 November 1799, *H.R.A.*, I, 2, pp. 395-6.

disgraced His Majesty's service; that he should consult the instructions from London on the evils of the traffic in spirits; that the Duke of Portland felt called upon by the sense of the duty he owed to the situation in which he had the honour to be placed to express his disapprobation of the manner in which the government of the settlement had been administered by Hunter in so many respects; that he had been commanded to signify the royal pleasure that Hunter should return by the first safe conveyance which offered itself after the arrival of Lieutenant-Governor King, who had been authorized by His Majesty to take upon him the government of that settlement immediately on Hunter's departure from it.[22] King was Hunter's junior officer, who had served under him on the first fleet, and was twenty-one years his junior.

With that dignity from which even under the most cruel and unjust wounds he never faltered, Hunter replied immediately. He assured the Duke that he would return promptly, and that he would assist King with every paper necessary for his guidance. After a somewhat waspish aside that whatever he might be deficient in, King's judgment would supply, he concluded by telling him that a most thorough consciousness of the strict justice and in-flexible integrity with which he had administered the government of New South Wales under the most arduous and difficult circumstances could not fail to relieve his mind in a very considerable degree from that pain and concern which his grace's letter would have otherwise occasioned him.[23] In the mean-time, King displayed all that indelicate impatience of the younger man to possess his office, and behaved in ways which Hunter found injurious to his character as an officer and a man.[24] As the days dragged on, Hunter, waiting for a suitable ship, began to brood over even darker thoughts for his dismissal.[25]

By 28 September 1800 all was in readiness. On that day Hunter proceeded to the wharf along a road lined on each side by troops, to find a large number of the inhabitants of the colony who, we are told, manifested by their de-portment the sense they entertained of the regard he had ever paid to their interests, and the justice and humanity of his government.[26] The civil and military officers gathered too to pay their tribute to his public worth and his private benignity.[27] The aborigines called goodbye to their *Be-an-na*, or father, for he had won their affections too, as indeed he had won the affections of the Europeans by being gracious and condescending to all without com-promising either his personal or official dignity.[28]

By 1810 he had forgiven John Macarthur for the evil he had done to him.[29] By 1812 when he gave evidence to the select committee on transportation, he remembered the material achievements and progress during his term of office

[22] Portland to Hunter, 5 November 1799, *H.R.A.*, I, 2, pp. 387-92.
[23] Hunter to Portland, 20 April 1800, *H.R.A.*, I, 2, p. 487.
[24] Hunter to King, 8 July 1800, *H.R.A.*, I, 2, p. 657.
[25] Hunter to Under Secretary King, 25 September 1800, *H.R.A.*, I, 2, p. 554.
[26] D. Collins: op. cit., vol. 2, p. 304.
[27] D. D. Mann: *The Present Picture of New South Wales* (London, 1811), p. 7.
[28] T. C. Croker (ed.): op. cit., vol. 2, pp. 85 and 156; A Literary Gentleman: *The History of New South Wales* (Newcastle-upon-Tyne, 1811), *passim*.
[29] Testimony of James Macarthur in S. M. Onslow (ed.): op. cit., p. 57.

rather than the drinking, the whoring and the gambling. By then time had softened the memory of those dark days when he had meditated on the horrid depravity of Macarthur's heart, when he had seen him as a man driven to put a crown of thorns on the head and drive the nails into the palms of the ones without sin. He remained to the end of his days as he had seen himself in a moment of self-discovery during those days of adversity in New South Wales, as a very plain man bred to the honourable and respectable profession of a seaman in His Majesty's navy, whose code of values and whose code of honour led him on to anguish and suffering, and in a measure to the derision of posterity, in a country which to the very end he loved passionately.[30] He died in London on 13 March 1821.

With him, on the *Buffalo*, the Reverend Richard Johnson and family returned to England, where Johnson took up parish work in London and later at Ingham in Norfolk. In September of 1826 he wrote his last will and testament in which he solemnly and devoutly committed his precious and mortal soul into the hands of a merciful and covenant-keeping God, humbly trusting in the atonement made by his dear and only begotten son the Lord Jesus Christ as his sole right and title to eternal life. His frail and mortal body he cheerfully committed to the dust of the earth.[31] He died the next year.

[30] Evidence of J. Hunter to the Select Committee on Transportation, 1812, p. 20, *P.P.*, 1812, II, 341.

[31] Photostat copy of the last will and testament of the Reverend Richard Johnson, 21 September 1826 (National Library, Canberra).

9

KING, FLINDERS, AND PORT PHILLIP

AFTER 1800 the outlines of two societies began to take shape in the settlements of New South Wales. One drew its wealth from trade, the other from land and sheep. One laid the foundations of bourgeois society, the other created the ancient nobility of New South Wales. At the same time the Protestant ascendancy continued to dominate the civilization in the colony, despite some desperate and anguished protests from the Irish Catholics; the relations between Europeans and aborigines rushed headlong towards their final tragedy; new settlements were begun at Port Phillip and in Van Diemen's Land. All these tendencies were strengthened when Philip Gidley King was Captain-General and Governor-in-Chief of the colony of New South Wales.

By birth, training and temperament, King was equipped to reap what others had sown, rather than to plant the first seed. By long tradition the Kings had belonged to the middle ranks of the officers, a tradition which King had neither the talent nor the ambition to upset. He was born in 1758, entered the navy in 1770, and in 1779 was dismissed his ship for ordering the ship's company to sign a power of attorney appointing an agent for prizes without the knowledge of the captain. All his life he was driven to find similar dodges to bridge the gap between desire and capacity, because he was not prepared to sustain his station in life by great thrift or meanness. In 1787, at the age of twenty-nine, he volunteered to serve in New South Wales, where he conducted himself with such distinction that even Phillip wrote of him as a man whose perseverance in the navy or any other service might fully be depended upon.[1]

In February 1788, Phillip appointed him commander of the settlement at Norfolk Island. In the beginning his aspirations were high-minded. He wanted to dispense with corporal punishment; within six weeks he had a boy of fifteen flogged with one hundred lashes for stealing rum. He was appalled by the sexual promiscuity and the drunkenness; within two years he had fathered two illegitimate children, and had begun to drink heavily. Yet he never lost faith in the piety which had sustained him before his fall, urging his illegitimate children later to say their prayers and not to forget their catechism, because then God would bless them and preserve them when they were fighting the French. Above all they must never forget God Almighty, and they must re-

[1] Anon.: *The Voyage of Governor Phillip to Botany Bay; with an Account of the Establishment of the Colonies of Port Jackson and Norfolk Island* (London, 1790), p. 60.

collect that He saw all their actions.[2] Gradually the flaws in his character converted the fresh open-faced young officer, who peered at the world with wonder and delight from the portrait of 1789, into the moody, maudlin, gout-ridden officer who took the oaths of office at Sydney Cove in September 1800. He had visited London in 1790 and returned to Norfolk Island from 1791 till 1796, when he received permission to return to England on sick leave. In 1797, with Sir Joseph Banks as his sponsor, he received a dormant commission as Governor of New South Wales in case of the death or during the absence of Captain John Hunter, but which did not carry the title of Captain-General and Governor-in-Chief, as King was intended to be a *locum tenens* or governor in probation.[3]

Observers had noted how time and circumstances had ravaged both his appearance and his character as soon as he arrived at Sydney Cove on the *Speedy* on 15 April 1800. One settler believed that his rheumatism almost incapacitated him for the active duties of a governor.[4] One noticed how his violent and intemperate disposition plunged innocent people into most distressing situations.[5] Another noticed how liberally King used such epithets as 'infernal scoundrel' or 'damned rascal' in addressing other people, and dismissed him as a man whose brutality and cruelty exceeded his courage.[6] Soon stories of King's eccentric behaviour began to circulate in the colony. There was a story of how a woman had asked him for a small quantity of rum from the store. When the woman would not take 'No' for an answer, King asked her her name: 'Bridget Kennedy, your Excellency,' she replied. 'Oh,' said he, 'you have another name; what do they call you?' 'The Pony, Sir,' said she. 'Trot, then, you hussy, trot,' said he, taking her by the shoulders and pushing her down the avenue. There was a story of how the Captain-General and Governor-in-Chief of the colony of New South Wales in a moment of drunken buffoonery had jumped into a basket of eggs.[7] Yet his behaviour and his vision of the world were still governed by that high-mindedness and humanity which informed his life before the rages and the buffoonery cheated him of the respect and esteem to which his talents and achievements entitled him.

He saw himself late in 1800 as a man sent to clean up a mess. Vice, dissipation and a strange relaxation seemed to pervade every class and order of people in New South Wales; from the better sort of people to the blackest characters amongst the convicts cellars were filled with the fiery poison; the

2 J. Hunter: *An Historical Journal of the Transactions at Port Jackson and Norfolk Island* (London, 1793), pp. 301-11; M. Bassett: *The Governor's Lady* (Oxford, 1940), p. 115.

3 *H.R.A.*, I, 2, pp. 340 and 605, and 3, pp. ix-x.

4 G. Mackaness (ed.): *Memoirs of George Suttor, F.L.S., Banksian Collector (1774-1859)* (Sydney, 1948), p. 44.

5 T. C. Croker (ed.): *The Memoirs of Joseph Holt* (London, 1838), vol. 2, p. 130.

6 M. Margarot to Under Secretary King, 1 October 1800, *H.R.N.S.W.*, vol 4, pp. 216-17.

7 *The Colonial Observer*, 9 March 1842, no. 23, vol. 1, p. 179; J. West: *The History of Tasmania* (Launceston, 1852), vol. 1, p. 32; *Hobart Town Almanack and Van Diemen's Land Annual for 1835*, pp. 122-3.

children were abandoned to misery, prostitution and every vice of their parents; prices were so high that it was more economical for the British government to send supplies of salt meat than to purchase private and public stock in the colony; there was upwards of one thousand five hundred people unnecessarily victualled from the public store who did no kind of labour or work for the public benefit. This and much more, he wrote, he had to rectify, adding that he knew full well he could not expect those to promote his plans of industry when the success of such plans must prove the infamy of their own conduct.[8]

Nor could he feel any measure of confidence in the men appointed to assist him. The senior military officer, William Paterson, he found a weak, honest man, who would do the right thing if he acted from his own ideas of right and wrong, but weakness made it easy for others to use him as a knave's tool.[9] As Judge Advocate he had Richard Atkins, who acquitted himself very well when not addicted to the bottle. In 1800 King reported that Atkins had made very fair promises, which he expected him to attend to as well as he could, for King, from his own experience and observations knew what was in man, though he had not seen that long unequal struggle between promise and performance which Atkins had put up ever since he arrived in the colony.[10] As senior chaplain he had the Reverend Samuel Marsden. King complimented Marsden as the best practical farmer in the colony, but was discreetly silent about his powers to wean his charges from vice, while Marsden's brother in Christ, the missionary Crook, believed his worldly interests and responsibilities were distracting him from his higher calling.[11]

King immediately tackled the traffic in spirits. He reduced the quantity of spirits landed, which did not please those vultures who had been enriching themselves at the expense and existence of their fellow creatures. He encouraged the settlers not to mortgage their crops to buy necessaries and spirits from the officers, by selling them goods which previously they had bought from the monopolizers at one thousand per cent on the prime cost.[12] By the end of 1802 Lord Hobart, who had taken over the seals of office from the Duke of Portland in 1801, described as laudable King's measures against monopoly and the traffic in spirits, as well as the measures he had taken to render the labour of the convicts as productive as possible.[13] It looked as though the measures of a well-intentioned eccentric had succeeded where the goodness and the innocence of Hunter had proved ineffectual and impotent.

Something more than a difference in character, something more than a difference in type, contributed to the success of King. Time played its part.

[8] King to Under Secretary King, 3 May 1800, *H.R.A.*, I, 2, pp. 505-6.

[9] King to Under Secretary King, 21 August 1801, *H.R.A.*, I, 3, p. 246.

[10] King to Under Secretary King, 10 March 1801, *H.R.A.*, I, 3, p. 75.

[11] King to Under Secretary King, 21 August 1801, *H.R.A.*, I, 3, p. 246; Crook to the London Missionary Society, 1 March 1804, *H.R.N.S.W.*, vol. 5, pp. 313-14.

[12] King to Hobart, 9 November 1802, *H.R.A.*, I, 3, pp. 647-8.

[13] Hobart to King, 29 August 1802, *H.R.A.*, I, 3, pp. 561-3.

DAVID COLLINS

From 'An Account of the English Colony in New South Wales'

Engraved by A. Cardon, from a Miniature by I.T.Barber.

JOHN HUNTER

Portrait by an unknown artist in the Nan Kivell collection, National Library, Canberra

So did luck, for King had the colossal good fortune to get rid of Mac-arthur, not by cunning or taking thought or superior intelligence, but by one of those singular strokes of chance which sometimes determines the deserts of a man in human history more decisively than moral worth. In July 1801, Lieutenant Marshall was tried before the criminal court of Judge Advocate and six military officers for assaulting his superior officers, Edward Abbott and John Macarthur. He was found guilty and sentenced to a fine of fifty pounds and one year's imprisonment. When Marshall alleged to King that the trial had been unfair, King, concluding that the six military officers had been motivated by vindictiveness and clannishness, remitted the fine and the imprisonment in the name not only of justice, humanity and equity but also strict propriety, provided Marshall left for England in two days, and reported to the Secretary of State.[14]

When the court flatly rejected King's request that they should consider Marshall's allegations of unfair trial, King was piqued, and called the court's decision a public insult to his legal commands. Second thoughts suggested a wider significance in the behaviour of the officers. He began to doubt whether there could be justice so long as the court was composed of the Judge Advocate and six military officers. So the idea for a reform of the system of administering the criminal law in New South Wales was the child of a governor's injured pride; the behaviour of the officers had forced King into the role of a reformer in the name of justice. Convinced as he was of the unjust and oppressive character of the existing system, he suggested that the civil officers should sit with the military officers and so strengthen the impartial and free administration of justice.[15] However, his thoughts on legal reform were pushed to the back of his mind by events which followed swiftly on his taking sides against the officers.

Macarthur immediately organized the officers to boycott King in their social life and, with the single-mindedness of the ambitious, com-manded his wife not to talk to the wives of officers who broke the boycott. Paterson, whose humanity as ever was warring with principle, continued to dine with King. When Macarthur published his correspondence with Paterson in an attempt to ostracize and punish the man who had dared to oppose him, Paterson challenged him to a duel, which took place on 14 September 1801. Paterson was wounded. King then decided to arrest Mac-arthur, whereupon Macarthur gave a dinner for the military detachment at Parramatta, at which the men were to drink spirits presented by Macarthur. When King refused to allow the spirits to be moved, the soldiers rallied forth with sticks to take it from the constabulary. Before the colony was plunged into utter confusion, Lieutenant Hobby and Ensign Moore ordered the soldiers back into their barracks.[16] Immediately both sides began to sling the mud. As in the times of Hunter, Macarthur concentrated on Atkins, alleg-ing that his character for low debauchery and every degrading vice, as well

14 King to Portland and the enclosures, *H.R.A.*, I, 3, p. 187 et seq.
15 *H.R.A.*, I, 3, p. 293.
16 King to Portland, 5 November 1801, *H.R.A.*, I, 3, p. 274 et seq.

M

as total want of every gentlemanly principle, was universally known throughout the settlement.[17] To this Atkins retorted with the traditional charges of the man who needs alcohol or religion to make the world bearable (and Atkins swallowed huge doses of both), by railing against Macarthur's infamous and diabolical conduct, his rapacity in accumulating a large fortune in so short a time, and his extortions on the industrious and laborious settler.[18] King, too, began to use strong language in his denunciations of Macarthur; he branded him as a perturbator, accused him of making a large fortune which he estimated at £20,000 in November of 1801, of helping his brother officers to make small ones at the public expense, and of sowing discord and strife. Experience, King added, had convinced every man in the colony that there were no resources which art, cunning, impudence, and a pair of basilisk eyes could provide that Macarthur did not exploit to obtain any point he undertook.[19]

An astonishing stroke of fortune forestalled a trial of strength between King and Macarthur. When King offered Macarthur release from arrest to be followed by a court martial, Macarthur refused to be released until he had received a written statement of the charges to be made against him. Whereupon King decided to send him to London to face a court martial and, for reasons on which both he and his family remained understandably silent, Macarthur left for London by way of Indonesia and India on 15 November 1801 on the *Hunter*. When Macarthur sailed out on to the high seas, there went with him all chance of destroying King as Governor of New South Wales. It was just in time, for King was beginning to show signs of strain, beginning to call on the Deity as support for his integrity, as Hunter had done when too weak to fight such an opponent. King, too, was beginning to rest his confidence on the supreme disposer of events, under the firm conviction of having acted an indispensable part.[20] Macarthur was content to rely on human contrivance, for on arriving in England he evaded court-martial by resigning his commission in the army, and used his influence in high places to promote his material interests in the colony of New South Wales.

In preparation for the celebration of the King's Birthday in June 1803, one of King's critics composed some doggerel verse in which he was described as a wicked, oppressive, notorious man who wanted to make everyone subservient, humble and poor, starve the convicts and sell all their rations. It was the sort of doggerel distinguished neither by wit nor venom, which King almost certainly would have laughed off, had not one reference to his investments in whaling touched him on a raw spot.[21] King had invested in whaling to supplement his income, not from greed but in a desperate attempt to plug the gap between getting and spending which was laying waste his

[17] King to Under Secretary King, 21 August 1801, *H.R.A.*, I, 3, pp. 245-6.
[18] *H.R.A.*, I, 3, p. 313.
[19] King to Under Secretary King, 8 November 1801, *H.R.A.*, I, 3, p. 322.
[20] King to Under Secretary King, 14 November 1801, *H.R.A.*, I, 3, p. 348.
[21] *H.R.A.*, I, 4, p. 170.

powers, as money, or the lack of it, bothered him all his days in New South Wales. Like most men under strain, a flick on a tender spot caused him to rage against his attackers. 'The dark and Concealed Assassins of my Reputation and Character' he called his vilifiers, and styled them as men who were destroying the character by which the colony was governed, and introducing general revolt, rapine, and murder. No man's life or property, he declared, could in future be considered safe.[22] King was not describing the scurrilities of the tavern tosspots; he was describing the men in the army appointed to maintain subordination in New South Wales. Without mutual trust and understanding between the two, order and good government must suffer. On 9 May 1803 King requested to submit the whole of his public and private conduct to a tribunal of civil, military and naval officers, and implored leave of absence to submit his conduct to his lordship's consideration.[23]

Again King was fortunate in the man to whom he had appealed. Lord Hobart had taken over the seals of office from the Duke of Portland in March 1801. He was born in 1760, and at the turn of the century enjoyed the reputation of being free from every vice, of being discreet without being close, and liberal without being extravagant, confidential, domestic, unsuspicious, a man of good temper, good nature and pleasantry whose mind was darkened by but one prejudice: that he was no friend to the Roman Catholics. To such a man King had appealed for sympathy and understanding.[24] Hobart told King of his great satisfaction that the general behaviour of the settlers and convicts had been peaceable and obedient, that agriculture had improved and the stock increased. At the same time he would not conceal that such satisfaction had been in a great degree alloyed by the unfortunate differences which had so long existed between King and the military officers. These considerations had led him to agree to King's request to return as soon as the important trust could be put in the hands of a person competent to exercise the important duties free from the spirit of party which had reached such an alarming height and might in its consequences be of material prejudice to His Majesty's service.[25] The case against King on that score was unanswerable. The absence of Macarthur in London probably saved him from a more ignominious end to his term as Governor.

The feud with the officers, however, bore some fruit as it forced King to do some thinking about the government of New South Wales. Ever since the decision in the Marshall case he had been unhappy about the administration of justice in New South Wales. In the civil court the members were not trained in the law; appeals were frequent; the only legal assistants to the Judge Advocate were Michael Massey Robinson, who had been transported in 1798 for writing threatening letters and had then committed a palpable perjury in the colony, where he enjoyed such a reputation as a bad character

[22] King to Hobart, 9 May 1803, *H.R.A.*, I, 4, pp. 159-85.

[23] Ibid., p. 244.

[24] *Dictionary of National Biography*, vol. 27, pp. 34-5; H. Grattan: *Memoirs of the Life and Times of the Rt. Hon. Henry Grattan, by his son, Henry Grattan* (London, 1849-59), vol. 3, p. 441, vol. 4, pp. 87-8.

[25] Hobart to King, 30 November 1803, *H.R.A.*, I, 4, p. 428.

that King questioned the propriety of using him in the courts, and George Crossley who, in 1798 had appeared for perjury in the pillory in front of Westminster Hall, London, before a vast concourse of people, dressed in professional black with a brown curled wig, to suffer the indignation of the populace, which, we are told, he endured with his countenance a little dismayed. In the same year he was transported to New South Wales where he began his career by selling goods which he had duped a ship's master to sell to him by fast talk about his agent in London. In 1801 King granted him a conditional pardon, despite his estimate of him as a disgrace to the honourable profession of the law.[26] King believed there was a case, too, for a change in the composition of the criminal court. The increase in numbers and what he called jarring interests were part of his objections. The core of the case against the criminal court however was that it was composed of one description of persons, which was a polite though less passionate way of saying that it was composed of the people who had opposed him, the military and naval officers. From his own experience of officer justice or lack of it, he went on to draw the lesson, indeed to suggest a reform, namely, that it would be more satisfactory to the inhabitants and colony at large to see every advance towards complete trial by jury.[27]

The quarrel with the officers pushed him into the definition of another principle. From the beginning the officers had disdained contact with the convicts, some even going so far as to refuse to co-operate in the administration of the system on the grounds that such work was not becoming to an officer and a gentleman. By this time some officers had even gone further and refused to have in the corps a man with a conditional pardon. This provoked King into a declaration of the legal rights of emancipists. He informed the commander of the New South Wales Corps, Major Johnston, that the colony was formed for the express purpose of receiving prisoners, that the king and the legislature's humanity, in giving the Governor power to emancipate, did not consign the offender to oblivion and disgrace for ever, that he would aver and support that the objects of that mercy became as free and susceptible of every right as free-born Britons as any soul in this territory, whether their emancipation were absolute or conditional.[28] So the first statements of the case for trial by jury and the case for the emancipists were both by-products of the angry exchange between the Governor and the military officers.

King was not the man to entertain the wider vision. This statement of the case for the emancipist was a rare example of dignity and nobility adorning his language. On other questions he did not break with the prejudices of his age. The relations between Europeans and aborigines provided one illustration of this. When King took up office in 1800 he was by pro-

[26] King to Hobart, 7 August 1803, *H.R.A.*, I, 4, pp. 350-3; H. G. Allars: 'George Crossley—An Unusual Attorney', R.A.H.S., *J. & P.*, 1958., vol. 44, pt. 5, pp. 261-300; *Madras Courier*, 28 March 1798 (Bonwick Transcripts, box 59, Mitchell Library).

[27] King to Hobart, 7 August 1803, *H.R.A.*, I, 4, p. 353; King to Hobart, 9 May 1803, *H.R.A.*, I, 4, p. 159 et seq.

[28] King to Johnston, 18 February 1803, *H.R.A.*, I, 4, p. 216.

fession a member of the kindness and amity school. In June 1802 he received instructions from Lord Hobart to pardon the five Europeans who had been found guilty by the criminal court on 18 October 1799 of wantonly killing two aborigines. Hobart added the rider that every means should be used to cultivate the goodwill of the natives. At that time King had not lost faith in the policy of amity and kindness. In a proclamation he announced that any future injustice or wanton cruelty against the natives would be punished as if it had been committed against the persons and estates of any of His Majesty's subjects. He went on to forbid any of His Majesty's subjects using any act of injustice or wanton cruelty against the natives. At the same time he pointed out that the settler was not to suffer his property to be invaded, or his existence endangered by the natives, qualifying this by adding that he was to use effectual though humane means of resisting such attacks. He ended by recommending a great degree of forbearance and plain dealing as the only means to avoid future attacks and to continue the present good understanding. That was on 30 June 1802.[29]

By 1805 King had joined the ever-increasing group of settlers who accused the aborigines of ungrateful and treacherous conduct. A native, while in the act of eating with one of the settlers and his labouring man, had scarce ended his meal before he took an opportunity of seizing the settler's musket and powder, and by a yell summoned his companions, who instantly put the unfortunate settler to death and left his servant, as they thought, in that state. On the same day, about three miles from where the first murder was committed, a house belonging to a settler was set on fire by the same band of natives. After a search the mangled and burned limbs of the settler and his man were found, some in the ashes and others scattered.[30] This finished King's faith in amity and kindness. To stop such barbarities he directed a party of soldiers to drive the natives from the area.

King, in fact, was beginning to wonder whether the aborigines' idea of revenge would not entail never-ending reprisals. A white man had struck an aborigine without provocation. For this he was sentenced to six months' imprisonment, which, as King put it, the white man would accept as sufficient atonement. To their everlasting irritation and despair the white men had found that the aborigines' thirst for revenge and atonement was insatiable, that their imaginations were heated and excited to action by the accidental recollection of an injury which had been expiated long past. This happened repeatedly in their relations with each other. It was not surprising therefore that the same ideas should obtain concerning real or imaginary evils they might have received from white people.[31] King's amity and kindness degenerated into a pessimistic innate racial characteristic explanation of the friction, which snuffed out all hope for any future improvement, and left him as a believer in force to protect the lives and property of the settlers. Amity and kindness pointed forward to equality; innate racial characteristics pointed

---

[29] *H.R.A.*, I, 3, pp. 592-3.
[30] King to Camden, 30 April 1805, *H.R.A.*, I, 5, p. 306.
[31] Ibid., p. 307.

to an eye for an eye and a tooth for a tooth, to force and terror as instruments of subordination.[32] In a calmer moment, nevertheless, King knew that the main cause of the trouble was that the white man had expropriated the original proprietors of the soil.[33]

King was not the first to drift from the benevolence and goodwill which informed the policy of amity and kindness to a belief in those innate and indelible characteristics of the aborigines which neither contact with civilization nor the beneficent influences of the Protestant religion could touch. More and more people were beginning to think of them as a permanent special case. Atkins was not prepared to admit aborigines as witnesses in the law courts of New South Wales, because the evidence of persons not bound by any moral or religious tie could never be considered as legal evidence, and because to admit them as either criminals or witnesses before a criminal court would be a mocking of judical proceedings and a solecism in law. The only mode of treating them for their excesses was to pursue them and inflict such punishment as they deserved.[34] Francis Barrallier, the son of a French *émigré*, who had arrived in the colony in 1800 as an ensign in the New South Wales Corps, found during his explorations to the west of Parramatta that the aborigines were strangers to feelings of gratitude, and that the most refined cruelty and barbarity were the principle features of their character.[35]

By 1805 less and less is heard of the early aspirations to civilize the aborigines as a preparation for their becoming members of the mystical body of Christ's Church. Experience was driving more and more settlers as well as civil and military officers, to explain the treachery, cruelty, revolting habits and inferiority of the aborigines, and the ineffectual results of all attempts to civilize them, by their innate characteristics as a race. Experience was also convincing more and more people that violence and reprisals were the only methods the aborigines could understand. No one contemplated the extinction of the aborigine with remorse, guilt or regret; nor did anyone testify to a common humanity, let alone to any sense that they too were made in the divine image. Not everyone accepted this fatalistic, hopeless view of the situation. Starting from quite a different premise, the French explorer Péron had reached an optimistic conclusion. He had reached Sydney in 1802 on a voyage of exploration in the south seas. He came to the conclusion that the material weakness and primitive culture of the aborigine were to be explained by his environment; that in the land of Diemen and New Holland the lack of food, its poor quality, and the excessive labour which the aborigine was compelled to employ to obtain it, seemed to be the causes of his weakness as well as the vices of his constitution. Péron went on to deduce that the perfection of the social state, by bringing abundance to such men, would probably be able to produce a more considerable development of their physical strength, and so cause the vices of their constitution to disappear. In this way the progress of civilization would become the two-fold source

[32] See the proclamation of 28 April 1805, *H.R.A.*, I, 5, p. 820.
[33] See King to Bligh, undated (ms. in Mitchell Library, Sydney).
[34] *H.R.A.*, I, 5, pp. 502-4.
[35] Ibid., p. 588.

of strength and physical perfection.[36] For Péron had derived his ideas on the nature of man from the enlightenment rather than from the Book of Genesis. With such ideas, the aborigine might have been saved from extinction and degradation, while the white man might have been saved from guilt and estrangement. King and the rest of his civil and military officers identified such ideas with Jacobin terror, with sedition, treachery and treason. The Reverend Samuel Marsden, the missionaries and the chaplains continued to explain the material weakness and the vices as a special punishment of their people for the role of their ancestors in that terrible drama between God and man in the garden of Eden. The European theft of the land, with the response of the aborigine to such a theft, and European ideas on the nature of man and his destiny, rushed both groups into a clash which doomed the culture of the aborigine, condemning him to destruction or degradation and the white man to peace, security and material success, at the price of a reputation in posterity for infamy.

This combination of material interest and an inherited ideology contributed also to the clash between the English Protestant and the Irish Catholic. On this issue King's mind mirrored the prejudices of his class and his country. In England the arguments for preserving the Protestant ascendancy had been put with all their prejudice and force by George III. No quiet could subsist in any country where there was not a church establishment. It was a subject, he said, on which he could scarcely keep his temper, because a change must inevitably unhinge Britain's excellent and happy constitution, and be most exactly following the steps of the French Revolution.[37] Lord Hobart trusted they would never see the parliament so debased as to yield to their insolent demands.[38] Others were beginning to have doubts on the wisdom and justice of such a policy. It was both a divided and a confused governing class, because the defenders of the Protestant ascendancy spoke at one time of the threat of Catholic tyranny and at another of Jacobin anarchy.

A similar confusion both in opinion and behaviour occurred in high places in the colony of New South Wales when the arrival of the convicts sentenced to transportation for their part in the Irish rebellion of 1798 roused the fears and prejudices of the Protestants. Three hundred and twenty-one Irishmen arrived in the *Minerva* and *Friendship* in January and February 1800, another two hundred and forty-four in the *Ann S. Luz* in February 1801, the *Minorca* in December 1801 and the *Hercules* in June 1802. King described them as ruthless, violent and turbulent characters with diabolical schemes for the destruction of all industry, public and private property, order and regularity.[39] Earlier, when rumours had begun to circulate in Sydney

36 M. F. Péron: *Voyage de découvertes aux terres australes* (Paris, 1807 and 1816), vol. 1, pp. 470-1.

37 G. Pellew: *The Life and Correspondence of the Right Honble. Henry Addington, First Viscount Sidmouth* (London 1847), vol. 1, p. 286.

38 *Dictionary of National Biography*, vol. 4, p. 367.

39 King to Portland, 10 March 1801, *H.R.A.*, I, 3, pp. 8-9; Government Order, 31 December 1800, *H.R.A.*, I, 3, p. 45.

and Parramatta in September 1800 of rebellions by the Irish, Governor Hunter, a firm believer in the Protestant ascendancy, had formed loyal associations in Sydney and Parramatta which were composed of fifty armed men in each, chosen from free men possessing property and good characters. William Balmain, a surgeon on the first fleet who had been raised to the rank of principal surgeon in September 1795, was appointed commandant in Sydney, and Andrew Thompson, an emancipist, was appointed commandant in Parramatta.[40] In a proclamation of December 1800, King referred to the constant state of alarm, and issued orders for handling any internal tumults.[41] When the fears had subsided, by July 1801, King disbanded both associations, only to enrol them again for one week in November 1802 to ensure a peaceful disembarkation of the two hundred odd Irish convicts who arrived on the *Atlas*.[42]

King also entertained other hopes. On 27 May 1801, when he received information from London of the union of England and Ireland, he appointed the King's Birthday for the public observation of this joyful event. On that day a royal salute from the batteries and ships, the unfurling of the new Union Jack, more salutes in honour of the day at noon and one o'clock, and other demonstrations of joy, celebrated the union of England and Ireland. Several of the Irish insurgents who had been in confinement were released on the same day.[43] Cautiously King began to move towards clemency, to grant conditional pardons to some of the Irish convicts because, somewhat to his surprise, the conduct of many of them had been uniformly good and highly deserving.[44] He began to toy with the idea of allowing the Irish Catholics to practise their own religion. But it was out of the question, he believed, to allow the Irish Catholic priests—O'Neal, Dixon and Harrold, who had arrived on the *Friendship*, the *Minerva* and the *Anne* in January and February 1800 and February 1801—to teach Catholic children in schools, because that would be the means of instilling improper ideas into the minds of their pupils.[45]

He was not too happy about allowing them to practise their religion, though he knew the Catholics were now one quarter of the population. The stumbling block, in his mind, was that no people was so bigotted in their religion and priests as the lower order of the Irish. As he saw it, their credulous ignorance was such that an artful priest might lead them to any action, good or bad.[46] For these reasons King was anxious to meet their grievances without allowing them to corrupt or disrupt the higher civilization. Perhaps, as he put it, the Reverend Mr Dixon, who was by natural disposition a peace-loving man, and quite unequal to the task either to incite or to

[40] *H.R.A.*, I, 3, pp. 768-9.

[41] Ibid., pp. 43-44.

[42] King to Hobart, 9 November 1802, *H.R.A.*, I, 3, p. 654.

[43] King to Portland, 21 August 1801, *H.R.A.*, I, 3, pp. 121-3; D. Collins: op. cit., vol. 2, p. 331.

[44] King to Portland, 21 August 1801, *H.R.A.*, I, 3, pp. 121-2.

[45] King to Hobart, 9 May 1803, *H.R.A.*, I, 4, p. 82.

[46] Ibid., p. 83.

repress sedition or revolt, might be trusted to hold religious services under certain conditions.[47] With such hopes he drafted the regulations to be observed by the Reverend Mr Dixon and the Catholic congregations: they were to observe that this extension of liberal toleration proceeded from the piety and benevolence of their most gracious sovereign, to whom, under Providence, they were indebted for the blessings they enjoyed; they were to ensure that no seditious conversations occurred at their places of worship or elsewhere; they were to manifest their gratitude and allegiance by detecting and reporting any such impropriety; Mr Dixon could perform his clerical functions at Sydney, Parramatta and the Hawkesbury in rotation; the priest was not to permit improper behaviour during the time of the service; a certain number of police would be stationed at or near the places of worship during the service to ensure strict decorum; the law already sufficiently provided for the punishment of those who might disquiet or disturb any assembly of religious worship or misuse any priest or teacher of any tolerated sect.[48] Under these regulations, masses were said first in Sydney on 15 May 1803, in Parramatta on 22 May, and on the Hawkesbury on 29 May.[49] The loyal associations were disbanded, as the restless spirit of Irish discontent seemed to have disappeared.

On 4 March 1804 an Irishman, William Johnston, who had been transported for his part in the rebellion of 1798, moved from house to house on Castle Hill urging his compatriots to join him in a bid for liberty. As he gathered his supporters, sometimes by cheering his men, sometimes by threatening those who refused to join his band to blow their brains out and set fire to their houses above their heads, and gathered arms by threatening to run through with the bayonet all who did not surrender their weapons, he told his followers of plans for an armed rebellion, in which the password, oddly enough for a people renowned for their savagery towards those who denied their leader, was 'St Peter'. In this way, by persuasion, charm, blarney and compulsion, Johnston gathered together a group of three hundred and thirty-three men, armed them at Castle Hill with rifles, improvised pikes and cutlasses, and planned to raise another three hundred at the Hawkesbury from where he proposed to march on Sydney and Parramatta using the catch-cry of liberty. His supporters were inspired by no social or religious programme, either for convicts, ex-convicts or settlers, but were united by a desire to hurt or take revenge on the Anglo-Saxon for all his outrageous cruelty and abominations against the Irish. One of Johnston's followers, Poor, an Irishman, showed a paper with the proposals for rebellion to Keo, while they were thatching at Castle Hill. Keo who had already suffered so much on account of the rebellion in Ireland, took fright and ran to Captain Abbott in Parramatta on 3 March 1804 to inform against his fellow-countrymen. In the meantime, blandly unaware of such treachery, the followers of William Johnston were making their way along the road from

47 P. F. Moran: *History of the Catholic Church in Australasia* (Sydney, 1896), p. 41.
48 *Sydney Gazette*, 24 April 1803.
49 P. F. Moran: op. cit., p. 38.

Castle Hill to Parramatta, shouting liberty, and death to tyrants, or sending up their petitions to the holy mother of God to pray for them in the hour of their death.

At 11.30 on Sunday night an express messenger from Captain Abbott arrived at Government House with the news that the convicts in government service at Castle Hill and the convicts assigned to settlers were in a state of insurrection, and had already committed many daring outrages. The alarm was immediately sounded in Sydney; the military and the inhabitants were put under arms, and all horses were held in requisition. At 12.30 a.m. on the Monday there was further alarming news of outrages at Castle Hill. King then set out for Parramatta, pausing at the house of Major Johnston to order him to take command of the company to be despatched against the rebels. King had arrived at Parramatta by 4 a.m., and Johnston an hour later. On that same day Governor King issued a proclamation declaring that every person who was seen in a state of rebellious opposition to the peace and tranquillity of the colony, and did not give himself up within twenty-four hours, would be tried by court martial. Johnston, after a hasty refreshment, set out with quarter-master Laycock and twenty-five non-commissioned officers and privates along the Castle Hill road, and reached Toongabbe, where he heard that the insurgents were making for the Hawkesbury. He promptly set out in pursuit. When they came up with the insurgents at 11.30 on that Monday morning at Vinegar Hill, seven miles out of Toongabbe, Johnston and Laycock, who had ridden ahead, advanced to within pistol shot of the rebels and called on them to surrender and take advantage of the mercy offered them in the proclamation. When they refused, Johnston asked to talk to their leaders, who with that incredible folly which characterized the Irish in their dealings with the English, met Johnston and Laycock half-way. Johnston presented his pistol at Philip Cunningham's head and Laycock presented his at William Johnston's head; both were driven into the detachment, while the men who had shouted for liberty offered no resistance.

In the meantime, the detachment of twenty-five soldiers had arrived on the scene. When Johnston ordered them to charge, they cut the insurgents to pieces. Within minutes nine of them lay dead, their leader, Cunningham, lay wounded, and the rest were in flight for the Hawkesbury. After Johnston caught up with them at 9 p.m. on the same night, retribution began. After taking the opinion of the officers about him, he directed Cunningham to be hanged on the staircase of the public store, which he had boasted in his march that he was going to plunder. On 7 March King announced that the principal leaders of the deluded and infatuated people had, through the arts and designs of some hidden characters, been induced to commit acts of rebellion, forgetting thereby the comforts and real liberty they enjoyed, and had given themselves up. He appealed to the rest to surrender. The trials began next day. Only leaders were tried, because in the official pattern of thinking the rank and file were deluded but not wicked men. Three hundred odd of the latter, who gave themselves up, were sent back to their work with a caution and a reprimand. With that zeal which he always used to serve the interests of the Protestant ascendancy, Marsden helped prepare the case for the prosecution. After a brief trial some were sentenced to death, some to a flogging, and some to transportation to one of the outer settlements of New South Wales. Hume, Hill and Place were immediately hanged at Parramatta, all acknowledging the justice of their sentence and hoping for that mercy from God which they had not received from man. Johnston, Harrington and Neale were hanged at Castle Hill on the following morning, after Johnston, as Hume before him, had given much important information and confessed his belief that the men engaged in the tumult were the victims of a very few contrivers and abettors of horrors. Brannon and Hogan were hanged at Sydney on Saturday, 10 March, after Burke and McCormick had been reprieved.[50] Five were flogged on 8 and 9 March when, according to Irish Catholic tradition, the Reverend Mr Dixon was forced to witness the scene, and placed his hand on the bleeding backs till he swooned away.[51] Thirty odd were sent to Coal River, which King decided to use as a penal settlement for the Irish. At the same time he announced that the name of the settlement was to be changed from Coal River to Newcastle, that the thirty-four Irish convicts were to cut coal and cedar on week days, while on the Lord's Day the commandant, Lieutenant Menzies, was to cause the prayers of the Church of England to be read with all due solemnity, and to enforce a due observance of religion and good order.[52] So the Protestant ascendancy reduced the Irish to subordination by force.

General orders were issued offering a pardon and a free passage to Great Britain, excluding Ireland, to any person giving information about the conspirators.[53] On 9 March, King published his thanks to His Majesty's loyal subjects in the colony, singling out the loyal association in Sydney, Captain Abbott, Major Johnston, Lieutenants Davis and Brabyn, quarter-master Laycock, the twenty-five soldiers, and the officers of the *Calcutta*, for special mention. In August King decided to withhold the salary from the Catholic priest, Dixon, for very improper conduct, as he believed seditious meetings had taken place in consequence of the indulgence and protection Dixon had received.[54] In retrospect King pinned the responsibility or part of it on Catholic teaching, or the machinations of the priests, rather than the other source of the Irish delusion, the rights of man, or just being Irish. Behind the words of abuse, the members of the Protestant ascendancy in New South Wales never paused to sort out the muddle in their own minds on the origins of the revolt, blaming indiscriminately the Irish, the priests, the Church of Rome, the ideas of 1789. Some hinted at an evil-minded machinator behind the rebellion; others wrote of it as the works of a few designing men.[55] The

[50] Description based on the *Sydney Gazette* account, 11 March 1804. See also King to Hobart, 12 March 1804, *H.R.A.*, I, 4, p. 563 et seq. Major Johnston's account is given in a letter to King of Monday, 5 March, at 5.30 p.m., printed in the *Sydney Gazette*, 11 March 1804.

[51] P. F. Moran: op. cit., p. 39.

[52] King to Hobart, 16 April 1804, *H.R.A.*, I, 4, pp. 611-12.

[53] *Sydney Gazette*, 11 March 1804.

[54] King to Hobart, 14 August 1804, *H.R.A.*, I, 5, p. 99.

[55] *Sydney Gazette*, 11 March 1804.

Protestant ascendancy was simply afraid that the two essential conditions of civilization, the Protestant religion and the British constitution, were menaced by these deluded, ignorant and wretched men. To the members of the Protestant ascendancy the blood spilt on Vinegar Hill was part of their long agony in raising the Irish from savagery to civilization. To the Irish it was part of that great river of blood spilt to rid their people of the Anglo-Saxon barbarian and keep alive those two most precious gifts of the Irish character and their holy faith. So in two of the major questions of the day, the relations between the Europeans and the aborigines, and the relations between the Protestant ascendancy and Irish Catholicism, evil stalked in the land, and New South Wales added its drips to the never-ending tears of humanity. One provided the setting for the material destruction of a culture, and a loss of dignity for its people; the other led to permanent bitterness, hatred and anger between those two views of the world which were to divide European civilization in Australia so long as its members were interested in questions of the nature of man and the meaning of his life.

At the same time there were events which contributed to the material development of that civilization as well as exhibiting man in all his tragic grandeur. In January 1801 the British Admiralty announced their intention of sending a new expedition of discovery to New Holland and New South Wales, partly to fill in the gaps in their knowledge about the coast, partly to allay the anxiety roused by the voyages of the French, and partly to continue their study of a land which had always appealed to their curiosity if not to their affection because of its unique vegetation, animal and human life.[56]

As commander of the expedition they appointed Lieutenant Matthew Flinders.[57] He was then just twenty-seven years old. He was born at Donington in Lincolnshire on 16 March 1774, and educated at a free school at Horfling which took him through the standard curriculum in English, Latin and Greek, to prepare a man for medicine. While at school he read *Robinson Crusoe* which inspired him with what an early biographer called 'the restless desire of peregrination'.[58] Against the wish of friends and the advice of relations who warned him of the unlikelihood of promotion in the navy without powerful interests, he determined to go to sea, first spending a year studying geometry and navigation at home. In 1790, at the age of sixteen, he volunteered for naval service, joined the *Bellerophon*, and in the very next year volunteered to go on an expedition with Captain Bligh to collect bread fruit. After surviving that test, he returned for a brief experience of active service under Howe, the patron of Hunter, in 1793. In July 1794 he volunteered to sail with Captain Hunter in the *Reliance* to New South Wales, being still fonder of voyages of discovery than of the regular routine of service.[59] There he was quickly absorbed in the voyages of discovery in Bass

56 *H.R.N.S.W.*, vol. 4, p. 677.

57 M. Flinders: *A Voyage to Terra Australis* (London, 1814), vol. 1, p. 3.

58 *Naval Chronicle*, vol. 32, pp. 178-9. See also *Biographie Universelle Ancienne et Moderne* (Paris, 1816), vol. 15, pp. 76-9.

59 *Naval Chronicle*. vol. 32, pp. 180-1.

Strait and Van Diemen's Land. In 1797 he was promoted to the rank of lieutenant after passing his examinations at the Cape of Good Hope. After he returned to England in 1800, he proposed to Joseph Banks a plan for completing the investigation of the coasts of New Holland, which Banks placed before Earl Spencer, First Lord of the Admiralty, who in turn obtained the sanction of His Majesty.[60]

When Flinders took command of the *Xenophon* in January 1801 with the rank of commander, he renamed it the *Investigator*. In April of the same year he married Ann, step-daughter of the Reverend William Tyler, rector of Brothertoft in Lincolnshire. Of the man we know very little. The writers of the obituary notices singled out his unabating ardour for the propagation of useful knowledge; his fellow-officers dubbed him the indefatigable. His one great passion was the love of discovery. Indeed, so strong was his predilection for such adventurous service, that he was frequently heard to say to his friends that if the plan of a voyage was read over his grave, he would rise up, awakened from death.[61] His private character was as admirable as his public one was exemplary; his integrity, uprightness of intention, and liberality of sentiment, were not to be surpassed; he possessed the social virtues and affections in an eminent degree; in conversation he was particularly agreeable, from the extent of his general information, and the lively acuteness of his observations.[62] On the inner man, there are the few peeps on the long voyage round Australia and during the even longer agony at Mauritius, when he rotted away as a prisoner-of-war those years which should have been the years of recognition.

The *Investigator* was a ship of three hundred and thirty-four tons, which came up to the description of vessels of discovery recommended by Cook. It was newly coppered and repaired. For crew, all the old men were replaced by young, while for the eleven vacancies the commander had the good fortune to choose from two hundred and fifty volunteers. The stores supplied by government were liberal, including articles for barter with the natives, a library of books of voyages to the south seas, a private library, the *Encyclopaedia Britannica*, and a copy of every chart in the possession of the Admiralty on the coasts of Terra Australis. In addition, the East India Company donated £600 for the table of the officers, with the promise of the same at the end of the journey, the directors being pleased to make this allowance because they expected the examinations and discoveries to prove advantageous to their commerce and the eastern navigation, and partly, as they said, as recognition of the former services of Flinders.[63]

He was instructed by the Admiralty to make a complete examination and survey of the whole coast of Australia. He was to sail from England to Madeira, to the Cape of Good Hope and on to the west coast of New Holland, and then to sail along the west coast to examine the harbours, where

60 This is Flinders' own account. See M. Flinders: op. cit., vol. 1, p. cciv.
61 *Naval Chronicle*, vol. 32, p. 191.
62 Ibid.
63 M. Flinders: op. cit., vol. 1, p. 6.

he was to look especially for an inland sea or strait, and to repair to Sydney Cove to refresh his crew and refit the ship. He was then to examine the north coast of New Holland, especially between the Trial Rocks and Timor, in the hope that great advantages might arise to the East India Company's ships, in case that passage should hereafter be frequented by them. Finally he was to examine very carefully the east coast of New Holland.[64]

There were eighty-eight on board when the *Investigator* sailed from Spithead on 18 July 1801. Following instructions, they touched both at Madeira and the Cape of Good Hope before sighting Cape Leeuwin on 6 December 1801. From there they sailed to King George's Sound, finding that the country they saw on this excursion had but little to recommend it. Nor had the natives. Indeed Flinders was surprised to find that the natives of the south-west coast of New Holland resembled the natives of New South Wales in everything except the extraction of a front tooth at puberty, and the use of the 'womerah' or throwing stick. The colour and texture of their hair, and their personal appearance were the same; their songs ran in the same cadence; their hair was worn in the same way; over their shoulders they wore short kangaroo skin cloaks in the manner of the inland rather than of the coastal natives of New South Wales. Flinders saw no signs of canoes, and noted that they were fearful of trusting themselves upon the water. Their manners were quick and vehement, and their conversation vociferous, like that of most uncivilized people. They seemed to have no idea of the superiority of the white man. They screamed with delight when the marines were exercised on shore, admiring their red coats and white crossed belts, expressing astonishment at the fife and drum, while the volleys from the rifles did not excite much terror.[65]

They left King George's Sound on 5 January 1802, to sail east for Récherche Archipelago, which they reached five days later. There was not a blade of grass, nor a square yard of soil from which the seed delivered to it could be expected back over those arid plains.[66] As they sailed along the shores of the Great Australian Bight, Flinders sorted out the puzzles of that voyage by de Nuyts in *'t Gulden Seepaart*, generously praising the Dutch map of 1627 as being as correct in form as could reasonably have been expected. He praised too the charting done on the French ship *Récherche*, which had sailed in the same waters in 1792, though he added with characteristic gentleness and modesty that his decision to publish his own charts sprang neither from a wish to depreciate those of his predecessor in the investigation, nor from an assumption of superior merit.[67]

When they reached the eastern extremity of the Great Australian Bight they began to search for a strait to an inland sea, or even to the Gulf of Carpentaria. Each trend of the coast to the north excited many conjectures,

[64] M. Flinders: op. cit., pp. 8-16.
[65] Ibid., pp. 60-6.
[66] Ibid., p. 81.
[67] Ibid., pp. 102-3.

and infused life and vigour into every man in the ship.[68] On such a quest they entered the port which formed 'the most interesting part of their discoveries'. Flinders named it Port Lincoln, in honour of his native province.[69] On 6 March they again sailed into a deep gulf, but the want of boldness in the shores and the shallowness of the water made Flinders doubt whether it belonged to a channel leading to the Gulf of Carpentaria or even any distance inland. By 9 March their prospect of finding a channel or strait cutting off some considerable portion of Terra Australis was lost. With a becoming simplicity, Flinders wrote the answer to the problem which had agitated the minds of people interested in New Holland ever since the *Duyfken* sailed into Carpentaria, and *'t Gulden Seepaart* to the islands of St Peter and St Francis. When the investigation of the gulf was terminated, to honour the respectable nobleman who presided at the Board of Admiralty when the voyage was planned and the ship put into commission, Flinders named it Spencer's 'Gulph'.[70]

From the gulf they sailed across to an island which they were astonished to find uninhabited by human beings, but infested with kangaroos. On that afternoon the whole ship's company was employed in skinning and cleaning kangaroos to prepare what Flinders called a delightful 'regale', after four months' privation from almost any fresh provisions. Half a hundred weight of heads, fore-quarters, and tails were stewed down into soup for dinner on this and the succeeding days. As much steaks were given, to both officers and men, as they could consume by day and by night. In gratitude for so seasonable a supply, he named this southern land Kangaroo Island.[71] They left Kangaroo Island on 24 March and sailed into another gulf on 30 March. Flinders, in language on the border between the dignified and the pompous, named it the 'Gulph' of St Vincent.[72]

On 8 April 1802 they sailed east to a long bay where they met the French seaman, N. Baudin, on the *Géographe*. On the evening after the first interview, Flinders wrote up his account in the taut language of a disappointed man, and in language which betrayed the provincial note in his mind on the French.[73] Baudin noted this reserve, and this coldness, in his account of the meeting, writing of the great reserve which Flinders displayed during the discussions.[74] When Flinders wrote his second account, the provincial prejudices had been soured into bitterness by the years of captivity on Mauritius, and by pique at the French claiming discoveries and renaming his work. By then he had read that the French called his Kangaroo Island, *L'Isle Decrés*, and Spencer's Gulf *Golfe Joséphine*. With an unwonted malice and absence of charity he charged the French with being liars, and gloated over the fact

[68] Ibid., pp. 132-3.
[69] Ibid., p. 142.
[70] Ibid., p. 167.
[71] Ibid., pp. 169-70.
[72] Ibid., pp. 179-80.
[73] Journal of H.M.S. *Investigator*, vol. 1; MS. in the Mitchell Library, Sydney.
[74] M. F. Péron: op. cit., vol. 1, p. 327.

that their area of prior discovery was only about fifty leagues of coast, in which there was neither river, inlet, nor place of shelter, nor did even the worst parts of Nuyt's Land exceed it in sterility.[75]

They sailed out of Encounter Bay on 9 April, and entered Bass Strait on 21 April and Port Phillip on 27 April. He explored the bay and climbed Arthur's Seat. The entrance to the port he found obscure, though with another unusual waspish remark he did wonder why M. Baudin had not entered it. The country was infinitely superior to anything they had seen on the south coast. It had a pleasing, and in many parts a fertile appearance, the grass being good, and the soil deep. It would be possible, he believed, to open a friendly intercourse with the natives who were the same people as those at King George's Sound and Port Jackson, though their language was completely different and their bodies were more fleshy and muscular, probably because they were better fed. Emus, kangaroos, black swans, ducks, and many varieties of birds abounded.[76] In this way Flinders described the site of the future city of Melbourne, without pondering on what man could do with it, for the land of New Holland and New South Wales excited no such vision in his mind.

On 3 May 1802 they sailed out of Port Phillip, past Cape Schanck, along the south coast of Phillip Island, where they passed a needle-like rock lying under the shore and Cape Wollamai, which Flinders explained, had been so named because Mr Bass was induced to give it that name when the shape of the headland bore a likeness to the head of a fish which the natives of Port Jackson called the Wollamai.[77] They sailed on past Wilson's Promontory, the Furneaux Islands, the Kent group and Cape Howe, and reached Sydney Cove on 9 May, with the officers and crew, generally speaking, in better health than on the day they sailed from Spithead, and not in less good spirits, for which fact a strict attention to cleanliness and a full circulation of air in the messing and sleeping places was chiefly responsible. With a becoming pride, Flinders reported that several of the inhabitants expressed themselves never to have been so strongly reminded of England, as by the fresh colour of many amongst the *Investigator's* ship's company.[78] For Flinders was young in the ways of the world, a man who took pride in health and cleanliness, a man who had no eye for human evil and madness.

On 4 June, to celebrate the King's Birthday, the ship was dressed with colours, a royal salute fired, and Flinders went with the principal officers of the *Investigator* to pay his respects to His Excellency, the Governor-in-Chief and Captain-General. On this occasion, a splendid dinner was given to the colony at which the number of ladies and civil, military and naval officers was not less than forty, who met to celebrate the birth of their beloved sovereign in this distant part of the earth.[79] On 20 June Baudin arrived in the

[75] M. Flinders: op. cit., vol. 1, p. 201.

[76] General Observations upon the port Number 16, 2 May 1802 (Journal of H.M.S. *Investigator*, Mitchell Library). See also M. Flinders: op. cit., vol. 1, pp. 218-9.

[77] M. Flinders: op. cit., vol. 1, pp. 221-2.

[78] Ibid., pp. 226-7.

[79] Ibid., p. 229.

PHILIP GIDLEY KING

Miniature by an unknown artist in the Mitchell Gallery, Sydney

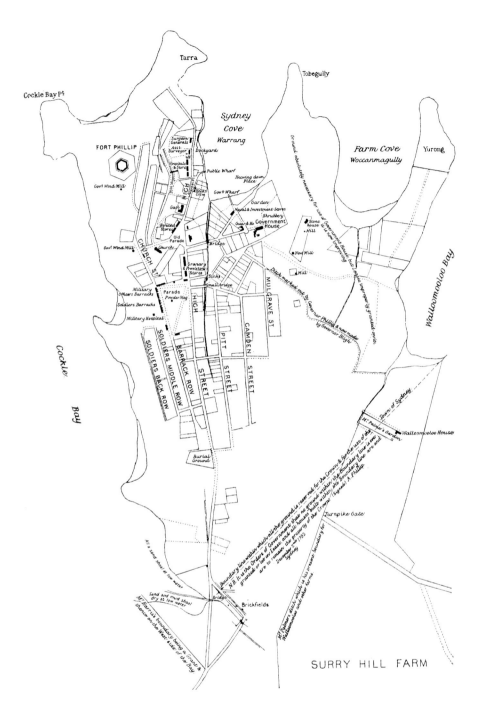

Tarra

Cockle Bay P.t

Tobegully

Sydney
Cove
Warrang

Farm Cove
Woccanmagully

Yurong

FORT PHILLIP

Surgeon
Generals
Ass.t
Surveyor
Hospitals
& Stores

Dockyard

Public Wharf

Heaving down
Place

Gov.t Wind Mill

Boats
Crew

Gov.t Wharf

Gaol

Garden

Naval & Investment Stores

Shrubbery

Guard Ho

Government
House

Stone
House

Mill

Bonded
Stores

Old
Parade

Church

Gov.t Wind Mill

Bridge

New Mill

Mill

CHURCH ST.

Granary
& Provision
Stores

Tanks

Small bridge

Military
Officers Barracks

Soldiers Barracks

Military Hospital

Parade
Powder Mag.

MULGRAVE ST.

CAMDEN STREET

PITT STREET

HIGH STREET

BARRACK ROW

SOLDIERS MIDDLE ROW

SOLDIERS BACK ROW

Cockle
Bay

Burial
Ground

Town of Sydney

Mr. Palmer's Garden

Walloomooloo House

Walloomooloo Bay

All a sand shoal at low water

Sand and mud shoal
dry at low water

Bridge

Brickfields

Turnpike Gate

SURRY HILL FARM

Boundary line within which all the ground is reserved for the Crown & for the use of the Government that no ground within the boundary line is ever granted or let on lease and all houses built within the boundary line are and are to remain the property of the Crown Sydney 20th Decemr. 1792 (signed) A. Phillip.

N.B. It is the Orders of Government that no ground within the boundary line is ever granted or let on lease and all houses built within the boundary line are and are to remain the property of the Crown.

Mr. Palmer's stile which is his present boundary for Walloomooloo and other farms

Ground absolutely necessary for use of Government House &c as now improving but been improperly granted into.

Dock marked out by Govr. Phillip & now made by Govr. Bligh

PLAN OF THE TOWN OF SYDNEY

From 'Historical Records of New South Wales', volume vii, based on a map prepared for Bligh in 1807.
High Street became George Street; the street running from the Old Parade towards Government House
became Bridge Street, and that running from Mulgrave (now Phillip) Street to Barrack Row became King
Street; Camden Street (previously Chapel Row) became Castlereagh Street.

Géographe. His men were so rotten with disease that only twelve were fit for duty out of one hundred and seventy, a fact which grieved Flinders. Baudin, Péron, other French officers and Colonel Paterson, the Lieutenant-Governor, did Flinders the honour of dining on the *Investigator* which received them under a salute of eleven guns. News of peace had just been received, and this contributed to enliven the party, making it more particularly agreeable. Encouraged by this friendly atmosphere, Flinders and Baudin exchanged charts, and even risked an exchange of views on how to make charts. Flinders later wrote cattily of Baudin's methods as extraordinary, and not worthy of imitation. Certainly, he concluded, these were never followed through the course of his voyage.[80]

They left Sydney again on 22 July 1802, and sailed north to complete Cook's chart of the east coast, to clear up the puzzles about early Dutch navigation of the north coast, and to examine the north-west coast between Trial Rocks and Timor for passages which might be used for the East India Company in their eastern commerce. Flinders continued to comment on the same things as in the first part of the voyage. They observed Hervey's Bay, Bustard Bay, Port Curtis, Keppel Bay, Port Bowen, Thirsty Sound, and Broad Sound, which they reached on 8 September. Each day they noted the tides, winds, position, soil, vegetation, and the aborigines, and encouraged the botanists to collect their samples. Some nights they passed disagreeably on shore amongst the mosquitoes, the sand flies, and the ants, in country which continued neither to excite nor delight them.[81] At Broad Sound, as earlier at Port Phillip, Flinders saw possibilities for a settlement growing wheat, maize, sugar and tobacco, if it ever were in contemplation to make an establishment in New South Wales, within the tropic.[82] They sailed on to the Percy Isles, and threaded the needle through the Barrier Reef, an experience which caused Flinders to warn posterity that only those with strong nerves should approach this part of New South Wales.[83]

Then they sailed into Torres Strait, reaching Murray Island on 30 October, where they noticed that the colour of the 'Indians' was a dark chocolate. They were active muscular men, of about the middle size, their countenances expressing a quick apprehension. They went quite naked except for the ornaments of shell-work, and plaited hair or fibres of bark, which they wore around their waists, necks and ankles. They used weapons, and their canoes were driven with the aid of a primitive sail.[84] At the Prince of Wales Islands they noticed high mounds of earth which at first they took for sentry boxes, but on closer examination found to be hills made by a sluggish feeble race of ants. They found too the common black flies to be excessively numerous, and almost as troublesome as Dampier had described them to be on the north-west coast.[85]

[80] Ibid., pp. 230-1.
[81] M. Flinders: op. cit., vol. 2, p. 66.
[82] Ibid., p. 71.
[83] Ibid., p. 104.
[84] Ibid., pp. 110-11.
[85] Ibid., p. 120.

They sailed down the west coast of Cape York peninsula into the Gulf of Carpentaria where Flinders, patiently, thoroughly and conscientiously worked out where the *Duyfken* had been in 1606, searching in particular for their Cape Keer-Weer, but when he could see nothing like a cape there, though the southern extreme of the land seen from the mast head projected a little, from respect to antiquity he announced that the Dutch name would be preserved there.[86]

They reached the Wellesley's Islands on 26 November 1802, where Flinders asked the master and the carpenter to report on the condition of the ship. To his dismay they reported that the ship was already totally unfit to encounter much bad weather; within twelve months there would be scarcely a sound timber in her; in fine weather, without accident, she might run six months longer without much risk. Flinders was so downcast that he could not express the surprise and sorrow which this statement gave him. As he saw it, on that hot sticky day in November, his hopes of ascertaining completely the anterior form of this immense and in many points interesting country, if not destroyed, would at least be deferred to an uncertain period. He had endeavoured to follow the land so closely that the washing of the surf upon it should be visible, and no opening, nor anything of interest escape his notice. He had hoped that, with the blessing of God, nothing of importance should have been left for future discoveries upon any part of these extensive coasts. But with a ship incapable of encountering bad weather he knew not how to accomplish the task.[87] So Flinders decided to speed up his return, and to sail for Port Jackson by the west and south coasts of New Holland.[88]

Just when all looked hopeless, Flinders' curiosity was aroused by a subject which might ensure his immortality as much as his meticulous charting of the coast. On the Wellesley's Islands he found earthen jars, trees cut with axes, remnants of bamboo lattice work, palm leaves sewn with cotton thread, and the remains of blue cotton trousers. He suspected them to be Chinese.[89] On Sweers' Island which he reached on 26 November he found more evidence. There were seven human skulls, a square piece of timber teak wood, trees felled with an axe, and the broken remains of an earthen jar. This time Flinders dropped the Chinese hypothesis, and suggested that some ship from the East Indies had been wrecked there.[90] On 5 January 1803 he sailed for Groote Eylandt, and on 5 February reached Caledon Bay. Here again he was convinced that strangers had been here before, because the natives had knowledge of fire arms. The natives had learned other lessons from visitors from over the seas as they had a propensity to steal; and they had learned the use of iron implements. Flinders believed that because of the example of his men, those who came after them would not be robbed with such effrontery,

[86] M. Flinders: op. cit., p. 129.
[87] Ibid., pp. 142-3.
[88] Ibid., p. 144.
[89] Ibid., pp. 172-3.
[90] Ibid., pp. 144-7.

and that the inhabitants of Caledon Bay would not avoid but be desirous of further communication with Europeans.[91]

On 17 February in a roadstead of an island to the south-west of Bramby's Isles, they saw a canoe full of men and at the southern extremity of that island six prows covered over like hulks. Flinders, fearing they might be pirates, sent a man to establish contact with them, who reported that they were from Macassar. Shortly after the six Malay commanders boarded the *Investigator*. They were Mohammedans who, on looking into the launch, expressed great horror to see hogs there; nevertheless they had no objection to port wine, even requesting to carry away a bottle with them at sunset. In the ensuing days they learned that the men were subjects of the rajah of Boni, who sailed with the north-west monsoon each season to fish for the trepang, and take it to Timor, where it was sold to the Chinese. They had no knowledge of any European settlement at Port Jackson; their only nautical instrument was a very small pocket compass apparently of Dutch design. After an exchange of presents, with Flinders giving them iron tools and a Union Jack, they parted. Flinders, to commemorate the occasion, decided to call the place where the *Investigator* anchored, Malay Road.[92] So Torres Strait continued its role as a site for great encounters, for there the aborigine had first met the European in 1606, the Moor had met the European in 1607, and now in 1803 the European met an Asian people who, like him, wanted to exploit the wealth of the country.

With ideas of trade with Asia fresh in their minds, Flinders' company began to investigate a suitable passage for ships between Timor and the Trial Rocks which could be used by ships of the East India Company. They arrived at Coepang Bay, Timor, on 31 March 1803, and left again on 8 April to examine the bank between the Trial Rocks and Timor, but sickness among his crew took Flinders' mind off the subject at hand, just as time and circumstance weaned the English from the idea that the wealth of the Indies could be exploited from ports in the north-west of New Holland. Sickness, too, was robbing Flinders of his chance to complete the examination of the west coast as the sickly state of his people from dysentery and fever, himself included, did not admit of anything to delay their arrival at Port Jackson.[93] So they sailed for the Leeuwin, and then along the south coast and east coast till they reached Port Jackson on 9 July 1803.[94]

With his usual zeal Flinders took measures to re-establish the health of the ship's company. There, except for the evidence he gave to the select committee on transportation in 1812, and the publication of his book in 1814, his association with the history of this country ended. He departed from Port Jackson in triumph as a passenger on the *Porpoise* on 10 August 1803, was wrecked on 17 August and returned to Port Jackson. He sailed again on the *Cumberland* on 21 September 1803, by way of Timor, where the

91 Ibid., p. 213.
92 Ibid., p. 228 et seq.
93 Ibid., p. 269.
94 Ibid., p. 272.

state of the ship caused him to make the fatal decision to call at Mauritius, with an imperfect passport and without having heard of the renewal of war between England and France. There he was detained as a prisoner-of-war, his journals were confiscated, and a mortal illness began. He was not permitted to leave till 13 March 1810, finally sailed on 13 June 1810, and returned to Spithead on 24 October 1810, where with what strength he had left he wrote his *Voyage to Terra Australis*. By then chance and a tragic blow had apotheosed the triumph of a clean-living, upright, almost priggish young man with a passion and a talent for discovery into a story of tragic grandeur.

Of the permanent contribution of Flinders little need be said. His own observations on the future of the colony were commonplace. Amongst the obstacles which opposed themselves to the more rapid advancement of the colony, the principal, he believed, were the vicious propensities of a large portion of the convicts, a want of more frequent communication with England, and the prohibition of trading with India and the western coasts of South America, in consequence of the East India Company's charter. As these difficulties became obviated and capital increased, the progress of the colonists would be more rapid. He had little doubt of New South Wales being one day a flourishing country, and of considerable benefit to the commerce and navigation of the parent state.[95] His voyage did not lead to the use of the northern coasts of New Holland for trade with the East. His charts of the coast of New South Wales, New Holland, and Van Diemen's Land, his proving conclusively that there was no sea separating New Holland from New South Wales, and his suggestion that the whole country should be called Australia, ensured him a permanent place in the history of European civilization in Australia. For by one of those odd ironies in human history, the country acquired its name[96] from a man who never delighted in the spirit of the land or its people, nor dreamed dreams of any singular contribution it might make to the history of civilization either in Europe or in Asia.

This fear of the French which led Flinders on to his destruction contributed also to the decision to begin a colony at Port Phillip. As early as 21 May 1802 in a letter to the Duke of Portland, King had mentioned the goodness of the soil and the natural advantages there, the need to separate the hardened criminals from the rest when peace was declared, and the probability of a French settlement on the north-west coast of Bass Strait, to support his proposal for a settlement at Port Phillip.[97] The British government did not quite see it in the same way: they agreed it was desirable to anticipate the French, because of the use the French might make of Bass Strait in the event of war between England and France; they were interested in the prospects for sealing and whaling; they agreed it would be necessary to relieve the settlements at Sydney Cove, Parramatta and the Hawkesbury

95 M. Flinders: op. cit., pp. 280-1.
96 See *Naval Chronicle*, vol. 32, p. 182, f.n.
97 King to Portland, 21 May 1802, *H.R.A.*, I, 3, p. 490.

of any convict surplus,[98] but their motive for this was the moral improvement of the convicts and not any concern for the material well-being of the other convict settlements. For by then Sydney opinion was beginning to be determined by the effect of the convicts on the economy, while London official opinion was beginning to be determined by concern for moral improvement.

So the British government decided to establish a convict settlement at Port Phillip. As Lieutenant-Governor they chose David Collins, who had left Sydney in 1796 on the *Britannia* to return to London. As chaplain they chose Robert Knopwood. Born in 1761, an M.A. of Cambridge, by persuasion and education a broad churchman, Knopwood was a man, it was said, who would have been valuable as a colonist, for he was a bon viveur, an ardent sportsman, a lover of animals, and had all the attributes for a secular calling, but no one would have suspected from his interests or his behaviour that his vocation was the eternal salvation of his fellow-man.[99] As Judge Advocate the British government appointed Benjamin Barbauld, who did not sail; so his duties were performed by the deputy Judge Advocate, S. Bate. As surgeons the government commissioned W. L'Anson and M. Bowden; as surveyor they commissioned G. P. Harris, and as mineralogist, A. W. H. Humphrey. All these were men of promise as well as being in the prime of life, between twenty-two and twenty-nine years of age. For ships they had the *Calcutta* and the *Ocean*, to carry four hundred and sixty-six all told, including forty-eight marines, nineteen settlers, twenty-six settlers' wives and children, two hundred and ninety-nine convicts, and twenty-nine convicts' wives and children.[100] Collins was told to choose a site in Port Phillip, to establish a settlement at King Island, to live in amity and kindness with the natives, to put the convicts to work, to use the products of convict labour for the subsistence of the convicts, their families, the marines and their families, to make land grants to officers, soldiers, settlers and ex-convicts on the same conditions as in New South Wales, to prohibit trade with the East, and to enforce a due observance of religion and good order among all the inhabitants of the settlement.[1]

The *Calcutta* and the *Ocean* sailed from Spithead on 24 April 1803 for Rio de Janeiro and Cape Town, with the settlers creating much disturbance while the demeanour of the convicts continued to be generally good.[2] They arrived at Port Phillip on 9 October 1803. While the ships were riding at anchor, Collins received his first unfavourable impression of Port Phillip in a report from John Mertho, master of the *Ocean*. With incredible folly he chose the long cove on the east shore of Port Phillip as the site for the settlement, because it had that great essential of fresh water. He decided

[98] Memorandum of a proposed settlement in Bass's Straights, n.d., *H.R.A.*, III 1, pp. 1-3.

[99] *H.R.A.*, III, 1, p. 782; and J. B. Walker: *Early Tasmania* 2nd impr. (Hobart, 1914), pp. 63-4.

[100] *H.R.A.*, III, 1, p. 783.

[1] Hobart to Collins, 7 February 1803, *H.R.A.*, I, 4, pp. 10-16.

[2] Collins to Sullivan, 15 and 16 July 1803, *H.R.A.*, III, 1, pp. 22-4.

to name the site Sullivan Bay after the Under Secretary for War and the Colonies.[3] They landed on 16 October. By the end of that month Collins had decided he ought to move the settlement. The bay, he decided, was unfit for commerce, being situated in a deep and dangerous bight. His surveyor, G. P. Harris, an incompetent and dissolute man, with the eye of the drunkard for the heart of things as they are, and the drunkard's failure to believe in man's power to change things for the better, had reported that the land in general round Port Phillip at a short distance from the shores carried a deceitful appearance of a rich country, that it was a dried-up country which seemed not to possess sufficient moisture for the smallest cultivation.[4] Collins had found the settlers a necessitous and worthless set of people.[5] He was having trouble too with absconders; twelve had deserted the settlement by 14 November, a fact which Collins explained by that restless disposition of man which was ever prone to change. Early in December, George Lee, a man superior to the rest in abilities and education, absconded. Here again, as in his judgments on Charles Williams at Parramatta, Collins wrote of these events with an Old Testament note of evil and retribution. As he saw it, George Lee, from the badness of his heart, had accused one of the superintendents and an overseer of some infamous conduct, which he could not support by any evidence. To escape punishment, he had persuaded a Scots lad to abscond with him for which imprudence Collins prophesied death as due retribution.[6] Not all the imprudent ones died, however, for one William Buckley absconded and was still alive when the white man came again in 1835. The only deterrent Collins knew for such evil and indiscipline was the fear of punishment. When Robert Andrews fell asleep while on sentry duty, he was sentenced to eight hundred lashes. He received four hundred, was taken down on doctor's orders, and ordered to receive the remaining four hundred on newly made skin. Though he survived that ordeal he was never able to do a day's work again, but went about doubled up for the rest of his days as a walking memorial to such brutality.[7]

By contrast the officers and their families lived quite agreeably under canvas. On Saturday, 12 November, at a parade attended by the Lieutenant-Governor, the officers, marines and convicts, the Reverend Knopwood read divine service, preaching a sermon in which he returned thanks to Almighty God for their safe arrival. As well he might, for Knopwood was enjoying dining with the officers off kangaroo, shooting the plentiful game, smoking a pipe and quaffing wine. If the weather proved inclement on the Lord's Day, the Reverend Knopwood plumped for comfort rather than duty, and cancelled the service.[8] Others enjoyed the natural beauties of the spot till, to their mortification, the whim and caprice of Collins caused them to abandon

[3] Collins to King, 5 November 1803, *H.R.A.*, III, 1, p. 26.

[4] *H.R.A.*, III, 1, p. 31 et seq.

[5] Collins to Hobart, 14 November 1803, *H.R.A.*, III, 1, p. 36.

[6] Collins to King, 16 December 1803, *H.R.A.*, III, 1, p. 49.

[7] Diary of J. P. Fawkner (MS. in the State Library of Victoria).

[8] Diary of Robert Knopwood, 6 November 1803. Published in First Survey and Settlement of Port Phillip. The Legislative Council of Victoria, *V. & P.* Paper 15, 1878.

the place.[9] The abscondings, the slackness of sentries such as Robert Andrews, the fear of being butchered by aborigines, the worthlessness of the settlers, and the failure to get on with tilling the soil, did not proceed from that restless disposition of man, or that badness of his heart, but rather reflected the lack of faith of the men in high places. Collins was quite determined to leave the settlement. To his relief King had written to him on 26 November 1803, accepting his view that Port Phillip was totally unfit in every point of view, and urging him to choose between the Derwent and Port Dalrymple. King's own preference was for Port Dalrymple, partly as a place for ships to touch at on their way from England to China or Sydney, partly because of the favourable reports on its soil by Bass and Flinders, and partly because such a settlement could protect sealers in Bass Strait.[10] By an odd coincidence he was writing when his traducers in Sydney were circulating doggerel verse accusing him of having a share in sealing and whaling. Collins, however, decided to sail for the Derwent. To understand the reasons for this decision it is necessary to sketch European contact with Van Diemen's Land since Tasman had hoisted the Dutch flag in Frederick Henry Bay in December of 1642 in order that those who came after them might know they had been there.

[9] Mrs Hartley to her sister, 23 May 1805, in E. H. Barker (ed.): *Geographical, Commercial and Political Essays; including Statistic details of various countries* (London, 1812), pp. 186-7.

[10] King to Collins, 26 November 1803, *H.R.A.*, III, 1, pp. 38-40.

VAN DIEMEN'S LAND AND THE
CIVILIZATION OF NEW SOUTH WALES

ALMOST one hundred and thirty years were to pass before any Europeans came to Van Diemen's Land after Tasman. The first was
a French explorer, M. Marion, who left Mauritius in October 1771
on a voyage of exploration in the south seas, and sailed into Frederick Henry
Bay on 3 March 1772. Next day some officers and soldiers landed to gather
wood, when they met the aborigines, who appeared to be of average height,
black in colour, both sexes quite naked. The women carried their children
on their backs, while the men were armed with pointed spears, and stones
shaped like hatchets. To the Frenchmen these savages appeared to have small
eyes, a bilious complexion, very wide mouths, very white teeth, and hair
like that of the kaffirs, tied into knots and powdered with red ochre. Several
of them wore engravings on their chests. In general they appeared a physic-
ally weak people. Their language seemed very harsh, as they seemed to draw
their sound from the depths of their throats.

The French tried to win them with small presents of mirrors, handkerchiefs and pieces of cloth, after which they showed them poultry and duck
in an attempt to get them to understand that they wanted to buy such things.
When the officers and the soldiers landed, one of the aborigines detached
himself from the others and approached holding out a bush as though inviting
M. Marion to light it. M. Marion, thinking that if he lit it he would show
his peaceful intentions, set alight to the bush, only to find such an act was
for the aborigine a declaration of war. When the aborigines withdrew swiftly
to a little hill from where they hurled their stone spears, M. Marion and
another officer were wounded. As the French retaliated by opening fire
and boarding the boats, the aborigines followed them to the water's edge,
uttering frightening yells, and hurling their spears. Again the French opened
fire, wounding several and killing one. In this way the first contact between
the European and the aborigine in Tasmania ended with death as the price
of misunderstanding. Six days later the French sailed on to New Zealand.[1]

On 24 January 1777 Captain Cook called at Adventure Bay in the *Resolution* on his way to explore the North Pacific. On the first evening, twenty
of the natives came to watch the Europeans filling their water casks. They
were entirely naked, and quite surprised by the clothing of the Europeans
which they at first thought was part of their bodies. Out of curiosity the
aborigines wanted to play with the water casks, but the Europeans insisted

---

[1] Anon.: *Nouveau Voyage à la Mer du Sud* (Paris, 1783), pp. 26-36.

they should stop. As the aborigines either would not or could not understand, an officer fired a musquet shot over their heads; the sudden and unexpected noise so alarmed them that one and all they clapped hands upon their heads, and fled.[2] Five days later, the aborigines returned to watch the white man load his boats, and Cook was able to observe their appearance and behaviour more closely. The colour of their skin was dark brown. Their hair, which was short and woolly, and their beards, were formed into small distinct lumps, with a mixture of reddish brown earth, and some kind of liquid, which appeared to be of an oily nature. Their teeth were in general bad, their noses flat, lips thick, foreheads low, and their eyes dark brown and lively. Their arms and breasts were marked with lines running in various directions, but totally different from any that the white man had ever seen before, the flesh being elevated or raised up as it were in little ridges. Some of them wore round their necks a kind of cord, about the thickness of a ship cord, which was very strong, and twisted in the European manner from three smaller cords. Their women were very plain, their heads shaved quite close, except for a very narrow circle of hair, which quite surrounded it. Some of them had an animal skin thrown over the shoulders, and fastened in front, which seemed to be merely for the convenience of carrying their children, two or three of which they had with them. Those who had no children were without this, or any other, covering. They readily accepted everything that was offered them, but set no particular value upon anything. Their language was entirely new to the white man, and they seemed to speak very fast. When anything pleased them, they expressed their satisfaction by a shout.[3]

Bligh, who called at Cape Frederick Henry in August 1788 on his ill-fated voyage to collect bread fruit at Tahiti, likened the voices of the aborigines to the cackling of geese, and complained of the prodigious clattering in their speech.[4] D'Entrecasteaux, who sailed into the south seas in 1792, with a commission to solve the mystery of the disappearance of La Pérouse, arrived at Adventure Bay in April of 1792, and returned again in 1793 when he discovered and explored the Derwent. At Adventure Bay, nature seemed in a generous mood after the sandy arid soil, the sameness, and the sterility he had observed on the south coast of New Holland. For him Adventure Bay was a harbour at the extremities of the world: the vegetation seemed as old as the world; nature untouched by man seemed more imposing and more picturesque than nature embellished by the industry of civilized man, for man in attempting to preserve its beauty, always destroyed its charm. Or so d'Entrecasteaux thought, as he mused on how man could maim, but could not adorn the natural world. Between April and June, 1793, Lieutenant John

---

2 W. Ellis: *An Authentic Narrative of a Voyage performed by Captain Cook and Captain Clerke, in His Majesty's Ships Resolution and Discovery During the Years 1776, 1778, 1779 and 1780* . . . (London, 1782), vol. 1, pp. 16-18.

3 Ibid., pp. 18-20.

4 W. Bligh: *A Voyage to the South Sea, undertaken by command of His Majesty, for the purpose of conveying the Bread-Fruit Tree to the West Indies, in His Majesty's Ship the Bounty* (London, 1792), pp. 45-52.

Hayes with the merchant ships *Duke of Clarence* and *Duchess* explored and named the Derwent.[5]

The first hopeful note of what man could do for Van Diemen's Land, as well as what Van Diemen's Land could contribute to the happiness and well-being of man, was expressed by Bass and Flinders when they circumnavigated the island in 1798 and 1799. Flinders was given command of the *Norfolk*, a colonial sloop of twenty-five tons, with instructions to find whether there was a strait between New South Wales and Van Diemen's Land and, if so, to sail through it and return by the south end of Van Diemen's Land.[6] From the Furneaux Islands, which they reached on 18 October, they sailed on to the north coast of Van Diemen's Land, where they were delighted to observe the contrast between the shores of the inlet, which were covered with grass and wood down to the water's edge, and the rocky sterile banks observed in sailing up Port Jackson. This spoke favourably for the country, and added to the satisfaction they felt in having made the discovery.[7] On 20 November they were off the entrance of a wide estuary which they explored over the next twenty odd days, Flinders deciding to name it Port Dalrymple after Alexander Dalrymple, late hydrographer to the Admiralty. The river which flowed into the estuary was named the Tamar by Colonel Paterson in 1804.[8] Flinders commented that anyone accustomed to the rocky banks of Port Jackson would be much delighted by the fertile appearance of the soil, the good covering of herbage, and the stronger grass of the valleys which was more particularly adapted to the bite of large cattle.[9] Flinders began to dream of the day when man would bring his civilization to the island which resembled the park lands and meadows of England rather than the harsh and sterile banks of Port Jackson. They sailed west along the north coast till 9 December, when they perceived a long swell coming from the south-west such as they had not been accustomed to for some time. It broke heavily upon a small reef, which lay a mile and a half from the point, and upon all the western shores. Although it was likely to prove troublesome, and perhaps dangerous, Bass and Flinders hailed it with joy and mutual congratulation, as announcing the completion of their long-wished-for discovery of a passage into the southern Indian Ocean.[10] In this way another mystery which had puzzled navigators and all that multitude of men from Tasman to Cook who did their business in deep waters, was cleared up by Flinders. In tribute to the great sea which rolled through the strait, and the wild desolate cape

[5] J.-A. B. d'Entrecasteaux: *Voyage de Dentrecasteaux, envoyé à la recherche de la Pérouse . . . rédigé par M. de Rossel* (Paris, 1808), vol. 1, pp. 54-5 and 222-3; R. W. Giblin: *The Early History of Tasmania* (London, 1929), vol. 1: The Geographical Era 1642-1804, p. 138 et seq.

[6] M. Flinders: *A Voyage to Terra Australis* (London, 1814), vol. 1, p. cxxxviii.

[7] Ibid., vol. 1, p. cliii.

[8] Ibid., vol, 1, p. clxiii f.n.

[9] M. Flinders: *Observations on the Coasts of Van Diemen's Land* (London, 1801), p. 21.

[10] M. Flinders: *A Voyage to Terra Australis*, vol. 1, p. clxxi.

which it pounded, he named the north-west cape of Van Diemen's Land Cape Grim.[11]

On the way down the west coast they sighted the two mountains mentioned by Tasman, which Flinders decided to name after Tasman's ships, the *Heemskerk* and the *Zeehaen*, in recognition of the achievements of the mighty dead.[12] From then on their task was to sort out the puzzles of where their predecessors had been, for they were now sailing in known waters to Adventure Bay, the Maatsuyker Islands, Storm Bay, and up the Derwent to Sullivan Cove and Risdon Cove. On the banks of the Derwent an aboriginal accepted a black swan with rapture. He seemed entirely ignorant of muskets, nor, according to Flinders, did anything excite his attention or desire except the swan and the red kerchiefs about the necks of the Europeans. In appearance he much resembled the inhabitants of New South Wales. He acceded to Flinders' suggestion of going to his hut, but took such a devious route and stopped so frequently that he tired their patience and they finally left him delighted with his swan. That was their only opportunity to communicate with the natives of Van Diemen's Land.[13] At the same time Bass was reflecting on the possible uses of the island. Both New South Wales and Van Diemen's Land were, he believed, poor countries. While Van Diemen's Land seemed to possess few or none of those vast depths of soil with which the happiest spots of New South Wales were blessed, it seldom sickened the heart of its traveller with those extensive tracts which left the warmest imagination without one beguiling prospect. In point of productive soil, Bass gave the preponderance to Van Diemen's Land. But both were deficient in water to facilitate the operations of man, and bring commerce to the door of the inland farmer.[14]

They sailed to Maria Island, which they reached on 4 January 1799, where the wind kept them off shore. By then shortage of provisions forced them to sail for Port Jackson which they reached on 11 January 1799. Fate or circumstance robbed Flinders of the chance of charting the one remaining unknown piece of coast of Van Diemen's Land, from Maria Island to the Furneaux Islands, as it robbed him later of doing all he hoped to do in his circumnavigation of New Holland and New South Wales in 1802-3. In his first major voyage to satisfy that all-consuming passion for discovery, this man with the talents and the virtues to finish a task to perfection, was cheated of it—possibly by chance, possibly also by that tragic flaw, that mote at his birth, which brought him later not to derision, but to an early death.

After the voyage of Bass and Flinders, the English knew almost all the coast of Van Diemen's Land, knew something of the aborigine there, knew of sites such as Port Dalrymple and Adventure Bay, where the appearance delighted the eye accustomed to the rocky banks of Port Jackson, or the

11 Ibid., vol. 1, p. clxxiii.

12 Ibid., vol. 1, p. clxxv.

13 Ibid., vol. 1, p. clxxxvii.

14 D. Collins: *An Account of the English Colony in New South Wales* (London, 1798 and 1802), vol. 2, pp. 189-90.

aridity and the sterility of New Holland, where soil and vegetation gave promise of greater wealth. But the only declared motive that played any part in the decision to occupy the island was fear of the French. In the latter part of 1802, Lieutenant-Colonel Paterson chatted over wine and dessert with French officers at Sydney Cove, who mentioned casually they might establish a base at Storm Bay. Paterson, for whom such a prospect was a commonplace in the gossip amongst the officers, reported the conversation to King. King took fright, and despatched the *Cumberland* to King Island in Bass Strait from where it was to sail to Port Phillip and Cape Otway to report on possible places for a settlement. In the meantime, Baudin disclaimed any intention of occupying any part of Van Diemen's Land.[15] But King went ahead with his plans. In this way, casual conversation, political gossip, rumour and the fear of the French, rather than any nobility of motive or grandeur of design, led to the settlement of Van Diemen's Land.

Between the conception and the creation there was a gap in time, during which other motives were added. When King proclaimed in May 1803 that it had become necessary to establish His Majesty's right to Van Diemen's Land, he declared that it was not only to prevent the French from gaining a footing on the east side of that island, but also to divide the convicts, to secure another place for procuring timber and other natural productions, as well as to raise grain and to promote the seal industry.[16] To achieve these objects he had appointed Lieutenant John Bowen to establish a settlement on the river Derwent.[17]

Bowen, who was only in his early twenties, had graduated from the Greenwich Naval College in 1798, had served in the navy and was commissioned as a junior lieutenant on the *Glatton* which arrived at Sydney Cove in March 1803. Bowen immediately won the good opinion of King, who appointed him Lieutenant-Governor of Norfolk Island, and then cancelled that appointment when he asked him to take command of the new settlement on the Derwent.[18] He was to take with him two officers, a serjeant and twelve men of the New South Wales Corps, three or four free settlers and their families, together with twenty to thirty male and twenty female convicts.[19] It was a tiny enough band with which to resist the French, let alone lay the foundations of European civilization in Van Diemen's Land. Yet this jealousy of a rival power apparently stimulated action which none of the other motives had been able to arouse, for neither the vices of the convicts nor the indolence and intemperance of the emancipists had hitherto prodded King into action.[20]

[15] King to Hobart, 9 November 1802, *H.R.A.*, I, 3, pp. 698-9, and King to Hobart, 23 November 1802, *H.R.A.*, I, 3, p. 737.

[16] King to Nepean, 9 May 1803, *H.R.A.*, I, 4, p. 249, and government order of March 1803, ibid., p. 338.

[17] *H.R.A.*, III, 1, p. 189 and ibid., p. 790.

[18] *H.R.A.*, III, 1, p. 790. For an opinion that Bowen was eighteen see *Hobart Mercury*, in September 1960.

[19] *H.R.A.*, I, 4, p. 672.

[20] King to Nepean, 9 May 1803, *H.R.A.*, I, 4, p. 249. See also J. West: *The History*

When they arrived in the Derwent on 12 September, Bowen chose Risdon Cove for the settlement, because of the stream of fresh water there. By 20 September he was finding every prospect in the Derwent pleasing, the banks of the river reminding him of a nobleman's park in England rather than an uncultivated country, for every part was beautifully green. Only man was vile, the soldiers in particular being discontented and corrupted by their previous life. All that Bowen wanted was a hundred men, with some good men among them, for with these he believed he could build a flourishing colony.[21] Just when he was laying plans for such a future by preparing to sow seed, and drafting the plan for a future town, two ships bringing Collins and his party from Port Phillip appeared in the Derwent on 15 February 1804, with orders to supersede Bowen. Bowen left in August 1804, and disappeared from the pages of Australian history when he sailed for England on the *Lady Barlow* in January 1805 in charge of King's despatches.

When Collins abandoned Port Phillip in December 1803, he decided to transfer to the Derwent simply because there was already a settlement there.[22] After the event, Collins found other reasons to justify the attraction of his heart for ease. The soldiers already at the Derwent, he argued, would promote a desirable spirit of emulation amongst his troops, while the Derwent was more adapted for whalers or traders from Europe, America or India.[23] All through December 1803, while abscondings, threats of insurrection amongst the soldiers, and the sullenness of the aborigines, seen as sinister silhouettes round their camp fires, convinced Collins both of the badness of men's hearts as well as of the urgency of action, the preparation for departure from Port Phillip continued. Collins, who had an almost superstitious reverence for sabbath observance, even permitted the loading of the ships to be continued on the day set aside by divine decree for devotion and rest, to hasten both their departure from that unpromising and unproductive country and the day when they could enjoy the comforts of a more fertile spot.[24]

Collins' company put to sea from Port Phillip on 30 January 1804, and after an unpleasant passage in which they were vexed both by calms and by foul winds accompanied by very bad weather, they arrived in the Derwent on 15 February.[25] In the very fine morning of the next day Collins, Knopwood and Lieutenant Lord went on shore to examine the Risdon Cove settlement. They quickly decided, as Knopwood put it, that it was not calculated for a town. On the following day Collins and Knopwood examined the south-west side of the river, where they found an extensive plain and a continual run of water coming from a lofty mountain, which reminded Knopwood of Table Mountain at Cape Town; it was a spot which he found

of Tasmania (Launceston, 1852), vol. 1, p. 27; R. W. Giblin: op. cit.; J. Fenton: *A History of Tasmania from its discovery in 1642 to the present time* (Hobart and Launceston, 1884).

21 Bowen to King, 20 September 1803, *H.R.A.*, III, 1, p. 198.
22 Collins to King, 16 December 1803, *H.R.A.*, III, 1, p. 46.
23 Collins to King, 28 February 1804, *H.R.A.*, III, 1, pp. 217-8.
24 General Orders, Sullivan's Bay, 31 December 1803, *H.R.A.*, III, 1, p. 85.
25 Collins to King, 29 February 1804, *H.R.A.*, III, 1, p. 221.

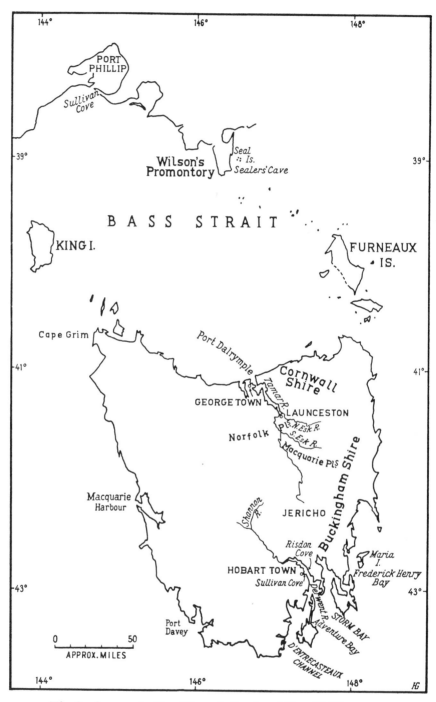

4 *The Settlements in Van Diemen's Land and Port Phillip, 1803–1820*

well suited for a settlement.[26] Collins chose this as the site, naming it Hobart Town. The landing, which began on 20 February 1804, was not celebrated by the drinking and the festivities which had marked the arrival at Sydney Cove. Nor did the first public ceremony assume a memorable character. At ten o'clock on the Sunday morning, the military, convicts, settlers, officers, and the Lieutenant-Governor all assembled to hear the Reverend Knopwood read divine service, preach on the prosperity of the new settlement, and pray to God for a blessing upon the increase of it.[27]

When they turned to pitch their tents, cut timber for huts and till the soil, some of their experiences reminded Collins of the desperate days at Sydney Cove. The axes were so soft that the commonest wood turned their edges; the shoes were of a bad quality; the soldiers were mutinous; the convicts were daring, flagitious and desperate characters.[28] Where Phillip had set the highest standards of humanity and moral rectitude, Collins soon lapsed. When the convicts were flogged, he stood by the triangles and took snuff in handfuls. Soon Collins had taken a convict woman as his mistress.[29] Though the few railed at the loose unchristian behaviour of the Governor, at his deliberate wickedness and his deeds of licentiousness,[30] those in high places showed that slackness and toleration, that absence of a spirit of emulation which pervades most small communities. Knopwood drank wine, smoked a pipe, hunted, fished, and enjoyed the world hugely, without any of that disgust for the depravity of his charges or that concern for their salvation which had bothered the Reverend Richard Johnson during the pioneer days at Sydney Cove. Collins won the affection of those who thought of the Ten Commandments as an aspiration rather than a command, by his warm heart and his amiable disposition.[31]

As on the mainland of New South Wales, they began by attempting to conciliate the affections of the aborigine and to treat them with amity and kindness. But when the aborigines perceived that the newcomers had stolen their land, they began their raids. The settlers promptly retaliated and killed three of the natives. Collins, who had lived through the same experiences on the mainland, believed that such indiscriminating savages would from then on consider every white man as an enemy, and take vengeance for the death of their companions upon those who had had no share in the attack. He still

[26] Diary of Robert Knopwood, 15, 16 and 17 February 1804. 7 February to 29 December 1804, MS. in Mitchell Library. 1805-8 in the possession of Miss Hookey. Republished in the Royal Society of Tasmania, *Papers and Proceedings*, 1946, pp. 51-125 (Hobart, 1947). See also W. H. Hudspeth: *An Introduction to the Diaries of the Rev. Robert Knopwood and G. T. W. B. Boyes* (Hobart, 1954).

[27] Ibid., 20 February 1804.

[28] Collins to Under Secretary Sullivan, 4 March 1804, *H.R.A.*, III, 1, pp. 232-3, and Collins to King, 24 April 1804, *H.R.A.*, III, 1, pp. 234-7.

[29] Rough Note Book of J. P. Fawkner, p. 30 (MS. in State Library of Victoria).

[30] Reminiscences of J. P. Fawkner, Second Book, p. 71 (MS. in State Library of Victoria).

[31] T. C. Croker (ed.): *The Memoirs of Joseph Holt* (London, 1838), vol. 2, pp. 252-4.

hoped, however, to obliterate the impressions such an affair might have left on the aborigines.[32] As on the mainland, the material interest of the settlers forced them more and more into deeds of hostility which belied all their protestations of goodwill.

While the settlers took up their farms in the upper reaches of the Derwent during 1804, the convicts began to till the soil on the government farm, and a plan for Hobart Town was drawn up. All that time food supplies continued to be so short that settlers, officers, soldiers and convicts lived off kangaroo and emu meat till well on into 1806.[33] In the meantime, observers were speculating on the settlement's future material prosperity. In 1804, one William Collins saw the Derwent to be most advantageously situated for the establishment and carrying on of a southern whale fishery. David Collins saw ships from England calling at Hobart Town with goods for sale. By September of 1806 the Lieutenant-Governor suggested that a respectable man and his wife might be sent out from England to start a school, and be supported by produce from a farm. He also had proposals to build houses for the officers.[34] Knopwood remained as dilatory as ever with his plans for a church and still allowed bad weather to absolve him from his duty on Sundays. By 30 June 1806 there were approximately four hundred and eighty in the settlement, of whom four hundred and sixty-five were victualled from the stores. Three hundred and twenty-seven were convicts, and six were emancipists. There were forty-nine free settlers, including their families, and ninety-nine civil and military officers, men and their families.[35] On 11 February 1807 a European walked into the settlement from the settlement at Port Dalrymple.[36]

The decision to establish this settlement at Port Dalrymple had been made in June of 1803, only a few months after the decision to establish a settlement on the Derwent. As at Port Phillip, the Derwent and King Island, though the immediate motive was to forestall the French,[37] other factors played a part. The great expense in administering Norfolk Island, in addition to the difficulties of communication between Port Jackson and Norfolk Island, made the British government decide to remove a proportion of the settlers and convicts from there to a place whose soil and climate recommended it as a site for a settlement. King believed Port Dalrymple answered these purposes.[38] As Lieutenant-Governor of the new settlement King appointed Lieutenant-Colonel Paterson. Paterson and his party left Port Jackson on 7 June 1804 but, after experiencing much bad weather, returned ten days later with most on board in ill-health, owing to confinement in the vessel's hold. While they

[32] Collins to King, 15 May 1804, *H.R.A.*, III, 1, p. 238.

[33] J. West: op. cit., vol. 1, pp. 38-42; T. C. Croker (ed.): op. cit., vol. 2, pp. 252-4.

[34] Collins to Hobart, 6 August 1804, *H.R.A.*, III, 1, pp. 275-8; Collins to Castlereagh, 2 September 1806, *H.R.A.*, III, 1, pp. 378-9.

[35] General Statement of the Inhabitants in His Majesty's Settlement, Hobart Town, 30 June 1806, *H.R.A.*, III, 1, p. 371.

[36] *H.R.A.*, III, 1, pp. 745-7 and n. 367, p. 847.

[37] King to Hobart, 7 August 1803, *H.R.A.*, I, 4, p. 359.

[38] Hobart to King, 24 June 1803, *H.R.A.*, I, 4, p. 304.

WILLIAM BLIGH

Portrait by George Dance, 1794, in the National Portrait Gallery, London

SYDNEY FROM THE EAST SIDE OF THE COVE, c. 1806

Lithograph in the Mitchell Library, Sydney, after a painting by John Eyre

waited the passing of winter to bring favourable weather for a passage to Bass Strait, on 1 October King defined the boundary between Collins' command on the Derwent and Paterson's in the county of Cornwall at Port Dalrymple. On 14 October Paterson and his wife, a captain, two subalterns, four serjeants, two drummers, fifty-eight privates and seventy-four convicts embarked on the *Buffalo*, the *Lady Nelson*, the *Integrity* and the *Francis* and reached Port Dalrymple on 5 November. On 11 November they hoisted His Majesty's colours after a royal salute from the *Buffalo*. Next day they began to clear the ground, to erect temporary buildings, and to cultivate the soil.

Civilization began there very much as it had begun at the other settlements of New South Wales. Paterson had been instructed to take measures for the observance of religion and good order, and in particular for the due and proper observance of the Lord's day. On the first Sunday divine service was read by a layman, the officers being told they were expected to attend. Paterson had been told to guard against the evils of indulgence in strong spirits; so he announced that spirits would not be issued to those found drunk. He was told to live in amity and kindness with the aborigines; but on 12 November the aborigines seized a serjeant and threatened to throw him over a rock into the sea, whereupon the guard fired, killing one and wounding another. He had been told to put the convicts to work; but the prisoners were so destitute of shoes, their tools were so unequal to the task, their disposition was so averse to labour, and the military, the means of subordination, so discontented and insubordinate, that the human means seemed pitifully inadequate to such ends.[39] And Paterson himself was so racked by gout that he could hardly withstand a breeze of wind without being affected.[40]

Paterson, who was born with a sanguine temperament and an inveterate distaste for difficult situations, tended to comment on their natural advantages. He wrote in despatches that the settlement would permit ships from the Cape of Good Hope to escape the boisterous passage round Van Diemen's Land, that they possessed an immense expanse of one of the most beautiful countries in the world, as well as a most superior tract of arable and grazing country.[41] What Paterson noticed was the success of three settlers from Norfolk Island in sowing their land with wheat, barley and potatoes, that the cattle were thriving, and that Laycock had left Launceston on 3 February 1807 to walk to the Derwent, and was back again on 22 February.[42] As far as his eye could tell, their world went well. Even King had stopped talking about the French, and was coming round to the view that the future of Bass Strait lay in its seals, and as a sea lane for trade,[43] though neither he nor Paterson could see then that on this latter point Port Dalrymple was to have a mighty rival over the water. Well before that time events at Sydney Cove

[39] Paterson to King, 14 November 1805, *H.R.A.*, III, 1, p. 644; and Paterson to King, 18 January 1806, *H.R.A.*, III, 1, p. 656.

[40] Paterson to King, 11 December 1805, *H.R.A.*, III, 1, pp. 650-1.

[41] Paterson to Castlereagh, 12 August 1806, *H.R.A.*, III, 1, pp. 663-5.

[42] Ibid., and Paterson to Sullivan, 21 April 1807, *H.R.A.*, III, 1, p. 669.

[43] Governor King's Instructions to Captain Kent, 1 October 1804, *H.R.A.*, 1, 5, pp. 222-4.

had brought Paterson into a disquiet with which he had neither the powers nor the temperament to cope.

This increase in the number of settlements reflected the changes in the economic situation of New South Wales. In the beginning the problem had been to produce and import enough food to win the battle for survival. This had been achieved by 1795; subsequent periods of shortage were brief, occasioned either by delay in the arrival of a ship or a natural disaster such as flood. With the achievement of subsistence, their problem was how to dispose of surplus grain. This question was coming up for discussion at the end of the Hunter period. It was referred to by King in his despatches to Lord Hobart in 1804,[44] and touched on in that most valuable source of what was in the mind of the people, the letters to the *Sydney Gazette*. As one writer put it, from the want of a staple, commerce could not be supported upon the principles of barter while, until an export could be provided, importation must necessarily drain the colony of its specie.[45] Side by side with this problem of a staple, there were the problems of high prices, the monopoly of the officers, and the traffic in spirits, or that unholy, unblessed trinity which King and his predecessor had attacked as a symptom of officer greed and a problem in human nature.

Developments in overseas trade probably contributed more than all the concern for human beastliness. In 1796 Campbell, Clark and Co. of Calcutta sent the *Sydney Cove* with a cargo of 7,000 gallons of spirits and general merchandise, which ran aground on 9 February 1797 at Preservation Island in the Furneaux Group.[46] Campbell, Clark and Co. then fitted out the *Hunter* with an assortment of Indian goods, cows and horses, to investigate first the wreck and then trade prospects at Sydney Cove. She arrived in Sydney on 10 June 1798, bringing with her as the main representative of the firm, Robert Campbell. Born on 28 April 1769 at Greenock, Scotland, the son of the last laird of Ashfield, Campbell had migrated to Calcutta in 1796 to enter the house of Campbell, Clark, and Co., in which his brother John was already a partner.[47] By 1798 Campbell was so impressed with trading prospects in Sydney that he purchased a house and land on the west side of Sydney Cove, and petitioned Hunter for permission to supply the colony with necessaries and to erect warehouses. While awaiting a reply, Campbell sailed for Calcutta, and returned in the *Hunter* with a cargo of wine, spirits, sugar, tea, candles, soap, china-ware, coffee, tobacco, rice, muslins, white rope and gunny bags,[48] which he sought permission to land. King, with one eye on Lord Hobart and another on the appetites of the locals, cautiously told him he could land the amount of spirits required for the domestic purposes of the officers and a few deserving industrious settlers, together with all other articles which

[44] King to Hobart, 20 December 1804, *H.R.A.*, I, 5, pp. 201-2.

[45] An Inquisitive Observer to the *Sydney Gazette*, 1 May 1803.

[46] Hunter to Portland, 6 July 1797, *H.R.A.*, I, 2, p. 82; and notes 35, 36, and 37 on pp. 709-10.

[47] J. K. S. Houison: 'Robert Campbell of the Wharf', in R.A.H.S., *J. & P.*, vol. 23, pt. 1, 1937, pp. 1-28.

[48] Campbell to King, 13 June 1800, *H.R.A.*, I, 2, pp. 548-9 and 572.

would be of use or comfort to the inhabitants.[49] Thus was the way opened for trade between India and Sydney. By December 1804, the government of New South Wales had bought nearly £18,000 worth of grain, live stock, spirits, and merchandise from Campbell.[50] Four years earlier he had erected a wharf and warehouses on the west side of Sydney Cove. In May 1803 he sent a trial consignment of seal skins and oil on the *Glatton* to England; by then Campbell had established an interest in whaling and sealing in Bass Strait.

He was not the first. In 1791 five English whaling ships carried convicts and stores to Sydney Cove on their way to the whaling grounds off the west coast of South America. The first American whaler arrived in 1802. By then it was a commonplace that a whale fishery was being established with Sydney Cove as a base. It was a commonplace, too, that the whalers might well help to lower the prices of English goods in the colony.[51] By 1803 King was discussing the possibility of allowing convict ships to go whaling or to trade with China after disembarking at Sydney. For the increase in trade led on not only to an increase in whaling, but to trade with China, which led King in turn to reflect on the desirable consequences of introducing Chinese into the settlements of New South Wales, as a people who would use their industrious character to raise cotton for the China market and so prevent that intercourse with and employment of Americans which he regretted that some contemplated.[52] It led, too, to a liberal encouragement and protection of those who wished to build ships to fish in and about the coast.[53] In 1804, for example, King granted Campbell permission to build a vessel of one hundred and thirty tons for sealing.[54]

To kill a young seal on the rocks a club was commonly used, and for the old ones, a lance. To overcome the largest bulls, a musket was necessary, loaded with a brace of balls. With this the sealer could advance in front of the animal, to within a few paces; the bull would rise on the forelegs or flippers, and at the same time open his mouth widely to send forth a loud roar. This was the moment to discharge the balls through the roof of the upper jaw into the brain, whereupon the creature fell forward, either killed, or so much stunned as to give the sealer sufficient time to complete its destruction with the lance. Seals were frequently discovered sleeping, in which case the muzzle of the piece was held close to the head, and discharged into the brain. The loudest noise would not awaken these animals when sleeping, and it was not unusual for the hunter to shoot one without awaking those alongside of it, and in this way proceed through the whole rookery, shooting

49 King to Campbell, 15 June 1800, *H.R.A.*, I, 2, pp. 549-50.

50 J. K. S. Houison: op. cit.

51 Marsden to W. Wilberforce, Parramatta, 1799 (Bonwick Transcripts, box 49, Missionary, vol. 2, p. 77, Mitchell Library, Sydney).

52 King to Hobart, 14 August 1804, *H.R.A.*, I, 5, p. 9.

53 King to Collins, 30 September 1804 (King Letter Book, 1797-1806, pp. 455-7, Mitchell Library, Sydney).

54 J. K. S. Houison: op. cit., p. 12.

and lancing as many as were wanted.[55] Of the life of the sealers at sea, and their life on land, little is known save from the remains at their camp sites on the south coast of Phillip Island, at Wilson's Promontory, King Island, the islands in the Furneaux Group, or Dusky Bay in the south island of New Zealand, at which latter place they suffered much from severe cold and incessant falls of snow, hail or rain, as they procured their skins with much hardship and difficulty.[56]

The skins were sold either on the China market, or in America or England, while the whale oil was sold in America or England. Between 1800 and 1806 imports and exports of whale oil and seal skins were as follows:[57]

Return of Oil and Seal skins imported into and exported out of His Majesty's colony of New South Wales, being procured by private Colonial vessels; also an account of the Oil and Sealskins imported in and exported out of the same in British South Whalers and Sealers from November, 1800, to the 19th day of August, 1806.

	IMPORTATION			EXPORTATION		
	Sperm oil *Tons*	Black oil *Tons*	Seal skins	Sperm oil *Tons*	Black oil *Tons*	Seal skins
Colonial vessels	—	711½	118,721	—	520½	98,280
British South Whalers and Sealers	2,831½	420	14,750	2,756½	420	14,750

In this way sealing and whaling contributed to economic activity in the colony, as men accumulated wealth from the trade. Robert Campbell had extended his activities to ship-building and sealing. So too had Simeon Lord. Born in 1770 and sentenced to transportation for seven years at Leeds in 1790 for stealing one hundred yards of muslin valued at sixpence and one hundred yards of calico valued at fourpence, Lord was assigned as a servant to Thomas Rowley an officer in the New South Wales Corps, and had become an employer of labour by 1798. In 1801 he was trading in coal and between 1801 and 1806 he had entered the seal skin, whale oil and Pacific islands trade. He took shares in American ships sealing and whaling in Bass Strait, stored their skins in his stores in Sydney, and reshipped them with sandalwood for Canton, where he disposed of them at good prices.[58] Lord was the first of the emancipists to find in trade a career open to talent. Both he and Campbell contributed to the creation of a commercial class in Sydney, a class trained in the tough school of competition with American traders, and with Chinese and Indian merchants. They were a class to whom the distinction between bond and free, or even previous occupation, was less relevant than success in building up for themselves treasures on earth. In this way avenues of employment were opened for emancipists and those born in the colony, as well

[55] E. Fanning: *Voyages Round the World, with selected sketches of Voyages to the South Seas, North and South Pacific Islands, China, Etc.* (New York, 1833), p. 347 et seq.

[56] *Sydney Gazette*, April and May, 1803.

[57] *H.R.N.S.W.*, vol. 6, p. 169.

[58] E. Fanning: op. cit., pp. 319-27; E. C. Rowland: 'Simeon Lord: a Merchant Prince of Botany Bay', in R.A.H.S., *J. & P.*, vol. 30, pt. 3, 1944; vol. 37, pt. 6, 1951.

as a path to wealth for those with the talents, the industry and the luck of a Simeon Lord.

When the *Lady Barlow*, despatched by Robert Campbell with a cargo of oil and skins, arrived in the Thames in July 1805, she was seized by officers of the East India Company for violating the clause in their charter which conferred on them the monopoly of trade in eastern seas.[59] This raised the question whether the East India Company should grant licences for trade with New South Wales, and so remove piecemeal or wholly the original restrictions imposed on the trade of New South Wales in order to preserve the monopoly of the company.[60] When a second ship arrived in the Thames 1806, one member of the British government, Lord Auckland, wrote to his colleague Lord Grenville, to tell him that a curious question had arisen at the committee of the council for trade on the subject of the Botany Bay establishment. A ship of nine hundred tons burden from Port Jackson, with oil and seal skins, was hourly expected. The people interested in the British fishery objected to this, as being ruinous to their whale fishery, and as producing no seamen for the navy. The East India Co. objected to it as an infringement of their charter, and also as having tended already to the building of ships calculated to follow the China trade, and eventually leading to the most alarming consequences. The short question, he went on, would be: Was it the intention and policy of government that these establishments should be considered as colonies, with all the privileges of colonists?[61]

At the same time, those with a contemplative mind in the colony were receiving peculiar pleasure from tracing how such developments were polishing and improving that remote part of the habitable world which, as they put it, might otherwise have remained to the end of time a wild waste. Their anticipating fancy dwelt with delight, too, upon the scene which would be enacted when edifices and warehouses arose to invite merchandise and traffic from the further corners of the globe.[62] In the meantime, another group was beginning to contemplate quite a different future for New South Wales, when wool had created their wealth and the possession of the land conferred on them the distinction of forming 'the ancient nobility' of New South Wales.

In December 1802 Macarthur had arrived in England to face court-martial, possible disgrace, and the consequent destruction of his career. By cunning, flattery, the use of influence on the men in high places, and chance, he turned impending disgrace to his own advancement. He became reconciled to Hunter, because Hunter could be used to influence the Earl of Camden, who had taken over the seals of office from Lord Hobart in May 1804. John Jeffreys Pratt, the second Earl of Camden, was born in 1759, and first achieved notoriety as Lord-Lieutenant of Ireland from 1795 to 1798, an office in which he was instructed to use his powers to conciliate the Catholics without

[59] *H.R.N.S.W.*, vol. 6, pp. 100-102.

[60] East India Company to Rt. Hon. G. Tierney, 5 February 1807, *H.R.N.S.W.*, vol. 6, pp. 240-1.

[61] Lord Auckland to Lord Grenville, 31 May 1806, *Dropmore Papers* (London, 1912), vol. 8, p. 165.

[62] *Sydney Gazette*, 10 April 1803.

abandoning the common cause of upholding the religion, the laws, and the constitution of the Protestant ascendancy. Camden's gift to the Catholics was the foundation of an ecclesiastical seminary at Maynooth, which in time was to influence a section of opinion in Australia as much as wool influenced its economy. In punishing the rebels of 1798 Camden at times displayed an unnecessary want of kindness and humane feeling. In June 1798 he had permitted the preparations for the execution of a member of the United party to take place within earshot of Lord Edward Fitzgerald, which threw him into a state of delirium, and deranged him for some time. Lady Louise Connolly threw herself on her knees before Camden to beg permission to see her relation before his execution, and in a flood of tears supplicated him to relent, but Camden remained inexorable. Some of those who found him cruel and cold-hearted, said he would have handed over the Irish to the rack and to torture and tolerated a system of bloodshed which would have disgraced savages. Others dismissed him as a piece of useless lumber in the ministry.[63] Such was the man to whom Macarthui presented his ideas. When he showed specimens of fine New South Wales wool to the manufacturers, he got from them an opinion that if they could procure a sufficient supply of it, it would enable them to surpass all other countries in the manufacture of the best woollen cloths. Armed with this opinion, he turned to Camden to convince him that with a suitable area of land and adequate convict labour, New South Wales could grow wool of a quality suited to the manufacture of fine cloth, at a price which the manufacturers in England could afford to give for that material.[64] On 14 July Camden issued instructions to the Governor of New South Wales to grant ten thousand acres of land to John Macarthur in the vicinity of the Cow Pastures, to provide him with thirty convicts, and to give him every encouragement to grow fine wool.[65] So Macarthur left London on the *Argo* at the end of 1804 to return triumphantly to that New South Wales which he had left in ignominy four years earlier.

When Macarthur arrived at Sydney Cove in June 1805 he found that King, who in 1802 had been prepared to warn all and sundry of the evil intent of that pair of basilisk eyes, was by then so debilitated by drink that his emotional responses had narrowed down to raging and weeping. When King first saw Macarthur after his return he burst into tears, and was un-able to conduct business. After soothing his pride with some petty malice, King announced that an obedience to the royal commands and his lordship's wishes would be his immediate and decided duty.[66] After recovering his

[63] W. Lord Auckland (ed.): *Journal and Correspondence of William, Lord Auckland* (London, 1862), vol. 4, pp. 243-4 and 387; *Gentleman's Magazine*, 1840, pt. 2, p. 651.

[64] The Memorial of Captain John Macarthur. To the Right Honourable the Lords of the Committee of His Majesty's most Honourable Privy Council appointed for the consideration of Matters of Trade and Foreign Plantations, quoted in S. M. Onslow (ed.): *Some Early Records of the Macarthurs of Camden* (Sydney, 1914), pp. 80-95.

[65] S. M. Onslow (ed.): op. cit., p. 96.

[66] King to Hobart, 20 December 1804, *H.R.A.*, I, 5, p. 206; and King to Camden, 20 July 1805, *H.R.A.*, I, 5, p. 511.

composure, King fussed over Macarthur, and granted him the ten thousand acres in the vicinity of the Cow Pastures, which Macarthur, in gratitude to the man who had set the seal of official approval on his plans, named Camden Park.

While King was seeking his own satisfaction in drunken rages or sobs, for which neither the pity nor the compassion of his contemporaries was extended to him, Macarthur was envisaging a day when the use of fine wool from New South Wales would enable the British manufacturers to sanction the universal use of machinery, which in turn would enable them so to reduce the price of their woollen cloths as to secure throughout the world the most complete monopoly that any people had ever possessed. The people of New South Wales would largely participate in the profits of this gainful trade, and enjoy the pleasing consolation that their labours were contributing to the support and prosperity of the parent country, to whom their debt of gratitude could never be paid.[67] At that time he had not conceived of the role in society of the men who owned the sheep, nor the connection between New South Wales as a grower of fine wool and New South Wales as a receptacle for the punishment and reformation of British convicts. What he saw then was the connection between his own interests, the interests of New South Wales, and the parent country. In time he began to confound his own interests with the welfare of society as a whole.

In the meantime, trade with India, China, North America, the Pacific islands and Europe, the increase in sealing and whaling in the south seas, the ship-building, the coal mining, the cedar cutting and the creation of settlements at Hobart Town and Port Dalrymple were gradually affecting the economy of New South Wales. Prices began to fall; the monopoly of the officers withered away; the traffic in spirits assumed a less prominent place in the economy, and even in the weekly pronouncements from the pulpit. King saw all this as the effect of his stern measures, while others saw it as the effect of expanding economic activity.[68] The area under crop had increased from 7,595 acres in 1800 to 11,254 acres at the end of 1806.[69] The proportion of people victualled from the government stores had decreased as the population increased, thus reducing the relative cost to government; in August 1806 there were seven thousand one hundred and twenty-six souls in the settlements of New South Wales—Sydney, Parramatta, the Hawkesbury and Newcastle—of whom only two thousand two hundred and fifty-four were victualled from the public store. There were six hundred and ninety-four persons on Norfolk Island, of whom little more than half, three hundred and seventy-two, were victualled from the public store. There were seven hundred and forty-seven persons in Van Diemen's Land at the settlements of Hobart Town and Port Dalrymple; of these, however, no less than seven hundred and thirty-three were still victualled from the public stores.[70]

67 J. Macarthur: A Report on the State of Mr McArthur's Flocks of Sheep, encl. no. 11 in King to Camden, 26 October 1805, *H.R.A.*, I, 5, p. 568.

68 King to Windham, 12 August 1806, *H.R.A.*, I, 5, p. 776.

69 *H.R.A.*, I, 2, p. 632, and vol. 5, p. 776.

70 Enclosures no. 4 and no. 5 in King to Windham, 12 August 1806, *H.R.A.*, I, 5, pp. 778-9 and 780-2.

By the end of 1806 the convicts had been organized into a system which remained unaltered in essentials until the abolition of transportation to New South Wales in 1840. They were divided between the government on the one hand and the military and civil officers and settlers on the other. Gunfire at daylight, followed by the tolling of a bell, marked the beginning of the day's work, which with intervals for breakfast and dinner continued for nine hours for the five week-days, and for five hours on Saturdays.[71] Convicts in government work were fed, clothed and lodged by the government, while those in assignment were victualled by their masters. The master was also required to provide them with a sheltered lodging on his farm or at his home from which they were not to absent themselves without leave; nor were they in any case to go from one settlement to another without a pass from a magistrate. For neglect of work, not obeying orders, or being absent without leave, the masters were to report the convicts to a magistrate who on conviction prescribed an appropriate punishment.[72] Judging by the number of times King reminded masters that they were not to chastise their servants by horsewhipping or beating them for real or supposed offences, or neglect of work, but rather that they were to bring delinquents to justice, the regulation seemed to be honoured more in the breach than the observance.[73] It was the same with the regulations for wages, which forbade masters to pay servants for work performed in regulation hours, and fixed rates for labour performed out of hours. The settlers found that in a choice between the lash and rewards as an incentive, the latter proved far more effective.[74]

Much of official time and effort was devoted to attempts to stamp out abuses of the system, to stop masters being bribed by convicts to permit them to sell their labour, to stop masters letting convicts out for hire,[75] to stop masters horsewhipping their servants,[76] to stop masters obtaining the labour of government convicts by offering them very high rewards,[77] and to stop that 'folly' of the prisoners and 'knavery' of the clerks in the government whereby the former bribed the latter with considerable sums of money, watches or other valuables, to alter their terms of transportation from life to shorter periods.[78] To prevent such abuses, corruption and malpractices, the regulations threatened punishments such as floggings, the tread-mill or transportation for the convicts, rewards for informers, and fines or loss of servants for offending masters. The abuses continued, despite the threats or the inducements and the floggings, and despite the humanity with which King used his power to reprieve and pardon. On each King's Birthday, King chose candidates to participate in His Majesty's mercy from those whose behaviour,

[71] *H.R.A.*, I, 3, p. 37.
[72] Ibid., pp. 36-7.
[73] Ibid., p. 43.
[74] Ibid., pp. 36-7 and vol. 5, p. 75.
[75] *H.R.A.*, I, 3, p. 254.
[76] Ibid., p. 43.
[77] Ibid., p. 467.
[78] Ibid., pp. 144-5.

merit and industry rendered them suitable. On 4 June 1802, for example, four men were granted full pardons, and twenty-nine received conditional emancipation, while on 4 June 1803 the royal grace and full pardon was extended to twenty-one soldiers and twelve men who had already received a conditional pardon, and sixty-seven others were conditionally emancipated. On the same day men were liberated from the gaol gangs, and the commissary was directed to issue the usual allowance of half a pint of spirits to each non-commissioned officer and private.[79] The settlers and the officers grumbled about the disastrous effect of such clemency on discipline and subordination; the articulate convicts groaned under what was to them a capricious and sentimental variation in a general theme of brutality and severity. The plain fact was that the system worked, and a civilization had been planted by convict labour.

Outsiders perceived this more clearly than those engaged in the day-to-day affairs of the colony of New South Wales and its settlements. Some wrote of the charm in seeing villages and churches and farms rising from a wilderness where civilized man had not previously set his foot since the creation of the world.[80] Others wrote of it as already England in miniature and of the flattering reformation wrought among the convicts on their arrival.[81] *The Times* sensed the possibility both of greatness and novelty in a country which had begun its history, like ancient Rome, as an asylum for fugitives and delinquents, and went on to predict that, like Rome, it might be destined to become the mistress of the world. The polished nations, they believed, should not look with contempt upon this people, the spirit of whose enterprise was nowhere more conspicuous than in the colony. Necessity, that mother of invention, might produce apparently miraculous effects amongst a people who came from a society worn with age and decrepitude, or debilitated by the indolence and apathy of modern luxury and refinement.[82]

It was this perception of the possibility of material advancement rather than any interest in the possibility of a society of men liberated from the effeteness and decadence of the old world, which caused Viscount Castlereagh, who had taken over the seals of office in 1807, to deem it expedient to encourage a certain number of settlers of responsibility and capital to emigrate to New South Wales. As he saw it, they might set useful examples of industry and cultivation, and from their property and education be fit persons to whose authority the convicts might be properly entrusted.[83] The encouragement offered was a free passage for the settler and his family, a large grant of land, and convicts to work it in the proportion of one to every hundred acres, such convicts to be fed and clothed by government for

[79] Ibid., p. 625 and vol. 4, p. 342.

[80] Review of volume two of D. Collins: *An Account of the English Colony of New South Wales*, in the *Edinburgh Review*, April 1803, vol. 2, pp. 30-42.

[81] Review of *A Concise History of the English Colony in New South Wales, from the Landing of Governor Phillip in January 1788, to May 1803*, in the *Gentleman's Magazine*, August 1804, vol. 74, pt. 2, pp. 754-5.

[82] *The Times*, 2 October 1807.

[83] Castlereagh to King, 13 July 1805, *H.R.A.*, I, 5, pp. 490-1. See also ibid., p. 830.

eighteen months on condition that the settler invested capital of up to six thousand pounds. The first permissions to settle under these terms were granted to Gregory and John Blaxland. Gregory Blaxland, born in Kent in 1771, was a gentleman farmer by birth, but threatened by material misfortunes to lose his position in society. John Blaxland, who was born in 1769, was also a farmer from Kent who faced the same problem as his brother. Migration became for both of them a promise of rescue from a slide down the social ladder in England. Gregory and his family arrived on the *William Pitt* on 14 April 1806, while John arrived on the *Brothers* on 4 April 1807.[84]

In the meantime a few ex-convicts, by the exercise of those same qualities of industry and cultivation, had raised themselves to a state of affluence. Andrew Thompson, who had arrived in the *Pitt* in 1792 under sentence of transportation for fourteen years for theft, was pardoned in 1797, obtained a lease of land in 1799, put up a granary, bought ships for trade with King Island, Van Diemen's Land, New Zealand and the Pacific Islands, and built both a salt-works and a bridge across the Hawkesbury.[85] James Larra, a French Jew, transported for stealing a silver tankard in 1790, worked to sustain himself during his days of poverty, obtained a grant of land, and married a Jewess who had also been led back to the habit of work by exile and misfortune. With their own hands they traced the first furrows on their land; with their own sweat they reaped abundant harvests. With his savings Larra invested in commercial speculations which succeeded beyond his hopes. By 1806 he was regarded as one of the wealthiest proprietors in New South Wales, while the regularity of his habits and the honesty of his character won for him genuine respect amongst the principal employers, both private and government, in the colony.[86] A few rose to a measure of affluence, though not to respectability, for though the successful emancipists coveted respectability as the crown of their endeavours, and began restlessly to accumulate for their families as well as for themselves all those outward and visible signs of respectability which wealth alone could not confer, there were few amongst the free prepared to overlook the stain of an emancipist's past.

Education was one of the ways to respectability. The education of the young had been begun under Hunter on the grounds of social utility to rescue the children from the evil influences of their parents and the consequences of idleness. It was continued and fostered as such by King. There was this difference, however, that whereas all previous education had been promoted as an insurance against crime as well as opening in the mind a perception of eternity, now, a faint note of idealism was sounded, that first faint note in Australia which would soon noise abroad the idea that learning was a foe to vice and that ignorance was generally the companion of guilt. There was also the hope that

[84] *H.R.A.*, I, 5, pp. 490-1, 748-9, and 754-5.

[85] J. V. Byrnes: 'Green Hills and Golden Grain . . .' (M.A. thesis in Fisher Library, University of Sydney); and *Australian Encyclopaedia* (Sydney, 1958), vol. 8.

[86] F. Péron: *Voyages de découvertes aux Terres Australes* (Paris, 1807-1816), vol. 1, p. 407 et seq.; G. T. J. Bergman: 'James Larra', in *Proceedings of the Australian Jewish Historical Society*, vol. 5, pt. 3.

in discovering every ornament concealed in the human breast, education might prepare the children of the affluent convicts for social preferment, even if it could not erase the convict stain from the parents.[87]

Another source of respectability was public religious piety. When Marsden preached at the opening of St John's, Parramatta, in April 1803, he traced the progress of religion in succeeding ages, and adverted to the many solid advantages the colony must derive from a proper observance of the duties of Christianity. In describing the becoming silence that prevailed, adding to the solemnity of the service, the writer in the *Sydney Gazette* singled out for special mention the many ladies of the first respectability who were present.[88] By a curious irony, Marsden, who courted the respect of the powerful with a desperation which exposed him to ridicule and his religious professions to the charge of hypocrisy, adopted a cold and haughty tone in his relations with the emancipists. In his sermons he was capable of saying that throne and altar fell together, or that religion was the great and essential comfort of the poor, the old and the sick, that in the sanctuary of God men learned the significance of those gradations of rank and wealth which in His infinite wisdom God had thought fit to establish in this transitory life as stimulants to the industry and energy of men. It was, he believed, true charity to give the poor the advantage and comfort of religious meditation, to open their eyes, and raise their hopes in those scenes of bliss which became brighter and more enchanting as they approached the confines of the grave.[89] Marsden could see no reason why the hopes of the poor or those whose families had been stained by crime should be raised in this world, where such people did not increase in divine things but remained permanently depraved. Towards the end of 1802 the chaise in which Mrs Eliza Marsden and her child were driving at Parramatta was overturned, and her dear child, as she put it, 'never stirred more'. To the Marsdens this melancholy death of the little boy was an affliction, but for the boy they believed that his was a happy translation from a world of depravity to a world of bliss.[90]

So ineluctable was the tie between public religious piety and respectability that most affluent ex-convicts ignored the snubs from Marsden. Early in 1803 another source of opinion in the colony began to propagate the connection between the religious and moral system of the. evangelicals and respectability. That was the *Sydney Gazette and New South Wales Advertiser*, which began publication on 5 March 1803 under the editorship of George Howe. He was born in 1769 at St Kitts, the son of a printer from the West Indies, worked in printing houses in London, and was sentenced to transportation for seven years, for the offence of shop-lifting.[91] Either in London or earlier in his career,

87 Letter by An Inquisitive Observer, *Sydney Gazette*, 8 May 1803.

88 *Sydney Gazette*, 17 April 1803.

89 Bigge Appendix (Mitchell Library collection, box 12, p. 109); and *Sydney Gazette*, 26 June 1803.

90 Mrs Eliza Marsden to Mrs Stokes, 13 November 1802 (Marsden Papers, Mitchell Library, Sydney).

91 J. A. Ferguson, A. G. Foster, and H. M. Green: *The Howes and Their Press* (Sydney, 1936); obituary in *Sydney Gazette*, 12 May 1821; and H.O. 13/12.

Howe came under the influence of the evangelicals, possibly through common ground on the slave trade and slavery. For when he obtained permission to publish the *Gazette* as a private speculation, on condition that the contents for each week's issue were inspected by an officer, Howe filled what space remained after inserting government notices and advertisements with material of an improving kind. In an early number he proclaimed that the utility of his paper was to open a source of solid information, that he had courted the assistance of the ingenious and the intelligent, and that he would open no channel to political discussion or personal animadversion, as information was his only purpose.[92] The pages of his newspaper between 1803 and 1823 mirrored faithfully the values of that Protestant cast of mind which rose to power and ascendancy in the period of Macquarie.

It was a religion which rejoiced in the blessings that Divine Providence seemed so wantonly to lavish on the English race. When news of the renewal of war with France was announced in December 1803, the *Gazette* reminded its readers that though they were too tender a branch of the British Empire to render actual assistance, nevertheless by tokens of affection they should show themselves worthy of so exalted a parentage.[93] When news of the victory at Trafalgar reached Sydney Cove on 13 April 1806, it was decided to observe Sunday 20 April as a day of general thanksgiving, when the community would render thanks to Almighty God for the mercy and goodness He had shown their most gracious sovereign and his dominions.[94] It was a view of the world which encouraged an insolent superiority to all other religious persuasions. One Thursday in March 1806 some Asiatic seamen marched in procession from the waterfront in Sydney Cove to a house at the lower end of Back Row East with torches, where they paraded round a fire, all the time uttering the most hideous howls. After they had ranged themselves in front of a temple they performed what the *Sydney Gazette* called wild and incredible extravagances amidst the odoriferous fumigation of sandalwood and other perfumes, till two of them seemed to pierce their cheeks, tongues, and thighs with peculiarly constructed instruments, at the same time bellowing with pain, as three tambourines beat time for the vocal accompaniment of the whole group. Howe, who each Sunday recited his belief in the communion of saints, the resurrection of the body, and the life of the world to come, dismissed their behaviour as very extravagant and bearing strong marks of unaccountable superstition.[95]

Their toleration did not extend beyond the other Protestant sects. When a dozen families from the Scottish border arrived as free emigrants, they received grants of one hundred acres each on the banks of the Hawkesbury at a place they called Ebenezer. They were Presbyterians, devout and God-fearing people, and much attached to the church of their fathers. Those in authority were prepared to allow the Presbyterians to worship God according to their

92 *Sydney Gazette*, 17 April 1803.
93 Ibid., 18 December 1803.
94 Ibid., 13 April 1806.
95 Ibid., 23 March 1806.

own lights under the guidance of their first elder, James Mein.[96] They were not, however, prepared to tolerate the practice of the Catholic religion, because they saw it as an instrument of mental slavery, a threat to their higher civilization, and a threat to liberty. All secular creeds were suppressed with an odd brutality for men committed by their faith to good-will to all men. For holding a meeting of freemasons, Henry Brown Hayes was sentenced to hard labour at the new settlement at Van Diemen's Land in May 1803. When Joseph Snodgrass uttered expressions of an inflammatory and seditious tendency in March 1806, he was sentenced to one hundred lashes and a term of public labour in the coal mines at Newcastle. On the journey from the Hawkesbury to Newcastle he was forced to hang a placard from his neck on which was written: Thomas Paine.[97]

They were not concerned, however, with debating or inquiring into the meaning of life: they knew it. They believed life to be a preparation for eternity. Paradoxically, their daily interests only extended from the trivial, or from crop news and weather news, to horror stories—of how, for example, one sultry Saturday in March 1803 an unfortunate woman attempted to commit the horrid crime of suicide with a cake knife which she drew across her throat with almost fatal success.[98] For the conviction that in the midst of life they were in death never left them. It was their all-consuming passion, the subject they fed on in all they read. Their scanty news space was filled with reports of women bearing still-born children, of men being struck by lightning, of men being drowned, and of women being cut down in the prime of life. For all of which they felt disposed to thank rather than quarrel with God, to admire while they dreaded Him. They interpreted all sudden deaths as a punishment for sin, as they believed passionately that what happened to a man was his just desert; the righteous, they believed, were launched by death into paradise, the evil were launched into everlasting damnation.

The supreme example of a just desert was death by hanging. One Monday in February 1804 the New South Wales Corps was under arms to attend to the execution of an unhappy malefactor, Charles Crump, who requested permission to walk to the place of atonement, attended by the Reverend Mr Marsden, and followed by a number of spectators who joined the solemn procession. When they arrived at the place of execution, the Reverend Mr Marsden in fervent prayer supplicated the throne of mercy for an extension of remission and divine grace to an unfortunate fellow-creature then about to expiate with his life an offence for which the law required a heavy retribution. Crump then ascended the cart, and a few moments after was left suspended. The *Sydney Gazette* described him as a young man of comely appearance, whose former character was by no means a bad one, who had recently entangled himself with such infamous company that he had lost sight of his duty and fell a victim

[96] J. Cameron: *The Centenary History of the Presbyterian Church in New South Wales* (Sydney, 1905), vol. 1, pp. 2-3; J. D. Lang: *A Historical and Statistical Account of New South Wales, from the founding of the colony in 1788 to the present day* 4th ed. (London, 1875), vol. 1, pp. 77-8.

[97] *Sydney Gazette*, 22 May 1803 and 30 March 1806.

[98] *Sydney Gazette*, 19 March 1803.

to the gratification of licentious appetites. The *Gazette* hoped that the aweful spectacle might serve as a lasting warning against the prosecution of crime, and therefore effectually promote the ends of moral rectitude.[99]

They interpreted great natural disasters as a divine punishment for human sin. On 20 March 1806 there were flood warnings on the Hawkesbury as rain was falling incessantly, and the river was discoloured and rising rapidly. In the next two days the river overflowed its banks, houses were submerged under the water, while wheat-stacks, pigs, dogs, cattle and horses floated out on to the swollen waters at Pittwater. Five people lost their lives. The hand of Providence, they believed, had chastised them: and the same hand of Providence had also extended itself in many instances miraculously to save lives. Or so they thought, for the idea of God's malice never darkened their minds. They praised God, believing that everything which had breath should praise the Lord. For them it was man who was vile. What they noticed in this disaster was the behaviour of unprincipled vagabonds pillaging private property, and thereby converting to their own depraved inclinations the most dreadful as well as the general disaster that had ever befallen this or any other so extensive settlement.[100]

The floods struck late in March 1806. In April King read first in the London newspapers, and then in a despatch, of His Majesty's entire approbation of his conduct as well as His Majesty's satisfaction at the great improvement of the colony under his superintendence. In the same despatch he read that his successor had sailed for New South Wales.[1] On 7 August, William Bligh arrived at Sydney on the *Lady Sinclair*, and took the oaths as Captain-General and Governor-in-Chief of the colony of New South Wales and its dependencies on 13 August. The next day George Johnston, for the military, Richard Atkins, for the civil officers, and John Macarthur presented King with an address in which they respectfully entreated him to accept their unfeigned wishes for his health, happiness and prosperity as well as a hope that His Majesty would duly appreciate his services. To which King replied on the same day, thanking them for their good wishes and hoping that their arduous exertions would forward the interests and establish the respectability of a colony whose prosperity would always be nearest the heart of their most obedient and faithful well-wisher, Philip Gidley King.[2] As he waited for his ship less worthy thoughts darkened his mind: he was piqued that he had heard of his successor from the newspapers; he wondered if his work would be adequately recognized; he wondered, too, whether the government would make him an *ex-gratia* payment to cover his losses during his term of office. He had seen himself earlier as the man who had reduced administrative expenditure, lowered prices, and gone a long way towards abolishing the monopoly of the officers and the traffic in

[99] *Sydney Gazette*, 26 February 1804.

[100] Ibid., 6 April 1806.

[1] Castlereagh to King, 20 November 1805, and encl. in Secretary Marsden to King, November 1805, *H.R.A.*, I, 5, pp. 623-4; Castlereagh to King, 13 July 1805, *H.R.A.*, I, 5, p. 489.

[2] *Sydney Gazette*, 24 August 1806.

spirits.[3] For King, on the eve of his departure, was preoccupied with what belonged to the dustbin of history, and was unaware that the developments in trade and sheep-breeding to which his own contribution had not been negligible had laid the material foundations of a civilization in both New South Wales and Van Diemen's Land. At two o'clock on the afternoon of Sunday 10 February 1807 he and his family embarked on the *Buffalo* after King had expressed his most sensible regret at taking leave. Half an hour later, to a salute from the *Porpoise*, the *Buffalo* sailed out on to the high seas with King's mind still on that material recognition for his services.[4] On his return to London he sent Castlereagh abstracts of the administration during his term as Governor.[5] His strength, however, had been so undermined by the severe attacks of gout which had wasted his powers since the days on Norfolk Island, that he died on 3 September 1808 before any official recognition of his nineteen years of service to the colony of New South Wales and its dependencies had been made.

[3] King to Camden, 15 March 1806, *H.R.A.*, I, 5, p. 642 et seq.
[4] *Sydney Gazette*, 15 February 1807.
[5] King to Castlereagh, 11 December 1807, *H.R.A.*, I, 5, p. 788 et seq.

II

BLIGH

FRIDAY, 8 August 1806, was a day of public rejoicing at Sydney Cove. At nine o'clock in the morning the New South Wales Corps and the loyal association marched out under arms, with the colours of the regiment flying, to line the avenue leading from Government Wharf to Government House. At ten, to a salute of fifteen guns, William Bligh left the *Lady Sinclair* to go to the *Porpoise* and *Buffalo*, on both of which he was honoured with a salute of guns. Then Philip Gidley King, attended by his civil staff, marched from Government House to Government Wharf, and received the military honours due to his rank. At the wharf the two men met and, after an exchange of compliments, repassed the line, when the same military honours were repeated in compliment to Bligh. On arriving at Government House, King presented Bligh to the civil and military officers: Bligh shook hands with Richard Atkins, Samuel Marsden, and two of his future opponents, Major Johnston and John Macarthur. At least one observer was extremely happy to state that Bligh was accompanied by his amiable daughter, Mrs Putland, a circumstance which conveyed the greatest pleasure, and could not, he believed, fail to be attended with the most beneficial consequences.[1] That night the Reverend Samuel Marsden went down on his knees with his usual fervour, to render thanks and praise to Almighty God for the great benefits he had received at His hands, and to ask for His blessing on the colony.

Bligh was then almost fifty-two years old. In stature he was short. His form erred on the side of the corpulent, but not from over-indulgence in food or drink, for he was neither a glutton nor a drunkard, being by nature temperate in all the passions of the flesh. On his cheek was a scar inflicted by his father who, when Bligh was young, had thrown a hatchet to turn a horse but struck his son instead.[2] He was born on 9 September 1754, probably at Plymouth. He entered the navy at the age of seven as servant to an officer, became an A.B. in 1770, a midshipman in 1771, and in March of 1776 was appointed by Cook to be master of the *Resolution* because of his promise and his talents.[3] At the Hawaiian Islands on 14 February 1779, an infatuated belief in his immunity to destruction had rendered Cook so deaf to the cries and entreaties of those who were imploring him to return to his ship and

[1] *Sydney Gazette*, 10 August 1806.
[2] G. Mackaness: *The Life of Vice-Admiral William Bligh*, new and rev. ed., (Sydney, 1951), p. 188, n. 7, and p. 530.
[3] Ibid., pp 3-8.

escape the vengeance of the natives, that the natives rushed on him with clubs and stones and murdered him.[4] Bligh spent that day neither reflecting on how overweening pride and arrogance could bring even the giants of this world to destruction, nor, as did other eye witnesses, in moralizing on the treachery of natives to representatives of a higher civilization.[5] That day Bligh was angry with King for believing his association with Cook would ensure his immortality, and with Lieutenant Phillips because he had done nothing but eat and sleep the whole voyage.[6]

After his return to London on the *Resolution* in 1780 he visited the Isle of Man, where he met Richard Betham, who introduced him to his daughter Elizabeth, whom Bligh married on 4 February 1781. Through his wife's uncle, Duncan Campbell, the contractor for transporting convicts to North America and the West Indies, Bligh obtained a position on ships sailing between England and the West Indies. On one such voyage one of the members of his crew was Fletcher Christian, who found Bligh very passionate, but flattered himself he knew how to humour him.[7] Campbell owned a ship called the *Bethia*; he also had an interest in providing bread-fruit to the West Indian islands. When, in 1787, the Royal Society for Promoting Arts and Commerce offered a gold medal for the first person to convey six plants of one or both species of the bread-fruit tree in a growing state to the islands of the West Indies, Bligh was offered the command of Campbell's ship, which was to be renamed the *Bounty*; one of the officers was Fletcher Christian. They sailed from Spithead on 28 November 1787. Near Tahiti, in April 1789, exasperated by the rages and the discipline of Bligh, a section of the crew of the *Bounty* led by John Adams and Fletcher Christian, seized Bligh in his cabin and put him in a long boat with his supporters, provisions and a compass. When Bligh asked Fletcher Christian if this treatment was a proper return for the friendship he had shown him in the West Indian days, Christian answered with much emotion: 'That—Captain Bligh,—that is the thing; —I am in hell—I am in hell.'[8]

It was not in Bligh's range to respond to such a remark. For him the mutineers were a set of sailors, most of them void of connections, led astray by the inducements of one of the finest islands in the world, where they did not need to labour, and where the allurements of dissipation were beyond anything that could be conceived.[9] In all this he discerned a moral about human nature, but not about himself. With that courage and determination

---

[4] W. Ellis: *An Authentic Narrative of a Voyage performed by Captain Cook and Captain Clerke* . . . (London, 1782), vol. 2, pp. 108-9.

[5] Anon.: *Journal of Captain Cook's Last Voyage to the Pacific Ocean* (London, 1781), p. 320.

[6] For extracts from the journal Bligh kept during the voyage, see G. Mackaness: op. cit., pp. 24-5.

[7] G. Mackaness: op. cit., p. 33.

[8] W. Bligh: *A Voyage to the South Sea, undertaken by command of His Majesty, for the purpose of conveying the Bread-Fruit Tree to the West Indies, in His Majesty's Ship the Bounty* (London, 1792), p. 161.

[9] Ibid., p. 162.

which he always displayed in the face of adversity, he sailed his long boat from Kotoo Island to the north-east coast of Australia, negotiated the Great Barrier Reef, and Torres Strait, and sailed on to Timor. There he sat down to write tenderly to his wife about his experiences, telling her of the emotion he felt in his heart and soul now that he once more had an opportunity of writing to her and his little angels, more particularly as they had all been so near losing the best of friends, when they would have had no person to regard them as he did, and they might have spent the rest of their days not knowing what had happened to him, as he might have been starved to death at sea or destroyed by Indians. All these dreadful circumstances he had combated with success and in the most extraordinary manner, never despairing from the first moment of his disaster but that he should overcome all his difficulties. 'Know then, my own dear Betsy,' he confessed, 'I have lost the *Bounty*.'[10] That was all his pride would permit him to tell his beloved Betsy and his little angels about the terrible humiliations and disgrace of losing his ship. When he arrived back in Portsmouth on ·14 March 1790 he wrote in his diary how it had pleased God that of the nineteen forced by the mutineers into the launch, twelve should surmount the difficulties and dangers of the voyage, and live to revisit their native country.[11]

For a while life flowed smoothly for Bligh. When he returned from his second voyage to collect bread-fruit, the crew cheered him heartily when he quitted the ship. At the mutiny at the Nore he was not one of the commanders removed for excessive severity to his crew. In February 1805, however, Bligh was tried for grossly insulting and ill-treating Lieutenant John Frazier publicly on the quarter-deck and generally for tyrannical, oppressive and un-officer-like conduct. He was reprimanded and admonished to be more circumspect and more correct in his language.[12] A month later, when Joseph Banks was asked whether he knew a man whose integrity was unimpeached, with a mind capable of providing its own resources in difficulties without leaning on others for advice, firm in discipline, civil in deportment and not subject to whimper and whine when severity of discipline was wanted to meet emergencies, he immediately answered he knew of no one but Captain Bligh who would suit. When he told this to Bligh, he added that if Bligh accepted he would live like a prince and have a chance of marrying his daughters more suitably than in England.[13] In this way Bligh became Captain-General and Governor-in-Chief of the colony of New South Wales, to exercise that important duty free from the spirit of party, and sailed for Sydney Cove on the *Lady Sinclair* in a convoy of ships under Captain Short on the naval ship *Porpoise* in February 1806.

Within a few days after sailing Short fired a warning shot across the bows of the *Lady Sinclair* because Bligh had ignored Short's orders on the course to

[10] Quoted in G. Mackaness: op. cit., p. 163.

[11] W. Bligh: op. cit., p. 264.

[12] Navy Black Book. Quoted in the *Australian Genealogist*, vol. 3, pt. 1, January 1939, p. 3.

[13] G. Mackaness: op. cit., p. 353.

be taken. Again Bligh was enraged, and called Short a specious and low character, a wicked and most violent man, a most irritating and insulting person.[14] They landed at Sydney Cove on 8 August 1806 to general rejoicing in the colony, while Bligh's mind was still consumed with his feud with Short, a dispute which he pursued with such tedious and petty ardour that he attempted to prevent Short landing from the *Porpoise*.[15] On 14 August, Richard Atkins administered to him the oaths of office, when Bligh swore, as all his predecessors had done before him, that he would preserve the Protestant succession, prevent dangers from popish recusants, observe the laws relating to trade and plantations, that he would display amity and kindness towards the aborigines, grant land, encourage religion, preserve subordination in society, and endeavour to educate the children of the convicts in religious as well as industrious habits.[16] On the same day George Johnston for the military, Richard Atkins for the civil officers and John Macarthur for the free inhabitants presented Bligh with an address of congratulation. A few weeks later Bligh received a second address from one hundred and thirty-five free inhabitants of Sydney, in which they repudiated Macarthur's right to speak for the free inhabitants, and accused him of being responsible for the high price of mutton by withholding a large flock of wethers from the market till the prices rose. At the same time a further two hundred and forty-four inhabitants sent another address to Bligh also repudiating Macarthur as spokesman for the free.[17] It so happened that at the same time Macarthur met Bligh at Government House, Parramatta, and moved the conversation round to sheep, whereupon Bligh exploded and asked him what he, Bligh, had to do with his sheep, sir, and what had he to do with his cattle, sir and was Macarthur to have such flocks of sheep and such herds of cattle as no man heard of before, and though Macarthur, sir, had five thousand acres of land in the finest situation in the country, by God sir, he would not keep it. King wept.[18] What Macarthur thought might be guessed from a remark in a letter Mrs Macarthur wrote to a friend in England, in which she described Bligh as violent, rash and tyrannical.[19]

Like his predecessors, Hunter and King, Bligh was appalled by the condition of the colony, and told Windham in London that in the customs and manners of the people much was to be corrected.[20] He was convinced that the immediate economic future lay in the encouragement of agriculture rather than in the development of the wool trade or the Bass Strait and over-

[14] Bligh to Banks, n.d., quoted in ibid., p. 358.

[15] Windham to Bligh, 30 December 1806, *H.R.A.*, I, 6, p. 80.

[16] *H.R.A.*, I, 6, pp. 1-19.

[17] The texts of these petitions are in the *H.R.N.S.W.*, vol. 6, pp. 188-92.

[18] S. M. Onslow (ed.): *Some Early Records of the Macarthurs of Camden* (Sydney, 1914), pp. 137-8; and evidence of J. Macarthur, in *Proceedings of a General Court-Martial . . . for the trial of Lieut. Col. Geo. Johnston . . . on a Charge of Mutiny . . .* (London, 1811), pp. 178-9.

[19] Mrs Macarthur to Miss Kingdon, 29 January 1807, S. M. Onslow (ed.): op. cit., p. 137.

[20] Bligh to Windham, 5 November 1806, *H.R.A.*, I, 6, pp. 26-7.

seas trade, or in manufactures, for they were extremely trifling.[21] He educated the farmers in methods of soil conservation; he taught them to sow rye
and clover grass to improve their pastures and, to the delight and approval
of the farmers on the Hawkesbury, and near Parramatta and Sydney, spoke
and wrote of them as the backbone of society in New South Wales;[22] those
with interests in wool, such as Macarthur, or trade, such as Simeon Lord,
were understandably less enthusiastic.

The man to whom he addressed these despatches, William Windham, was
described by his contemporaries as the model of a true English gentleman.
He was born in 1750 of an old family in Norfolk. In the country he was
fond of field sports and of all manly exercises. In the town he delighted in
the pursuits of a scholar, and sought the company of men of distinction in
the literary world. As Samuel Johnson lay dying, Mr Windham placed a
pillow conveniently to support him. Johnson thanked him and said it would
do all that a pillow could do. To all public and private affairs he brought a high
and chivalrous sense of humour.[23] Windham took over the seals of office in
1806, but by the time Bligh was engulfed in his whirlpool the chivalrous Mr
Windham had been replaced by a man with ice in his heart, Robert Stewart,
Viscount Castlereagh.

At the same time Bligh took steps to improve moral standards. Although
he did not subscribe to the view of one moralist that all preferment of place
and wealth in the colony was to be obtained through harlots,[24] he did con-
clude that the bartering in spirits was the root of much evil. In a tour through
the colony he lamented to find that the most calamitous evils had been produced
by the system of barter and the habit of paying in spirits for grain of all
kinds and the necessaries of life in general, and to labourers for their hire.
Such proceedings were depressing the industrious, and depriving the settlers
of their comforts. To remedy these grievous complaints, he issued general
orders to prohibit the exchange of spirits or other liquors as payment for grain,
animal food, labour, wearing apparel, or any other commodity whatever to
all descriptions of persons in the colony and its dependencies. For a breach
of the order a prisoner was to receive one hundred lashes and twelve months'
hard labour, an emancipist was to be deprived of all indulgences from the
crown and sentenced to three months' imprisonment and a fine of twenty
pounds, and a free settler, or any other free inhabitant, masters of ships, or
any other persons on board ships or vessels, were to lose all indulgences
granted by the crown and pay a fine of fifty pounds, a portion of which was
to be granted to the informer. The order ended with an appeal to all the

[21] Bligh to Windham, 7 February 1807, *H.R.A.*, I, 6, pp. 121-3.

[22] Bligh to Windham, 31 October 1807, *H.R.A.*, I, 6, pp. 146-7.

[23] P. H. Stanhope: *Life of the Right Honourable William Pitt* (London, 1861-2),
vol. 2, pp. 251-2; J. Boswell: *The Life of Samuel Johnson* (London, 1867), pp. 442,
487 and 490.

[24] Anon.: 'Present State of the Colony of New South Wales, related to me February 14, 1809, by the Rev. Mr. Marsden, the Chaplain' in E. H. Barker (ed.):
*Geographic, Commercial and Political Essays; including statistic details of various
countries* (London, 1812), p. 185.

civil and military officers to assist in carrying it into execution, because it would tend to relieve the distresses of the people, and give credit and stability to the settlement at large. That was on 14 February 1807.[25]

A month earlier, the Reverend Samuel Marsden, being aware, as he put it, that a great political storm was fast gathering in the colony, sought an interview with Bligh in which he prophesied such an upheaval. When Bligh replied that he fully relied on the authority of His Majesty's commission to protect him, Marsden added that he could not believe that so many among the rising generation who were strangers to the fear of God would honour the commands of the King. Marsden, discerning in the turn of events yet another of those highly favourable dispensations of Providence towards himself, decided to use the opportunity both to gratify his desire to preach the gospel in New Zealand as well as to secure his own quiet, by asking for leave of absence from the colony.[26] So Marsden sailed away from trouble in the *Buffalo* on 8 February 1807, bearing with him Bligh's recommendation that he was an authority on the nature and soil of the colony[27] while, purblind as ever to the fruits of his own behaviour, Bligh paid no heed to the warning.

As far as he could see material conditions were improving.[28] He was not altogether happy about the colonists' morals; the expirees were still addicted to their vicious habits; the emancipists could not be expected to advance to morality until the next or later generations; the free settlers were a thoughtless set of people addicted to liquor and disposed to get in debt; the larger settlers, such as the Blaxlands, only thought of making money. The acting Judge Advocate, Atkins, was so accustomed to inebriety that he had become the ridicule of the community; he had pronounced sentences of death in moments of intoxication, his determination was weak, and his opinion floating and infirm.[29] The inhabitants in general were contented, except for a very few who had been in the habit of turning everything to their own interest.[30] In Bligh's mind they were clearly negligible and of no account. That was in October 1807.

By that time Bligh was known as Caligula to some people in Sydney. Some were angered by the ruthless changes he had introduced at Government House and the surrounding area. Shrubs replaced lawns; the tomb of a young officer was annihilated; all the rocks in the garden were blown up and carried away; carriage roads were constructed on Bennelong Point and Farm Cove; all dogs were ordered to be shot; in July 1807 a row of houses occupied by emancipists was ordered to be demolished at the cost of what looked like the total ruin of the wretches who inhabited them. Some were disgusted by the vile, abusive and degrading language which Bligh used to the prisoners and other vagrants. Some were nauseated by the pleasure Bligh seemed to

25 *Sydney Gazette*, 15 February 1807.

26 J. R. Elder (ed.): *The Letters and Journals of Samuel Marsden, 1765-1838* (Dunedin, 1932), p. 42.

27 Bligh to Windham, 7 February 1807, *H.R.A.*, I, 6, p. 123.

28 Bligh to Windham, 31 October 1807, *H.R.A.*, I, 6, p. 160.

29 Ibid., pp. 148-50.

30 Ibid., p. 160.

derive from signing a death warrant. Some were repelled by what appeared to be his singular lack of generosity in the use of the power to pardon, for under his government only two men were pardoned. If anyone dared to object or remonstrate with him, he lost his senses and his speech, his features became distorted, he foamed at the mouth, stamped on the ground, shook his fist in the face of the person so presuming, and uttered a torrent of abuse in language disgraceful to him as a governor, an officer and a man. On 28 September 1807 when Bligh complained that vile wretches of soldiers had laughed at his daughter in the church on Sunday, Lieutenant Minchin explained they were laughing at a drummer putting a feather in a cap. Bligh got warm and swore that if any dared to offer him an insult he would have his head off as they might as well say the drummer had put a feather into the man's ——![31] People who had had such an experience were inclined to agree with Mrs Macarthur that there was a tyranny in the land, that liberty had retired into the pathless wilds amongst the poor native inhabitants.[32]

Not all of the colonists of New South Wales shared these views. As late as January 1807 eight hundred and thirty-three people, including such diverse people as Richard Atkins, Robert Campbell, John Palmer the commissary, Henry Fulton the acting chaplain-general, Andrew Thompson the emancipist farmer and merchant on the Hawkesbury, Rowland Hassall—Marsden's agent during his voyage to London, and George Crossley the emancipist attorney, signed an address to Bligh in which they eulogized the extensive rising greatness and enterprising spirits of the colonists over which Bligh governed, how they rested their welfare and their desires in the fullest confidence in his wisdom and goodness to direct, and how they prayed for a long continuance of His Excellency's happy and benign government.[33] By then, Bligh had had the singular folly to convince both Simeon Lord and John Macarthur that the comparison with Caligula was not inept.

On 10 August Simeon Lord, together with his business associates, Kable and Underwood, wrote to Bligh for permission to trans-ship goods from the *Commerce* to the *Sydney Cove* without landing them. Bligh, suspicious as ever of any request to evade the letter of the regulations, not only refused permission but prosecuted Lord, Kable and Underwood on 11 August before a special bench of magistrates for writing a letter couched in improper terms, and highly derogatory to His Excellency's high rank and authority. The bench dutifully returned a verdict of guilty, ordered each of them to be imprisoned for one calendar month, and pay a fine of one hundred pounds. On that day Richard Atkins, as Judge Advocate, wrote out an order to the common gaoler in Sydney, Daniel McKay, to receive into his custody Messrs

[31] Surgeon Harris to Mrs King, 25 October 1807, *H.R.N.S.W.*, vol. 6, pp. 342-9; Surgeon Harris to P. G. King, 25 October 1807, *H.R.N.S.W.*, vol. 6, pp. 336-42; Lieutenant Minchin to P. G. King, 20 October 1807, *H.R.N.S.W.*, vol. 6, p. 331; J. Blaxland to the Earl of Liverpool, 27 November 1809, *H.R.N.S.W.*, vol. 7, pp. 230-8; *H.R.N.S.W.*, vol. 6, pp. 588-9.

[32] Mrs Macarthur to Miss Kingdon, 21 October 1807, S. M. Onslow (ed.): op. cit., p. 137.

[33] The Address of the Settlers to Governor Bligh, 1 January 1807, *H.R.N.S.W.*, vol. 6, pp. 410-11.

Lord, Kable and Underwood for one calendar month.[34] In this way Lord, whose business interests in sealing and whaling in the south seas and trade in salt pork in the Pacific islands Bligh had snubbed earlier, had the mortifying experience of being reduced once again to the company of common criminals by the same arbitrary behaviour.

In October, as Bligh read through the manifest of the ship *Dart*, he noticed that two stills had been imported by John Macarthur and Edward Abbott. With his usual punctilious attention to detail, Bligh ordered that the stills should be returned to bond. Whereupon Macarthur asked that he be allowed to appropriate the copper on the stills to some domestic use. Again Bligh refused, and ordered Robert Campbell junior, the nephew of Robert Campbell, to take possession of the stills, which he did on 22 October. Macarthur then sued Campbell for removing two copper boilers from his house contrary to the laws of the realm. When the case began in Sydney on 24 October, Major Johnston, the commander of the New South Wales Corps, Judge Advocate Atkins, and Palmer, the commissary, were on the bench. With that high seriousness and fanaticism which characterized all his actions when his interests were threatened, Macarthur had elevated a question of trespass into a question of fundamental rights, and told the court it was for them to determine whether this was the tenure on which Englishmen held their property in New South Wales. Johnston and Atkins found for Macarthur: Palmer found for Campbell.[35]

At the same time Bligh took another action which convinced his supporters that his government was just if not gracious, and confirmed them in their hope that God would long continue it.[36] He dismissed D'Arcy Wentworth from his position of surgeon to the hospital for alleged corrupt practices.[37] His opponents, the ones who had suffered the rages and the torrents of abuse, again likened Bligh to the despots of old. When the armed schooner *Parramatta* returned to Sydney Cove in December 1807, a board consisting of Bligh, Atkins and Campbell decided that the owners must forfeit their bond of £900 for leaving Sydney Cove earlier with an escaped convict on board. Macarthur, who was a part owner of the *Parramatta*, then announced he had abandoned the ship. When the crew came ashore to obtain rations, Atkins wrote to Macarthur to ask him to appear in Sydney to show cause why the crew had violated the regulations by coming ashore. Macarthur refused. Whereupon Atkins issued a warrant to the chief constable at Parramatta to arrest Macarthur and charge him before a bench of magistrates on 15 December with illegally stopping the provisions of the crew of the *Parramatta*, thereby compelling them to come on shore contrary to the regulations. When the chief constable, Oakes, served the warrant on Macarthur, Macarthur told him in a great rage to inform the persons who had sent him that he, Macarthur, would never submit to the horrid tyranny that was attempted until he was

---

[34] S. Lord and Co. to Bligh, 10 August 1807, *H.R.N.S.W.*, vol. 6, pp. 277-8.

[35] Bligh to Windham, 31 October 1807, *H.R.A.*, I, 6, p. 160 and encl. no. 11 in ibid., *H.R.A.*, I, 6, pp. 174-8.

[36] *H.R.N.S.W.*, vol. 6, pp. 410-11.

[37] Bligh to Windham, 31 October 1807, *H.R.A.*, I, 6, p. 188.

forced; that he would consider it with scorn and contempt, as he considered the persons who had directed it to be executed; that he had been robbed of ten thousand pounds; that he had not committed a criminal act; but to let his accusers alone, because they would soon make a rope to hang themselves.[38]

Oakes returned to Sydney to swear before a bench of magistrates about the contemptuous and disrespectful manner in which Macarthur had treated the warrant. Whereupon the bench issued a second warrant to the chief constables at Sydney and Parramatta and all other His Majesty's peace officers and all others whom it might concern, to take into their custody the body of the said John Macarthur, Esq., and lodge him safely in His Majesty's gaol until he should be discharged by due course of law. On 16 December, Macarthur, who in the meantime had proceeded to Sydney, was arrested; he promptly appealed for bail, which was granted after the court had heard from Oakes that Macarthur had used the Governor's name with a great deal of disrespect.[39] The night before the trial began, the son of John Macarthur, several of his partisans, and the six military officers appointed to try him for inciting the people to hatred and contempt of the government and certain high misdemeanours, dined together at a public dinner, with the band of the regiment playing till a late hour.[40] When the trial began on 25 January 1808, Macarthur asked that Atkins should step down from the bench, because a suit was pending between them, because Atkins had cherished a rancorous inveteracy against him for many years, because he was the victim of the vindictive malice of Atkins, and because Atkins was a swindler. When Atkins refused to budge, Macarthur told the court they had to decide whether law and justice should finally prevail against the contrivances of the convict attorney George Crossley, for in his eyes the reputable were then on trial before the disreputable in some low mockery of justice. The eyes of an anxious public, he told the members of the bench, were upon them: the public were trembling for the safety of their property, their liberty, and their lives; to them had fallen the lot of deciding a point which perhaps involved the happiness or misery of millions yet unborn. He conjured them in the name of Almighty God, in Whose presence they stood, to consider the inestimable value of the precious deposit with which they were now entrusted. The court broke up in confusion.

The following day was 26 January, the anniversary of the foundation of the colony, a day traditionally observed by the soldiers, the emancipists, the expirees and the convicts in drinking and merriment. Early that morning the soldiers, whom in a moment of great foolishness Bligh had described as wretches, adding that if any one of the villains offered him an insult he would have the man's head off, paraded in their barracks as usual. Early that same morning Macarthur was arrested on an escape warrant and placed in Sydney gaol. At ten, the six military officers who had sat with Atkins on the bench on the previous day asked Bligh to restore Macarthur to bail, and appoint an

[38] *H.R.N.S.W.*, vol. 6, pp. 471-7.

[39] Ibid., pp. 476-7.

[40] Ibid., p. 432.

impartial person as Judge Advocate to replace Atkins. Bligh consulted Atkins, who hastily wrote a memorandum which summarized events and concluded by accusing the six military officers—Anthony Fenn Kemp, John Brabyn, William Moore, Thomas Laycock, William Minchin, and William Lawson— of committing crimes which amounted to a usurpation of His Majesty's government, and tended to incite or create rebellion or other outrageous treason in the people of this territory. Bligh then wrote a note to each of the six military officers informing them they were charged with certain crimes, and requiring them to appear at Government House at nine on the following morning.

Bligh also sent a note to Major Johnston, who had asked to be excused from coming to Sydney as he was scarcely able to move because of a violent hurt received when a gig overturned. In the note, Bligh mentioned the Atkins' memorial against the six military officers for practices deemed to be treasonable. When Johnston received this note at four in the afternoon he set off for Sydney, the communication of such extraordinary measures occasioning a temporary forgetfulness of his bruises. He arrived at five, assumed the title of Lieutenant-Governor, and, as Lieutenant-Governor and major commanding the New South Wales Corps, signed an order to the keeper of His Majesty's gaol in Sydney requiring and directing him to deliver into the custody of Garnham Blaxcell and Nicholas Bayly the body of John Macarthur, on the grounds that the bail entered into by those two remained in full force. Macarthur went to Barrack Square where he wrote this letter to Johnston:

Sir,
      The present alarming state of this colony, in which every man's property, liberty and life is endangered, induces us most earnestly to implore you instantly to place Governor Bligh under an arrest and to assume the command of the colony. We pledge ourselves, at a moment of less agitation, to come forward to support the measure with our fortunes and our lives.

We are, with great respect, Sir,
Your most obedient servants

Jno. Macarthur	Gregory Blaxland
Jno. Blaxland	James Badgery
James Mileham	Nicholas Bayly
S. Lord.	

and upwards of one hundred other inhabitants of all descriptions, whom Bligh later described as coming from the worst class of life.[41] At the same time martial law was proclaimed to be in force until such time as the civil government could be restored on a permanent foundation.[42]

Johnston wrote to Bligh to tell him he had been called upon to execute a most painful duty, as Bligh had been charged by the most respectable inhabitants of crimes that rendered him unfit to exercise the supreme authority for another moment in the colony, and as in that charge all the officers under his command concurred, he therefore required Bligh in His Majesty's sacred name to resign his authority, and to submit to that arrest under which he was

[41] Ibid., p. 434.
[42] Ibid.

placing him by the advice of all the officers and by the advice of every respectable inhabitant in the town of Sydney.[43] When Bligh refused, John Macarthur, John and Gregory Blaxland, James Mileham, Simeon Lord, some soldiers, and a band of the curious who were probably seeking revenge for the insults and the abuse as well as those who delighted to see the mighty taken down from their seat, entered Government House to find Atkins with a glass in his hand, Robert Campbell behaving with dignity, and Bligh in a situation, according to Johnston, three months later, too disgraceful to be mentioned. This suggestion understandably caused Bligh to burn with indignation. The three were arrested. That evening Johnston announced the arrest, and told the inhabitants of Sydney and Parramatta that in future they were to obey him. All night the carousing, the cheering, and the singing went on in Barrack Square, while no one so much as lifted a finger to help Bligh, as he raged into the night, impotent and alone except for the company of his faithful daughter, and his secretary, Griffin.

The next day the secretary to his honour the Lieutenant-Governor, Nicholas Bayly, announced that Atkins had been replaced by Edward Abbott as Judge Advocate; that A. F. Kemp, J. Harris, T. Jamison, C. Grimes, W. Minchin, G. Blaxland, J. Blaxland and A. Bell had been appointed magistrates in place of the existing ones, who were to consider themselves dismissed; that J. Palmer the commissary and R. Campbell the naval officer and collector of taxes, were also dismissed. On the same day the public peace being happily and, he trusted in Almighty God, permanently established, Nicholas Bayly proclaimed the cessation of martial law. In future, he continued, no man would have just cause to complain of violence, injustice or oppression; no free man would be taken, imprisoned, or deprived of his house, land, or liberty but by the law; justice would be impartially administered, without regard to or respect of persons; and every man would enjoy the fruits of his industry in security. As for the soldiers, their conduct had endeared them to every well-disposed inhabitant in the settlement.[44] On that day, too, eighty-three officers and private individuals wrote to Johnston to hail him as the protector of their property, their liberty, their lives, and their reputation.[45]

It was also arranged that the trial of John Macarthur would resume from the point when the proceedings in the court had broken up in confusion and disorder two days earlier. It soon became clear, however, that Bligh and his accomplices were actually on trial rather than Macarthur. Atkins, in a desperate effort to win the favour if not the respect of the new men in high places, began by making a candid offer to disclose every improper measure he had been forced to sanction through being completely under the influence of the Governor and of the wickedness in Government House. He testified how Bligh had stooped so low as to use the services of George Crossley, a man who had been convicted of wilful and corrupt perjury, and whose conduct was notorious during his residence in this country. So Atkins paid his price to

---

[43] Johnston to Bligh, 26 January 1808, *H.R.N.S.W.*, vol. 6, p. 434.

[44] *H.R.N.S.W.*, vol. 6, pp. 453-4.

[45] Ibid., pp. 454-5.

win the respect of the man who despised him as a drunkard.[46] The court of six officers, with Charles Grimes as Acting Judge Advocate, unanimously and fully acquitted Macarthur of all the charges laid in the information against him and fully discharged him.[47] On 30 January, a government order announced that C. Grimes would act as Judge Advocate as E. Abbott had declined the post; that H. Fulton was suspended from performing his function as chaplain; and that the civil and military officers were ordered, and any well disposed person requested, to attend divine service on Sunday 7 February, when they would all join in thanks to Almighty God for His interposition in their favour by relieving them without bloodshed from the awful situation in which they stood before the memorable twenty-sixth.[48]

On that Sunday they meekly went down on their knees while Crook, the missionary from Tahiti, read a special prayer for divine blessing on Johnston composed by Macarthur for the occasion. On the following day, when the soldiers and the towns-people were filled with liquor, a bellman was heard crying in the streets that a meeting would be held in the church that night to celebrate victory. All the leaders attended: John Macarthur, Simeon Lord, Nicholas Bayly, Gregory Blaxland, Edward Macarthur, William Minchin, and Garnham Blaxcell. Bayly, Blaxcell and Lord proposed that a sword should be given to Major Johnston, not under the value of one hundred guineas, for the wise and salutary measures which he had adopted to suppress the tyranny which had ruled their country, with a vote of thanks added to their motion. The meeting passed a vote of thanks to the members of the New South Wales Corps for their spirited conduct, and another vote of thanks to John Macarthur as having been chiefly instrumental in bringing about the happy change which had taken place, and then elected Macarthur as their delegate to present their case to the British government. Amidst vociferous cheering and drunken enthusiasm Macarthur rose to his feet to call Bligh's supporters a band of bloody-minded and blood-thirsty butchers and villains who wanted to drink his blood, but of policy or principle he could say nothing beyond repeating platitudes or such catch-cry words as liberty, property and life, all of which were greeted with thunderous applause. The night ended in drunkenness while the shouts, the hurrahs, the stamping and the clapping wafted over to Government House where Bligh spent an anxious night expecting violence every hour.[49] For it never occurred to Bligh to reassure himself through such a ghastly night that his being alive was the best asset Macarthur had, as by his actions he was bound to provide abundant evidence of the case for his deposition.

Within a week a canny Scot, to whom Macarthur had granted a licence to sell spirits, had erected a sign outside his premises showing Major Johnston with one foot on a snake and his sword through it, and a female figure

[46] Encl. no. 9 and no. 16 in Johnston to Castlereagh, 11 April 1808, *H.R.A.*, I, 6, p. 279, and p. 317. For the examination of the accomplices of Bligh by the officers, which probably began on the night of 26 January, see *H.R.N.S.W.*, vol. 6, pp. 435-53.

[47] Encl. no. 16 in Johnston to Castlereagh, 11 April 1808, *H.R.A.*, I, 6, p. 352.

[48] *H.R.N.S.W.*, vol. 6, p. 458.

[49] Bligh to Castlereagh, 30 June 1808, *H.R.A.*, I, 6, pp. 530-2.

presenting a cap of liberty to the highlander. On the reverse, the sign read: 'The ever memorable 26th of January, 1808.' Another man wrote on the inside wall of his house: 'Success to Major George Johnston; may he live for ever! Our Deliverer and the Suppressor of Tyrants.'[50]

On 17 February, D'Arcy Wentworth was acquitted on the charges of improper practices, and restored to his position in the hospital at Parramatta. Such spoils of office as were in the gift of the victors were distributed amongst their supporters, who also clamoured for grants of land, but Johnston was in no hurry to satisfy such greed. At the same time the supporters of the vanquished were punished. For asserting that the officers who had taken part in the arrest of Bligh would be capitally punished for their traitorous behaviour, Sir Henry Brown Hayes was sent to the coal mines.[51]

In the meantime, news of the arrest began to spread abroad. On 1 March, the Reverend Knopwood was lying very ill in his bed at Hobart Town when three non-commissioned officers called from Port Dalrymple and gave him the information that there was a new government at Port Jackson; and at one o'clock on the same day Lieutenant-Governor Collins and Lieutenant Lord called on him to discuss the news.[52] By September the news had reached London. The Reverend Samuel Marsden had no hesitation in blaming Macarthur for the upheaval, as his great wealth gave him influence, and his unbounded ambition made him turbulent and his natural ability dangerous to the government. What bothered Marsden was that as the rebels had silenced the only clergyman, there were eight thousand British subjects without any person duly authorized to perform the sacred rites of religion. He could not estimate the evils which would arise from such a melancholy situation; for himself he was happy to be in the land of liberty where the violent hand of oppression could do him no injury.[53] At the same time he wrote off in haste to Castlereagh to express his apprehensions lest his property should have received injury during the late commotion in New South Wales.[54] By that time Castlereagh had a more difficult problem on his hands than the protection of the property of the Reverend Samuel Marsden; he had read both Major Johnston's and Captain Bligh's explanation of the events on that memorable twenty-sixth of January.

Major Johnston had written his explanation on 11 April. For him the case for deposing Bligh was threefold: Bligh had betrayed the high trust and confidence reposed in him by his sovereign, and acted upon a predetermined plan to subvert the laws of the country, to terrify and influence the courts of justice, and to bereave those persons who had had the misfortune to be obnoxious to him of their fortunes, their liberty, and their lives; Bligh had to be arrested to prevent an insurrection of the inhabitants, and to secure him and

[50] Ibid., pp. 533-4.

[51] *H.R.N.S.W.*, vol. 6, p. 673.

[52] Diary of Robert Knopwood, Thursday 1 March 1808 (MS. in Royal Society of Tasmania, Hobart).

[53] Marsden to Banks, 28 September 1808 (Banks Papers vol. 20, Australia and South Sea Islands, 1774-1809, Mitchell Library).

[54] Castlereagh to Paterson, 8 October 1808, *H.R.A.*, I, 6, p. 668.

the persons he had confided in from being massacred by the incensed multitude; Bligh had engaged in an implacable feud against Macarthur. Johnston saw himself as a man who had sacrificed comparative ease, and taken on a great responsibility rather than permit His Majesty's sacred name to be profaned and dishonoured by deeds of injustice and violence.[55] Of policy he had none; for on the following day, when he wrote his first business letter to Viscount Castlereagh, he described his measures to reduce expenses and to improve the quality of the cattle, of his attentions to the needs of the large free settlers, and his regard for the trust which uncontrollable circumstances had placed in his hands.[56] The man who saw himself as called to depose a tyrant, could only repeat platitudes on economy and integrity when the time came for him to show what he affirmed.

Bligh saw it all in quite a different light. The welfare of the colony was continuing to the infinite satisfaction of every good person until 26 January. The country was becoming well cultivated: the settlers and land-holders had a market for whatever their labours produced: the convicts had become reconciled and contented in their situations as servants, feeling no oppression or wanton punishment: the people in the country could relieve their wants without being subject to the wicked monopolizing persons who heretofore had been making themselves rich on the vitals of the poor. On 1 January just on nine hundred persons had signed a dutiful address, though it should be noted that the persons who had been checked in the enormous practice of bartering spirits did not sign, nor any of the military officers. The arch-fiend John Macarthur had so inflamed the minds of these last two groups as to make them dissatisfied with the government and to trick them into misfortunes, even to his own advantage, and finally led them on to the iniquity of treason and rebellion to the state. The very breath of Macarthur was sufficient to contaminate a multitude, as the man always had been a disturber of public society and a venomous serpent to His Majesty's governors. Macarthur had overcome Bligh's predecessors with artifice: the dignity and firmness pursued by Bligh had forced him to descend to low and illiberal falsehoods and a most cowardly force of arms. He felt it was his duty to represent his thoughts that it was absolutely necessary for him to repair to England to show what measures were necessary for the security of the colony.[57]

The man to whom both Johnston and Bligh had written their despatches had a peculiar horror of mutiny. Robert Stewart, Viscount Castlereagh, who was born in 1769 in Ireland, had taken over the seals of office from Windham in March 1807. In person he was tall and handsome and much admired by both sexes. His manners were exquisitely and unfailingly courteous, though his dress, like his personal bearing, was plain and simple. He was a man of eminent ability, spotless integrity, a high sense of humour, comprehensive and enlarged views, sound practical knowledge, ready despatch of business and perfect discretion and temper in the conduct of the most arduous public

---

[55] Johnston to Castlereagh, 11 April 1808, *H.R.A.*, I, 6, pp. 208-21.
[56] Johnston to Castlereagh, 12 April 1808, *H.R.A.*, I, 6, pp. 407-10.
[57] Bligh to Castlereagh, 30 April 1808, *H.R.A.*, I, 6, pp. 420-40.

affairs. Or so his friends and supporters esteemed him.[58] Others were not so sure: 'As for my friend Lord Castlereagh,' said Lord Cornewallis, 'he is so cold that nothing can warm him.'[59] Those who abhorred his policy of repression in Ireland and England were more scathing. Byron called him an intellectual eunuch. To him Castlereagh was the most despotic in intention and the weakest in intellect that ever tyrannized over a country, and a man who deemed the chain the fit garb for man. To such a man Johnston had appealed, not knowing that no feeling dwelt in that ice when questions of law and order were involved.[60]

In the meantime, Bligh's hopes ran high. By April 1808 the people who had deposed him were hopelessly divided, and beginning to reproach each other. The free-holders and cultivators of land in the County of Cumberland, Sydney Cove and its hinterland, petitioned Johnston on 11 April to remove Macarthur from the office of Colonial Secretary as a scourge of the colony and a fermenter of quarrels between His Majesty's officers, servants and subjects, as well as the creator of a system of monopoly and extortion which had been highly injurious to the inhabitants of every description.[61] Paterson and Collins had expressed their highest indignation at the proceedings of the memorable twenty-sixth.[62] But Paterson dallied at Port Dalrymple because the rum and the gout were engaging his attention more closely than mutiny at Sydney Cove, while at Hobart Town the ageing Collins showed no inclination to allow his way of life to be disturbed.

On 28 July Lieutenant-Colonel Joseph Foveaux arrived at Sydney Cove on the *Sinclair* from England. Foveaux was senior in rank to Johnston. He was born in 1765, enlisted in the New South Wales Corps in 1789 with the rank of lieutenant, became a captain in 1792, a major in 1796 and a lieutenant-colonel in 1802. In 1800 King sent him to Norfolk Island which he left in 1803 to return to England. He was on his way back to Norfolk Island when he called at Sydney in July 1808. The convicts at Norfolk Island knew him as the man who laughed when they asked for mercy during a flogging, as a man who had ordered so many floggings for one man that his back was bare of flesh and his shoulder blades exposed like two ivory polished horns. He had also permitted the female convicts to be sold openly to free settlers and convicts, the young and attractive ones fetching as high a price as ten pounds.[63] People who mixed in Government House society in Sydney found him pleasant-looking and handsome, though very corpulent, indeed quite a man of business and extremely attentive and obliging.[64]

[58] *Dictionary of National Biography* (London, 1898), vol. 54, p. 357; A. Alison: *Lives of Lord Castlereagh and Sir Charles Stewart* (Edinburgh, 1861), *passim.*

[59] *Dictionary of National Biography*, vol. 54, p. 357.

[60] G. S. Truman (ed.): *Byron: Don Juan* (Austin, Texas, 1957), vol. 2, p. 18 and vol. 3, pp. 3-4.

[61] Encl. no. 21 in Bligh to Castlereagh, 30 June 1808, *H.R.A.*, I, 6, pp. 572-3.

[62] Bligh to Castlereagh, 30 April 1808, *H.R.A.*, I, 6, p. 438.

[63] R. Jameson Buckley: 'Recollections of 13 Years Residence in Norfolk Island and Van Diemen's Land, Sydney 1823' (note book in Mitchell Library).

[64] Ellis Bent to his mother, Sydney, 4 March 1810 (MS. letters from Ellis Bent, in National Library, Canberra).

Bligh, believing Foveaux had arrived in the colony with authority to re-instate him,[65] immediately sent three of his supporters, Griffin, Palmer and Fulton, to present his compliments to Lieutenant-Colonel Foveaux, who de-clined to see them. Foveaux, no friend of the convicts, was astonished that Bligh should send an emancipated convict on such a mission, an event which confirmed his suspicion that Bligh had been chiefly guided by persons of that class. The next day Foveaux received Johnston, Macarthur and others on board the *Sinclair*, where they presented their case with such force that Foveaux wrote to Bligh to excuse himself from taking action on the grounds that he had no authority to reinstate him. He informed Bligh that he had de-cided to keep him under house arrest, but was prepared to allow him, as Johnston had offered before, to sail to England as a prisoner on the *Porpoise*.[66] To this Bligh replied with the haughtiness and righteous indignation which had bedevilled his whole career, saying he would travel in command of His Majesty's ship *Porpoise* bearing his broad pennant, which was at the peril of anyone to tarnish or deprive him of.[67] That was on 4 August. Bligh was storming and raging at the man whom seven days earlier he had welcomed as his liberator from ignominy. Within a month Foveaux had written to Castlereagh that Bligh had so violated private property, and so tyrannized over the colonists, that nothing but his removal from the government could have prevented an insurrection, with all its attendant miseries.[68]

Within six weeks, however, Foveaux was bewailing the state of New South Wales in much the same way as all his predecessors had done. He de-nounced the traffic in liquor, the number of illicit stills, and the clandestine imports of liquor not because of its pernicious effects on behaviour, but rather on the novel grounds that through the sale of such liquor a class of persons, many of whom ought never to have been raised beyond the condition of labourers, amassed large properties in the country. The way of life of the female convicts confirmed them in the practice of vice rather than contributed to their amendment. The colony was so short of skilled labour that the cargoes of ships could not be loaded satisfactorily.[69] People of quality would not take office. He had offered the office of Judge Advocate to several people, but all had declined till, as he put it, necessity alone and not personal pre-ference had obliged him to have recourse to Mr Atkins who, after enduring as best he could the humiliation of seeing the office hawked around, was not offered the post but ordered to resume his duties.[70] While Bligh believed Foveaux was abusing his power distributing land to swell the numbers with a vested interest in the rebel cause, or distributing liquor to the plebs,

[65] Bligh to Castlereagh, 31 August 1808, *H.R.A.*, I, 6, pp. 588-9.

[66] Ibid., p. 590.

[67] Bligh to Foveaux, 4 August 1808; encl. no. 11, in Bligh to Castlereagh, 31 August 1808, *H.R.A.*, I, 6, pp. 594-5.

[68] Foveaux to Castlereagh, 4 September 1808, *H.R.A.*, I, 6, p. 624.

[69] Foveaux to Castlereagh, 6 September 1808, *H.R.A.*, I, 6, pp. 641-3.

[70] *Sydney Gazette*, 18 December 1808; and Foveaux to Castlereagh, 20 February 1809, *H.R.A.*, I, 7, p. 2.

Foveaux was in fact desperately anxious to wash his hands of the mess he had inherited from Johnston as quickly as possible.

To hasten that day he wrote to Paterson at Port Dalrymple urging him to come to Sydney,[71] and telling him of Bligh's plans to violate private property and infringe personal liberty so as to occasion universal terror amongst all classes of people from the highest to the most obscure. For these reasons he had no choice but to maintain the government in the way he found it. In the meantime he was anxious to be relieved from such embarrassments either by Paterson's árrival, or by receiving instructions from His Majesty's ministers, because he was convinced Bligh was acting on a settled plan to destroy and ruin the better class of inhabitants. Eight days earlier Bligh was also beseeching Paterson to come, telling him how the country had been in peace and happiness, and the settlers highly satisfied with his administration, and how on this unparalleled occasion he called on him as Lieutenant-Colonel of His Majesty's New South Wales Corps, and Lieutenant-Governor of the territory, to use his utmost endeavours to suppress this mutiny of the Corps he commanded.[72] Sickness, wrote Paterson to Castlereagh, had so shattered his frame that the voyage would have completed his destruction.[73] It was not till the end of December that Paterson sailed from Port Dalrymple for Sydney, still uncertain whether to support Bligh or Foveaux.

As the ship on which he was sailing was tossed like a cork by the violence of the weather outside the heads of Port Jackson, on 1 January Paterson, to his great indignation, received a message from Foveaux that Bligh proposed to arrest him, though Paterson had in no instance given him the most trifling cause to contemplate what Paterson called such unjustifiable violence.[74] By contrast Foveaux sent a carriage to the heads, and in this Paterson was conveyed up to town where Foveaux had prepared a reception for him suitable to his honour's high rank.[75] By this act of egregious folly Bligh had estranged yet another man who might have released him from the indignity of his arrest. Within ten weeks of Paterson's assuming the government of the colony on 9 January,[76] he was writing to Castlereagh telling him Bligh had borne the most rancorous ill-will to every officer and inhabitant whom he had conceived could have interfered in the remotest manner possible with a matured plan of exercising the high command with which he had been honoured, in the purposes of gratifying his insatiably tyrannic disposition and advancing his pecuniary interest.[77] So Bligh remained a prisoner in Government House, with his spy glass still trained on the waters of Sydney Cove, looking

[71] Foveaux to Paterson, 16 August 1808; encl. in Foveaux to Castlereagh, 4 September 1808, *H.R.A.*, I, 6, pp. 632-4.

[72] Bligh to Paterson, 8 August 1808; encl. A. in Bligh to Castlereagh, 31 August 1808, *H.R.A.*, I, 6, pp. 601-2.

[73] Paterson to Castlereagh, 12 March 1809, *H.R.A.*, I, 7, p. 17.

[74] Ibid., pp. 17-18.

[75] *Sydney Gazette*, 1 January 1809.

[76] Foveaux to Castlereagh, 20 February 1809, *H.R.A.*, I, 7, p. 3.

[77] Paterson to Castlereagh, 12 March 1809, *H.R.A.*, I, 7, p. 18.

desperately for the arrival of a ship which would confound his enemies.[78] In the meantime he poured out his anger and his hatreds on to that make-shift paper with which he was now reduced to conduct his correspondence with his gaolers and would-be-rescuers, for Foveaux had deprived him of the use of official notepaper.[79]

There was worse to come. Paterson ordered him to cease giving orders to ships in the harbour. Paterson also ordered him to leave on the *Porpoise* under supervision. Bligh would have none of this, as no man could remove the flag of a British flag officer, and Captain Bligh would unfurl his broad pennant on the mast of the *Porpoise* and sail over the seas to hear His Majesty's pleasure.[80] On 30 January, Paterson ordered Bligh to be removed from Government House to the barracks, where he was attended by his daughter and the faithful Griffin. Before that, as Bligh put it in a letter to Castlereagh, fresh insults came on. On 30 January—anniversary of the martyrdom of King Charles—the sentinels, much heated with liquor, bellowed 'All's well' with peculiar tones of hellish composition. At the barracks they were overwhelmed by the heat, while the officers seemed afraid to pay any respects for they all passed Bligh without removing their hats. On 4 February, Bligh finally accepted Paterson's terms, and returned to the comfort and dignity of Government House, having given an assurance that when he sailed on the *Porpoise* he would not call at any of the outer settlements of New South Wales. He sailed on 17 March.[81]

At the same time, the minds of the other leaders in the drama were turning towards England. Johnston was preparing to leave, but was having trouble in persuading Atkins to accompany him to present evidence in London of the oppressive and tyrannical conduct of the late Governor, for the drunk are often more sensitive to the direction of the wind than the sober.[82] Macarthur, too, was preparing to leave with Johnston on the *Admiral Gambier*, taking with him in his baggage the books and papers he had violently seized from Bligh on the memorable night of the twenty-sixth.[83] By then, Macarthur was beginning to chafe under the maddening complacency of Paterson. For whereas all his predecessors had been incensed by the moral filth in the settlements of New South Wales, and some overwhelmed by their unexpected impotence in the face of such evil, Paterson remained incurably optimistic and complacent, telling Castlereagh in March 1809 that he had never known the colony to be more tranquil, or the people more disposed to exertion in their different pursuits. His sincerest wish and most earnest desire was to so conform his conduct as to ensure the approbation of his gracious sovereign.[84]

[78] Bligh to Pole, 31 August 1808, *H.R.A.*, I, 6, p. 616.

[79] Bligh to Castlereagh, 12 November 1808, *H.R.A.*, I, 6, p. 702.

[80] Bligh to Castlereagh, 10 June 1809, *H.R.A.*, I, 7, pp. 118-31.

[81] Johnston to Atkins, 4 March 1809, *H.R.A.*, I, 7, p. 61, and Atkins to Johnston, 4 March 1809, *H.R.A.*, I, 7, p. 63.

[82] *H.R.A.*, I, 7, p. 54. See also Macquarie to Castlereagh, 8 March 1810, *H.R.A.*, I, 7, pp. 219-20.

[83] Paterson to Castlereagh, 12 March 1809, *H.R.A.*, I, 7, pp. 24-5.

[84] Bligh to Castlereagh, 10 June 1809, *H.R.A.*, I, 7, pp. 125-6.

The approbation of their gracious sovereign was what Johnston, Foveaux, Paterson and Bligh most passionately pursued in life, though the mole in their clay, their past and chance, were all conspiring to cheat them of such a satisfaction. Bligh, despite his undertaking to Paterson not to call at any ports, decided to appeal to Lieutenant-Governor David Collins at Hobart Town to restore him to his lawful position at Sydney Cove. He excused himself for this lapse from an officer and a gentleman's code of honour on the grounds that no oath to a usurper was binding. On 29 March, David Collins, the Reverend Knopwood, some military and civil officers, the marines, and a few poor inhabitants of Hobart Town gathered on the banks of the Derwent to cheer Bligh as Captain-General and Governor-in-Chief of the colony of New South Wales. The triumph was short lived. What Bligh craved was display, grandeur and recognition. When he moved into Government House on 8 April, he found it a poor miserable shell of three rooms with the walls a brick thick, neither wind nor water proof, and without conveniences. Collins heard everything Bligh had to say, but said very little, while in particular parts of etiquette he was inattentive, as likewise in decorum.[85] When Bligh placarded the gum stumps on the parade ground with notices that all who felt aggrieved were to come to him for redress, Collins withdrew the guard from Government House. Whereupon Bligh, in high dudgeon, returned to the *Porpoise* where, within a few weeks, in another of those incredible acts of madness and folly, he had the son of Lieutenant-Governor Collins tied up and flogged with two dozen lashes for insubordination.[86] Towards the end of May, Collins ordered Knopwood to read in church the proclamation by Paterson commanding all His Majesty's subjects within the territory of New South Wales not to communicate or correspond with Bligh, as all such would be dealt with as abettors of sedition and enemies of the peace and prosperity of the colony.[87]

Bligh turned to that behaviour with which he punished all those who had thwarted his plans. He attempted to interfere with the shipping on the Derwent;[88] he formed a pattern in his mind of his enemies as the rulers of a wicked and unjust society, of how in Hobart Town all the indulgences were put into the hands of a few to accumulate wealth while the poor suffered, and how the poor wallowed in vice and wickedness at Sydney Cove, while the usurpers practised iniquity.[89] By June, Bligh had given way to despair, and in a moment of self-pity, but not self-awareness, he wrote to Castlereagh: 'I now remain, my Lord, under the most embarrassed Situation that can be conceived, in a small Ship, without power to relieve myself, but which I am reconciled to in doing my Duty to the utmost, and conscious of the

[85] Encl. no. 2, in Paterson to Castlereagh, 26 March 1809, *H.R.A.*, I, 7, pp. 73-4; and Bligh to Pole, 31 July 1809, *H.R.A.*, I, 7, p. 171.

[86] J. Hobbs to Calder, St Kilda, Melbourne, 26 May 1873 (Calder Papers, State Library of Victoria).

[87] *H.R.A.*, I, 7, pp. 156 and 175-6.

[88] Bligh to Banks, 8 July 1809 (Bligh Papers, Miscellaneous, 1808-10, Mitchell Library).

[89] Bligh to Castlereagh, 10 June 1809, *H.R.A.*, I, 7, p. 131.

support I shall receive from your Lordship.'[90] By then, his behaviour had degenerated from the haughty to the petty, for the man who yearned for the dignity of Captain-General and Governor-in-Chief was spending his days protesting against such trifles as the withdrawal of ink from his room in Government House, or so consumed by suspicions, as to be tempted to open letters not addressed to him, or conjuring up in his mind schemes of revenge against those who had despitefully used him.[91]

Even when relief arrived from England, chance and his own behaviour robbed him of what little comfort that might have afforded. When the whaler *Albion* entered the Derwent with news that Bligh's successor had probably arrived at Sydney Cove, Bligh, with his daughter and the faithful Griffin, sailed on the *Porpoise* for Sydney. But he was too late. For when his successor told the civil and military officers, the clergy, the soldiers and the respectable inhabitants of Sydney Cove on 1 January 1810 of his painful duty to be thus compelled publicly to announce His Majesty's high displeasure and disapprobation of the mutinous and outrageous conduct displayed in the forcible and unwarrantable removal of his late representative, William Bligh, and of the tumultuous proceedings connected therewith, Bligh was not there to hear it.[92]

When the *Porpoise* did arrive at Sydney Cove, however, on 17 January, Bligh was saluted by His Majesty's ships and from the battery at Dawes Point. On the same day the acting major of the brigade issued orders that Commander Bligh, as late Governor of this territory, was to be received with presented arms from all guards and sentinels, while the drums were to beat a march. When he landed the next day, the ships in the harbour again saluted him, while on shore he and Mrs Putland were received by the Governor-in-Chief and his lady with every possible mark of attention and respect.[93] Once more his broad pennant flew at the mast of His Majesty's ship *Porpoise* in Sydney Cove; but another man slept at Government House, while Bligh resided in the town of Sydney, protected, at his own request, by a guard of the seventy-third regiment.

There Bligh was busily employed at the one occupation which gave him deep satisfaction; selecting papers and evidence to substantiate the charges he proposed to prefer against Johnston and Macarthur. There too he pored over the petitions from his supporters, from civil officers such as Robert Campbell, Henry Fulton, William Gore, and John Palmer, from the settlers of Norfolk Island, and from the settlers on the Hawkesbury who wrote again of the blessings they had received under his firm, upright and impartial administration, and of their hopes that he would soon return armed with power to enforce his authority;[94] other settlers wrote how they abhorred

[90] *H.R.A.*, I, 7, p. 153 and p. 176.

[91] Macquarie to Castlereagh, 8 March 1810, *H.R.A.*, I, 7, p. 218, and encl. no. 1 in ibid., pp. 226-7.

[92] *Sydney Gazette*, 21 January 1810.

[93] Macquarie to Castlereagh, 8 March 1810, *H.R.A.*, I, 7, p. 219.

[94] For text of these petitions see *H.R.A.*, I, 7, pp. 137-51, and 159-60.

and detested the rebellion, its aiders and abettors, and of their confidence in his wisdom, justice and humanity. But Bligh wanted more than sympathy, agreement, and understanding: he wanted revenge.

All those who worked closely with him during the days while he was waiting for a ship for England were shocked by his motives. Ellis Bent, who had arrived to take up duty as Judge Advocate, began by being sympathetic to Bligh and his daughter. He soon found that both had violent and ungovernable tempers. Mrs Putland was very small, had a nice figure and rather a sensible face, dressed with some taste, if very thinly, and compensated for the want of petticoats by wearing breeches, or rather trousers. She was, he found, conceited and affected to a greater degree than any woman he had ever seen before: everything was studied about her, her walk, her talk, everything. To observe her mode of sitting down was to see this part of her character at once. She was extremely violent and passionate, and, according to the tittle-tattle of her father's enemies, now and then flung a plate or a candlestick at his head.[95] As for Bligh, he was a broad, stout little man, considerably past the prime of life, revengeful in the extreme, a man who would be delighted to hang, draw and quarter all those who had deprived him of his government.[96]

To his successor, Lachlan Macquarie, Bligh quickly became a great plague. Macquarie found him a most disagreeable person to have any dealings or to transact public business with, as he had no regard whatever for his promises or engagements however sacred, and his natural temper was uncommonly harsh and tyrannical in the extreme. Although Macquarie could not discover any crime or act of tyranny during Bligh's administration that could in the smallest degree excuse or justify the rebellious and mutinous conduct of those who arrested him and subverted his government, he was convinced that Bligh was a very improper person to be employed in any position of trust or command. He was convinced, too, that he was very generally detested by high, low, rich and poor, but more especially by the higher classes of people. Macquarie for one was heartily glad to get rid of him when he finally left Sydney Cove.[97]

All through April there were rounds of farewells, beginning with a ball and supper on the *Porpoise* on 8 April, when the ship was elegantly decorated;[98] the atmosphere resounded with royal airs from a large band, and the dancing continued till three in the morning.[99] On 11 April, Robert Campbell put on a splendid farewell fete.[100] On 28 April, Government House was neatly

[95] E. Bent to J. H. Bent, 2 May 1810 (MS. letters from Ellis Bent, National Library, Canberra) and E. Bent to his mother, 4 March 1810 (National Library, Canberra).

[96] E. Bent to his mother, 4 March 1810 (MS. letters from Ellis Bent, National Library, Canberra).

[97] L. Macquarie to C. Macquarie, 10 May 1810 (photostat in National Library, Canberra). See also Macquarie to Castlereagh, private, 10 May 1810, *H.R.A.*, I, 7, p. 331.

[98] *Sydney Gazette*, 14 April 1810.

[99] Ibid.

[100] *Sydney Gazette*, 28 April 1810.

decorated and brilliantly lighted for Macquarie's farewell. The ballroom was hung round with festoons of flowers encircling the initials of Mrs Putland and Commodore Bligh in a very neat device. There was dancing, and fireworks, and no single circumstance was omitted which could convey the idea of the respect entertained by Macquarie for the distinguished persons in compliment to whom the entertainment had been given.[1]

There was just as fulsome a display of respect on the day he embarked on the *Hindostan*. Bligh proceeded to Government House to take farewell of the civil and military officers; then, accompanied by Macquarie and Mrs Putland, after the military had presented arms and the band of the seventy-third regiment had played 'God Save the King', they proceeded to the waterfront where, to the accompaniment of salutes, Bligh and Mrs Putland entered the barge in which they proceeded to the *Hindostan*.[2]

Three days later, to the universal sorrow of the whole colony, Mrs Putland left the *Hindostan* to make what Ellis Bent called a cursed match with Lieutenant-Governor O'Connell.[3] They gathered at Government House again, this time in the sight of God, to see the two joined together in holy matrimony by the Reverend Samuel Marsden. When Bligh returned again to the *Hindostan* only Griffin was with him; all the others had forsaken him, and he sailed out on the high seas on 12 May with only the madness of revenge to comfort him during his long journey across the ocean until such time as the approval of His Majesty's ministers and his gracious sovereign should atone for what he had endured.

In the meantime, on 1 May, at eleven in the morning, Colonel William Paterson and his lady had taken leave of a numerous company of civil and military officers at the end of the wharf and boarded the *Dromedary* to a salute of guns and cheers by the spectators which were echoed from each vessel as their pinnace passed. As the party passed the public landing wharf a numerous body of inhabitants burst into cheering, while crowded boats followed the colonel's pinnace to the *Dromedary*, cheering all the way in a public demonstration of respect towards an officer whose urbanity of manners, joined to a true benevolence of disposition, had endeared him to all classes of the inhabitants.[4] The cheering, the shouting, the displays of grief at parting, all the unmistakable signs that they were saying farewell to a likeable man drifted over the waters to the *Hindostan*, to be heard by an unloved man, who was probably comforting himself with dark and monstrous thoughts about his enemies, rather than advancing in wisdom by examining the causes of his cruel fate. Fate, however, was more cruel than man to Paterson; he died on 20 June, during the passage of the *Dromedary* around Cape Horn, and was buried in the great water of the south seas.[5]

---

[1] Ibid.

[2] *Sydney Gazette*, 5 May 1810.

[3] E. Bent to J. H. Bent, 2 May 1810 (MS. in National Library, Canberra).

[4] Ibid., 22 December 1810.

[5] Lieutenant Lord to Macquarie, 31 March 1810; encl. no. 10 in Macquarie to Castlereagh, 30 April 1810, *H.R.A.*, I, 7, pp. 288-90; E. Bent to his mother, 27 April 1810 (MS. in National Library, Canberra).

Fate also snatched away another actor in the drama before the judgment of the powers that be was proclaimed. Towards the end of 1809 and in the beginning of 1810, an unwonted melancholy began to descend on David Collins at Hobart Town. The news from England early in the new year with the rebuke from Castlereagh about his extravagance sharpened his depression, till, as his successor put it, Divine Providence was pleased to remove him from this world in a very sudden manner after a short indisposition. His funeral on 24 March was attended by upwards of six hundred persons, including the civil and military officers, who showed every mark of attention and respect to the remains of a man who had been nearly a quarter of a century in that part of the world. No expense was spared, for in a somewhat fulsome outward display of grief his successor spent five hundred and seven pounds, eight shillings and three pence—including special waistcoat fronts, stockings, shoes, a lavish pall, trimmings for the pantaloons of the sergeants, black gowns for the marines' wives, and black handkerchiefs for all the official mourners. Ellis Bent described the funeral rather cattily as a complete job.[6]

Some time after the funeral, the church in which Collins was buried was blown down in a great gale. Some said his satanic majesty had taken both the church and the Governor; some said it was a pity Satan did not take the clergyman as well, as they were much alike in deliberate wickedness, indulged equally in deeds of licentiousness, and gave a most villainous example in a society where good men were scarce, and the people only too ready for evil.[7] Others had averred that Collins had been overcome by an excess of anxiety after reading Castlereagh's rebukes for his conduct to Bligh.[8] Collins believed from his own experiences that sin consumed a man's life as a moth fretted a garment, and knew in his heart that every man was but vanity. Yet when his body was committed to the earth enough had been done to show those who came after him that the European had been there.

In the meantime Bligh, Johnston and Macarthur, with their supporters and their accomplices, prepared to face the judgment of man. On 7 May 1811, a general court martial began at the Royal Hospital, Chelsea, at which Lieutenant-Colonel Johnston was arraigned for beginning, exciting, causing and joining in a mutiny.[9] Time had mellowed some of the antagonists. The technicalities of the law drained off the heat from the exchanges, as both parties testified to their memory of events leading up to the memorable twenty-sixth. Even Bligh, with surprising magnanimity, told the court that if Johnston's actions could be vindicated by the need to stop an insurrection he would be the first to rejoice at his acquittal.[10] Feeling as he put it too

6 E. Bent to his mother, 27 April 1810 (MS. in National Library, Canberra).

7 Reminiscences of John Pascoe Fawkner, Second Book, p. 171 (MS. in State Library of Victoria).

8 *Proceedings of a General Court-Martial . . . for the trial of Lieut. Col. Geo. Johnston, . . . on a Charge of Mutiny . . .* (London, 1811), pp. 408-9.

9 Ibid., p. 407.

10 Ibid., pp. 388-9.

deep a personal interest to sum up the case for the prosecution with the calmness and self-possession suited to the occasion he asked the court to indulge him by allowing the Judge Advocate to read his statement.[11] The court completed the taking of evidence on 5 June and on 2 July, after having duly and maturely weighed the evidence both for the prosecution and the defence, pronounced Lieutenant-Colonel Johnston guilty of the act of mutiny and sentenced him to be cashiered.[12] At the same time the Commander-in-Chief explained that in passing a sentence so inadequate to the enormity of the crime the court had apparently been actuated by a consideration of the mood and extraordinary circumstances which might have appeared to them to have existed during the administration of Governor Bligh, both as affecting the tranquillity of the colony, and calling for some immediate decision.[13] In the sequel, Johnston was allowed to return to the colony as a settler in October 1812, when he took up land at Annandale, farmed quietly somewhat to the surprise of Macquarie, and died on 3 January 1823 just when the War Office was getting round to giving sympathetic consideration to his appeals for compensation. Macarthur was not granted permission to return till the end of 1816; for a season, he wrestled with the peculiarity and untowardness of a fate which separated him from his beloved wife and his dear girls, for at that time he could see no hope that he would ever be permitted to reside in New South Wales exempt from danger and persecution, while if he brought them to England he might have to reproach himself for depriving them of plenty and comparative affluence and embittering the remainder of their lives with pinching penury.[14] He finally arrived at Sydney Cove in February of 1817.

For a brief season Bligh's enemies were confounded, and he was rewarded, for on 31 July 1811 he was promoted to Rear Admiral of the blue squadron, and in 1812 to Rear Admiral of the white.[15] Bligh continued to get on in the world while that other satisfaction he craved, getting on with the world, eluded him as unmistakably as ever. When news of his death in London, on 7 December 1817, at the age of sixty-five reached Sydney Cove, neither then nor at any subsequent time did the *Sydney Gazette* write of regret, of grief, of loss, or of achievement.[16] Nor did a generation which so frequently and so lavishly indulged in displays of public grief bestir itself. The clergy were silent while the officers, both civil and military, were indifferent. For Bligh had not touched even the morbid imagination of his contemporaries, who seemed determined on the contrary to obliterate the few surviving signs of his unhappy life in the colony. On 5 August 1819 Macquarie proclaimed

11 *The Times*, 6 June and 5 July 1811.

12 Ibid., 5 July 1811.

13 Ibid.

14 J. Macarthur to E. Macarthur, London, 16 October 1812, S. M. Onslow (ed.): op. cit., pp. 224-5.

15 G. Mackaness: op. cit., p. 524.

16 *Sydney Gazette*, 2 May 1818.

that the deed by which King had granted land to Bligh was absolutely void and of no effect in law or equity.[17]

The other memorials did not confer great credit on his heart. Bligh had been niggardly in the granting of land: he was also singularly ungenerous in the use of the power to pardon, granting only two pardons during his term of office. His picture of his opponents as a group of men motivated purely by the desire for filthy material gain had reflected that baseness which he detected in all human behaviour. Johnston made only seven land grants, of which not one was to a leader of his side; Foveaux made five. Paterson was more lavish, but some of these were made to compensate settlers for flood losses on the Hawkesbury, and some to reward his supporters. Of the one hundred and fifty odd who signed the request to Johnston to arrest Bligh, thirty-five received land grants. Amongst them was Gregory Blaxland, Atkins, Mrs Paterson, James Meehan, D'Arcy Wentworth, and Charles Throsby, but not Macarthur, not Foveaux, not Johnston, and not Paterson, except possibly through his wife.[18] So chance and circumstance connived to ensure once again in the history of human affairs that the man who was angry without cause bequeathed no monument of achievement to posterity, and tasted deep damnation on earth as the fruit of his disquiet. For Macquarie's creation was built not on any incomplete foundations left by Bligh, but on the ideas and work begun by King.

[17] *Sydney Gazette*, 14 August 1819.

[18] App. A to J. V. Byrnes: 'Green Hills and Golden Grain, or the Life and Times of Andrew Thompson' (M.A. thesis in Fisher Library, University of Sydney). For a different opinion see H. V. Evatt: *Rum Rebellion*, 4th ed. (Sydney, 1944), pp. 255-6.

12

THE SOCIETY OF NEW SOUTH WALES
IN 1810

WHILE the actors in the centre of the stage were creating all this sound and fury from the day Phillip landed till Bligh sailed out on to the high seas in May 1810, other developments were occurring in the colony of New South Wales and its dependencies. The settlement gradually spread: population increased: a convict system was created: the natural wealth was exploited: the rudiments of a civilization began to take shape.[1]

The first main expansion of the settlement occurred in the district of the Hawkesbury River. On 6 June 1789 Phillip, with Hunter, Collins, Johnston, White and others entered Broken Bay in a boat, investigated the bays and inlets for two days, and on the third came across the mouth of a river, up which they rowed for twenty miles before returning to Sydney. On 28 June, Phillip returned with Johnston, rowed sixty or seventy miles up the river to a waterfall, examined the surrounding country, climbed and named Richmond Hill, gazed west at the range of mountains on the horizon which he named the Blue Mountains, and returned to that noble river, on which he conferred the name of Hawkesbury.[2] Two days earlier, on 26 June, Tench had set out from Rose Hill to journey westward till he reached a river which he named the Nepean.[3] As early as January 1794, a few farmers had squatted on the banks of the Hawkesbury. Grose made land grants to twenty-two settlers in April 1794, and by June 1795 there were about four hundred persons settled along both banks of the river. By 1802 there were two main settlements on the Hawkesbury, one at Green Hills (later called Windsor) with nine hundred and thirty-seven, and the other at Portland Place.[4]

[1] By July of 1790 there were settlements at Sydney Cove, Norfolk Island, and Parramatta. From 1790 to 1800 settlements were established in the vicinity of Sydney at Bulanaming, February 1793; Hunter's Hill 1793, Petersham Hill January 1794, Eastern Farms February 1794, Yorke Place August 1796, Mulgrave Place December 1796, George's River June 1798, Banks Town August 1798, Dundas District April 1799. In the same period settlements were established in the vicinity of Parramatta at Northern Boundary August 1791, Prospect Hill July 1791, The Ponds July 1791, Field of Mars January 1792, Kissing Point February 1792, Toongabbe July 1792, Liberty Plains, so named because it was first settled by free settlers, February 1793 and Concord during the same year. (Lists compiled from the *H.R.A.*, I, vols. 1-3. The date given is the date of the first land grant in the district.)

[2] Phillip to Sydney, 13 February 1790, *H.R.A.*, I, 1, pp. 155-7.

[3] W. Tench: *A Complete Account of the Settlement at Port Jackson in New South Wales* (London, 1793), p. 26 et seq.

[4] Encl. in King to Hobart, 9 November 1802, *H.R.A.*, I, 3, p. 615.

The needs of the gaol contributed to the next expansion of settlement. In 1798 a lieutenant on the *Nelson* had sighted Hunter's River. In May 1801 a small settlement was established there for convicts undergoing secondary punishment—that is punishment for serious offences committed in New South Wales, and for those hardened criminals deemed likely to contaminate other convicts, or deemed dangerous on other grounds. In this way the penal settlements of New South Wales began their sombre history. At the end of 1801 the Hunter's River settlement was abandoned, but it was begun again in March 1804 when some deluded Irish insurgents from the Castle Hill rising were sent down the coal mines to mend the error of their ways, and to protect their fellow countrymen against their corrupting influence. At the same time King changed the name of the settlement from Coal River to Newcastle.[5]

The need to divide the convicts, the fear of the French, and the hope of material gain played a part in the creation of the abortive settlement at Port Phillip in 1803, and the settlements at Hobart Town in 1804, and Port Dalrymple in 1804. These latter remained farming and trading settlements until 1810, where both settlers and the government farmed on both banks of the Derwent as far as New Norfolk, and in the hinterland of York Town on the banks of the Tamar. In the same year, 1804, John Macarthur took up his land grant to grow wool at Camden, and so settled a district which was to cradle the 'ancient nobility' of New South Wales. By 1810 there were five main settlements on the mainland; administrative and convict settlements at Sydney and Parramatta, the farming settlement on the Hawkesbury, the pastoral settlement at Camden, and the penal settlement at the Coal River. In addition there was a settlement at Norfolk Island, which was under orders to be evacuated, and the two settlements in Van Diemen's Land.

The population of the settlements of New South Wales at Sydney, Parramatta, the Hawkesbury and Newcastle, was 10,454—5,513 men, 2,220 women and 2,721 children. These included the Governor and Lieutenant-Governor, 35 civil officers (one of whom had a wife and three children); 1,416 on the military establishment, together with their 219 wives and 414 children; 307 free men, with 183 women and 198 children, all victualled from the public stores; fourteen orphans receiving rations from government; and the convicts —1,132 men, 151 women and 154 children, similarly supported by government. Finally there were those who supported themselves—2,621 men, 1,666 women and 1,938 children. By contrast, excepting the Governor and Lieutenant-Governor, a total of 4,227 people were victualled from the public stores. The convicts comprised 13.7 per cent of the population. There were roughly two and a half times as many men as women, and three adults to every child in the colony.

The population at Norfolk Island was only 177—127 men, 26 women and 24 children. All were victualled by the government. There were 6 civil officers, and the military establishment consisted of 35 men, 7 women and

---

[5] King to Hobart, 16 April 1804, *H.R.A.*, I, 4, pp. 611-12.

5 children. Ninety-five free persons (61 men, 18 women and 16 children), 3 orphans, and 25 men and 1 woman convict made up the remainder. It was a strongly masculine community—about five men to every woman—and there were six adults to every child in the island. The convicts made up 14.6 per cent of the total population.

In Van Diemen's Land there were in all 1,321 persons in the two settlements at Hobart Town and Port Dalrymple—702 men, 273 women and 346 children. Two Lieutenant-Governors, 19 officials, 8 women and 4 children made up the civil establishment, while the military establishment was composed of 108 men, 29 women and 58 children. A surprisingly large number of orphans—37—were supported by the government; and a high proportion of free persons (294 men, 161 women, 243 children) also received rations from the public stores. The convict population consisted of 221 men, 23 women and 4 children. Only 58 men and 52 women supported themselves. Excluding the two Lieutenant-Governors, there were 1,209 persons victualled by government, compared with the 110 who were not. The proportion of men to women—two and a half to one—and of adults to children—three to one—were roughly the same as in New South Wales, but the convicts comprised a higher proportion—18.7 per cent—of the total population of the island.[6]

The simplest classification between people was that between the bond and the free. One other classification was the quantities in the ration they received from the government stores, which was calculated not according to needs or wealth, but according to station in society. As an outward and visible sign of the prestige and power of the military in the early period, the ration of a military officer exceeded that of a civil officer.[7] From the time of Bligh, however, both civil and military officers received a weekly ration of ten pounds of wheat or eight pounds of flour maize, three pounds or three pints of pease, seven pounds of beef or four pounds of salted pork, six ounces of sugar or one pound of rice, or one pound of wheat,[8] while the non-commissioned officers, the clerks in government service, their wives and children, the privates in the New South Wales Corps, and the convicts in government service received proportionate amounts.[9]

Classifications made by contemporaries divided society into six groups. First there were the military officers; second, the civil officers; third, the settlers, including both those from England and those who had taken grants of land after receiving their pardons. Emancipist settlers were treated by the military officers as socially inferior to the free settlers, but a convict past was not regarded by all the free settlers as a perpetual bar to a social future. Fourth, there were the landholders, men paying rent, a class which included

---

[6] *H.R.A.*, I, 7, pp. 280-1 and 284-5.

[7] Evidence of W. Bligh to the Select Committee on Transportation, 1812, p. 35, *P.P.*, 1812, II, 341.

[8] Ibid., pp. 35-6.

[9] Ibid.

some ticket-of-leave men; fifth, the free workers; and sixth, the ticket-of-leave workers and the convicts.[10]

At the base of the social pyramid were the men and women undergoing the punishment of transportation, a punishment of exile and forced labour designed to punish, to reform, and to provide a work force for the colony. In the beginning there had been no system. From 1717 to 1776 shipping contractors had purchased convicts sentenced to transportation from gaolers in the British Isles and sold them at so much per head to plantation owners in the West Indies or the southern colonies of North America, who thus acquired a property in their labour during the period of their servitude.[11] As the indigenous population of New South Wales had no interest in acquiring a property in the services of convict labour, an imperious necessity dictated the creation of a new system from the two vague principles in the instructions to the governor. The first was that he should proceed to the cultivation of the land, distributing the convicts for that purpose in such manner, and under such inspectors or overseers, and under such regulations as might appear to him necessary and best calculated for procuring supplies of grain and ground provisions.[12] The second was that he was granted full power and authority to emancipate and discharge from their servitude any of the convicts under his superintendence who, from their good conduct and a disposition to industry, were deserving of favour, and to grant them land—thirty acres for a single man, twenty acres more if married, and ten acres for each child residing in the colony.[13]

By 1810 the economic needs of the colony, rather than abstract aims of punishment and reformation, had influenced both the regulations and the conventions of the system. The officer in charge of the convicts was called the superintendent of convicts. His first duty was to supervise their distribution. On the arrival of a convict ship in Sydney Harbour the regulations forbade employers or their agents negotiating with the convicts until after the inspection by the superintendent of convicts. As soon as the supply of labour trailed demand, employers or their agents rowed out to the ship, promising indulgences to those who succeeded in becoming their servants. The early inspections of the convicts were perfunctory because of the paucity of information sent with them; but by 1806 the inspection had settled into a routine. The Home Office sent a record of every convict, his place of birth, age, occupation, religion, crime, previous record, behaviour on the hulks, and on the convict ship. The superintendent inspected the ship, and then permitted the convicts to lodge any complaints about their treatment. Sometimes the Governor explained how good behaviour in the colony could hasten their

[10] This account is based on the evidence of W. Bligh to the Select Committee on Transportation, 1812, p. 35. For a different classification see the evidence of A. Riley to the Select Committee on the State of the Gaols, 1819, p. 19, *P.P.*, 1819, VII, 579.

[11] See A. E. Smith: *Colonists in Bondage. White Servitude and Convict Labor in America, 1606-1776* (Williamsburg, 1947).

[12] Instructions to Phillip, 25 April 1787, *H.R.A.*, I, 1, p. 11.

[13] Ibid., p. 14.

emancipation and their return to that station which they had forfeited by their crimes, and warned them that vicious habits and evil associations would lead inevitably to dire punishment and physical and mental suffering. The superintendent then proceeded to distribute the convicts to their place of servitude. In this distribution, the wealth, social position, and capacity of the convict to labour, rather than his criminal record, were generally decisive.

Convicts with money or property capable of being converted into money were granted a ticket-of-leave, which meant they were free to work for wages and to find their own board and lodging, free in all ways except that they could not move out of their police district, return to any part of the United Kingdom or any British colony, or exercise any legal rights in the law courts of New South Wales. The gentlemen convicts were also given a ticket-of-leave.[14] All the other convicts were drafted into servitude. As the government had first choice, the skilled men were distributed to their trades in government service, the educated to clerical work in the government service, or the commissariat, and the Governor's service, while the uneducated and the unskilled were distributed to the government farms, road work, or wharf labour.

Most of the rest were assigned to employers. In Sydney the distribution to employers was done by the superintendent of convicts. In other districts the distribution was performed by the magistrates. As soon as demand by the settlers exceeded the supply, the magistrates were compelled to adopt some criterion of selection. This differed from magistrate to magistrate, and from district to district. The regulations of 1811 prescribed that convicts were only to be assigned to those settlers who were considered most in want and best entitled to receive them.[15] In general, however, the settlers obtained their convicts by lot. Yet the magistrates had a wide discretion. Marsden at Parramatta gave free settlers the preference, and then allowed settlers who had been convicts to draw by lots, as he considered it to be a degradation to the honest part of society to be put on the same level with the class that had been convicts.[16] No such distinction was made by the magistrates for the Hawkesbury district, for there the society was too predominantly ex-convict to permit such discrimination. Those who were not wanted by the settlers were distributed to unskilled government work. In addition, those who had been returned by private employers either for some crime or for their general attitude were drafted into government work.

The same principles were observed in the distribution in Van Diemen's Land. Up to January 1810 those convicts not wanted at Sydney or the other settlements on the mainland were sent by ship to Hobart Town or Port Dalrymple, where the government again had first choice, then the settlers, while the left-overs worked for the government. For these reasons complaints about the quality of convict labour were if anything more frequent in the

14 J. T. Bigge: The Colony of New South Wales, pp. 17-18, and evidence of A. Riley to the Select Committee on the State of the Gaols, 1819, p. 69.

15 J. T. Bigge: The Colony of New South Wales, p. 18.

16 Ibid.

settlements of Van Diemen's Land.[17] When the distribution was completed the convicts landed. In the noisy and joyous recognition of their friends and acquaintances, in the tumult of hasty and unequal bargains, or in disappointments for the loss of their property and bedding, they proceeded from the boats to the shore. In the countenances and demeanour of a few, especially of those who had been in the higher ranks of life, some indications of shame and of sorrow might be discovered, though most were overwhelmed by the pleasures of the moment.[18]

The regulations and practices for the distribution of the women differed little from the men. The Governor's secretary and the superintendent of convicts conducted the muster on the ship. Women with property were immediately granted tickets-of-leave, and women with husbands in the colony were assigned to them. The rest were assigned for domestic service either in Sydney or one of the settlements, or sent to work in the female factory at Parramatta which opened in 1804 on the first floor of the new gaol there. These were taken by boat from Sydney Cove to Parramatta. This journey lasted from morning till evening in fair weather, but with an adverse wind darkness came down before the end of the journey, when great irregularities took place and the women frequently arrived at Parramatta in a state of intoxication and plundered of their property, to begin their servitude the next day in destitution and on a hangover. By an odd irony this was generally their first experience of life in a colony which had been created for their reformation as well as their punishment.[19]

In the period before 1800 the convicts in government service worked in the main to grow food, put up the public buildings and build roads. The development of trade, the expansion of settlement, and the increase in population created a greater variety of occupations for convicts in government service. At the mainland settlements of Sydney, Parramatta, the Hawkesbury, Toongabbe and Castle Hill, in 1805, two hundred and eighty-six of the men convicts were employed in government farms, one hundred and eighty-three in the building trades, as brick and tile makers, bricklayers, plasterers, builders' labourers, blacksmiths, shingle-, pale- and lathe-splitters, stone cutters and layers, sawyers and timber measurers, house carpenters and labourers, painters, lime and charcoal burners, thirty-seven as boat builders, four hundred and twenty-five in various employments, and one hundred and forty-eight as servants to officers. At the same time sixty-eight women were employed in the manufacture of wool, and a few in such occupations as spinning and picking oakum, husking corn, picking weeds, sail-making, caring for orphans, hospital nursing, dairying and midwifery. The remainder in the complement of women victualled by the government was made up of the sick, the convalescent, the blind, the insane, the invalids, and the women in domestic service to the New South Wales Corps.[20]

[17] J. T. Bigge: The Colony of New South Wales, pp. 19-20, 42-4.
[18] Ibid., p. 17.
[19] Ibid., p. 20.
[20] H.R.A., I, 5, pp. 662-4.

In the year 1805 the convicts gathered, husked and shelled maize, broke up ground, sowed and planted wheat, barley, maize, flax and potatoes, or took care of government stock as herdsmen or watchmen. In Sydney, the building labourers were building Fort Phillip, a wharf, a brick house for the Judge Advocate, a brick house for the main guard, a brick printing office, a repairing store, and houses; at Parramatta they were making alterations to the brewery, building a brick house for the Reverend Samuel Marsden, and repairing storehouses and officers' and soldiers' barracks; others were building a school house at the Hawkesbury. The boat and ship builders were fitting the *Investigator* for service, working on the *Buffalo*, the *Lady Nelson*, the *Francis*, the *Integrity* and the *Resource*, building rowing and long boats for the use of all the settlements, keeping the punts in repair, and squaring some 5,500 feet of ship timber. The wheel and millwrights were making and repairing carts, timber and gun carriages, ploughs and harrows, or repairing the mills. Those who worked on colonial ships helped to establish the new settlement of Port Dalrymple, or carried supplies between Sydney and Norfolk Island, Sydney and Hobart Town, Sydney and the Hawkesbury, or carried coal, cedar and salt from Newcastle. The town and gaol gangs built and repaired roads and loaded and unloaded boats, while those employed in manufacturing in hemp, flax, and wool, made canvas, sacking, girthing, linen, blankets, flannel, coarse cloth and collar cloth.[21] In the same year the labour at the outer settlements of Newcastle, Norfolk Island, Hobart Town and Port Dalrymple was confined to the production of food, public works, and, in the case of the two new settlements of Hobart Town and Port Dalrymple, building their own huts. For until 1810 the supplies of the outer settlements, other than food, came from Sydney Cove, and what Sydney could not provide was shipped from England or Ireland through Sydney Cove.

The hours of their labour were prescribed in the regulations governing convict discipline. In summer and winter they worked from sunrise to three in the afternoon with an hour's interval for a meal. At least those were the regulation hours, though those on task work finished work as soon as their task for the day was performed, while convicts at Port Dalrymple worked for shorter hours to give them time to work on the construction of their own lodgings. On Saturdays, work stopped between one and two in the afternoon, while on Sundays all labour, either coercive or profitable, was forbidden. After regulation labour the convicts could, if they so wished, work for either the government, a civil or military officer or a settler for wages, paid either in money or kind or both. As skilled labour was short, there was ample opportunity for the skilled worker to earn good wages. There was a career in the colony for the skilled and the industrious, an economic advancement which had little if anything to do with moral behaviour. In this way the economic needs of the colony created a hierarchy within the convict society which bore no relation to previous criminal record or conduct in the colony. The skilful and immoral men were indulged and rewarded while the in-

21 *H.R.A.*, I, 5, pp. 664-5; see also J. T. Bigge: The Colony of New South Wales, pp. 21, 24-5, 27, and 41.

expert and well-conducted men were made uneasy and discontented.[22] Or so critics said, who assumed too lightly that there was justice in the world, let alone that it was reasonable to find a just system of rewards in a convict society.

The convicts in government service were divided into gangs, and for every two or three gangs there was a superintendent, frequently chosen from among the convicts with a good-conduct record.[23] They were fed and clothed by the government, and so had to endure such inconvenience and distress as was caused by the irregularity of supply of both food and clothing from England. With the increase in local production and the more regular sailings of convict supply ships, both food and clothing were abundant, and the convict began to enjoy a standard of living higher than that afforded by a life of crime in the British Isles. Paradoxically, this reduced the terrors of transportation as a punishment, while creating a more favourable material setting for their reformation. Also, although the government issued a clothing ration for both men and women in government service in a distinctive colour of yellow and grey, it was only possible in Newcastle to force the convicts to wear their distinctive dress. In Van Diemen's Land in particular there was such a great variety that it was impossible to distinguish between bond and free by dress.[24]

In Sydney the convicts in government service were expected to make their own arrangements for lodging, and to pay for it out of the earnings from their work after 3 p.m. and on Saturday afternoons. By 1810 the fashionable site for convict lodgings was at the Rocks.[25] At Parramatta and Hobart Town, too, both men and women in government service had to hire their own lodgings, which encouraged the men to lodge with the drinkers and the gamblers, and encouraged the women to continue their career of prostitution. At George Town and Norfolk Island, on the government farms on the mainland, and along the Hawkesbury, they lived in huts put up by their own hands.[26]

For misconduct during work the superintendent had no power to inflict punishment, but was obliged by the regulations to take offenders accused of a minor offence before a single magistrate, who could order a punishment of twenty-five lashes. For a more serious offence the convict was tried before a bench of at least three magistrates who could order as many as three hundred lashes. This punishment could not be executed, however, without the concurrence of the Governor. A convict could also be sentenced to work for

[22] J. T. Bigge: The Colony of New South Wales, p. 48.

[23] Report of the Select Committee on Transportation, 1812, p. 11, *P.P.*, 1812, II, 341.

[24] J. T. Bigge: The Colony of New South Wales, pp. 49 and 60-3; evidence of J. Hunter and W. Bligh to the Select Committee on Transportation, 1812, pp. 19 and 30, *P.P.*, 1812, II, 341.

[25] J. T. Bigge: The Colony of New South Wales, p. 21.

[26] Evidence of J. Hunter, W. Bligh and J. Duce Harris to the Select Committee on Transportation, 1812, pp. 19, 31 and 50, *P.P.*, 1812, II, 341.

a number of days in the gaol gang, where he laboured at some public work from six in the morning till six at night, and no hours were allowed to him for profit or amusement. He could also be sentenced to transportation to Norfolk Island or, after 1801, to the Coal River. For any breaches of criminal law he was tried by the criminal court consisting of the Judge Advocate and six military officers, and sentenced to any punishment known to the criminal law.[27]

Of their leisure, most contemporaries wrote with lamentations in the spirit of the Old Testament prophets, but without their conviction that the days of Sodom and Gomorrah were numbered. They complained of their drinking, their gambling, their sexual promiscuity, and their addiction to the vices of 'the cities of the plain'. They lamented that their life was brutish and short, that it was one of wretchedness and squalor. It was a life in which only a few were vouchsafed a vision of higher things, for after the departure of Richard Johnson in 1800 no clergyman of the Protestant persuasion told them in their huts of the message of divine love, while no priest was permitted to administer the sacraments as a means of grace, except for the few months before the Irish rebellion at Castle Hill in 1804. Of other means to soften the harshness of their lives, education, reading, and theatre, they knew nothing, for, except for Richard Johnson's library of improving literature, books were not provided for them. After 1803 the literate could read from time to time cautionary tales in the *Sydney Gazette* to illustrate the punishment of wickedness and vice, of those launchings into eternity which cut short most lives of crime in this world, and of the awful fate awaiting sinners in the next. The religious faith was kept alive by the Irish Catholic convicts, while in their songs the convicts mixed defiance and sentimentality in a vision of the world which helped to make their own lives bearable, while giving them the strength to survive.

Not all were sunk irredeemably in debauchery and dissipation or driven to despair. By 1810 some were beginning to rise from the ranks of the convicts to positions of affluence and prosperity. For most convicts, getting on in the world was no easier than for the camel to pass through the eye of the needle. Although there were abundant opportunities for skilled and unskilled to work in their leisure moments for high wages, the system provided as many opportunities for their dissipation. Environment worked hand in hand with innate disposition to ensure that few convicts in government service rose out of the working class.

After their servitude they returned to that station in society which their life of crime had caused them to forfeit. While in servitude they were abused for their indolence, which officials from Phillip to Bligh explained by their innate aversion to labour. This created a dilemma for officials in New South Wales: how could men and women with an innate aversion to labour, which was the psychological cause of their pursuit of a life of crime, be expected to labour without the incentive of material reward? All use of material rewards, of payments in money or kind, during their compulsory working

27 Report of the Select Committee on Transportation, 1812, p. 7, *P.P.*, 1812, II, 341.

hours, was incompatible with the punishment of forced labour. So between the incentives and indulgences on the one hand and coercion or the use of the lash on the other, the men in charge of convict labour pursued their Sisyphean task of extracting labour from the convicts.

In addition to complaints about indolence, there were also complaints about the quality of the workmanship. Some complained, for example, that the wheat was reaped in a slovenly manner, and a good deal left scattered on the ground, that this was the inevitable concomitant of using a working class which possessed neither the ability nor the incentive to work for a living.[28] For this was an alienated working class, a class with no spiritual or material interest in the products of its work. It quickly developed that habit of defiance and that spirit of resentment which characterize people driven or terrorized into labour. The men sought escape from the squalor and wretchedness of their lives in drinking, gambling, and sexual licence. Their behaviour towards each other reflected the fear, the terror and the coercion by which they were surrounded in their working days, and their alienation from the fruits of their labour. Contemporary critics attributed some of their vicious behaviour to the close association of so many depraved and desperate characters, and added that the treachery of the convicts towards each other flowed from such association.[29] Such treachery, however, was nourished by the atmosphere of terror, as all the officials—the Governor, the military and civil officers, the chaplains, the magistrates, the superintendents and the overseers —believed one and all that physical terror was the one effective restraint.

For the convicts seemed to provide abundant evidence of man's sinful nature. The men in the road parties plundered travellers on the road from Sydney to Parramatta, an operation more often than not made easy by the intoxicated condition of the travellers.[30] The convicts in the commissariat were bribed by the settlers to gain admission for their grain to the stores, used the bribe to buy alcohol, and then were punished for drunkenness. The mechanics stole building materials from the government stores because high prices presented an irresistible temptation to secrete and purloin them. Convicts bribed the flogger.[31] All the rules and regulations of the society were designed to protect the few against the evil machinations of the many: the use of passes to proceed from one settlement to another; the restriction of movement after sounding taptoo; control of firearms; orders against inflammatory libels, and seditious assemblies; punishments for hiding convicts and deserters; orders against forgery, perjury and gambling; punishments for vagrants and idlers; general musters of the population; formation of loyal associations; provisions for watchmen and town police; the forbidding of loitering on the wharf; even the denying of rumours of a settlement beyond

28 A short account relative to the proceedings in New South Wales, from the year 1800 to 1803, with hints and critical remarks, by George Caley addressed to Sir Joseph Banks, *H.R.N.S.W.*, vol. 5, pp. 292-4.

29 J. T. Bigge: The Colony of New South Wales, p. 33.

30 Ibid., p. 38.

31 Ibid., pp. 35-42.

the mountains.[32] Here, indeed, was a society in a state of siege, with human depravity in the attack, and force, terror, fear, spying, prying, rumour and meddling the weapons for its defence.

Assignment of convicts to private employers was begun by Phillip in 1789 to ensure that at least some convicts were employed by those who had a material interest in their labour.[33] To encourage the officers and later the settlers to employ convicts, the assigned convicts were at first fed, clothed, and if necessary housed by the government. By 1798 the shortage of labour caused by the very few convicts arriving between 1794 and 1797, as well as by the ever-pressing need to reduce the cost to government of the maintenance of convicts, caused the Duke of Portland to instruct Hunter to publish regulations under which the convict in assignment was to be fed, clothed and housed by his employer.[34] Although tentative attempts were made to fulfil these instructions in the regulations of 1798 and 1799, it was not until 1804 that the principle was effectively embodied in the system when King published an order which required all persons applying for convicts to sign an indenture by which they covenanted to clothe and maintain them according to the rate of allowance made by government. In return the convict was to labour for ten hours a day for five days of the week, and for six hours on Saturday. Those who finished their allotted tasks before the regulation time could work for their employers for the prescribed wage, or, if their employers either did not want or could not pay for their services, they could work for government or another employer for the prescribed wage.[35] This was £10 and board for a year's labour; or 6s. per week, together with provisions at least equal to the ration issued from the stores; or 1s. per day, with board, or 2s. 6d. per day without board. For clothing, those at public labour received annually, when the clothing in the stores allowed of that distribution, one frock, one shirt, one pair of trousers, one pair of breeches, and one pair of shoes in December, and two jackets, two shirts, one pair of trousers or breeches, one hat and two pairs of shoes in June.[36]

The condition of the assigned servant varied from employer to employer. Broadly, the condition of the man assigned to an opulent settler was superior. He was housed in separate huts built of wood, while his employer was able to pay him for extra labour in cash, which afforded some protection from the practice of grossly over-estimating the value of such articles of consumption

[32] See *New South Wales General Standing Orders: Selected from the General Orders issued by former Governors from the 16th of February, 1791, to the 6th of September, 1800, also General Orders issued by Governor King, from the 28th of September, 1800, to the 30th of September, 1802* (Sydney, 1802).

[33] Phillip to Sydney, 12 February 1790, *H.R.A.*, I, 1, p. 146; Phillip to Sydney, 13 February 1790, *H.R.A.*, I, 1, p. 157.

[34] J. T. Bigge: The Colony of New South Wales, pp. 74-5; Portland to Hunter, 31 August 1797, *H.R.A.*, I, 2, pp. 107-8.

[35] Government and General Orders, 6 January 1804 and 14 January 1804, in *H.R.A.*, I, 5, pp. 73-5.

[36] Proclamation of 14 January 1804, encl. in King to Hobart, 14 August 1804, *H.R.A.*, I, 5, pp. 74-5.

as tea, sugar and tobacco when they were used for payment in kind. The convict was not encouraged to wander from his master's farm, as by exertion he could accumulate wealth and obtain property. By contrast the convicts assigned to the less opulent settlers perforce wandered in search of extra labour, and in such wanderings were exposed to temptations. They generally inhabited the same houses as their masters, and frequently the same apartments. But whether assigned to the opulent or to the poorer settler, few possessed habits of cleanliness and order. The regulations did not compel a settler to provide soap; the scarcity of water and the distance from settlements also contributed to brand the convicts in assignment with all the appearances of the unwashed.[37]

English opinion welcomed assignment for its contribution to reformation. The English dwelt with approval on an idyll of two or three convicts domiciled in a family, removed from their former companions, and forced into habits of industry and regularity, which opened up the possibility of their becoming prosperous and respectable settlers.[38] By contrast the employers in New South Wales tended to discuss assignment in terms of its costs. All their talk on assignment was how a convict cost them forty pounds a year, and a free worker seventy pounds a year, though the free man did nearly twice as much work. On the other hand the convict could be compelled to work while the free man could only be subjected to persuasion.[39] The convict was singularly disinterested in any concern for his soul, generally indifferent to the incentive to acquire respectability, but prepared to endure any punishment rather than be assigned to an avaricious or cruel master. For them, some masters were generous and considerate, while others were unfeeling monsters.[40] As for the women the assignment system, in much the same way as government service, tended to operate as an encouragement to general depravity, for their employers received them as prostitutes rather than servants, a way of life little calculated to minister to the reform of their morals, let alone to counter their addiction to crime.[41]

The regulations for the punishment of assigned servants were very similar to those for the punishment of convicts in government service. For a minor offence against convict regulations the employer was required to lay a charge against his servant before a magistrate who could punish with anything up to twenty-five lashes; for more serious offences for which the punishments were floggings up to three hundred lashes, sentence to a gaol gang, or a penal settlement, the employer had to prefer the charge before a bench of three magistrates. The regulations also prescribed offences and penalties for employers. For thrashing a servant, for wanton cruelty or injustice an employer

[37] J. T. Bigge: The Colony of New South Wales, pp. 75-8.

[38] Report of the Select Committee on Transportation, 1812, p. 12, *P.P.*, 1812, II, 341.

[39] Evidence of J. Palmer and R. Campbell to the Select Committee on Transportation, 1812, pp. 63-4, 70-1, and Report, p. 12, *P.P.*, 1812, II, 341.

[40] *Memoirs of J. Hardy Vaux. Written by himself* (London, 1819), vol. 2, pp. 116-21.

[41] Report of the Select Committee on Transportation, 1812, p. 12, *P.P.*, 1812, II, 341.

could be deprived of the right to employ convicts; for under-paying him he could be fined. For presenting frivolous or vexatious complaints against employers a servant could be flogged.[42] The regulations, like the magistrates, were concerned to administer justice impartially for the punishment of wickedness and vice, but always in the context of a society whose first principle was subordination and whose agent was terror.

The system, however, provided incentives to climb towards affluence and respectability, as well as deterrents. For those who displayed a disposition to industry and good conduct during servitude there were indulgences such as tea, tobacco, extra allowances of food, and from private employers there was payment of wages which, although strictly forbidden in the regulations, had become so universal an incentive as to require frequent regulations condemning the practice. Another incentive was the ticket-of-leave, which contained a declaration of the Governor's pleasure to dispense with the attendance at government work of the convict holding it, and of his being permitted to engage in any lawful occupation within any given district for his own advantage during good behaviour, or until the Governor's further pleasure should be made known. There were certain restrictions on his freedom of movement, however, and limits on his legal rights; he could not leave his police district without permission; he could not sue or be sued in the law courts; he could not own though he could lease land. For a breach of the regulations governing the behaviour of ticket-of-leave holders he could be deprived of his ticket; his employer could prefer a charge carrying such a penalty against him.[43] Tickets-of-leave were granted, on their arrival, to convicts who possessed property or social standing, or had been transported for an action not involving criminal turpitude. They made it possible for convicts to return to that position in society which through their follies, their passions or their crimes, they had temporarily forfeited. Tickets were also granted for industry and good conduct. This encouraged the convicts to bribe the clerks, the overseers, the superintendents, and all officials placed in immediate authority over them to use their influence with the superintendent of convicts to obtain a ticket. From time to time the governors published regulations warning convicts against such traffic in tickets.[44] In general the tickets acted as a powerful incentive to industry, if not to good conduct. Through them, some climbed towards respectability, if not affluence. Up to 1810 observers praised them as an incentive. By 1820, men of a conservative cast of mind were beginning to wonder whether they had enabled men to climb not only to the rank in society they had forfeited but to much higher ranks, and whether or not the incentives of the convict system were subverting the traditional hierarchies in society.[45]

---

[42] Government and General Order of 2 October 1800, *H.R.A.*, I, 2, pp. 623-4. Government and General Order of 6 February 1802, *H.R.A.*, I, 3, pp. 472-3. Report of the Select Committee on Transportation, 1812, p. 11, *P.P.*, 1812, II, 341.

[43] J. T. Bigge: The Colony of New South Wales, pp. 130-1.

[44] See *New South Wales General Standing Orders* . . .

[45] J. T. Bigge: The Colony of New South Wales, pp. 149-50.

The major incentive to reformation was the prospect of a pardon. The power to pardon was granted to Phillip in his second commission of 2 April 1787,[46] and defined more specifically in the instructions of 25 April by which he was empowered to pardon those convicts who, from their good conduct and a disposition to industry, were found to be deserving of favour.[47] In 1790 this power was given the authority of statute law.[48] Pardons were of two kinds—absolute or conditional. An absolute pardon by the Governor of New South Wales and, after 1804, by the Lieutenant-Governor of Van Diemen's Land, contained a declaration that the unexpired term of transportation was absolutely remitted. The fee for such a pardon was five shillings to the principal clerk and after 1804, six-pence to the Government Printer. A conditional pardon contained a declaration that the unexpired term of the convict's sentence was remitted to him on condition that he continued to reside within the limits of New South Wales (including Van Diemen's Land) for the remainder of the original sentence, under pain of all the penalties he would have received by returning to Great Britain during the term of his original sentence of transportation.[49] In practice, pardons were granted for displays of bravery, such as the behaviour of some convicts when the *Guardian* sank,[50] for performing essential work within a prescribed time, for convicts transported for political offences such as Muir, Margarot, Skirving, Palmer and Gerrald, for persons sentenced to transportation during a period of crisis such as 1798—the year of troubles in Ireland. King granted many conditional pardons in the first years of his office. The other major occasion for the granting of a pardon was the celebration of the King's Birthday. On 4 June 1802, for example, King granted four full pardons and twenty-nine conditional pardons, but added that in future full and conditional pardons would only be granted on the King's Birthday and on extraordinary occasions.[51] But King's soft heart suppressed such scruples and principles; over one hundred and fifty received full or conditional pardons in 1803. Bligh, on the other hand, was niggardly, pardoning only two during his period of office. When Macquarie declared the pardons granted by Johnston, Foveaux and Paterson null and void, the ones who petitioned for their recognition were careful to argue that they had received them for their good conduct and their disposition to industry. Thomas Baker argued that he had received his pardon in consideration of his general good character and long service to his king and country, that he had sought it to enable him to minister to the great joy and comfort of his unhappy relatives. John Austin argued that he had enjoyed an unimpeachable character for sobriety, honesty and general good behaviour, that he wanted his pardon to

46 *H.R.A.*, I, 1, p. 4.

47 Ibid.

48 30 Geo. III, c. 47. *H.R.A.*, I, 1, pp. 208-12.

49 J. T. Bigge: The Colony of New South Wales, pp. 119-29.

50 *H.R.N.S.W.*, vol. 1, pt. 2, pp. 414 and 542; Grenville to Phillip, 16 November 1790, *H.R.A.*, I, 1, p. 213; encl. no. 4 in Phillip to Grenville, 15 December 1791, *H.R.A.*, I, 1, p. 325.

51 *H.R.A.*, I, 3, p. 625.

restore him to the bosom of his family and friends in his native land, for without that 'a very gloomy prospect succeeded to that refulgent one'.[52]

Emancipists and expirees who elected to stay in the colony were eligible for a land grant if, in the opinion of the Governor, they were deserving of favour. To such people the Governor granted thirty acres of land, with twenty acres more for a married man and ten acres for each child in the colony. They were to be victualled for twelve months from the government stores, supplied with an assortment of tools and utensils and such proper proportion of seed, cattle, sheep, and hogs as could be spared from the general stock of the settlement.[53] By 1810, opinions differed on the success of the system. Some believed that it provided an opportunity for the emancipist to establish himself in independence, and by proper conduct to regain a respectable place in society, and such instances, they believed, were not infrequent.[54] Some emancipists, however, failed to prosper. They fell into debt and lost their land to their creditors. Some said this was the appropriate desert for their viciousness, that they had borrowed on the security of their land to indulge in such beastly gratifications as drinking and gambling, and that it was through their own grievous faults that they were degraded from the level of respectability conferred by the possession of land to that of hirelings for wages. Some looked on them with the eyes of pity, believing them to be more the victims of economic conditions and environment than their own folly, that prices, soil, climate and lack of capital rather than thirst and greed had brought them to their destruction.[55] Whatever the cause, it was to be a member of their own group, Samuel Terry—rather than one of the free settlers or the much-maligned officers, who waxed fat in the land from their misfortunes.

Some by their behaviour while convicts, some by their failure as land-holders, and some from choice, became hirelings for wages. Tradesmen were much in demand in the building trade; others found employment in the small industries of the colony, in the pottery, the hat-manufactory, the tannery, the brewery, or with the shoe-maker, the tailors or the tin smiths; others took to the sea, on vessels fishing in the south seas, on coastal vessels, or on a ship trading with the islands. For up to 1810 the convict stain did not cause emancipist, expiree or free worker to shun any occupation; and until the time of Macquarie it was impossible, by clothing, lodging, or way of life, to distinguish the bond from the free workers. Nor within the free group was it possible to distinguish the ex-bond from the native-born and the free immigrant. Up to 1810 the men with pretensions, the men of sentiment, and the men sensitive to family ties or the tug of 'the old dart', or indeed any haunt for which they felt strong affection, worked their passages to England or Ireland, while the women prostituted themselves to the officers and sailors on ships sailing for

[52] Colonial Secretary of New South Wales archives (In letters, February 1810, Mitchell Library, Sydney).

[53] *H.R.A.*, I, 1, pp. 14-15.

[54] Report of the Select Committee on Transportation, 1812, p. 13, *P.P.*, 1812, II, 341.

[55] Report of the Reverend Samuel Marsden and assistant surgeon Arndell, March 1798, encl. in Hunter to Portland, 2 March 1798, *H.R.A.*, I, 2, pp. 140-6.

England or Ireland. Up to 1810 no emancipist or native born talked of the colony as peculiarly his own, let alone of 26 January as a day of general significance in his life. Nor was any emancipist stung to retort by the epithets of abuse about his morals and character which the official and more opulent classes so gratuitously propagated. No emancipist had yet thought to boast that by the labour of their hands the convicts had laid the foundations of European civilization in Australia, nor of the wealth possessed by the successful few amongst the ex-convicts.

Like that of the emancipists, the story of the settlers included successes as well as failures. The settlers were recruited from all sorts and conditions— from men such as Macarthur who had resigned their commissions in the army, or like Alt and Arndell who had received land grants in recognition of their services as civil officers in the colony of New South Wales. Chance, too, connived with circumstance to push some towards affluence and respectability, and others to wander as vagabonds free both of property and reputation. In 1796, Rowland Hassall sailed, with his wife Elizabeth and their two-year-old son Thomas, as a carpenter on the ship *Duff*, which, with a number of high-minded men sailed for the Pacific islands to bring the blessings of Christianity to those heathen lands where 'thick darkness' brooded. Under the threat of having their heads removed by the natives, Hassall and his party sailed for Sydney Cove, which they reached in 1798. There he quickly won a reputation for religion and piety by preaching the gospel in all the districts of the colony; he began, too, to acquire property, both of which activities won him the esteem of the Reverend Samuel Marsden. When Marsden was dejected by the fate of the soul of a negro convicted of rape in November 1804, Hassall comforted him.[56] When Marsden left for England in 1807, Hassall acted as his agent. By 1808, Hassall had acquired one thousand three hundred acres of land, including a grant of four hundred acres on the Nepean at Camden.[57] Despite his high calling neither his charity nor his loving kindness were very fully developed, and for the lack of these qualities he was often reproved by the convicts to whom he lectured on Christian qualities.[58]

Alexander Riley, a man of liberal education, arrived at Sydney Cove on the *Experiment* on 25 June 1804 with instructions from Lord Hobart to King that he was to be placed upon the most favourable footing as a settler in the colony.[59] As King rather tartly pointed out, this instruction cost the colony one hundred and fifty pounds odd more than for an ordinary settler.[60] Riley chose to take up his land at Port Dalrymple where he also held the office of storekeeper from 1 October 1804, at an allowance of five shillings per day. That brought him into contact with Paterson who found him of infinite use and proposed to mark out the most advantageous spot of land for

[56] *Sydney Gazette*, 25 November 1804.

[57] *Missionary Chronicle*, March 1821. *Australian Encyclopaedia* (Sydney, 1958), vol. 4.

[58] *The Atlas*, 28 December 1844.

[59] *H.R.A.*, I, 4, pp. 438-9.

[60] *H.R.A.*, I, 5, p. 127.

him.[61] Within a year Paterson had nominated him for the post of deputy-commissary, and for an additional land grant as a civil officer. During the same year, when he and some other whites were ambushed by the aborigines, Riley received a severe spear wound in the hip. That year, too, most of his crop on his land was ruined by flood.[62] In 1806 Paterson again favoured him by granting him the contract to supply the government stores with kangaroo meat. By 1807 he enjoyed the reputation of being a modest, hard-working and fairly successful settler.[63] Then the rebellion against Bligh swept him from the ranks of the fairly successful into the ranks of the opulent. Paterson took Riley with him when he sailed for Sydney Cove at the end of December 1808 and appointed him secretary to the acting commander-in-chief and administrator. The year 1809 brought halcyon days for Riley, as Paterson granted him one thousand acres at Cabramatta and a thousand more at an unspecified place, as well as confirming his previous grants at Port Dalrymple.[64] Though Macquarie obliged him to surrender the largesse he had received from Paterson, nevertheless the wealth he had accumulated permitted Riley in 1810 to begin his career in Sydney as a respectable merchant, in which he was to win eminence both as a magistrate and a business man in the era of Macquarie.

By contrast, one Andrew Hamilton Hume, dogged by ill-luck and some fatal flaw in his character, earned neither riches nor the esteem of his fellow-men. In England, Hume had been employed by Duncan Campbell as a super-intendent of convicts at Woolwich where he also enjoyed a reputation for understanding farming, an experience and knowledge which stood him in good stead when he applied for and was chosen to be one of the nine superintendents to be sent to Sydney Cove at a salary of forty pounds a year plus rations. He left in the *Guardian*, was wrecked off the Cape of Good Hope, and transferred to the *Lady Juliana*, which arrived in Sydney on 3 June 1790. He was promptly sent to Norfolk Island to superintend the cultivating and processing of flax. Again things began to go wrong, for which Hume blamed the inadequate tools and equipment, and he returned to Sydney Cove in March 1793 having decided to become a settler.[65] In addition to his attempts to become a settler he took a position in the granary at Parramatta, and appeared before the criminal court in 1798 for malversation of public property and for rape. He was acquitted on both charges, but dismissed from his office for impropriety in his conduct.[66] From 1800 to 1810 he was dismissed from a variety of positions as a man of bad character. So the search for a respectable condition in life, and the esteem of his fellow-men eluded him, and continued to elude him even after Macquarie granted him land at Appin in 1812. When his

[61] *H.R.A.*, III, 1, p. 629.

[62] *H.R.A.*, III, 1, p. 639 and pp. 649-51.

[63] *H.R.A.*, III, 1, pp. 745 and 749-51.

[64] *H.R.A.*, I, 7, pp. 26, 308 and 315; *H.R.A.*, III, 1, p. 701.

[65] D. Collins: *An Account of the English Colony in New South Wales* (London, 1798 and 1802), vol. 1, pp. 130, and 277; J. White: *Journal of a Voyage to New South Wales* (London, 1790), pp. 114-15, and 127. *H.R.A.*, I, 1, pp. 233 and 394.

[66] *H.R.A.*, I, 2, pp. 672-3 and 717.

son Hamilton, who was born in the colony in 1797, achieved glory and honour in 1824 by walking from Sydney to Port Phillip and back, Andrew Hamilton Hume had settled into obscurity.[67]

George Suttor was born in Chelsea, England, in 1774. In his twenties he decided that his native land had few bright and many dark prospects for the peaceful civilian. His older brothers would, he believed, absorb all his father's property by their own improvidence. This misgiving, the raging of parties, and the unsettled state of the times, turned his mind towards Australia. In 1798 he sought an interview with Sir Joseph Banks who agreed to send him out. He reached Sydney in November 1800, where King told him to look on every man as a rogue and that he, King, would not be troubled with his affairs. He took up land near Parramatta and slowly prospered till the mutiny of 1808 when, in his eyes, anarchy and idleness spread over the land. For writing a contumelious letter to Foveaux he spent six months in Sydney gaol, while his wife had to endure many fears and privations. After the arrival of Macquarie he was sent to London to testify for Bligh, and from his return to the colony in May 1812 he and his family began to prosper, for chance had put him on that side whose political fortunes could minister to his success.[68]

While Riley, Hassall and Suttor were climbing towards affluence and respectability, others were reaching the same position by different methods. Robert Campbell reached it by trade with Calcutta and Madras, the islands of the Pacific and Van Diemen's Land, and the Bass Strait fisheries. By 1808 he was so firmly entrenched that not even being on the wrong side after the deposition of Bligh could bring him to ruin. The Blaxland brothers were to reach affluence and respectability by virtue of their social station in England; but by 1810 their homes still lacked the grandeur and their manners, deportment and values the firmness, to distinguish them from the ordinary settlers. The one family displaying such grandeur and firmness was the Macarthurs.

In May of 1810 Ellis Bent wrote to his brother in England telling him that in New South Wales unless a man was connected with the government he was nobody.[69] Social prestige and eminence belonged, both at Sydney Cove and Hobart Town, to the civil and military officers, with the Governor or the Lieutenant-Governor at the head of each little world. Some of these lived in opulent squalor and some lived in comfort and abundance. Atkins, who had continued as Acting Judge Advocate till the arrival of Ellis Bent, lived near Government House in a house in very bad order, surrounded by an old and extremely shabby paling; the out-houses were extremely decayed and shabby and the yard itself was filthy. The entrance to the house was mean, narrow and shabby, and the house itself, to Ellis Bent's great grief, was but one storey high. The windows and doors were all bordered with low and vulgar caricatures: the doors were painted with alternate colours of blue and white: the furniture was very poor, and very dirty, and the house itself a

[67] *H.R.A.*, I, 2, p. 609; I, 6, p. 408; I, 7, p. 654. *Australian Encyclopaedia*, vol. 5.
[68] G. Mackaness (ed.): *Memoirs of George Suttor* (Sydney, 1948), *passim*.
[69] E. Bent to J. H. Bent, 2 May 1810 (MS. in National Library, Canberra).

perfect pig-stye.[70] Or so it appeared to Bent, who was surprised to find Atkins a very fine looking man of sixty-three, very prepossessing in his appearance, engaging and easy in his manners, a gentleman in his deportment, who plainly showed he was in a situation beneath him and that he was accustomed to polished and higher classes of life. By then, as Bent put it, Atkins was a most inordinate drinker of spirits, and was constantly intoxicated in the house where he was surrounded by his three illegitimate children, his old house-keeper, and at times, his legal assistant—an Irishman of the name of Fleming who was transported for passing a forged note, was very attentive and quick by day, but apt to drink at night, and be indecorous in the street.[71]

By contrast the house and way of life of the Chaplain General and civil magistrate, the Reverend Samuel Marsden, was as spotless as his moral reputation. In 1802 Marsden drove the French explorer Péron in a very elegant cabriolet seven or eight miles from Parramatta where he showed Péron with the most attentive kindness his farm with its spacious and well-built buildings, its flocks of sheep, its horses, pigs and goats, and its garden in which most of the European fruit trees were growing.[72] No wonder Marsden could write later: 'In the midst of all difficulties, God has always blessed my basket and my store, and prospered me in all that I have set my hands unto . . . We may trust God with all we have. I wish to be thankful to Him who has poured out His benefits upon me and mine.'[73]

In general the people in society were, as Ellis Bent put it rather waspishly, of the common run, neither good, bad nor indifferent. He knew of none worthy of extraordinary mention, and thought the whole bunch of them could not furnish matter to fill six pages for a letter.[74] The one possible exception was the Governor. He was the centre of the social life, for by 1810 the crown of social success was to dine at his table in Government House, Sydney, Parramatta or Hobart Town. He enjoyed the highest income and enjoyed great privileges—free meat, a boat to catch his fish, a farm at Parramatta to supply him with milk, butter, poultry and vegetables, and the right to import his groceries, his wines, his spirits and his ales free of freight. Convicts in government service made his furniture, and repaired his two houses. Horses were kept and found for him. The doings of the Governor and his circle challenged the ingenuity of the gossips, while observers described him as in a most excellent situation, or thought of him as an absolute master, as one who could do what he liked, with no one to say him nay.[75]

For the Governor enjoyed power over things both great and small. He

[70] E. Bent to his mother, 4 March 1810; E. Bent to J. H. Bent, 9 March 1810 (MS. in National Library, Canberra).

[71] E. Bent to his mother, 4 March 1810; E. Bent to J. H. Bent, 9 March 1810 (MS. in National Library, Canberra).

[72] F. Péron and L. Freycinet: *Voyage de découvertes aux Terres Australes*, vol. 1, (Paris, 1807), p. 402.

[73] Marsden to the Reverend J. Pratt, 2 July 1825. Quoted in J. R. Elder (ed.): *The Letters and Journals of Samuel Marsden* (Dunedin, 1932), p. 35, n.

[74] E. Bent to his mother, 4 March 1810 (MS. in National Library, Canberra).

[75] Ibid.

prescribed the times of all religious services held according to the rites of the Church of England, the length and form of that service, and the conditions under which people conducted services according to the rites of other religious persuasions. He defined the rights of assembly and publication; he issued orders about drinking water and about trespass; he decided when the corn was ripe for harvesting; he decided whether a man and a woman were 'proper objects of holy matrimony'; he decided when a man was sane or not; he decided how much men should drink and how much those victualled by the government stores ate; he decided what the children were taught in school; he granted land; he appointed to positions in the colony; he influenced if he did not decide the promotions of the civil and military officers under his command; and he pardoned convicts and criminals.[76]

Yet except for the rather noisy and by no means disinterested whig principles which Macarthur invoked to depose Bligh, few people in the colony were bothered by these powers. Up to 1810, the governors such as King and even Bligh had done all the thinking on a future constitution for the colony of New South Wales and its dependencies. The witnesses from the colony who gave evidence to the 1812 committee on transportation were not bothered by the powers of the Governor. Up to the time of Macquarie this was a subject which bothered only the theorists in England. In 1803 Jeremy Bentham wrote a pamphlet in which he pleaded for a constitution, showing the enormities and the oppressions of the innocent as well as the guilty, the breach of Magna Carta, of the Petition of Right, Habeas Corpus and the Bill of Rights, in the colony of New South Wales.[77] The 1812 committee observed that where so much authority and responsibility were thrown into the hands of one man it could not be expected that his will, however just, and his administration, however wise, would not at times create opposition and discontent amongst men unused, in their own country, to see so great a monopoly of power.[78]

That was not the way in which the articulate ones in the colony discussed their politics. A few perceived that the dilemma of those in authority was how to combine the discipline required in a gaol with the freedom of publication and action observed in England. To preserve the discipline of the gaol, meetings were forbidden except with the permission of the Governor, and petitions to the Governor were illegal unless signed by three magistrates; supreme legislative, executive and judicial powers were vested in the Governor; political questions were not discussed in the *Sydney Gazette*; the criminal court was controlled by the military officers; the doffing of caps to military officers, the presenting of arms and the drum salute to senior officers encouraged obedience and conformity rather than dissent, or an atmosphere in which people could agree to differ. Until 1810 no great issues divided that society, for although the officers and the more opulent classes had been split

[76] Based on orders published in the *Sydney Gazette* between 1803 and 1810.

[77] J. Bentham: *A Plea for the Constitution* (London, 1803).

[78] Report of the Select Committee on Transportation, 1812, p. 8, *P.P.*, 1812, II, 341.

into two factions by the behaviour of Bligh, the split did not correspond with any differences of interest or of principle.

The inhabitants spent part of their time in ceremonies which reminded them of their homeland. On St Patrick's day the Governor gave an entertainment for the government labourers and artificers, on which day, according to the *Sydney Gazette*, British hospitality displayed itself, and every heart was filled with sentiments of respect and gratitude.[79] Each year the anniversary of the birthday of their most gracious sovereign was ushered in with the ringing of bells and display of flags. Flags flew from the mastheads of all the ships in the cove, while the royal standard waved conspicuously at Fort Phillip, and the Union Jack at Dawes Point. In June 1810 the military paraded at noon for an inspection by the Governor, with more salutes. At one o'clock there was a levée at Government House when the civil and military officers came to pay their compliments, and Michael Massey Robinson delivered this ode in a very impressive style:

> Tho' far from Albion's hallow'd Coast
> Ocean's first Pride, and Nature's Boast
> . . .
>
> Still shall the Muse prefer her tribute Lay,
> And *Australasia* hail her George's Natal Day!
> Auspicious Morn! to Britons Dear:
> The pride of each Revolving Year!

At night, eighty or ninety persons from the civil and military officers and gentry sat down to a dinner at Government House of such elegance and style as to afford the utmost gratification to those partakers in the festivity. Toasts were drunk to the King, the Queen, the Prince of Wales, the Duke of York, and the rest of the royal family, to Lord Mulgrave and the navy, to Sir David Dundas and the army, to success to their arms by sea and land, to Governor Phillip the founder of the colony, to prosperity to the colony of New South Wales ('and may harmony and unanimity ever reign'), to Commodore Bligh and the squadron that lately left, to the immortal memory of the Right Honourable William Pitt, of Lord Nelson, and of Sir Ralph Abercromby, to Lord Castlereagh, Lord Wellington, the Archbishop of Canterbury, Mr Wilberforce, 'May British commerce ever flourish all over the globe', and 'May the single be married, and the married happy'. In the evening the lawns in front of Government House were crowded with an immense number of the inhabitants who looked at the decorations on the verandah, the festoons of rich foliage, and the lamps, and listened to the numerous airs and pieces performed by the band of the seventy-third regiment which, according to the *Sydney Gazette*, rendered their fascination complete.[80]

Officers and settlers were still perplexed and puzzled by the behaviour of the aborigines. Their religion taught them that the Creator had made all nations of the earth of one blood, from which they inferred that all people would in the fulness of time adopt their religion and their civilization. But by 1810

[79] *Sydney Gazette*, 17 March 1810.
[80] Ibid., 9 June 1810.

the original gesture of goodwill towards the aborigine had changed into one of disgust and reproach. They reproached the aborigine for being too indolent to provide for his common wants, for preferring a state of nakedness instead of the most trivial protection from the weather, for not cultivating a single herb or plant and contenting himself with whatever chance contributed to the immediate calls of appetite, for devouring the most nauseous insects in the most nauseous filth, and for not making the slightest attempt to alleviate the misery of his condition.[81] The only effect of contact with civilization was that the adults became despicable and loathsome degenerates while the children either conceived an utter abhorrence for the society and language of their countrymen, or deserted the European utterly. By 1810 few amongst the whites esteemed the aborigines worthy of the slightest notice or regard, except those whites with a relish for sanguinary cruelty who wantonly provoked the rancour of the aborigines against each other. The serious-minded were either expecting the aborigines to withdraw themselves from the areas of white settlement, or meditating how to raise the aborigine from barbarism to civilization.[82]

The serious-minded spent even more of their time propagating the ideas of the evangelicals on morality and social order. For them such a religion was, as the *Sydney Gazette* put it, the bond of society, and the ground of all civil order amongst men. As they believed that a good example was universally acknowledged to have a powerful and salutary effect upon the minds and conduct of all, it was, in their view, much to be wished, especially for the rising generation and the general prosperity of the colony, that all ranks of the community should unite in the highly meritorious service of suppressing vice in all its forms, and in pointing out to their offspring and servants the paths of virtue by themselves uniformly regarding the sabbath day and regularly attending church.[83] But church attendances remained so pitifully low as to present a perpetual challenge to the missionary zeal of the evangelicals. In the meantime, the clergy and the *Sydney Gazette* taught their listeners and readers to detect the divine plan in all human events. Marsden, for example, reminded them in a sermon that while in the sight of the unwise the decision to found a settlement at Botany Bay was motivated by the need to find a receptacle for the criminal population of Britain, He who governed the universe had had another object in view: God had provoked the Americans against the English in 1776 because the time had drawn near for the poor heathen nations of the south seas to be favoured with the knowledge of divine revelation.[84]

In such sermons Marsden likened himself to a man sent by God to deliver threatenings to a wicked generation, and to warn sinners that they would be cast into hell to suffer the vengeance of eternal fire. By painting lurid pictures

[81] *Sydney Gazette*, 14 July 1810.

[82] Ibid., 28 July 1810.

[83] Ibid., 11 August 1810.

[84] S. Marsden: Observations on the Introduction of the Gospel into the South-Sea Islands. MS. undated, but probably written just after his first voyage to New Zealand in 1814. (Marsden Papers, Mitchell Library, Sydney.)

of eternal torment he appealed to the wicked and unrighteous to forsake their ways and to purify their thoughts and return unto the Lord for He would have mercy and would abundantly pardon. There was little in his sermons of charity and the love of God, and much about fire and brimstone.[85] The Judge Advocate also reminded the guilty in his court of the connection between the law and morality. In sentencing Terence Flynn to death for murder, Ellis Bent admonished him to turn his thoughts seriously aside from the objects of this life, and to endeavour by an earnest repentance to evince a solicitude for his welfare in a world which was eternal. After an execution early in 1805 the *Sydney Gazette* wrote that by the example common charity inspired the hope that others might be hereafter deterred from crime.[86]

The *Sydney Gazette* from time to time published cautionary tales to illustrate the punishment of wickedness and vice in this world. On 10 March 1810, it told the story of Clorinda, a girl of more than ordinary beauty and an understanding far from contemptible, who had reached the colony in her fifteenth year in what the *Gazette* with becoming propriety termed unfortunate circumstances, and the fatal persuasion that a character once blighted must remain for ever irretrievable. She yielded to the addresses of a young man, but did not secure the relationship by the sacred bonds of marriage, and so cut off the hapless offspring of their unlicensed intercourse from society. After emancipation they raised their condition by industry and care. Five blooming babes, as the *Gazette* put it, adorned their table with the smiles of innocence, and no circumstance seemed wanting to complete their earthly bliss. But, with the rose of health still upon his cheek, the destinies willed that her partner should be drowned. Clorinda's transports of grief were much heightened by the terrible reflection that her children had no rights in law to her partner's wealth while she herself was excluded from the benefits she would have enjoyed had she been married. When an uncle of her partner successfully claimed his worldly goods, the widow and the five orphans were ejected. 'Ill-fated Orphans!' the *Gazette* asked, 'when Reflexion's torch shall kindle sad regret within your bosom, will filial love retain its vast ascendancy, and plead a mother's cause? and when maturer age shall flush conviction of your birth debased, and hold ye forth the contumelious outcasts of a licentious passion, say whether ye will most regret your being, or deprecate the want of common charity in those, whose preference to immoral habits hath intailed calamity on you?'[87]

One of the expedients to prevent such a calamity was education. In England, the three types of education corresponded with the three main classes in society—education by tutor for the children of the aristocracy; education at the grammar school for the children of the middle and professional classes; education at the charity school for the children of the lower classes. The English system could not be used as a model; there were no children of the aristocracy, most of the children of the lower classes belonged to convict

[85] MS. of sermons of S. Marsden (Marsden Papers, Mitchell Library, Sydney).
[86] *Sydney Gazette*, 3 March 1805.
[87] Ibid., 10 March 1810.

families, and the children of Irish Catholic parents were forbidden by the teachings of their church to receive religious instruction from heretics. Until 1800 at the earliest there were not sufficient children of middle class or professional parents to create a demand for a grammar school. There were twenty-six children in 1788, forty-two in October 1789, nine hundred and fifty-eight in 1800, and two thousand three hundred and four in 1810 out of a total population of eight thousand two hundred and ninety-three.[88]

Up to a point the creation of schools kept pace with the increase in the number of children. Phillip had been instructed to reserve two hundred acres in or near every town for a school and a schoolmaster. By March 1792, Johnson reported that schools had been opened in Sydney, Parramatta, and Norfolk Island where children were instructed in religion, morality and reading, writing and arithmetic. For they aimed high, though the men entrusted with the discharge of such a high calling stumbled into drunkenness on their ten pounds a year. By September 1800 King had decided that the peculiar composition of society in New South Wales required special measures. To save the youth of the colony from the destructive examples of abandoned parents, he proposed to create an orphan school in Sydney to provide asylum for them. This school, financed by voluntary subscriptions and the duties collected on the entrance and clearance of vessels landing articles for sale at Sydney Cove, was opened by the Reverend Samuel Marsden on 8 August 1801.[89] Keeping pace with the expansion of settlement, government schools, under the supervision of the government chaplain, were opened at Parramatta in 1796, and at the Hawkesbury in 1804. Each Christmas the children attending the several schools in the town of Sydney with their respective teachers appeared at Government House where the Governor examined them, presented each of them with a suit of clothing, and addressed them on the desirable attainment of a moral and religious education which imparted a sense of their duty to their country and their God.[90]

In the meantime some attempts had begun to provide a grammar school education. In September 1804, D. Parnell, who had been a schoolmaster at Norfolk Island, announced in the *Sydney Gazette* the opening of an academy for the instruction of youth in the principles of the English language, writing and arithmetic.[91] In January 1805 John Mitchell, assisted by James MacConnell, opened an academy in which grammar, writing, bookkeeping after the Italian mode, French and mathematics were taught. In August 1807, a Mrs Dorothy Marchant opened a school for young ladies, and on 2 April 1809 Mrs Mary Hodges announced the opening of a school for ladies in which she would carefully attend to the improvement of the pupils in the various kinds of needlework, a principal but too much neglected branch of female accomplishment,

[88] *H.R.A.*, I, 2, p. 535; Evidence of W. Bligh to the Select Committee on Transportation, 1812, p. 40, *P.P.*, 1812, II, 341; *H.R.A.*, I, 12, p. 313.

[89] King to Portland, 9 September 1800, *H.R.A.*, I, 2, pp. 532-3.

[90] *Sydney Gazette*, 6 January 1805; V. W. E. Goodin: 'Public Education in New South Wales before 1848', in R.A.H.S., *J. & P.*, 1950, vol. 36, pts. i-iv.

[91] *Sydney Gazette*, 9 September 1804.

while with the inculcation of moral principles she would studiously attend to the necessary routine of reading, writing and arithmetic.[92]

Such high-mindedness, however, was the preserve of the few; for while the clergy and the schoolmasters conceived of education as a means to salvation as well as to rescue the young from the examples of their parents, or from contracting habits of idleness,[93] the people spent their leisure quite oblivious of their divine destiny. In June 1810, the Whitsuntide holidays were kept up with great spirit at Parramatta. A cockpit was prepared at the upper end of the town, and a number of good battles were fought. Those who fancied bull baiting were elegantly amused with a very refined diversion in the course of which, according to the *Sydney Gazette*, a number of useless dogs were killed or crippled and in the end the provoked animals, breaking from their tether, rushed in amongst a group of the spectators, and nearly gave a tragic termination to the sports of the day.[94] The night ended in drunkenness and debauchery. But by then the first steps had been taken to raise the evangelical from the voice crying in the wilderness to a position of ascendancy in New South Wales.

92 Ibid., 23 December 1804.
93 Ibid., 10 March 1810.
94 Ibid., 16 June 1810.

PART IV

THE AGE OF MACQUARIE

13

MACQUARIE, 1810-1815

SHORTLY after midday, on 1 January 1810, on the parade ground at Sydney Cove, in a short and very animated speech, Lachlan Macquarie told his fellow-citizens and fellow-soldiers that His Majesty having been graciously pleased to honour him with the chief command and government of the colony of New South Wales he thought it was his duty to assure them it was his firm intention to exercise the authority with which he was thus vested with strict justice and impartiality.[1] To many who listened to those high-minded sentiments or had an eye for candour, sincerity and talent on that hot sticky day in January, it appeared that the man to bring together the two factions into which the upper classes of New South Wales were divided, the man to rescue the lower classes from their idleness and dissipation, as well as the man to reassure those in England who were questioning the wisdom of establishing a colony consisting entirely of the outcasts of society and the refuse of mankind, had that day taken office as Captain-General and Governor-in-Chief of the colony of New South Wales.[2]

He was born into a society which by tempering the inhumanity of Calvinist teaching with some of the common-sense of the enlightenment had put forward the upright man as the ideal of human behaviour. He was born in 1761 on the island of Mull, the son of a farmer. His mother imbued him with a respect for social rank and order, and he was endowed by nature with great gifts of industry and courage. He entered the army as an ensign in 1776 and between that date and his appointment to New South Wales in 1808 served with distinction in North America, India, Egypt, and Europe. He had seen the influence of rum, sugar and slavery in the new world, and the influence of Islam, Hinduism and Buddhism on the older civilizations of India, Ceylon and Egypt, all of which confirmed the principles he had imbibed in his homeland that the Protestant religion and British institutions were indispensable both for liberty and a high material civilization.

Things had not passed smoothly for him. By 1800 he was complaining that he had served twelve years as a captain in the army without promotion to a major.[3] When his first wife died in 1796 he told his brother Charles that

[1] *Sydney Gazette*, 7 January 1810; E. Bent to his mother, 4 March 1810 (MS. in National Library, Canberra).

[2] Sir G. Romilly in the House of Commons, 9 May 1810, *Hansard*, 1st series, vol. 16, col. 945.

[3] L. Macquarie to C. Macquarie, 12 March 1800 (photostat in the National Library, Canberra).

his days of happiness were past forever,[4] and in the following year he was toying with the idea of sequestering himself from the world and public society so that he might indulge his grief.[5] But by 1801 he was confiding to his brother that he was now reconciled to life.[6] After serving in England between 1803 and 1805, he returned to Bombay in 1805 where he learned that he had been appointed commander of the seventy-third regiment which was on its way back to England. He returned from India by way of Persia and Russia, and arrived in England in October of 1807, to marry Elizabeth Campbell a month later. In 1809 Castlereagh appointed Brigadier-General Miles Nightingall as Governor of New South Wales, and decided to send the seventy-third regiment under the command of Macquarie, who was designated Lieutenant-Governor.

When Nightingall resigned because of ill-health, Macquarie wrote to Castlereagh offering himself as a candidate for the governorship, promising to discharge the duties with zeal, fidelity and attention. As he put it, his one claim for so high and honourable an appointment was his long and faithful services; he had served in the four quarters of the globe with credit and with the approbation of the officers under whom he had had the honour to serve. He took the liberty of reminding his lordship that he had been recommended both by the Duke of York and by his friend, Sir Arthur Wellesley. He therefore indulged a fond hope that he would not be thought unworthy of the appointment of Governor of New South Wales. That was written on 11 April.[7] When he was presented to the king as Lieutenant-Governor elect on 26 April, he noted in his diary how he had seen four men made Knights of the Bath, and ended his entry with the words: 'I was present during this Ceremony.'[8] The next afternoon he met Lord Castlereagh by chance in Berkeley Square, who informed him that he was to be appointed Governor of New South Wales, and, as Macquarie wrote it in his memoranda book that night, 'His Majesty had already approved thereof!!!'[9]

On 14 May 1809 Castlereagh instructed him on what he was to do on his arrival in the colony. If Bligh were still there he was to liberate him from arrest and replace him in the government, but at the same time he was to intimate to Bligh that from the circumstances which had taken place, and the numbers of complaints against him, his continuance in the colony might tend to keep alive dissatisfaction, and it was His Majesty's pleasure that he should give up the government into Macquarie's hands immediately and return to England. He was to place Major Johnston under immediate arrest, and send

[4] L. Macquarie to C. Macquarie, 9 February 1799 (photostat in National Library, Canberra).

[5] L. Macquarie to C. Macquarie, 12 March 1800 (photostat in National Library, Canberra).

[6] L. Macquarie to C. Macquarie, 28 February 1801 (photostat in National Library, Canberra).

[7] Macquarie to Castlereagh, 11 April 1809 (Macquarie's private letter book, 1808-1810, Mitchell Library, Sydney).

[8] Macquarie's Memoranda, p. 3 (Mitchell Library, Sydney).

[9] Ibid.

him to England for trial. As Bligh had represented Mr Macarthur to be the leading promoter and instigator of the mutinous measures he was to arrest him for criminal acts against the Governor and his authority and bring him to trial before the criminal court. He was to restore the deposed officers, appoint Ellis Bent as Judge Advocate, send Atkins to England, send every officer of the New South Wales Corps back to England with that regiment, restore to Bligh his papers, declare informal all trials held during the usurpation of the government, and revoke the land grants and pardons made in the same period. The great objects of his attention were to be to improve the morals of the colonists, to encourage marriage, to provide for education, to prohibit the use of spirituous liquors, and so to increase agriculture and stock as to ensure the certainty of a full supply to the inhabitants under all circumstances. Castlereagh attributed the previous failure of these ends to the want of example and co-operation in the higher classes of the settlement. Macquarie was also to consider whether it would not be most advisable to allow markets to find their own level by abolishing price control; he was also to consider whether it was good policy to continue to maintain a government farm and government cattle. Finally, he was to adopt precautionary measures to prevent the recurrence of famine occasioned by the inundations of the Hawkesbury and to consider the expediency of forming a public granary.[10]

Five days earlier, on 9 May, he had received a commission and instructions appointing him Captain-General and Governor-in-Chief in and over the territory of New South Wales. These repeated the instructions to his predecessors. He was to proceed to the cultivation of the lands, distributing the convicts for those and other purposes as might appear to him necessary and best calculated to render their services most useful to the community; to make voyages of discovery; to conciliate the affections of the aborigines, enjoining all subjects to live in amity and kindness with them; to enforce a due observance of religion and good order, and to take particular care that all possible attention be paid to the due celebration of public worship. He was to grant land to all emancipists who from their good conduct and a disposition to industry were deserving of favour, and assist them with seed and stock; he was to grant land to free settlers, to assign convicts to settlers, and to form townships, reserving four hundred acres in each town for a church and the maintenance of a clergyman and two hundred acres for a schoolmaster.[11]

Macquarie and his party sailed on the storeship *Dromedary* on 22 May 1809, which was convoyed by the *Hindostan*. Ellis Bent, the new Judge Advocate, and his wife were with him. Born in 1783 and educated at Peterhouse, Cambridge, Bent had practised at the bar from 1805 to 1809, when severe family misfortunes forced him to accept the position in New South Wales. He was a tall and rather heavy man, and his health was poor. In the beginning Macquarie wrote of him with enthusiasm as a man who united the mildest and gentlest disposition with the most conciliating manners, great

10 Castlereagh to Macquarie, 14 May 1809, *H.R.A.*, I, 7, pp. 80-3.
11 *H.R.A.*, I, 7, pp. 183-97.

good sense and accurate legal knowledge.[12] From his behaviour it looked as though Bent had something to contribute towards the improvement of the morals of the colonists, and the Protestant ascendancy. On the first Sunday possible on the voyage he read prayers publicly on board the ship, churched a woman and christened a child.[13] The name of England brought a tear to his eye; he was happy and young, believed himself healthy and lived in the hope of returning to England with independence and honour.[14] At Madeira, Bent wrote with condescension in his diary of a people of such superstition that they knelt and cried and offered almost their all to kiss the dress of a doll representing the Virgin Mary, made in London by their own order and at their own expense.[15]

Fortune seemed to be favouring them, for at Rio de Janeiro they heard that Johnston and Macarthur had just left that port on their way to London. Macquarie, with his usual candour, wrote to tell his brother how happy he was to be quit of such troublesome gentry.[16] Over four months later, on 29 December, the night before they landed in Sydney Cove, the wind blew a hurricane, the rain fell in torrents, the ships rolled heavily, and the cabins were filled with water. The next day the sky was serene, the wind as fresh and fair as it could blow. As the band on the *Dromedary* struck up 'God Save the King', Bent wept, as he thought tenderly of his mother and brother in England, and felt a tremendous verbal impotence to convey to his mother a mixture of anxiety, fear, hope, and joy such as he had never experienced before.[17]

At ten o'clock on the morning of Sunday, 31 December, as Macquarie stepped from the ship into the landing barge, the guns of the ships in the harbour fired salutes which were answered by the battery at Dawes Point. At the wharf, Macquarie and his wife were received by Colonel Paterson, Colonel Foveaux, and all the principal civil and military officers, who accompanied him to Government House. At noon on the following day at a grand parade before the officers and men of the seventy-third and the one hundred and second regiments, the civil officers, and a large gathering of the respectable inhabitants of Sydney and its settlements, Ellis Bent as Judge Advocate read Macquarie's commission and administered the usual oaths of such office on the Protestant succession, popish recusants, the due and impartial administration of justice, and the due observance of the laws relating to trade and plantations.[18]

[12] *Australian Encyclopaedia* (Sydney, 1958), vol. 1; Macquarie to Liverpool, 18 October 1811, *H.R.A.*, I, 7, p. 395.

[13] E. Bent: Journal of a Voyage from England to the Cape of Good Hope being part of a Voyage to New South Wales, including Sketches of Madeira, Porto Praya and the City and Harbour of St. Sebastian's Rio Janeiro, pp. 24-5 (MS. in the National Library, Canberra).

[14] E. Bent to his mother, 15 June 1809 (MS. in National Library, Canberra).

[15] E. Bent: Journal of a Voyage from England, pp. 118-19.

[16] L. Macquarie to C. Macquarie, Rio de Janeiro, 14 August 1809 (photostat in National Library, Canberra); E. Bent: Journal of a Voyage from England, pp. 62-3.

[17] E. Bent to his mother, 4 March 1810 (MS. in National Library, Canberra).

[18] *Sydney Gazette*, 7 January 1810; *H.R.A.*, I. 7, p. 184.

After the military had fired three volleys, Macquarie spoke with animation and peculiar energy to the citizens and soldiers of his intention to exercise strict justice and impartiality. He trusted he would enjoy the cordial support of the civil and military gentlemen placed at the head of the several departments of government. He was sanguine that all the dissensions and jealousies which had unfortunately existed would now terminate for ever and give way to a more becoming spirit of conciliation, harmony and unanimity among all classes and descriptions of the inhabitants. To attain this desirable object it was necessary that the upper ranks of society should hold out a good example to the lower orders by conducting themselves with propriety and rectitude and readily conforming to the laws and regulations established for the benefit of the colony. He most strongly recommended to all classes of the community, giving one of his characteristic emphases to classes, a strict observance of all religious duties and a constant and regular attendance at divine worship on Sundays and holy days, at the same time urging the magistrates and all other persons in authority to exert themselves to the utmost to check and prevent all forms of vice and immorality. He hoped he need not express the wish that the aborigines would not be molested, but that on the contrary they might always be treated with kindness and attention. From the troops he would expect a vigilant discharge of duty, adding the hope that their steadiness, sobriety and strict discipline would be so exemplary as to preclude the painful necessity of resorting but very rarely to punishment. As it was the earnest wish of their most gracious sovereign and his ministers to promote the welfare and prosperity of this rising colony, so it would be not only his duty but also his chief happiness to pursue it. The honest, sober and industrious inhabitant, whether free settler or convict, would ever find in him a friend and protector. When he ceased, the crowd broke into three cheers, and the band again played 'God Save the King'. That night the town of Sydney and the ships in the harbour were brightly illuminated. To observers it appeared a very brilliant spectacle pervaded by a sentiment which promised the fulfilment of that conciliation of classes, that improvement in morals, as well as that welfare and prosperity which Macquarie, in the full flood of the generous emotions and enthusiasms of that day, had declared to be both his ardent wish and his duty to promote.[19]

On the same day the inhabitants of Sydney read on all government notice boards a proclamation in which Macquarie expressed the utmost regret and high displeasure of His Majesty on account of the late tumultuous and mutinous proceedings to depose Bligh, his anxiety for the complete restoration of quiet and harmony, and that Bligh's absence had made it impossible for Macquarie to restore him to the government for a day. He went on to express the hope that all party spirit which had unfortunately resulted from the late unhappy disturbances would end, and that the higher classes would set an example of subordination, morality and decorum, and that those in an inferior station would endeavour to distinguish themselves only by their loyalty, their sobriety and their industry, by which means alone the welfare and happiness

[19] Ibid.

of the community could be effectually promoted. The *Sydney Gazette* published the proclamation on 7 January.[20] By the end of January it was clear in all the settlements of New South Wales and Van Diemen's Land, that Caligula had been succeeded by an improver.

The celebrations continued all through the month. On the night of 16 January an address was presented to Macquarie. Again the houses of Sydney and the ships in the harbour were brilliantly illuminated. At Mr Underwood's house two transparencies were displayed, one representing the Crown, the other representing commerce, for with affluence the emancipist was quick to adopt the symbols of respectability. A large bonfire blazed in front of the house as a band played 'God Save the King', 'Rule, Britannia!' and other loyal airs. After a display of fireworks the house was thrown open for the entertainment of the spectators. The tables were covered to profusion with refreshments. The guests danced merrily and festively until dawn when some of the stragglers probably saw a ship sweep in full sail into the harbour. It was the *Porpoise*. On it was Captain Bligh, still raging inwardly against those who had despitefully used him. With that dignity and generosity of sentiment that success and good fortune generate, Macquarie received him with every possible mark of respect and attention.[21]

Within a month a doctor in Sydney was complaining to his brother in England that Macquarie and his lady were Scotch and consequently close fisted, that he kept a shabby table, and very rarely had visitors.[22] A few months later Ellis Bent gossiped about the same tightness in a letter to his mother, telling her that Mrs Macquarie's dinners were much too small, and that the service was so stingy that one might have danced a reel between dishes.[23] As the gossip began, Macquarie, not knowing of it, published his plans for the welfare and happiness of the community; no one could as yet hazard even a guess on how he would respond to vilification let alone opposition.

He began by implementing his instructions on the actions of Johnston, Foveaux and Paterson. On 4 January he dismissed all the officers appointed by Johnston, Foveaux and Paterson, restored those who had been dismissed, and declared all trials and investigations held between 26 January 1808 and 31 December 1809 invalid, and all grants and leases of land null and void.[24] In a consequential order on 7 January, John Palmer was restored to the office of commissary, Robert Campbell as naval officer, William Gore as provost marshal and the Reverend Henry Fulton as assistant chaplain.[25] In an order dated 27 January, all absolute and conditional pardons granted by Johnston, Foveaux and Paterson were declared void and of no effect.[26]

[20] *Sydney Gazette*, 7 January 1810; *H.R.A.*, I, 7, p. 184.

[21] Macquarie to Castlereagh, 8 March 1810, *H.R.A.*, I, 7, p. 219.

[22] Dr J. Arnold to his brother, 25 February 1810 (letters of J. Arnold, Mitchell Library, Sydney).

[23] Ellis Bent to his mother, 27 April 1810 (MS. in National Library, Canberra).

[24] *Sydney Gazette*, 7 January 1810.

[25] Ibid., 14 January 1810.

[26] Ibid., 4 February 1810.

He then turned to improve the morals of the people, especially those of the lower orders. On 27 January he also published a proclamation in which he referred to the very shameful and indecent custom of settlers and other inhabitants carrying on their usual avocations on a Sunday. He prohibited such indecent profanation of the sabbath in the future, proclaiming that all public houses were to be shut during divine service, and that anyone selling liquors during such times was to lose his licence.[27] On 16 February, in an attempt to reduce profligacy of manners, dissipation and idleness, he reduced the number of licensed houses.[28] He also placed an import duty on spirits in the hope that high prices would reduce drunkenness and idleness.[29] On 24 February he addressed a proclamation against the scandalous and pernicious custom so generally and shamefully adopted throughout the territory of persons of different sexes cohabiting and living together unsanctioned by the legal ties of matrimony, which was a scandal to religion, decency and all good government. He warned of the consequences of such behaviour: the woman had no valid title to the property of the man if he died intestate; and neither favour nor patronage would ever be extended to them. But those whose lives were sober, decent, and industrious might ever look up to His Excellency for all reasonable encouragement.[30]

To instruct the rising generation in those principles which, he believed, could alone render them dutiful and obedient to their parents and superiors, honest, faithful and useful members of society, and good Christians, he established several schools in Sydney and the subordinate settlements. Within a few months he wanted chaplains of respectable, good and pious character to minister to the people who were dispersed over the country without, as he put it, any awe of religious restraint over them.[31] To improve the religious tendency and morals of all classes in the community Macquarie issued an order on 19 May that convicts of all religious persuasions must attend divine worship on Sundays, conducted according to the rites of the Church of England, with instructions to the constables to arrest all vagrants on the sabbath and to commit to gaol all people drinking or rioting in disorderly houses during the hours of divine service.[32] On the first Sunday of compulsory church for the convicts, Macquarie attended their service in person, when he was pleased to bestow the highest commendation upon the whole convict body for their clean and neat appearance.[33]

At the same time he began a vigorous programme of public works which again was motivated by the same high moral purpose. The making of roads and bridges was, as he put it, one of the first steps towards improving a new country. He justified new buildings on the grounds of necessity, as he had

[27] Ibid.
[28] Ibid., 17 February 1810.
[29] Macquarie to Castlereagh, 30 April 1810, *H.R.A.*, I, 7, pp. 250-4.
[30] *Sydney Gazette*, 24 February 1810.
[31] Macquarie to Liverpool, 27 October 1810, *H.R.A.*, I, 7, p. 346.
[32] *Sydney Gazette*, 26 May 1810.
[33] Ibid.

found all the public buildings in a state of rapid decay. He began work on new barracks, on a new hospital (the present one being in a most ruinous state), granaries and other public stores. At that time he was aware of the wide field for improvement, aware too of the hope that in responding to this challenge his own services might not be unimportant, that, as he put it, they would ultimately meet with the approbation of his sovereign and His Majesty's ministers, and thereby confirm the opinion they did him the honour to form in his favour.[34] By October his conception of the new hospital was more grandiose as he began to write of an elegant and commodious building —adding that government would not pay a penny, as the contractors, William Broughton, Garnham Blaxcell, Alexander Riley and D'Arcy Wentworth, had undertaken to build it in three years in return for the exclusive right to import spirits during that time. The greater the achievement the more anxiously he looked for approval from London, which, in his usual candour, he described as 'so interesting to my Feelings'. He ended a description of his achievements with the hope that his lordship would give his administration credit at least for rectitude and integrity of principle.[35]

By November the record was one of achievement. Ever since he had had the honour of taking charge of the government the colony had been in a state of the utmost peace and tranquillity.[36] By October 1810 he was writing of how he rejoiced to have it in his power to inform his lordship that there was already within the short period of his government a change for the better in the religious tendency and morals of all the different classes of the community.[37] The material improvements were just as substantial. There were turnpike roads from Sydney to the Hawkesbury and from Sydney to Parramatta, with a plan to extend the latter to Liverpool.[38] There was a partly executed plan for the ornament and regularity of the streets of Sydney, to secure the peace and tranquillity of the town as well as reduce the number of disorderly and ill-disposed persons, by which the centre of Sydney received the lay-out and street names it has preserved to this day.[39] For the grandeur was part and parcel of the concern for order and morality. In December he announced plans to erect a township for each settlement— at Richmond, Windsor, Pitt Town, Wilberforce, Castlereagh and Liverpool —with a church, a school-house, a gaol and a guard house in each as the outward and visible signs of what Macquarie understood by civilization.[40]

On 16 November, Macquarie and his wife set out from Parramatta on a tour of the outer settlements, visiting the Cow Pastures, George's River and the Hawkesbury. On the whole he was delighted with the natural fertility and beauty of the country, with the progress in clearing the land, the increase

34 Macquarie to Castlereagh, 30 April 1810, *H.R.A.*, I, 7, pp. 254-5, 275 and 277.
35 Macquarie to Liverpool, 18 October 1811, *H.R.A.*, I, 7, pp. 384-97.
36 Ibid., p. 378.
37 Macquarie to Liverpool, 27 October 1810, *H.R.A.*, I, 7, p. 346.
38 Ibid., pp. 342-3.
39 *Sydney Gazette*, 6 and 27 October 1810.
40 Ibid., 22 December 1810.

in the area under grain, and the industry of the settlers. He could not, how-ever, forbear expressing his regret that the settlers had not paid proper attention to their domestic comfort by erecting commodious residences for themselves and suitable houses for the reception of their grain and cattle. He regretted too their neglect in providing decent apparel for themselves, as well as their disregard for economy and temperance, in all of which he hoped that by his next annual tour they would pay such attention to these objects as to enable him to give a more unqualified approbation to their exertions. To encourage such behaviour in future he proposed to grant land and other indulgences to those who could procure unquestionable vouchers to their honesty, industry and sobriety.[41]

In the meantime Macquarie had noticed that the men who had originally been sent out as convicts had, by long habits of industry and total reformation of manners, not only become respectable but by many degrees the most useful members of society. Yet these persons had never been countenanced or received into society. Conceiving that emancipation when united with rectitude and long-tried good conduct should lead a man back to that rank in society which he had forfeited, and believing that such would be the greatest inducement towards a reformation of manners as well as consistent with the gracious and humane intentions of His Majesty and his ministers in favour of this class of people, Macquarie, with great caution and delicacy, invited four emancipists to his table: Mr D'Arcy Wentworth, principal sur-geon, Mr William Redfern, assistant surgeon, Mr Andrew Thompson, an opulent farmer and proprietor of land, and Mr Simeon Lord, an opulent merchant. Three of them had acquired property to a large amount; all had conducted themselves with the great propriety; all gave most liberal assistance to government.[42] He also appointed Andrew Thompson a Justice of the Peace and a magistrate at the Hawkesbury, and planned to confer the same marks of distinction on Lord and Wentworth when vacancies occurred.[43]

In the *Sydney Gazette* on 31 March, Macquarie announced the appoint-ment of Marsden, Simeon Lord and Andrew Thompson as trustees and com-missioners for the turnpike road to be built between Sydney and the Hawkes-bury.[44] Marsden, who had only recently returned to the colony on the *Anne* on 27 February 1810, believed his superiors in England would never approve of his associating with ex-convicts, who still lived in scenes of immorality, and might therefore not only besmirch his sacred character but also cause him to lose the respect of the people under his care.[45] He was therefore much astonished when he read of his appointment in the *Sydney Gazette*, and considered it a degradation to his office as senior chaplain in the colony. He

[41] Macquarie to Liverpool, 18 October 1811, *H.R.A.*, I, 7, pp. 398-401.
[42] Macquarie to Castlereagh, 30 April 1810, *H.R.A.*, I, 7, pp. 275-6.
[43] Ibid., p. 276.
[44] *Sydney Gazette*, 31 March 1810.
[45] Marsden to Macquarie, 2 April 1810 (Bigge Appendix, box 12, p. 347, Mitchell Library); Marsden to the Archbishop of Canterbury, 2 May 1810 (Bonwick Tran-scripts, Missionary vol. 1); and Marsden to Wilberforce, 27 July 1810 (Bonwick Transcripts, Missionary vol. 1).

waited on Macquarie and immediately requested permission to decline the appointment. Whereupon Macquarie told him he considered the refusal an act of hostility to his government, and of disrespect to his person. Marsden withdrew, convinced that Macquarie's feelings of indignation betrayed a man for whom obedience to his commands was essential. A few days later Macquarie sent for Marsden, who again regretted his inability to comply with Macquarie's request. Whereupon Macquarie flew into a rage, shouting it was just as well Marsden held a civil commission, or he would have had him tried for disobedience by court martial. When Marsden retired this time he was fully aware of the great gulf between their points of view. Macquarie, as Marsden saw it, believed people should obey his commands. Marsden believed his first duty was to protect the reputation of his sacred office.[46] Macquarie then began to identify himself all the more ostentatiously and flamboyantly with the cause of the emancipists.

When Andrew Thompson died on 22 October 1810, at the age of thirty-seven, Macquarie attended the funeral as chief mourner, while Simeon Lord led the funeral procession. The Reverend Cartwright told them man that is born of woman hath but a short time to live, and the Reverend Samuel Marsden stayed on his glebe at Parramatta, for not even death could persuade him to give public recognition to a notorious evil-liver. A few days later the *Sydney Gazette*, which was edited by an emancipist, wrote of Thompson's success in accumulating considerable property after his lapse from rectitude, and how his success in winning the confidence and esteem of some of the most distinguished people enabled him to surmount the private solicitude of revisiting his native country and led him to yield to the wish of passing the evening of his life where his manhood had been meritoriously exerted, rather than return to the land which gave him birth.[47] As Macquarie put it, this most useful and valuable man closed his earthly career on the twenty-second day of October at Windsor, of which he was the principal founder, in the thirty-seventh year of his age with the hope of eternal life.

In this way, Thompson's death became the occasion for the first statement that the country belonged to deserving emancipists. At the same time Macquarie identified himself more closely with their aspirations by writing the epitaph for the headstone over the grave, in which he pointed out that by persevering industry and a diligent attention to the command of his superiors, Thompson had raised himself to that state of respectability and affluence, which had caused Macquarie to appoint him a Justice of the Peace, and to restore him to that rank in society which he had forfeited[48] (and this in time had made so deep an impression on the grateful heart of Thompson that he had bequeathed one quarter of his fortune to the Governor). So a headstone on a grave became a memorial of the case for the emancipist and Macquarie, who had dedicated himself to the destruction of faction in the colony, was

46 S. Marsden: *An Answer to Certain Calumnies in the late Governor Macquarie's Pamphlet, and the third Edition of Mr. Wentworth's Account of Australasia* (London, 1826), pp. 5-6.
47 *Sydney Gazette*, 27 October and 3 November 1810.
48 Epitaph on A. Thompson's tomb.

driven by his passions into a warm defence of the interests and aspirations of one group in the community. At that time he had no idea that such behaviour could provoke opposition; far less that such opposition could stand on moral principle.

In the meantime, Macquarie's correspondence with London had uncovered more of the tragic flaw in his make-up. His early despatches ended with almost desperate appeals for recognition. By chance these early statements of his hopes, his achievements, and his craving for such recognition, were answered by a man singularly lacking in those qualities of generosity and understanding which the occasion demanded. For in 1809 Lord Liverpool had taken over the seals of office from Viscount Castlereagh. Liverpool was conspicuous for his unruffled temper, his ever-ready and unvarying courtesy, his affability and his tact. He had never been known to utter a word at which anyone could take exception. He was, however, sensitive to extravagance with government money. He believed that government expenditure in England had become so enormous that all must look to economy. He believed, too, that there were insuperable objections to every proposal for reform or change.[49]

In the beginning Liverpool wrote with approval, though not with the warmth that Macquarie craved. He told Macquarie in a despatch of July 1811 that he had been commanded to signify the general approbation of His Royal Highness the Prince Regent of Macquarie's conduct in his civil capacity. Liverpool was not altogether happy, however, about Macquarie's policy on spirits, because he believed inveterate habits of drunkenness and dissipation among the lower orders of the people were more likely to be increased than checked by the facility of indulgence. He also urged Macquarie to exercise the utmost vigilance to prevent unnecessary expenditure in the execution of the works in progress. For the rest, Liverpool was content to instruct Macquarie on such questions as the evacuation of Norfolk Island and making Port Dalrymple dependent on Hobart Town.[50] Within a year Liverpool was asking Macquarie for a better explanation than any he had thought of so far for the deplorable increase in expenditure, and repeating to him the positive commands of His Royal Highness that while he remained in charge of the colony of New South Wales he should use the most unremitting exertions to reduce the expense at least to within its former limits, and that he should undertake no public buildings or works of any description without having the previous sanction of His Majesty's government for their construction.[51] Macquarie was deeply hurt. In reply, he wrote of the sincere sorrow and mortification he felt on account of the severe censure and strong animadversions. With all the passion of which he was capable he insisted on the integrity and rectitude and honourable purity of his motives, adding with pride that he might also without vanity and with great truth assert that he

[49] C. D. Yonge: *The Life and Administration of Robert Banks, second Earl of Liverpool, K.G. late First Lord of the Treasury* (London, 1868), vol. 1, pp. 315-16, vol. 3, p. 458.

[50] Liverpool to Macquarie, 26 July 1811, *H.R.A.*, I, 7, pp. 361-6.

[51] Liverpool to Macquarie, 4 May 1812, *H.R.A.*, I, 7, pp. 477-8.

had already done more for the general amelioration of the colony, the improvement of the manners, morals, industry and religion of its inhabitants, than his three predecessors during the several years they governed it.[52]

Up to the end of 1812, however, such wounds to his pride were as rare as the rages to which he had been provoked by the opposition of the Reverend Samuel Marsden. Both in England and in the colony, if one may judge by contemporary opinion, he was by then on the crest of the wave of success. Perhaps his reputation in England was even higher than in the colony. In England, a few were attacking New South Wales as the most unpromising project possible for establishing a new colony, consisting as it did of the outcasts of society and the refuse of mankind. Others spoke of it irresponsibly as a place where the great cement of society, morals, were thrown underfoot, where the government was corrupt, and the subjects licentious. Others thought of it as a place where pickpockets were reformed, simply because there were no pockets to pick.[53] Most, however, were so indifferent that it took two years of agitation by the humanitarians and the criminal law reformers before the House of Commons was prepared to appoint a select committee to inquire into the manner in which sentences of transportation had been executed, and into the effects which had been produced by that mode of punishment.[54]

After taking evidence from Hunter, Bligh, Palmer, Campbell, George Johnston, Richard Johnson, Flinders, Margarot, and two other returned convicts, as well as from officials in England and Ireland responsible for the selection and despatch of convicts, the committee brought down a report which summarized the recent history of the transportation system, of New South Wales, and of Van Diemen's Land. It described the economy of the two colonies, and unequivocally condemned the manner in which the criminal courts were composed. This system, as the report put it, resembled a court martial rather than the mode of trial they were accustomed to see and enjoy in their own country.[55] Members of the committee recommended the establishment of courts of justice in Van Diemen's Land.[56] They were unhappy about the powers of the Governor, because when so much power and responsibility were thrown into the hands of one man it could not be expected that it would not at times create opposition and discontent amongst men unused in their own country to see so great a monopoly of power. To prevent these evils the committee recommended the creation of a council to share with the Governor the responsibility for the measures necessary for the security or prosperity of the colony, but they were vague about the precise powers, the numbers, and the method of appointment of such a council.[57]

On the religious, moral and educational life of the colony the committee reported with a bland optimism. They found that the erection of places of

---

[52] Macquarie to Liverpool, 9 November 1812, *H.R.A.*, I, 7, pp. 525-6, and 532.

[53] *Hansard*, 1st series, vol. 16, cols. 833-5, 944-8.

[54] Report of the Select Committee on Transportation, 1812, p. 1, *P.P.*, 1812, II, 341; *Hansard*, 1st series, vol. 21, col. 761.

[55] Ibid., p. 7.

[56] Ibid., p. 8.

[57] Ibid.

THE REVEREND SAMUEL MARSDEN

Portrait by Richard Read, Senior, in the Mitchell Gallery, Sydney

ELLIS BENT

Portrait by an unknown artist in the National Library, Canberra

worship had not been neglected, and that no restraint was imposed on those practising forms of worship other than that of the Church of England. They found that the education of youth appeared by no means to be neglected.[58] They were just as enthusiastic in their estimate of the incentives to reformation in the convict system. They singled out for special mention the principle adopted by Macquarie that tried good conduct should lead a man back to that rank in society which he had forfeited. In general the colony was answering the ends proposed by its establishment.[59] When the report was tabled in the House of Commons on 10 July the brief debate did not challenge the opinions of the committee. This was interpreted later by Macquarie to mean that parliament supported his policy—not only for the material and moral progress of the colony but also for the emancipists.[60]

At the same time a throw of chance in British politics contributed to Macquarie's ascent to the pinnacle of success. For in 1812, Earl Bathurst had taken over the seals of office from Lord Liverpool. Henry Bathurst, third Earl of Bathurst, born on 22 May 1762, succeeded to the family title in 1794, and had held various offices in the governments of Pitt and Liverpool when he took office as Secretary of State for War and the Colonies in 1812. By nature he was more amiable than Liverpool. In behaviour he was nervous and reserved, with a good deal of humour, and an habitual jester, as his conversation consisted of a series of jokes. In conviction he was greatly averse to changes; he opposed all proposals to reform the English constitution on the grounds that any change would not only change but destroy it. In politics he was a High Churchman and a high Tory who happened by great good fortune for Macquarie to share his views on the utility of religion and moral education in achieving subordination in society.[61]

In commenting on the recommendations of the select committee on transportation, Bathurst used language which underlined his spiritual affinities with Macquarie. He wrote of his desire to promote the prosperity of the settlement, to advance its civilization and to raise its character. He wrote too of the anxiety of His Majesty's government to encourage a religious feeling in the colony.[62] On changes in the administration of justice he outlined what was to be done without bothering about abstract arguments on justice or rights. In civil cases there were to be three courts for the colony of New South Wales. There was to be a Governor's Court, presided over by the Judge Advocate, which would hear suits in which the amount at issue did not exceed fifty pounds. In such cases their decision was to be final. There was to be a similar court for Van Diemen's Land, presided over by a deputy Judge Advocate, with the same upper limit of fifty pounds, all suits exceeding that amount to be pleaded before the Supreme Court in Sydney. The Supreme

58 Ibid., p. 9.

59 Ibid., p. 14.

60 Macquarie to Bigge, 6 November 1819, encl. in Macquarie to Bathurst, 22 February 1820, *H.R.A.*, I, 10, p. 222.

61 L. Strachey and R. Fulford (eds.): *The Greville Memoirs, 1814-1860* (London, 1938), vol. 3, pp. 65-6; Bathurst to Macquarie, 23 November 1812, *H.R.A.*, I, 7, pp. 675-6.

62 Bathurst to Macquarie, 23 November 1812, *H.R.A.*, I, 7, pp. 675-6.

T

Court was to consist of a Chief Justice and two persons chosen by the Governor in rotation from among the magistrates of the territory. Solicitors were to be employed in either side of a plea. There was to be a right of appeal to His Majesty in Council in all suits exceeding three thousand pounds.[63]

For criminal cases, the Supreme Court, comprising the Chief Justice and two magistrates, was to hear all criminal proceedings. That was a step away from the court martial in the preceding system of trial by the Judge Advocate and six military officers. But he drew the line at introducing trial by jury, after considering gravely how far the peculiar circumstances of colonial society would allow it. There were not sufficient settlers capable and willing to undertake jury duties; the principle of trial by peers might be infringed if free settlers judged convicts; it would not be prudent to allow convicts to act as jurymen; the settlers would not be happy if ex-convicts acted as jurymen. Bathurst said better not, as all conservatives must and do, by conjuring up all the difficulties in the way of change, and the dangers of rousing the passions of mankind.

The same caution informed his discussion of the powers of the Governor. No one living in an intellectual climate in which the British constitution and the Protestant religion were extolled as the creators of liberty, political stability and the higher civilization could be happy about such powers. Here again Bathurst moved cautiously, picking out one facet of it, the power to pardon. He informed Macquarie that he should in future recommend pardons to the Crown, because the power was liable to great abuse. On the recommendation which the committee had made of assisting the Governor by a council, he told Macquarie that His Majesty's government felt no disposition to accede. He foresaw many difficulties—the dissensions and disputes to which a council's opposition to the Governor must give rise, the parties which would arise in the colony, the length of time during which the public tranquillity would be interrupted before a communication could be received from home, and the danger of weakening the higher authorities in a society composed of such discordant materials.[64] It was Burke's warning—that if society was tampered with by human beings, the result was certain to be disastrous.

In the meantime success seemed to be crowning Macquarie's efforts in the colony. In his own eyes the colony never had been in such a flourishing condition as it was in November 1812. The colonists were taking greater pleasure than previously in honest industry and labour, and in cultivating their lands. They were becoming more regular in their conduct, more temperate in their habits, and infinitely more moral and religious than they had been on his arrival in the colony.[65] At six on the evening of 29 January 1813 one hundred and fifty people, including many gentlemen of the first respectability, sat down to an excellent dinner in a spacious tent in the front garden of Mr Jenkins to celebrate the anniversary of Macquarie's assuming command. William Gore, the provost marshal, acted as president, and William Cox, the magistrate at Windsor, as vice-president, each supported by a clergyman

[63] Bathurst to Macquarie, 23 November 1812, *H.R.A.*, I, 7, pp. 672-4.
[64] Ibid., pp. 674-5.
[65] Macquarie to Liverpool, 17 November 1812, *H.R.A.*, I, 7, p. 581.

on the right, while the rest of the company placed themselves promiscuously without respect to rank or difference of condition. This challenge to 'hob nob' was accepted with cordiality. After-dinner toasts were drunk to the King, the Prince Regent, the Queen and the rest of the royal family; success to the British arms by sea and land; a bumper toast to Governor Macquarie —May the anniversary of his assuming the command of the territory be commemorated and reverenced by our latest posterity! with three times three; Governor Phillip the founder of the colony; Earl Bathurst; Mr Wilberforce, the friend of the colony and of mankind in general, may religion and virtue be the foundation whereon the superstructure of our colony will be reared, unanimity! May all hearts be united for mutual benefit and general good; prosperity to the commerce and agriculture of New South Wales; the speedy establishment of an export trade, with three times three; the intending library: may every inhabitant of our colony unite in promoting the general diffusion of useful knowledge; the seventy-third regiment, and finally, good night. It was near eleven when the last toast was drunk, and the guests dispersed on the universal wish that such a commemoration might be repeated each year.[66]

All through 1813 the record of achievement continued. As early as 1810 the settlement had begun to expand along the valley of the Hunter River as ex-convicts began to take up their land grants on Wallis's, Paterson's, and Patrick Plains. At the same time the settlement expanded to the south-west towards Bringelly and the Cow Pastures, though further expansion was discouraged by the grant held by Macarthur in the district before the land deteriorated into the hills at Picton and the scruffy country of the Bargo Brush. Expansion west of Penrith was still blocked by the Blue Mountains.[67] From the time when they were first seen as a blue line against the horizon by Phillip and his party of officers at the Hawkesbury in 1789, until 1810, all attempts to cross them had failed. By 1811, however, the motives of curiosity and fame were strengthened by the need to find more grass for the sheep and cattle. In that year Gregory Blaxland, who had taken up land at South Creek in 1806, could not find sufficient food for his stock in the country east of the mountains, as caterpillars were eating what grass he had; nor could he find any adequate unoccupied space of good pasturage anywhere on the east side of the mountains. As he put it later, being fully convinced of the necessity of a further extension of pasturage, he made every inquiry in his power respecting the practicality of discovering a passage over the Blue Mountains. When told it was impossible, he began to fear that Port Jackson being so circumscribed would soon become a place of small importance. To dispel such pessimism he set out in 1811 with a party of three Europeans and two aborigines, and came back convinced that it would be possible to cross the mountains by keeping to the crowning ridge.[68]

[66] *Sydney Gazette*, 30 January 1813.

[67] T. M. Perry: 'The Spread of Rural Settlement in New South Wales, 1788-1826', in *Historical Studies*, May 1955, vol. 6, no. 24, pp. 376-95.

[68] G. Blaxland: *A Journal of a Tour of Discovery Across the Blue Mountains in New South Wales* (London, 1823).

The drought of 1812-13 quickened his desire to find more grass. To assist him he chose William Charles Wentworth and William Lawson. Wentworth was the son of D'Arcy Wentworth and a convict girl Catherine Crowley, who had been transported to Norfolk Island where Wentworth was born, probably in October 1790. He moved to Sydney in 1796, and left for England in 1803 for his education. On his return to Sydney in 1810 he was appointed acting provost marshal by Macquarie, and thus became the first of the native born to hold an office of importance in the colony. At the same time he received a land grant of one thousand seven hundred and fifty acres on the Nepean, and so had an interest in the search for grass.[69] Lawson, who was born in 1774, joined the New South Wales Corps and reached Sydney in 1800, and then served for a time at Norfolk Island. By an odd irony of history he was one of the officers on the court martial to try D'Arcy Wentworth in 1807, but came round later to the side of the opponents of Bligh. He went to England for the court martial of Johnston but returned before the proceedings began, to take up land. He was probably chosen by Blaxland because of his knowledge of surveying.[70] With these two, together with four servants, five dogs, and four horses laden with provisions and ammunition, Blaxland set out from his farm at South Creek on 11 May 1813. By 31 May, after enduring great hardships which had sapped their strength, they were looking down on the plains to the west at forest and grass land sufficient to support the stock of the colony for the next thirty years. Years later Wentworth remembered it as the day when the boundless champaign burst upon their sight like Canaan opening on rapt Israel's view, and in his mind's eye he saw the plains of Australasia as a new Arcadia. As provisions were almost used up, however, they turned back, and reached their homes on 6 June.[71] On 12 February in the following year Macquarie, desiring to confer on them substantial marks of his sense of their meritorious exertions in being the first Europeans who had accomplished the passage over the Blue Mountains, presented each of them with a grant of one thousand acres in this newly discovered country.[72]

In November 1813 Macquarie chose G. W. Evans to lead a party of five, including one of the servants who had accompanied Blaxland, over the mountains. Evans had had a rather mixed career in the colony. He was born in Warwick, England, in 1775 and apprenticed to an engineer and architect, from whom he learned the essentials of cartography. He migrated to the Cape of Good Hope in 1796 and from there to Sydney in 1802, where for a time he acted as surveyor-general and storekeeper at Parramatta, from which latter post he was dismissed by King for fraud in 1805. He then took up land on the Hawkesbury, came out in support of Bligh in 1808, was sent to Port

[69] *Australian Encyclopaedia*, vol. 9.

[70] Ibid., vol. 5.

[71] G. Blaxland: op. cit.; W. C. Wentworth: *A Statistical, Historical, and Political Description of the Colony of New South Wales, and Its dependent Settlements in Van Diemen's Land* . . . (London, 1819), pp. 60-5; W. C. Wentworth: *Australasia: A Poem written for the Chancellor's Medal at The Cambridge Commencement July 1823*, (London, 1823), pp. 13-14.

[72] *Sydney Gazette*, 12 February 1814.

Dalrymple as a surveyor in 1809, but did not sail there till 1812. Macquarie recalled him from Port Dalrymple to take charge of this second expedition across the Blue Mountains.[73] He performed this task with distinction, by following Blaxland's track to Mount Blaxland, from where he descended into the plains till he reached a river on which he conferred the name of Macquarie. In consideration of the importance of these discoveries, Macquarie presented Evans with a grant of one thousand acres in Van Diemen's Land, where he was to be stationed as deputy surveyor, and paid him one hundred and thirty pounds out of the colonial funds.[74]

As soon as Macquarie heard of this beautiful country of very considerable extent and great fertility, he decided to build a road across the mountains.[75] He appointed William Cox, the chief magistrate at Windsor, to supervise the work, and offered pardons to those convicts who volunteered to work on it provided the road was finished in a prescribed time. The road, which followed closely the Blaxland and Evans route, was begun in July 1814 and finished six months later.[76] On 25 April Macquarie set out to see for himself the real value and capabilities of the new district, taking with him his wife, Cox, J. T. Campbell, Captain Antill, Lieutenant Watts, Redfern, Oxley, the surveyor-general, and Evans. On Sunday, 7 May, on the west bank of the Macquarie River, Macquarie fixed on a site suitable for the erection of a town, to which he gave the name of Bathurst in honour of the Secretary of State for the Colonies. For here, as he saw it on that Sunday, was a very great acquisition to the colony in as much as it furnished an outlet for the increases and redundancy of its population for a century to come. When he returned to Sydney he saw it as an opportunity for sober industrious men with small families from the middling class of free people to receive from fifty to one hundred acres of land according to the number of the family. He saw it too as a country where there was abundance of fine grazing land where gentlemen of the upper class of settlers and great graziers might receive grants of land. In the meantime he would make no grants until he had received the commands of His Majesty's ministers. Here, indeed, was the opportunity, and the man with the imagination to dream the great dream. For when he returned to Sydney, on 19 May 1815, Macquarie was at the apogee of his achievement.[77]

When Evans returned to Bathurst for his second journey, in May 1815, he travelled over one hundred miles to the west of Bathurst, where he discovered a river flowing to the south-west to which he gave the name of Lachlan. The country, he wrote to Macquarie, was good indeed. On 31 May Evans and his party came on an aborigine who was quite terrified. The aborigine ran up a tree in a moment, where he hollered and cried so much that he could have

[73] *Australian Encyclopaedia*, vol. 3.
[74] *Sydney Gazette*, 12 February 1814.
[75] Macquarie to Bathurst, 28 April 1814, *H.R.A.*, I, 8, p. 150.
[76] Macquarie to Bathurst, 7 October 1814, *H.R.A.*, I, 8, pp. 314-15.
[77] Encl. no. 3 in Macquarie to Bathurst, 24 June 1815, *H.R.A.*, I, 8, pp. 568-76; L. Macquarie: *Journals of his Tours in New South Wales and Van Diemen's Land, 1810-1822* (Sydney, 1956), Sunday 7 May 1815, p. 101.

been heard a mile away: the more Evans spoke to him the more he cried.[78] By a curious coincidence this cry of fear was uttered on the Bathurst Plains at a time when Macquarie was beginning to make his bid to conciliate the affections of the aborigines and to civilize them, so as to render them industrious and useful to the government, as well as to improve their own condition. At that time he was full of hope. He told Bathurst the aborigines had scarcely emerged from the remotest state of rude and uncivilized nature, that they appeared to possess some qualities which if properly cultivated and encouraged might render them not only less wretched and destitute by reason of their wild wandering and unsettled habits, but progressively useful to the country either as agricultural labourers or a lower class of mechanics.[79] It seemed, he thought, only to require the fostering hand of time, gentle means, and conciliatory manners, to bring these poor unenlightened people into an important degree of civilization, and to instil into their minds, as they gradually opened to reason and reflection, a sense of the duties they owed their fellow kindred and society. What he hoped to do was to teach them a sense of duty as the first and happiest advance to a state of comfort and security, so that acts of hostility by the aborigines against the settlers might gradually cease.[80]

To civilize the aborigines Macquarie proposed to establish a native institution at Parramatta under Mr William Shelley in which the native youth of both sexes would be educated in habits of industry and decency, beginning with six boys and six girls. He also proposed to allot a piece of land bordering on the sea shore of Port Jackson where adult natives could settle and cultivate the land, till they had learned to prefer the productive effects of their own labour and industry to the wild and precarious pursuits of the woods.[81] The native institution was opened on 18 January 1815; but the parents immediately enticed some of the children away, for, as Macquarie noted with regret, the natives, timid and suspicious as they were by nature, had not sufficient confidence in Europeans to believe that the institution was solely intended for their advantage and improvement. But, given time, he believed that their repugnance to civilization would be entirely overcome. Sixteen adult natives entered the farm on the north side of the harbour.[82]

At the same time Macquarie continued with unflagging zeal to promote the moral well-being of the inhabitants of New South Wales. In the new towns of Liverpool, Windsor, Richmond and Wilberforce he built school houses, believing that the establishment of respectable clergymen and school masters greatly contributed to the morals of the lower orders of the people and to the implanting of religious principles in the minds of the rising generation.[83] In the following year, 1815, he promoted in the colony the work of

[78] Encl. in Macquarie to Bathurst, 30 June 1815, *H.R.A.*, I, 8, pp. 611-19.

[79] Macquarie to Bathurst, 7 October 1814, *H.R.A.*, I, 8, p. 313.

[80] Macquarie to Bathurst, 8 October 1814, *H.R.A.*, I, 8, p. 367.

[81] Ibid., pp. 369-70.

[82] Macquarie to Bathurst, 24 March 1815, *H.R.A.*, I, 8, p. 467.

[83] Macquarie to Bathurst, 28 April 1814, *H.R.A.*, I, 8, p. 154.

two movements aiming at moral progress. The first was the British and Foreign Bible Society, which had been founded in London in 1804. The founders believed that every man should be made capable of reading the Bible, because its sacred truths produced a unity of sentiment and a correction of the most ferocious manners. They believed too that such an improvement in morals was the promise of prosperity as from the fountain of morality flowed the greatest worldly comforts.[84] The second movement was the Sunday School movement, which had been begun by Robert Raikes in Gloucester, in 1783. Like the British and Foreign Bible Society, its supporters believed in the benefits to be derived by mankind from religious education, and proposed to promote this great object among the children.[85] In this way, under the patronage of Macquarie, the children in the settlements of New South Wales and its dependencies were encouraged to attend Sunday School where, under the guidance of teachers such as Rowland Hassall they sang the words:

> Happy the child whose tender years
> Receive instruction well:
> Who hates the sinner's path, and fears
> The road that leads to hell.[86]

At the very pinnacle of his achievement Macquarie began to follow the road that would lead him to his private hell. As early as November 1812, when criticism of his emancipist policy trickled back to him, he wrote with some warmth of those people who found it advantageous to their interests and illiberal prejudices to consider emancipists as outcasts beneath their notice and doomed to oblivion for ever.[87] By 1813 such opposition had pushed him into a warm defence of the policy. This, he argued, was a convict country, and people who were too proud or too delicate in their feelings to associate with the population of the country should bend their course to some other country in which their prejudices in this respect would meet with no opposition. The government in London should decide whether the policy was to be conducted to please the minds of the free people or to hold out the greatest possible rewards to convicts for the reformation of manners.[88] On the same day he wrote off another despatch to Bathurst in which he contrasted the emancipist surgeon Redfern with the free surgeon Luttrell: Redfern had the talent to justify him looking forward to filling the highest situation in the medical department in New South Wales; Luttrell was sordid and unfeeling, and did not afford any medical assistance to any person who could not afford to pay him well for it.[89] By then the drive to defend his policy had rendered Macquarie blind to the faults of Redfern as a man, and the strength of his feelings had caused his judgment to falter. From that it was

[84] *Sydney Gazette*, 30 September 1815.
[85] Ibid., 14 October 1815.
[86] Hymns for the Eighth Anniversary of the Parramatta Sunday School 1816 (MS. in Mitchell Library, Sydney).
[87] Macquarie to Liverpool, 17 November 1812, *H.R.A.*, I, 7, pp. 616-17.
[88] Macquarie to Bathurst, 28 June 1813, *H.R.A.*, I, 7, pp. 775-6.
[89] Ibid., pp. 787-8.

but a step to the language of righteous indignation, for the man who believed that truth and humanity were on his side was beginning to feel a righteous anger against those in the colony who would destine a fellow creature who had once defected from the path of virtue to an eternal badge of infamy. 'I am happy,' he went on, 'in feeling a Spirit of Charity in Me, which shall ever Make Me despise such Unjust and illiberal Sentiments.'[90] When John Macarthur heard during his exile in London that Macquarie was associating with and bringing to his table men who had been convicts, who had amassed fortunes by the most infamous frauds, and continued to set the most shameful examples of the dissoluteness and vice, he believed Macquarie had been misled and was involved in a mist by the artifice and falsehood of persons who had guided him on his first arrival.[91] But by 1815 the mist in Macquarie's mind could not be puffed away by the winds of enlightenment.

This preoccupation with the righteousness of his own position, as well as the drive to defend it, became so over-powering that it engulfed more and more of his time and energy. The first fruits of this had appeared during those days of his greatest triumphs. On 13 June 1813, Philip Connor and Archibald McNaughton, both officers of the seventy-third regiment, one dressed in a coatee, the other in a great coat, and both much intoxicated, followed Elizabeth Winch down Pitt Street using indecent expressions to her. She entered the house of Mr and Mrs Holness and closed the door in their faces. Connor began to beat loudly on it with his stick, whereupon Holness asked his wife what the gentlemen wanted, and opened the door saying, 'Oh, oh, if it's f——g you want, I can give you enough if you do not be off.' Connor then struck Holness with his cane, and as a result of the fight which ensued Holness died; whereupon McNaughton said, 'If he is dead let him die, and be d——d.' In the trial which followed the Judge Advocate's court, consisting of the Judge Advocate, Ellis Bent, and six military officers, found Connor and McNaughton not guilty of murder, but guilty of feloniously slaying and killing William Holness, fined them one shilling each, and sentenced them to imprisonment for six months in the Parramatta gaol.[92]

Macquarie was appalled by the verdict. Little justice, he wrote, could be expected towards the poor while the court consisted of brother officers of the prisoner at the bar. He wrote too of the fatal consequences attendant on a life of drunkenness, debauchery and riot, which inevitably tended to the debasement and degradation of the upright and manly character of a British soldier. To him this was a melancholy and disgraceful occasion.[93]

Both the strengths and the weaknesses were revealed in his handling of the affairs of Van Diemen's Land and Lieutenant-Governor Thomas Davey. Macquarie had arrived in Hobart for his first tour of Van Diemen's Land on 23 November 1811. Everywhere he went he saw how things could be im-

[90] Macquarie to Bathurst, 7 October 1814, *H.R.A.*, I, 8, p. 316.

[91] J. Macarthur to E. Macarthur, 21 April 1811, S. M. Onslow (ed.): *Some Early Records of the Macarthurs of Camden* (Sydney, 1914), pp. 215-16.

[92] Encl. no. 2 in Macquarie to Bathurst, 31 July 1813, *H.R.A.*, I, 8, pp. 7-26; *Sydney Gazette*, 3 July 1813.

[93] Macquarie to Bathurst, 31 July 1813, *H.R.A.*, I, 8, pp. 1-5.

proved. At Hobart Town he regretted much the irregularity of the buildings, and the inattention to any established plan in the formation of the town, and issued instructions for a plan to be made so that the convenience and beauty of the place might be greatly improved. He had ideas, too, for the improvement both of agriculture, and the houses of the settlers and their stockyards. After travelling from Hobart Town to Port Dalrymple he suggested military posts to protect the settlers against the natives, while he proposed to move Port Dalrymple to George Town.[94] He even had ideas on a suitable replacement for Collins, putting forward his own brother Charles as a man of good sound sense, high honour and integrity, conciliatory in manners and thoroughly acquainted with business in civil as well as in military affairs.[95] Liverpool had other ideas, and in March 1812 he told Macquarie he had decided to offer the position to Lieutenant-Colonel Thomas Davey.[96]

Davey was probably born in 1760, took a commission in the marines in 1778, became a lieutenant in 1780, volunteered for service in New South Wales in 1786, returned to England in 1792, was promoted captain in 1795, major in 1809, and lieutenant-colonel in 1812, when Liverpool, under pressure from Davey's aristocratic patron, appointed him Lieutenant-Governor of Van Diemen's Land. Liverpool's successor at the Colonial Office, Bathurst, privately warned Macquarie that Davey's financial honesty was doubtful,[97] so Macquarie was on his guard when Davey arrived in Sydney on the *Minstrel* on 25 October 1812. During his stay of four months, Macquarie lectured him to use unremitting exertions to keep expenditure at a minimum. He warned Davey that the moment he sanctioned any peculation of the public property, or applied any part thereof or any public money he might be entrusted with to his own use, he as Governor would take immediate measures to prevent a repetition thereof.[98] During that four months Macquarie formed quite a low opinion of Davey, observing, as he put it later, an extraordinary degree of frivolity and low buffoonery in his manners.[99]

Before an open breach occurred, Davey sailed for Hobart Town, while Macquarie nursed his misgivings till such time as Davey's behaviour cloaked his personal disgust with the higher purpose of duty.

Davey arrived at Hobart Town on 20 February, to face problems which he had neither the capacity nor the inclination to handle. The settlers were plagued by bushrangers and the natives, while crimes of violence were all too common. Public works languished because of the indolence and negligence of the convict workers, for at this time both government and settlers had to be content with the rejects from the mainland. Davey himself was appalled with the magnitude of his task; the most deplorable chaos prevailed, the stores

---

[94] Encl. no. 1 in Macquarie to Liverpool, 17 November 1812, *H.R.A.*, I, 7, pp. 618-21.

[95] Macquarie to Liverpool, 31 January 1812, *H.R.A.*, I, 7, p. 456.

[96] Liverpool to Macquarie, 13 March 1812, *H.R.A.*, I, 7, p. 459.

[97] See Macquarie to Goulburn, 30 June 1813, *H.R.A.*, I, 7, pp. 789-90, and *Australian Encyclopaedia*, vol. 3.

[98] Macquarie to Goulburn, 30 June 1813, *H.R.A.*, I, 7, p. 790.

[99] Macquarie to Bathurst, 22 March 1815, *H.R.A.*, I, 8, p. 458.

were pillaged of their contents, little regard was paid to religious worship, Government House resembled a barn, the troops lacked a barracks and the sick a hospital, the settlers were exposed to depredations by the convicts, and subordination was not observed.[100] Within three years Davey had certainly improved the material conditions. In the meantime, however, he was winning notoriety for his eccentricities of behaviour. 'Mad Tom' or the 'Mad Governor' the locals called him. By day and by night he caroused at The Bird in Hand, in Argyle Street, frequently with convicts as his drinking companions. He was equally unconventional in dress and manner of speaking, walking the streets in his shirt sleeves, calling all and sundry by their Christian names or even by their nicknames, dropping in at the first house he came to for a drink, and cohabiting openly and unashamedly with convict women.[1]

By the beginning of 1815 every person arriving from Van Diemen's Land brought fresh reports of Davey's dissipation and profligacy. As Macquarie put it, it came to his ears through a variety of channels, that Davey spent almost his entire time in drinking, and every other form of low depravity, in company with the basest and meanest of the people. What rendered this debasement the more gross and offensive to Macquarie was that Davey was a married man, and his wife and daughter, who lived with him, were both very amiable and highly respectable. Davey was also venal and corrupt in his public life, as he was privy to and sanctioned the smuggling of spirits. Significantly, Macquarie omitted all reference to the improvement in material conditions generally. For Macquarie's judgment on Davey tended to focus so much on his personal behaviour, that Davey spent the rest of his days trying to persuade people in high places not to allow his conduct as an officer and a gentleman to suffer from the foul stigma uncharitably heaped upon it by Macquarie.[2] In Macquarie's mind these traits of dissipation, venality and downright fraud and imposition rendered Davey unfit and unworthy of his position. He therefore suggested the propriety of Davey being immediately relieved or superseded by some other person of greater energy of mind and of more honourable principles. Macquarie added a plea of provision for Davey's amiable but unfortunate wife and daughter, whose situations were, he believed, at best much to be pitied.[3]

The time taken to communicate with London gave Davey many months more for drinking and promiscuity; finally, in a despatch to Macquarie in April 1816, Bathurst made the point that when the state of society was good the immorality and profligacy of a superior officer might not cause harm, but in Van Diemen's Land society was composed of persons who had but lately, if at all, renounced their former vicious habits. There, the effect of bad example in a superior officer had a direct tendency to defeat that purpose of punishment

[100] The memorial of T. Davey to Bigge, 29 February 1820 (Bigge Appendix, C.O. 201/137).

[1] Oldham Papers, vol. 3, p. 348, Royal Society of Tasmania, Hobart.

[2] The memorial of T. Davey to Bigge, 29 February 1820 (Bigge Appendix, C.O. 201/137).

[3] Macquarie to Bathurst, 22 March 1815, *H.R.A.*, I, 8, pp. 458-61.

and reformation of criminals for which the colony had been founded. Bathurst had decided to remove Davey, and to appoint Colonel Sorell in his place. Macquarie was to grant land to Davey in the neighbourhood of Port Jackson as that appeared the only way to afford relief to his wife and family.[4] It was not till 9 April 1817 that Davey handed over to Sorell, after which he took up his land grants, but being no more successful as a farmer than as Lieutenant-Governor, he sailed for England in 1821, where he died on 2 May 1823, bequeathing to his wife and daughter the land which had been intended to console them for all the humiliations and indignities they had suffered from his waywardness.

So far, Macquarie could sing with the psalmist that the ungodly were trapped in the work of their own hands, and the wicked turned into hell. He could not draw the same lesson from the story of his relations with Marsden. Despite the heat engendered during 1810, Marsden rejoiced to have so moral a man as Captain-General and Governor-in-Chief of the colony of New South Wales.[5] In February 1814, when Macquarie asked the chaplains to read a government notice in church urging settlers to send their grain to the government stores because of the scarcity, Marsden refused on the grounds that the sacred should not be confounded with the profane. Macquarie was incensed, and cautioned Marsden to beware of resisting *his* commands in the future, as Marsden should answer for it at *his* peril, as Macquarie believed that it could not be improper to make public during worship any information to benefit the community in a material degree. To him, Marsden's objections were both frivolous and ill-founded, arising from the illiberal sentiments and bigoted principles which, he added, had on all occasions pervaded Marsden's conduct both on political and religious subjects.[6]

In June and July 1814, Marsden, who had received from the London Missionary Society copies of Dr Goode's version of the Psalms, had them sung in the churches of New South Wales to the exclusion of those attached by authority to the Bible and the Book of Common Prayer. Macquarie prohibited the use of the Goode version, because he believed this to be an unwarrantable violation of the services of the Established Church, and one which would probably lead to still further and greater innovations in its sacred ceremonies, as Mr Marsden and some of the assistant chaplains were originally of low rank, and not qualified by liberal education in the usual way for the sacred functions entrusted to them. They were also much tinctured with methodistical and other sectarian principles, which disposed them to a hasty adoption of new systems, or at least of new forms, to the exclusion of the old establishment of the Church of England.[7] On this point Bathurst supported Macquarie, enjoining him to enforce a strict adherence to the forms and services prescribed by the competent authority.[8] When Macquarie read these words in the middle

[4] Bathurst to Macquarie, 18 April 1816, *H.R.A.*, I, 9, pp. 113-14.
[5] J. S. Hassall: *In Old Australia* (Brisbane, 1902), p. 152.
[6] Macquarie to Bathurst, 24 May 1814, *H.R.A.*, I, 8, pp. 255-6.
[7] Macquarie to Bathurst, 7 October 1814, *H.R.A.*, I, 8, pp. 336-7.
[8] Bathurst to Macquarie, 2 December 1815, *H.R.A.*, I, 8, p. 637.

of 1816, his objections to Marsden were stronger than an anxiety about his methodistical tendencies. By the end of 1814 it looked as though Macquarie was claiming for the Governor as great a power in things spiritual as in things temporal. Marsden was not the man to challenge this claim, not only because he accepted without question the principle that the powers that be had been ordained by God, but because by temperament he was prepared to cringe before the temporal power.

Before the clash sharpened the authoritarianism in Macquarie, or the servility in Marsden, the latter sailed away on a mission to the Maoris in New Zealand, for in obedience to what he believed were the commands of God the behaviour of the man changed. From 1794 to 1814, the more he examined the national character of the Maoris, the more he felt interested in their temporal and spiritual welfare. Their minds appeared like a rich soil that had never been cultivated, and only wanted the proper means of improvement to render them fit to rank with civilized nations. He knew that they were cannibals, that they were a savage race, full of superstition, and wholly under the power and influence of the prince of darkness. There was, as he saw it, only one remedy which could effectually free them from their cruel spiritual bondage and misery, and that was the gospel of a crucified saviour. But, as St Paul observed, how could those who had not heard believe on Him, and how could the missionaries preach except they be sent?[9] He decided to go to England to persuade missionaries to go to New Zealand, noting, with honesty, that he could at one and the same time fulfil his desire to have the gospel preached as well as secure his own quiet, for a great political storm was brewing in the colony of New South Wales. He sailed for England in February 1807 and returned in 1810 to hear that the captain and crew of the *Boyd* had been murdered and eaten by the natives of Whangaroa in New Zealand. Yet, fearing cannibalism less than the wrath or reproach of men in high places in his own society, he continued his preparations to evangelize the Maori.[10]

Towards the end of 1814 he was ready, and Macquarie granted him leave of absence. On 28 November 1814 the brig *Active*, with thirty-five on board, including the missionaries Kendall, Hall and King, their wives and children, eight Maoris, two Otaheitans, various mechanics and one runaway convict, together with horses, cows, one bull, sheep and poultry, weighed anchor in Sydney Cove and sailed out on to the Tasman Sea where Marsden, as ever, suffered much from sickness. On 16 December they sighted the Three Kings off the north-west coast of the north island of New Zealand, and sailed round the northern extremity, then down the east coast to Whangaroa Bay, and the Cavallis Islands. There, on the night of 19 December, Marsden and some of his party slept on the beach. The night was clear, the stars shone brightly, and the sea was smooth. Around them numerous spears stood upright in the ground, while groups of natives lay in all directions like a flock of sheep upon the

[9] S. Marsden: 'Observations on the Introduction of the Gospel into the South Sea Islands: Being my first visit to New Zealand in December, 1814'; printed in J. R. Elder (ed.): *The Letters and Journals of Samuel Marsden, 1765-1838*, (Dunedin, 1932), p. 60.
[10] Ibid., pp. 61-2.

grass, as there were neither tents nor huts to cover them. Surrounded by cannibals, who had massacred and devoured his countrymen, Marsden wondered much at the mysteries of Providence, and how these things could be. Never had he beheld the blessed advantages of civilization in a more grateful light. That night he slept little as his mind was too much occupied by the scene around him and the new and strange ideas it naturally excited.[11]

On Christmas Day, from the decks of the *Active*, Marsden saw the English flag flying which, as he said, was a pleasing sight signalling the dawn of civilization, liberty and religion in that dark and benighted land. Never had he viewed the British colours with more gratification, and he flattered himself they would never be removed till the natives there enjoyed all the happiness of British subjects.[12] They formed the men, women and children into a circle. As Marsden rose and began the service by singing the Old Hundredth psalm a very solemn silence prevailed. He felt his soul melt within him as he viewed the congregation and considered the state they were in. After reading the service, during which the natives stood up and sat down at the signal given by the motion of Korokoro's switch, Marsden preached to them, taking as his text the tenth verse of the second chapter of St Luke's gospel: 'Behold I bring you glad tidings of great joy.' When the natives told the interpreter, the Maori Duaterra, they could not understand what he meant, Marsden replied that they were not to mind that now, for they would understand by and by. When the service ended the natives, to the number of three or four hundred, surrounded Marsden and the other Europeans, and began a war dance, yelling and shouting in their usual style. One eye-witness took this performance to mean that a furious demonstration of joy was the most grateful return they could make for the solemn spectacle they had witnessed.[13] While this was going on Marsden was praying that the glory of the gospel would never depart from the inhabitants till time was no more.[14]

For at that time his mind was sustained by the vision that trade and European civilization would stimulate the industry of the Maori and lay a solid foundation not only for their civilization and what he called their mental improvement in the civil arts, but also for the introduction of Christianity, and thus mitigate the miseries of those poor heathen who lived without hope because they knew not God. He wanted to rouse the British nation, which already enjoyed these infinite blessings of the gospel, which rendered her the envy and glory of all nations, to feel a lively interest in the temporal and eternal welfare of so great a nation as New Zealand.[15] On 26 February 1815, after signing a bill of sale by which the Maoris sold land near the bay of Te Puna to the committee of the Church Missionary Society in London, they weighed anchor, leaving behind twenty-five Europeans to civilize and evangelize the

[11] Ibid., p. 89.

[12] Ibid.

[13] J. L. Nicholas: *Narrative of a Voyage to New Zealand performed in the years 1814 and 1815, in company with the Rev. Samuel Marsden, Principal Chaplain of New South Wales*, (London, 1817), vol. 1, p. 206.

[14] J. R. Elder (ed.): op. cit., p. 94.

[15] Ibid., pp. 130-1.

natives.[16] They returned to Sydney Cove on 23 March 1815.[17] Within a few weeks Marsden the visionary, Marsden the missionary, had drifted back to the role of principal chaplain of the colony of New South Wales. In June, Macquarie dashed off a rather ungenerous reference to his achievement in New Zealand in a despatch, telling Bathurst he had given each of the chiefs who had returned with Marsden a dress, some live stock and a few other articles as presents as it was his wish to conciliate them to the British nation.[18] These were the people on whom Marsden believed he had conferred the most precious gift of all, the gift of eternal salvation.

Within a few months Marsden and Macquarie were needling each other again. On 15 July 1815, Marsden addressed a memorandum to Macquarie on morals and crime at Parramatta, in which he pointed out the daring crimes of the men, and the vices of the women, and reminded Macquarie how as their minister he must account, ere long, at the bar of divine justice for the discharge of his duty to these objects of vice and woe. He had often felt an inexpressible anguish of spirit at the moment of their approaching dissolution, on his own and their own account, and followed them to the grave with awful forebodings, lest he should be found at last to have neglected any part of his public duty as their minister and their magistrate, and by so doing contributed to their eternal ruin.[19] Macquarie replied promptly, thanking him for the information and suggestions and agreeing with him, and telling him of the steps he proposed to take to reduce crime and immorality. On the surface it appeared a polite exchange, but appearances deceive, for unwittingly Marsden had sown in Macquarie's mind the idea that Marsden held him responsible for the vices and miseries of these people. By then other events had planted in his mind the dark thought that Marsden's motives were unqualified opposition to him and his government. That emerged from his quarrel with the Bents.

In the beginning, Macquarie had treated Ellis Bent with generosity and benevolence, granting him twelve hundred acres of land at Bringelly near Camden, with seed, and convict servants, and in return he had expected gratitude and respect. But this was what Bent was not inclined to show. He wanted from Macquarie those outward and visible signs of the importance of his office, which was precisely what Macquarie did not have it in his power to give, partly because by temperament he wanted inferiors and not equals in the colony, and partly because the pomp and circumstance which Bent craved meant expense. When Bent asked for a court house worthy of his rank and station, Macquarie proposed to build it by subscription, but the amount raised fell short of the sum required. Bent blamed Macquarie for the delays, caused, he claimed, by Macquarie not putting enough artificers and labourers on the work. On 16 December 1813, when they discussed the progress on the building at Government House, Bent lost his temper and, in what Macquarie called a very passionate and unbecoming manner, accused the Governor of showing

16 J. R. Elder (ed.): op. cit., pp. 123-5.
17 Ibid., p. 127.
18 Macquarie to Bathurst, 24 June 1815, H.R.A., I, 8, p. 561.
19 Quoted by A. Riley in evidence to the Select Committee on the State of the Gaols, 1819, p. 79 et seq., P.P., 1819, VII, 579.

a great want of feeling for his situation and personal comfort as Judge Advocate in not having a suitable and comfortable court house erected at Sydney for his accommodation. From that day Bent never visited Government House except on official business, and shortly afterwards rudely declined an invitation to dine there with Macquarie.[20]

From that time Macquarie detected a slight to his person and his position in everything Bent did. When Bent disobeyed the Governor's orders that officers of the government of New South Wales should not go to their farms without his permission, Macquarie took this as evidence of Bent's spirit of insubordination and hostility. To Bent, obedience would have symbolized what he was resisting, the notion that a Judge Advocate was subject to military discipline. Out of a quarrel begun by outraged pride and vanity, an issue of great moment began to take shape. Bent sold his land grant without, as the regulations required, asking the permission of the Governor. In church, as a mark of respect, all the laity rose when the Governor entered, but after the quarrel in December Bent remained in his seat in a quaint outburst of non-conformity in the service of human vanity. All through 1814 Bent pro-crastinated over the drafting of the port regulations, a delay which Macquarie interpreted as disrespectful to his wishes. Towards the emancipists Bent acted as though nothing could ever restore a man to his former rank in society. From this principle, according to Macquarie, he never deviated except where his own pecuniary interest or other personal accommodation was concerned.

Macquarie was puzzled by this. As he saw it his best endeavours had been uniformly and strenuously exerted to produce the welfare and prosperity of all the inhabitants. He had served in the army for thirty-eight years with honour and credit. He had never been actuated by any sinister or private motive of enmity to make an unfavourable representation of the character of any officer under his command. Indeed, Ellis Bent was the only officer with whom he had ever had any serious disagreement on points of public duty. As Macquarie saw it, he had behaved with moderation and forbearance towards Bent. What worried him was that the spirit of insubordination, resistance to authority, and personal disrespect was fraught with the most dangerous consequences in a colony so remote from any appeal to superior authority at home. The rank and situation of Bent might bring odium on the executive government for it might spread a dangerous contagion amongst those persons with a natural disposition against the measures of government. Macquarie asked Bathurst to instruct and admonish Bent to behave with more respect and deference, and tell him plainly how far he was subject to Macquarie's orders.[21]

This was what Bent at the same time was urging Bathurst not to do. In defence of his behaviour he explained how he had worked long hours drafting the port regulations, not to pique Macquarie as a man, but to resist their tendency to increase the powers of the Governor. He objected to the Governor confounding the right to issue ordinances with the right to make laws. He objected to the Governor's use of the power to pardon, because it weakened the

[20] Macquarie to Bathurst, 24 February 1815, *H.R.A.*, I, 8, pp. 389-92.
[21] Ibid., pp. 392-9.

majesty of the law. He often met in the streets of Sydney with persons upon whom but shortly before he had been under the necessity of passing the sentence of death, or of some other sentence intended to be exemplary. He did not believe emancipists should be forced forward into office or society contrary to the current of feeling. The utility of a magistrate depended upon his general respectability, which determined his influence on the minds of others. To appoint a man like Simeon Lord degraded the magistracy in the public estimation, produced no benefit to the community, and did not raise the character of the individual on whom the office was conferred.

Bent was groping his way towards a statement of a position which would separate the judicial and executive powers. The Governor, he wrote, considered the Judge Advocate as a subaltern officer, a cypher, a person sent out simply for his convenience, and merely to execute his commands as one of his staff. Macquarie, he said, saw the court as a species of court martial, assembled by a brigade order issued from head-quarters. As he saw it, Macquarie's behaviour filled him with alarm and anxiety. He too protested the correctness of his conduct and the purity of his motives. He did not take his thinking past that point, though as a portent of future disaster he mentioned casually in his first letter to Bathurst that a poor court house had damaged his health.[22] His brother, with clearer head and that single-mindedness which outraged vanity so often confers, thought his position through to its logical conclusion and, unlike Ellis, had no memories of happier days with Macquarie to restrain him.

On 7 February 1814 Jeffery Hart Bent was commissioned in London as Judge of the new Supreme Court of New South Wales. He was born in 1780, educated at Mr Barnes' school in Manchester and at Trinity College, Cambridge, before being called to the bar in 1806. He sailed from Plymouth on the *Broxbornebury* on 21 February 1814. During the voyage Bent kept a diary in which he noted that when sailors got into a country where the wine was cheap, they made themselves strange beasts; that it was no very pleasing sight to stand by and watch a man flogged, and listen while he hallooed loudly; or to see a woman convict sentenced to be displayed in the pillory throw herself down on the deck when being led to her punishment, dash her head against it, and hold her breath with a determination to suffocate herself till she was black in the face, when the captain, upon the surgeon's entreaty, forgave her.[23] For Bent was endowed by nature with a sensitive mind and a horror of cruelty and, like most sensitive people, he had acquired all the courtesy, the love of etiquette and ceremonial to protect himself against the world. Like most sensitive people too he was insatiably vain and arrogant. For when he arrived at Sydney Cove on 28 July, to his mortification Macquarie would not take the hint Bent had given him and receive him with an appropriate ceremony. Bent wanted a salute of guns on shore as well as on ship when he landed, but Macquarie at first jibbed at this with his usual reluctance to allow a ceremony

[22] E. Bent to Bathurst, 14 October 1814, *H.R.A.*, IV, 1, pp. 100-8; Bent to Bathurst, 1 July 1815, *H.R.A.*, IV, 1, pp. 122-42.

[23] J. H. Bent: Journal of a voyage performed on board the ship Broxbornebury, Captain Thomas Pitcher, from England to New South Wales (MS. in National Library, Canberra).

JEFFERY HART BENT

Portrait by an unknown artist in the National Library, Canberra

LACHLAN MACQUARIE, 1805

Portrait by John Opie in the Mitchell Gallery, Sydney

which might convey false ideas of importance. Macquarie finally permitted a salute of thirteen guns, and sent his aide-de-camp to meet Bent, who was also met at the wharf by his brother Ellis, and Jeffery Hart Bent offered a prayer for a happy meeting with all his friends and a safe return.[24]

On Friday 12 August the new charter of justice was formally published at Government House. There were to be three courts of civil jurisdiction in New South Wales. The Governor's Court, consisting of the Judge Advocate and two fit and proper persons inhabiting the territory and appointed by the Governor, was to hear and determine in a summary way all civil pleas where the sum in dispute did not exceed fifty pounds. The Lieutenant-Governor's Court, consisting of the Deputy Judge Advocate of Van Diemen's Land and two fit and proper persons inhabiting that island and appointed by the Lieutenant-Governor of Van Diemen's Land, was to hear and determine all civil pleas in that island where the sum in dispute did not exceed fifty pounds. The Supreme Court was to consist of a judge appointed by commission under the royal sign manual and was to hear and determine in a summary way all civil pleas where the sum in dispute exceeded fifty pounds. There was to be an appeal from the Supreme Court to the Governor, and in cases where the amount at issue exceeded three thousand pounds the parties could appeal to the King in Council.[25] After the reading of the letters patent, Ellis Bent was sworn in as Judge Advocate and Jeffery Hart Bent was sworn in as the Judge of the Supreme Court, but to vain men the choice of day was unfortunate, for in the levée and festivities which followed, the importance of the Bents was lost in the celebrations in honour of the Prince Regent.[26] In the following month Macquarie showed Bent two of the largest wards in the general hospital which he proposed to fit up as a temporary court house. When Bent was not impressed, Macquarie was stung into describing his disapproval as very selfish and very unreasonable.[27]

By February 1815, the *Sydney Gazette* was writing with enthusiasm of the commodious size, the air of solemnity, the massive pillars of stone and wood, and the many other objects in the stately Court House, which laid claim to praise because of the solemn impression the mind received on entering it.[28] Bent, however, was still not prepared to be grateful, let alone impressed, for by then his relations with Macquarie were strained to the point where anger and folly governed the behaviour of both of them. When Bent refused to summon the Supreme Court because no solicitor had arrived from England, Macquarie snorted at it as a frivolous and ridiculous reason.[29] In April, Macquarie asked Bent to permit emancipist attorneys such as George Crossley and Edward Eagar to practise in the Civil Court, partly because it would be a severe measure

24 Ibid., and *Sydney Gazette*, 30 July 1814.

25 Letters Patent to establish Courts of Civil Judicature in New South Wales, 4 February 1814, *H.R.A.*, IV, 1, pp. 77-94.

26 *Sydney Gazette*, 13 August 1814.

27 Macquarie to Bathurst, 30 November 1814, *H.R.A.*, I, 8, p. 380.

28 *Sydney Gazette*, 4 February 1815.

29 Macquarie to Bathurst, 24 March 1815, *H.R.A.*, I, 8, p. 466.

to debar them from their only means of subsistence, and partly because it would be a breach of propriety to deprive their clients of their services. To Macquarie these men were persons of a respectable profession.[30] To Bent they were men who had been convicted of crimes of an infamous nature. In his eyes both statute and case law warranted him in assuring Macquarie that they were no longer members of that profession to which they pretended to belong. As Bent saw it, Macquarie had subjected the judiciary to an influence which ought never to be applied to it, an influence inconsistent with the independent deliberations of an English court of justice, as Macquarie had been guilty of an open, avowed and direct communication of the opinion of the executive government on a point under judicial discussion. It was his object and duty to render the supreme court of judicature in his territory as respectable as possible in the eyes not only of the colony, but of the world, an object, he believed, which must be defeated by compliance with the request of the petitioners.[31]

At the first meeting of the Supreme Court, on 1 May, Broughton and Riley were sworn in as assistants to Mr Justice Bent before the court was adjourned till 5 May. When Crossley, Eagar and Chartres presented their petitions at the adjourned meeting on 5 May, Bent, after describing Eagar's petition as irregular as it was underscored and reproving him for using argument in his petition, adjourned the court till 11 May, having arranged to discuss the petitions with Broughton and Riley in chambers on 9 May. At this meeting in chambers Bent lectured them on the law, and the injury to his personal feelings as well as the feelings and interests of the solicitors Moore and Garling who had been promised the exclusive practice of the Governor's Court and the Supreme Court and that no person who had been prisoner would practise with them. To which Broughton and Riley replied that they considered that the philanthropy of the British government had established this colony more under the benevolent hope of effecting reformation in the principles of the unfortunate characters who were sent to it than to render it a place solely of perpetual punishment and irremoveable degradation. To prevent a man practising his profession would take from prisoners the most active of all stimulus to reform, the hope of once again recovering by good conduct the privileges they had formerly enjoyed in their native country. They went on to reply in detail to the arguments of Bent, who, in turn, recapitulated all his own arguments before they separated.[32]

When the Supreme Court met on 11 May Crossley immediately rose to present his petition. Bent ordered him to stop. Crossley persisted; whereupon Bent threatened to commit him. Broughton managed to get in a word that he had understood the petitioners were to be given a chance to present their

[30] Macquarie to J. H. Bent, 18 April 1815, encl. no. 1 in Macquarie to Bathurst, 22 June 1815, *H.R.A.*, I, 8, pp. 489-91.

[31] Bent to Macquarie, 20 April 1815, encl. no. 5 in Macquarie to Bathurst, 22 June 1815, *H.R.A.*, I, 8, pp. 495-500.

[32] General Minutes of the Proceedings of the Supreme Court on 1st, 5th, 9th and 11th May 1815, *H.R.A.*, I, 8, pp. 510-14.

arguments, and Riley added that that was the sense in which he had understood it. To which Bent replied that if that was the sense in which he saw it, then he must be devoid of common-sense. Riley retorted he was sorry Mr Justice Bent had so little sense as to tell him so publicly, and added that he thought it necessary to declare unequivocally that he did not consider the simple circumstances of any man having unfortunately come to this colony as a prisoner was in itself a sufficient bar to his being ever permitted to practise in the court as an attorney, provided his abilities rendered him capable and his character was in all other respects pure and without blemish. As Bent called: 'Order, Order,' Broughton added that he agreed with Riley. With such dignity as he could muster, Bent said that the most insidious and improper means had been exercised to force the petitioners on the court. The opinions of the executive government had been promulgated. Two men who would not allow their wives and daughters to be contaminated by associating with emancipists were attempting to offer an insult to his feelings and the dignity of this court. He repeated his most solemn determination to adjourn the court until the opinion of His Majesty's government could be obtained.[33]

Then the paper war began. Bent began it on 15 May with a letter to Riley and Broughton in which he told them that the convict attorneys had not only been transported as felons, but were persons who had never been admitted to the society of gentlemen, and with whom no gentleman or officer could or would associate, and that Chartres in particular was entirely out of the question as, in addition to other objections, he was a publican.[34] On 31 May he defended his actions to Macquarie on quite different grounds—that he was defending the honour of his profession, and that he could only discuss the issue in terms of the equality and independence of each other.[35] To which Macquarie replied briefly that he would not write again as a continuation of the correspondence would probably subject him to further insult.[36] By that time Macquarie detected a deeper significance in the brawl; the Bents, he believed, were attempting to raise a party against the measures of his government. Therefore, either they or he should be removed. If the Prince Regent, he told Bathurst, approved of the Bents, then he must ask his lordship to do him the favour to move His Royal Highness to be graciously pleased to accept his resignation as Governor of this territory.[37] To support the Bents, he concluded, would be to inflict a wound on the minds of seven-eighths of the inhabitants of this colony, a wound that could never be healed. The consequence would be that the country never could achieve that pitch of general improvement, commercial importance, wealth and respectability that might otherwise be expected.[38]

[33] Ibid., pp. 515-16.
[34] J. H. Bent to Riley and Broughton, 15 May 1815, encl. no. 9, and encl. nos. 10-14 in Macquarie to Bathurst, 22 June 1815, *H.R.A.*, I, 8, pp. 517-31.
[35] J. H. Bent to Macquarie, 31 May 1815, Ibid., pp. 538-40.
[36] Macquarie to J. H. Bent, 2 June 1815, Ibid., p. 540.
[37] Macquarie to Bathurst, 1 July 1815, *H.R.A.*, I, 8, pp. 620-1.
[38] Ibid., p. 621.

In August, Macquarie perforce began a correspondence with Bent about the payment of tolls on the turnpike road between Sydney and Parramatta. Bent had refused to pay, partly because if the Judge paid, and the Governor did not, this would contradict Bent's claim that as a judge he was the equal of the Governor, and partly because he argued that the Governor possessed no legal authority to levy taxes upon the subject. Again Macquarie was incensed by so insolent and disrespectful a letter, and told Bent that he must decline all 'further epistolary correspondence' with him.[39] When Bent reached the toll gate on 5 September, he was, as he saw it, subjected to personal outrage when the farmer of the tolls, in a state of intoxication, asked him to pay a toll. To which Bent shouted that he was the judge of this colony, that he would pay no toll while he was in it, and that if the toll-keeper did not let him go he would send him to gaol. When the farmer of the tolls reported the episode, D'Arcy Wentworth issued a summons for Bent to appear before a magistrate's court. To this Bent replied that he was not subject to criminal jurisdiction except for treason and felony.[40]

So matters stood when Ellis Bent became dangerously ill with a dropsy of the chest. When Jeffery offered to deputize for him, provided all sentences of death were passed on to the Prince Regent for consideration, Macquarie rudely declined, because of Bent's tendency to treat his authority with such marked disrespect.[41] In the meantime Macquarie waited anxiously at Government House for a call to the bedside, too proud, too concerned for his dignity and honour, to go himself without an invitation from the dying Bent. Macquarie was hoping for some expression of regret for the part Ellis had played in opposition to Macquarie and his measures, but Bent died on 11 November without appeasing Macquarie's vanity. Macquarie immediately announced his intention to attend the funeral, to mark both his sincere regret for the event and his high sense of the severe loss to the colony in the death of a gentleman who had presided in the law courts for nearly six years with honour to himself and equal advantage to the public. He requested all the civil and military to join him on that solemn occasion.[42]

On Monday 13 November the Reverend Samuel Marsden, the two assistant chaplains, followed by the principal surgeon, Luttrell, and Redfern (who, though an emancipist, had attended Bent in his last illness), the Lieutenant-Governor, John Piper, the officers of the seventy-third regiment, and Macquarie, lined up to the front and on the sides of the hearse, while Jeffery Hart Bent walked behind followed by civil officers, military officers, merchants and a numerous train of the respectable inhabitants of Sydney. They walked solemnly to the church of St Philip, where the Reverend Cowper read the service, after which the procession formed up again to walk slowly towards the burial ground to pay their last respects to a man whose virtues, as the *Sydney Gazette* put it,

[39] Macquarie to Bathurst, 20 February 1816, and enclosures, *H.R.A.*, I, 9, pp. 7-15.

[40] Ibid., pp. 19-22.

[41] Ibid., pp. 8-9.

[42] *Sydney Gazette*, 11 November 1815; Macquarie to Bathurst, 20 February 1816, *H.R.A.*, I, 9, pp. 3-4.

would never be effaced from the memory of the public, while their poet proclaimed that he would survive in the Australian record as a prototype of magisterial grace.[43]

On 19 November they all gathered again at St John's Church, Parramatta, to hear the Reverend Samuel Marsden preach a panegyric. After they had sung a hymn, and a psalm in which they were reminded that God turned man to destruction, and had confessed in unison that they had erred and strayed from God's ways like lost sheep, Marsden climbed the three-decker pulpit, and pronounced his text from the twenty-ninth chapter of the Second Book of the Chronicles, verses ten to eleven, on God's wrath, and how it might be turned against them. Those in authority, he began, should use that authority to promote virtue and religion. God, he went on, had used Bent for His purposes. Sin was invariably the object of God's abhorrence. God's wrath, he thundered, was waxed hot against them. They were suffering from famine as a punishment for their wickedness. Bent's death was a most serious calamity and an aweful token of the divine displeasure, for, just as God removed an upright judge from the Israelites, so He had taken Bent from them to punish them for their sins. Bent had relieved the oppressed, judged the fatherless, and pleaded for the widow. A pious feeling pervaded his every look, word and gesture. Bent had been very anxious to know the way to glory, for the word of God appeared very precious to him. Therefore, though their loss might be Bent's gain, Marsden urged them to consider the death in a humbling point of view. Let them tremble and fear when they saw the hand of God raised against them; let them cry unto the Lord, for on Him alone rested all their hopes of a glorious immortality. Sorrow might continue for a night, but joy would come in the morning. Rejoice therefore, in the Lord, he counselled them, O ye righteous, and again rejoice.[44]

These grounds for rejoicing escaped Macquarie. He left the church not in love and fellowship with his neighbour, but aware that he had enemies in the land. Within a week or ten days he sent for Marsden and in the presence of the Reverend Cowper and Major Antill, lectured him severely on the content of the sermon, stating that it was blasphemous to speak so highly of any man.[45] Almost before the official days of mourning ended, Macquarie's mind was darkened with thoughts of treachery. The man who had dreamed the dream of material and moral greatness on the bank of the Macquarie River at Bathurst in May 1815, had turned to the lonely defence of his honour and his reputation.

[43] *Sydney Gazette*, 18 November 1815.

[44] Essays and Sermons of Reverend Samuel Marsden (Marsden Papers, Mitchell Library).

[45] Ibid.

14

MACQUARIE, 1816-1819

ON THE MORNING of Thursday, 17 January 1816, news of great moment reached Sydney Cove. Under the Duke of Wellington, the British army had won the sanguinary but decisive battle of Waterloo. That night a gay assemblage graced a room at the new general hospital for a ball and supper. The floor was painted with emblems of martial glory with a figure of fame in the centre sounding her trumpet and holding in her right hand a scroll on which were inscribed the words 'Waterloo', 'Wellington', and 'Victory'. Stars, insignia and mottoes ornamented the arches and pillars, while the royal arms appeared at the upper end of the room through an elegant transparency. Native shrubs, evergreens and flowers hung in graceful festoons. The dancing, the drinking, and the general merriment continued till dawn. On the Saturday, Macquarie proceeded to Hyde Park to witness a *feu de joie* by his regiment in honour of the signal and glorious victory. The firing was preceded by a grand salute from the battery at Dawes' Point, while the royal standard waved from Fort Phillip, and the Union Jack from Dawes' Point. On the Sunday, psalms of praise and thanksgiving were sung in all the churches.[1] It was a memorable moment not only in the history of British civilization in the old world, but also in the new. For by then the colony of New South Wales had begun to face problems whose solution was to influence its history until the discovery of gold in the middle of the century.

Not the least of these was to find land for the increasing number anxious to become settlers. Up to 1810, four hundred all told had come as free immigrants to the colony, apart from the civil and military officers. By 1820, nine hundred and forty-three men, together with three hundred and thirty-three women and six hundred and sixty-five children (most of the latter being the wives and children of convicts) had come free to New South Wales and Van Diemen's Land, together with a tiny group of men with property.[2] By April 1817, Macquarie was telling Bathurst that no very great quantity of Crown Land remained unappropriated on the Sydney side of the Blue Mountains, or the east side of the Nepean. Consequently, he continued, future settlers would have either to cross the Blue Mountains to the newly discovered country, or proceed south to Illawarra. Natural increase, grants to civil and military officers, grants to emancipists, and second grants, had left very little elsewhere for the new settler.[3]

[1] *Sydney Gazette*, 20 and 27 January 1816.
[2] See R. B. Madgwick: *Immigration into Eastern Australia* (London, 1937), p. 30 and p. 32.
[3] Macquarie to Bathurst, 4 April 1817, *H.R.A.*, I, 9, p. 350.

This provided the incentive to discover further land, an incentive which was sharpened by hope and curiosity about the destination of the inland rivers, as well as the command by the Secretary of State to continue such exploration. In March 1817 Macquarie fitted out an expedition to follow up the discoveries by Evans to the west of the Blue Mountains. As leader, he chose John Oxley, the surveyor-general of lands who, Macquarie believed, was well qualified from his general and scientific knowledge and liberal education.[4] Born in 1783 at Kirkham Abbey near Westow in Yorkshire, Oxley had entered the navy in 1799, sailed to Sydney as master's mate on the *Buffalo* in 1802, visited England in 1807 and 1810, where on 1 January 1812 he was appointed surveyor-general of lands, arriving in Sydney on the *Minstrel* in October of 1812 on the same ship as Lieutenant-Colonel Davey.[5]

As second-in-command, Macquarie appointed G. W. Evans, in consideration of his meritorious exertions in making the first discoveries, despite Bathurst's rather ungenerous description of him as a man not qualified by his education to report on the country, for the English disdain for the man who had bush lore, but lacked refinement and book learning had a long history.[6] He also accepted the offer of Allan Cunningham, a botanist who had arrived in the *Surry* on 20 December 1816, to join other persons of inferior ranks in various subordinate positions.[7] They were supplied with good clothing, bedding, and arms, and furnished with five months' provisions, carried by thirteen strong pack horses. The point of departure was to be a depot erected at Macquarie's orders on the Lachlan about one hundred miles south-west of Bathurst.[8]

Oxley left Sydney for Bathurst on 4 April, Evans and the baggage carts having arrived there a few days earlier.[9] They then proceeded from Bathurst on 20 April through a dull uninteresting country to the depot on the Lachlan, from where on 27 April they began their expedition down the river, finding to their chagrin that it was constantly dissipating in lagoons and swamps. Their hopes of finding fertile river valleys in the inland, their fantasies of an inland sea, as well as of the river as a source of life for generations yet unborn, were dashed. They left the river on 14 May and travelled south-west but found only a barren and desolate country without any water except such rain water as remained in holes and crevices of rocks, which caused at least Oxley to write more in sorrow than in anger about their difficulties and privations. On 4 June, the King's Birthday, Mr Cunningham planted acorns, peach and apricot stones, and quince-seeds under Mount Brogden, in the hope rather than the expectation that they would grow and serve to commemorate the day and situation, should these desolate plains ever again be

[4] Ibid., p. 356.

[5] *Sydney Gazette*, 24 October 1812.

[6] Macquarie to Bathurst, 4 April 1817, *H.R.A.*, I, 9, p. 356, and Bathurst to Macquarie, 18 April 1816, *H.R.A.*, I, 9, p. 114.

[7] Macquarie to Bathurst, 4 April 1817, *H.R.A.*, I, 9, pp. 343, and 356-7.

[8] Ibid., pp. 356-7.

[9] Ibid.

visited by civilized man. But Oxley thought there was very little probability of that.[10] The next day they decided to proceed north-west to the river, as the want of water and grass for the horses might become serious. By 14 June Oxley noted down how irksome it was to make a tedious day's journey through country in which there was not the smallest variety, each day's occurrences and scenes being but a recapitulation of the day before's. Their patience, he added, would have been exhausted long since were it not that their spirits were daily reanimated by the hope that the morrow would bring them to a better country.[11]

On 18 June a new peril beset them as rain began to fall, and transformed the valley along which they were travelling into a complete bog.[12] On 23 June they arrived back at the river, and decided to proceed further down it along the edge of extensive morasses covered with water, as the land to the south was a barren scrub.[13] For seven days there was not the least appearance of natives; nor was bird or animal of any description seen during the day, except a solitary native dog. As Oxley put it, nothing could be more melancholy and irksome than travelling over wilds which nature seemed to have condemned to perpetual loneliness and desolation. They seemed, indeed, to be the sole living creatures in those vast deserts.[14] It was the same for the next four days, the same dead level country still prevailed; the sandy deserts of Arabia, Oxley thought, could not boast a clearer horizon. By that day too the country afflicted them in yet another way, as the decaying vegetation gave off a putrid sour smell.[15] On 5 July the state of their provisions determined Oxley to return to Bathurst. By then he believed he had placed beyond all question the impossibility of a river falling into the sea between Cape Otway and Spencer Gulf.

On 9 July they set out on their return eastward, everyone feeling no little pleasure at quitting a region which had offered nothing but disappointment and desolation. Before leaving they cut the words 'Dig Under' into the bark of a tree, and buried in the ground a bottle containing a paper on which Oxley outlined their journey, their arrival, their departure, and the names of the members of their party. He noted pessimistically in his journal that he could not flatter himself with the belief that European eyes would ever trace the characters either on the tree or the paper. They had, however, deposited the scroll as a memorial that the spot had at least once been visited by civilized man, and so that, should Providence forbid their safe return to Bathurst, the friends who might search for them should at least know the course they had taken.[16] With that certainty that despair nurses in the human heart, he

[10] J. Oxley: *Journals of Two Expeditions into the Interior of New South Wales, undertaken by order of the British government in the years 1817-18* (London, 1820), p. 58.

[11] Ibid., pp. 65-6.

[12] Ibid., pp. 68-72.

[13] Ibid., pp. 78-9 and 87.

[14] Ibid., p. 91.

[15] Ibid., pp. 96-8.

[16] Ibid., p. 108.

told Macquarie by letter that they had demonstrated, beyond shadow of doubt, that no river whatever could fall into the sea between Cape Otway and Spencer Gulf, and that most of the land east of 147° 30′ was uninhabitable, and useless for all purposes of civilized man.[17] The prophecies of despair were no more perceptive than the guesses about the facts of geography, for in time the European was to discover that the very river which inspired these words eventually ran into the sea between Spencer Gulf and Cape Otway. The European was in time to live west of this point. It was, however, to take great courage, endurance, and heroism to solve that mystery of the inland which caused Oxley to call halt in anguish on the banks of the Lachlan. The first man who had followed the Dutch advice of 1644, that he who might wish to know this country must first walk over it, had sent up a cry of despair.

For days together, as they proceeded up stream, the sky was not obscured by a single cloud, and the air was cold and sharp, for sky and climate had their monotonies too, though by then Oxley had even ceased to wonder about the purpose of these barren wastes. His mind was concentrating on more mundane things, on the difficulties of following the Lachlan to Bathurst, and how tedious the journey would be. On 20 July he decided to cross the Lachlan, make for the Macquarie and follow it to Bathurst. On 4 August, with men, horses, and baggage ferried over the vast expanse of water on improvised rafts and canoes,[18] they proceeded north-east by east till by 15 August they had crossed a country peculiarly adapted for sheep grazing. On 19 August they came to the long-sought Macquarie River, the sight of which, Oxley wrote, amply repaid them for all their former disappointments. The banks of this river were low and grassy, the blue gums on its banks extremely fine. This river, which rendered fertile a great extent of country, was not like that other river over which they had toiled and which was constantly diffusing the waters it originally received over low and barren deserts, creating only wet flats and uninhabitable morasses.[19] They reached Bathurst between eight and nine o'clock in the evening of 29 August, where the hospitable reception from Mr Cox, the superintendent of Bathurst, caused them almost to forget in the hilarity of the moment that nineteen harassing weeks had elapsed since they had set out on their journey.[20]

On 30 August Oxley wrote to Macquarie from Bathurst and set down his impressions. A week later, Macquarie summed up his own conclusions in a letter to Earl Bathurst, stating that the Oxley report on the morasses of the Lachlan was a great disappointment and mortification to him, as he had entertained the best-grounded hopes that the river would have emptied itself into the sea on the south-west coast of the continent. He had marked the spot for a future settlement, which would combine local advantages for both internal trade and for foreign trade with Europe and India. He added

[17] J. Oxley to Macquarie, 30 August 1817, encl. in Macquarie to Bathurst, 5 September 1817, *H.R.A.*, I, 9, pp. 479-84.

[18] J. Oxley: op. cit., pp. 109-12, 114-16, 137-8, 142-5 and 150.

[19] Ibid., pp. 185-90.

[20] Ibid., p. 201.

that this disappointment was in some degree compensated for by the very gratifying account of the country Oxley had discovered on his return from the morasses.[21]

Still entertaining the most sanguine expectation that a communication with the ocean or interior navigable waters would be discovered by following the course of the Macquarie, Macquarie fitted out another expedition under the command of Oxley, with surgeon Harris, Evans, Frazer—the colonial botanist, twelve men, eighteen horses, two boats and provisions for twenty-four weeks.[22] The party gathered for the occasion in the Wellington valley in May and June of 1818 from where, on 4 June, they set out with Oxley scarcely in doubt of their ultimate success. In their attempt to trace the Macquarie to its mouth, however, they failed, for by early July that river, like the Lachlan, seemed to terminate in an inland sea, and again Oxley despaired of throwing light on the obscurity in which the interior of this vast country was still shrouded.[23] For this reason they turned east towards the coast, and by August came into a beautiful and fertile country, a land of plenty to compensate them for the miserable harassing deserts of the inland.[24] They met aborigines whose appearance was most miserable, whose features approached deformity, and whose persons were disgustingly filthy; their small attenuated limbs seemed scarcely able to support their bodies, and their entire person formed a marked contrast to the fine and manly figures of their brethren in the interior.[25] After crossing the mountains with such hardships that the sight of the ocean caused Oxley to compare Balboa's ecstasy with their own, they descended with difficulty to the plains where they came on a river, on which Oxley conferred the name of Hastings in honour of the Governor-General of India. They followed this river till the night of 4 October, when their ears heard the welcome murmurs of the ocean on the beach. They entered the bay on which Oxley conferred the name of Port Macquarie, in honour of the original promoter of the expedition, and then turned homewards with, as Oxley put it, all those feelings which that word could inspire even in the wilds of Australia.[26] By 1 November they had reached Port Stephens, from where Oxley wrote to Macquarie of the country over which they had walked in the latter half of their journey, which promised at no very remote period to prove of material advantage to their rising colony.[27]

By the middle of 1819 prospects of expansion to the south-west were opened up by the journey of Charles Throsby from the Cow Pastures to Bathurst. Throsby, who was born at Leicester in England in 1771, arrived in the colony as a surgeon in 1802, served at Newcastle, took up land at

[21] Macquarie to Bathurst, 5 September 1817, *H.R.A.*, I, 9, pp. 478-9.

[22] J. Oxley: op cit., p. 209; *Sydney Gazette*, 5 December 1818.

[23] J. Oxley: op. cit., pp. 241-7.

[24] Ibid., pp. 275-6.

[25] Ibid., pp. 289-90.

[26] Ibid., pp. 309-29.

[27] Ibid., pp. 381-7; *Sydney Gazette*, 5 December 1818.

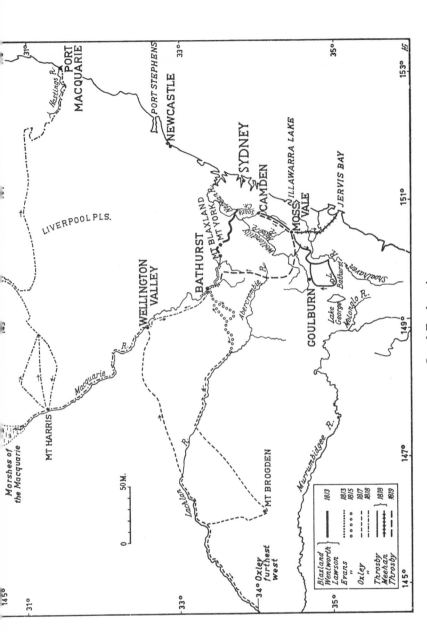

5　*Land Exploration*

PORT MACQUARIE

Hastings R.

PORT STEPHENS

NEWCASTLE

LIVERPOOL PLS.

SYDNEY

CAMDEN

ILLAWARRA LAKE

MOSS VALE

JERVIS BAY

Marshes of the Macquarie

MT HARRIS

WELLINGTON VALLEY

BATHURST

MT BLAXLAND
MT YORK
Nepean
South Ck.
Warragamba
Wollondilly R.

GOULBURN

Lake George
Bathurst?
Wollondilly R.
Shoalhaven
Molonglo R.

Macquarie R.

Abercrombie R.

Lachlan R.

MT BROGDEN

34° Oxley furthest west

Murrumbidgee R.

50 M.

0

Blaxland	
Wentworth	1813
Lawson	
Evans	1813
"	1815
Oxley	1817
"	1818
Throsby	1818
Meehan	1818
Throsby	1819

31°

33°

35°

145°

147°

149°

151°

153°

Cabramatta in 1808, became agent to Sir John Jamison in 1811, returned to England for a visit, and then returned to Sydney where he spent some of his time exploring the Moss Vale, and Sutton Forest district. In March 1818, he had set out with Meehan to discover a land route to Jervis Bay. The immediate motive for the journey of 1819 was not to discover more land, but rather a new route to the rich and extensive plains of Bathurst, because the communication with the western country was over a long and difficult range of mountains, alike uncongenial to man and cattle because of their parched and barren state.[28] Throsby set out on 25 April, accompanied by John Rowley, two servants, and two aboriginal guides, Cookoogong and Dual, passing through the Cow Pastures. Fifteen days later, on 9 May, they arrived at the hut of Lieutenant Lawson on the Campbell River within a short distance of Bathurst. Throsby had found the country over which he had passed rich, fertile, and luxuriant, abounding with fine runs of water, and highly suitable to all the purposes of pasturage and agriculture. Macquarie was so delighted that he offered to Throsby a public tribute of acknowledgment, and one thousand acres in any part of the new country, to John Rowley two hundred acres, to the two servants, Joseph Wait and John Wild, one hundred acres each, and to the two aborigines for their very meritorious services a remuneration of clothing and bedding, appointing Cookoogong chief of his tribe, together with a badge of distinction, and conferring on Dual the badge of merit.[29] By July he detected a wider significance in the discovery, believing the rich country between the Cow Pastures and Bathurst Plains would be fully equal to meet every increase in the population, that it would provide opportunities for the speculative grazier and farmer, and that it would increase intercourse with the mother country by furnishing wool, hides and tallow.[30] By 1819 New South Wales promised to be a land of opportunity for free settlers in the areas discovered by Oxley in the hinterland of Port Macquarie, in the valley of the Hunter River, in the land between Bathurst and the Cow Pastures, at Illawarra, and Jervis Bay. All of those, except for Illawarra and Jervis Bay, presented opportunities for the grazier, for the large estates, for dispersion of settlement, for an economy and a way of life clean different from a convict farm.

At the same time, the sudden increase in the number of convicts arriving also contributed to this change in the material setting. Between 1810 and 1813 the number of convicts arriving in New South Wales each year varied between three hundred and twenty and six hundred and nineteen. In 1814, however, the number jumped to one thousand and thirty-two, back to seven hundred and ninety-four in 1815, to twelve hundred and eighty-seven in 1816, and to sixteen hundred and twenty-one in 1817.[31] This increase was caused both by the wave of crime in the United Kingdom in a disturbed

---

[28] Government and General Order of 31 May 1819; *Sydney Gazette*, 5 June 1819.

[29] *Sydney Gazette*, 5 June 1819.

[30] Macquarie to Bathurst, 19 July 1819, *H.R.A.*, I, 10, pp. 178-9.

[31] App. Q to the Report of the Select Committee on the State of Gaols, 1819, *P.P.*, 1819, VII, 579.

post-war society, and by the greater number of ships available to transport convicts.[32] In May 1818 Macquarie pointed out to Bathurst that five convict ships had arrived at Sydney within one month and five days, bringing no less than one thousand and forty-six male convicts into the colony in that short time. The settlers, he believed, could not employ them as they were suffering from the preceding year's scarcity, and the government would have to employ and feed as many as it could, and send the surplus in two ship loads to Van Diemen's Land without landing them in Sydney.[33]

In March 1819, Macquarie returned again to the problem, pointing out to Bathurst that sixteen ships conveying upwards of two thousand six hundred male and female convicts had arrived within the short space of less than ten months. Again the settlers were unable to take more than a small portion because of their poverty, though Macquarie hoped that when the settlers recovered they might take convicts off the store for their agricultural and grazing purposes. In the meantime he proposed to employ them either in Van Diemen's Land, or in large gangs on the public works in Sydney and the other settlements, on public buildings, and in constructing new roads and bridges to make travelling safe, easy and commodious.[34]

The increase in the number of convicts caused a great number and variety of public works to be begun. In Sydney, convicts worked on a new barracks for convicts, a house and offices for the Judge of the Supreme Court, the fort on Bennelong Point, and a new burial ground. In Windsor and Liverpool new churches were built, and in Parramatta a new hospital, a soldiers' barracks, and a factory for the female convicts.[35] To give grace and distinction to some of these buildings Macquarie had the extraordinary good fortune to have the services of Francis Howard Greenway as civil architect. Greenway, who was born probably in 1777, had practised as an architect of some eminence in Bristol and Bath where in 1812 he was charged with forging part of a building contract, and sentenced to death, a sentence which was commuted to fourteen years transportation. He sailed for Sydney where he arrived in February 1814 with a letter of recommendation from Phillip to Macquarie who, on 30 March 1816, appointed him civil architect and assistant to the engineer, Capt. Gill, to superintend and direct the planning and execution of government works at a salary of three shillings per day.[36] So, by an act of folly, regency Bath was transported to parts of Sydney and its settlements, while churches were built to the greater glory of God which evoked that majesty and simplicity appropriate to a religion such as Protestant Christianity which abhorred all intercessors, and images between man and God.

Most of the buildings ministered to a more mundane purpose, for by another odd irony in human affairs this convict labour was also used to

[32] M. Clark: 'The Origin of the Convicts transported to Eastern Australia, 1787-1852', in *Historical Studies*, May 1956, vol. 7, no. 26, and November 1956, vol. 7, no. 27.

[33] Macquarie to Bathurst, 16 May 1818, *H.R.A.*, I, 9, p. 794.

[34] Macquarie to Bathurst, 24 March 1819, *H.R.A.*, I, 10, pp. 88-9.

[35] Ibid., p. 96.

[36] *Sydney Gazette*, 30 March 1816.

create conditions which changed beyond recall their previous way of life. The convict barracks in Sydney was intended by Macquarie as a commodious spacious building with all the necessary offices to render it convenient and healthy for five to six hundred convicts.[37] On the King's Birthday, 4 June, in company with the Lieutenant-Governor, the Judge Advocate, the Judge of the Supreme Court, and his own wife and son, Macquarie dined at the barracks with six hundred convicts who were enjoying material comforts which to the general class of prisoners had been before unknown. Their ration was much increased, while their comfortable lodging and clothing were amply provided for. As they ate their meal of beef and plum pudding Macquarie told them the prospect of favour and indulgence would be ever in the view of the well-behaved. The convicts gave him three cheers when he left the dining room to join the other distinguished guests in a glass of wine drunk, at his suggestion, to the health, future comfort, well-being and extension of future favour and indulgence to those whose deserts should entitle them to such benefits. As Macquarie and his family departed peals of cheers burst from the convicts, who then had the gratification of drinking good punch to the 'sanctified remembrance of their beloved sovereign'.[38]

Within seven weeks Macquarie put forward a more high-minded motive for the convict barracks. Over and above what it would contribute to their health and happiness it would gradually improve their morals, and prevent nocturnal robberies, thefts, and various depredations.[39] It was typical of him that in deciding what was good for others he should lose sight of what they valued, for their material and moral well-being were being achieved at the price of regimentation. Macquarie simply could not perceive that their previous life of filth, squalor, and licentiousness carried with it the great boon of independence, and the complete absence of that regimentation of their daily lives which life in a barracks entailed. Nor did he pause to consider that such labour could be used to exploit the wealth of the older districts and the new country discovered by Oxley and Throsby. Such a vision was not vouchsafed to Macquarie, because by then he was so engrossed in answering criticism, so wounded by criticism, and so consumed by his own righteousness in punishing the wicked, and so lacking in charity to the men driven by forces over which they had no control, that he was left with little time or energy with which to do creative thinking on the problems of the colony.

All through 1816 Macquarie feuded with Bent while they both waited anxiously for Earl Bathurst's comment on Bent's refusal to open the Supreme Court. Once again Macquarie saw himself as the victim of the wanton and unprovoked insults and arbitrary conduct of Bent, while Bent saw himself as fighting the adoption of maxims suited only to a military despotism. They fought over the ownership and custody of a set of statutes, and over the dismissal of Riley and Broughton from the Supreme Court. In November of

---

[37] Macquarie to Bathurst, 24 March 1819, *H.R.A.*, I, 10, p. 96.
[38] *Sydney Gazette*, 5 June 1819.
[39] Macquarie to Bathurst, 20 July 1819, *H.R.A.*, I, 10, p. 193.

1816 a row began over the eviction of Mrs Ellis Bent from the house of the Judge Advocate; Macquarie smartly delegated the correspondence to his secretary, J. T. Campbell, whereupon Mrs Bent immediately charged Campbell with displaying in his correspondence with her a pettiness which would hardly be excuseable in one of her own sex. In the heat of her anger she had asked whether a tenant had a property in the door locks of the house she was leasing! In December 1816, with understandable relish, Macquarie proclaimed His Royal Highness's high displeasure at all the serious evils which had followed in the train of Bent's suspending the Supreme Court, and forbade Bent to exercise any further his functions as a judge.[40]

Bent's legal casuistry, however, was by no means exhausted. He claimed that his commission was not determined till the arrival of his successor. He complained too of Macquarie's vindictiveness towards him, of his carrying discourtesy so far as to affect not only the style and form of address used to him, but also the occupation of the usual pew in church reserved for the Judge of the Supreme Court. In February of 1817 Bent asked Macquarie's permission to remove the remains of his brother from the old burial ground to the church. On 15 February he wrote a letter which began with an appeal to Macquarie as a man of honour and feeling, then threatened that if His Excellency intended to carry enmity beyond the grave, or to punish the surviving relations by persisting in the refusal he would cause the request and denial to be inscribed on the present tomb, that when those who knew his brother should chance to read the inscription, the sigh they would breathe over departed worth might bear a silent malediction upon what he should be authorized to call and ever should consider Macquarie's despicable conduct. But Macquarie did persist. So the remains of Ellis Bent were transferred to Garden Island in 1825, and later to the graveyard of St Thomas' in Sydney. Even the departure of Bent in May of 1817 led to another sordid exchange.[41]

With all the purblindness of the self-righteous, Macquarie was slow to see that Bent had his sympathizers, let alone understand why this should be so. He himself had noted that his efforts to restore to society convicts who conducted themselves well instead of dooming them for the period of their whole lives to odium, infamy and disgrace, had provoked the opponents of this policy into forming a party. What he did not foresee was that this group would sympathize with every person he singled out for criticism or attack. Thus to this group Macquarie's measures against Bent gave very great offence.[42] On 19 February 1816, an American schooner the *Traveller* arrived in Sydney Cove with a cargo from Canton, and a clearance and pass

[40] Encl. nos. 1, 2, 3 in Macquarie to Bathurst, 3 April 1819, *H.R.A.*, I, 9, pp. 281-317; Bathurst to J. H. Bent, 12 April 1816, encl. no. 2 in Bathurst to Macquarie, 18 April 1816, *H.R.A.*, I, 9, pp. 112-13; Government and General Order of 11 December 1816, ibid., pp. 312-14.

[41] The disputes between J. H. Bent, Mrs E. Bent and Macquarie are contained in the enclosures to Macquarie to Bathurst, 3 April 1817, *H.R.A.*, I, 9, pp. 279-323. Some more additional facts on the grave incident are given in note 65, on p. 864 of *H.R.A.*, I, 9. For the departure of Bent see *Sydney Gazette*, 17 May 1817.

[42] Ensign Bullivant to Macquarie, 15 July 1817, encl. in Macquarie to the Duke of York, 25 July 1817, *H.R.A.*, I, 9, pp. 473-5.

for the port of Sydney from the supercargoes of the East India Company. Macquarie granted it a right of entry, and permission to trade, before proceeding on his tour of the interior. When he returned to Sydney on 26 February he found with much surprise that the ship had been seized as a lawful prize under the Navigation Act by the Reverend Benjamin Vale, one of the assistant chaplains, who had arrived in the colony on the *Broxbornebury* in 1814 on the same ship as Jeffery Hart Bent, and W. H. Moore, one of the solicitors sent out by the British government on a salary of three hundred pounds per annum to practise in the colony under the charter of justice. After Macquarie removed the arrest and restraint on the *Traveller*, he sent for Mr Vale on 27 February and told him his behaviour in seizing the vessel during his absence was highly disrespectful, insolent and insubordinate. He admonished him as his Governor and Commander-in-Chief and told him candidly he was entertaining hopes of an apology. When Vale, instead of apologizing or expressing regret, proceeded to vindicate his conduct, Macquarie, believing Vale's profession should have taught him to support and maintain authority, ordered Vale into military arrest to face court martial for his obstinate resistance. Macquarie believed that Vale and Moore persevered in their most factious and illiberal principles on the private advice and recommendation of Judge Bent.[43]

Under the strain of opposition, the tone of Macquarie's comments on the weak became more and more censorious. In 1815 the folly and extravagance of a Mr Parker had caused his family and friends to send him to New South Wales. By March 1816, Macquarie wrote of Parker as an incorrigible drunkard, a man addicted to low company and too dissipated ever to be able to do anything for himself in this country.[44] He was just as severe on the aspirations of the trading classes to acquire social station by settling on the land. Early in 1816, a Mr Ingle asked him for a land grant. Macquarie refused: 'Mr. Ingle', he wrote, 'is a low Vulgar Man Who has Accumulated a Considerable Property by Carrying on Trade at the Derwent.'[45] In 1816 Connor, who made his previous appearance in this history in a drunken brawl, applied to Macquarie as Governor for permission to marry. Macquarie refused because he sincerely believed Connor was not worthy of such a calling, as he had consorted with prostitutes and drunkards.[46] In April 1816, this concern for the moral well-being of others led him to actions which his enemies construed as evidence of his arbitrary disposition. The shrubbery on the government domain in Sydney was, he knew, much frequented by both men and women for most improper purposes. He had wanted for a long time to put a stop to these disgraceful indecencies, as well as, he added, to save the shrubs and the trees. To achieve this he issued a proclamation threatening to punish future trespassers. On Thursday, 18 April, Daniel Read walked across the domain on his way to work, and William Blake had also slipped into the

43 Macquarie to Bathurst, 8 March 1816, *H.R.A.*, I, 9, pp. 42-8.
44 Macquarie to Bathurst, 18 March 1816, *H.R.A.*, I, 9, p. 58.
45 Ibid., p. 64.
46 *H.R.A.*, I, 9, pp. 886-7; and ibid., pp. xiv-xv.

LACHLAN MACQUARIE, 1822

Portrait by Richard Read, Senior, in the Mitchell Gallery, Sydney

PARRAMATTA, c. 1824

Lithograph from Joseph Lycett's 'Views in Australia or New South Wales and Van Diemen's Land'

domain. On the following morning, for an undisclosed reason, William Henshall also crossed the domain over the broken-down wall. They were arrested and Macquarie summarily ordered all three to receive twenty-five lashes. That day at noon the gaoler ordered first Read, then Henshall, then Blake to strip to receive their twenty-five lashes, and to pay the fee of a free man, three shillings per day, to the gaoler. All three found their way promptly to Bent, where they made sworn depositions before him, in one of which Henshall, probably prompted by the learned judge, wound up with these words: 'I have no knowledge of what I was punished for than I have said, than that It was the Governor's will.' Bent promptly sent these depositions to Bathurst in a semi-official letter on 12 June 1816. Macquarie was convinced that the punishment had had the desired effect as it had put a complete stop to the trespassers, and had prevented the breaking down of the government wall, as well as the gross indecencies.[47]

Once again Macquarie believed he was cleaving to that which was good, and abhorring that which was evil. Once again his enemies believed that his every action illustrated his authoritarian, if not despotic personality. This time they took action. They listed his arbitrary actions in a petition to the House of Commons. He had influenced the decisions of a jury at an inquest in which his coachman was interested; he had personally given orders for corporal punishments without any previous magisterial inquiry; he had sold pardons to convicts; he had prohibited banns of marriage; he had arbitrarily pulled down houses; he had seized upon lands which were presumably private property; he had influenced the courts of justice.[48] Vale took the indictment with him when he sailed for England in June of 1816. Macquarie was incensed, and said it was the work of a mischievous and mean faction, the work of Bent, a man, he said, of a weak head and a bad heart. Its charges, he went on, were false and malicious, while the signatures of several persons had been put to the memorial without their having any knowledge of it. These people had since sworn on oath that they did not sign their own names.[49]

At the same time Macquarie began to use his powers to punish those who had signed the Vale petition. In November 1816, William Stewart, a master mariner, applied for a land grant. Macquarie told him that his conduct in having signed a petition lately sent to England by a few despicable, factious and malignant individuals, and well-known to contain the most false, libellous, and seditious matter was an instance of such unprincipled depravity that he could not think Stewart deserving of any indulgence whatever.[50]

[47] For Macquarie's defence see Macquarie to Goulburn, 15 December 1817, *H.R.A.*, I, 9, pp. 732-6. For the three depositions, see note 162 in *H.R.A.*, I, 9, pp. 883-6.

[48] The text of the petition has been lost. For a summary of it see *H.R.A.*, I, 9, note 77, p. 866. For Macquarie's comments on it see Macquarie to Bathurst, 3 April 1817, *H.R.A.*, I, 9, pp. 330-1.

[49] Macquarie to Bathurst, 3 April 1817, *H.R.A.*, I, 9, p. 330 and W. H. Moore to Macquarie, 18 September 1816, encl. no. 1 in ibid., p. 331.

[50] J. T. Campbell to W. Stewart, 18 November 1816, quoted in H. G. Bennet: *A Letter to Earl Bathurst, Secretary of State for the Colonial Department, on the Condition of the Colonies in New South Wales and Vandieman's Land, as set forth*

Three years later Macquarie told George Howe, the printer of the *Sydney Gazette*, that as one George Williams had affixed his signature to a scandalous, rebellious and libellous paper directed to the House of Commons against Macquarie's person and government, and as it was Macquarie's determination that no such infamous incendiary should be employed in any department under government in this colony, he hereby commanded and directed Howe that he would retain Williams in his employ at his peril.[51] That, however, is to anticipate the degree of spite and vindictiveness to which Macquarie descended as the confounding of his enemies became the consuming passion of his life.

By the end of 1816 Macquarie was complaining of the disrespectful, insulting and insubordinate conduct of the officers of the regiment. This began with the Sanderson affair. Soon after the arrival of the 46th regiment, in 1815, Captain Edward Sanderson was provoked into using most unbecoming and disrespectful language when charged with a misdemeanour. When Macquarie admonished and reproved him for this, Sanderson resented the criticism and, according to Macquarie, formed a mutinous licentious faction amongst his brother officers who scoffed and reviled at the actions and policies of the civil government so immodestly that Colonel Molle lectured them on the bold licence they were giving to their tongues. In July of 1816, Ensign Bullivant drew on the wall of the guard room in Sydney a full caricature of Macquarie in a position of ignominy with indecent scurrilous labels under it. At the same time the officers began to decline invitations to dine at Government House.

A scurrilous lampoon which reflected in unjust and malicious terms against Molle, was dispersed through the town of Sydney in 1816. At a court of inquiry into the authorship of that and a second lampoon, D'Arcy Wentworth announced that the author of the first was his son, William Charles, who was then on the high seas on his way to England to study at Cambridge. On 13 June 1817 the officers gave a dinner for Molle to congratulate him on the revelation of authorship. They also presented him with an address in which they presumed in a most illiberal, unjust and malicious manner to reflect in sarcastic though indirect terms on the measures of Macquarie's government. The attacks on Molle, they said, had issued from the pens of men so much their inferiors in rank and situations, from that promiscuous class which had ever been excluded from intercourse with them. They praised their policy of exclusion, the benefits of which they had reaped with advantage to themselves as officers and gentlemen. How different from the standards of the other side, who had stooped to that vile and mean practice of anonymous scurrility, and had perverted their talents to do the degrading work of dark assassins! They for their part welcomed the prospect of leaving a country in no point of view congenial to military feelings.[52]

---

in the evidence taken before the Prison Committee in 1819 (London, 1820), pp. 129-30.
[51] Macquarie to G. Howe, 21 February 1819, quoted in ibid., p. 116.
[52] Captain Sanderson, Surgeon Forster and Lieutenant Grant to Colonel Molle, 13 June 1817, encl. no. 3 in Macquarie to the Duke of York, 25 July 1817, *H.R.A.*, I, 9, pp. 453-4.

Again Macquarie was incensed, and dashed off a letter to Molle which bore all the signs of a hurt and exasperated man. Addresses of congratulations, he wrote, were all very well, but when the officers presumed to make strictures on a political measure long since adopted and acted on by government for the benefit and improvement of the great bulk of the inhabitants of the colony, sanctioned by the House of Commons (meaning that the report of the 1812 committee on transportation, in which his emancipist policy was approved, had been received by the house) and approved by His Majesty's ministers, then it became his imperious duty to express his strongest reprobation of such disrespectful and insubordinate conduct.[53] For once again Macquarie could find only one answer for the motives of people who opposed a policy based on the principles of justice, humanity and benevolence. As for his own motives, his conscience was clear. His sole object on this occasion, as he put it to the Duke of York in demanding the withdrawal of the 46th regiment, was to restrain that dangerous principle of insubordination which had insulted and tended to degrade the honour and dignity of the government, most graciously confided to him by his sovereign, and at the same time to support and secure discipline, so essential to the welfare of His Majesty's service and the maintenance of good order in society.[54] This was dangerously close to saying that all who did not agree with him were guilty of insubordination.

As the quarrels with the judiciary, the army officers and some of the clergy darkened his mind, he extended a fulsome welcome to the men who replaced the Bent brothers, and expressed extravagant hopes both for the success of their work in the colony and their co-operation with him. The new Judge Advocate, John Wylde, born probably in 1780 into a family of some prominence in the English legal world, arrived on the *Elizabeth* on 5 October 1816. The new Judge of the Supreme Court, Barron Field, arrived on the *Lord Melville* on 24 February 1817. Born in 1786, the son of a doctor, educated as a barrister, and called to the Inner Temple in 1814, Field was well known in literary circles in London, where he enjoyed the friendship of Lamb, the acquaintance of Wordsworth and Leigh Hunt, and was for a time a theatrical critic for *The Times*. A versifier himself in his spare time, he promised to add a modicum of distinction to such literary life as the colony enjoyed, and possibly even to pen poems for official occasions more worthy of attention than the flatulent verse of Michael Massey Robinson.

The new Lieutenant-Governor of Van Diemen's Land, William Sorell, arrived on the *Sir William Bensley* on 10 March 1817.[55] Sorell was born in England in 1775, the eldest son of an army officer, joined the army in 1790, served in the West Indies, fought in the revolutionary and Napoleonic wars, married, separated from his wife, and served in South Africa where he fell in love with the wife of another army officer, Lieutenant Kent, who later

53 Macquarie to Molle, 23 June 1817, encl. no. 1 in *H.R.A.*, I, 9, pp. 451-2.

54 Macquarie to the Duke of York, 25 July 1817, *H.R.A.*, I, 9, p. 451.

55 Macquarie reported the arrival of all three in the despatch Macquarie to Bathurst, 4 April 1817, *H.R.A.*, I, 9, pp. 343-4.

sued him for criminal conversation with his wife. Yet so desperate was Macquarie at the beginning of 1817 for support that when Sorell·arrived at Sydney Cove with Mrs Kent, Macquarie hailed his arrival with sincere pleasure. Despite Sorell's flagrant flouting of the seventh commandment Macquarie wrote of him as a man of good understanding, firmness and integrity.[56] On Wylde and Field he was even more enthusiastic and hopeful, predicting to Bathurst in April 1817 that they would prove a great blessing and acquisition to the colony, that they appeared to be men of superior talents and conciliating manners, and that Wylde in particular, had evinced not only industry but in addition every possible desire to support Macquarie's government, and to assist him with his advice and counsel.[57]

For it was becoming clearer all through 1816 and 1817 that Macquarie confounded all criticism and opposition with insubordination. What he craved was approval, even possibly applause. Men who advocated and supported both by precept and example the vision closest to his heart, the moral regeneration of a wicked and an adulterous generation, became the victims of his hatred and contempt if they dared to show publicly that the dictates of their heart and mind suggested different conclusions than those of Lachlan Macquarie for the government of New South Wales. With no one did this emerge more sharply than in his relations with the Reverend Samuel Marsden. On 4 January 1817, the secretary to the Governor, J. T. Campbell, exasperated in general, he claimed later, by Marsden's marked disrespect to the measures of Macquarie's government, and in particular by his failure to attend a ceremony at the native institution at Parramatta,[58] wrote a letter to the *Sydney Gazette*, signed Philo Free, in which he denounced Marsden as the Christian Mahomet who under the cloak of religion supplied the natives of the south seas with Bibles and booze, to his own pecuniary profit as well as his glory as an evangelizing hero. Their spirit, he wrote, was spirituous rather than spiritual, while the human vessels of the holy spirit arrogated to themselves airs of importance for acts of public benefit which they had never displayed in their private lives, as these evangelizing heroes had not exhibited any zeal to help the abject natives of New South Wales. Philo Free concluded with some digs at the failure of the evangelical heroes to dispel the dark and gloomy clouds of ignorance under which it had pleased Providence to permit the aborigines of the colony to remain, and an appeal to men of liberal and generous disposition to open the eyes of all to a sense of duty and Christian charity towards their adopted country, and its harmless though uncivilized natives.[59]

Macquarie immediately disclaimed all responsibility for the publication of the letter in a Government and General Order in the *Sydney Gazette* on 18 January 1817, in which he also took the opportunity to express his disapprobation of the letter as well as his regret that from the great pressure of gov-

[56] Ibid., p. 347.

[57] Ibid., p. 345.

[58] Campbell to Macquarie, 31 March 1819, encl. in Macquarie to Bathurst, 31 March 1819, *H.R.A.*, I, 10, pp. 140-1.

[59] *Sydney Gazette*, 4 January 1817.

ernment business in the secretary's office it should inadvertently have appeared in the *Sydney Gazette*.[60] Marsden was not so sure, for by that time both he and Macquarie put the basest possible construction on each other's behaviour. Suspecting malice towards him in everything Macquarie did, he concluded that Campbell had acted in collusion with Macquarie, and decided to begin an action for libel against Campbell, calculating, as do the men consumed with the problems of power, that in taking his adversary to court he might damage a person in a higher place.[61] In using the courts to satisfy his spite, however, Marsden was playing into the hands of his enemies, who were only too anxious to believe that the clerical garb all too inadequately concealed his greed and his ambition. To his enemies it was sanctimonious hypocrisy for a man to preach love to mankind when his passion and his wealth were dedicated to bringing another human being to destruction. On 21, 22 and 23 October 1817 the libel suit in which Marsden sued Campbell with having written and published in the *Sydney Gazette* on 4 January a letter signed Philo Free which contained libellous matter against him in his clerical and magisterial capacities, and as the agent and representative of certain religious societies, was heard before the Judge Advocate and six military officers. The court, according to the *Sydney Gazette*, went through the whole of this complicated inquiry in all its various hearings and stages with great patience, and the most solemn and cautious circumspection. On the third day they pronounced their verdict, finding the defendant guilty of having permitted a public letter to be printed in the *Sydney Gazette*, which tended to vilify the public character of the prosecutor as the agent of the Missionary Societies for propagating the gospel in the south seas. Marsden then appealed to the Supreme Court which awarded him two hundred pounds damages, which the *Sydney Gazette* interpreted as not unfavourable to Campbell.[62]

That was not the end as far as Marsden was concerned. With a singular lack of charity and a rash disregard of the warning against taking one's adversary to the law courts, he continued his campaign against Campbell by writing a letter to Jeffery Hart Bent in England. On 3 August Bent replied, telling him how greatly he rejoiced to hear of Marsden's success in bringing the shameless author of Philo Free to his well-merited punishment, and how the trial had done more to open the eyes of ministers to Macquarie's conduct than anything else. Doubtless, Bent concluded, Campbell had acted in collusion with Macquarie, whose spirit was that of an arbitrary and cruel man, who in other times would have been more intolerably despotic.[63]

[60] Ibid., 18 January 1817.

[61] For Marsden's motives see Marsden to the secretary of the Church Missionary Society, 26 September 1818, quoted in J. R. Elder (ed.): *The Letters and Journals of Samuel Marsden 1765-1838* (Dunedin, 1932), p. 48, n.

[62] This was Campbell's point. See J. T. Campbell to Macquarie, 31 March 1819, encl. in Macquarie to Bathurst, 31 March 1819, *H.R.A.*, I, 10, pp. 140-1; J. T. Bigge: Judicial Establishments, pp. 25-7; Report of Select Committee on the State of Gaols, 1819, pp. 96-7, *P.P.*, 1819, VII, 579.

[63] J. H. Bent to Marsden, 3 August 1818 (Marsden Papers, vol. 6, pp. 228-31, Mitchell Library, Sydney).

Towards the end of 1817 the relations between Marsden and Macquarie were further damaged by two despatches which Macquarie received from Earl Bathurst. In one of these, written on 6 February 1817, Bathurst censured Macquarie for attempting to court martial the Reverend Vale. Military chaplains, he pointed out, could only be court-martialled for absence from duty, drunkenness, or scandalous and vicious behaviour derogatory of the sacred character with which a chaplain was invested. The whole of Macquarie's proceedings against Vale were therefore illegal. Bathurst concluded by lamenting that Macquarie should in a moment of irritation have been betrayed into an act which exposed him to considerable risk and could not fail to diminish his influence among the more respectable part of the community, who justly looked upon the law as the only true foundation of authority.[64] There was worse to follow, for on 22 April 1817 Bathurst wrote instructing Macquarie to reinstate Moore as a solicitor.[65]

This expression of Bathurst's displeasure and censure had truly mortified Macquarie's feelings. In a short reply he repudiated the suggestion that he had been influenced by sentiments of irritation or passion. So very different, he said, was his conduct towards this worthless man that he had given him every opportunity to explain away or apologize for his insolent, and insubordinate conduct. He was not going to allow his authority to be trampled on by anyone. He had been bred in the school of subordination too long not to respect it, and was assured that his lordship would not want to see him degraded by tamely submitting to the subversion of his authority as Governor-in-Chief of this colony by Mr Vale or any other seditious unprincipled person.[66] On the same day he dashed off a reply to Bathurst about Moore, connecting his action with a seditious and violent cabal headed by Mr Justice Bent and some other disaffected persons then in the colony, and refused to reinstate him. After brooding over Bathurst's censure for another week, Macquarie decided to tender his resignation as Governor-in-Chief of the colony of New South Wales.

The private and confidential letter in which he announced this intention to Bathurst began in the mood of a man asking for pity. He had hoped, he wrote, to hold office for two or three years more, to see the matured effects of his system of government for the reformation of the inhabitants, and for their improvement and their prosperity. So long as he enjoyed the support of Bathurst he had combated the men in the colony who had at all times attempted a most indecent and insubordinate interference with the governors by opposing their measures and writing home false and malignant representations. Now Bathurst's attitude had changed, and he must consider this as one of those mortifying trials to which human nature was liable. He had been looking forward to a period of repose at the termination of perhaps one of the most arduous and troublesome commands under the British Crown. Even this hope had been dashed by the harsh tenor of his lordship's late letters. This utterly

[64] Bathurst to Macquarie, 6 February 1817, *H.R.A.*, I, 9, pp. 206-7.
[65] Bathurst to Macquarie, 22 April 1817, *H.R.A.*, I, 9, p. 385.
[66] Macquarie to Bathurst, 24 November 1817, *H.R.A.*, I, 9, pp. 491-3.

unmerited change was achieved by those with the rank of gentlemen, those secret but not avowed enemies, those deep designing men whose delight it was to sow the seeds of discord and insubordination.

At the head of this list of malcontents stood the Reverend Samuel Marsden. He had shown Marsden and his family every civility, kindness and attention. His enmity was therefore the more unaccountable. He could only ascribe it to a deep-rooted malevolence and to his avidity for power and consequence. The ill-will had begun when Macquarie did not consult him on everything as his predecessors had done. This malevolent man, he believed, was clothed in the garb of humanity and hypocritical religious cant. The letter ended with a list of the persons who had all along been discontented, intriguing or seditious, and had written home the most gross misrepresentations: the Reverend Marsden, with Dr Townson, Nicholas Bayly, John Blaxland, Gregory Blaxland, Doctor Throseby (*sic*), Mr John Horseley, Sir John Jamison, Mr David Allan, Mr John Oxley, Mr W. H. Moore, Mr Thomas M. Moore.[67]

On the same day he wrote a public despatch tendering his resignation, and three days later on 4 December another despatch in which he let slip the reason for making Marsden the villain of the piece: that he had written the letter written by Bayly, an inference he made because, as he put it, Marsden was the only person, *in the character of a gentleman* in the whole colony, capable of writing and making such unfounded and malicious representations with a view to injuring him, Macquarie, in the eyes of His Majesty's ministers. He then launched into a lengthy and tedious defence of himself against the Bayly criticism, impugned the motives of his opponents, and composed a peroration on the purity of his own which suggests he was losing his grip. He was proud to add that as far as precept and example went he could defy the most en-venomed malice to tax him justly with omitting any opportunities or means within his power to restrain and repress vice and immorality through all the classes of the community, or of neglecting to encourage virtue and religion conformable to the high sentiments he entertained of their importance both in his public station and private capacity.[68] Early in 1818 Macquarie sent for Marsden. As soon as Marsden entered the room at Government House, he realized immediately that he was in a pretty mess, because when he objected to Macquarie making observations upon his public conduct in front of the Reverend Cowper, Mr J. T. Campbell, and the aide, Lieutenant J. Watts, Macquarie was much agitated. Then, when Marsden attempted to leave, Mac-quarie, with much warmth, as Governor of the colony, commanded him to sit down. After Marsden had sat down very quietly and answered Macquarie's questions, Macquarie read him a long reprimand. He had long known Mr Marsden, he began, as a secret enemy, but so long as Marsden remained only a secret enemy he had despised his malicious attempts to injure his character too much to take notice of his treacherous conduct. He could not, however, pass over unnoticed a recent most daring act of insolence and insubordination—

67 Macquarie to Bathurst, 1 December 1817, *H.R.A.*, I, 9, pp. 499-501.

68 Ibid., pp. 501-2 and Macquarie to Bathurst, 4 December 1817, *H.R.A.*, I, 9, pp. 502-10.

namely taking depositions from the three men who had been flogged. When Marsden answered that he did not consider he had done anything wrong, Macquarie launched into a long train of invective and abuse, calling Marsden's actions insolent, impertinent, insubordinate, and seditious. The conduct, he said, would be highly seditious in any man, but more so in a magistrate and a clergyman who ought to be the first to set an example of loyalty, obedience and proper subordination. If he ever dared to interfere again, or investigate any part of Macquarie's conduct, as Governor of the colony, Macquarie would consider it his indispensable duty, as a measure of necessary precaution, alike to preserve his own high station, the support of his authority, and the tranquillity of the country, to suspend him as a clergyman and a magistrate till he wrote to the Prince Regent. He concluded:

> Viewing you *now*, Sir as the *Head of a seditious low—Cabal*—and consequently unworthy of mixing in Private Society—or intercourse with me, I beg to inform you, that, I never wish to see you *except on Public Duty*; and I cannot help deeply lamenting, that, any Man of your *Sacred Profession* should be *so much* lost to every good feeling of Justice, generosity, and gratitude, as to manifest such deep rooted malice, rancour, hostility and vindictive opposition towards one who has never injured you—but has, on the contrary, conferred several acts of kindness on both yourself and family.[69]

At parting, Macquarie shouted 'I command you, sir, that you never set foot in Government House except upon public duty.' To which Marsden replied that His Excellency might rest assured that he would be very particular in not violating His Excellency's command in this respect. Later he told Riley in a letter that as he was conscious of his own entire innocence, Macquarie might as well have beat an anvil as to hope to excite fear in his heart where no fear was.[70] A few weeks later Macquarie sent the Judge Advocate, Wylde, to question the prisoners in the gaol on the severity of Marsden as a magistrate. Marsden interpreted this as a move to court the vilest of men at the expense of the authority of the magistrates. When Macquarie wrote direct to the gaoler without consulting the magistrate, Marsden wrote to Macquarie that he would not act another day as a magistrate. Macquarie then announced in the *Sydney Gazette* that he was pleased to dispense with the services of the Reverend Samuel Marsden as a Justice of the Peace and a magistrate.[71] Thus ended Marsden's career as a magistrate, that service to Caesar which he had first assumed in 1796 when he saw himself as a man not born of noble birth, nor heir to any great inheritance, but as a man whom God had highly exalted from his low station and rank, and had given this opportunity to support the measures of government, and do everything in his power for the good of His Majesty's service.[72] By contrast, when the Reverend Cartwright

[69] Macquarie to Marsden, 8 January 1818 (Macquarie Letters, 1809-1820, Mitchell Library, Sydney).

[70] Marsden to Riley, 19 May 1818, quoted in H. G. Bennet: op. cit., pp. 122-6.

[71] *Sydney Gazette*, 28 March 1818.

[72] Marsden to the Reverend M. Atkinson, 16 September 1796, in J. R. Elder (ed.): op. cit., pp. 29-30.

resigned as a magistrate Macquarie referred fulsomely to his work in the public notice, how his work had conferred much credit on himself and much advantage to the public service, adding some words on his able, zealous, and upright manner, and a concluding word of praise for his faithful and meritorious services as well in his sacred capacity of chaplain as in that of magistrate of this colony.[73]

In the meantime Macquarie continued his work for the material and moral progress of the inhabitants of New South Wales. In 1815 and 1816 he continued his efforts to civilize the aborigines. At the end of the year 1816 he invited the natives to a friendly meeting at Parramatta, assuring them they would be kindly received, and plentifully furnished with refreshments of meat and drink.[74] At ten o'clock on the morning of Saturday, 28 December, the natives formed a circle in the market place at Parramatta, with the chiefs placed on chairs, and the rest on the ground. In the centre of the circle, several large tables groaned under the weight of roast beef and potatoes, bream, and a large cask of grog, which, as the *Sydney Gazette* put it, lent its exhilarating aid to promote the general festivity and good humour which so conspicuously shone through the sable visages of this delighted congress. Macquarie arrived at ten thirty, with all the members of the Native Institution, and several of the magistrates and gentlemen of the district, but not the Reverend Samuel Marsden. After he had met the chiefs, he confirmed the rank to which their own tribes had raised them, and conferred badges of distinction on them. Then came Mrs Macquarie and after her the fifteen children of the Institution, who looked very clean, well clothed and happy. There followed an oral examination in which the children displayed their progress in learning and civilized habits of life, while the chiefs clapped the children on the head, and one turned to Macquarie with extraordinary emotion and exclaimed: 'Governor,—that will make good Settler—that's my Pickaninny.' Some of the aboriginal women shed tears at seeing the infant and helpless offspring of their deceased friends so happily sheltered and protected by British benevolence. Or so the *Sydney Gazette* believed, for who could tell what moved any woman to tears, let alone a woman from the aboriginal natives of New South Wales. Shortly after the feasting began, Macquarie took his departure, to the long and reiterated acclamations and shouts of the aborigines present. All told one hundred and seventy-nine of them took part in the feast which commemorated Macquarie's attempt to open the path to their future civilization and improvement.[75]

They met again on 1 January 1818 when Macquarie expressed himself much gratified by the very improved decent and orderly appearance of the tribes. Again the children displayed their progress in reading and writing, while the girls demonstrated their progress in needle-work. But while the *Sydney Gazette* was commenting on how the philanthropist and the Christian could contemplate with satisfaction the peculiar advantages of an institution founded

[73] *Sydney Gazette*, 31 January 1818.
[74] Ibid., 21 December 1816.
[75] Ibid., 4 January 1817.

on such liberal and praise-worthy principles, one of their readers was expressing his disdain for joining the black cattle, as well as contempt for all such mummery.[76] When they met again, on 28 December 1818, an intensely warm day, to partake of the kindness and hospitality of the government, the numbers had swollen to nearly three hundred, including aborigines from the country west of the Blue Mountains, who were distinguishable from the rest by the feathers decorating their hair, and the teeth of wild animals suspended over their foreheads, their bodies and faces being painted with a red and white ochre, which gave them a wild and *outré* appearance. They had a degree of confidence in their manner which at least one observer interpreted as indicating a consciousness of security in the protection of European friendship. There were other tribes there from the new settlements to the north and south of Sydney. To the European, all this symbolized improvement and approach to civilization in a wild and improvident race, as well as their awareness of the comfort and advantages inseparable from the protection of the British government. Again Macquarie awarded his badges of distinction, and the children displayed their progress in letters, in an examination which so delighted some chiefs that they burst out laughing, leapt in the air, and made other wild gesticulations which the *Sydney Gazette* called the spontaneous offerings of uncultivated nature. Again the natives feasted off roast beef and plum pudding washed down with a fair proportion of strong drink, and rose and gave Macquarie three cheers as he left the gathering.[77]

In April, 1819, prizes were distributed to the European and aboriginal school children who had excelled in the early rudiments of moral and religious education. The *Sydney Gazette* stated it was pleasing to remark, in answer to the erroneous opinion that the aborigines were not susceptible to any mental improvement which could adapt them to the purposes of civilized association, that a black girl of fourteen years who had been in the school for three or four years had won the first prize. True, they went on to argue, some natives had retreated to the wilds after tasting the fruits of European civilization. But this was not surprising, for the whites had used them in the meanest offices of drudgery, and had shown them a want of attention of which the very dogs and horses of the whites had not to complain. What if the native took up more congenial pursuits, what if he rose above the role of kitchen boy? The doubt of their capacity and quality of their intellect must now wear off. Or so the *Sydney Gazette* argued.[78]

It might have been the grain of mustard seed. But the fruits of everyday experience were producing a climate of opinion quite unfavourable to the aspirations of the high-minded. In the country settlements the clash between aborigine and settler, the murders, robberies and slaughter of live stock continued, till the whites became convinced that their only protection lay in driving the aborigines away by force. In the towns, the aborigines were figures of cruel fun for young and old. On 31 May 1817, for example, some boys

76 *Sydney Gazette*, 3 January 1818.
77 Ibid., 2 January 1819.
78 Ibid., 17 April 1819.

from the Rocks began to torment some aborigines who were a little intoxicated. They began by throwing dirt, then moved on to stones. If the natives had retaliated they would have been prosecuted for assault. So they retired and bore in silent anguish all their hurts and bruises.[79] One Sunday sport for both young and old was to give the aborigines in towns drink, and then encourage them to fight by the promise of a reward for the victor. The *Sydney Gazette* branded this as that most shameful, cruel and barbarous custom of encouraging black people to murder or mangle one another for the sport of the learned, the polite and the refined Europeans.[80] Despite government orders prohibiting natives carrying weapons with which they could hack or hew one another,[81] and despite the attempts of the worthy to prevent their access to alcohol,[82] the sport went on and with it the degradation of the aborigine, as well as the strengthening of the conviction in the minds of the Europeans that these people were special victims of divine wrath, or at any rate exiles by birth, temperament and disposition from a higher civilization.

For many years it had been customary to celebrate the anniversary of the foundation of the colony with a dinner. On Monday, 27 January 1817, a party of about forty sat down to dinner at 5 p.m. in the house of Isaac Nichols. Nichols, who had been transported in 1791, had accumulated fourteen hundred acres of land by 1815, held the licence of a successful inn in George Street, and had held minor offices in the government of New South Wales such as chief overseer of convicts 1799, and first postmaster, 1809. At the dinner a Mr Jenkins sang some verses of his own composition to the tune of 'Rule Britannia', in which he sang not only of the day when Australia first rose to fame, and seamen brave explored her shore, but of one difference between Europe and Australia for here was a country free from the old world scourge of war.[83] So the early sentiments of Australian patriotism, even the use of that name, were expressed at gatherings of ex-convicts. In the same year Macquarie, sensitive as ever to the emancipist mind, recommended that Australia should be the name given to the country instead of the very erroneous and misapplied name of New Holland which properly speaking, only applied to a part of the immense continent.[84]

At the same time important developments had occurred in the economy and political life of the colony. As early as March 1810 Macquarie had recommended the creation of a colonial government bank, but when the Secretary of State did not deem it expedient, Macquarie dropped the idea. In 1816 Macquarie decided to call a meeting of the magistrates, principal merchants and gentlemen of Sydney, which was held in the Judge Advocate's chambers

[79] Ibid., 31 May 1817.
[80] Ibid., 7 November 1818.
[81] Ibid., 31 October 1818.
[82] Ibid., 7 November 1818.
[83] Ibid., 1 February 1817.
[84] Macquarie to Goulburn, 21 December 1817, *H.R.A.*, I, 9, p. 747. See note 84 in *H.R.A.*, I, 9, pp. 867-9, and A. Lodewyckx: 'De benamingen van het vijfde werelddeel, historisch en taalkundig toegelicht', *Tijdschrift van het Koninklijk Nederlandsch Aardrijkskundig Genootschap*, series 2, vol. lxvi, pp. 704-18.

on 22 November; among those present were Lieutenant-Governor Molle, Judge Advocate Wylde, D. Wentworth, R. Jones, A. Riley, T. Macvitie, R. Jenkins, J. R. O'Connor, R. Brooks, C. Hook, J. T. Campbell, Simeon Lord, and T. Wylde, and the following seven resolutions were passed:

1. That the present Meeting is desirous that a Sterling Currency should take place in this Colony under such Regulations and Provisions, as His Excellency the Governor may deem proper and applicable to a reduced price of Labour and rate of Sterling Charges in every kind of Dealing and Trade within the Colony.

2. That a Sum of not less than Twenty Thousand Pounds, in Shares of not less than One Hundred Pounds each invested in a Public Colonial Bank, transferable by assignment or otherwise in due course of Law, will be necessary for supplying a circulating medium for the uses of the Colony.

3. That every Subscriber of £100 have a right of a single Vote at every Meeting to be assembled . . . in every Year upon all general Questions, with regard to the Government and general Interests of the Bank, and upon the appointment of the Committee and Officers, and passing of the Accounts:—no Subscribers being allowed to have, in Right of any number of Shares in the said Bank, more than . . . Votes upon any Question submitted to the Meeting.

4. That the internal Management of the Bank and its immediate Concerns be committed to a Chairman and . . . Persons, chosen by the Subscribers yearly and appointed Directors of the Same.

5. That the general object and Business of the Bank be to advance, upon due Interest and the credit of the Bank, pecuniary assistance to the Colonial Trader, Agriculturalist and Settler, as well as to afford a Safe Depository of Money committed to its Security and charge.

6. That no Dividends shall ever take place or be made upon the Fund of £20,000 as first established:—but that the same shall be made upon the Interest of the Bank Capital at such rate and times, as a Public Meeting shall authorize upon Suggestion from the Directors in that Respect.

7. That, in conviction of the beneficial results that would be thus given to the Colony in every view of its best Interests, as well as to put an end to the destructive consequences and embarrassment of the present Colonial Currency, the Undersigned thus voluntarily pledge themselves as approving the measure of a Sterling Currency as above suggested, the Establishment of a Colonial Bank upon proper Regulations, as hereafter to be considered and adopted, and to become Subscriber thereto and to support the measure with all their Influence and Interest, provided His Excellency the Governor be pleased to Sanction the Same with his general Approbation and Permission.[85]

On 7 February 1817 a full meeting of the subscribers was held at the Court House, when the rules and regulations of the bank were adopted; D'Arcy Wentworth, J. Harris, R. Jenkins, T. Wylde, A. Riley, W. Redfern, and J. T. Campbell were elected as directors, with J. T. Campbell unanimously appointed president of the board. It was named the Bank of New South Wales.[86] With his usual flair for the historical significance of an occasion, Macquarie predicted that the bank would be productive of incalculable benefit to the mercantile and agricultural interests in the colony, would redound to its future credit and form an era in its true respectability which would hereafter be looked back

[85] Note 56 in *H.R.A.*, I, 9, pp. 861-2.
[86] *Sydney Gazette*, 8 February 1817.

to with public gratitude, and relieve the expenses of the mother country by releasing the relatively depressed energies of the colony.[87]

At the same time Macquarie entertained high hopes for the improvement in the material and moral well-being of the inhabitants of Van Diemen's Land. Sorell arrived at Hobart Town on 8 April 1817, and was received by Lieutenant-Governor Davey, the deputy Judge Advocate, and the civil and military officers. On the following day he assumed the command of His Majesty's settlements in Van Diemen's Land. On 14 April he issued his first proclamation against the bushrangers,[88] and established a system of passes for people wishing to proceed to the country districts. By then the situation was desperate. For after perpetrating enormous crimes against the inhabitants of the country districts, and in some cases venturing into Hobart Town, the bushrangers, with cheek and effrontery, now offered to return to civilization in exchange for a pardon. By then individuals ran great risks if they attempted to convey property from one settlement to another. Michael Howe had become a terror to traveller and settler alike. For some of the bushranger vengeance against society was stiffened by the concept of a higher purpose, of bushranging as a calling in which the Irish could punish the Anglo-Saxon for the wrongs of Ireland.[89] By chance, or possibly by greater zeal, Sorell pursued his campaign with success. In March 1818 the *Sydney Gazette* could announce that Michael Howe was the only desperado still alive, and predicted that from his present forlorn and miserable condition he could not much longer elude the punishment due to his crimes.[90] On 21 October of that year William Pugh, a soldier of the 48th regiment, shot Howe at a place near the Shannon River.[91] It looked as though zeal had destroyed the bushrangers, but this was only a lull before the storms to come, for no man could have removed the causes driving such men to the bush.

With the natives, Sorell's policy of amity and kindness bore little fruit. They avoided the settlements, and they destroyed live stock, as their hatred for the white man appeared to be fixed and ineradicable. The musket and the sword remained the only weapons the Europeans believed the natives could understand. So long as terror was the instrument of policy no attempts such as had been begun on the mainland to civilize them could ever start, and no man on the island dreamed such dreams as had sustained the few on the mainland. While the aborigine in Van Diemen's Land faced doom and disaster, the material prospects for the white man began to improve. As the tactics of terror lessened the disturbances from the aborigines, the settlers accepted its superiority over the tactic of amity and kindness.

In 1818 Port Davey and Macquarie Harbour were discovered.[92] At Mac-

87 Macquarie to Bathurst, 29 March 1817, *H.R.A.*, I, 9, p. 221.

88 Macquarie to Bathurst, 16 May 1817, *H.R.A.*, I, 9, p. 404 and *Sydney Gazette*, 17 May 1817.

89 *Sydney Gazette*, 22 February 1817, and *Hobart Town Gazette*, 23 November 1816.

90 *Sydney Gazette*, 14 March 1818.

91 Ibid., 12 December 1818.

92 Macquarie to Bathurst, 16 May 1818, *H.R.A.*, I, 9, pp. 795-6.

quarie Harbour the huon pine grew in abundance, while plenty of good coal was also found there. They were moving close to the country where Tasman had first sighted Van Diemen's Land, and finding a different wealth from that for which the Dutch had searched in vain. Lieutenant-Governor Sorell proposed to form a small settlement at Macquarie Harbour to supply the other settlements with coal and huon pine, and as a place of banishment and security for the worst description of offenders. In the autumn of 1819 Sorell reported the finest wheat harvest in the history of the colony.[93] So between 1816 and 1819 the settlers of Van Diemen's Land gradually ceased to be plagued by bushrangers, or to be harried by the natives; and in high places, zeal and enterprise replaced the sloth and the indulgence of the Davey period. Perhaps Sorell's success, or good fortune, might be measured by the singular fact that rarely was a voice raised to reproach or revile him for publicly flouting the seventh commandment.[94]

The curious thing was the response from Macquarie to all these advances. By the last quarter of 1817 he had been so wounded by opposition to his policies, and so hurt by censure when by nature he desperately needed approval and cooperation, that much of his enthusiasm began to drain out of his official comments on the colony. When John Macarthur returned on the *Lord Eldon* with two of his sons on 30 September 1817, Macquarie, who had written three years earlier of the precautions he proposed to take to prevent George Johnston inciting people to mischief, now contented himself with recording the fact without flourish or embellishment. Within two months he was handling the problem of O'Flynn, a Catholic priest, who had arrived on the *Duke of Wellington* on 9 November 1817.[95]

Before leaving England O'Flynn had petitioned Bathurst for permission to minister to Catholics in New South Wales, so that he might teach the members of his congregation their duties to God and their neighbour, to conform to the laws of their country, and practise habits of religion, decency, and regularity.[96] As O'Flynn did not receive Bathurst's formal permission, Macquarie decided he was an impostor, and ordered him to leave. After all, as he put it to Bathurst, Catholics could attend Protestant services, and the people were quiet, but they might be worked on by a designing artful priest, who could excite a spirit of resistance, insubordination and insurrection similar to what took place under Governor King.[97] By then he had had enough of insubordination. In the meantime, Macquarie waited to see whether O'Flynn's credentials arrived by the next ship. When O'Flynn broke his promise by celebrating mass, preaching to Catholics, and disseminating resistance to the orders of the government, especially the regulations enforcing a sabbatarian Sunday, Macquarie

---

[93] *Sydney Gazette*, 24 April 1819.

[94] Macquarie to Bathurst, 12 December 1817, *H.R.A.*, I, 9, pp. 717-18; A. F. Kemp to Alan H. Broughnson, March 1818, A. F. Kemp to Macquarie, April 1818, A. F. Kemp to Bathurst, November 1818 (Oldham Papers, vol. 3, p. 346, Royal Society of Tasmania, Hobart).

[95] Macquarie to Bathurst, 12 December 1817, *H.R.A.*, I, 9, p. 710.

[96] For the petition of O'Flynn see note 146 in *H.R.A.*, I, 9, p. 881.

[97] Macquarie to Bathurst, 12 December 1817, *H.R.A.*, I, 9, p. 710.

again ordered him to leave. O'Flynn, however, slipped off to what Macquarie called a skulking place in the country, where he gave further offence by attempting to convert Protestants by promising he could cure all their bodily disorders, and treated a Protestant clergyman, the Reverend Cartwright, with what Macquarie termed low and vulgar insolence. This so exasperated Macquarie that he arrested O'Flynn as the only means of getting rid of a muddling, ignorant, and dangerous character, on 15 May, and deported him on the *David Shaw*. By that time O'Flynn, in his opinion, had infused into the colony a bigotry which would not be easily eradicated.[98] For Macquarie accepted the common-place of the Protestant ascendancy that Irish Catholicism menaced the higher civilization, both by its bigotry and its superstitious practices.

At the same time his language in describing the behaviour of those he despised became more haughty and censorious. The country, he told Bathurst in the middle of 1818, was already swarming with needy, idle and profligate people.[99] For time did not soften his tendency to condemn the weak. Early in 1819 the provost marshal of Van Diemen's Land, Martin Tims, arrested a man, and then drank himself into such a state of stupefaction that he could not give evidence in court when the man applied for bail. Macquarie promptly dismissed him from office as a very illiterate, low, vulgar man, much addicted to drunkenness and low company, vices, he believed, which rendered him altogether unfit and unworthy of holding so respectable and important an office.[100]

By one of those odd throws of chance in human affairs, Macquarie's desire to confound his enemies and reproach the weak engulfed him at a time when the despatches from England should have soothed his injured pride. Early in 1819 he had received a despatch from Bathurst approving his dismissal of Moore for affixing a signature to a petition without the signatory's consent.[1] In March Macquarie read of the considerable satisfaction the Prince Regent had derived from his assurances of the peace, tranquillity and progressive improvements of the colony placed under his administration. He read too that the barracks for the convicts, the factory and the churches had Bathurst's entire approbation.[2] A few months later he should have read a private despatch in which Bathurst disavowed any imputation upon his character or the uprightness of his intentions and discounted the attacks to which in common with other public men Macquarie had been exposed. As a proof of the confidence he reposed in him he would not appoint a successor until he had learned that Macquarie still persisted in his determination to return to England.[3] By some extraordinary mischance Macquarie did not read this despatch till he returned to England.[4]

---

98 Macquarie to Bathurst, 18 May 1818, *H.R.A.*, I, 9, pp. 799-801.
99 Macquarie to Bathurst, 16 May 1818, *H.R.A.*, I, 9, pp. 796-8.
100 Macquarie to Bathurst, 4 March 1819, and enclosures, *H.R.A.*, I, 10, pp. 36-9.
1 Bathurst to Macquarie, 24 July 1818, *H.R.A.*, I, 9, p. 822.
2 Bathurst to Macquarie, 24 August 1818, *H.R.A.*, I, 9, pp. 830-3.
3 Bathurst to Macquarie, 18 October 1818, *H.R.A.*, I, 9, pp. 838-40.
4 Macquarie to Bathurst, 10 October 1823 (photostat of MS. in Mitchell Library, Sydney).

It was too late by then, for the initiative in the colony was passing to other hands, while Macquarie's dark thoughts were encouraged by the announcement that a commissioner had been appointed to inquire into the conditions of the colony of New South Wales. In January of 1819 Macquarie gave permission to the gentlemen, clergy, merchants, settlers and other free subjects to convene a meeting at the court room in the new general hospital, to prepare a petition to make an appeal to the foot of the throne.[5] When the first meeting was held on 19 January, Sir John Jamison was elected to the chair. Jamison was born in 1776, educated as a surgeon, joined the navy, and helped to cure an outbreak of cholera in the Swedish army for which he was made a knight of the order of Gustavus Vasa. In 1814 he arrived in the colony to take up his father's property, on the Nepean. His father had arrived as surgeon's mate on the *Sirius* in 1788. At the first meeting the following resolutions were agreed to:

1. That a regular Demand does exist in this Colony for British Manufactures of nearly all Descriptions, greater than the Established mercantile Houses here have supplied, or are likely to supply regularly; and that from the rapid Increase of our Population, this Demand may be considered as yearly increasing.

2. That the Restrictions which prevent Merchants from employing Ships of less than three hundred & fifty Tons Burthen, in the Trade from the Mother Country to this Colony, operate so as to amount almost to a prohibition; as few mercantile Adventurers here are willing or able to employ the large Capital necessarily required for the Cargoes of vessels of this Magnitude; and we are consequently left ill supplied with many Articles of British Manufactories, which Habit has rendered necessary to our Comfort.

3. That it is therefore expedient that an Application should be made, by Petition, to HIS MAJESTY'S GOVERNMENT, through His EXCELLENCY GOVERNOR MACQUARIE, praying that the Navigation between Great Britain and the Colony may be opened (as to British Manufactures and Colonial produce) through the Medium of Vessels of one hundred and fifty Tons Burthen, and upwards.

4. That it is also highly expedient, that the Subjects, of Trial by Jury: the Distillation of Spirits from Grains; the Repeal of the Duties imposed in England upon Oils, Skins, Wool, Timber &c. imported there from the Colony, as well as certain Drawbacks upon Colonial Export Duties, be embodied in the same Petition; and thereby solicited from His Majesty's Government.

5. That a Committee be now appointed to draw up a Petition to the foregoing effect; and that the same be composed of the following Gentlemen, viz.

Sir John Jamison	W. Cox, Esq.
W. Browne, Esq.	R. Brooks, Esq.
J. Harris, Esq.	R. Jenkins, Esq.
Mr. E. Eagar	F. Garling, Esq.
S. Lord, Esq.	Mr. E. S. Hall
G. Blaxland, Esq.	W. Redfern, Esq.

R. Townson, Esq.

Five of whom shall form a quorum.

[5] Macquarie to Bathurst, 22 March 1819, *H.R.A.*, I, 10, p. 52.

SOUTH-WEST VIEW OF HOBART TOWN, 1819

Lithograph in the Mitchell Library, Sydney, after a watercolour by G. W. Evans

JOHN MACARTHUR

Miniature by an unknown artist in the possession of Lady Stanham at Camden Park

6. That the Committee are instructed to prepare the aforesaid Petition, and lay it before the Public Meeting, to be held pursuant to Ajournment, on Thursday the 11th of February next.

7. That the grateful Thanks of this Meeting be presented to His Excellency Governor MACQUARIE, for the Privilege granted by him to the Inhabitants of the Colony in the Convening of the present Meeting, by which they have an Opportunity of entering upon Matters affecting their vital Interests, and of freely discussing the same; and they cannot but express their Gratification at the Confidence manifested by HIS EXCELLENCY in the political Integrity and Discretion of the Colonists, in acceding to the Requisition which stated the Objects of the Meeting in such general Terms.

The Chairman is requested to communicate this Resolution to HIS EXCELLENCY by an early Opportunity.

8. The Thanks of the Meeting having been returned to the Chairman, for his able and impartial Conduct in the Chair, it was adjourned to Thursday the 11th Day of February next, at 11 o'Clock, in the Forenoon, at the General Hospital; when the Gentlemen, Clergy, Landholders, Merchants, and other respectable Inhabitants are earnestly requested to attend.

9. That these Proceedings be published thrice in the Sydney Gazette.[6]

On 12 February 1819 they met again in the court room at the new general hospital to debate the petition which was read, and, after a considerable discussion, adopted. The petition began with matter-of-fact, common-sense requests for changes in the administration of justice, written in language which reflected the minds of money changers and tillers of the soil rather than men with philosophical or religious conceptions of the rights of man. They started by repeating the commonplace that the Judge Advocate's court appeared to be a court martial rather than a court of law, then moved on to denounce it as contrary to all their habits, feelings and opinions as Englishmen. From this point they asserted there were now a great number of free respectable inhabitants, sufficient and competent to act as jurymen, and named the men on their side in the past, tossing in the point that the Hindus, the Hottentots, and the negro slaves had it, before they reverted to what they were worthy of as Englishmen and the sons of Englishmen—namely that great safeguard of British rights, trial by jury. For the rest they concentrated on ways and means to facilitate the making of wealth—the need for a market for their grain; the suggestion that surplus grain could be used to distil ardent spirits, with an aside on colonial morals; how the moral habits and sobriety of their numerous and rapidly rising generation were such as would reflect the highest credit on any people and do honour to any country which was an early colonial brag and boast on touchy questions; the need to abolish statutory restrictions on shipping; the way colonial trade was harmed by paying duties on whale oil, wool, etc.; and the employment problem for the colonial born.[7] All this was written in a respectful, hopeful tone by men who saw the future of the colony in the expansion of its trade, and perceived vaguely that there was a connection between trade and the rights of Englishmen.

6 *Sydney Gazette*, 23 January 1819.
7 Encl. in Macquarie to Bathurst, 22 March 1819, *H.R.A.*, I, 10, pp. 55-65.

w

The meeting also appointed Jamison, Brooks, Browne, and Simeon Lord as a deputation to wait on the Governor, and the clergy and magistrates as their agents to collect signatures. They concluded by slipping back to the problem of liberty, or rather touched on the problem of free discussion, an inalienable right in the mother country, but here only a boon conferred by the grace of the Governor, which, before they could draw together their ideas on such rights, swept their minds back to sentiments of gratitude to Macquarie, which they asked their deputation to convey to him when they met him on 20 March.[8] On 20 March, signed by twelve hundred and sixty persons who represented in Macquarie's words, all the men of wealth, rank or intelligence throughout the colony, the petition was presented to Macquarie who passed it on to Bathurst with a note on the good disposition of the people.[9] So ended the first move of the merchants and landowners to sketch their ideas on the future of the colony. They were men for piece-meal reforms, rather than men of vision, with the Protestant clergy as the agents of men whose one declared aim was material gain.

For the Protestant religion was their means of grace as well as their hope of glory. In Government House circles it was supported for its social utility. At the inaugural meeting to institute an Auxiliary Bible Society, held in the court room on Friday 7 March 1817, Macquarie gave the opening address, in which he expressed his wish that the institution should receive that support it was entitled to from its object, as it should ever receive that reverential attention and encouragement which as a man and a Christian, he was bound to give it. Marsden followed with an equally fulsome and vague speech. Then Judge Advocate Wylde declared that the value of a Bible society was that it would correct the growth of vice, and, at the same time, extend the knowledge of that sacred volume whose inestimable contents were alone capable of regulating and restraining the passions, and of bringing man to a nearer acquaintance with his Creator.[10] The effect of Bible reading on behaviour was *the* great assumption of the period. As the Bible, wrote one letter-writer to the *Sydney Gazette*, urged natural affection, so all Bible readers had strong family feelings, in contrast with the non-Bible readers, who were the deepest sunk into sensuality and vice, and furthest removed from family affection.[11] On 8 May a branch of the New South Wales society was inaugurated at Hobart Town under the patronage of Lieutenant-Governor Sorell; for between intention and performance there were gaps.

From such a faith, two practical conclusions were drawn. The first was to educate the young in these principles. At the inaugural meeting of the New South Wales branch, the resolution passed stated that the education of the young was of the first importance to the best interests of this colony, as it

[8] *Sydney Gazette*, 20 March 1819.

[9] Macquarie to Bathurst, 22 March 1819, *H.R.A.*, I, 10, pp. 52-4.

[10] *Sydney Gazette*, 8 March 1817.

[11] Ibid., 23 October 1819. See also A T. Thompson: *Australia and the Bible. A Brief Outline of the Work of the British and Foreign Bible Society in Australia, 1807-1934* (London, 1935); and *The First Report of the Auxiliary Bible Society of New South Wales* (Sydney, 1817).

afforded a sure hope of the advantages which the general circulation of the holy scriptures tended to bestow. The second was to establish public schools in different parts of the territory for the instruction of those children whose parents could not afford to send them to school.[12] The other duty was to attend to the relief of the poor and other benevolent purposes, as religion was the source and origin of their benevolence. It was at a meeting of the New South Wales Auxiliary Bible Society that the chairman, Judge Advocate Wylde, drew the attention of members to the want of any adequate means of relief, and their duty to create a society worthy of their general character and philanthropy.[13] So the Benevolent Society of New South Wales was founded as a duty of Christian charity, at the next meeting of the Bible Society on 6 May 1818.[14]

Their faith was strictly sabbatarian. At Parramatta, in September 1818, the magistrates admonished persons for driving carts on the roads on the sabbath day, pointing out that market day had been moved from Saturday to Friday to prevent so improper a practice.[15] Their faith held constantly before the reading and sermon-listening public the notion of divine punishment for transgression. In 1818 a man was accused of the murder of a boy whose body could not be found. The man was acquitted, but before he left the dock the Judge Advocate, according to the *Sydney Gazette*, expatiated with much energy on the mysterious circumstances of the case, which though unfathomable to human investigation, could not escape the knowledge of an avenging God.[16] In December 1818 a woman was accused of child-murder. The Judge Advocate addressed the prisoner at considerable length in a language so truly impressive as to affect her almost to a state of convulsion. The *Sydney Gazette* regretted the lack of space in which to print the speech, not because of the unhappy duty of exposing to public odium the wretchedness of a fallen creature, but because it would be a polished mirror to show readers their duties to society.[17] The man who delivered that speech on an avenging God was the chairman of the Auxiliary Bible Society of New South Wales.

These lessons were constantly presented to the minds of the readers of the *Sydney Gazette*, often with a gruesomeness which might have offended readers not sympathetic with their aims. On 17 April 1819, the *Sydney Gazette* described the execution of three men who were taken to the foot of the scaffold in a cart, followed by another cart bearing their three coffins. The men were all penitent, confessed to the justness of their punishment, and appeared to be stricken with the infallibility of the law in the detection of vice.[18] For penitence was what the establishment wanted. The *Sydney Gazette* wrote with disapproval of John Brennan who met death by hanging with a hardihood

---

12 *Sydney Gazette*, 15 March 1817.
13 Ibid., 25 April 1818.
14 Ibid., 9 May 1818.
15 Ibid., 3 October 1818.
16 Ibid., 31 January 1818.
17 Supplement to the *Sydney Gazette*, 5 December 1818.
18 *Sydney Gazette*, 17 April 1819.

and a counterfeit courage which, they believed, must be known to result from the deepest depravity and the worst influence of moral turpitude. The crowd was disgusted too; for impenitence had driven out their pity. By contrast, the other men, the *Sydney Gazette* was pleased to report, had met their death with decent deportment and becoming resignation.[19]

Death by hanging was, as it were, the penultimate punishment for vice. There were, however, other punishments in this world for those who practised the minor vices. Of these the clergy, the magistrates, and the *Sydney Gazette* lingered longest on the consequences of intemperance. On 11 January 1817 the *Gazette* published a poem about a man who drank to stupefaction, returned home, and struck his wife, whereupon her naked infants pressed to her breast, and screamed in lamentation:

> In pity spare our mother dear, nor take her precious life!
> She gives us bread, by her we're fed; oh! father she's your wife!

But their screams were in vain, for in a drunken rage he murdered his wife, and then contemplated his fate:

> Repentance now too late obtrudes; no hope remains to thee;
> Remorse, poor wretch, must be thy scourge:—thy dread, Eternity![20]

Indeed, the *Sydney Gazette* never wearied of reminding its readers of the horrid fates of the over-bibulous. On 9 May they reported that a drunken carpenter on the ship *Minerva* had fallen overboard and drowned.[21] Nor did it weary of printing stories of how respectable people, by contrast, met suffering and death with Christian fortitude and died universally regretted and lamented.[22] They also printed stories to illustrate how unbelievers did not enjoy the same respect as believers; how, for example, the testimony of an unbeliever in a law court was received with diminished credit.[23] By contrast again, the clergy were the vessels of all attempts to improve the human lot. They were the ones who urged parents at baptism to have their children vaccinated against small pox, telling them they were bound by religion no less than by ties of affection to guard the child from every impending evil, and especially from infectious diseases endangering its life.[24]

The Protestant way of life enjoyed, they believed, a superiority over that of all other faiths and persuasions. The Asian they were told, was sunk in the most revolting practices. In March 1819, the readers of the *Sydney Gazette* read of how some Hindus began a religious ceremony with a barbarous jangle of harsh sounding drums and pipes, and by a sort of beastly play, somewhat resembling the plays of dogs or monkeys.[25] The Irish Catholics came from the lowest ranks of life, and were sunk in ignorance and

19 *Sydney Gazette*, 24 April 1819.
20 Ibid., 11 January 1817.
21 Ibid., 9 May 1818.
22 Ibid., 13 March 1819.
23 Ibid., 11 April 1818.
24 Ibid., 21 February 1818.
25 Ibid., 6 March 1819.

idolatry.[26] Jews were people who haggled about money, and were indifferent to the things of the spirit.[27] In the news of the outside world the same tendency prevailed. The *Sydney Gazette* reported all the revolts, barbarities, and cruelties committed in the non-British part of the world, as well as the disgusting religious practices of the heathen.[28] They reported French attempts to efface the inconsistencies of revolutionary innovation to secure France from a renewal of her past misfortunes, and the revolts in South America.[29] By contrast, the British enjoyed a blessed calm. No wars, no battles, no human carnage appeared in the columns of British newspapers; manufactures were beginning again to flourish—'Great and miraculous Providence!' exclaimed the editor of the *Sydney Gazette*, 'the Author of all Good! how are we indebted to your saving Power!'[30]

The pride and pleasure in being British was symbolized in their ceremonies to commemorate events in the life of the royal family. Each year the Queen's and the King's Birthdays were celebrated with pomp and gaiety. On 4 April 1818 the *Sydney Gazette* was published with black borders. The hopes of the country were dashed to the earth, it informed its readers. For instead of tidings of great joy, instead of proclaiming the birth of a future sovereign of these realms, of England's future hope and glory, they had the painful task of announcing that Princess Charlotte had died after being delivered of a still-born child. The colony plunged into the deepest mourning. Flags flew at half-mast, the church bells tolled for one hour; all places of amusement were shut up; all shops except butchers and bakers were closed; all public labour ceased; all officers wore mourning; everyone was invited to humble themselves before the throne of divine mercy on the following Sunday,[31] when the Reverend Cowper preached an affecting and most impressive sermon, and a special hymn and anthem were sung which heightened the general feeling of melancholy.[32] Macquarie wrote of it as the most fatal national calamity that could possibly have happened.[33] At a public meeting of the officers, gentlemen and settlers of the colony of New South Wales at the court room on 14 May 1818 an address was prepared for transmission to the Prince Regent.

TO HIS ROYAL HIGHNESS THE PRINCE REGENT
May it please Your Royal Highness,
We, HIS MAJESTY'S GOVERNOR, LIEUTENANT GOVERNOR, JUDGES, CIVIL and MILITARY OFFICERS, and other BRITISH INHABITANTS of New South Wales, deeply feeling the heavy Rod with

[26] Evidence of A. Riley to the Select Committee on the State of Gaols, 1819, p. 61, *P.P.*, 1819, VII, 579.
[27] *Sydney Gazette*, 28 November 1818.
[28] Ibid., 24 April 1819.
[29] Ibid., 21 February 1818 and 7 March 1818.
[30] Ibid., 3 July 1819.
[31] *Sydney Gazette*, Extraordinary, 2 April 1818.
[32] *Sydney Gazette*, 11 April 1818.
[33] Macquarie to J. Drummond, 18 May 1818 (Macquarie Letters, 1809-1820, Mitchell Library, Sydney).

which the whole civilized World in either Hemisphere has been chastened, in the premature Death of HER ROYAL HIGHNESS the Princess CHARLOTTE AUGUSTA, humbly presume to offer the Assurances of our Grief, under this Dispensation of the Divine Will, and our undiminished Attachment to YOUR ROYAL HIGHNESS, and HIS MAJESTY'S August FAMILY; and we devoutly pray to that GOD, by whom Kings reign and Princes decree Justice, and who is equally present at the uttermost Parts of the Sea, that that Consolation which we have not to bestow, but of which we stand in Need ourselves; that that Peace which the World cannot give, the Peace of God which passeth all Understanding, may have been poured abundantly into your Royal Breast; so that the invaluable Life of YOUR ROYAL HIGHNESS may be preserved and prolonged, to be a Blessing to Great Britain, in the Colonies, and to the universal World.

(By Desire of the Meeting)
LACHLAN MACQUARIE, Chairman[34]

There were signs that some of the graces of civilization were taking root in New South Wales. For over and above the concerts, the dances, the horse-racing, the yachting, the picnics, and the hunts of the kangaroo, other activities were beginning. In January 1818, T. Florance announced his intention to open a boarding school for young gentlemen at 74 Pitt Street where they would be instructed in English, Latin, Greek, Reading, Writing, Arithmetic, Book-keeping, Geography, Geometry, Algebra, Surveying, Navigation, and Nautical Astronomy for a fee of forty pounds per year with extra charges for French, Italian, Fencing, Dancing, Music, and Drawing.[35] The next year Mrs Hickey opened a boarding and day school for young ladies at Bent Street to instruct them in English Grammar, Writing, Geography and the French Language, promising speedy improvement in pupils at twenty pounds a year.[36] On 16 October 1819, the first number of a literary magazine appeared which was called appropriately the *Australian Magazine*, and contained agricultural and commercial reports, original essays, British intelligence, domestic occurrences and philosophical, moral and poetical essays. The models were the *Annual Register*, and the *Gentleman's Magazine*.[37]

In the same year a volume of verse by Barron Field was published in Sydney with the title: *First Fruits of Australian Poetry*. Some thought the poetry execrable:

> Thy poems, Barron Field, I've read
> And thus adjudge their meed—
> So poor a crop proclaims thy head
> A *barren field* indeed![38]

Whatever its quality as verse, the significant thing was that Field was writing about Australia, and seeing its harsh country, and its curious animals, through the eyes of an exile from civilization:

[34] *Sydney Gazette*, 16 May 1818.
[35] Ibid., 3 January 1818.
[36] Ibid., 8 May 1819.
[37] Announced in *Sydney Gazette*, 5 June 1819.
[38] Note 37 in *H.R.A.*, I, 10, p. 814.

The Kangaroo

—'mixtumque genus, prolesque biformis.'

VIRG. *Aen.* vi

Kangaroo, Kangaroo!
Thou Spirit of Australia,
That redeems from utter failure,
From perfect desolation,
And warrants the creation
Of this fifth part of the Earth,
Which would seem an after-birth,
Not conceiv'd in the Beginning
(For GOD bless'd His work at first,
    And saw that it was good),
But emerg'd at the first sinning,
When the ground was therefore curst;—
And hence this barren wood![39]

At the same time the native born were becoming aware of themselves as Australians. Observers noticed that they were tall in person, and slender in their limbs, and of fair complexion and small features. They were capable of undergoing more fatigue than people born in Europe. In habit they were active, but awkward in their movements. In their tempers they were quick and irascible, but not vindictive. They had evinced a strong disposition for a sea-faring life. Most of the older ones regarded the colony as their future home. Some of them believed the colony belonged to themselves and their descendants. In speech they had taken over the flash and giddy language of their parents, and were developing their own distinctive pronunciation, though not as yet a distinctive vocabulary or turn of phrase in which to communicate their sense of place or the meaning of their lives. By 1820 these early sentiments of belonging to the country went hand in hand with ideas of exclusive ownership, for their passion of patriotism was fed by xenophobia.

For xenophobia has had a long history, and its origins, both in its nobler and in its baser manifestations might be traced to the passions and aspirations of the convicts. From this idea that the colony belonged to the convicts and their descendants stemmed both the notion that the Australians could create a society free from the evils of the old world and that the enjoyment of such an achievement should be reserved for the native born. From the start it was accompanied by a sensitivity to criticism, and a touchiness which expressed itself in a species of bragging. In the same year as Bent was commenting on the aspirations of the convicts and their families, a writer in the *Sydney Gazette* was defending the 'currency lads'[40] against English aspersions on

[39] Barron Field: *First Fruits of Australian Poetry*, p. 7 (Sydney, 1819).

[40] The origin and use of the term 'currency lad' is explained in P. Cunningham: *Two Years in New South Wales*, 2nd ed. (London, 1827), vol. 2, p. 46:

'Our colonial-born brethern are best known here by the name of *Currency*, in contradistinction to *Sterling*, or those born in the mother country. The name was originally given by a facetious paymaster of the seventy-third regiment quartered here,—the pound currency being at that time *inferior* to the pound sterling. Our Currency lads and lasses are a fine interesting race, and do honour to the country whence they originated. The name is a sufficient passport to esteem with all the well-informed and right-feeling portion of our population;

their drinking, profane swearing, gambling, cock fighting, horse-racing and sabbath-breaking, not by ridiculing such Puritanism and philistinism, but by bragging that the principles of virtue and integrity were as frequently found to adorn the youth of New South Wales, as those of the mother country.[41]

The most successful of the ex-convicts was Samuel Terry who, by 1820, had accumulated 19,000 acres. Terry was born in 1776 and transported in 1801, it was said, for stealing geese. He was placed in a stone-mason's gang at Parramatta, where he also opened a shop, in which convict servants exchanged worn clothes for spirits and tobacco. This began Terry's reputation as a man who higgled with convicts for their dirty clothes. In 1811 he moved to Sydney where he obtained a licence for an inn and continued his retail shop business. From that time and possibly earlier he began his traffic in the exchange of liquor for land grants. He advanced spirits and tobacco on the security of the land grant, and when the grantee could not pay his debt, either foreclosed or bought the land when the sheriff auctioned it as a bankrupt estate. So the man of perfectly sober and frugal habits profited by exploiting human weaknesses. The clergy denounced him as a grasping man; the poorer settlers complained of his extortions; inborn niggardliness deprived him of all charity in his relations with the fraternity of thieves. It was said that when he was robbed of a chest containing some thousand sovereigns, he promised his convict servant, who had been capitally convicted, that he would obtain his pardon if he disclosed the spot in the garden where the chest was hidden. The boy trusted Terry, who recovered the sovereigns and then let the boy hang. By 1823 Terry was known to his enemies as the richest outlaw in Australia, or the Botany Bay Rothschild, and to his friends as the man who entertained them each year on the anniversary of the founding of the colony with such a liberal hand that his 'festive board actually groaned under its ponderous weight of true British hospitality'.[42]

A few of the emancipists established their families in that independence which ownership of land conferred. George Best, a farmer in Sussex, was transported in 1792 for petty theft. For his servitude he worked as an overseer and seedsman on the government farm at Toongabbe, at the end of which he received a grant of thirty acres as a man deserving encouragement. By 1820 he had cleared one hundred and sixty of the four hundred and sixty-five acres he had accumulated at Toongabbe. By that time four convicts were working for him on his land, while he was paying two free workers to put up posts and rails, one free man as a shepherd and two ticket-of-leave men to clear stumps. He was married in 1797, and had nine children, all of whom

---

but it is most laughable to see the capers some of our drunken old Sterling madonnas will occasionally cut over their Currency adversaries in a quarrel. It is then, "you saucy baggage, how dare you set up your *Currency* crest at me? I am *Sterling*, and that I'll let you know!"'
See also *Australian Encyclopaedia*, vol. 3.

[41] Evidence of J. H. Bent to the Select Committee on the State of Gaols, 1819, p. 125, *P.P.*, 1819, VII, 579; J. T. Bigge: Agriculture and Trade, pp. 81-2.

[42] Anon.: *The History of Samuel Terry, in Botany Bay, who died lately, leaving a princely fortune of nearly one million sterling* (London, 1838), by A.L.F., late of New South Wales; *Sydney Gazette*, 6 February 1823.

were born in wedlock. Two of his sons were educated by Crook the missionary, a daughter at a school in Sydney, and the rest by a hired schoolmaster. A daughter married one of his convict servants, and Best put him on the land, too, where they prospered. In this way Best used the wealth of the land, his industry, and his sobriety to pass from servitude to respectability. The proportion of those who extended their grants by purchase was not large. Most of the emancipists who took up their grants lived in abject poverty until they sold their precarious source of independence and became workers for wages. Only those such as a Terry and a Larra, who supplemented their income from land by entering the retail trade, especially the trade in spirits, were able to use the convict system to rise out of the social class to which they had belonged in the United Kingdom.[43]

The other possibility was to invest savings accumulated during servitude in manufacturing. By 1820 Simeon Lord had turned the profits of marriage, fishing in the south seas and trade in the Pacific Islands into a manufactory at Botany Bay where he employed convicts and from fifteen to twenty colonial boys making blankets, stockings, wool hats, kangaroo hats, seal hats, opossum skin hats, all of them shoddy but cheaper than the imported English hats, boot leather, trousers, shirts, thread, kettles and glass tumblers.[44] The bulk of the wool grown in New South Wales was shipped direct by the growers to England, and Lord was the exception to the principle that the settlers should use their great natural advantages of grass and climate to grow food and wool and import the other goods they needed. Between 1810 and 1820 the numbers of sheep trebled, and some settlers were finding it profitable to sell the fleeces rather than the carcases.[45] They imported manufactured goods from England; sugar, spirits, soap and cotton goods from Bengal; sugar candy, silks and wearing apparel from China. They exported sandal wood, pearl shells and bêche de mer to China and Java. With the islands in the Pacific they exchanged coarse cottons and ironware for coconut and salt pork.[46]

Between 1816 and 1819 some thinking had occurred in the colony on its probable or desirable future, in the public discussion of which the usual passions had been aroused. Over the same years the question of its future had become a subject of public debate in the British Isles. This debate was conducted in the journals and newspapers, which were quick to report and comment on the significance of the voyages of discovery. As early as December of 1816 the London press contained reports of the journey of Evans across

[43] Evidence of G. Best to Bigge, 4 September 1820 (Bigge Appendix, C.O. 201/123); J. T. Bigge: Agriculture and Trade, pp. 10-11, p. 36; evidence of J. Larra to Bigge, 6 January 1821 (Bigge Appendix, C.O. 201/120).

[44] Account of Mr Lord's manufactures, submitted to Bigge, 1 February 1821 (document no. K14, Bigge Appendix, C.O. 201/129).

[45] J. T. Bigge: Agriculture and Trade, pp. 16-18, 28 and 53. John Blaxland had a small wool manufactory on his property. See his evidence to Bigge, 18 August 1820 (Bigge Appendix, C.O. 201/123). See also evidence of E. Riley to Bigge, n.d. (Bigge Appendix, C.O. 201/129).

[46] J. T. Bigge: Agriculture and Trade, p. 57.

the Blue Mountains.[47] In February 1817 the *Gentleman's Magazine* wrote that the report of this journey would be read not only as an object of curiosity, but from a consideration of the important advantages which this rising colony might hereafter derive from the discoveries now made.[48] By November 1819 the English readers were presented with the report of how Throsby had travelled through lands of the finest description.[49] The idea of New South Wales as a land of opportunity began to take root, especially in families with a vested interest in the future of the colony, who began to discuss New South Wales as a good capital investment because of the cheap land and the cheap convict labour.[50]

At the same time the feuds and brawls in the colony drifted over the seas to be metamorphosed into rumours of convict insubordination, caused by the mild and amicable manners of Governor Macquarie, while alarmist reports of this contagion spreading to the soldiery were reported in the journals.[51] By March 1817, these reports were being debated in the House of Commons. From 1810 to 1812 the House of Commons had been asked from time to time to debate the failure of transportation as a punishment. In April 1816, H. G. Bennet assumed the role of jeremiad of the convict system in a debate on a bill to amend several laws relative to the transportation of offenders, in which he trotted out all the well-established arguments about expense, failure to reform, and the low morals in the colony, before letting slip that he was basing his condemnation on the figures given to the house in 1810. The government replied with an assurance that the number of crimes in the colony had decreased, that marriage had become frequent, and depravity less common.[52] In March 1817, when Bennet presented the Vale-Moore petition to the house, in which the petitioners complained of the mode in which the laws were administered by the Governor, Castlereagh defended Macquarie as a distinguished officer.[53] The house could not rouse much interest in the affairs of such a remote colony.

They were, however, prepared to look into the transportation system, because that affected the incidence of crime in the United Kingdom. On 18 February 1819, Bennet moved for the appointment of a committee to inquire into the management of the hulks, the general conduct of the transportation system, the voyage to New South Wales, and the general government of New South Wales. After a debate in which thirteen others spoke, he was defeated by ninety-three ayes against one hundred and thirty-nine noes.[54]

Eleven days later, on 1 March 1819, when Castlereagh moved for the appointment of a committee to inquire into the state and description of gaols and other places of confinement, and into the best method of providing for

[47] *Annual Register*, 2nd ed., December 1816, vol. 58, pp. 193-5.

[48] *Gentleman's Magazine*, February 1817, vol. lxxxvii, pp. 117-22.

[49] *Annual Register*, November 1819, vol. 61, pp. 88-90.

[50] See, for example, the evidence of J. Macarthur jr, to the Select Committee on the State of Gaols, 1819, p. 137, P.P., 1819, VII, 579.

[51] *Gentleman's Magazine*, January 1817, vol. lxxxvii, pt. 1, p. 75.

[52] *Hansard*, 1st series, vol. 33, cols. 987-92, 5 April 1816.

[53] Ibid., vol. 35, cols. 920-1, 10 March 1817.

[54] Ibid., vol. 39, cols. 464-509, 18 February 1819.

the reformation as well as the safe custody and punishment of offenders, the motion was carried without dissent, probably because it directed attention to the domestic problem of the increase in crime. Castlereagh added that it would be a fit subject for the committee to inquire whether Botany Bay had not outgrown the object for which it was originally intended. The debate as usual encouraged the wild men to have their say. Bennet asked whether it was the intention of the government to start a settlement to which only the worst characters would be sent, and Fowell Buxton forged his generalization for the historian, when he stated that the English prisons were the schools and seminaries of the worst vices.[55]

The committee[56] had before them the report respecting sentences of transportation, presented on 10 July 1812, the report on prisons presented on 1 May 1815, the reports on the police of the metropolis, presented on 1 July 1816, 2 May, 8 July 1817, and 5 June 1818, the statement of number of persons capitally convicted, which had been presented on 23 February, and the annual returns of commitments, presented on 25 February and 1 March.[57]

The committee, known for short as the select committee on the state of gaols, took evidence in 1819, when they heard from A. Riley, J. H. Bent, S. Bate, and R. Jones, first-hand reports on conditions on the mainland and in Van Diemen's Land. They questioned witnesses on the system, its success or failure as a punishment, and a means of reformation, on public morality in New South Wales and Van Diemen's Land, the administration of justice, and the powers of the Governor. Unlike the 1812 committee on transportation, they did not draw any conclusions to guide the historian of New South Wales, for the report was very short and did not touch on the colony, though the evidence and the appendices add substantially to the corpus of knowledge of this period. While the committee was sitting, the house again had before it complaints against the conduct of Governor Macquarie, presented on 23 March 1819 by Brougham on behalf of the two free settlers, Blake and Williams. Members tended, however, to defend rather than condemn Macquarie, Brougham himself suggesting that his behaviour, if culpable, was the fault of the system rather than of the man, while Manning presented the case for a Governor enforcing the greatest subordination in a society composed such as New South Wales. Wilberforce presented the case for an inquiry, while recognizing Macquarie to be a gallant and respectable officer, an encomium capped by Sir James Mackintosh who described him as a man of high honour and humanity. Goulburn wound up for the government by conceding that the condition of New South Wales was such as to render some reform necessary, but insisted that imperfections in the administration were to be attributed to the system rather than the personality of the Governor.

55 Ibid., vol. 39, cols. 740-60, 1 March 1819.

56 Members were Lord Castlereagh, Sir James Mackintosh, Mr Canning, Mr Fowell Buxton, Mr Bathurst, Mr Bennet, Sir W. Scott, Mr Brougham, Mr Serjeant Copley, Lord Binning, Sir Arthur Piggott, Mr Henry Clive, Mr Wilberforce, Mr Vesey Fitz-Gerald, Sir John Newport, Sir W. Curtis, Mr Eastcourt, Mr Holford, Mr Wilmot, Mr Stuart Wortley, and Mr Attorney General.

57 *Hansard*, 1st series, vol. 39, cols. 740-60, 1 March 1819.

He concluded by referring to the decision to appoint a commissioner to inquire into conditions in the colony.[58]

The appointment of such a commissioner had been made in January 1819, though, as Goulburn reminded the house, the decision to make such an appointment had been made as long ago as 1817, well before the house heard from the vilifiers and traducers of Macquarie. It arose from a doubt in the mind of Lord Bathurst whether the settlements were calculated to satisfy the object for which they were originally established, namely the punishment and reformation of criminals. By 1817 permission to settle in New South Wales had, he believed, become an object to all who desired to leave their native country and had capital to apply to the improvement of the land. It was this very circumstance which appeared to Bathurst to render it less fit for the enforcement of regulations which were suitable for a penitentiary and therefore interfered with the exercise of rights to which as British subjects they conceived themselves entitled in every part of His Majesty's dominions. Nor could he conceal from himself that transportation was becoming neither an object of apprehension in the United Kingdom nor the means of reformation in the colony. For these reasons he had decided to appoint commissioners to investigate all the complaints about the treatment of convicts and the general administration of the government, as well as to recommend improvements and alterations.[59]

By the time he got round to issuing a commission his ideas on its work had changed somewhat. He decided to appoint one commissioner rather than two or three. For that office he chose John Thomas Bigge, who had been born at Linden, Northumberland, on 8 March 1780, educated at Westminster School and Christ Church, Oxford, admitted to the bar in 1806, and appointed Chief Justice at Trinidad in 1815.[60] As secretary, Bathurst appointed a well-connected man, Thomas Hobbes Scott, who was born in either 1773 or 1783, became a wine merchant, and then a late matriculant at Oxford in 1813.[61] In defining the purposes of the inquiry Bathurst stressed the need to inquire whether transportation was any longer efficient as a punishment. The colony was to be considered primarily as a receptacle for offenders, and to be judged by its success in sustaining a peculiar apprehension of transportation in the United Kingdom, and in all classes of the community. If the existing system was failing, Bigge was to recommend other places on the coast where the suffering of the convicts would not be divested of all salutary terror.[62]

These instructions were supplemented in two other letters by Bathurst to Bigge, written on the same day. In the first of these Bigge was instructed to inquire into the conduct of all the officials in the colony no matter how

[58] *Hansard*, 1st series, vol. 39, cols. 1124-38, 23 March 1819.

[59] Bathurst to Sidmouth, 23 April 1817, note 5 in *H.R.A.*, I, 10, pp. 807-8.

[60] Note 3 in *H.R.A.*, I, 10, p. 806; *Australian Encyclopaedia*, vol. 1; J. Dennis: 'Bigge versus Macquarie', in R.A.H.S., *J. & P.*, 1937, vol. 23, pt. 6.

[61] R. T. Wyatt: 'Wine Merchant in Gaiters', in R.A.H.S., *J. & P.*, 1949, vol. 35, pts. 3, 4 and 5.

[62] Bathurst to Bigge, 6 January 1819, encl. no. 2 in Bathurst to Macquarie, 30 January 1819, *H.R.A.*, I, 10, pp. 4-8.

exalted their rank or how sacred their character, but he was not to reveal his opinion in the colony.[63] In the second, he was instructed to inquire into a variety of topics relevant to the advancement of those settlements as colonies of the British Empire. He was to inquire whether the courts of justice were adequate, whether Van Diemen's Land needed a judicial system altogether separate from that of New South Wales, whether it was consistent with safety in a population compounded as that of New South Wales to dispense with any of those more severe provisions which had frequently given rise to complaints and which could not but be irksome to the free inhabitants of New South Wales, the possibility of diffusing religion and education (bearing in mind always that the two branches ought to be inseparably connected), the agricultural and commercial interest of the colony, whether to permit distillation of spirits within the colony (bearing in mind the dangers of the indiscriminate and unrestrained dissemination of ardent spirits throughout a population inclined already to an immoderate use of them, and too likely to be excited by the use of them to acts of lawless violence), the actual and probable revenues of the colony, and the propriety of admitting into society persons who originally came to the settlement as convicts. The Governor, Bathurst explained, favoured this, but the policy had drawn the hostility of some who held association with convicts to be a degradation against the Governor.[64] In the official commission Bigge was instructed to examine all the laws and regulations of the territory, everything connected with its administration, the superintendence and reform of the convicts, and the state of the judicial, civil and ecclesiastical establishments, while the Governor, his officers and ministers were instructed to assist him in carrying out such inquiries.[65] In his letter to Macquarie, on 30 January, Bathurst wrote briefly of the appointment of Bigge, instructed Macquarie to appoint him a Justice of the Peace and a magistrate to enable him to take evidence on oath, and to implement any reforms recommended by Bigge unless he had strong reasons against them.[66]

Bigge and Scott left, with 142 male convicts and 31 soldiers of the 59th Regiment, on board the *John Barry* and arrived in Sydney on 26 September 1819.[67] Macquarie was at Windsor when he arrived, so Bigge travelled to meet him over the road Macquarie himself had built. In these first few days relations between them were cordial. Macquarie, as ever, set himself to impress the newcomer, giving orders for Bigge to be accommodated in quarters appropriate to his rank and station.[68] On 4 October Bigge commented in a letter to Bathurst on the disposition and cordiality manifested by Governor Macquarie, as well as the anxiety Macquarie had expressed for an impartial investigation of his conduct. This anxiety led Bigge to express the hope that

[63] Bathurst to Bigge, 6 January 1819, encl. no. 3 in *H.R.A.*, I, 10, p. 8.

[64] Bathurst to Bigge, 6 January 1819, encl. no. 4 in *H.R.A.*, I, 10, pp. 9-11.

[65] Commission of John Thomas Bigge, 5 January 1819, encl. no. 1 in *H.R.A.*, I, 10, pp. 3-4.

[66] Bathurst to Macquarie, 30 January 1819, *H.R.A.*, I, 10, pp. 2-3.

[67] Macquarie to Bathurst, 28 February 1820, *H.R.A.*, I, 10, p. 277.

[68] Macquarie to Bathurst, 22 February 1820, *H.R.A.*, I, 10, pp. 211-12.

he could execute that most arduous and delicate part of his duty without creating any hostility in the mind and heart of Macquarie.[69]

In the beginning, the public exchanges were just as cordial. Early in October 1819, in the great saloon of Government House in Sydney and before a large assemblage consisting of the Governor, the Lieutenant-Governor, the Judge, the reverend chaplains, the magistrates and the civil and military officers, the Judge Advocate administered the oaths of allegiance, abjuration, supremacy, and office to Bigge. Then Macquarie spoke with that dignity, fulsomeness and enthusiasm with which he greeted every newcomer to his government, and assured him of every aid and assistance in conducting an investigation into the affairs of the colony over which he had so long had the honour to preside. The investigation, Macquarie concluded, was designed to place these settlements in a state of progressive happiness and prosperity, and that, after all, would accomplish the first and most earnest wish of his heart. In reply Bigge adopted the tone and the manner of the man who did not wear his heart on his sleeve. He explained how the increase in the number transported and doubts about the efficacy of secondary punishment, had led to his appointment, and how it was his duty to inquire and ascertain how far the rapid improvement in agriculture, and the several attainments in the various branches of civilized life had disqualified the settlements from answering the original purpose of their institution. After hinting that there were other subjects of inquiry, but refraining from disclosing them, he concluded by reminding his distinguished audience that the strictest impartiality to all, facility of access to all, and the attainment of truth would be his principal objects. Nothing, he added, would be gained from concealing the truth for private purposes, or from the gratification of malignant feelings and personal resentment.[70]

Within a few weeks the Reverend Samuel Marsden wrote to Bigge, that calumnies against him had been sent out into the world with the apparent public sanction of the Governor, that he was in danger of forfeiting the good opinion of the Christian world, and that he was not prepared quietly to suffer his public reputation to be torn to pieces by the hand of power and scattered in blotted scraps by an official engine over the face of the whole earth.[71] This was the sort of thing Macquarie believed a man had to endure as part of his fate in being a man. Marsden had his delusions too. His motive, he believed, was to promote the good of His Majesty's service and the eternal welfare of the inhabitants of the settlements of New South Wales. He thanked Almighty God in His superintending providence for raising up friends to advocate the cause in which the future welfare of the colony was involved.[72] For that was now the subject, and Bigge the man whom the men with ideas in their minds as well as the men with madness in their hearts wanted to bend to their purposes.

[69] Bigge to Bathurst, 4 October 1819 (Bigge Appendix, C.O. 201/142).

[70] *Sydney Gazette*, 9 October 1819.

[71] Marsden to Bigge, 28 December 1819 (Bigge Appendix, C.O. 201/142).

[72] Marsden to Reverend J. Pratt, 14 January 1820 (Bonwick Transcripts, Missionary vol. 2, box 50, pp. 576-8, Mitchell Library, Sydney).

MACQUARIE, 1820-1821

B Y THE TIME Bigge arrived in New South Wales, Macquarie's vision for the future of the colony was fading fast as his mind fed more and more on schemes to confound his enemies, and to win recognition for his work from the people in high places in London. To achieve this, Macquarie had first of all to win the approval of Bigge. Macquarie, who had not conceded equality let alone superiority to a judge or a minister of Christ's Church during his nine years in the colony, was asked to submit himself to the judgment of a man who was twenty years his junior in age, as well as being his junior in the service of government. The man who was incapable of believing there could be any other point of view than his own, was to be judged by a man who enjoyed in abundance the ability to be fair-minded, by a man who understood everyone's point of view and was endowed by nature with the gift of thinking himself into the mind of another person. So fate and the past afflicted his heart with a suffering which Macquarie could not reconcile with his notions of just deserts.

It began on 30 October, when Bigge let Macquarie know that he objected to the appointment of Redfern as a magistrate. On 1 November Macquarie called on Bigge who, somewhat to Macquarie's surprise, told him the appointment would not be approved at home, that it would give great offence, and might be annulled. To withhold the appointment was precisely what Macquarie could not do consistently with his honour, because on 1 September he had promised Redfern to appoint him a magistrate. Nor was Macquarie prepared to expose himself to the humiliating and mortifying reproach of a dereliction from that principle on which he had uniformly acted for the last ten years in the colony. They parted after agreeing that any further discussion on the appointment would be in writing.[1] In his first letter, Bigge urged Macquarie to avert a measure so replete with danger to the community and mischief to himself, and not to be swayed by any fear of affording a triumph to his enemies, but rather to disarm their malignity by setting a noble example of devotion to the higher interests of government by making a magnanimous sacrifice of his personal feelings to his public duty.[2] Macquarie replied, on 6 November, that he was gratified to be working with a man who, like himself, had the one object of the faithful discharge of their duty to their sovereign and their country in view. Redfern, he went on, possessed the qualifications. Experience had convinced him that some of the

[1] Macquarie to Bathurst, 22 February 1820, H.R.A., I, 10, pp. 215-16.
[2] Bigge to Macquarie, 2 November 1819, encl. no. 2 in Macquarie to Bathurst, 22 February 1820, H.R.A., I, 10, pp. 219-20.

most meritorious men in the colony had been convicts. As for the factious ones who had fattened themselves on the labours of the convicts, they had been bad subjects. Nine-tenths of the population had been convicts. They were the men who had tilled the land, built the houses and the ships, and made wonderful efforts in agriculture, maritime speculations and manufactures. With these arguments, he appealed to Bigge not to let the disposition with which nature seemed to have endowed him for doing good be overwhelmed by an over-strained delicacy, or too-refined a sense of moral feeling. He appealed to him too to avert the blow he appeared to be too much inclined to inflict on those unhappy beings, and let souls now in being as well as millions yet unborn, bless the day on which he had landed on their shores and given them when they deserved it what he so much admired—namely freedom.[3]

In reply Bigge expressed his painful regret at Macquarie's determination. He went on to set out the grounds which had persuaded him to interpose so early in his mission the authority of his advice and suggestions. As early as 3 February 1814 Bathurst had stigmatized such appointments as injudicious in a despatch to Macquarie. Besides, Bigge continued, Bathurst had said that with respect to the readmission of convicts to society, His Majesty's government entirely concurred with him in the propriety of the general principle. But this principle might be carried too far, and he was not prepared to say it would be judicious, unless under very peculiar circumstances to select convicts for the office of magistrates as this would violently incite the illiberal though not unnatural prejudice Macquarie had aroused when he admitted them to society.[4] There was no need for another magistrate in the Liverpool district; the faithful discharge of the duties of assistant surgeon could never form a claim to the honours of the magistracy; the crime for which Mr Redfern was transported was that of the most foul and unnatural conspiracy that ever disgraced the pages of English history, and though it might be forgiven it could never be forgotten; his exclusion from offices of trust and dignity must be continual or those offices would be contaminated by his admission; the appointment would promote a perpetual reproach to the magistracy and encourage the lower orders to hold that office in contempt; to appoint Redfern would prejudge one of the subject of his inquiry, that appointment of convicts to the magistracy which had been the distinguishing feature of Macquarie's administration. In conclusion he wished to assure Macquarie that he would not yield even to him in sentiments of feeling and compassion towards the convicts, and that he could subdue those objections which must arise in the breast of every man to an association with them. But if Macquarie insisted on appointing Redfern he must solemnly protest against being forced in the course of his duties into any public association with him.[5]

Macquarie did insist, at the same time enjoining Redfern not to attend any bench of magistrates where there might be the least chance of meeting

[3] Macquarie to Bigge, 6 November 1819, encl. no. 3 in Macquarie to Bathurst, 22 February 1820, *H.R.A.*, I, 10, pp. 220-4.

[4] Bathurst to Macquarie, 3 February 1814, *H.R.A.*, I, 8, pp. 134-5.

[5] Bigge to Macquarie, 10 November 1819, encl. no. 4 in Macquarie to Bathurst, 22 February 1820, *H.R.A.*, I, 10, pp. 224-31.

with Bigge.[6] Bigge then put pen to paper to let Bathurst know that Macquarie had been so little accustomed to and showed so little disposition or aptitude for the temperate discussion of any subject wherein his feelings had already been engaged, that he, Bigge, had nearly abandoned the hope of being able to influence him in the adoption of any one of the changes that he was certain would meet with his lordship's approbation as well as be of immediate advantage to the colony.[7] A month later, when Macquarie apologized for his intemperate language, Bigge wondered whether Macquarie's illness had caused a temporary aberration.[8] Macquarie's behaviour, however, quickly rid his mind of such a charitable explanation.

Early in January 1820, Macquarie read the letter by H. G. Bennet to Viscount Sidmouth in which the writer described New South Wales as a colony where reformation was the purpose, corruption the result, and where the government was so arbitrary, and the people so discontented, that a colony of Englishmen was living without morals, liberty, or laws.[9] To Macquarie this was another example of those cruel attacks on his public and private character, and his mind ran on to consider how to counter the damage to his honour and reputation. Believing as he did that the facts would vindicate him he decided to collect information on the state of New South Wales to confound his enemies, and sent a circular to the magistrates and chaplains on 15 January 1820 asking them to collect such information. When Bigge heard of the circular he wrote to Macquarie to protest against this improper interference with his own inquiry, adding that in support of his authority, he must from that day decline all private intercourse with him.[10] Macquarie needed Bigge's approval so desperately that he was prepared to humble himself to ask Bigge to reconsider his decision. He asked Bigge's secretary, T. H. Scott, to act as mediator, accepted Bigge's terms for a reconciliation, and then, when Bigge's pride was still unassuaged, agreed to send a circular to the magistrates and chaplains in which he unambiguously declared that he would not use their information during Bigge's stay. For, as he concluded, he had rarely met in public life any gentleman of whom he thought more highly, nor any whose friendship and good opinion he was more solicitous to cultivate and possess.[11]

In the meantime Bigge had begun to collect his evidence, and sort out his ideas on the colony. By the middle of October 1819 he was commenting on Macquarie's extravagance on public buildings, and expressing his astonishment to Bathurst about what he called the useless magnificence of the plan for new government stables at Sydney. In the same letter he wrote about

[6] Macquarie to Bigge, 12 November 1819, encl. no. 5 in *H.R.A.*, I, 10, pp. 233-4.

[7] Bigge to Bathurst, 20 November 1819 (Bigge Appendix, C.O. 201/142).

[8] Bigge to Bathurst, 19 December 1819 (Bigge Appendix, C.O. 201/142).

[9] H. G. Bennet: *Letter to Viscount Sidmouth, Secretary of State for the Home Department, on the Transportation Laws, the State of the Hulks, and of the Colonies in New South Wales* (London, 1819), pp. 112-13.

[10] Macquarie to Bathurst, 22 February 1820, *H.R.A.*, I, 10, pp. 235-7.

[11] See Macquarie to Bathurst, 22 February 1820, and the enclosures which contain the correspondence between Bigge and Macquarie, *H.R.A.*, I, 10, pp. 235-46.

x

the pernicious effects of the imperfect confinement of the women convicts
at Parramatta, and the urgent need for another building.[12] At the same time
he was giving some thought to the problem of employment for the large
numbers of convicts who had arrived between 1817 and 1819. In November,
he visited Port Macquarie with Oxley and Mr Gyles, of the London Missionary Society, who had earlier established a sugar manufactory at Otaheite.
Gyles believed the soil and climate were favourable for the cultivation of
sugar, and Bigge immediately perceived a connection between a sugar plantation and the excess supply of convict labour. As he put it, the labours of
a sugar estate, excepting always the manufacture of rum and spirit (for he
believed in temperance for the lower orders), offered the best means of
constant as well as profitable employment for the convicts.[13]

While Macquarie so disquieted himself in vain attempts to avenge his
private wrongs that he had almost ceased to use his imagination on the problems of the colony, Bigge was sketching his ideas on the function of convict
labour. As he saw it, the aim of reformation could serve the economic needs
of the colony by using the convicts to clear land in the country where they
would be both removed from the contamination of town vices, and provide
the means to promote that extension of settlement rendered so necessary by
the increase of population.[14] This idea was conceived, too, before Bigge had
taken evidence from the larger settlers, indeed well over a year before Macarthur developed the idea with special reference to the growth of wool.
Indeed, it was conceived at a time when the only evidence he had before
him from a person of any weight in the colony was that rather long bilious
letter which gave the history of the Macquarie period through the eyes of
Samuel Marsden.[15] But Bigge remained receptive to, though uninfluenced
by, gossip; for what interested him was the future of the colony. He also
remained uninfluenced by, if not indifferent to, any considerations of the
pain any of his opinions and recommendations might cause to its inhabitants
and its officials.

He sailed for Hobart Town early in 1820 to collect evidence there, arriving on 21 February.[16] In addition to his general instructions, he had to conduct a mission of great delicacy—reporting on Sorell's consorting at Government House with Mrs Kent. He reported that most of Van Diemen's Land
society continued to attend Government House even after knowing of Mrs
Kent's presence there, and that the moral feelings of the respectable portion
of the inhabitants had been much hurt, while the worthless portion had found
in it a pretext for their own open and repeated disregard of moral decency
and domestic obligations. He paid a high tribute to Sorell's ability and the
regard in which he was held in Van Diemen's Land. Indeed, as he pointed
out later to Bathurst, he took every opportunity consistent with his honour

[12] Bigge to Bathurst, 18 October 1819 (Bigge Appendix, C.O. 201/142).

[13] Bigge to Bathurst, 20 November 1819 (Bigge Appendix, C.O. 201/142).

[14] Bigge to Bathurst, 19 December 1819 (Bigge Appendix, C.O. 201/142).

[15] Marsden to Bigge, 28 December 1819 (Bigge Appendix, Papers relative to New
Zealand, C.O. 201/130).

[16] Sorell to Lt. Col. Cimitière, 29 February 1820, *H.R.A.*, III, 3, p. 90.

of showing his respect for Sorell's character and authority. But he would not enter Government House, because, as he put it, its walls had been compromised.[17]

Through late February, March, April and May of 1820 Bigge collected evidence in Van Diemen's Land. The men with a private grievance interviewed him. One day in March, Bigge heard from Lieutenant-Colonel Thomas Davey how grievously Macquarie had misrepresented him, and was besought to write to Bathurst in his favour. Bigge, who believed both the character and authority of Sorell had been compromised by consorting with Mrs Kent, agreed to enclose Mad Tom's petition to Bathurst in a letter in which he supported Macquarie's decision on Davey, but regretted the insinuations and invective in Macquarie's correspondence with Davey.[18] In contrast with the mainland there were no contentious public issues. He listened to the merchants of Hobart Town on the future of trade.[19] He sent Oxley to inspect Port Davey and Macquarie Harbour.[20] From Sorell and his officials he heard how the convict system worked.[21] He heard too the case for a separate court of criminal jurisdiction in Van Diemen's Land, and found it obvious. He heard how the settlers were plagued by sheep and cattle stealing, and agreed that something should be done about it.[22] In Hobart Town and Port Dalrymple there was a society where geniality and comradeship were achieved at the expense of that subordination, that hierarchy, those exacting standards of dress and deportment, and that absence of familiarity on official occasions which Bigge believed to be the essentials of civilization. Bigge's imagination, however, was not touched by what he saw and heard, probably because no great issues were agitating that society. For in Van Diemen's Land there was no public discussion of the expediency of admitting ex-convicts to society or office, and no problem of surplus convict labour. Van Diemen's Land presented only the elemental problems of how to prevent a society lapsing into anarchy, together with the attendant problems of bushranging, depredations by the aborigines, and the vices of officials, which Bigge disdained. Bigge was bored, and in all his letters from Van Diemen's Land he betrayed an impatience to return to a society with issues of some importance and persons of some stature.[23]

On 4 June 1820 he returned to Sydney.[24] All that he saw and heard during his last eight months in the colony strengthened the impressions formed before his journey to Van Diemen's Land. He saw no reason to change his mind on the inexpediency of appointing ex-convicts to public office. All

[17] Bigge to Bathurst, 3 February 1823 (Bigge Appendix, C.O. 201/142).

[18] *H.R.A.*, III, 3, pp. 649-51, and Bigge Appendix, C.O. 201/137, and Bigge to Bathurst, 12 February 1823 (Bigge Appendix, C.O. 201/142).

[19] *H.R.A.*, III, 3, p. 652.

[20] Ibid., pp. 644-5.

[21] Ibid., p. 648 et seq.

[22] Bigge to Macquarie, 16 June 1820, encl. in Bigge to Bathurst, 24 August 1820 (Bigge Appendix, C.O. 201/142).

[23] Bigge to Bathurst, 24 August 1820 (Bigge Appendix, C.O. 201/142).

[24] Macquarie to Bathurst, 31 August 1820, *H.R.A.*, I, 10, p. 346.

that he saw of the consequences of Macquarie's policy of employing the surplus convict labour on public works in the towns convinced him of the wisdom of employing them with the settlers. He received many letters from settlers expressing their wish to employ such labour which convinced him that Macquarie's argument that such labour could only be employed in the towns was refuted by the facts.[25] So one of the main themes in the report grew in Bigge's mind. And just as his ideas on the future of the colony were diverging from those of Macquarie, relations between them again became strained by an angry exchange of letters on the best site for the town of Launceston.

Once again a *modus vivendi* was reached before Bigge set out for Bathurst in October of 1820, having arranged to meet Macquarie at Lake Bathurst on 26 October. Bigge was not impressed. The land there, he wrote to Lord Bathurst, could not be considered as a valuable acquisition to the colony.[26] The man who was to recommend the unrestricted use of convict labour for the pastoral industry was indifferent to the country which would contribute so much to its wealth. On 28 October they met on the shores of a large sheet of fresh water which Macquarie named Lake George in honour of His Majesty. On the following day, a Sunday, the party moved to the shores of Lake Bathurst. At four that afternoon Macquarie, Bigge, Oxley, their servants and a few aborigines gathered on the shores of the lake to hear the Reverend Cartwright read prayers and preach a very excellent sermon in which he stressed the justice, good policy and expediency of civilizing the aborigines and settling them in townships, for God and man would judge failure in this harshly. Bigge's mind, however, did not respond to the tragic grandeur of the occasion. He did not foresee that the white man's civilization and religion would doom the aborigine, nor despair of the prospect of raising a civilization in the wilds. His mind knew nothing of doom and disaster, let alone of guilt. Indeed, the scene made so little impression on him that he did not even refer to it in his letters to Bathurst or in his report. The aborigines were not mentioned in the commission he had received.[27]

After his return to Sydney the pattern in his mind took firmer shape as the evidence from the settlers poured in. As early as January 1820, Marsden had suggested to him the importance of the pastoral industry, and the part convicts could play in that industry. Sheep, he wrote to Bigge, would be the source of unknown national wealth, if government supplied convicts of the most experience and best characters to sheep farmers as opportunity offered.[28] By January 1821 this had become such a commonplace of Bigge's

[25] Bigge to Bathurst, 24 August 1820 (Bigge Appendix, C.O. 201/142).

[26] Bigge to Bathurst, 31 July 1821 (Bigge Appendix, C.O. 201/142).

[27] Remarks on the Country between Bathurst and Lake George, including the Country South West of the Cowpastures, 1820 (Bigge Appendix, C.O. 201/123); and Journal of a Tour of Inspection to the Western and Southern Countries some time since discovered by Chas. Throsby Esq. in Octr. to Novr. 1820, in *Lachlan Macquarie, Governor of New South Wales: Journals of his Tours in New South Wales and Van Diemen's Land, 1810-1822* (Sydney, 1956), p. 160.

[28] Marsden to Bigge, 31 January 1820 (Bigge Appendix, Opinions of Individuals upon the Management and discipline of Convicts, Document A49, C.O. 201/118).

thinking that he was asking the settlers who gave evidence whether they had observed and were of the opinion that agricultural occupations in their most extended sense afforded better means of employing convicts and had a greater tendency to reform than any other species of labour.[29] At the same time others were making some sharp comments on Macquarie's use of convicts on government works, especially buildings. By this system, they told Bigge, the labour of an immense proportion of the persons banished to these shores was retained solely for the use of government, and at enormous public expense. Nor was this prodigious expenditure from the public purse the only ruinous effect of the monopoly of the useful labour of the country. The settlers, and the community generally were precluded from the means of improvement, and while the most puerile and frivolous works were being carried on by government, as if for the mere purpose of finding employment for their over-teeming and idle gangs of labourers, the house of the settler was shutterless and miserable, and without barn or out-house.[30]

In February, 1821, John Macarthur told him in some detail what could be done. The labours which were connected with the tillage of the earth, and the rearing and care of sheep and cattle, he told Bigge, were best calculated to lead to the correction of vicious habits. When men were engaged in rural occupations their days were chiefly spent in solitude. They had much time for reflection and self-examination, and they were less tempted to the perpetration of crimes than when herded together in towns, amidst a mass of disorders and vices.[31] Macarthur went on to sketch the sort of society that ought to develop in New South Wales. He suggested a body of really respectable settlers, not needy adventurers but men of real capital, with estates of not less than ten thousand acres, a body of proprietors who would become powerful as an aristocracy, in contrast to the democratic feeling which had already taken deep root in the colony in consequence upon the absurd and mischievous policy pursued by Governor Macquarie. These settlers would employ convict labour and supply Great Britain so abundantly with wool of the finest quality that the price must considerably diminish.[32]

Earlier, in his oral evidence, he had uncovered what was in his mind on the state of the colony and its future. The convicts, he told Bigge, were less respectful than in 1809, because they now claimed indulgences as a matter of right where before they had accepted them as a reward of merit. Admitting convicts into society had not been productive of those good consequences which the Governor's humanity induced him to expect. Emancipated convicts did not deserve to have convicts assigned to them. He himself employed eighty convict servants. He dreaded his convicts marrying, because convict

[29] W. Howe to Bigge, 22 January 1821 (Opinions of Individuals upon the Management and discipline of Convicts, Document A49, Bigge Appendix, C.O. 201/118).

[30] H. Kitchen to Bigge, 29 January 1821 (Bigge Appendix, C.O. 201/133).

[31] J. Macarthur to Bigge, 7 February 1821 (Opinions of Individuals upon the Management and discipline of Convicts, Document A49, Bigge Appendix, C.O. 201/118).

[32] Memorandum of 19 December 1821, quoted in S. M. Onslow (ed.): *Some Early Records of the Macarthurs of Camden* (Sydney, 1914), pp. 349-50.

women were too depraved and were the cause of much disorder. He opposed the creation of a distillery. The 'currency lads' lacked fields for their industry, but were sober and honest. The fierceness and impatience of restraint in the native youth were the bad consequences of their copying their parents and becoming disorderly. Great confusion and disorder would ensue if trial by jury were introduced, as it would be an act of temerity to remove the lawful incapacity of men to sit as jurors who had been convicts. Ex-convicts felt the highest malignancy towards those who had not suffered a similar degradation, their greatest satisfaction being to utter calumnies against the respectable and bring them down to their own level.[33]

Bigge heard these opinions on the eve of his departure. In the last week of January 1821 a dinner was given in his honour at the house of Sir John Jamison in the presence of a large party of officers, civil and military, including Governor Macquarie.[34] On 3 February Bigge publicly acknowledged his debt to the reverend chaplains and the civil and military officers for their ready assistance in pursuing the objects of his inquiry. He went on to say that a general disposition had been shown in all ranks of the community to give entire effect to his authority, and not to interfere with the testimonies of good respect which it had been his good fortune to receive, that the powers confided in him had not been abused, that the security of no individual, however humble, would be compromised by his disclosures, and that he entertained sanguine hopes that the interests of the colony would, through his means, be rightly understood and effectually promoted.[35] That day he joined a procession with the Governor, the Lieutenant-Governor, and the civil and military officers, preceded by the full band of the 48th regiment, to the Governor's private landing-place at Bennelong Point, where he boarded the *Dromedary* to a salute from the battery at Dawes' Point and the guns of the *Dromedary*, and sailed out on to the high seas on 14 February.[36]

A few weeks later the Reverend Samuel Marsden put down on paper his hopes for the inhabitants. He wanted to prevent the lower classes becoming a drunken race. He wanted the female orphan institution at Parramatta not to be like a boarding school for young ladies who had some prospects in life, but like a house of industry. As for himself, he told Bigge, he had met with many unmerited kicks from those in authority, when he ought to have met with their countenance and support, but then sacred and profane history had taught him that it was very dangerous to offend a lady in power—John the Baptist lost his head for this. Things in time would find their level. Then, begging Bigge's pardon for troubling him so much, he told him he had 'the honour to be, honoured sir, his most obedient servant Sam¹ Marsden'.[37]

Bigge had taken with him enough material to write both a survey of the

[33] Evidence of J. Macarthur to Bigge (Bigge Appendix, C.O. 201/120).

[34] *Sydney Gazette*, 3 February 1821.

[35] Ibid.

[36] Ibid., 10 and 17 February 1821.

[37] Marsden to Bigge, 15 March 1821 (Document G2, Bigge Appendix, C.O. 201/127).

colony and its history from its foundation to the end of 1820. From the day of his return to England in the middle of 1821 until the publication of his reports between June 1822 and March 1823 he discussed in letters to Bathurst such things as the need to send salt meat with the convicts, the need to replace the 48th regiment, the need for more chaplains, the news of a proposal to attack Sydney from South America, the site for a new convict settlement, and the request of Germans to migrate to New South Wales. But he always came back to his theme that the need for reforming the convicts and reducing the expense of convict labour could best be met by sending the convicts to work for the settlers in the interior.[38] In these letters, as in all he wrote, he did not descend from principle to the petty and the vulgar, nor abandon that determination not to become involved, which he had observed throughout the whole inquiry. On the eve of the publication of the first report he urged Bathurst not to publish the supplementary documents and evidence lest they should stir up feelings in the colony.[39] To understand more fully what was in those reports, the responses to them in the colony, their effect on Macquarie, and how far the British government was prepared to accept Bigge's view on the future of the colony, it is necessary to examine events in the colony and the United Kingdom while Bigge was collecting and sifting his evidence.

Life on the mainland and in Van Diemen's Land had gone on very much as before: the convicts expiated their crimes by forced labour for the government or the settlers; the men in high places planned and laboured for the welfare of the colony; Marsden, as ever, was torn between his call to work for the eternal salvation of those in his charge and the desire for vengeance against those who had despitefully used him; the problem of what to do with the convicts still perplexed the officials; the settlement was expanding along the valley of the Hunter, west of Bathurst, south-west of the Cow Pastures to Moss Vale, and south to Illawarra and Jervis Bay. This expansion increased the problems of administration. It also spelt doom to the aborigines, for as the population increased, settlement expanded, and the aborigines were driven from these remoter stations. This flight brought relief to the settlers from depredations, but it disturbed the consciences of the few, who put forward schemes for the civilization of the aborigine. In December of 1819 the Reverend Cartwright put his ideas on this subject to Macquarie. As the British nation, he wrote, enjoyed a distinguished character for benevolence, justice and piety, it would be an additional gem to the British Crown to admit the sable proprietors of this land to the rank of British subjects. Let not the British government, he went on, leave this abject, wretched race entirely destitute of the means of grace and salvation, for buried in the intellect of these savages in Augean filth the British, he believed, might yet find

[38] See the letters from Bigge to Goulburn, 31 October 1821, and Bigge to Bathurst, 3 July 1821 and 5 May 1822; Bigge to Goulburn, 17 August 1821 and 31 October 1821; Bigge to Wilmot, 5 June 1822 and 2 December 1822 (Bigge Appendix, C.O. 201/142).

[39] Bigge to Bathurst, 5 May 1822 (Bigge Appendix, C.O. 201/142).

gems of the first magnitude and brilliance. The faith which sustained Cartwright was simply that if the aborigines were civilized and christianized then in competition with what he called the more highly favoured of Albion's sons they might bear away the prize of merit.[40] By then, this was already a vain dream, because the forces of destruction, the forces driving the natives from the hunting grounds, and the forces conducing to their humiliation and degradation in the towns, were stronger than such forces of construction. What Cartwright recommended was a grant of land near the Cow Pastures where the aboriginal boys could be trained till they were ready in man's estate to become settlers.[41]

Each year, on the occasion of the annual conference of the chiefs and tribes of the aborigines at Parramatta, the *Sydney Gazette* reminded its readers of the role of that institution, and of its glorious and humanizing conception of beholding these children snatched from the wilds of barbarism, ignorance, and misery. They assembled again on 28 December when Macquarie conferred badges of honour and merit on the most deserving, and exhorted them to continue on terms of amity with the Europeans, before the aborigines were again regaled with roast beef, plum pudding and beer in abundance. The occasion prompted the *Sydney Gazette* to reflect on the vast and glorious object of the civilization and salvation of thousands at present involved in gross darkness, and how the work of the native institution would tend to accelerate and hasten the period when righteousness covered the earth as the waters covered the deep.[42] At that time there were twenty-three children in the native institution of whom ten read and spelt well, one was improving in reading and spelling, two were learning to read, seven could repeat the alphabet, one could repeat double letters, and one could spell four syllables as well as read in the Bible.[43]

They might have been the grain of mustard seed, though not all entertained the hope that civilization would rescue them from darkness and ignorance. A few argued that contact with civilization degraded the aborigine. On 12 August 1821 an aborigine named Andrew Sneap Hammond Douglass White died at the home of James Squire, Kissing Point. He had been taken from the woods as a child in 1788 by surgeon John White, when his parents died of the small-pox which was one of the first afflictions the aborigines suffered from the white man's invasion of their land. After White's departure he served as a seaman on the *Reliance*, then went on the voyage with Flinders in the *Investigator*. Upon his return he took to the bush where he remained, despite all the tender attempts of his protector, Mr Squire, to rescue him from such wretchedness. As the *Sydney Gazette* commented rather wistfully, ancestral habits were too indelibly engendered ever to be eradicated by human effort, however strained in its benevolent design. So Andrew Sneap Hammond

[40] See Macquarie to Bathurst, 24 February 1820, and enclosures, including Cartwright to Macquarie, 6 December 1819, and 18 January 1820, *H.R.A.*, I, 10, pp. 263-70.

[41] Ibid., p. 265.

[42] *Sydney Gazette*, 30 December 1820.

[43] Minutes of Evidence taken before the Committee on the Aborigines Question, 1838, p. 56, the Legislative Council of New South Wales, *Votes and Proceedings*, 1838.

Douglass White was buried in the same grave with Bennilong and his wife in Squire's garden, as one of the many who had rejected the higher civilization after tasting its fruits.[44] He at least had escaped that degradation which provided evidence for the European of the inferiority of the aborigine, just as the raids, the thefts, the acts of incendiarism, all the deeds of violence provoked by the loss of their land, convinced those Europeans not touched by the hopes which sustained the few, that expulsion, if not total destruction, provided the only permanent solution to the problem of the aborigine. The settlers were not prepared to wait for the day when righteousness covered the earth.

According to the testimony of Captain Bellingshausen, one of the Russian officers who visited Sydney Cove and Hobart Town in 1820 on a voyage of exploration in the Pacific, the natives of Van Diemen's Land lived in a state of perpetual hostility against the Europeans. They destroyed flocks of sheep not for food but to inflict material damage upon their enemies. They hated all Europeans because of what Bellingshausen called the inexcusable behaviour of the first English settlers at the Derwent.[45] On the day after they arrived at Sydney Cove, Boongaree, one of the native chiefs, clambered on board the *Discovery* and, pointing to the country, told Bellingshausen: 'This is my Land.' When he and his wife and some other fellow-countrymen cadged tobacco, old clothes and anything they happened to notice, and shouted horribly, Bellingshausen was disgusted by their display of vulgarity. Within a few weeks he had come to the conclusion that contact with European civilization had been disastrous to the natives as they had borrowed all the bad language habits of the Europeans, the oaths and the curses in currency amongst the English rabble, and had learnt to lie, to steal, to smoke, and to drink alcohol. Their thirst for alcohol was so great that despite their prodigious laziness they would work at anything to obtain it. They had no material possessions. They had made no progress in education in thirty-three years, and had not even the elementary notions of Christianity. All that was left to them was a memory of their former independence, and a spark of vengeance smouldering in their hearts.[46]

Those in high places in Sydney were more concerned with the problems created by the sudden increase in the number of convicts. Between 24 August 1819 and 28 January 1820, fifteen convict ships arrived at Sydney bringing a further two thousand five hundred and fifty-nine male and female convicts from England and Ireland, all of whom arrived in good health and without complaints about their treatment on their respective ships. It added greatly to the expense of the colony. It also raised again the problem of how to employ them. As Macquarie believed the settlers required very few of them, he sent as many to Van Diemen's Land as were needed by the settlers and government there. The rest he employed on the public buildings and streets in Sydney, on building roads and bridges in the interior, and the residue on

[44] *Sydney Gazette*, 8 September 1821.

[45] F. Debenham (ed.): *The Voyage of Captain Bellingshausen to the Antarctic Seas, 1819-1821* (Hakluyt Society, London, 1945), vol. 2, p. 355.

[46] Ibid., vol. 1, pp. 162-3, vol. 2, pp. 329-39.

the government farm at Emu Plains which was opened in 1819, partly to absorb surplus convict labour, partly to employ convicts in useful labour, and partly to improve their morals and make them good and useful servants.[47] Macquarie's solution to the problem of surplus convict labour was made at a time when the settlers were developing the argument that an assigned convict could be reformed, and contribute to the wealth of the colony without costing government a penny, and when Bigge was beginning to be shocked by the extravagance of the building programme. For by then Macquarie had lost touch if not with the creative forces in society, then certainly with the powerful forces in that society and, like all men who have walked into the night, he was devoting more and more of his time and energy to answering his critics, as events were beginning to pass him by.

Two Catholic priests arrived on the *Janus* on 3 May 1820. Until the peace of Amiens, in 1802, Rome's interest in New South Wales, in the conversion of both heathen and heretics, and ministering to the faithful, had been negligible. Individual priests had petitioned for permission to practise their religion, without touching on the mission theme. In 1818 the Roman Curia appointed Edward Bede Slater, Vicar Apostolic of the Cape of Good Hope, with the title of Bishop of Ruspa *in partibus infidelium*, with jurisdiction over the Cape of Good Hope, Madagascar, Mauritius, New Holland and the adjacent islands.[48] In April 1819 Bishop Slater visited Ireland to persuade priests to go to Botany Bay.

For one priest this was not a new idea. Walking one day in the streets of Cork a waggon passed him, which contained a number of Irishmen who were handcuffed and under a military escort. On inquiry he found they were convicts bound for New South Wales. With that generosity and compassion for the afflicted, the distressed and the oppressed which he displayed to the end of his days, he rushed into a neighbouring bookshop, bought some twenty or thirty prayer books, flung them on to the cart, and vowed there and then that one day he would follow these men to New South Wales.[49] He was John Joseph Therry, who was born in Cork in 1790 of parents with worldly comforts and pious habits, educated for the priesthood partly by Dr Doyle, and ordained priest by Archbishop Troy in 1815. He served as a priest in Cork, where he met Father O'Flynn, who told Bishop Slater of Therry's interest in New South Wales, who in turn wrote to Therry telling him he had heard that his charity led him to wish to render assistance to the spiritual welfare of his fellow-countrymen expatriated to New South Wales. Therry replied protesting his unworthiness, his indolence, his ignorance of the things a missioner should know, and added that he was utterly destitute of any acquaintance with the Irish language. What he did possess, he believed, was a zeal for the glory of God and a solicitude for the salvation of his fellow-men. This con-

---

[47] Macquarie to Bathurst, 28 February 1820, *H.R.A.*, I, 10, pp. 278-9.

[48] See Dom Birt: *Benedictine Pioneers in Australia* (London, 1911), vol. 1, pp. 7 and 14; and E. O'Brien: *Life and Letters of Archpriest John Joseph Therry* (Sydney, 1922), p. 11.

[49] See Dr Comerford: *Recollections of the Diocese of Kildare and Leighlin*, vol. 1, p. 179, quoted in O'Brien: op. cit., p. 13.

fession caused Slater to accept him with pleasure. As his companion Bishop Slater appointed the Reverend Philip Conolly, a native of the diocese of Kildare.[50]

On 20 September 1819, Bishop Slater issued the faculties to Therry and Conolly, granting them power throughout the whole of New Holland and the island usually called Van Diemen's Land. He added a letter to Therry in which he exhorted him to win back the stray sheep rather by the example of Christian sweetness than by harsh and angry exhortations, and urged him not to be disheartened for God's grace would be his aid, while after the planting of the seed he would send other workers to help bring in the harvest.[51] On 20 October 1819 Bathurst wrote to Macquarie telling him to pay Therry and Conolly an allowance of one hundred pounds per annum each, in consideration of their attendance on the prisoners of the Roman Catholic persuasion. The difference between that sum and the sum paid to the Anglican chaplains was made because Bathurst knew they did not require more, as the Catholic laity were more generous than others in supporting their clergy.[52]

They left Cork in the convict ship *Janus* on 5 December 1819, for a voyage in which the officers and sailors debauched the women into prostitution. When Therry was questioned on arrival, he assured the court of inquiry that he did not agree with the suggestion that the Irish Catholic girls had willingly entered into the illicit intercourse; for Therry was not only Irish in his loyalty, but had learned not to expect too much from those whose imagination was evil from the start.[53] They arrived in Sydney on 3 May 1820. On 7 May, Father Conolly celebrated the mass in a temporary chapel in a house in Pitt Row, and on 8 May Father Therry offered holy mass for the glory of God and St Michael from which day the belief spread amongst priests and laity that he had found that the sacred particles of the host consecrated by Father O'Flynn had remained free from corruption. The Catholic community hailed this as a miracle of their holy faith.[54] For the Catholic population of Sydney, the arrival of the priests was the day of mercy they had yearned for, and an answer to prayers that God would not allow them to be for ever shut out from the blessings of His Holy Church. For them, too, it meant at least the temporary supremacy of that priest-ridden, puritanical, superstitious, credulous Irish Catholicism in which priesthood and laity had united in an unbreakable alliance to avenge an ancient wrong. It meant, too, a Catholicism in which charity, compassion, the love of God and the preservation of the faith, were entangled with the worldly aspirations of the Irish people.

Though in time the Protestants sneered at such beliefs as evidence of an

50 E. O'Brien: op. cit., pp. 12-16.

51 Quoted in Dom Birt: op. cit., vol. 1, pp. 19-20.

52 Ibid., and Bathurst to Macquarie, 20 October 1819, *H.R.A.*, I, 10, p. 204.

53 Encl. no. 7 in Macquarie to Bathurst, 19 July 1820, *H.R.A.*, I, 10, pp. 328-9; cf. with the reaction of Therry's biographer who described this experience as a 'violent and disgusting initiation. . . .' E. O'Brien: op. cit., p. 22.

54 e.g. P. F. Moran: *History of the Catholic Church in Australasia* (Sydney, 1896), pp. 64-7; but cf. W. B. Ullathorne: *Autobiography* (London, 1891-2), pp. 166-7; and E. O'Brien: op. cit., p. 24.

attachment to a disgusting superstition, the arrival of Therry and Conolly in 1820 provoked neither anxiety nor dismay. Marsden had already told Bigge of his hope that priests would never be seen in New South Wales. Macquarie at the height of the controversy with O'Flynn had seen himself as a man if not sent by God, then sent at least by the British to protect the higher civilization against the corrupting influence of popish superstition and Irish squalor. This time, however, Macquarie confined himself to reporting to Bathurst that Roman Catholic chaplains had, with the permission of government, come out as passengers in the *Janus*.[55] For the rest, the Protestant community seemed disposed to assist rather than frustrate the work of the Catholic chaplains. A Protestant, John Piper, helped them to find board and lodging.[56] At a public meeting held on 30 June at the court house, Protestants agreed to unite with Catholics to raise funds to build a church, and three of the Protestants present were appointed to collect funds from the members of their own persuasion.[57] For the memories, the anger, and the bitterness engendered by 1798 and 1803-4 had faded, while the sectarian sentiment stirred up by the tractarian movement and the Catholic revival were still in the womb of time. So the Catholic clergy began their pastoral work in what was to prove to be, in Australia, one of those rare calms between sectarian storms.

On 6 June 1820, Macquarie informed Conolly and Therry of the restrictions on their freedom in New South Wales. They could celebrate mass; they could marry two Catholics, but not a Catholic and a Protestant; they could baptize the children of Roman Catholic parents; they were to endeavour not to make converts from the Established Church, or generally from the Protestant Church; they were not to interfere with the religious education of orphans in the government charitable institutions of the colony, who were to be instructed in the faith and doctrine of the Church of England.[58]

Macquarie's authority was the laws of the mother country. Conolly and Therry owed their allegiance to the laws of God. There was much in what Macquarie prescribed for them which, according to the teaching of their church, contravened the laws of God. There was much, too, in the laws and practices of the colony which contravened the teaching of the Roman Catholic Church. Some of these the Roman Catholic community touched on in a petition to Bigge on 30 August 1820. The tenets of their faith, they pointed out, would not admit them to be governed in their religious offices by the ministers of any other religion or sect. In the colony there were ten public schools. In those schools the Protestant chaplains were zealously initiating the children of Catholics in the services and ceremonies of the Established Church. This system of taking advantage of the unwary debarred numerous Catholics from being educated, as it was contrary to their religious principles. They therefore petitioned Bigge to excite the compassion of their prince and ministers to look with sympathy on the dejected religious state of His Majesty's Catholic

[55] Macquarie to Bathurst, 1 September 1820, *H.R.A.*, I, 10, p. 365.
[56] E. O'Brien: op. cit., pp. 23-4.
[57] Resolutions passed at this meeting are printed in the *Sydney Gazette*, 1 July 1820.
[58] Quoted from the Therry Papers in E. O'Brien: op. cit., pp. 28-32.

subjects whom he had been pleased to place in this distant land, to sanction three Roman Catholic clergymen to come out to this colony, and to select such men whose exemplary lives and learning would entitle them to their affections and reverence (presuming to say such men were to be found in Ireland) and to sanction the free exercise of their sacerdotal functions, to build houses of worship, and to open seminaries for the education of their children, with such other indulgences peculiar to their calling as might be deemed expedient.[59]

This petition did not mention all the religious grievances of the Catholic community. Neither the compulsory attendance of Catholics at Protestant religious services on convict transports, nor the career disabilities of Catholics were brought up for discussion. For in British societies in general, there was a career in the law, in the services, and in the administration, for Protestant men of talent but not for Catholics. Over and above these religious and personal disabilities, Conolly and Therry were dedicated by the laws of God and the teaching of their church, to work for the day when there was one fold and one shepherd, and all heretics, schismatics, unbelievers and heathen had made their peace with Christ's Church. Some of those aspirations were incompatible with the restrictions Macquarie had imposed, and some were incompatible with the laws and practices of the colony of New South Wales. Also, at least one of the practices exhorted by these priests, the practice by which Catholics were forbidden to join with their Protestant fellow-countrymen in any Protestant act of worship, was bound to cause offence, just as their teaching on the Reformation as the work of Antichrist was bound to be a puzzle, if not to appear as wanton foolishness, to those who believed that the Protestant religion had assured the survival of the two essential conditions for their higher civilization—liberty and British institutions.

In the meantime Father Conolly had left for Van Diemen's Land, where he soon created a reputation for indolence and self-indulgence not unlike that of the Reverend Knopwood. The Catholics, Knopwood had told Bigge earlier in the same year, were not reluctant to attend a Protestant service, and Catholic parents were bringing their children to be baptized by him as readily as Protestants. Catholics were buried in the same burying ground.[60] Therry remained on the mainland, and dedicated himself to the work of ministering to the religious needs of the faithful, saying mass every Sunday at Parramatta and Liverpool and twice at Sydney, giving public instruction in the mysteries of his faith, visiting the sick, and attending all persons professing the Catholic religion who might be in danger of dying within a circuit of two hundred miles. Once word was brought to Father Therry that a convict sentenced to death wanted to see him for confession. After a long ride Therry came to a river in flood, and shouted to a man on the opposite bank to give help in the

[59] The Humble Petition and Remonstrance of the Roman Catholics of His Majesty's Settlements in New South Wales to the Honorable John Thomas Bigge Esquire Commissioner of Enquiry &c, &c, &c. (Document G1, Bigge Appendix, C.O. 201/127).

[60] Evidence of R. Knopwood to Bigge, 3 April 1820, *H.R.A.*, III, 3, p. 364; *H.R.A.*, III, 4, pp. 233-4.

name of God and a departing soul. The man threw over a rope which Therry tied round his waist and plunged into the river to be hauled across to the other side, where without pausing for a rest or a change of clothing he mounted another horse and arrived in time to bring the consolation of religion to the convict before he was launched into eternity.[61] By such acts of heroism and devotion and a boundless charity Therry demonstrated that the image of Christ lived in the sons of the Church.

By contrast, the Protestant community was wedded to the existing political institutions; its leaders both lay and clerical were committed to the defence of the *status quo*, and its religious ceremonies were placed at the service of the state.' When news of the death of George III reached Sydney by the *Neptune* on 15 July 1820, Macquarie invited the magistrates, clergy, and principal inhabitants of the colony to join in a solemn procession at 11 a.m. on Sunday, 23 July, from Government House to the church of St Philip for divine service to return humble thanks to Almighty God that in the lamented dispensation of His all-wise Providence in removing from this scene of worldly care their late beloved and highly exalted sovereign lord King George III of sacred memory, He had softened down and mitigated the sorrows of a nation in assigning to rule over them his present majesty, King George IV, as matured in wisdom and experience and as filled with ardent zeal to promote the interest, prosperity and happiness of the nations happily placed under his paternal government. Those who attended were to be dressed in the deepest mourning. A salute of eighty-two guns was fired in commemoration of the years of the late king; flags flew at half mast; from the Saturday to the Monday the bells of the churches were tolled twice a day; all places of amusement were shut up, and shops were closed; courts of justice were suspended; public labour was at a stand-still; all civil and military officers were to wear mourning till further notice.[62] By such outward displays of grief the Protestant community displayed its veneration for the Crown as a part of the British constitution.

On 7 August of the same year, fourteen days after these demonstrations of grief ended, Charles Throsby set out on another journey to explore the country to the south-west of Moss Vale. In August 1817, with Hamilton Hume, John Rowley and Joseph Wild, Throsby had travelled west from Sutton Forest towards the Wollondilly River. This journey was worthy of note not because of its achievement, which was meagre, or its promise, but because one of the immortals in the history of land exploration, Hamilton Hume, began his career on this journey as a servant to Throsby. Hume, born at Parramatta on 18 June 1797, the eldest son of Andrew Hume, was educated by his mother, and began his career as an explorer in 1814 and 1815 when in company with his brother he walked over the country near Bong Bong and Berrima. On 3 March 1818, Throsby, J. Meehan—the surveyor, J. Wild—a freeman, two unnamed convict servants of Throsby, J. Glynn—a shoemaker, H. Hume—servant to Meehan, G. Grimes—son of the former Surveyor-General, three other convicts and two aborigines—Bundell and Broughton, set out on an expedition to the

[61] E. O'Brien: op. cit., p. 39.
[62] *Sydney Gazette*, 22 and 29 July 1820.

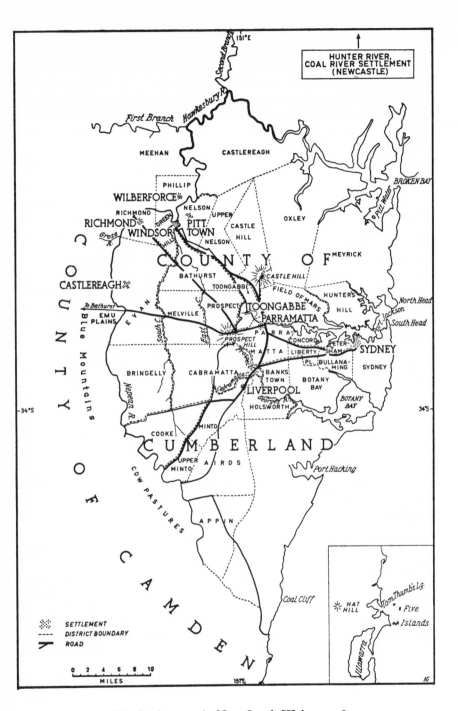

6 *The Settlements in New South Wales, c. 1820*

south. They reached the Shoalhaven River, where the party split, Throsby returning home by way of Jervis Bay, while Meehan with Hume and some servants travelled inland towards Bungonia, where on 3 April 1818 they came on a lake, later named Lake Bathurst, and then proceeded north-west for four days to the Goulburn Plains before turning for home, which they reached on 14 April. On 24 March 1820, Throsby, W. Macarthur and Hume visited the Goulburn Plains again.

On 7 August 1820, Throsby with Wild and others attempted to open up a road to the south from Bong Bong to Cookbundoon. While working at this the natives told him of another lake to the south. Throsby fitted out Wild and two of the road party to look for the lake, which they found on 19 August. When Throsby reported the discovery to Macquarie on 4 September, he told him he had heard from the natives of a river which they called MUR RUM BIDGIE. On 16 October 1820, Macquarie set out to visit the Goulburn Plains, taking with him Throsby, Meehan and others. They had arranged to meet Commissioner Bigge, who had set out from Bathurst with Oxley, Scott and others, on the shores of Lake Bathurst on 26 October. Both parties proceeded from there to Lake George two days later. While at Lake George, Throsby attempted unsuccessfully to find 'Murrumbidgie', but found instead a creek which he named the Boongaroon. On 17 November 1820, on Macquarie's instructions, Throsby sent J. Wild, C. T. Smith, and J. Vaughan to proceed to the Boongaroon and trace it, but the party did not find it. On this journey Wild and his party entered the country which is now part of the Australian Capital Territory, on 7 December, on a hill north of Gungahlin, from where they came to the Molonglo River, camped at a site probably near Duntroon, and climbed the next day what Wild called a very high hill, probably Black Mountain, from where they could see the Molonglo running to the south-west past Yarralumla. On 9 December they returned to Lake George where one of the party, C. T. Smith, who was Throsby's nephew, wrote the first description of the district, writing of a beautiful forest as far as the eye could see, thinly wooded with gums and bastard box, the tops of the hills stone and sand, but in the valleys a fine rich soil, and in the night it was fine and clear.[63] On their return the irascible Throsby quarrelled with Smith, not taking kindly to Smith's suggestion that the Murrumbidgee did not exist. The men who saw themselves as eagles in the sky had no patience with the incredulous.

On 20 March 1821, with two companions, Throsby left Throsby Park at Moss Vale to search again for the Murrumbidgee, travelling to Lake George, past Bungendore to the Molonglo, and then to the present site of Queanbeyan, where he followed the river till it joined the Murrumbidgee near Tharwa. Like Oxley on the Lachlan, Throsby was puzzled about the outlet of this river. From its direction and the mountains he concluded it was unlikely that it flowed to the south-east coast. He suspected that it probably terminated in the same way as Oxley had already ascertained the Lachlan and Macquarie to do, and threw out the hint that perhaps it was a branch of the Lachlan,

[63] The description by Smith is quoted in F. Watson: *A Brief History of Canberra the capital city of Australia* (Canberra, 1927), pp. 7-9.

adding that wherever they effected a junction, their united streams must form a river of considerable magnitude. By chance, Hume, the man who learned his bushcraft from Throsby, discovered that river of considerable magnitude in 1824; while Charles Sturt, a settler from the territory Throsby had opened up, was to prove the accuracy of Throsby's prediction in 1830.[64] On the quality of the country Throsby wrote to Macquarie on 12 May with enthusiasm. It was well watered, with extensive meadows of rich land in the river valleys; it contained very fine limestone, slate, sandstone and granite fit for building, with sufficient timber for every useful purpose; from the appearance of the country there was an unbounded extent of it to the westward; to the south-east there were very high mountains, which did not present that aspect of barrenness as did the mountains near Sydney—they were thinly timbered, with a pleasant appearance of verdure between the trees.[65] In these words a white man wrote down the first description of the Australian Alps, in a mood clean different from the despair of the men who first saw the country round Sydney, or the despair of Oxley on first seeing the Australian wilds.

While Therry and Conolly were beginning their ministry to the faithful, and Throsby, Wild, Meehan, Hume, Smith and their companions were exploring the country to the south, a political storm was brewing in the colony. On 1 January 1820 in the court room at Parramatta the judge, Barron Field, turned in exasperation to one of the litigants and said: 'You have made seditious Speeches, And you have reared up the Standard of Disaffection and party. You are a revolutionist.'[66] The litigant he addressed was Edward Eagar, who then sued Barron Field for damages on 4 April 1820. Field wanted to protect himself and the court against a tedious, vexatious litigant, but the method he chose threatened to engulf the legal rights of the group to whom Eagar belonged. Also, as so often happens in human history when a question of the rights of the individual is raised, the creator of the controversy was unworthy of his cause and his supporters. Eagar had been an attorney in Ireland when he was sentenced to transportation for life at Cork in 1809 for perjury. He sailed in the *Providence*, which arrived at Sydney on 2 July 1811. On the strength of a testimonial from the gaol chaplain, Marsden had him appointed a teacher in the family of the Reverend Cartwright. Eagar rewarded his trust by writing to a Methodist Society in London impugning Marsden's religious zeal and expatiating on his devotion to the object of accumulating wealth, and his indifference to the interests of religion. Bigge called this an act of treachery.[67] Marsden, who knew nothing of this reward for his pains, con-

[64] For Throsby's account see the *Australian Magazine*, 1821, vol. 1, pp. 60-1. For a discussion of the problem of working out where Throsby was, see F. Watson: op. cit., pp. 10-12.

[65] *Australian Magazine*, 1821, vol. 1, pp. 60-1. My account of the explorers is based on R. H. Cambage: *Exploration between the Wingecarribee, Shoalhaven, Macquarie and Murrumbidgee Rivers* (Sydney, 1921); supplemented by F. Watson: op. cit.; *H.R.A.*, I, 10, *seriatim*; the *Sydney Gazette*, and the *Australian Magazine*, 1821, vol. 1.

[66] Encl. no. 4 in Macquarie to Bathurst, 1 September 1820, *H.R.A.*, I, 10, p. 354.

[67] Bigge to Bathurst, 7 February 1823 (Bigge Appendix, C.O. 201/142).

fessed later that he had been much deceived by the apparent piety and moral conduct of Eagar, who, while professing concern for the eternal salvation of the natives of the Pacific Islands showed neither benevolence nor Christian consideration, but lively interests in the profits to be made from trade.[68] The closer people got to know Eagar the more they became aware of his treachery.

Macquarie, however, who was peculiarly gullible to the men who professed publicly to their high-minded aspirations, continued to lend Eagar his support. To him Eagar was an emancipist whose material success entitled him to a restoration to that place in society which he had forfeited by the commission of a crime. By 1817 Eagar had accumulated enough wealth to entitle him to a directorship in the Bank of New South Wales. But the bank rule by which all directors had to be absolutely and unconditionally free debarred him, as Eagar was still a convict. To soothe him for this hurt to his pride, as well as the injury to his pocket, Macquarie pardoned him on 31 January 1818.[69] Eagar repaid this gesture of confidence by indulging in a plethora of legal suits which so tried the patience of Barron Field that he made one outburst against Eagar as a grasping Jew before finally losing his temper in the court at Parramatta on that day in January when he used the words which prompted Eagar to bring his suit for damages.

When the hearing began on 4 April, Barron Field's solicitor, W. Moore, a man with a long anti-emancipist record in the colony, raised the question: Who was capable of suing in the colony? He argued that no act of pardon could remove the disability of suing once it had been incurred. Eagar replied in person that a pardon in the colony entitled the holder to all the benefits of a statute pardon—i.e. full restitution of his legal rights, including the right to sue, and added that the argument for Barron Field was as odious as an argument for slavery. So the issue was fairly joined, with the legal rights of nine-tenths of the population of New South Wales depending on a legal technicality raised in a suit brought by an unctuous, sanctimonious hypocrite. The court was adjourned to send to Ireland to obtain proper evidence of the plaintiff, Eagar, having been transported to New South Wales as a convict attaint, the court assuming that the question of the right of emancipists to sue would be referred to His Majesty's ministers. In the meantime, they adjudged that persons holding instruments of absolute or conditional remission of their terms of transportation were not thereby restored to any civil rights of free subjects, nor put in the capacity to acquire, hold or convey property, to sue or give evidence in a court of justice, unless and until their names should be inserted in some general pardon under the great seal of England.[70] When Eagar brought another suit before the Court on 15 September 1820 the same plea was advanced for the defence, and again the court adjourned

[68] Marsden to Bathurst, 21 July 1821 (Bigge Appendix, Papers relative to New Zealand, C.O. 201/130).

[69] For Eagar's career see *H.R.A.*, I, 10, p. 557.

[70] Wylde to Macquarie, 1 September 1820, encl. no. 5 in Macquarie to Bathurst, 1 September 1820, *H.R.A.*, I, 10, pp. 362-4; and encl. in Macquarie to Bathurst, 22 October 1821, *H.R.A.*, I, 10, p. 553.

to await the arrival of the evidence that Eagar had been transported as a convict attaint.[71]

These actions forced the emancipists to appeal from the courts to the Crown, and both houses of parliament. Simeon Lord and eight emancipist house-holders requisitioned the secretary to the Governor for permission to convene a public meeting of those persons emancipated by servitude, or by absolute or conditional pardons, for the purpose of humbly petitioning His Majesty, and both houses of parliament for relief from the consequences of certain principles of law lately pronounced in the British courts, affecting the civil privileges of the above-mentioned colonists. On 6 January 1821, Campbell granted permission for the meeting to be held in the court house.[72] The meeting, which was held on 23 January, was very respectably attended. Indeed the *Sydney Gazette* had never witnessed a more numerous, orderly and well-conducted gathering. After William Redfern was unanimously called to the chair, those present proceeded to pass a series of resolutions: first, that by the humane and benevolent policy of His Excellency, Governor Macquarie, a policy hitherto sanctioned by their mother country, the emancipated colonists had been encouraged and protected, and were now possessed of the larger moiety of the property of the colony, and were become the middle class of society therein; second, that from the foundation of the colony till April 1820 it had been assumed that those who obtained their pardon either by service of the term, or by absolute or conditional pardon, might and could acquire and possess landed and other property, and enjoy all the civil rights of free citizens; third, that by a recent decision in the law courts the vital interests of the emancipated colonists were exposed to infinite prejudice and danger, and their restoration to their rights, as citizens, protracted beyond the period that either justice or policy could require; fourth, that this state of the law affected not only the liberty, property and civil rights of the emancipists but also a considerable part of the property of the emigrant colonists who had acquired their property from emancipated colonists; fifth, that impressed with a deep sense of the injurious consequences to their personal liberty, their property, their civil rights as citizens, the rights and properties of their children, and the properties of their fellow colonists, they would now humbly address the throne and parliament by petition; sixth, that they should appoint an agent to send to London and raise a fund to pay his expenses; seventh, that a standing committee consisting of William Redfern, Simeon Lord, the Reverend Henry Fulton, James Meehan, S. Terry, Edward Eagar, James Underwood, William Hutchinson, and D. Cooper be appointed; eighth, that the Governor be requested to forward their petition; ninth, that this meeting, impressed with a deep sense of the protection and encouragement invariably afforded by Governor Macquarie to the emancipated colonists of New South Wales, begged leave to present to His Excellency the just tribute of their most sincere thanks and heartfelt gratitude with the assurance that His Excellency's name would live in the grateful remembrance of generations yet unborn as the founder and

71 Ibid.
72 *Sydney Gazette*, 20 January 1821.

promoter of benevolent principles, and the best interests alike of this colony, and of the mother country as connected with it; tenth, that Redfern, Fulton, Lord, Eagar, Meehan and Terry wait on Macquarie to express to him their thanks and gratitude; and eleventh, that the thanks of the meeting be given to Redfern for his able, upright and impartial conduct in the chair. All these resolutions were carried unanimously; the ninth, which expressed their sincere thanks and heartfelt gratitude to Macquarie, was carried with repeated acclamation.[73] When the deputation presented the petition and the expressions of gratitude to Macquarie on the following day, he returned a most gracious answer. It was no small gratification, he told them, for him to find that their conduct ever since he had been honoured with the administration of the colony had been such as to merit the sentiments they had expressed in their resolution. To those sentiments he would ever adhere, so that they would find protection in their persons and properties such as the British government afforded to all its subjects. He had only been fulfilling the duties delegated to him by his sovereign.[74]

On 29 January Charles Thompson wrote to him about the real enemies of his person and government, to tell him the truth about the writing of the Vale petition of 1816 to the House of Commons. Vale had written the first draft, and had shown it to Bent, who had declared it 'a mimming pimming' one, and not half severe enough; he, Bent, would write one himself. If it had not been for Vale and Bent such a document would never have been sent to England. His Excellency had many enemies who for reasons not at all to the credit of their character or their heart had endeavoured to throw a false light upon His Excellency's praiseworthy intentions, for the purpose of raising a party cabal in the colony to the destruction of good order and government, and to gratify their own ambitious, sordid views. Trusting that he, Thompson, would ever retain the high sense he now felt of the humane and benevolent views of His Excellency towards them as colonists, and that the gratitude of his heart would never cease to flow at the recollection of the benefits from the steadiness of His Excellency's perseverance for their welfare, and that emancipists might ever return to the rank they formerly held in society, he, had the honour to subscribe himself, His Excellency's most respectful, most obedient and most obliged servant, Cha⁸ Thompson.[75]

When Macquarie finally got round to forwarding the petition of the emancipists in October 1821, he strongly recommended it to Bathurst's humane and favourable consideration after assuring Bathurst that there was nothing improper or in the smallest degree disrespectful in it. In the same despatch, he remained strangely silent both on their achievements as well as on his own passionate defence of their right to be restored to the position in society they had forfeited by the commission of a crime.[76] Perhaps he thought the petition spoke for itself; perhaps by then his mind was preoccupied with that other

[73] *Sydney Gazette*, 27 January 1821.

[74] Ibid.

[75] C. Thompson to Macquarie, 29 January 1821 (Document A89 Bigge Appendix, C.O. 201/119).

[76] Macquarie to Bathurst, 22 October 1821, *H.R.A.*, I, 10, p. 549.

problem which devoured more and more of his time as 1821 wore on—the vindication of his work in New South Wales. Certainly the arguments in the petition, the tone of it, the sense of outraged justice which informed every word in it, and the underlying assumption that the teachings of religion, the dictates of humanity and decency were on their side, suggested that it was the sort of document he himself would have written if he had been the author. The petition began by reciting the same arguments as Macquarie had used in his dispute about Redfern: that the emancipists constituted the far greater majority of the free inhabitants, being 7,556 in number, and having 5,859 children, compared with the 1,558 adults and 878 children of those who originally came free; that the emancipists were those persons by whose labour and industry the colony had been cleared, and cultivated, its towns built, its agriculture and commerce carried on; that the emancipists had acquired and possessed the far greater portion of the real and personal property—for example, emancipists possessed 29,028 acres of land in cultivation, while the free emigrants possessed only 10,787 acres in cultivation, and they produced other figures to illustrate this superiority in wealth; that emancipists filled offices of rank, trust and importance under the colonial government; that their behaviour was such as to render them not unworthy of the character of useful and respectable citizens; that the system of encouragement to deserving emancipists, such as land grants, had contributed to a general reformation in the moral character and conduct of emancipists, and a higher tone of moral feeling and a sense of worth in their children; that they were proud to state there was not a more industrious and loyal youth in any part of His Majesty's empire; that by the labour of the emancipists the colony of New South Wales had been converted from a barren wilderness of woods into a thriving British colony; that the effect of a pardon had restored an emancipist to all the civil rights and privileges of free subjects—to own or lease land, to sue or be sued, to give evidence in a law court—until the decision in the cases of *Eagar* v. *Field* and *Eagar* v. *de Mestre* subverted the personal liberty, the right and possession of property, and all the civil capacities, rights and privileges of those who composed the far greater majority of the population of the colony and who possessed the greater proportion of its property; that unless this disability was removed party distractions, unpleasant discussions, irritable feelings, jealousies, heats, animosities and diversions would be introduced and perpetuated in the colony; that the colony would also revert to that state of immorality, poverty, and distress which had prevailed during the early period of its establishment. All told, 1,367 signed the petition, beginning with the chairman, W. Redfern, followed by Fulton, Samuel Terry and all the principal emancipists of New South Wales.[77]

On 25 October 1821 Eagar sailed with the emancipist petition for London on the *Duchess of York*. With him went Redfern, whose presence on the ship might explain Macquarie's restraint, in forwarding the petition to Bathurst. For while the emancipist crisis was developing, Macquarie had opened despatches from Bathurst in which he was told that Redfern's name was not to

[77] Encl. in Macquarie to Bathurst, 22 October 1821, *H.R.A.*, I, 10, pp. 549-56.

appear in the new commission for the peace to be issued when George IV ascended the throne. In giving his reasons Bathurst mentioned the general inconvenience which had been found to result from the former nominations to the magistracy made by Macquarie, and the importance of not unnecessarily resorting to such appointments.[78] This time Macquarie showed no fight, confining himself to reporting to Bathurst with becoming dignity that the king's commands had been carried into effect in respect to the removal of that gentleman from the office of magistrate.[79] At the same time he atoned in some measure to Redfern as a man by telling Bathurst that however unjustifiable Redfern's dereliction from the duty and allegiance he owed to his King had been in his participating in the Nore mutiny, he had, in Macquarie's opinion, amply atoned for that much to be lamented single indiscretion by subsequent good conduct and unimpeachable loyalty.[80] Yet so gullible was Macquarie where emancipists were concerned, so blind to their faults, that on the same day he wrote a testimonial for Eagar to Bathurst in which he eulogized his strong sound good sense and superior understanding, and warned Bathurst not to be deceived by Barron Field's criticisms, because Eagar had dared to criticize the high fees charged by Field in the Supreme Court.[81]

At the same time Macquarie read a despatch from Bathurst which reproved him for granting a pardon to the school-teacher Laurence Halloran. Halloran was born in 1765, had published two volumes of verse, had acted as a chaplain in the navy, and taught as chaplain and rector in South Africa where he was charged by the commander of the forces as an encourager of discord and duelling. After his return to England he was charged with forging a frank of the value of ten pence, pleaded guilty and was sentenced to transportation for seven years.[82] Macquarie, as Bathurst saw it, had erred in enabling Halloran to establish himself as an instructor of youth before he had proved by his good conduct his contrition for his past offences or his disposition to reform. By such an extension of mercy Halloran had not only been relieved from the effect of his previous misconduct, but had been permitted to exercise the profession of a schoolmaster, in which above all others he had the means of disseminating the evil principles by which his conduct had heretofore been actuated. This, concluded Bathurst, had excited additional pain in the breast of every one who was acquainted with Halloran's previous character or took an interest in the real welfare of the settlements.[83] This time Macquarie was stung into a firm reply. When Halloran arrived, he said, he had viewed him in the light of a very old man deserving sympathy. He had not remitted his sentence, but merely granted him a ticket-of-leave, which he had done in all similar cases to gentlemen convicts who could by their industry or finances maintain themselves without being a burden to the Crown. Halloran had since

[78] Bathurst to Macquarie, 10 July 1820, *H.R.A.*, I, 10, pp. 310-11.
[79] Macquarie to Bathurst, 20 March 1821, *H.R.A.*, I, 10, pp. 477-8.
[80] Macquarie to Bathurst, 22 October 1821, *H.R.A.*, I, 10, pp. 557-8.
[81] Ibid., p. 557.
[82] *Australian Encyclopaedia*, vol. 4.
[83] Bathurst to Macquarie, 14 July 1820, *H.R.A.*, I, 10, pp. 312-13.

conducted himself with the strictest propriety, and was by far the best and most admired instructor of youth in the colony.[84]

By then it was clear that Macquarie's policies of promoting emancipists to positions of social rank and the employment of convicts on public works and government farms rather than as workers for the settlers were doomed. The rapid increase in the wealth and population to which Macquarie had contributed so much, itself created the need for a change in the method of administration. When Bathurst agreed with Macquarie's suspension of W. Gore as provost marshal, and his suggestion that J. T. Campbell should fill the vacant place, he took the opportunity to change the title of Campbell's previous office from that of secretary to the Governor to that of Colonial Secretary. In the same despatch he announced the appointment of Major Frederick Goulburn, the younger brother of the right honourable Henry Goulburn, Under-Secretary for the Colonies, as the first Colonial Secretary. Goulburn was born in 1788, and served in the army from 1805 to 1820, where he attained the rank of major in 1816. He arrived in Sydney on the *Hebe* on 31 December 1820. His commission as Colonial Secretary and registrar was read at Government House on 1 January 1821, though he did not take over from Campbell till 1 February. This change occurred at the height of the emancipist agitation and on the eve of Bigge's return to London. Nor did the occasion pass without a generous tribute by Macquarie to the work of Campbell, in which he expressed publicly his sense of the meritorious, zealous and useful services of that officer, and went on to use language which showed to all who had ears to hear his awareness that a whole era was passing, as well as his joy that Campbell had not betrayed or forsaken him.[85] Indeed, perhaps as a gesture of loyalty, when Campbell retired to his estate and the less onerous duties of provost marshal, he named his estate 'Mount Philo' in memory of his attack on one of the most inveterate enemies of Macquarie—the Reverend Samuel Marsden.[86]

Before Campbell retired he gave Bigge some account of the emoluments and duties of the secretary to the Governor. He received fees and emoluments from registering grants of land, marriage licences, colonial vessels and their clearance; head money for persons leaving the colony; fees per folio for the transcripts of reports from law courts of appeal, for licences to colonial coast craft (excluding Van Diemen's Land), and on receiving and on affixing the colonial seal to appeals to the King-in-Council. His duties, in addition to those enumerated in the collection of fees and emoluments, were: to conduct the correspondence of the Governor throughout the colony and its dependencies, and with the governments of India, Ceylon, Isle of France, Cape of Good Hope, and all other places; to assist in preparing the Governor's despatches for England, and to collect and prepare all the documents to be transmitted therewith; to prepare, when ordered, all pardons and tickets-of-leave by making the necessary extracts from deed polls or indents; to prepare grants

84 Macquarie to Bathurst, 20 March 1821, *H.R.A.*, I, 10, p. 478.

85 Government and General Order of 6 January 1821, in *Sydney Gazette*, 26 January 1821.

86 Bigge Appendix, D, Agriculture, document no. 31, Copy of a Grant of an Estate 'Mount Philo' to Mr Campbell, C.O. 201/123.

and leases; to superintend the publication of the *Sydney Gazette*, and to prepare proclamations, government and general orders, public notices &c. &c. for the press; on arrival of convict ships from England and Ireland, to muster the convicts on board and to inquire minutely into their conduct and treatment during the voyage; to muster the crews and passengers of all ships or vessels leaving Port Jackson and therein to have frequent reference to the indents and colonial black book assisted by the gaoler; to grant permits for the friends of convicts under sentence at Newcastle to send them by the government vessels little necessaries and articles of comfort therein enumerated free of freight; to muster at the secretary's office and describe the persons sent to the colony from the Cape of Good Hope, the Isle of France, the several governments of India and from Ceylon—adding a *nota bene* for Bigge that the persons of European convicts were in like manner described when mustered.[87]

While Bigge prepared for his departure, while the emancipists were drafting their petition, and the Reverend Samuel Marsden returned on the *Dromedary* in December 1820 after an absence of ten months sedulously engaged in the cause of the church mission in New Zealand,[88] Macquarie remained strangely withdrawn. On 26 January 1821, with W. Redfern as president and Simeon Lord as vice president, and eight well-known emancipists such as Samuel Terry and James Meehan as stewards, the emancipists held their anniversary dinner at Gandell's Rooms, Hyde Park, to celebrate the foundation of what they had come to call *their* colony at a time when the lawyers, the scribes and the pharisees among the officials and the free emigrants as far as they could see were threatening to take it from them.[89] Their claims and clamour were not lost on Bigge. Redfern, whom he had described as guilty of the foulest crime known to man, and Simeon Lord, whom he had disdainfully described as a man who sold things, were presiding over a group who in the heat and passion of the moment were drinking toasts proclaiming that the colony belonged to them and their posterity. It was in the main a patriotism of convenience, of men driven by the hope of material gain, and not by any lofty convictions that the man who lost connection with his country lost his gods and walked into the night.[90] This was the group who had shouted from the housetops their debt to Macquarie. Yet Macquarie remained not so much untouched by their expressions of gratitude, but strangely remote, no longer showing his heart like Samson and no longer writing those passionate despatches to Bathurst in defence of the cause he had espoused. For by then his mind was on other things.

On 26 September 1819 Macquarie had received a letter from Under-Secretary Goulburn advising him to accommodate matters with solicitor Moore. On 19 November of the same year, at Government House Sydney, in the presence of Lieutenant-Governor Erskine, Judge Advocate Wylde, Mr Justice Field, J. T. Campbell, and Lieutenant Macquarie, aide-de-camp to the Governor, Moore told Macquarie that as it was a highly improper act for

[87] Evidence of J. T. Campbell to Bigge (Bigge Appendix, C.O. 201/120).
[88] *Sydney Gazette*, 23 December 1820.
[89] Ibid., 20 and 27 January 1821.
[90] On the latter idea see the letter by N. Stavrogin in F. M. Dostoevsky: *The Possessed*, Everyman ed., (London, 1931), vol. 2, p. 307.

him to have affixed his brother's signature to the Vale petition in 1816, he did hereby express his unfeigned sorrow and regret, and requested Macquarie to accept these sentiments as an apology for the same. They then shook hands. Macquarie was exultant; one of his bitterest enemies had been disposed of. But, as he put it, he found he still had a great many to subdue 'at home', and he was more anxious than ever to return to England for that purpose.[91] This impatience to vindicate his name and honour became the ruling passion of his life during his last two years as Governor. In this way Macquarie became reconciled with some of his mortal enemies in the colony. All that remained of the old Macquarie was the upright man who could not conceal his contempt for the lazy, the dissipated, the turbulent and the discontented.[92]

When he heard, in March 1821, that Bathurst had at last accepted his resignation, and named his successor, he took Bathurst's condescension as very gratifying, because, as he put it, after the many indignities and mortifications he had experienced for the last eighteen months, the early arrival of a successor would be a source of sincere pleasure.[93] From that day until his departure he toured the settlements to receive the thanks and praise of officials and settlers for his work. On 4 April 1821, accompanied by his wife and son, he set sail for Hobart Town, was driven back by adverse winds, set sail again on 13 April, and arrived on 24 April to be received with every attention and respect. He was delighted with the industry and spirit of enterprise, the improvements in the town, and the contribution of Sorell to public and private building. On 26 April the magistrates, public officers, landholders and principal inhabitants met to draft an address to Macquarie, which he graciously received on the following day at Government House in the presence of Lieutenant-Governor Sorell, the Judge Advocate of New South Wales, and the leading officials of Van Diemen's Land. In it they expressed their gratitude to Macquarie for the great benefits they had received at his hands, the progress of agriculture, the reduction in the price of labour, the foundation of noble and useful institutions for the advancement of religion and morals, for the instruction of youth, and for the relief of the aged and the poor. Macquarie replied that as it had ever been his study to benefit these settlements by every means in his power, it was highly satisfactory to him that his efforts towards that end had not escaped their observation. The progress due to Sorell would confer on them and their posterity every lasting benefit which could be enjoyed by the inhabitants of one of the most highly favoured abodes for the residence of man in the habitable world.[94] Similar sentiments were exchanged at Launceston, where he was greeted on 12 May with an address from the magistrates, public officers and inhabitants, in which

---

91 Macquarie to Under Secretary Goulburn, 29 February 1820, *H.R.A.*, I, 10, p. 292.

92 See, for example, Macquarie to Bathurst, 31 August 1820, *H.R.A.*, I, 10, p. 344.

93 Macquarie to Bathurst, 20 March 1821, *H.R.A.*, I, 10, p. 479. Bathurst accepted the resignation in his despatch to Macquarie of 15 July 1820, which was acknowledged by Macquarie on 20 March 1821: see *H.R.A.*, I, 10, pp. 314-15. The news of his successor was conveyed in the despatch by Goulburn of 10 November 1820, *H.R.A.*, I, 10, p. 371.

94 *Sydney Gazette*, 26 May 1821.

they thanked him for the many benefits they had received at his hands, in particular for the improvement of morals, the encouragement of industry, and the general happiness of the people. Their remote situation from the seat of government, however, deprived them of the full benefits of his policy. This was the one oblique reference to their political disabilities he heard before he returned to Hobart Town, to prepare for the return to Sydney.

When Macquarie and his party arrived at Sydney Cove on 12 July the town burst into rejoicing to greet them. That night Macquarie Place and Barrack Square were brilliantly illuminated; the residences of the most distinguished individuals displayed testimonials of rejoicing by exhibiting a conspicuous blaze of light; the humble cottager vied with the proud and liberal merchant in displays of esteem and affection to their beloved Governor. Joseph Underwood, with his usual liberality, threw his house open to all. The officers, merchants and inhabitants gave a ball in the premises of Mrs Reibey, in George Street, where the utmost hilarity and harmony prevailed. On the Friday night the towns of Parramatta and Liverpool were illuminated in demonstrations of joy and satisfaction. Every house in Liverpool had tokens of affection in the windows, while those who were precluded from that mode of testifying their respect and attachment lit ample and cheering bonfires, the roarings of which were heard for the most part of the night amidst the display of fireworks, and the almost uninterrupted discharge of musketry and other firearms, in the intervals of which the shrill and martial sound of the clarion could be heard, as Sydney and the neighbouring towns displayed their esteem and their affection.[95]

It was the same in the northern settlements which he farewelled in the month of November, for there too the people gathered to demonstrate both their gratitude and their affection.[96] He returned to Sydney to hear of the arrival of his successor. On 30 November he sat down to write his last despatch as Governor of New South Wales; next day he was to deliver over charge of the government to Sir Thomas Brisbane. After reporting with pleasure that the colony continued to improve progressively and was in a state of perfect tranquillity, he wound up with an odd remark for a man of vision; he would be obliged, he wrote, to pay an exorbitant sum for his passage if he travelled on a merchant ship.

Next day, on the parade ground, he bade farewell to the people who had gathered for the ceremony to swear in Brisbane. His constant maxim, he told them, had been to reward merit and punish vice without regard to rank, class or description of persons. He had found the colony in a state of rapid deterioration: threatened with famine, discord and party spirit prevailing, and the public buildings in a state of decay. He had left it in a very different condition: the face of the country was greatly improved; agriculture flourished; manufactories had been established; commerce had been revived; roads and bridges had been built; the inhabitants generally were opulent and happy. It was a source of sincere delight to him to have been instrumental in bringing

95 *Sydney Gazette*, 14 and 21 July 1821.
96 Ibid., 24 November 1821.

about so favourable a change. He was not arrogating to himself any questionable merit by talking of his exertions of mind and body. Every man in public life must make enemies. It would be perhaps unreasonable to expect to have been exempted from the virulent attacks of party and disaffection. But he was buoyed above this fear of base calumny, vindictive slander and malicious reproach by the knowledge that he had devoted forty years of service to such honourable pursuits, and that his life was stained with no emotion which would cause remorse. He therefore confidently expected not only the approbation of his sovereign, but also the applause of posterity for the purity of his motives and the rectitude of his actions. He then spoke of his affection for the country, and how he would encourage in his son who had been born there the strongest affection for his native Australian land. He would pray for the prosperity of the country and for the happiness of its inhabitants, and would recommend it to the attention of His Majesty and his ministers, confidently anticipating that it would be in fifty years one of the most valuable appendages of the British Empire. They were fortunate to have Brisbane as his successor. The *Gazette* believed his speech would pave its own way into the grateful heart.[97]

From that day till his departure the round of tributes and farewells continued. On 15 December the magistrates, clergy, public officers, merchants, landholders and free inhabitants presented an address in which they thanked him for his work for the advancement of religion, of benevolent institutions, of social order, and of expanding happiness, adding their hope that he would receive his just reward from the King for his long and faithful services. When Macquarie replied, he began by reminding them he was speaking not as their governor but as a man. As it was not compatible with the frail nature of man that any mortal should attain perfection, the comforts of the gospel and the mild dispensations of the Christian religion had been set forth as their greater exemplar and guide through life. In these holy comforts and divine dispensations, he would repose in Christian charity towards his frail fellow-creatures, conscious of the rectitude of his own purposes. He thanked them for their kindness and attention and assured them that it would be the study and pride of his future days to press for their welfare. He concluded by urging the different classes to forbear with one another, and to cultivate harmony in all their transactions, with a determined resolution to submit themselves to the guidance and protection of their governor.[98]

On Wednesday 12 February 1822 the shores of Sydney Cove were lined with innumerable spectators on whose countenances, as the *Sydney Gazette* put it, there was an indication of feeling too big and too sincere for utterance. As Macquarie and his family left Government House for the last time to pass down to the landing barge, he noted with obvious satisfaction the immense numbers who were manifesting by melancholy looks a sincere and undisguised regret at their departure. So Australia, as the *Gazette* put it, saw her benefactor treading 'her once uncivilized unsocial shores' for the last time.

[97] Ibid., 1 December 1821.
[98] Ibid., 15 December 1821.

As the *Surry* moved down the harbour boats loaded with respectability and opulence farewelled the man whose chief principal aim and happiness had been the good of the colonists.[99] The *Surry* sailed out on to 'that very vast sea', with Macquarie still wanting that something more, that something he could never have while he was alive—the vindication of his name and honour as well as the recognition, from those whom he had served, that what had happened to him was unjust.

[99] *Sydney Gazette*, 15 February 1822; L. Macquarie: Journal of A Voyage from New South Wales to England in 1822. 12 February 1822 (ms. in Mitchell Library).

16

MACQUARIE AND MR COMMISSIONER BIGGE
IN ENGLAND

WHEN MACQUARIE arrived in London in July 1822 he believed the time was at hand when he and his friends would taste the wages of their virtue, and all his foes the cup of their deservings. Consuming his energy on what was unattainable, not only for Macquarie, but for any man, he rushed on to his dissolution and destruction. He wanted vindication of his name and honour; Bathurst wanted a policy for the colony. This simple but vital difference only aggravated the hurts and anguish which he had begun to suffer as soon as his fatal decision to answer his critics stretched him on the rack of the world. As soon as he arrived in England he became one of the many trying to influence the mind of Earl Bathurst.

Three years before, in 1819, Bennet had propagated his view that in the colony of New South Wales reformation had been the purpose, but corruption the result; that there was arbitrary power in the government, discontent in the people and, in general, a colony of Englishmen without morals, liberty or laws.[1] In 1820 he had returned to the attack in a letter to Bathurst which alleged that transportation was no longer dreaded as a punishment, that it was expensive and burthensome, that it was neither equal nor exemplary, nor reformatory, that there had been petty corruption in the granting of tickets-of-leave, land, and jobs, that those bold enough to differ with the public authorities had been persecuted, and that some had been oppressed, while all had been badly governed.[2] Ever since he had returned to London, Jeffery Hart Bent had been using every opportunity to poison Bathurst's mind against Macquarie. Macquarie certainly had his supporters; there were Eagar and Redfern who had arrived in 1821 to plead for the legal rights of emancipists. But both were vulnerable men, for Eagar was haunted by that most terrible fear that his mask of piety might be stripped off and the worldliness of his motives exposed, while Redfern's irritability of temper did not ingratiate him with the men who held the fate of the emancipists in their hands.

Until Bigge presented his report, no decision either by government or parliament could be made. He arrived in London in 1821 to continue work

[1] H. G. Bennet: *Letter to Viscount Sidmouth, Secretary of State for the Home Department, on the Transportation Laws, the State of the Hulks, and of the Colonies in New South Wales* (London, 1819), pp. 112-13.

[2] H. G. Bennet: *A Letter to Earl Bathurst, Secretary of State for the Colonial Department, on the Condition of the Colonies of New South Wales and Vandieman's Land, as set forth in the evidence taken before the Prison Committee in 1819*, (London, 1820), pp. 114-15.

on it. Before him he had copies of his own letters to Bathurst, letters written to him, the oral and written evidence he had collected in New South Wales, including Van Diemen's Land, and the statistical evidence he had collected, as well as the evidence of his eyes, and the intimations of his heart. The first part of his report, the 'Report of the Commissioner of Inquiry into the State of the Colony of New South Wales and its Government, Management of Convicts, their Character and Habits', was presented to Bathurst on 19 June 1822. The second part, the 'Report of the Commissioner of Inquiry on the Judicial Establishments of New South Wales and Van Diemen's Land' was presented on 21 February 1823, and the third part, the 'Report of the Commissioner of Inquiry on the State of Agriculture and Trade in the Colony of New South Wales', on 4 July 1823.

The letters by Bigge, the reports, and the appendix, contained his view of the history of New South Wales in the period of Macquarie. He wrote with insight on the character and work of the individuals in that society. He praised, for example, the great zeal, disinterestedness and piety of the Reverend Cowper. He praised too the lofty principles by which his life was guided, for, as he pointed out, Cowper had not thought it consistent with his sacred character and duties as a clergyman to engage in any secular employment. But, as Bigge put it, Cowper's long and diffuse discourses, delivered extempore and frequently interrupted with inept quotations from scripture, exhausted his hearers, weakened the effect of his open and loud denunciations of the vicious and depraved habits of the people, and deterred the higher and middle classes from attending church.[3] On Marsden he wrote with the same insight and understanding. He listed the charges against him—that his opposition to the government of Macquarie arose from worldly considerations and not from moral religious duty, that the ardent pursuit of a fortune was unworthy of a clergyman, that he was miserly in payments to people, and that he had acted with undue severity as a magistrate. As Bigge saw it Marsden's agricultural and pastoral interests were evidence of a restless disposition rather than a desire to accumulate wealth, while his severity as a magistrate did not belong to his natural character, but arose from the habitual contemplations of the depravity of the people brought before him, and the sense he gradually acquired of the inefficiency of any other punishment than that which was severely and corporally felt by them.

Bigge understood Macquarie's belief that Marsden was a secret critic of his government, and a sanctimonious hypocrite, for Macquarie had that impatience, natural to those in the possession of uncontrolled power, of any act which had a tendency to expose or repress what was wrong in the exercise of that power. To Macquarie, as Bigge saw it, Marsden was first a secret maligner and detractor and later an open and avowed enemy. To Marsden, as Bigge saw it, Macquarie was a man who was incapable of making sufficient allowances for varieties of opinion, a man who considered as opponents of his government all those who did not at once make a surrender of their judgment and feeling to his upon that most delicate question, the estimate

[3] Bigge to Bathurst, 27 February 1823 (Bigge Appendix, C.O. 201/142).

of moral character. On such questions, Macquarie interpreted humble remonstrances as rebellion.[4] Bigge understood both Macquarie and Marsden. But Macquarie wanted something more than understanding: he wanted personal vindication.

He wanted also vindication of his policy, but Bigge had little to say for that. To begin with, Bigge recommended radical changes in the methods used in the punishment and reformation of the convicts. Macquarie believed in leniency; Bigge recommended a maintenance of that degree of severity and vigour by which alone, in his view, the punishment of transportation might be made a subject of dread even to the worst offenders.[5] Macquarie believed in the ticket-of-leave as one of the means of restoring a man to the rank in society which he had forfeited; Bigge acknowledged its success as an incentive to industry, but frowned on its quick and abrupt elevation of convicts from a condition of punishment to a condition of enjoyment. Their industry, he believed, so fed their vanity as well as their vices that they lost speedily that sense of humility and contrition which was essential to a state of punishment and reform. The ticket also placed them in a state of equality with those who came to the colony free. To mitigate such evils Bigge recommended that ticket-of-leave holders should be allowed to be tenants but not owners of land, and be admitted to the law courts to defend their property at the discretion of the courts of justice.[6]

Macquarie believed both in the legal and social rights of emancipists; Bigge recommended the protection of their legal right to maintain actions in the law courts, and their right to protect the property they had acquired, as both were, he believed, consistent with the aim of reformation as well as the principles of humanity.[7] But he recommended the abolition of land grants to emancipists except those with capital, so that the emancipists in general would remain in the class to which they belonged, the class of labourers, where their hope of future success would depend more on their own industry and exertion than on the early disposal and abuse of the indulgences of the Crown. Macquarie wanted to restore the emancipist to the condition in society he had forfeited; Bigge believed that all such restoration which implied an entire oblivion of former transgressions was impracticable, because other men could not be united to give effect to this encouragement without violating the independent exercise of their own judgment.[8] Macquarie, that is, had been thinking of it as a colony for the convicts; Bigge was thinking of it as a colony for the free settlers.

Macquarie believed in appointing emancipists to positions of trust and responsibility; Bigge believed that such a policy was dictated by motives of humanity rather than reason, and was hazardous in practice. The circumstances of Mr Simeon Lord's domestic life, for example, were notorious

---

[4] Bigge to Bathurst, 7 February 1823 (Bigge Appendix, C.O. 201/142). Bigge to Marsden, 20 January 1821 (Marsden Papers, Mitchell Library, Sydney). J. T. Bigge: The Colony of New South Wales, pp. 90-6.

[5] J. T. Bigge: The Colony of New South Wales, p. 175.

[6] Ibid., pp. 125-31.

[7] Ibid., pp. 144 and 147.

[8] Ibid., pp. 173-5.

at the time when Macquarie appointed him a magistrate. He had lived with a female convict on some property in Sydney and by the profits of her trade in baking as well as by his own industry, he had acquired sufficient means to embark in larger speculations both to India and in the south sea fisheries. At the time Macquarie arrived in the colony it was rumoured that Lord had attempted to seduce two girls at the orphan school. After his elevation to the magistracy, his former irregularities were in part redeemed by the respectability of his domestic life, though he still consorted with low company in Sydney in his work as an auctioneer. As a magistrate he was sagacious and shrewd, but his want of education and of feelings of self-respect had on more than one occasion exposed the magisterial office to contempt.[9] Fulton on the other hand had been no discredit to the bench of magistrates, while Redfern by his irritability of temper, and by forward and obtrusive behaviour, had betrayed an entire forgetfulness in himself of that occurrence in his life which Bigge believed he would not be able to erase from the memory or feelings of others.[10]

Macquarie believed in the distribution of convicts to government work; Bigge recommended that the employment of convicts in the management of sheep might be made highly conducive to their improvement and reform, and that the rest of the convicts should be employed in new settlements at Moreton Bay, Port Curtis and Port Bowen to effect their entire separation from the mass of the population.[11] Macquarie believed in selecting and retaining the best of the mechanics and labourers for the government service, and that the settlers refused to take bad and inexperienced convicts; Bigge believed the settlers ceased to ask for mechanics because of repeated refusals and disappointments, as pretexts for refusal of mechanics multiplied with the buildings undertaken. Bigge believed that a more judicious and more liberal distribution would have been preferable to the government monopolizing the useful convicts, subsisting them at government expense and forcing upon the settlers a mass of useless and expensive labourers from whom they were at all times desirous of relieving themselves.[12]

Macquarie had encouraged Simeon Lord in the manufacture of coarse cloths, stockings, blankets and hats; Bigge recommended that this should be discouraged because Lord was engaging in the manufacture of goods which could be exported from the mother country.[13] Macquarie believed New South Wales was a colony founded for the punishment and reformation of convicts; Bigge believed that the future of New South Wales was highly favourable to the production of delicate breeds of wool by the character of its soil, climate and pasture, and that in such work, the convict would be removed from the evil example of the towns.[14] Macquarie believed in substituting trial by jury for trial by Judge Advocate and six military officers; Bigge believed it was highly inexpedient and dangerous to submit the property or

9 J. T. Bigge: The Colony of New South Wales, pp. 82-3.
10 Ibid., pp. 83-9.
11 Ibid., pp. 161-3.
12 Ibid., p. 52.
13 Ibid., p. 158.
14 Ibid., pp. 161-3.

the life of a free person in New South Wales to the verdict and judgment of a jury of remitted convicts, or that of a remitted convict to a jury of free persons. He believed in an educational mission to the sons of the bond before conferring on them the birth-right of Englishmen; he believed in separating them first from the vicious habits and bad examples of their parents, and in giving the most liberal and marked encouragement to their enterprises and industry.[15]

On the future of Van Diemen's Land there was no such clash because of the absence of fundamental issues. From the earliest times the Lieutenant-Governors had complained that only the profligate and useless convicts were sent there from Sydney.[16] In 1820 the settlers complained to Bigge that artificers never came to Van Diemen's Land.[17] The settlers were aggrieved by the adverse effect on their economic interests of decisions made in Sydney. In 1816, for example, they lost the market in New South Wales for their wheat when Macquarie ordered a large amount from India by contract.[18] The settlers complained too of the difficulty, inconvenience and expense of having to sue for the recovery of debts in the Sydney courts, and to prosecute in Sydney for crimes punishable by death.[19] Bigge wrote the case for the administration and the settlers of Van Diemen's Land in a language to which they could not aspire. He wrote of the evils arising to the settlement from the unchecked commission of crime, and from the extensive schemes of plunder in which the remitted convicts and those whose terms of service had expired were then tempted to engage. He wrote too of the temptation to personal redress of civil injuries that was held out to the free inhabitants, as well as to strangers, from the distance and long absence of any controlling judicial authority. These evils were only partially and insufficiently corrected by the occasional and annual circuit of the judges from Sydney. For these reasons he recommended the early establishment of a separate civil and criminal judicature in Van Diemen's Land, as a measure essential to its tranquillity and to the prosperity of its inhabitants.[20] At that time the administration and the settlers had asked for the removal of their difficulties, but Sorell was not then convinced that the only way to achieve this lay in independence from New South Wales.[21]

While Bigge might assume for the historian the role of publicist for a pastoral society exploiting convict labour for the creation of its wealth, the instructions issued by Bathurst to Macquarie's successor, Brisbane, ignored all the larger issues. Bigge had written of the first principles of human society; Bathurst began by informing Brisbane that he had authorized Edward Barnard to assume the duties of agent in London for New South Wales and Van

[15] J. T. Bigge: The Judicial Establishments, pp. 34-41.

[16] Collins to King, 29 February 1804, H.R.A., III, 1, p. 226; Davey to Bathurst, 1, April 1816, H.R.A., III, 2, p. 147.

[17] Evidence of A. W. H. Humphrey to Bigge, 13 March 1820, H.R.A., III, 3, p. 278.

[18] Davey to Bathurst, 13 April 1816, H.R.A., III, 2, pp. 148-9.

[19] Ibid., p. 147; H.R.A., III, 3, pp. 525-6; evidence of A. F. Kemp to Bigge, 9 November 1819, H.R.A., III, 3, pp. 218-19.

[20] J. T. Bigge: The Judicial Establishments, p. 46.

[21] J. West: *The History of Tasmania* (Launceston, 1852), vol. 1, pp. 87-8.

Diemen's Land at a salary of six hundred pounds per annum.[22] Bigge had written of the expediency of using public money for the construction of works of urgent necessity, or of solid utility to the colony, and the great inexpediency of prematurely introducing into a new colony a taste for ornamental and expensive modes of building.[23] Bathurst contented himself with telling Brisbane that he should constantly and prominently bear this principle in mind upon every occasion.[24] On the employment of convicts, Bathurst concentrated on detail rather than principle. No convict was to be assigned to a settler with less than fifty acres of land; convicts were to be compelled to place their savings in a bank till their conduct warranted permission to withdraw it; every endeavour should be made to separate the convicts from the general mass of the population; industry and sustained good conduct, rather than skill, should bring rewards to the convict; good behaviour was to be the sole claim for a ticket-of-leave, and convicts holding it were not to be permitted to acquire property; emancipists possessed of property were to receive land grants of ten acres; it was inexpedient to encourage manufacturers in the towns;[25] to prevent convicts participating in the comforts and advantages produced by the progress of colonization, by which the terrors of transportation had been diminished, Brisbane was instructed to order Oxley to examine sites suitable for a penal settlement at Port Bowen, Port Curtis, and Moreton Bay; Brisbane was to investigate the names, condition and property of expirees who had been convicted of felony in the colony; the additional duty on the import of wool into the United Kingdom from New South Wales was abolished, and the duties on some of its products reduced in the hope that the industry and perseverance of the colonists of New South Wales and Van Diemen's Land would do justice to the encouragement so liberally extended to them.[26] Nine months later, Bathurst instructed Brisbane on the parts of the reports on the judicial establishments and on agriculture and trade which were to be implemented. Brisbane received instructions on such diverse subjects as the salaries of petty constables, licences to publicans, the numbering of houses in towns, the need to improve communications, the reservation of land for clergy and schoolmasters, licences for tanning in Van Diemen's Land, the state of the water tanks, licences to brew, the need for clergymen in Van Diemen's Land, the state of education, leases for the coal mines, the salary of the colonial secretary, and horses for the principal surgeon.[27] The recommendations which could only be implemented by statute were written into the bill for the administration of justice in New South Wales and Van Diemen's Land. On this Bathurst had before him a variety of opinions.

By 1823 it was a commonplace of English opinion that the colony of New South Wales had ceased to be exclusively a gaol for the punishment and re-

[22] Bathurst to Brisbane, 1 September 1822, *H.R.A.*, I, 10, p. 728.
[23] J. T. Bigge: The Colony of New South Wales, p. 51.
[24] Bathurst to Brisbane, 9 September 1822, *H.R.A.*, I, 10, p. 786.
[25] Ibid., pp. 784-90.
[26] Ibid., pp. 792-3.
[27] Bathurst to Brisbane, 31 July 1823, *H.R.A.*, I, 11, pp. 95-102.

formation of British criminals. As early as 1819, *The Times* was reminding its readers that the inhabitants were producing all the necessaries of life and had begun to export their surplus produce.[28] In the next year they were advising people thinking of emigrating that they would be well directed to the settlements in New South Wales.[29] In April 1822, the *Quarterly Review* informed its readers that the government no longer considered New South Wales and Van Diemen's Land as the mere resort of felons, and that, with the removal of such a stigma, not only had the reluctance felt by many to emigrate there disappeared, but an influx of a better description of people to both of them had begun. Van Diemen's Land, they said, was England with a finer sky, with less of its winter frosts and of its autumnal and spring moisture, where all the fruits and vegetables of an English kitchen garden were raised without difficulty.[30] Letter writers in the press, speakers in parliament and pamphleteers were busy discussing the type of constitution suitable for a society exploiting convict labour. In addition, Bathurst had before him the recommendations for trial by jury and a legislative council made by the 1812 committee on transportation, the petition of 1819 for trial by jury and a legislative council, and the petition of 1821 by the emancipists for the protection of their legal rights, as well as the reports in which Bigge had recommended protection for the legal rights of the emancipists, a separate judiciary for Van Diemen's Land, and the postponement of the introduction of trial by jury.

Two men in the Colonial Office in London then worked on this material to draft a bill for the better administration of justice in New South Wales and Van Diemen's Land. They were Francis Forbes, who had been Chief Justice in Newfoundland before he returned to London to be promised the first Chief Justiceship of New South Wales, and James Stephen, a barrister by profession and a sound evangelical by persuasion, who had been appointed counsel to the Colonial Office. These two worked in with Robert John Wilmot, the Parliamentary Under-Secretary for the Colonies, who spoke for the Colonial Office in the House of Commons and who, in May 1823, in accord with a request made in his father-in-law's will, obtained a royal writ to change his name to Wilmot Horton. As early as January 1823, Forbes submitted a first draft which contained no provisions for a legislative council, but did contain a provision requiring the Governor to lay each bill first before the Chief Justice who would decide whether the proposals were repugnant to the laws of England. On 3 April 1823 Eagar submitted a memorandum on behalf of the emancipists to Bathurst. Later he was granted an interview with Horton, who assured him that the legal rights of the emancipists would be protected, though trial by jury would not be included. By the time the Forbes-Stephen-Wilmot ideas, with some promptings from Eagar, were written into a bill in June 1823, the proposal for a legislative council had been added as an after-thought, in the sense that it came late in the day, though it was central to the idea behind the act.

28 *The Times*, 3 November 1819.
29 Ibid., 10 January 1820.
30 *Quarterly Review*, April 1822, pp. 99-110.

When Wilmot Horton defended the bill at its second reading before the House of Commons, he began by insisting that whereas in its previous measures with respect to this settlement government had always treated it as the destination of certain individuals who were sentenced on account of particular offences to be transported thither from the mother country, this bill treated New South Wales as a British colony. This also dictated their decision to separate the convicts as much as possible from the free population. They were not, however, prepared to go as far as trial by jury, because they believed it unwise to select juries from the peculiar population of New South Wales. At least one speaker in the debate regretted the latter decision, stating that trial by jury had always been justly considered as one of the proudest marks of freedom. For the most part the few speakers accepted the Horton proposals, especially after the speaker in the house for the cause of the emancipists persuaded Horton to withdraw the Governor's power to deport, and to limit the operation of the bill for five years. An amendment moved on the floor of the house by Sir J. Mackintosh to substitute for a trial by officers of the army and the navy, trial by a jury of twelve men duly qualified to serve, was defeated by forty-one votes to thirty. After some minor amendments in the House of Lords the bill received the royal assent on 19 July 1823.[31]

The act had the omnibus title—'An Act to Provide, until the First Day of *July* One thousand and eight hundred and twenty-seven, and until the End of the next Session of Parliament, for the better Administration of Justice in *New South Wales* and *Van Diemen's Land*, and for the more effectual Government thereof; and for other purposes relating thereto, 4 Geo. IV, c. 96.'[32] After stating that it might be necessary to make laws and ordinances for the welfare and good government of the colony, and that it was not expedient to summon a legislative assembly, the act created a legislative council to consist of not more than seven nor less than five men appointed by His Majesty, prescribing no qualifications for them and not requiring that they be officials. The right to initiate legislation was reserved to the Governor, who in the case of emergency could pass an act of the legislative council with the consent of only one member, and in the event of rebellion, on his own authority, as the act required him only to give an account of his reasons to His Majesty-in-Council. By section twenty-nine, the Governor was required to obtain a statement from the Chief Justice, before presenting a bill to the council, that it was not repugnant to the laws of England but was consistent with such laws so far as the circumstances of the said colony would admit. By section thirty the Crown might disallow any law within three years of its enactment. By sections twenty-seven and twenty-eight the council was empowered to impose duties provided it stated the reasons clearly in the act. By section one the act provided for a Supreme Court of New South Wales and a Supreme Court of Van Diemen's Land, under a Chief Justice in each, appointed by the

[31] For the preparation of the Bill and its passage through the House of Commons, see A. C. V. Melbourne: *Early Constitutional Development in Australia: New South Wales, 1788-1856* (London, 1934), pp. 88-97; and *Hansard*, 2nd series, vol. 9, cols. 1400-5, 1447-52, 1456-8.

[32] *Statutes at Large*, vol. 9.

Crown. The trial of all crimes, misdemeanours and offences was to be held in prosecution by the Attorney-General in each colony, with questions of fact referred to a jury of seven commissioned officers of His Majesty's sea or land forces. For civil actions the trial was to be conducted by the Chief Judge and two assessors who were to be chosen from the justices of the peace, and nominated by the Governor. By section thirty-four the Governor's pardons were to have such like force and effect in the law, to all intents and purposes, as any general pardon issued in the United Kingdom under the great seal, which included the names of such felons. So the legal rights of emancipists were protected in perpetuity. Sections thirty-six to thirty-nine dealt with convict discipline. Section forty-four gave the Crown the power to create a separate colony in Van Diemen's Land, while section forty-five limited the operation of the act until 1 July 1827.[33]

In the meantime the news of what was in the Bigge reports trickled through to the colony of New South Wales in dribs and drabs. The *Sydney Gazette* on 29 November 1822 apologized sarcastically to its readers that although five or six copies had arrived on the *Eliza* they could not get hold of a copy of this highly important and deeply interesting volume, though they promised their readers rather fulsomely a 'future gratifying perusal of the long expected characteristical promulgation'.[34] On 13 December 1822 they were ready, as they put it, 'to drop a few remarks', and complimented Bigge on the dignity of his observations. Their one quarrel with him was his impugning the morals of the emancipists on the evidence of the reverend clergy. They were careful to point out that although Bigge had criticized Macquarie's policy of restoring emancipists to that position in society which they had forfeited, he had argued for their full legal rights. As the *Sydney Gazette* saw it, Bigge had viewed the colony with a benignant eye. His first report confirmed their opinion that the colony of New South Wales, including the dependencies, would, at no very remote period, form a valuable and also honourable acquisition to the mother country.[35] In the main, however, their interest was confined to the gossip value in the reports. There was quite a 'have you heard' note in the way in which they reported all the Bigge news from London. It is rumoured among respectable circles, they began their news item on 23 October 1823, that important alterations would almost immediately take place in some of the principal, and many of the subordinate, situations under the Crown.[36] The discussions of fundamental principles were not for them. On 22 November 1822 when the *Eliza* arrived in Sydney bringing copies of the first report, Macarthur was at Camden entertaining Brisbane to sheep shearing. Within a few days Macarthur was reading how the Bigge report had been productive of much pleasure to his sons in England, and of much land to himself,[37] for Bigge knew, even if Macarthur did not, the meaning of the

[33] Ibid.

[34] *Sydney Gazette*, 29 November 1822.

[35] Ibid., 13 December 1822.

[36] Ibid., 23 October 1823.

[37] S. M. Onslow (ed.): *Some Early Records of the Macarthurs of Camden* (Sydney, 1914), pp. 380-8.

promise that unto him that hath it shall be given. As for Marsden, he rejoiced that his long, laborious and praiseworthy exertions on behalf of religion and morality had at last received some recognition, while he comforted himself for the aspersions on his severity as a magistrate with the text, 'All that will live godly in Christ Jesus shall suffer persecution.' Lying and slander and all manner of evil speaking, he believed he must submit to, but the day was coming when the Judge of all the earth would do right. The divine promises, he concluded, were his comfort.[38]

In London one man was deeply hurt. That was Macquarie. He had arrived in England on the *Surry* on 4 July 1822 and immediately sought an interview with Bathurst, who extended him a kind and gracious welcome,[39] but not that vindication of his name and honour which he craved. On 27 July he wrote to Bathurst his own estimate of his achievement: how he had found the colony barely emerging from infantile imbecility, the population in general depressed by poverty, the morals of the great mass of the population in the lowest state of debasement, and religious worship almost totally neglected, and how he had left it reaping incalculable advantages from his extensive and important discoveries in all directions. How far this change might be ascribed to the natural operation of time and events on individual enterprise, and how far to measures originating with himself he left it to His Majesty's ministers to decide.

To help them he proceeded to describe his work for the general amelioration of the colony, and the improvement and reformation of the manners and morals of its inhabitants. To reward merit and punish vice wherever he found them, without regard to rank, class or description of persons had been his unerring principle. Twelve years experience of the effects of his emancipist policy on the manners and habits of the motley part of the population of New South Wales had fully justified his most sanguine expectations. He had endeavoured to inspire a religious feeling amongst all classes of the community, to excite sentiments of morality, and to inculcate habits of temperance and industry. He had endeavoured to improve education and public building. He had created a bank. He had endeavoured to ameliorate the condition of the aborigines, and to civilize them as far as their wandering habits would admit. He had laboured for the paupers, the aged and the infirm. He had 'created' a convict system, and attempted to reduce expense. Despite all this, turbulent characters had represented his administration as oppressive, and the people as discontented. Even the work which he would ever value as the most meritorious part of his administration, his work of charity and sound policy in endeavouring to restore emancipated and reformed convicts to a level with their fellow subjects, had not escaped their animadversion. They had even had the audacity to insinuate that he had increased his fortune by improper means.

---

[38] S. Marsden: *An Answer to Certain Calumnies in the late Governor Macquarie's pamphlet, and the third Edition of Mr. Wentworth's Account of Australasia* (London, 1826), pp. 85-6: and Marsden to E. D. Coates of the Church Missionary Society, 17 September 1825 (Marsden Papers, Mitchell Library, Sydney).

[39] L. Macquarie: Journal of A Voyage from New South Wales to England in 1822. 4 July 1822 (MS. in Mitchell Library).

Though their persons and their malice were beneath his contempt, he could not afford to be indifferent to them because he had been and was deeply wounded by them. So he asked Bathurst to judge. He expressed in addition the anxious and fervent hope that his long, faithful and arduous services would receive the approbation of his gracious sovereign, which, if accorded, would be to him the most gratifying and highest reward that could be bestowed upon him.[40]

On 10 September 1822 Bathurst replied, telling him of the sense which His Majesty was pleased to entertain of the assiduity and integrity with which Macquarie had administered the colonial interests of New South Wales. He told him, too, that its great increases in agriculture, trade and wealth could not but be highly creditable to his administration. And if, he went on, it has not answered all the purposes for which it was intended that was not due to any deficiency of zeal or solicitude by Macquarie. The rapid and unprecedented succession of convicts appeared to have embarrassed his government, and required a change of system not contemplated in its earlier period, the necessity for which had continued to increase by such slow and imperceptible degrees, as not necessarily to force itself upon his attention.[41] He refrained from the cruel point of speculating whether Macquarie might have perceived the need for a change of system if he had bothered less about his critics and exercised his zeal and solicitude on the problems of the colony. What Bathurst could not bring himself to do was to express his sympathy to him for what he had suffered from those who had despitefully used him. On that—the ruling passion of Macquarie's life—Bathurst was silent.

When Macquarie returned from a tour of the Continent which had begun in November 1822 and ended early in 1823, he sat down to read Bigge. Again he was deeply wounded. He sought an audience with the King; he saw friends with influence in high places. On 10 October 1823 he wrote to Bathurst forty-two folio pages in defence of his administration, in which he explained how his anxiety for his honour and his name had been greatly increased by the publication and extensive circulation of unfounded statements most injurious to his reputation. He trusted his lordship would feel that he could not, in justice to himself, remain silent under such public and private attacks upon that fair and honourable character which he had had the pride and the pleasure to maintain during a career of forty-seven years in His Majesty's service in every quarter of the globe, having had in the course of that period the honour of holding seven high staff situations, all of which had been conferred on him unsolicited, while during the whole of his long service he had had the good fortune not once to incur the censure of his superiors. He had 'the honour to be, with great respect, my lord, his lordship's most obedient and most faithful humble servant, Lachlan Macquarie'.[42]

But, carried away as he was by that passion for a true recognition of his achievement, he nowhere showed any awareness that he and Bigge had really

[40] Macquarie to Bathurst, 27 July 1822, *P.P.* 1828, XXI, 477.
[41] Bathurst to Macquarie, 10 September 1822, *H.R.A.*, I, 10, pp. 793-4.
[42] Macquarie to Bathurst, 10 October 1823 (photostat in Mitchell Library, Sydney).

differed in their conception of what the colony should be, and that, in this sense, he was fighting not so much his traducers as the trend of events, for which he was entitled to understanding, even to sympathy and pity, but not to approval and support. This time Bathurst did not even bother to reply, and Macquarie withdrew to Mull for the winter of 1823-4.

He returned to London in April of 1824, and on 26 April, with his usual candour and enthusiasm for his successes in high society, he listed the people he had visited that day:

1. H.R.H. the Duke of York.
2. H.R.H. the Duke of Clarence.
3. H.R.H. Prince Leopold.
4. Earl Bathurst.
5. Earl of Harrington.
6. Sir Henry Torrens.
7. Colonel Macdougal.

Bathurst was flattering, kind and friendly. On succeeding days Macquarie dined at the club, attended royal levées, and spent the evenings pleasantly in the salons of London. He applied for a pension, and was awarded one thousand pounds a year. He spent an evening with Sir Robert Peel, during which he explained to him his error in supposing that he, Macquarie, had been too lavish in granting pardons. There was only one terrible darkness amidst the gaiety, and the pleasure: that vile and insidious Bigge report was everywhere, and in the hands of everyone, and had gone all over the world. He asked for a title as a mark of his sovereign's approval, and a means to clear his name. He heard on 25 May that such was not to be. Then a greater darkness descended, as his physical powers wasted away in a mortal illness, ending in the silence of death on 1 July. His face expressed both exhaustion and resignation at the end.[43]

When the news reached the colony, late in October 1824, J: T. Campbell and D. Wentworth invited the friends of the late Major-General Macquarie to meet at Campbell's house at twelve noon on 5 November to consult on such measures as might be deemed expedient to mark their respect to the memory of a man who, as they put it, would long be cherished in the utmost tenderness of affection and veneration. In the *Australian* a correspondent proposed mourning for six months by the friends of the late esteemed Governor, and a subscription to erect a monument to his memory.[44] On the next Sunday in November most of the higher civil officers and magistrates, some of the military, and nearly the whole of the more respectable inhabitants paid their last tribute of respect to his memory at a special service at St Philip's, where the Reverend Cowper, ignoring the secular features of the government of Macquarie, dwelt with much feeling and at considerable length on the great moral and religious improvements which he had effected in the colony. The whole service was conducted with that solemnity and deep feeling which commonly attended the loss of a much esteemed and valued individual. Or so his supporters felt, but even for such a solemn service, unity about Mac-

43 L. Macquarie: Journal Commencing on Thursday 15 Apl 1824. See especially 26 and 29 April, 14, 17 and 25 May (MS. in Mitchell Library, Sydney); M. H. Ellis: op. cit., pp. 584-7.

44 The *Australian*, 28 October 1824. The origins, ownership and policy of this paper will be discussed in the next volume of this history.

quarie was not achieved, because the principal surgeon refused permission to toll the bell of St James's Church on the plea that it might have an injurious effect on the sick in the general hospital.[45]

For neither contemporaries nor posterity agreed on the significance of the man and his work. To his friends and supporters the whole colony was a monument to his work and he the father of Australia.[46] To his friends he was the man with the benevolent heart and the sagacious head, who counteracted distress and misery, who gave employment to the convicts, improved the streets, erected buildings of the highest utility and ornament, built the roads, befriended popular freedom, sowed the seeds for the reformation of the convicts and the civilization of the aborigine. They saw him as a man not without faults, indeed, as a man who had committed arbitrary acts, which, his friends said, were the fault not of the man but of the system. They saw him as a man subjected to obloquy, misrepresentation, and incessant vituperation, who passed through that fiery ordeal unscorched. They saw him as a man who united the greatest kindness of heart to the most captivating urbanity of manner, who left a chasm in the domestic and social circle of the colony which could never be filled up. So those who viewed his passing with grief but not with malice detected neither what came up from inside the man to lead him on to his destruction, nor the tragedy of a man whose very creation swept him aside. Those who eulogized his work or execrated his memory as a tyrant were all unaware that his errors were those of the understanding rather than of the heart; they lacked that eye of pity with which an historian should contemplate those who are powerless to avoid the anguish in their last days.[47] Though he did not lack the strength to endure such suffering with dignity, in fighting for what he believed to be his true deserts, he almost brought himself to derision.

[45] The *Australian*, 18 November 1824.

[46] See, for example, W. C. Wentworth: *A Statistical, Historical, and Political Description of the Colony of New South Wales, and Its dependent Settlements in Van Diemen's Land* . . . (London, 1819), pp. 188-9.

[47] J. D. Lang: *An Historical and Statistical Account of New South Wales*, 1st ed. (London, 1834), vol. 1, pp. 142-3; J. West: op. cit., vol. 2, pp. 170-2; R. Flanagan: *History of New South Wales* . . . (London, 1862), vol. 1, pp. 214, 221, and 231; G. W. Rusden: *History of Australia* (London, 1883), vol. 1, pp. 498, 543, 549, 560, and 567.

17

A RETROSPECT

WHEN MACQUARIE died it seemed that chance and circumstance had colluded to award the palm of success amongst all the peoples who had dreamed of planting their civilization in the south seas to those who believed in the Protestant religion and British institutions. The Hindus had dreamed of the islands of gold, and had likened the fate of a man to a voyage across the terrible ocean of life, but had succumbed to the Muslim conqueror. The Chinese had searched for spices, for gold, and for precious woods, but at the time when their quest brought them to the frontiers between barbarism and civilization, events at home ended their expansion into the south seas. The Muslim had advanced as far as the west of New Guinea when his quest for gold and spices and souls for his God was ended by the coming of another conqueror. The Catholics had dreamed of a day when the people walking in darkness would see a pure light, and had been tormented by the fear that the English and the Dutch might infect countless numbers of Gentiles with the depravity of their apostasy. By the time Macquarie died the men who believed their church had been entrusted by Christ with the keys of the kingdom of heaven depended on a Protestant governor for permission to perform their religious rites in the colony of New South Wales and its dependent territories.[1]

The Protestants, too, had dreamed that a 'wealth of terrestrial laurel and a crown of celestial glory' would be their reward for following the 'lovely paths of virtue'.[2] By the time Macquarie died it seemed that at least some of this dream had come true. By then some of them believed that they had begun a journey which was leading them forward not only to moral and religious but also to material prosperity.[3] Some in the colony were even looking forward to a day when the convict blot would be forgotten, and Australasia would become a new Britannia in another world.[4] Yet within three generations the Protestant ascendancy was crumbling to its ruins, and the dream of the brotherhood of man was taking possession of men's minds. For just as the history of a man turns some to a tragic vision of life, the history of men's dreams prompts others to work for the day when that wealth of love which used to be lavished on Him is turned upon the whole of nature, on the world, on men, and on every blade of grass.

[1] *Sydney Gazette*, 3 November 1821.   [2] Ibid., 22 December 1821.
[3] Ibid., 4 August 1821; Ibid., 27 December 1822.
[4] W. C. Wentworth: *Australasia: A poem written for the Chancellor's Medal at the Cambridge Commencement, July 1823* (London, 1823), pp. 14-16 and 22.

APPENDICES

The Population of New South Wales in 1820

(Taken from the Bigge Appendix, C.O. 201/130, document No. L3.)

District	Came free		Born in the colony		Free by servitude		Absolutely pardoned		Conditionally pardoned		Ticket-of-leave		Convicts		Children		On colon. vessels	Total
	M	F	M	F	M	F	M	F	M	F	M	F	M	F	M	F		
Sydney	378	320	401	490	857	696	67	18	353	28	519	234	4,308	149	1,703	1,338	220	12,079
Parramatta	77	82	46	69	275	245	25	4	157	3	198	13	1,165	265	461	495	—	3,581
Liverpool	96	62	35	44	181	143	16	2	129	3	174	14	975	55	346	290	—	2,566
Castlereagh & Evan	34	21	36	46	82	35	5	—	45	1	48	1	434	21	77	81	—	967
Windsor	49	24	62	61	165	116	10	1	101	3	103	6	600	23	180	140	—	1,644
Wilberforce	53	23	62	48	167	77	7	—	50	2	61	1	262	9	137	114	—	1,073
Richmond	38	27	22	55	95	80	3	—	81	1	47	1	174	—	130	120	—	874
Bathurst	3	1	4	3	8	2	1	—	2	—	2	—	74	1	8	7	—	116
Newcastle	17	2	8	3	22	9	—	—	3	—	—	—	799	64	23	18	—	968
Government stockkeepers	—	—	—	—	—	—	—	—	—	—	—	—	71	—	—	—	—	71
Totals	745	562	676	819	1,852	1,403	134	25	921	41	1,152	270	8,864	587	3,065	2,603	220	23,939

APPENDIX II

The Population of Van Diemen's Land in 1820

(Taken from the Bigge Appendix, C.O. 201/135, document No. X9.)

District	Came free or born in the colony				Free by pardon, emancipat. or expiration of sentence				Children of convicts		Total No. of free people	Convicts		Total No. of convicts	Total No. of souls
	Adults		Children		Adults		Children								
	M	F	M	F	M	F	M	F	M	F		M	F		
Cornwall	75	39	66	49	142	48	42	55	18	13	547	712	71	783	1,330
Buckinghamshire	342	217	138	158	385	141	136	90	36	45	1,688	1,679	204	1,883	3,571
Totals	417	256	204	207	527	189	178	145	54	58	2,235	2,391	275	2,666	4,901

APPENDIX III

The Principal Landholders in New South Wales in 1820

(Taken from the Bigge Appendix, C.O. 201/123, document No. D36.)

Note: The same man may have held land in more than one district. Individual holdings of less than 1,000 acres have not been noted.

SYDNEY	*Acres*	LIVERPOOL	*Acres*
W. Campbell	1,700	C. Hook	1,100
C. Thompson	1,500	James Meehan	2,750
— Henderson	1,300	Wm. Howe	7,120
S. Terry	3,700	Col. Molle	4,000
S. Levy	1,000	Wm. Campbell	4,000
G. Johnston	5,592	W. J. Drummond	1,000
W. Connell	1,000	Robert Lowe	1,280
W. Underwood	1,000	Matthew Norton	2,400
J. Clarkson	2,000	Jas. Badgery	1,950
A. Riley	5,400	J. Oxley	4,400
N. Bailey	2,100	W. Brown	5,100
W. Minchin	1,060	C. Throsby	2,520
J. Chisholm	2,696	W. Redfern	2,360
F. Garling	1,200	Thos. Caine	1,365
R. Jenkins	1,399	Richard Brook	6,330
R. Campbell Snr.	3,328	John Blaxland	6,850
Mrs Reibey	2,000	Wm. Broughton	1,700
B. Field	2,000	Joseph Sappish	1,750
G. S. Hall	1,400	Thos. Laycock	1,200
J. Piper	2,000	J. T. Campbell	2,030
G. Panton	1,100	John Jamison	1,205
W. Hutchinson	1,400	Thos. Moore	4,200
J. Wylde	1,479	Ex'ors of Andrew Thompson	1,580
S. Lord	4,165		

RICHMOND	*Acres*
A. Bell	1,739
Wm. Cox Jnr.	1,270
W. Faithful	1,300

PARRAMATTA	*Acres*
J. Williamson	1,150
J. McArthur	9,600
J. Harris	1,382
R. Rouse	1,300
R. Kelley	1,000
Rev. S. Marsden	4,500
Mrs King	3,000
Dr Townson	2,682
W. Wentworth	30,100
R. Hassall	2,360
W. Chapman	1,000
— Sherwin	1,150
J. Palmer	1,900
Capt. O'Connell	5,155
Col. Erskine	3,000
J. Harris	3,734

WINDSOR	*Acres*
Wm. Cox	4,000
G. & H. Cox	4,500
J. Brabyn	1,477
G. Hall	1,500
Rd. Fitzgerald	2,442

CASTLEREAGH & EVAN	*Acres*
Sir John Jamison	11,206
Rev. H. Fulton	1,000
W. Martin	1,000
John Wood	2,250
W. N. Chapman	1,300

APPENDIX IV

The Principal Landholders in Van Diemen's Land in 1820

(Taken from the Bigge Appendix, C.O. 201/134, document No. X7.)

Note: The same man may have held land in more than one district. Only holdings of more than 100 acres have been noted.

KINGBORO'	*Acres*	YORK	*Acres*
James Clysold	130	Robert Evans	110
Thomas Lucas Snr.	180	James McCawley	200
		Samuel Tharn	200
GLOUCESTER			
Thomas Pennington	200	**CLARENCE PLAINS**	
Peter Mills	170	Daniel Stanfield Jnr.	210
John Wade	300	Edward Kimberley	180
Roland W. Loane	400	William Nicholds Snr.	160
A. W. H. Humphrey	400	Clergyman's Glebe	400
Robert Allums	130	William Atkins	110
Samuel Sedrick	110	Edward Weetlake	105
Robert Nash	200	Richard Morgan Snr.	190
Arnold Fisk	500	J. Clarke	195
Bart. Reardon	200	Wm. Gangel	210
Thomas Kent	1,230		
		HARRINGTON	
ARGYLE		Hy. St John Young	500
Wm. Thompson	110½	Lieut. Chas. Jeffries	800
Wm. Blyth	180	John Ingle	400
Robt. Jillet	140	Wm. Hopley	300
Noah Mortimore	170		
Wm. Mitchell	103	**CAMBRIDGE**	
Thos. Rd. Preston	654	Thos. Wm. Birch	500
NEW NORFOLK		**MACQUARIE**	
Abraham Hands	105	Richard Barker	1,000
		John Hy. Cawthorn	1,000
MELVILL		John Ford	800
Lieut. G. B. Forster	800	Geo. Salter	260
Danl. Stanfield	310		
G. W. Evans	370	**DRUMMOND**	
John Beamont	500	Richard Fryatt	200
James Salmon	200	Andrew Whitehead	200
Alex. Noble	400	Rev. R. Knopwood	500
Edward Westwood	110	John Ingle	200
Geo. Smith	120	Henry Thrupp	1,200
Geo. Karley	140	George Gatehouse	400
John Taylor	110		
		GREEN PONDS	
GLENURCHY		Thomas Ransome	400
Jos. Berresford	140	Martin Timms	500
John Berresford	140	Anty. Fenn. Kemp	800
Robert Littlejohn	120	John Ingle	400

JARVIS	Acres
John Ingle	800

FORBES	
Edward Abbott	2,000
Andrew Geils	500
George Guest	• 300

ULVA	
G. W. Gunning	1,300
Leonard Fosbrook	500
Richard Stynes	140
Robert Troy	140
G. W. Evans	1,000
W. Sorell Esq.	710

CALEDON	
Charles Murray	600
Francis Williams	625
Lieut. Col. Thos. Davey	3,000

CALEDON—*continued*	Acres
Wm. Davis	180
Edward Lord	1,500

STAFFA	
Pat. Gould Hogan	600

ORMIAG	
John Drummond	800
Edward Lutterell	600
Richard Lewis	400

SUSSEX	
John Lakeland	300
James Gordon	600
Mary Giels	860
Nathl. Ayres	300
Thos. Allan Lascells	800

STRANGFORD	
John Ingle	400

APPENDIX V

Land Held by Former Convicts in New South Wales in 1820

(Taken from the Bigge Appendix, C.O. 201/123, document No. D5.)

(A) Abstract of returns from the several districts in New South Wales, showing the quantity of land held by emancipated convicts, either by servitude or the Governor's remission of sentence, in 1820.

Class of Persons by whom land is held	Grand total of land held by these persons
	Acres
Free by servitude	54,693
Free pardon	8,585
Conditional pardon	19,459
Ticket-of-leave	765
Total	83,502

(B) Statement showing the number of acres of land that have been held by emancipated convicts in the several districts of New South Wales, either by grant or purchase, in 1820.

District	Grant	Purchase
	Acres	Acres
Sydney	9,837	28,309
Parramatta	7,445	8,240
Liverpool	2,099	2,811
Bringelly, Cook, Minto, Airds, Appin and Cabramatta	1,080	1,190
Castlereagh & Evan	2,582	1,132
Windsor	5,881	4,405
Richmond	2,605	1,750
Wilberforce	3,780	3,047
Total	35,309	50,884

AA

(C) The most important emancipist landholders in New South Wales in 1820.

District	Name	Condition	By grant (acres)	By purchase (acres)	Total (acres)
SYDNEY					
	Charles Thompson	Free by servitude	—	1,500	1,500
	Samuel Terry	Free by servitude	2,000	17,000	19,000
	Thomas Clarkson	Free by servitude	150	2,000	2,150
	Mrs Reibey	Free by servitude	500	500	1,000
	Thomas Rose	Free pardon	—	930	930
	Solomon Levy	Condit. pardon	—	1,000	1,000
	Daniel Cooper	Condit. pardon	—	400	400
PARRAMATTA					
	George Best	Free pardon	90	360	455
	John Pye	Free by servitude	—	800	800
	John Bennett	Free by servitude	—	800	800
	James Harrox	Condit. pardon	200	1,182	1,382
	Hugh Kelly	Free by servitude	60	940	1,000
	Mary Cable	Free by servitude	100	280	380
	James Lara	Free by servitude	380	—	380

LIVERPOOL, BRINGELLY, COOK, MINTO, AIRDS, APPIN, CABRAMATTA

	Joseph Ward	Condit. pardon	200	300	500
	Michael Dwyer	Free pardon	100	520	620

CASTLEREAGH & EVAN

	Rev. H. Fulton	Free pardon	1,000	—	1,000
	Charles Hadley	Free pardon	—	400	400

Mr Hadley received an absolute pardon, returned to England and came back to the colony as a free settler.

HAWKESBURY

	Henry Kable	Free pardon	700	250	Now holds 90 acres & is tenant to Mr Murray for 30 acres
	Richard Fitzgerald	Free by servitude	1,730	712	2,442

A SELECT BIBLIOGRAPHY

For the convenience of students as well as general readers the lists of books, pamphlets, articles, newspapers and manuscripts are arranged under subject headings.

1. BIBLIOGRAPHIES AND INDEXES

Adam, M. I., Ewing, J. and Munro, J.: *Guide to the Principal Parliamentary Papers Relating to the Dominions, 1812-1911.* Edinburgh, 1913.
Cambridge History of the British Empire, vol. vii, pt. 1, p. 647 et seq. Cambridge, 1933.
Ferguson, J. A.: *Bibliography of Australia*, vol. 1, 1784-1830. Sydney, 1941.
General Index to the Accounts and Papers, Reports of Commissioners, Estimates &c. &c., 1801-1852.
General Index to the Reports of Select Committees, 1801-1852.
Hendy-Pooley, G.: Index to the *Sydney Gazette*, 1803-1825 inclusive. Sydney, 1913. Typescript in National Library, Canberra.
Library of Congress of the United States of America: A Selected List of References on Australia. Washington, 1942.
Library of the Parliament of the Commonwealth of Australia: Catalogue of the Books, Pamphlets, Pictures and Maps in the Library of Parliament to September, 1911. Melbourne, 1912.
List of the Colonial Office Records preserved in the Public Record Office. London, 1911.
Petherick, E. A.: *Bibliography of Australian Historical Material, 1870-1921.* National Library, Canberra.
References to 'Australia' in *The Times* newspaper between 1791 and 1829. Typescript in National Library, Canberra.

2. BOOKS OF REFERENCE

Australian Encyclopaedia. 10 vols. Sydney, 1958.
Cambridge History of the British Empire, vol. vii, pt. 1. Cambridge, 1933.
Dictionary of National Biography. 63 vols. London, 1885-1900.
Serle, P.: *Dictionary of Australian Biography.* 2 vols. Sydney, 1949.

3. ABORIGINES

Berndt, R. & C.: *The First Australians.* Sydney, 1952.
Childe, V. G.: *Man Makes Himself.* London, 1936.
——: *What Happened in History.* London, 1942.
Cree, E. D.: *The Australian Native: His Capabilities and the Power of Christianity in Mission Life.* London, 1872.
Elkin, A. P.: *The Australian Aborigines.* 3rd ed. Sydney, 1954.
Flower, W. H.: *The Aborigines of Tasmania, an extinct race.* London, n.d.
Foxcroft, E. J. B.: *Australian Native Policy: Its History, especially in Victoria.* Melbourne, 1941.

Gribble, R. B.: *The Problem of the Australian Aborigine*. Sydney, 1932.

Lindsay, H. A.: 'The First Australians', in *Science News*, no. 43, pp. 54-61. London, 1957.

Mathew, J.: *Eaglehawk and Crow. A Study of the Australian Aborigines including an inquiry into their origin and a survey of Australian languages*. London, 1899.

Tindale, N., and Birdsell, J.: 'Results of the Harvard-Adelaide Universities Anthropological Expedition, 1938-9; Tasmanian Tribes in North Queensland', in *Records of the South Australian Museum*, vol. 7, Adelaide, 1941-3.

Warner, W. L.: 'Malay Influence on the Aboriginal Cultures of North-Eastern Arnhem Land', in *Oceania*, June 1932, vol. 2, no. 4, p. 476 et seq.

——: *A Black Civilization*. New York, 1937.

Worsley, P. M.: 'Early Asian contacts with Australia', in *Past and Present*, no. 7, April, 1955.

4. HINDU-BUDDHIST COLONIZERS

Bernier's Travels in Constable's *Oriental Miscellany of Original and Selected Publications*, vol. 1. 5 vols. Westminster, 1891-3.

de Haan, F.: *Priangan: de Preanger-Regentschappen onder het Nederlandsch bestuur tot 1811*. 4 vols. Batavia, 1910-12.

de Kat Angelino, A. D. A.: *Colonial Policy*. 2 vols. Chicago, 1931.

Goedes, G.: *Les états Hindouisés d'Indochine et d'Indonésie*, Paris, 1948.

Nilakantasastri, K. A.: *History of Sri Vijaya*. Madras, 1949.

——: *South Indian Influences in the Far East*. Bombay, 1949.

Panikkar, K. M.: *Asia and Western Dominance*. London, 1953.

Penzer, N. M. (ed.): *The Ocean of Story*. 10 vols. London, 1924-8.

Rumphius, G. E.: *Het Amboinsche Kruid-Boek, dat is, Beschryving van de . . . Boomen, Heesters, Kruiden, . . . in Amboina en de omleggende Eylanden, . . .* 6 vols. Amsterdam, 1741-55.

Vlekke, B. H. M.: *Nusantara: A History of the East Indian Archipelago*. Harvard, 1945.

5. MUSLIM MERCHANTS

de Goeje, M. J. (ed.): *Bibliotheca Geographorum Arabicorum*. 5 pts. Lugduni Batavorum, 1870-85.

Encyclopedia of Islam. Articles on Shihab/al/din and Sulaiman/al/majri.

Ferrand, G.: 'L'élément persan', in *Le Journal Asiatique*, vol. 204, 1924.

—— (ed.): *Rélations, Voyages et Textes Géographiques Arabes, Persans et Turks Rélatifs à l'Extrême-Orient*. Paris, 1914.

Hitti, P. K.: *History of the Arabs*. London, 1951.

Hourani, G. T.: *Arab Seafaring in the Indian Ocean in ancient and early mediaeval times*. Princeton, 1951.

Stutterheim, W. F.: *De Islam en zijn Komst in den Archipel*. Batavia, 1935.

6. CHINESE COLONIZERS

Duyvendak, J. J. L.: *China's Discovery of Africa*. London, 1949.

——: *The True Dates of the Chinese Maritime Expeditions in the Early Fifteenth Century*. Leiden, 1939.

Fitzgerald, C. P.: 'A Chinese Discovery of Australia?' in T. I. Moore (ed.): *Australia Writes*. Melbourne, 1953.

Forster, W. (ed.): *Early Travels in India*. London, 1921.

Fuchs, W.: *The 'Mongol Atlas' of China by Chu-Ssu-Pen and the Kuang-Yü-T'u*. Peking, 1946.

Groeneveldt, W. P.: *Notes on the Malay Archipelago and Malacca. Compiled from Chinese Sources*. Batavia, 1876.

Hirth, F. & Rockhill, W. W.: *Chau-Ju-Kua*. St Petersburg, 1911.

Ma Touan Hin: *Ethnographie des Peuples Etrangers à la Chine, XIIIᵉ siècle*. Traduit par le Marquis d'Hervey de Saint Denis. Méridinienaux, 1883.

Marré, A.: *Malais et Chinois. Coup d'oeil sur leurs rélations mutuelles à l'arrivée des Portugais dans les Indes Orientales*. Paris, 1892.

Mills, J. V.: 'Notes on Early Chinese Voyages', in *Journal of the Royal Asiatic Society of Great Britain and Ireland*, 1951, pp. 3-25.

Rockhill, W. W.: 'Notes on the Relations and Trade of China', in *T'oung Pao*, vols. 15 and 16. Leiden.

7. THE BUGIS SEAMEN

Cense, A.: 'De Tripang-Visscherij'. *Bijdragen Koninklijk Instituut*, vol. 108, 1952, pp. 248-64.

Dalrymple, A.: *A Plan for Extending the Commerce of this Kingdom, and of the East India Company*. London, 1769.

Doorduyn, J.: 'Een Achttiende-Eeuwse Kroniek Van Wadjo', *Buginese Historiografie*. 's-Gravenhage, 1955.

Earl, G. W.: *The Eastern Seas, or voyages and adventures in the Indian Archipelago in 1832-33-34*. London, 1837.

Forrest, T.: *A Voyage from Calcutta to the Mergui Archipelago*. London, 1792.

Heeren, H. J.: 'Indonesische Cultuurinvloeden in Australie', *Indonesie*, vol. 6, 1952-3, pp. 149-59.

Le Roux, C. C. F. M.: 'Boegineesche Zeekaarten van den Indischen Archipel', *Tijdschrift van het Koninklijk Nederlandsch Aardrijkskundig Genootschap*, 1935, vol. 52.

Ligtvoet, A.: 'Transcriptie van het Dagboek der Vorsten van Gowa en Tello met Vertaling en Aanteekeningen', *Bijdragen tot de Land, Taal en Volkenkunde*, 4th series, vol. 3, 1880.

Raffles, T.: *The History of Java*. 2 vols. London, 1817.

8. PORTUGUESE AND SPANISH VOYAGES

Amherst of Hackney and Thomson, B. (eds.): *The Discovery of the Solomon Islands by Alvaro de Mendaña*. 2 vols. Hakluyt Society, London, 1901.

Bayldon, F. J.: 'Voyage of Luis Vaez de Torres from the New Hebrides to the Moluccas', in R.A.H.S., *J. & P.*, 1926, vol. 11, pt. 3.

Beaglehole, J. C.: *The Exploration of the Pacific*. London, 1934.

Beazeley, C. R.: *The Dawn of Modern Geography*. 3 vols. London, 1897.

Birch, W. de G. (ed.): *The Commentaries of the Great Alfonso Dalboquerque*. 4 vols. Hakluyt Society, London, 1875-84.

Boxer, C. R.: *The Christian Century in Japan, 1549-1650*. Berkeley, 1951.

Burney, J.: *A Chronological History of the Discoveries in the South Sea or Pacific Ocean.* 5 vols. London, 1803-17.

Collingridge, G.: *The Discovery of Australia.* Sydney, 1895.

Corney, B. (ed.): *The Quest and Occupation of Tahiti by emissaries of Spain during the years 1772-1776.* 3 vols. London, 1913-19.

Cortesao, A.: *Historia Expansao Portuguesa no Mundo.* Lisbon, 1939.

—— (ed.): *The Suma Oriental of Tomé Pires, and the Book of Francisco Rodriques.* 2 vols. Hakluyt Society, London, 1944.

Dalrymple, A.: *An Account of the Discoveries made in the South Pacifick Ocean, previous to 1764.* London, 1767.

Greenwood, G.: *Early American-Australian Relations.* Melbourne, 1944.

Grose, J. H.: *A Voyage to the East Indies.* 2 vols. London, 1766.

Kelly, C.: *The Terra Australis: a Franciscan quest.* 2 vols. New York, 1948.

Major, R. H. (ed.): *Early Voyages to Terra Australis, now called Australia.* Hakluyt Society, London, 1859.

Markham, C.: *Progress of Discovery on the Coasts of New Guinea.* London, 1884.

—— (ed.): *The Voyages of Pedro Fernandez de Quiros, 1595-1606.* 2 vols. Hakluyt Society, London, 1904.

Moran, P. F.: *The Discovery of Australia by De Quiros in the year 1606.* Sydney, 1906.

Robertson, J. A. (ed.): *Magellan's Voyage around the World.* 3 vols. Cleveland, 1907.

Spate, O. H. K.: 'Terra Australis—Cognita?' in *Historical Studies*, vol. 8, no. 29, November 1957.

Thomson, J. O.: *The Story of Ancient Geography.* Cambridge, 1948.

Wood, G. A.: *The Discovery of Australia.* London, 1922.

9. THE RUSSIAN VOYAGES

Golder, F.: *Russian Expansion on the Pacific 1641-1850* . . . Cleveland, Ohio, 1914.

10. THE FRENCH VOYAGES

Bougainville, Comte L. A. de: *Voyage autour du monde par le frégate du roi La Boudeuse, et la flûte L'Etoile en 1766-69.* 2nd ed. 2 vols. in 1 Neuchatel, 1773.

Entrecasteaux, J.-A. B. d': *Voyage de Dentrecasteaux, envoyé à la recherche de la Pérouse . . . rédigé par M. de Rossel.* 2 vols. Paris, 1808.

Nouveau voyage à la mer de Sud, commencé sous les ordres de M. Marion, et achevé sous M. Duclesmeur, (avec) un extrait de celui de M. Surville dans les mêmes parages. Paris, 1783.

Péron, F. and Freycinet, L.: *Voyage de découvertes aux Terres Australes.* 2 vols. Paris, 1807-16.

Scott, E.: *Terre Napoléon: a history of French explorations and projects in Australia.* London, 1910.

Triebel, L. A. and Batt, J. C.: *The French exploration of Australia: with special reference to Tasmania.* Hobart, 1957.

Voyage de La Pérouse autour du monde: publié conformément au décret du 22 Avril 1791 et rédigé par M. L. A. Milet-Mureau. 4 vols. Paris, 1797.

11. EARLY ENGLISH VOYAGES

Dampier, W.: *A New Voyage round the World* . . . 3rd ed. 2 vols. London, 1698.

——: *A Voyage to New Holland, &c. in the Year, 1699*, vol. III. London, 1703. And 2nd ed. containing part 2. London, 1709.

Kerr, R.: *A General History and Collection of Voyages and Travels.* 18 vols. Edinburgh, 1811-24.

Rowse, A. L.: *Sir Richard Grenville of the Revenge: An Elizabethan Hero.* London, 1937.

Taylor, E. G. R.: *Tudor Geography, 1485-1583.* London, 1930.

Temple, R. C. (ed.): *The World Encompassed by Sir Francis Drake.* London, 1926.

Wright, I. A. (ed.): *Documents Concerning English Voyages to the Spanish Main, 1569-1580.* Hakluyt Society, London, 1932.

12. THE DUTCH VOYAGES

Beaglehole, J. C.: *The Discovery of New Zealand.* Wellington, 1939.

Boer, M. G. de: *Van oude Voyagien.* 3rd impr. Amsterdam, 1939.

Brosses, C. de: *Histoire des Navigations aux Terres Australes.* 2 vols. Paris, 1756.

Chijs, J. A. van der: *Geschiedenis der Stichting van de Vereenigde Oost Indische Compagnie.* Leiden, 1857.

Halligan, G. H.: 'Tasman's Landing Place', the Royal Society of Tasmania, *Papers and Proceedings,* 1925, pp. 195-202.

Harlow, V. T. (ed.): Journal of a voyage made from the town of Batavia in East India for the discovery of the unknown Southland (1642), in *Voyages of Great Pioneers.* London, 1929.

Heeres, J. E.: *The Part Borne by the Dutch in the Discovery of Australia, 1606-1765.* London, 1899.

—— and Stapel, F. W.: *Corpus Diplomaticum Neerlando-Indicum* . . . 5 vols. 's-Gravenhage, 1907-1938.

——and Van Bemmelen, W.: *Abel Janszoon Tasman: Journal of his discovery of Van Diemen's Land and New Zealand in 1642, with documents relating to his exploration of Australia in 1644.* Amsterdam, 1898.

Hocken, T. M.: *Abel Tasman and his journal.* Otago, 1895.

Leupe, P. A.: 'Kaartje van de Banda-eilanden vervaardigd door Emanuel Godinho de Eredia in 1601'. *Bijdragen tot de land, taal, en volkenkunde,* 3rd series, vol. xi, 1876, pp. 386-91.

Lord, C.: 'On the planting of the Dutch flag in Tasmania in 1642', in the Royal Society of Tasmania, *Papers and Proceedings,* 1926, pp. 25-34.

Meyjes, R. P.: *Abel Janszoon Tasman: De Reizen van Abel Janszoon Tasman en Franchoys Jacobszoon Visscher ter nadere ontdekking van het Zuidland in 1642/43 en 1644,* Linschoten Vereeniging, vol. 17. 's-Gravenhage, 1919.

Mooij, J.: *Geschiedenis der Protestantse kerk in Nederlandsch Indië.* Batavia, 1923-31.

Mulert, F. E. Baron (ed.): *De Reis van Mr. Jacob Roggeveen ter ontdekking van het Zuidland, 1721-1722,* Linschoten Vereeniging, vol. 4. 's-Gravenhage, 1911.

Stapel, F. W.: *De Oostindische Compagnie en Australië*. Amsterdam, 1937.

Swart, J. (ed.): *Journaal van de reis naar het onbekende Zuidland, in den Jare 1642, met de schepen Heemskerck en de Zeehaen*. Amsterdam, 1860.

Tiele, P. A. and Burnell, A. C. (eds.): *The Voyage of John Huyghen van Linschoten to the East Indies*. 2 vols. Hakluyt Society, London, 1885.

Valentijn, F.: *Oud en Nieuw Oost-Indië*. 5 vols. in 8 vols. Amsterdam, 1724-6.

Van Dijk (ed.): *Mededeelingen uit het Oost-Indisch Archief*, no. 1, Twee togten naar de Golf van Carpentaria: J. Carstenz, 1623. Amsterdam, 1859.

Villiers, J. A. J. de (ed.): *The East and West Indian Mirror, being an account of Joris van Spielbergen's voyage round the world, and the Australian navigations of Jacob le Maire*. Hakluyt Society, London, 1906.

Walker, J. B.: *Abel Janszoon Tasman: his life and voyages*. Hobart, 1896.

Wieder, F. C. (ed.): *Monumenta Cartographica. Reproductions of unique and rare maps, plans and views . . .* 5 vols. The Hague, 1925-33.

Wroth, L. C.: 'The Early Cartography of the Pacific', in *The Papers of the Bibliographical Society of America*, vol. 38, no. 2, 1944.

13. COOK AND HIS TIMES

I MANUSCRIPTS

For the history of the manuscripts of Cook's first voyage see J. C. Beaglehole (ed.): *The Journals of Captain James Cook on his Voyages of Discovery: The Voyage of the Endeavour*, p. cxciv et seq., Cambridge, for the Hakluyt Society, 1955.

Journal on board His Majesty's Bark *Endeavour*, May 27th, 1768-July 11th, 1771. Original MS. in National Library, Canberra.

Journal of the proceedings of His Majesty's Sloop *Resolution* in exploring the South Atlantic, Indian and Pacific Oceans. By James Cook, Commander, Jy 13, 1772-March 21, 1775. Original MS. in the Public Record Office, London. Photostat copy in the Mitchell Library, Sydney.

Journal of Captain James Cook's Voyage in His Majesty's Ship *Resolution*, 1772-5. Original MS. in the National Maritime Museum, Greenwich. Microfilm copy in the National Library, Canberra.

Journal on board His Majesty's Sloop *Resolution*, February 10th, 1776-January 6th, 1779. Original MS. in the British Museum. Photostat copy in the Mitchell Library, Sydney.

II BOOKS, PAMPHLETS AND PERIODICALS

Anon.: *An Epistle from Mr. Banks, Voyager, Monster-Hunter, and Amoroso, to Oberea, Queen of Otaheite*. Transferred by A. B. C. Esq. second Professor of the Otaheite and of every other *unknown* Tongue. Enriched with the finest Passages of the Queen's Letter to Mr. Banks. 2nd ed. Printed at Batavia and sold in London, n.d.

Anon.: *An Epistle from Oberea, Queen of Otaheite to Joseph Banks, Esq.* Translated by T. Q. Z. Esq. 3rd ed. London, 1774

Anon.: *An Epistle (Moral and Philosophical) from an Officer at Otaheite to Lady Gr-s-n-r*. With Notes, Critical and Historical, by the author of the rape of Pomona. London, 1774.

Anon: *An Historic Epistle, from Omiah, to the Queen of Otaheite; being his Remarks on the English Nation.* With Notes by the Editor. London, 1775.

Anon. (Rickman, J.): *Journal of Captain Cook's last Voyage to the Pacific Ocean, on Discovery; performed in the Years 1776, 1777, 1778, 1779, . . .* London, 1781.

Anon.: *Seventeen Hundred and Seventy-Seven, Or, A picture of the Manners and Character of the Age. In a poetical epistle from a lady of quality.* London, 1777.

Beaglehole, J. C.: *The Exploration of the Pacific.* London, 1934.

Burney, J.: *A Chronological History of the Voyages and Discoveries in the South Sea or Pacific Ocean.* 5 vols. London, 1803-1817.

Callander, J.: *Terra Australis Cognita: or Voyages to the Terra Australis, or Southern Hemisphere, during the Sixteenth, Seventeenth, and Eighteenth Centuries.* 3 vols. Edinburgh, 1766-8.

Cook, J. and King, J.: *A Voyage to the Pacific Ocean . . . In his Majesty's Ships the Resolution and Discovery. In the Years 1776, 1777, 1778, 1779 and 1780.* 3 vols. Vols. I and II written by Captain Cook, vol. III written by Captain King. 3rd ed. London, 1785.

Cragg, G. R.: *From Puritanism to the Age of Reason.* Cambridge, 1950.

Dalrymple, A.: *A Plan for Extending the Commerce of this Kingdom and of the East India Company.* London, 1769.

Ellis, W.: *An authentic Narrative of a Voyage performed by Captain Cook and Captain Clerke, in His Majesty's Ships Resolution and Discovery During the Years 1776, 1777, 1778, 1779 and 1780 . . .* 2 vols. London, 1782.

Forster, G.: *A Voyage round the World, in His Britannic Majesty's Sloop, Resolution, commanded by Capt. James Cook, during the years 1772, 3, 4 and 5.* 2 vols. London, 1777.

Harlow, V. T.: *The Founding of the Second British Empire.* London, 1952.

Harris, J.: *Navigantium atque itinerantium bibliotheca; or, a complete collection of voyages and travels.* Rev. ed. 2 vols. London, 1744-8.

Hawkesworth, J.: *An Account of the Voyages . . . for making Discoveries in the Southern Hemisphere, And successively performed by Commodore Byron, Captain Wallis, Captain Carteret, and Captain Cook, in the Dolphin, the Swallow and the Endeavour . . .* 3 vols. Dublin, 1773.

Hooker, J. D. (ed.): *Journal of the Right Hon. Sir Joseph Banks during Captain Cook's First Voyage in H.M.S. Endeavour in 1768-71.* London, 1896.

Lloyd, C.: *Captain Cook.* London, 1952.

Lyons, H. T.: *The Royal Society 1660-1940. A History of its Administration under its Charters.* Cambridge, 1944.

Parkinson, S.: *A Journal of a Voyage to the South Seas, In his Majesty's Ship, The Endeavour.* London, 1773.

Scott, E.: 'English and French Navigators on the Victorian Coast', in *Victorian Historical Magazine*, 1912, vol. 11.

Spratt, T.: *The History of the Royal Society of London, For the Improving of Natural Knowledge.* London, 1702.

Tewsley, U. and Anderson, J. C. (eds.): Zimmermann's *Account of the third voyage of Captain Cook, 1776-1780.* Wellington, 1926.

Wood, G. A.: *The Discovery of Australia.* Sydney, 1922.

Zimmermann, H.: *Reise um die Welt mit Capitain Cook.* Mannheim, 1781.

14. THE BRITISH BACKGROUND

I GENERAL

Brosses, C. de: *Histoire des Navigations aux Terres Australes.* 2 vols. Paris, 1756.

Callander, J.: *Terra Australis Cognita: or, Voyages to the Terra Australis, or Southern Hemisphere, during the Sixteenth, Seventeenth, and Eighteenth Centuries.* 3 vols. Edinburgh, 1766-8.

Dalrymple, A.: *An Historical Collection of the Several Voyages and Discoveries in the South Pacific Ocean.* 2 vols. London, 1770.

——: *A Plan for Extending the Commerce of this Kingdom and of the East India Company.* London, 1769.

Fortescue, J.: *The Correspondence of King George the Third.* 6 vols. London, 1928.

Johnson, S.: *Thoughts on the Late Transactions respecting Falkland's Islands.* 2nd ed. London, 1771.

Schuyler, R. L. (ed.): *Josiah Tucker, A Selection from his Economic and Political Writings.* New York, 1931.

Smith, A.: *The Wealth of Nations.* Everyman ed. London, 1954.

II ENGLAND

Anon.: *An address to the public from the philanthropic society, instituted in 1788, for the prevention of crimes, and the reform of the criminal poor.* London, 1791.

Anon.: *A Review of the Policy, Doctrines and Morals of the Methodists.* London, 1791.

Anon.: *The Dispute Adjusted, about the Proper Time of Applying for a Repeal of the Corporation and Test Acts, by shewing That No Time Is Proper.* 2nd ed. Oxford, 1790.

Barrington, G.: *An Account of a Voyage to New South Wales.* London, 1810.

Bean, J.: *Zeal without Innovation: or the Present State of Religion and Morals Considered; with a view to the Dispositions and Measures required for its Improvement.* London, 1808.

Berington, J.: *An Essay on the Depravity of the Nation, with a view to the Promotion of Sunday Schools.* Birmingham, 1788.

——: *The State and Behaviour of English Catholics, from the Reformation to the Year 1780. With a View of their Present Number, Wealth, Character &c.* London, 1780.

Blackstone, W.: *Commentaries on the Laws of England.* 5th ed. 9 vols. Oxford, 1773.

Colquhoun, P.: *A Treatise on the Police of the Metropolis.* 4th ed. London, 1797.

Haslam, J.: *Convict Ships. A Narrative of a Voyage to New South Wales, in the year 1816* . . . London, 1819.

Howell, T. B.: *State Trials.* 11 vols. London, 1811-14.

Kippis, A.: *A Sermon preached at the Old Jewry, on the Fourth of November, 1788, before the Society for Commemorating the Glorious Revolution.* London, 1788.

Madan, M.: *Thoughts on Executive Justice, with respect to our Criminal Laws, particularly on the circuits.* London, 1785.

More, H.: *An Estimate of the Religion of the Fashionable World. By one of the laity.* 3rd ed. Dublin, 1791.

——: *Modern Politicians: a word to the working classes of Great Britain, by Will Chip, a country carpenter. Newly edited for the present time by his grandson.* 2nd ed. London, 1848.

——: *Thoughts on the Importance of the Manners of the Great to General Society.* 4th ed. London, 1788.

Rawson, G.: *The Strange Case of Mary Bryant.* London, 1938.

Romilly, S.: *Observations on a late publication, intituled, thoughts on executive justice.* London, 1786.

——: *Thoughts on the Probable Influence of the French Revolution on Great Britain.* London, 1790.

Vaux, J. H.: *Memoirs.* 2 vols. London, 1819.

Wakefield, E. G.: *Facts Relating to the Punishment of Death in the Metropolis.* London, 1831.

Whately, R. B.: *Thoughts on Secondary Punishment.* London, 1832.

Wilberforce, W.: *A Practical View of the Prevailing Religious System of Professed Christians . . .* London, 1797.

Williamson, J.: *A Defence of the Doctrines, Establishment, and Conduct, of the Church of England . . .* Oxford, 1790.

The Whole Proceedings on the King's Commission of the Peace, Oyer and Terminer, and Gaol Delivery for the City of London, and also the Gaol Delivery for the County of Middlesex . . . London, 1786-93.

III SCOTLAND

Anon.: *Authentic Biographical Anecdotes of Joseph Gerrald, a delegate to the British Convention in Scotland from the London Corresponding Society.* 2nd ed. London, 1795.

Anon.: *An Account of the Trial of Thomas Fyshe Palmer, Unitarian Minister, Dundee . . . September, 1793 . . .* Perth, n.d.

Anon.: *Gerrald, A Fragment; containing some account of the life of . . . a Delegate to the British Convention at Edinburgh . . . Transported to Botany Bay for Fourteen Years!!!* London, 1795.

Anon.: *The Trial of Maurice Margarot, delegate from London, to the British Convention.* Edinburgh, 1794.

Brown, R.: *Strictures and Remarks on the Earl of Selkirk's Observations on the Present State of the Highlands of Scotland.* Edinburgh, 1806.

Galt, J.: *Annals of the Parish.* Edinburgh, 1821.

Palmer, T. F.: *A Narrative of the Sufferings of T. F. Palmer, and W. Skirving, during a voyage to New South Wales, 1794, on board the Surprize Transport.* Cambridge, 1797.

IV IRELAND

Alexander, J.: *Some Account of the late Rebellion in the County of Kildare, and an adjoining part of the King's County.* Dublin, 1800.

Anon.: *An Answer to the Right Hon. P. Digenan's Two Great Arguments against the full enfranchisement of the Irish Roman Catholics. By a Member of the Establishment.* Dublin, 1810.

Anon.: *History of the Rebellion in Ireland, in the year 1798* . . . Workington, 1806.

Anon.: *A Test of Roman Catholic Liberality, submitted to the Consideration of both Roman Catholics and Protestants.* London Derry, 1792.

Anon.: *The Year Ninety-Eight: being another and a truer ballad version of the events of the year of the Great Irish Rebellion.* London, 1844.

Barrow, J.: *Serious Reflections on the Present State of Domestic and Foreign Affairs.* London, 1757.

Curtis, E. and McDowell, R. B.: *Irish Historical Documents, 1172-1922.* London, 1943.

Curwen, J. C.: *Observations on the State of Ireland, principally directed to its Agriculture and Rural Population* . . . 2 vols. London, 1818.

Gordon, J.: *A History of Rebellion in Ireland in the Year 1798.* Dublin, 1801.

Lewes, G. C.: *Our Local Disturbances in Ireland; and on the Irish Church Question.* London, 1836.

Reports from Commissioners for inquiring into the State of the Poorer Classes in Ireland, *P.P.* 1835, XXXII, 369; 1836, XXX, 43; 1837, XXXI, 68.

Report of the Select Committee on the State of Ireland, *P.P.* 1831-2, XVI, 677.

Report of the Select Committee of the House of Lords on the State of Ireland in respect of Crime, *P.P.* 1839, XI, 486.

Statutes Revised. Northern Ireland. 16 vols. Belfast, 1956.

Trant, D.: *Considerations on the Present Disturbances in the Province of Munster, their Causes, Extent, Probable Consequences, and Remedies.* 2nd ed. Dublin, 1787.

Troy, J. T.: *Pastoral Instruction to the Roman Catholics of the Archdiocese of Dublin.* Dublin, 1798.

——: *To the Reverend Pastors and other Roman Catholic Clergy of the Archdiocese of Dublin.* Dublin, 1798.

Wakefield, E.: *An Account of Ireland, Statistical and Political.* 2 vols. London, 1812.

V THE NUMBER OF CONVICTS

(a) *Official sources*

Historical Records of Australia, series I, vols. 1-10.

Indents of convict ships from England and from Ireland, in the Mitchell Library, Sydney.

Convict transportation registers, in H.O. 11/1, 11/2, 11/3, 11/4, 11/5.

Lists of convicts on board the First Fleet ships prior to sailing, in C.O. 201/2.

Lists of convicts on board the *Lady Juliana* and the second fleet ships prior to sailing, in C.O. 201/4.

Entry books of correspondence, no. 1. Alphabetical lists of convicts with particulars, 1788-1825, in C.O. 207/1.

A List of the Ships hired by this Department between the Year, 1794, and the present time, and employed in the Conveyance of convicts, settlers, Provisions and Stores to the Settlement at New South Wales, Transport Office, 5th September 1810, in H.O. 28/38.

A List of Convicts arrived from England, Ireland, East Indies, Cape of Good Hope &c. from 1812 to 1820 inclusive. . . . in the Bigge Appendix, document no. A 22, C.O. 201/118.

Return of Boys, Prisoners (of the Age of 18 Years and under) arrived in this Colony from January 1818 to December 1820 Inclusively, in the Bigge Appendix, document no. A 54, C.O. 201/119.

List of Ships that have sailed from Great Britain and Ireland to New South Wales with Convicts, distinguishing the number they have conveyed . . . together with the number of deaths that have occurred in each, and the number of convicts landed sick at their conclusion, in the Bigge Appendix, document no. A 85, C.O. 201/119.

Return of the number of Convicts embarked for New South Wales, and Van Diemen's Land, from the year 1810 to the year 1820, distinguishing Males from Females, and shewing the number that Died on the Passage, and the number that were Landed Sick at its termination, in the Bigge Appendix, document no. A 86, C.O. 201/119.

Statement of the number of Female Convicts arrived in New South Wales from the 13 Jany 1814 to 12 September 1820, shewing both the total number that arrived, the number sent by Government to the Factory, and to the Hospital as Nurses—and also those sent to Van Dieman's (sic) Land, in the Bigge Appendix, document no. A 87, C.O. 201/119.

Return of the Number of Convicts transported from this Country to New South Wales since the establishment of that Colony up to the 31 Jany 1818 distinguishing the Males from Females & the Numbers that have been transported in each year, in the Bigge Appendix, document no. L 4, C.O. 201/130.

Accounts and Papers relative to convicts on board the Hulks and those transported to New South Wales, . . . P.P., 1792, XXXV, no. 751.

A Return of the Number of Persons, Male or Female, who have been transported as criminals to New South Wales since the first establishment of the colony, specifying the term for which each Person was transported; the Date and Place of Conviction; and the Time of Embarkation for New South Wales. (Except 607 Persons, who were Transported as Criminals to New South Wales in the Spring of 1787). P.P., 1810, XIV, 45 and 1812, X, 97.

An Account of the number of Convicts who have died in the Passage to New South Wales, since the year 1795; distinguishing the names of the Ships in which the deaths have occurred, Appendix no. 29, p. 110, of the Report from the Select Committee on Transportation, P.P., 1812, II, 341.

An Account of the number of Convicts landed in New South Wales, since the year 1795; distinguishing the Ships by which they were conveyed from this Country, Appendix no. 30, p. 111, of the Report from the Select Committee on Transportation, P.P., 1812, II, 341.

An Account of the Number of Convicts who have died in their Passage to New South Wales, since the year 1810; distinguishing the Names of the Ships in which the Deaths have occurred, P.P., 1816, XVIII, 314.

An Account of the Number of Convicts Landed in New South Wales, since the Year 1810; distinguishing the Ships in which they were conveyed from this Country:—So far as the same has been received, P.P., 1816, XVIII, 315.

Convicts transported to New South Wales since 1812. P.P., 1817, XVI, 276.

Return of the Total number of Convicts transported from this Country to New South Wales, since the establishment of that Colony up to the 31st

January 1818; distinguishing the Males from the Females, and the Numbers
that have been Transported in each Year, Appendix Q, p. 554, of the Report
from the Select Committee on the State of Gaols, *P.P.*, 1819, VII, 579.

Number of Convicts sent from Ireland to New South Wales, *P.P.*, 1821, XX,
172.

Convicts sent to New South Wales from the United Kingdom, *P.P.*, 1822,
XXII, 136 and 281.

Report of the Commissioner of Inquiry, on the State of Agriculture and
Trade in New South Wales, *P.P.*, 1823, X, 136.

The Number of Convicts sent out to New South Wales, 1793 to 1837; and
the Number of Convicts sent out to New South Wales and Van Diemen's
Land in each year since the commencement of the Colony, in *P.P.*, 1837-8,
XXII, 669.

(b) *Books and Periodicals*

Bateson, C.: *The Convict Ships, 1787-1868*. Glasgow, 1959.

Bennet, H. G.: *Letter to Viscount Sidmouth, Secretary of State for the
Home Department, on the Transportation Laws, the State of the Hulks,
and of the Colonies in New South Wales*. London, 1819.

Clark, M.: 'The Origins of the Convicts Transported to Eastern Australia,
1787-1852', in *Historical Studies: Australia and New Zealand*, vol. 7 no.
26, May 1956, and vol. 7 no. 27, November 1956.

Kiernan, T. J. *Transportation from Ireland to Sydney, 1791-1816*. Canberra,
1954.

O'Brien, E.: *The Foundation of Australia*. 2nd ed. Sydney, 1950.

Shaw, A. G. L.: Review of T. J. Kiernan: Transportation from Ireland to
Sydney, 1791-1816, in *Historical Studies: Australia and New Zealand*, vol.
7 no. 25, November 1955.

VI SECONDARY SOURCES

Abbey, C. J. and Overton, J. H.: *The English Church in the Eighteenth
Century*. 2 vols. London, 1878.

Adam, Margaret: 'Highland Emigrations of 1783-1803', in *Scottish Historical
Review*, 1919-20, vol. 17.

Barton, G. B. and Britten, A.: *History of New South Wales from the Records*.
2 vols. Sydney, 1889-94.

Blake, J. W.: 'Transportation from Ireland to America, 1653-60', in *Irish
Historical Studies*, 1942-43, vol. 3.

Bogue, D. and Bennett, J.: *The History of Dissenters from the Revolution to
the Year 1808*. 2nd ed. 2 vols. London, 1833.

Bonwick, J.: *Australia's First Preacher*. London, 1898.

Connell, K. H.: 'Land and Population in Ireland, 1780-1845', in *Economic
History Review*, 1950, vol. 11, no. 3.

Currey, C. H.: 'An Argument for the Observance of Australia Day on the
Seventh Day of February and an Account of the Ceremony at Sydney
Cove, February 1788', in R.A.H.S., *J. & P.*, 1957, vol. 43, pt. 4.

Dakin, A.: *Calvinism*. London, 1940.

Dallas, K. M.: 'The First Settlement in Australia, considered in relation to Sea-power in World Politics', in the Tasmanian Historical Association, *Papers and Proceedings*, 1952, no. 3.

Dixon, W.: 'The First Landing', in R.A.H.S., *J. & P.*, 1923, vol. 9, pt. 2.

——: 'The Official Landing Place of Governor Phillip', in R.A.H.S., *J. & P.*, 1920, vol. 6, pt. 6.

Eldershaw, M. Barnard: *Phillip of Australia; An Account of the Settlement at Sydney Cove, 1788-1792*. London, 1938.

Elliott, B.: *James Hardy Vaux. A Literary Rogue in Australia.* Adelaide, 1944.

Ferguson, J. A., Foster, A. G. and Green, H. M.: *The Howes and their Press.* Sydney, 1936.

Froude, J. A.: *The English in Ireland in the Eighteenth Century.* 3 vols. 2nd ed. London, 1881.

Graham, H. G.: *The Social Life of Scotland in the Eighteenth Century.* London, 1937.

Halevy, E.: *A History of the English People in the Nineteenth Century.* 6 vols. London, 1949-52.

Harlow, V. T.: *The Founding of the Second British Empire, 1763-93.* London, 1952.

Hazard, P.: *La Pensée Européenne en XVIIIe Siècle de Montesquieu à Lessing.* 2 vols. Paris, 1946.

Holdsworth, W.: *A History of English Law.* 13 vols. London, 1932-52.

Lecky, W. E. H.: *A History of Ireland in the Eighteenth Century.* 5 vols. London, 1902-6.

Lee, A.: 'The Landing of Governor Phillip in Port Jackson', in R.A.H.S., *J. & P.*, 1901, vol. 1, pt. 1.

Lilburn, R.: *Orangeism, its Origin, Constitution and Objects.* London, 1866.

Lincoln, A.: *Some Political and Social Ideas of English Dissent, 1763-1800.* Cambridge, 1938.

Macdonagh, O.: 'The Irish Catholic Clergy and Emigration During the Great Famine', in *Irish Historical Studies*, 1946-7, vol. 5, p. 292 et seq.

Mackaness, G.: 'Australia Day', in R.A.H.S., *J. & P.*, 1960, vol. 45, pt. 5.

——: *The Life of Vice Admiral William Bligh.* 2nd ed. Sydney, 1951.

——: 'Some Proposals for Establishing Colonies in the South Seas', in R.A.H.S., *J. & P.*, 1943, vol. 29, pt. 4.

Manning, H. T.: *British Colonial Government after the American Revolution, 1782-1820.* New Haven, 1933.

Murphy, H. R.: 'The Ethical Revolt against Christian Orthodoxy in Early Victorian England', in *American Historical Review*, July 1955, vol. 60, no. 4.

Newman, J. H.: *History of My Religious Opinions.* London, 1865.

O'Brien, E.: *The Foundation of Australia.* 2nd ed. Sydney, 1950.

Oldham, W.: The Administration of the System of Transportation of British Convicts, 1763-1793. Thesis in the Library of the Australian National University, Canberra.

Pastor, L. F. von: *The History of the Popes from the Close of the Middle Ages.* 40 vols. London, 1923-53.

Rawson, G.: *The Strange Case of Mary Bryant.* London, 1938.

Shaw, A. G. L.: Review of T. J. Kiernan: *Transportation from Ireland to Sydney, 1791-1816, in Historical Studies*, vol. 7, no. 25, November 1955.

Smith, A. E.: *Colonists in Bondage. White Servitude and Convict Labour in America, 1607-1776*. Chapel Hill, 1947.

Stanhope, P. H.: *The Life of the Right Honourable William Pitt*. 4 vols. London, 1861-2.

Yarrington, W. H.: 'Some particulars concerning Phillip's arrival', in R.A.H.S., *J. & P.*, 1918, vol. 4, pt. 6.

Ward, B.: *The Dawn of the Catholic Revival in England, 1781-1803*. London, 1909.

Whitington, F. T.: *William Grant Broughton, Bishop of Australia*. Sydney, 1936.

Wood, G. A.: 'Australia's First Clergyman', in R.A.H.S., *J. & P.*, 1926, vol. 12, pt. 5.

15. THE BEGINNING OF SYDNEY COVE

I MANUSCRIPTS

Bonwick Transcripts in the Mitchell Library, Sydney.

Bowes, A.: Diary. MS. in the Mitchell Library, Sydney.

Browne, R.: Log of the *Fishburn*. MS. in Mitchell Library, Sydney.

Clark, R.: Journal. MS. in the Mitchell Library, Sydney.

Johnson, R.: Letters. MS. in the Library of St Paul's Cathedral, Melbourne.

King, P. G.: Journal, 1786-1790. MS. in the Mitchell Library, Sydney.

Southwell Papers: MS. in the Mitchell Library, Sydney.

Worgan, G. B.: Journal. MS. in the Mitchell Library, Sydney.

II BOOKS AND PAMPHLETS

Anon.: *An Historical Narrative of the Discovery of New Holland and New South Wales*. London, 1786.

Anon.: *The History of Botany Bay in New Holland*. London, 1790.

Anon.: *The History of New Holland, from its first discovery in 1616, to the present time*. London, 1787.

Anon.: *A Short Review of the Political State of Great Britain at the Commencement of the Year One Thousand and Seven Hundred and Eighty-Seven*. 6th ed. London, 1787.

Anon.: *The Voyage of Governor Phillip to Botany Bay; with an Account of the Establishment of the Colonies of Port Jackson and Norfolk Island*. London, 1789.

Collins, D.: *An Account of the English Colony in New South Wales*. 2 vols. London, 1798-1802.

Dalrymple, A.: *A Serious Admonition to the Public, on the Intended Thief-Colony at Botany Bay*. London, 1786.

Gardenstone, F. W.: *Miscellanies in Prose and Verse*. 2nd ed. Edinburgh, 1792.

Hunter, J.: *An Historical Journal of the Transactions at Port Jackson and Norfolk Island*. London, 1793.

K— G—: *Proposals for employing Convicts within this Kingdom*. London, 1787.

Tench, W.: *A Narrative of the Expedition to Botany Bay*. London, 1789.

White, J.: *Journal of a Voyage to New South Wales*. London, 1790.

Wraxall, N. W.: *Historical Memoirs of His Own Time*. 4 vols. London, 1836.

——: *A Short Review of the Political State of Great Britain*. London, 1787.

16. PHILLIP TO BLIGH

I COLLECTIONS OF SOURCES

Historical Records of Australia

Series I, 26 vols.: Governor's despatches to and from England.

Series III, 6 vols.: Despatches and papers relating to the settlement of the States: vol. 1, Port Phillip, Victoria, 1803-4; Tasmania, 1803—June 1812. vol. 2, Tasmania, July 1812—December 1819. vol. 3, Tasmania, January—December 1820. vol. 4, Tasmania, 1821—December 1825.

Series IV, 1 vol. Legal papers, vol. 1, 1786-1827.

Historical Records of New South Wales

vol. I, pt. 1, Cook, 1762-80. vol. I, pt. 2, Phillip, 1783-92. vol. 2, Grose and Paterson, 1793-5. vol. 3, Hunter, 1796-9. vol. 4, Hunter and King, 1800, 1801, 1802. vol. 5, King, 1803-5. vol. 6, King and Bligh, 1806-7, 1808. vol. 7, Bligh and Macquarie, 1809, 1810, 1811.

II MANUSCRIPTS

For a list of the manuscript material covering this period see M. H. Ellis: *John Macarthur*, pp. 533-7. Sydney, 1955.

Banks Papers, Brabourne Collection, Mitchell Library, Sydney.

Australia, 1786-1800.

Australia, 1801-20.

Bligh, 1805-11.

Caley, 1795-1808.

Miscellaneous Documents.

Miscellaneous Correspondence, 1766-1818.

Australia and the South Sea Islands, 1774-1809.

Captain Bligh and Captain Short, 1805-8.

Documents relating to Captain Bligh and Captain Short, 1806-11.

Miscellaneous Papers relating to Australia.

Letters to Sir Joseph Banks, 1790-1805.

Buckley, R. Jameson: Recollections of 13 Years Residence in Norfolk Island and Van Diemen's Land, Mitchell Library, Sydney.

Calder Papers, State Library of Victoria.

Diary of Robert Knopwood, 7 February to 29 December 1804, Mitchell Library, Sydney. 1805-8 in possession of Miss Hookey. Published in the Royal Society of Tasmania, *Papers and Proceedings*, 1946. Hobart, 1947.

Diary of Richard Atkins, 6 April 1792 to 16 May 1810, National Library, Canberra.

Diary of J. P. Fawkner, State Library of Victoria.

Fawkner, J. P.: Rough Note Book, in State Library of Victoria.

Letters of the Reverend Richard Johnson, Library of St Paul's Cathedral, Melbourne.

Journal of *H.M.S. Investigator*, Mitchell Library, Sydney.

Last will and testament of the Reverend Richard Johnson, 21 September 1826. Photostat in the National Library, Canberra.

Palmer, T. F.: Letter to the Reverend Disney, 13 June 1795. Photostat in the National Library, Canberra.

Reminiscences of J. P. Fawkner, Second Book, State Library of Victoria.

III CONTEMPORARY BOOKS AND PAMPHLETS

Anon.: *An Authentic and Interesting Narrative of the late expedition to Botany Bay . . . Written by an Officer . . . who visited that Spot with Captain Cook and Dr. Solander . . .* London, 1789.

Anon.: *A Concise History of the English Colony in New South Wales from the Landing of Governor Phillip in January 1788, to May 1803.* London, 1804.

Anon.: *Journal of Captain Cook's Last Voyage to the Pacific Ocean.* London, 1781.

Anon.: *A Missionary Voyage to the Southern Pacific Ocean, performed in the years 1796, 1797, 1798, in the Ship Duff, Commanded by Captain James Wilson.* London, 1799.

Anon.: *The Voyage of Governor Phillip to Botany Bay, with an Account of the Establishment of the Colonies of Port Jackson and Norfolk Island.* London, 1789.

Barker, E. H. (ed.): *Geographic, Commercial and Political Essays; including statistic details of various countries.* London, 1812.

Barrington, G.: *The History of New South Wales . . . from the Original Discovery of the Island . . . to the Present Time.* London, 1802.

Bentham, J.: *A Plea for the Constitution.* London, 1803.

Biographie Universelle Ancienne et Moderne. vol. 15: Vie de Flinders. Paris, 1816.

Bligh, W.: *A Voyage to the South Sea, undertaken by command of his Majesty, for the purpose of conveying the Bread-Fruit Tree to the West Indies, in His Majesty's Ship the Bounty.* London, 1792.

Collins, D.: *An Account of the English Colony in New South Wales.* 2 vols. London 1798 and 1802.

Croker, T. C. (ed.): *The Memoirs of Joseph Holt.* 2 vols. London, 1838.

Elder, J. R. (ed.): *The Letters and Journals of Samuel Marsden, 1765-1838.* Dunedin, 1932.

Ellis, W.: *An Authentic Narrative of a Voyage performed by Captain Cook and Captain Clerke, in His Majesty's Ships Resolution and Discovery during the Years 1776, 1777, 1778, 1779, and 1780 . . .* 2 vols. London, 1782.

Entrecasteaux, J.-A. B. d': *Voyage de Dentrecasteaux, envoyé à la recherche de la Pérouse . . . rédigé par M. de Rossel.* 2 vols. Paris, 1808.

Fanning, E.: *Voyages Round the World, with selected sketches of Voyages to the South Seas, North and South Pacific Islands, China etc.* New York, 1833.

Flinders, M.: *Observations on the Coast of Van Diemen's Land.* London, 1801.

——: *A Voyage to Terra Australis.* 2 vols. London, 1814.

Hunter, J.: *An Historical Journal of the Transactions at Port Jackson and Norfolk Island . . . since the publication of Phillip's Voyage.* London, 1793.

Johnson, R.: *An Address to the Inhabitants of the Colonies, established in New South Wales and Norfolk Island.* London, 1794.

Literary Gentleman, A: *The History of New South Wales.* Newcastle-upon-Tyne, 1811.

Mackaness, G. (ed.): *Memoirs of George Suttor, F.L.S. Banksian Collector, (1774-1859).* Sydney, 1948.

Mann, D. D.: *The Present Picture of New South Wales.* London, 1811.

Marsden, S.: *An Answer to Certain Calumnies in the late Governor Macquarie's Pamphlet, and the Third Edition of Mr. Wentworth's Account of Australasia*. London, 1826.

Memoirs of J. Hardy Vaux. Written by himself. 2 vols. London, 1819.

Naval Chronicle. vols. 6 and 32.

Péron, F. and Freycinet, L.: *Voyage de découvertes aux Terres Australes.* 2 vols. Paris 1807-16.

Proceedings of a General Court-Martial . . . for the trial of Lieut. Col. Geo. Johnston . . . on a Charge of Mutiny . . . London, 1811.

Report of the Select Committee on Transportation, P.P., 1812, II, 341.

Tench, W.: *A Complete Account of the Settlement at Port Jackson in New South Wales.* London, 1793.

——: *A Narrative of the Expedition to Botany Bay.* London, 1789.

Thomson, G.: *Slavery and Famine, Punishments for Sedition; or, an Account of the Miseries and Starvation at Botany Bay.* London, 1794.

White, J.: *Journal of a Voyage to New South Wales.* London, 1790.

IV NEWSPAPERS AND PERIODICALS

Amsterdamsche Courant
Annual Register
Edinburgh Review
Gazette de Leyden
General Evening Post
Gentleman's Magazine
Hobart Town Gazette
Lady's Magazine or Entertaining Companion for the Fair Sex
London Chronicle
London General Evening Post
Morning Chronicle and London Advertiser
Morning Post and London Advertiser
Scots Magazine
Sydney Gazette and New South Wales Advertiser
The Times
Whitehall Evening Post
Note: The London newspapers are collected in the Burney collection in the British Museum.

V SECONDARY SOURCES

Alison, A.: *Lives of Lord Castlereagh and Sir Charles Stewart.* 3 vols. Edinburgh, 1861.

Allars, H. G.: 'George Crossley—An Unusual Attorney', R.A.H.S., *J. & P.*, 1958, vol. 44, pt. 5.

Auckland, W. Lord (ed.): *Journal and Correspondence of William, Lord Auckland.* 4 vols. London, 1861-2.

Becke, L. and Jeffrey, W.: *The Naval Pioneers of Australia.* London, 1899.

Bassett, M.: *The Governor's Lady.* Oxford, 1940.

Bergman, G. T. J.: 'James Larra', in the Australian Jewish Historical Society, *Proceedings*, vol. 5, pt. 3.

Brougham, Henry Lord: *Historical Sketches of Statesmen who flourished in the time of George III.* First series. 2nd. ed. London, 1839.

Butlin, S. J.: *Foundations of the Australian Monetary System, 1788-1851.* Melbourne, 1953.

Byrnes, J. V.: Green Hills and Golden Grain. Thesis in the Fisher Library, University of Sydney.

Cameron, J.: *The Centenary History of the Presbyterian Church in New South Wales.* 2 vols. Sydney, 1905.

Eldershaw, M. Barnard: *Phillip of Australia: An Account of the Settlement at Sydney Cove, 1788-1792.* London, 1938.

Ellis, M. H.: *John Macarthur.* Sydney, 1955.

Evatt, H. V.: *Rum Rebellion.* 4th ed. Sydney, 1944.

Ferguson, J. A., Foster, A. G. and Green, H. M.: *The Howes and their Press.* Sydney, 1936.

Fitzpatrick, B. C.: *British Imperialism and Australia, 1783-1833: An Economic History of Australia.* London, 1939.

Giblin, R. W.: *The Early History of Tasmania, vol. 1, The Geographical Era, 1642-1804.* London, 1929.

Goodin, V. W. E.: 'Public Education in New South Wales before 1848', in R.A.H.S., *J. & P.*, 1950, vol. 36, pts. 1-4.

Grattan, H.: *Memoirs of the Life and Times of the Rt. Hon. Henry Grattan, by his son, Henry Grattan.* 5 vols. London, 1849-59.

Houison, J. K. S.: 'Robert Campbell of the Wharf', in R.A.H.S., *J. & P.*, 1937, vol. 23, pt. 1.

Hudspeth, W. H.: *An Introduction to the Diaries of the Rev. Robert Knopwood and G. T. W. B. Boyes.* Hobart, 1954.

Lang, J. D.: *A Historical and Statistical Account of New South Wales from the founding of the colony in 1788 to the present day.* 2 vols., 4th ed. London, 1875.

Lecky, W. E. H.: *A History of England in the Eighteenth Century.* 8 vols. London, 1890.

Mackaness, G : *Admiral Arthur Phillip, Founder of New South Wales, 1738-1814.* Sydney, 1937.

——: *The Life of Vice-Admiral William Bligh.* Rev. ed. Sydney, 1951.

Moran, P. F.: *History of the Catholic Church in Australasia.* Sydney, 1896.

Onslow, S. M. (ed.): *Some Early Records of the Macarthurs of Camden.* Sydney, 1914.

Pellew, G.: *The Life and Correspondence of the Right Honble. Henry Addington, First Viscount Sidmouth.* 3 vols. London, 1847.

Rowland, E. C.: 'Simeon Lord: a Merchant Prince of Botany Bay', in R.A.H.S., *J. & P.*, 1944, vol. 30, pt. 3, 1951, vol. 37, pt. 6.

Stanhope, P. H.: *Life of the Right Honourable William Pitt.* 4 vols. London, 1861-2.

Truman, G. S. (ed.): *Byron: Don Juan.* 4 vols. Austin, 1957.

Walker, J. B.: *Early Tasmania.* Hobart, 1914.

West, J.: *The History of Tasmania.* 2 vols. Launceston, 1852.

17. THE AGE OF MACQUARIE

There is a comprehensive bibliography of the age of Macquarie in M. H. Ellis: *Lachlan Macquarie, His Life, Adventures and Times*, p. 596 et seq. Sydney, 1947.

I MANUSCRIPTS

Arnold, J.: Letters, Mitchell Library, Sydney.

Bent, E.: Journal of a Voyage to New South Wales, including Sketches of Madeira, Porto Praya and the City and Harbour of St. Sebastian's Rio Janeiro, National Library, Canberra.

——: Letters of Ellis Bent, National Library, Canberra.

Bent, J. H.: Journal of a voyage performed on board the ship *Broxbornebury*, Captain Thomas Pitcher, from England to New South Wales, National Library, Canberra.

Bigge Appendix. These items are collected under the following headings:

C.O. 201/118. Convicts. Documents, A 1-50.

C.O. 201/119. Convicts. Documents, A 51-93.

C.O. 201/120. Convicts. Evidence, A 1-33.

C.O. 201/121. Police. Evidence B 1-7. Documents B 1-46.

C.O. 201/122. Tasmania. Examinations C 1-70.

C.O. 201/123. Agriculture. Evidence D 1-15.
Agriculture. Documents D 1-51; 53-60.

C.O. 201/124. Medical. Evidence E 1-16. Documents E 1-30.

C.O. 201/125. Judicial. Evidence F 1-19. Documents F 1-37.

C.O. 201/126. Judicial. Documents F 38-56; 58-87.

C.O. 201/127. Ecclesiastical Establishments, Schools and Charitable Societies. Evidence G 1-7. Documents G 1-25.

C.O. 201/128. Commissariat. Evidence I 1-8. Documents I 1-39. Case of Deputy Commissioner Drennan.

C.O. 201/129. Trade. Evidence K 1-7. Documents K 1-8; 10-29.

C.O. 201/130. Population, Colonial Expenditure and Estimates, New Zealand, Otahiti, Documents and Returns.

C.O. 201/131. Memorials and Complaints. Documents and Returns. O.

C.O. 201/132. Miscellaneous and Military. Evidence Q 1-8. Documents Q 1-17.

C.O. 201/133. Mr. Greenway. Public Buildings.

C.O. 201/134. Tasmania. Documents X 1-8.

C.O. 201/135. Tasmania. Documents X 9-11.

C.O. 201/136. Tasmania. Memorials and Complaints. Mr. Kemp, Mr. Loane. Mr. Timms, Mr. Yonge.

C.O. 201/137. Tasmania. Memorials and Complaints. Mr. Barker, Lt.-Col. Cimitière, Lt.-Col. Davey, Mr. Hogan.

C.O. 201/138. Returns of Births, Marriages and Deaths.

C.O. 201/139. Case of Deputy Commissioner Allan.

C.O. 201/140. Memorials and Complaints. Mr. Campbell, Mr. Cox, Mr. Fitzgerald, Mr. Hutchinson, Mr. Roberts.

C.O. 201/141. Commissioner Bigge's correspondence in the colony.

C.O. 201/142. Commissioner Bigge's despatches, 1819-1823.

Journal of J. M. Hudspeth, January 1822-March 1823, Royal Society of Tasmania, Hobart.

Letter-book of John Hudspeth, 31 August 1811 to 14 December 1822, Royal Society of Tasmania, Hobart.

Macarthur Papers, Mitchell Library, Sydney. (See M. H. Ellis: *John Macarthur*. Sydney, 1955.)

Macquarie Papers, Mitchell Library, Sydney.
These include:
    Journals, 1787-92, 1794-1807. 5 vols.
    Memoranda, 1808-14.
    Diary, 1816-18, 1818-22, 1822-23, 1824. 6 vols.
    Visit to Van Diemen's Land, 1811.
    Tour in New South Wales, April 1815; October 1815. 2 vols.
    Visit to Newcastle, 1815.
    Visit to Western and Northern Districts.
    Visit to Bathurst, 1821.
    Visit to Van Diemen's Land, 1821.
    Visit to the Northern Settlements, 1821.
    Tour to the Cowpastures, 1822.
    Letter-books, 1793-1820. 11 vols.
    Commission as Governor.
    Commissions and Instructions.
    Address to, 1821.
    Letters and reports, 1822-3.
    Letter-books, 1809-21. 2 vols.
    Journal of a Tour of Inspection, Nov. 6-Dec. 19, 1810.
    Memoranda, 1819-22.
    Journal of a Voyage from New South Wales to England, 1822.
    Memoranda, July 29-October 26, 1822.
    Journal (of a trip to the continent of Europe, commencing at London) Nov. 30, 1822-Jy 26, 1823.
    Diary of a visit to London, April 15-June 11, 1824.
Letters of Macquarie to his brother. Photostats in National Library, Canberra.
Marsden Papers, Mitchell Library, Sydney.
These include:
    Letters to Rev. S. and Mrs. Marsden, 1794-1837.
    Letters and reports by, 1810-37.
    New Zealand Missions: Letters to Marsden, 1816-37.
    Letters from the London Missionary Society, 1802-36.
    Letters from South Sea Missionaries, 1810-36.
    Journals, 1814-23.
    Replies to accusations, 1825-8.
    Essays and sermons, 1810-13.
    Miscellaneous documents, 1802-37.
Marsden, S.: Diary, July 1793-July 1794, Mitchell Library.
Oldham Papers, Royal Society of Tasmania, Hobart.
Wentworth Woodhouse Muniments, Sheffield City Libraries. (These letters and papers of the Second Marquis of Rockingham contain some letters to Earl Fitzwilliam from and concerning D'Arcy Wentworth and his sons D'Arcy and William Charles, 1796-1834.)

II CONTEMPORARY BOOKS AND PAMPHLETS

Anon.: *The History of Samuel Terry, in Botany Bay, who died lately, leaving a princely fortune of nearly one million sterling, by A.L.F., late of New South Wales.* London, 1838.

Bennet, H. G.: *Letter to Viscount Sidmouth, Secretary of State for the Home Department, on the Transportation Laws, the State of the Hulks, and the Colonies in New South Wales.* London, 1819.

——: *A Letter to Earl Bathurst, Secretary of State for the Colonial Department on the conditions of the colonies in New South Wales and Vandieman's Land, as set forth in the evidence taken before the prison committee in 1819.* London, 1820.

Blaxland, G.: *A Journal of a Tour of Discovery Across the Blue Mountains in New South Wales.* London, 1823.

Debenham, F. (ed.): *The Voyage of Captain Bellingshausen to the Antarctic Seas, 1819-1821.* 2 vols. Hakluyt Society, London, 1945.

Field, Barron: *First Fruits of Australian Poetry.* Sydney, 1819.

First Report of the Auxiliary Bible Society of New South Wales. Sydney, 1817.

Macquarie, L.: *Journals of his tours in New South Wales and Van Diemen's Land, 1810-1822.* Sydney, 1956.

——: *A Letter to the Right Honourable Viscount Sidmouth . . .* London, 1821.

Marsden, S.: *An Answer to certain Calumnies in the late Governor Macquarie's Pamphlet, and the Third Edition of Mr. Wentworth's Account of Australasia.* London, 1826.

Nicholas, J. L.: *Narrative of a Voyage to New Zealand performed in the years 1814 and 1815, in company with the Rev. Samuel Marsden, Principal Chaplain of New South Wales.* 2 vols. London, 1817.

Oxley, J.: *Journals of Two Expeditions into the Interior of New South Wales, undertaken by order of the British Government in the Years 1817-18.* London, 1820.

Report of the Select Committee on the State of Gaols, P.P., 1819, VII, 579.

Report of the Select Committee on Transportation, P.P., 1812, II, 341.

Reports of Commissioner J. T. Bigge:

Report of the Commissioner of Inquiry into the State of the Colony of New South Wales, P.P., 1822, XX, 448.

Report of the Commissioner of Enquiry, on the Judicial Establishments of New South Wales, and Van Diemen's Land, P.P., 1823, X, 33.

Report of the Commissioner of Inquiry, on the State of Agriculture and Trade in the Colony of New South Wales, P.P., 1823, X, 136.

Copy of the Instructions given by Earl Bathurst to Mr. Bigge, on his proceeding to New South Wales, P.P., 1823, XIV, 532.

Copy of a Report, and Extract of a Letter of Major General Macquarie, relating to the said colony, P.P., 1828, XXI, 477.

Wentworth, W. C.: *Australasia: A Poem Written for the Chancellor's Medal at the Cambridge Commencement, July 1823.* London, 1823.

——: *A Statistical Account of the Colony of New South Wales and its Dependent Settlements.* 3rd ed. 2 vols. London, 1824.

III NEWSPAPERS AND PERIODICALS

Annual Register
Australian, 1825-
Australian Magazine, 1821
Gentleman's Magazine
Hobart Town Gazette and Southern Reporter, 1816-

Scots Magazine
Sydney Gazette and New South Wales Advertiser
The Times
Van Diemen's Land Gazette and General Advertiser, 1814

IV SECONDARY SOURCES

Birt, Dom.: *Benedictine Pioneers in Australia*. 2 vols. London, 1911.

Cambage, R. H.: *Exploration between the Wingecarribee, Shoalhaven, Macquarie and Murrumbidgee Rivers*. Sydney, 1921.

Dennis, J: Bigge versus Macquarie', in R.A.H.S., *J. & P.*, 1937, vol 23, pt. 6.

Elder, J. R. (ed.): *The Letters and Journals of Samuel Marsden*. Dunedin, 1932.

Ellis, M. H.: *John Macarthur*. Sydney, 1955.

——: *Lachlan Macquarie: His Life, Adventures and Times*. Sydney, 1947.

Flanagan, R.: *History of New South Wales*. 2 vols. London, 1862.

Giblin, R. W.: *The Early History of Tasmania*. Vol. 2: The Penal Settlement Era 1804-28. Melbourne, 1939.

Hartwell, R M.: *The Economic Development of Van Diemen's Land, 1820-1850*. Melbourne, 1954.

Hassall, J. S.: *In Old Australia*. Brisbane, 1902.

Lang, J. D.: *An Historical and Statistical Account of New South Wales*. 2 vols. London, 1834.

Lodewyckx, A.: 'De benamingen van het vijfde werelddeel, historisch en taalkundig toegelicht,' *Tijdschrift van het Koninklijnk Nederlandsch Aardrijkskundig Genootschap*. vol. lxvi, no. 6.

Madgwick, R. B.: *Immigration into Eastern Australia*. London, 1937.

Melbourne, A. C. V.: *Early Constitutional Development in Australia: New South Wales, 1788-1856*. London, 1934.

O'Brien, E.: *Life and Letters of the Archpriest John Joseph Therry*. Sydney, 1922.

Perry, T. M.: 'The Spread of Rural Settlement in New South Wales, 1788-1826', in *Historical Studies*, May 1955, vol. 6, no. 24.

Rusden, G. W.: *History of Australia*. 3 vols. London, 1883.

Stiles, H.: *A Sermon, preached at St. John's Church, Parramatta, May 20th, 1838, on the occasion of the death of the reverend Samuel Marsden at Parramatta*. Sydney, 1838.

Strachey, L. and Fulford, R. (eds.): *The Greville Memoirs, 1814-60*. 8 vols. London, 1938.

Thompson, A. J.: *Australia and the Bible. A Brief Outline of the Work of the British and Foreign Bible Society in Australia, 1807-1934* (London, 1935).

Ullathorne, W. B.: *Autobiography*. London, 1891-2.

Watson, F.: *A Brief History of Canberra, the capital city of Australia*. Canberra, 1922.

Wools, W.: *A Short Account of the Character and Labours of the Reverend Samuel Marsden, formerly principal chaplain of the Church of England in New South Wales*. Parramatta, 1844.

Wyatt, R. T.: 'Wine Merchant in Gaiters', in R.A.H.S., *J. & P.*, 1949, vol. 35, pts. 3, 4, 5.

Yonge, C. D.: *The Life and Administration of Robert Banks, second Earl of Liverpool, K.G., late First Lord of the Treasury*. 3 vols. London, 1868.